An Introduction to Programming with

C++

Diane Zak
College of DuPage

COURSE
TECHNOLOGY

ONE MAIN STREET, CAMBRIDGE, MA 02142

an International Thomson Publishing company I(T)P®

Cambridge • Albany • Bonn • Boston • Cincinnati • London • Madrid • Melbourne • Mexico City
New York • Paris • San Francisco • Singapore • Tokyo • Toronto • Washington

An Introduction to Programming with C++ is published by Course Technology.

Managing Editor	Kristen Duerr
Product Manager	Cheryl Ouellette
Developmental Editors	Kim T. M. Crowley and Janice Jutras
Production Editor	Jean Bermingham
Text and Cover Designer	Douglas Goodman
Cover Illustrator	Douglas Goodman

Preface

An Introduction to Programming with C++ is designed for a beginning programming course. This book uses the C++ programming language to teach programming concepts. Although the book assumes that the student is using the Microsoft Visual C++ 5.0 compiler, the student will be able to create the programs in the book using any C++ compiler, often with little or no modification.

Organization and Coverage

An Introduction to Programming with C++ contains 11 tutorials that present hands-on instruction. In these tutorials, students with no previous programming experience learn how to plan and create well-structured programs. By the end of the book, students will have learned how to write programs using the sequence, selection, and repetition structures, as well as how to create and manipulate sequential access files, structs, classes, and arrays.

Approach

An Introduction to Programming with C++ distinguishes itself from other textbooks because of its unique approach, which motivates students by demonstrating why they need to learn the concepts and skills. This book teaches programming concepts using a task-driven, rather than a command-driven, approach. By working through the tutorials—which are each motivated by a realistic case—students learn how to create programs that solve problems they are likely to encounter in the workplace. This is much more effective than memorizing a list of commands out of context.

Features

An Introduction to Programming with C++ is an exceptional textbook because it also includes the following features:

- **"Read This Before You Begin" Page** This page is consistent with Course Technology's unequaled commitment to helping instructors introduce technology into the classroom. Technical considerations and assumptions about hardware, software, and default settings are listed in one place to help instructors save time and eliminate unnecessary aggravation.
- **Tutorial Cases** Each tutorial begins with a programming-related problem that students could reasonably expect to encounter in business.
- **Lessons** Each tutorial is divided into two lessons—A and B. Lesson A introduces the programming concepts that will be used to solve the problem outlined in the Tutorial Case. In Lesson B, the student creates the program that solves the Tutorial Case problem.
- **Step-by-Step Methodology** The unique Course Technology methodology keeps students on track. They click or press keys always within the context of solving a specific problem or the Tutorial Case. The text constantly guides students, letting them know where they are in the process of solving the problem. The numerous illustrations include labels that direct students' attention to what they should look at on the screen.

- **Help?** paragraphs anticipate the problems students are likely to encounter and help them resolve these problems on their own. This feature facilitates independent learning and frees the instructor to focus on substantive conceptual issues, rather than on common procedural errors.

- **TIPs** provide additional information about a procedure—for example, an alternative method of performing the procedure.

- **OOP Concepts** give the student a gentle introduction to the terms and concepts used in object-oriented programming and show how these concepts are implemented in the C++ language. Giving the students a basic understanding of OOP terms and concepts from the very beginning will help them better understand how to create and manipulate the objects they create in Tutorial 11.

- **Mini-Quizzes** are strategically placed to test the student's knowledge at various points in each lesson. This allows the student to determine if he or she has mastered the material covered thus far before continuing with the lesson.

- **Summaries** Following each lesson is a Summary, which recaps the programming concepts and commands covered in the lesson.

- **Questions and Exercises** Each lesson concludes with meaningful, conceptual Questions that test students' understanding of what they learned in the lesson. The Questions are followed by Exercises, which provide students with additional practice of the skills and concepts they learned in the lesson.

- The answers to the even-numbered exercises (except Discovery and Debugging exercises) can be found at www.course.com in the "Downloads" section.

- **Discovery Exercises** The Discovery Exercises, which are designated by the word "Discovery" in the margin, encourage students to challenge and independently develop their own programming skills.

- **Debugging Exercises** One of the most important programming skills a student can learn is the ability to correct problems, called "bugs", in an existing program. The Debugging Exercises, which are designated by a Debugging icon, provide an opportunity for students to detect and correct errors in an existing program.

Microsoft Visual C++ 5.0 Learning Edition

Microsoft Visual C++ 5.0 Learning Edition is an optional item available with this text. The Learning Edition of the Visual C++ development system (formerly called the Standard Edition) targets developers learning the C++ language. It is designed for entry-level programmers who want to take advantage of the powerful C++ language and the Microsoft Foundation Classes (MFC). The Visual C++ 5.0 Learning Edition includes step-by-step tutorials, wizards, and MFC object-oriented libraries that make it easy to create powerful Windows-based applications. Version 5.0 includes a variety of professional tools to help the programmer learn C, C++, and many other professional technologies such as MFC, OLE, ODBC, DAO, ActiveX, and COM.

There are some differences between the Learning Edition, which is an optional item available with this book, and the Enterprise and Professional Editions, which are offered by Microsoft. The Professional Edition targets professional software developers who need features such as code optimization and statically-linked libraries. These features are not found in the Learning Edition. The Enterprise Edition was developed for corporate developers. It provides a complete toolset for developing C++ applications and components that access remote databases, including SQL databases, and takes advantage of the latest Internet and ActiveX technologies.

The Supplements

• **Instructor's Manual**   The Instructor's Manual has been quality assurance tested. It is available in printed form and through the Course Technology Faculty Online Companion on the World Wide Web. (Call your customer service representative for the URL and your password.) The Instructor's Manual contains the following items:

• Cases that can be assigned as semester projects.

• Answers to all of the questions and solutions to all of the exercises. Suggested solutions are also included for Discovery Exercises.

• Tutorial Notes, which contain background information from the author about the Tutorial Case and the instructional progression of the tutorial.

• Technical Notes, which include troubleshooting tips as well as information on how to customize the students' screens to closely emulate the screen shots in the book.

• **Course Test Manager Version 1.21 Engine and Test Bank**   Course Test Manager (CTM) is a cutting-edge Windows-based testing software program, developed exclusively for Course Technology, that helps instructors design and administer examinations and practice tests. This full-featured program allows students to generate practice tests randomly that provide immediate on-screen feedback and detailed study guides for questions incorrectly answered. Instructors can also use Course Test Manager to create printed and online tests. You can create, preview, and administer a test on any or all chapters of this textbook entirely over a local area network. Course Test Manager can grade the tests students take automatically at the computer and can generate statistical information on individual as well as group performance. A CTM test bank has been written to accompany your text and is included on the CD-ROM. The test bank includes multiple-choice, true/false, short answer, and essay questions.

• **Solutions Files**   Solutions Files contain every file students are asked to create or modify in the tutorials, Exercises, and Debugging Techniques and Exercises.

• **Student Files**   Student Files, containing all of the data that students will use for the tutorials, Exercises, and Debugging Techniques and Exercises, are provided through Course Technology's Online Companion, as well as on disk. A Readme file includes technical tips for lab management. See the inside covers of this book and the "Read This Before You Begin" page before Tutorial 1 for more information on Student Files.

Acknowledgments

I would like to thank all of the people who helped to make this book a reality, especially Kim Crowley, my Development Editor. You have been so kind, patient, understanding, helpful, and fun. I know I could not have made it without you.

Thanks also to Kristen Duerr, Managing Editor; Cheryl Ouellette, Product Manager; Jean Bermingham, Production Editor; Janice Jutras, Development Editor; Brian McCooey, Quality Assurance Project Leader; and Alex White, Quality Assurance Manuscript Reviewer. I am grateful to the many reviewers who provided invaluable comments on the manuscript, in particular: Ronald Carlisle, Oglethorpe University; Tom Farrell, Dakota State University; Roger Lignugaris, DeKalb Technical Institute; and Howard Pyron, University of Missouri—Rolla.

Finally, I dedicate this book to the loving memory of Mary Clare Karnick. We all loved you more.

Diane Zak

Contents

t u t o r i a l   3

VARIABLES, CONSTANTS, AND EQUATIONS *85*

t u t o r i a l   4

BUILT-IN FUNCTIONS AND PROGRAMMER-DEFINED FUNCTIONS *143*

t u t o r i a l   5

THE SELECTION STRUCTURE   *201*

tutorial 8

ARRAYS *387*

tutorial 9

TWO-DIMENSIONAL ARRAYS *457*

Read This Before You Begin

To the Student

Using Your Own Computer

If you are going to work through this book using your own computer, you will need:

- **Computer System** Microsoft Visual C++ 5.0 Professional Edition, Learning Edition, or Enterprise Edition for Windows 95 or Microsoft Windows NT Workstation 4.0 or later must be installed on your computer. This book assumes a complete installation of Microsoft Visual C++.

- Microsoft Visual C++ 5.0 Learning Edition is an optional item with your book. The following system requirements apply.

  - Personal computer with a 486/66 or higher processor
  - Microsoft Windows 95 or Windows NT Workstation version 4.0 or later
  - 20 MB of memory (32 MB recommended) if running Windows 95
  - 24 MB (32 MB recommended) if running Windows NT Workstation
  - VGA or higher-resolution monitor (Super VGA recommended)
  - Microsoft Mouse or compatible pointing device
  - Hard Disk Requirements:
    - 20 MB of free disk space required during installation
    - 10 MB required once the installation is complete
  - A CD-ROM drive with 32-bit protected mode CD-ROM drivers
  - Modem or other connection to the World Wide Web (recommended)

- **Student Files** Ask your instructor or lab manager for details on how to get student files. You will not be able to complete the tutorials or exercises in this book using your own computer until you have student files. The student files may also be obtained electronically through the Internet. See the inside front or back cover of this book for more details.

Visit Our World Wide Web Site

Additional materials designed especially for you are available on the World Wide Web. Go to **www.course.com**.

To the Instructor

To complete the tutorials in this book, your students must use a set of student files. These files are included in the Instructor's Resource Kit. They may also be obtained electronically through the Internet. See the inside front or back cover of this book for more details. Follow the instructions in the Readme file to copy the student files to your server or standalone computer. You can view the Readme file using a text editor such as WordPad or Notepad.

Course Technology Student Files

You are granted a license to copy the student files to any computer or computer network used by students who have purchased this book.

TUTORIAL

1

An Overview of a Microcomputer System and Programming

case ▶ In May of each year, the Computer Science department at Adolphus College offers a one-day seminar to local high school students. The purpose of the seminar is to introduce the students to the Computer Science curriculum at the college, as well as to inform the students about the growing demand for computer programmers. During the seminar, the students learn about hardware and software, which are the components of a microcomputer system. The seminar also gives the students a brief introduction to computer programming. In this tutorial, you will experience some of the material covered in the seminar. You will find this knowledge helpful as you progress through this book, learning how to use the C++ programming language to write computer programs.

In this lesson you will learn how to:

- Describe the components of a microcomputer system
- Explain the relationship between hardware and software
- Understand the history of programming languages
- Understand the terminology used in object-oriented languages

An Introduction to Hardware and Software

An Introduction to a Microcomputer System

In 1977, the first **microcomputers**, also called **personal computers**, appeared in the marketplace. Since then, the microcomputer has become so popular that it is difficult to imagine what a person ever did without one. Imagine typing a letter on a manual typewriter, or keeping track of your investments manually, or drawing the blueprints for a house without the aid of a computer!

Since the arrival of the microcomputer, situations and tasks that were at one time considered impossible are now commonplace. For example, **telecommuting**, where an employee works from home and uses a microcomputer to communicate with his or her office, is now an option available to many business professionals. Microcomputers also allow you to access information from around the world, via the Internet and the World Wide Web, from the comfort of your home.

Figure 1-1 shows a typical microcomputer system found in most businesses and homes.

software

3.5" floppy disk drive

screen or monitor

system unit

CD-ROM

3.5" storage media

keyboard

hard disk drive

CD-ROM drive

mouse

printer

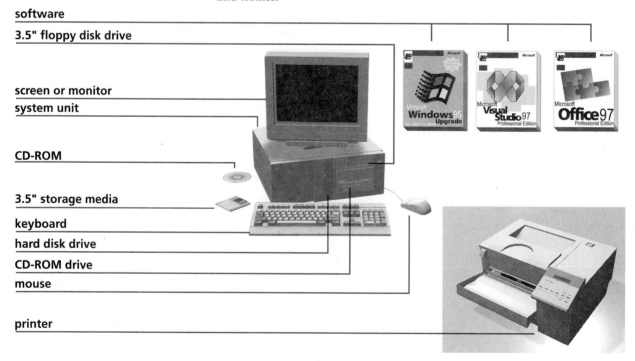

Figure 1-1: A typical microcomputer system

Notice that a **microcomputer system** is composed of both hardware and software. **Hardware** refers to the physical components of the microcomputer system. **Software** refers to the programs (step-by-step instructions) that tell the hardware how to perform a task. In the next section, you will learn about the relationship between the hardware and software found in a microcomputer system.

The Relationship between Hardware and Software

As Figure 1-1 shows, the hardware in a microcomputer system consists of a system unit, which is the case or box that holds the main circuit boards and storage devices, as well as other devices, called peripheral devices. A **peripheral device** is a device that is attached to the system unit; its purpose is to extend the capabilities of the computer system and to provide the user a means for communicating with the computer. The three categories of peripheral devices are input devices, output devices, and auxiliary storage devices. An **input device** allows you to communicate with the computer by entering data into it. Examples of commonly used input devices are a keyboard, mouse, and scanner. You will use an input device—the keyboard—to enter your C++ program instructions into the computer. An **output device** allows the computer to communicate with you by displaying or printing information. Examples of commonly used output devices are a monitor and printer. You will use an output device, a monitor, to display the results of your C++ programs; you will use a printer to print the results. **Auxiliary storage devices**, the third category of peripheral devices, are the devices that allow you to store information permanently. For example, after you enter the program instructions into the computer, you will typically use an auxiliary storage device to save the program so that you can use it again without retyping it. Floppy disk drives and hard disk drives are the two most common auxiliary storage devices. These storage devices use an auxiliary storage media—either a floppy disk or a hard disk—to store the information.

Now look inside the system unit to see what it contains. See Figure 1-2.

tip

Auxiliary (which means "additional" or "secondary") storage devices and auxiliary storage media are so named because they provide storage capability in addition to that available in the internal memory of the computer.

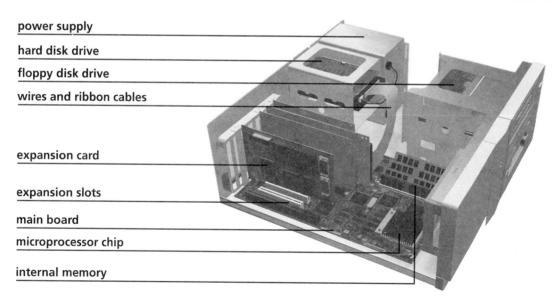

power supply

hard disk drive

floppy disk drive

wires and ribbon cables

expansion card

expansion slots

main board

microprocessor chip

internal memory

Figure 1-2: The inside of the system unit

The system unit houses an area called **internal memory**, which is simply an ordered sequence of memory cells contained on chips—integrated circuits residing on silicon. Internal memory is like a large post office, where each memory cell, like each post office box, has a unique address, and each can contain mail. Figure 1-3 illustrates this relationship.

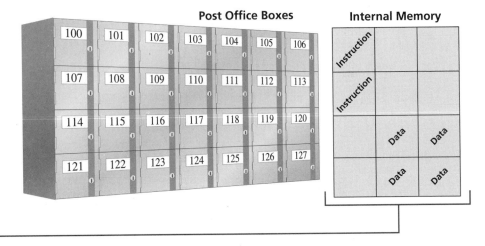

each memory cell has
a unique address

Figure 1-3: Comparison of post office boxes to internal memory

However, unlike a post office box, which can contain many pieces of mail at the same time, a memory cell can store only one piece of mail at any time. The mail found in a memory cell is typically either a program instruction or an item of data. **Data** refers to the information processed by a program. The data may be input by the user, such as the number of hours an employee worked, or it may be the result of a calculation made by the computer, such as an employee's gross pay.

Some of the chips in internal memory are **Random-Access Memory (RAM)** chips; others are **Read-Only Memory (ROM)** chips. Two major differences exist between a RAM chip and a ROM chip. First, while the computer is on, the user can both write information to and read information from the memory cells located on a RAM chip. In contrast, a user can only read information from a ROM chip's cells; he or she cannot write information to the memory cells on a ROM chip. Second, a RAM chip is volatile, which means that any information stored on a RAM chip is temporary; the information is lost when the computer is turned off or unexpectedly loses power. A ROM chip, on the other hand, is nonvolatile; instructions remain on a ROM chip even when the computer is not turned on.

The memory cells located on ROM chips contain instructions written there by the manufacturer. When you turn a computer on, these instructions perform an automatic self-test of the computer. The self-test makes sure that the different components of the computer are working properly. If all is well, the instructions contained on the ROM chips search either the computer's hard drive or a floppy drive for a set of instructions known as the operating system. The **operating system**, a collection of software programs, is the link between you and the computer; it manages the computer and its peripheral devices and allows both you and the computer to communicate with each other. Windows 95, DOS, OS/2, and UNIX are popular operating systems.

The instructions on the ROM chips direct the computer to read the operating system instructions from either the hard disk or a floppy disk. As the instructions are read, they are written to the RAM chips in internal memory, where they are stored until the computer is turned off (or loses power). When you use the keyboard to enter a program, or when the computer reads a program previously saved on a disk, the program instructions are also written to and stored on the RAM chips in internal memory. The RAM chips also store any data entered using the keyboard or read from a file stored on a disk.

In addition to internal memory, the system unit also houses the **Central Processing Unit (CPU)**, which is the brain of the computer. The CPU resides on a microprocessor chip, which is a single integrated circuit, and it contains two components—the control unit and the Arithmetic/Logic Unit (ALU). The **control unit** is like a traffic officer; it directs the flow of information from one part of the computer to another. The control unit is responsible for making sure that the computer correctly processes the program instructions and data stored in internal memory. The **Arithmetic/Logic Unit (ALU)**, on the other hand, performs the arithmetic calculations and logic operations for the computer. For example, if a program instructs the computer to add two numbers, the ALU performs the addition. The ALU is also the unit that makes comparisons. For example, if a program instructs the computer to compare an employee's hours with the number 40 to see if the employee should receive overtime pay, the ALU would perform this task. The ALU is also the unit that would compare two names—for example, "Smith" and "Jones"—to determine which name comes first alphabetically.

The hardware component of a computer system isn't of much use without software. Recall that the term *software* refers to the instructions that tell the computer how to perform a task. You have already learned about operating system software, which is essential for the computer's hardware to work properly. In addition to including the operating system software, a computer system typically includes application software.

Application software acts as an interface between the user and the system software. It allows the user to perform a specific task, such as typing a letter or creating a computer program. Included in application software are word processors, spreadsheets, databases, and graphics programs. Application software can also include programming languages, which you will learn about in the next section.

mini-quiz

Mini-Quiz 1

1. The two components of a microcomputer system are _____ and _____ .

2. The step-by-step instructions that tell the hardware how to perform a task are called _____ or _____ .

3. The three categories of peripheral devices are _____ , _____ , and _____ .

4. The information processed by a program is called _____ .

5. When you enter a program into the computer, the program is stored on _____ chips in internal memory.

6. The _____ , which is the brain of the computer, contains the ALU and the control unit.

7. Word processors and programming languages belong to a group of software called _____ software.

8. The _____ is a collection of programs (software) that manages the computer and its peripheral devices and allows both you and the computer to communicate with each other.

A Brief History of Programming Languages

Although computers appear to be amazingly intelligent machines, they cannot yet think on their own. Computers still rely on human beings to give them directions. These directions are called **programs**, and the people who write the programs are called **programmers**.

Just as human beings communicate with each other through the use of languages such as English, Spanish, Hindi, or Chinese, programmers use a variety of special languages, called **programming languages**, to communicate with the computer. Some popular programming languages are COBOL (Common Business Oriented Language), Pascal, C, BASIC (Beginner's All-Purpose Symbolic Instruction Code), Visual Basic, C++, and Visual C++. In the next sections, you will follow the progression of programming languages from machine languages to assembly languages, then to high-level procedure-oriented languages, and finally to object-oriented languages.

Machine Languages

A computer represents each character in its **character set**—the letters, numerals, and special symbols that can be entered into the computer—by a series of microscopic electronic switches. Like the light switches in your house, each electronic switch can be either on or off. Computers use the binary number system to represent the two switch states. Unlike the decimal number system, with which you are familiar, the **binary number system** uses only the digits 0 and 1, rather than the digits 0 through 9. A 0 indicates that the switch is off; a 1 indicates that it is on. Each character in the computer's character set is represented by a series of these off and on switches—in other words, by a series of 0s and 1s.

Each switch—each 0 and 1—is called a **bit**, which is short for *binary digit*. Most computers use eight switches—in other words, eight bits or binary digits—to represent each number, letter, or symbol. Which of the eight switches are on and which are off is determined both by the character being represented and by the coding scheme used by the computer. Microcomputers typically use a coding scheme called **ASCII** (pronounced *ASK-ee*), which stands for American Standard Code for Information Interchange. The letter X, for example, is represented in the ASCII coding scheme by the eight bits 01011000. The collection of eight bits used to represent a character is called a **byte**. Appendix A in this book shows the ASCII codes for the letters, numerals, and special symbols included in your computer's character set.

Because computers can understand only these on and off switches, the first programmers had to write the program instructions using nothing but combinations of 0s and 1s. Instructions written in 0s and 1s are called **machine language** or **machine code**. The machine languages (each type of machine has its own language) represent the only way to communicate directly with the computer. Figure 1-4 shows a program written in a machine language.

As you can imagine, programming in machine language is very tedious and error-prone; it also requires highly trained programmers.

```
0100
001101 100000 001101 110001
00101 10001 10000
01110
111001
111001 001 11000 001
11000
0011100
100010 00110
```

Figure 1-4: A program written in a machine language

Assembly Languages

Slightly more advanced programming languages are called **assembly languages**. Figure 1-5 shows a program written in an assembly language.

```
main proc pay
        mov ax, dseg
        mov ax, 0b00h
        add ax, dx
        mov al, bl
        mul bl, ax
        mov bl, 04h
```

Figure 1-5: A program written in an assembly language

The assembly languages simplify the programmer's job by allowing the programmer to use mnemonics in place of the 0s and 1s in the program. **Mnemonics** are memory aids—in this case, alphabetic abbreviations for instructions. For example, most assembly languages use the mnemonic ADD to represent an add operation and the mnemonic MUL to represent a multiply operation. The mnemonic MOV is used to move data from one area of memory to another. Programs written in an assembly language require an **assembler**, which is also a program, to convert the assembly instructions into machine code—the 0s and 1s the computer can understand. Although it is much easier to write programs in assembly language than in machine language, programming in assembly language still is tedious and requires highly trained programmers.

The next major development in programming languages was the introduction of the high-level languages. High-level languages are either procedure-oriented or object-oriented. The first high-level languages were procedure-oriented.

High-Level Procedure-Oriented Languages

High-level languages allow the programmer to use instructions that more closely resemble the English language. In **high-level procedure-oriented languages**, the emphasis of a program is on *how* to accomplish a task. The programmer must instruct the computer every step of the way, from the start of the task to its completion. The programmer determines and controls the order in which the computer should process the instructions. COBOL, BASIC, Pascal, and C are popular procedure-oriented languages.

Figure 1-6 shows a program written in BASIC. Notice how closely most of the instructions resemble the English language. Even if you do not know the BASIC language, it is easy to see that the program shown in Figure 1-6 tells the computer, step by step, *how* to compute and display an employee's net pay.

```
input "Enter name";names$
input "Enter hours";hours
input "Enter rate";rate
gross = hours * rate
f edtax = .2 * gross
socsec = .07 * gross
state = .06 * gross
net = gross—fedtax-socsec-state
print names$, net
end
```

Figure 1-6: A program written in BASIC—a high-level procedure-oriented language

Almost everyone, at one time or another, has used top-down design to create a solution to a problem. You probably used top-down design when you planned your last vacation. Your overall goal was to "take a vacation." In order to accomplish that goal, you divided the solution into small tasks, such as "choose vacation spot," "make hotel reservations," "make airline reservations," "call kennel," and so on.

Some high-level languages—for example, some versions of the BASIC language—use an interpreter to convert the English-like instructions into machine code. An **interpreter** translates the high-level instructions into machine code, line-by-line, as the program is running.

In all procedure-oriented programs, the order of the instructions is extremely important. For example, in the program shown in Figure 1-6, you could not put the instruction to display the net pay before the instruction to calculate the net pay and expect the computer to display the correct results. When writing programs in a procedure-oriented language, the programmer must determine not only the proper instructions to give the computer, but the correct sequence of those instructions as well. A programmer will typically use a design methodology called top-down design to assist him or her in planning a procedure-oriented program.

When using **top-down design** to create a procedure-oriented program, the programmer begins with a statement that describes the overall purpose or goal of the program—in other words, it describes what the program is supposed to do. The purpose of the payroll program shown in Figure 1-6, for example, is to determine the amount an employee should be paid. Notice that the program's purpose states *what* needs to be done, but it does not tell *how* to get it done. The programmer tells *how* to accomplish the program's purpose by dividing the solution into small, manageable tasks. The payroll program shown in Figure 1-6, for example, is broken up into small tasks that input the employee name, hours, and pay rate; calculate the gross pay; calculate the taxes; calculate the net pay; and display the employee name and net pay. These tasks describe how to reach the program's goal—in this case, determining how much to pay the employee. You will learn more about top-down design in Tutorial 2.

High-level procedure-oriented languages require a compiler to convert the English-like instructions into the 0s and 1s the computer can understand. Like assemblers, compilers are separate programs. A **compiler** translates the entire program into machine code before running the program.

High-level procedure-oriented languages are a vast improvement over the low-level machine and assembly languages. Some of the high-level procedure-oriented languages—for example, the BASIC language—do not require a great amount of technical expertise to write simple programs.

Object-Oriented Languages

Recently, more advanced high-level languages, referred to as object-oriented languages, have become popular. C++ and Visual Basic are two popular object-oriented languages. Unlike procedure-oriented languages, which view a problem solution simply as a set of ordered steps, **object-oriented languages** view a problem solution as a set of interacting objects. A programmer typically uses a design methodology called **object-oriented design (OOD)** to assist him or her in planning an object-oriented program. As with top-down design, the programmer begins with a statement that describes the purpose of the program. Rather than breaking up the program into one or more tasks, the programmer divides the program into one or more objects, resulting in programs whose code is very different from those created using the procedure-oriented approach.

The objects in an object-oriented program can take on many different forms. For example, the menus, option buttons, and command buttons included in many Windows programs are objects. An object can also represent something encountered in real-life. For example, a payroll program may include objects such as a time card object, an employee object, and a date object. The partial program shown in Figure 1-7 shows how you can use the C++ language to create a date object named payDay.

```
class date                                        //defines what a date object looks like
{
public:
        void changeDate(int month, int day, int year);   //changes the month, day, and year
        void displayDate( );                      //displays the month, day, and year
private:
        int month;                                //a date object contains a month,
        int day;                                  //a day, and a year
        int year;
};

date payDay;                                      //creates a date object named payDay
```

Figure 1-7: A partial program written in C++—an object-oriented language

All but the last instruction shown in Figure 1-7 simply describe what a date object looks like. You describe an object by specifying its characteristics and behaviors. In this case, a date object is composed of a month, day, and year. The date object's month, day, and year can be both changed and displayed. The last instruction shown in Figure 1-7—date payDay;—uses the object's description to create the object named payDay. (You will learn more about objects and object-oriented programming later in this lesson.)

The object-oriented languages offer two advantages over the procedure-oriented languages. First, object-oriented languages allow a programmer to use familiar objects to solve problems. The ability to use objects that model things found in the real world makes problem solving much easier. Assume, for example, that your task is to create a program that handles the checking account transactions for a bank. Thinking in terms of the objects used by the bank—checking accounts, withdrawal slips, deposit slips, and so on—will make this problem easier to solve. Second, because each object is viewed as an independent unit, an object can be used in more than one application, with either little or no modification; this saves programming time and money. For example, you can use the date object shown in Figure 1-7 in any program that requires a date. In a personnel program, for instance, you could use a date object to represent a hire date. In an airline reservation program, on the other hand, a date object might represent a departure date.

Many object-oriented languages, such as C++ and Visual Basic, are direct descendants of existing procedure-oriented languages. The C++ language, for example, is a superset of the procedure-oriented C language; the procedure-oriented predecessor of Visual Basic is the QBasic language. Because both C++ and Visual Basic are based on procedure-oriented languages, you can use either C++ or Visual Basic to create not only object-oriented programs, but procedure-oriented programs as well.

tip

· · · · · · · · · · · · ·

Many object-oriented languages, like C++ and Visual Basic, are referred to as hybrid languages because you can use them to create either procedure-oriented or object-oriented programs.

mini-quiz

Mini-Quiz 2

1. The collection of letters, numerals, and symbols that you can enter into a computer is called the computer's _____ .

2. Instructions written in 0s and 1s are called _____ languages.

3. _____ languages allow a programmer to use mnemonics in place of the 0s and 1s in a program.

4. In _____ languages, the emphasis of a program is on how to accomplish a task.

5. In _____ languages, the programmer breaks up a problem into interacting objects.

6. When designing programs, procedure-oriented languages use a design methodology called _____ , whereas object-oriented languages use a design methodology called _____ .

Like procedure-oriented languages, object-oriented languages need a compiler to translate the high-level instructions into machine code.

As you can see, programming languages have come a long way since the first machine languages. What hasn't changed about programming languages, however, are the three basic control structures used by programmers: sequence, selection, and repetition. These structures are referred to as **control structures** because they control the flow of the program—in other words, the order in which the program instructions are processed. You will learn about these three structures in Lesson B. Before doing so, however, learn about the terminology used by object-oriented programmers.

OOP Terminology

Although you may have either heard or read that object-oriented languages are difficult to learn, don't be intimidated. Admittedly, creating object-oriented programs does take practice, but most of the concepts upon which object-oriented programming is based are concepts with which you are already familiar. Much of the fear of object-oriented programming stems from the terminology used when discussing it. Many of the terms are unfamiliar because they are not used, typically, in everyday conversations. This section will help to familiarize you with the terms used in discussions about object-oriented programming. Don't be concerned if you don't understand everything right away; you will see further explanations and examples of these terms in OOP Concept boxes throughout this book.

When discussing object-oriented programs, you will hear programmers use the terms OOP (pronounced like *loop*) and OOD (pronounced like *mood*). **OOP** is an acronym for object-oriented programming and simply means that you are using an object-oriented language to create a program that contains one or more objects. **OOD**, on the other hand, is an acronym for object-oriented design. Like top-down design, which is used to plan procedure-oriented programs, OOD is also a design methodology; but it is used to plan object-oriented programs. Unlike top-down design, which breaks up a problem into one or more tasks, OOD divides a problem into one or more objects.

An **object** is anything that can be seen or touched. You deal with objects every day. This book, for example, is an object, and so is your car. The advantage of using an object-oriented language is that it allows the programmer to use familiar objects, such as a book and a car, to solve problems. You can use a book, for example, to learn C++; you can use a car to get to school.

Every object has attributes and behaviors. The **attributes**, also called **data**, are the characteristics that describe the object. For example, when you tell someone that your car is a red Pontiac Firebird, you are describing the car (an object) in terms of some of its attributes—in this case, its color, manufacturer, and model type. Your car also has many other attributes, such as a steering wheel, tires, an engine, and so on. An object's **behaviors**, on the other hand, are the operations (actions) that the object can either perform or have performed on it. Your car, for example, can accelerate and brake; it can also be steered and have its oil changed.

You will also hear the term "class" in OOP discussions. A **class** is simply a pattern or blueprint for creating an object. A class contains all of the attributes and behaviors that describe the object. The object that you create from a class is referred to as an **instance** of the class. Notice that a class is not an object; an instance of a class, however, *is* an object. The blueprint that the manufacturer used to create your car is a class; your car, as well as any other car that is made from that blueprint, is an instance of the class—an object. Here is another analogy that may help to differentiate between a class and an instance of a class: think of a class as being similar to a cookie-cutter, and an instance of a class (an object) as being similar to a cookie that is made using the cookie-cutter.

Human beings typically don't use the word "encapsulation" in everyday conversations. "Encapsulation" is a derivative of the word "encapsulate," which means "to enclose in a capsule." **Encapsulation** in the context of OOP refers to the combining of an object's attributes and behaviors into one package—a class. The manufacturer of your car, for example, encapsulated the car's attributes (color, manufacturer, model type, steering wheel, tires, engine, and so on) and behaviors (accelerate, brake, steer, tune-up, and so on) into one package—a blueprint of your car.

Another OOP term that is not used much in everyday conversations is "abstraction." **Abstraction** refers to the hiding of the internal details of an object from the user which helps prevent the user from making inadvertent changes to the object. Car manufacturers, for example, hide much of a car's internal details—engine, spark plugs, and so on—under the hood. Also hidden from the driver is how the transmission takes rotary motion from the engine and converts it to forward motion of the wheels. Attributes and behaviors that are not **hidden** are said to be **exposed** to the user. For example, a car's steering wheel, gas pedal, and brake pedal are exposed to the driver. The idea behind abstraction is to expose to the user only those attributes and behaviors that are necessary to use the object, and to hide everything else.

Another OOP term, **inheritance**, refers to the fact that you can create one class from another class. The new class, called the **derived class**, inherits the attributes and behaviors of the original class, called the **base class**. For example, your car's manufacturer might create a blueprint of a 1999 Firebird from a blueprint of a 1998 Firebird. The 1999 blueprint (the derived class) would inherit all of the attributes and behaviors of the 1998 blueprint (the base class), but it could be modified to fit the new design for the 1999 Firebird. For example, the blueprint for a 1999 Firebird may contain an additional option—for instance, a passenger-side air bag—that may not be included in the 1998 blueprint. Figure 1-8 uses the car example to illustrate most of the OOP terms discussed in this section.

base class

A car's attributes and behaviors are encapsulated into the blueprint. Some attributes and behaviors are hidden; some are exposed.

derived class inherits properties of base class

objects—instances of a class

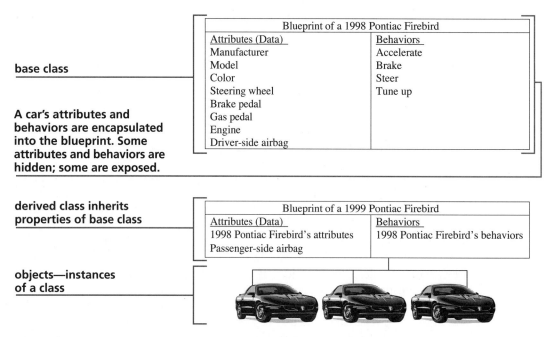

Blueprint of a 1998 Pontiac Firebird	
Attributes (Data)	Behaviors
Manufacturer	Accelerate
Model	Brake
Color	Steer
Steering wheel	Tune up
Brake pedal	
Gas pedal	
Engine	
Driver-side airbag	

Blueprint of a 1999 Pontiac Firebird	
Attributes (Data)	Behaviors
1998 Pontiac Firebird's attributes	1998 Pontiac Firebird's behaviors
Passenger-side airbag	

Figure 1-8: Illustration of OOP terms

You have now completed Lesson A. You can either take a break or complete the end-of-lesson questions and exercises.

SUMMARY

The first microcomputers, also called personal computers, appeared in the market-place in 1977. Microcomputers can now be found in almost every home and business. A microcomputer system contains both hardware and software. Hardware refers to the physical components of the system, and consists of the system unit, input devices, output devices, and peripheral devices. The system unit contains internal memory, which is composed of both RAM and ROM chips. The system unit also contains the Central Processing Unit (CPU).

Software refers to the step-by-step instructions, called programs, that tell the hardware how to perform a task. Operating system software and application software are two categories of software. The operating system software manages the computer and its peripheral devices and allows both you and the computer to communicate with each other. Application software, which includes word processors, spreadsheets, databases, graphics programs, and programming languages, allows the user to perform a task.

A computer represents each character in its character set—the letters, numerals, and special symbols that can be entered into the computer—by a series of microscopic electronic switches that can be either on or off. Computers use the binary number system to represent the two switch states. The binary number system uses the digit 0 to indicate that a switch is off; it uses a 1 to indicate that the switch is on.

Each switch—each 0 and 1—is called a bit, which is short for *binary digit*. Most computers use eight bits, referred to as a byte, to represent each number, letter, or symbol. Which of the eight bits are on and which are off is determined both by the character being represented and by the coding scheme used by the computer. Microcomputers typically use a coding scheme called ASCII (pronounced ASK-ee), which stands for American Standard Code for Information Interchange.

Programs are the step-by-step instructions that tell a computer how to perform a task. Programmers, the people who write computer programs, use various programming languages to communicate with the computer. The first programming languages were machine languages, also called machine code. Machine languages use combinations of 0s and 1s to communicate directly with the computer. Slightly more advanced programming languages, called assembly languages, allow the programmer to use mnemonics in place of the 0s and 1s in the program. Programs written in an assembly language require an assembler, which is also a program, to convert the assembly instructions into machine code. The next major development in programming languages was the introduction of the high-level languages, which allow the programmer to use instructions that more closely resemble the English language. High-level languages require a separate program, called a compiler, to convert the English-like instructions into the 0s and 1s the computer can understand. The first high-level languages were procedure-oriented. In high-level procedure-oriented languages, the emphasis of a program is on *how* to accomplish a task. When planning a procedure-oriented program, programmers typically employ a design methodology referred to as top-down design. Recently, more advanced high-level languages, referred to as object-oriented languages, have become popular. Object-oriented languages allow the programmer to write computer programs using objects that model things found in the real world. The design methodology employed when creating object-oriented programs is called object-oriented design (OOD). Many object-oriented languages, such as C++ and Visual Basic, are direct descendents of existing procedure-oriented languages.

Most of the concepts upon which object-oriented programming is based are concepts with which you are already familiar; only the terminology may be unfamiliar to you. For example, OOP (pronounced like *loop*) is an acronym for object-oriented programming and simply means that you are using an object-oriented language to create a program that contains one or more objects. OOD (pronounced like *mood*) is an acronym for object-oriented design—the design methodology that divides a problem into one or more objects. A class is simply a pattern or blueprint for creating an object—referred to as an instance of the class. Every object has attributes and behaviors. In the context of OOP, a class encapsulates the attributes and behaviors of an object. Some of the attributes and behaviors are hidden from the user, while others are exposed. The hiding of the internal details of an object from a user is referred to as abstraction.

Another OOP term, inheritance, refers to the fact that you can create one class from another class. The new class, called the derived class, inherits the attributes and behaviors of the original class, called the base class.

ANSWERS TO MINI-QUIZZES

Mini-Quiz 1

1. hardware, software **2.** software, programs **3.** input devices, output devices, auxiliary storage devices **4.** data **5.** RAM **6.** CPU **7.** application **8.** operating system

Mini-Quiz 2

1. character set **2.** machine **3.** Assembly **4.** high-level procedure-oriented **5.** object-oriented **6.** top-down design, object-oriented design

QUESTIONS

1. The ability of an employee to work from home and use a microcomputer to communicate with his or her office is called _____ .
    a. homecomputing
    b. microconferencing
    c. microcommuting
    d. telecommuting
    e. teleworking

2. Which of the following is not a peripheral device?
    a. auxiliary storage device
    b. input device
    c. output device
    d. system unit
    e. all of the above are peripheral devices

3. _____ are devices that allow you to store information permanently.
    a. Auxiliary storage devices
    b. Input devices
    c. Internal memory devices
    d. Output devices
    e. RAM chips

4. The hardware in a microcomputer system consists of _____ .
    a. auxiliary storage devices
    b. input devices
    c. output devices
    d. a system unit
    e. all of the above

5. A computer's system unit contains _____ .
    a. the ALU
    b. the control unit
    c. internal memory
    d. all of the above

6. A storage cell in the internal memory of a computer can store _____ at a time.
    a. one instruction
    b. one piece of data
    c. two or more instructions
    d. two or more pieces of data
    e. either a or b

7. While the computer is on, you can both write information to and read information from a storage cell located on _____ .
   a. a RAM chip
   b. a ROM chip
   c. either a RAM chip or a ROM chip

8. While the computer is on, you can read information from _____ .
   a. a RAM chip
   b. a ROM chip
   c. either a RAM chip or a ROM chip

9. You cannot write information to _____ .
   a. a RAM chip
   b. a ROM chip
   c. either a RAM chip or a ROM chip

10. If the computer loses power, the information stored on _____ is lost.
    a. the RAM chips
    b. the ROM chips
    c. both the RAM and ROM chips

11. If the computer loses power, the information stored on _____ remains in internal memory.
    a. the RAM chips
    b. the ROM chips
    c. both the RAM and ROM chips

12. _____ are volatile.
    a. RAM chips
    b. ROM chips
    c. Both RAM and ROM chips

13. The _____ chips contain the instructions that perform a self-test of the computer, and also load the operating system program.
    a. RAM
    b. ROM

14. _____ software is a collection of programs that manage the computer and its peripheral devices.
    a. Application
    b. Internal memory
    c. Operating system
    d. RAM
    e. ROM

15. Which of the following is an example of an operating system?
    a. DOS
    b. UNIX
    c. Windows 95
    d. OS/2
    e. All of the above are examples of an operating system.

16. The _____ , which is the brain of the computer, resides on a microprocessor chip.
    a. ALU
    b. control unit
    c. CPU
    d. internal memory unit
    e. ROM chip

17. The _____ is responsible for making sure that the program instructions, which are stored in internal memory, are processed correctly.
a. ALU
b. control unit
c. CPU
d. internal memory unit
e. RAM chip

18. The _____ performs the arithmetic calculations and logic operations for the computer.
a. ALU
b. control unit
c. CPU
d. internal memory unit
e. ROM chip

19. Which of the following is not an example of application software?
a. database
b. spreadsheet
c. word processor
d. operating system
e. programming language

20. The set of step-by-step directions given to a computer is called _____ .
a. computerese
b. commands
c. a collection
d. a program
e. rules

21. In the binary number system, only the digits _____ are used to represent the characters in a computer's character set.
a. 0 and 1
b. 0, 1, and 2
c. 1 and 2
d. 1, 2, and 3
e. 0, 1, 2, and 3

22. Using the binary number system, a _____ indicates that a switch is off.
a. 0
b. 1
c. 2
d. 3

23. Each 0 and 1 in memory is called a _____ .
a. bit
b. byte
c. character
d. number

24. Using the ASCII coding scheme, how many bits are in a byte?
a. 1
b. 2
c. 4
d. 8

25. _____ , which are used in assembly languages, are alphabetic abbreviations for instructions.
    a. Abbreviators
    b. Identifiers
    c. Machine coders
    d. Mnemonics
    e. Procedures

26. _____ languages allow the programmer to use instructions that more closely resemble the English language.
    a. Assembly
    b. High-level
    c. Low-level
    d. Machine

27. A(n) _____ is a program that translates high-level instructions into machine code.
    a. assembler
    b. compiler
    c. source program
    d. translator

28. A(n) _____ is a program that converts assembly instructions into machine code.
    a. assembler
    b. compiler
    c. interpreter
    d. program
    e. translator

29. In object-oriented languages, the emphasis of a program is on *how* to accomplish a task.
    a. True
    b. False

30. When planning a procedure-oriented program, programmers typically employ a design methodology referred to as _____ design.
    a. object-oriented
    b. procedure-oriented
    c. top-down
    d. vertical

31. When planning an object-oriented program, programmers typically employ a design methodology referred to as _____ design.
    a. object-oriented
    b. procedure-oriented
    c. top-down
    d. vertical

32. Many object-oriented languages are based on existing procedure-oriented languages.
    a. True
    b. False

33. Which of the following is not an attribute that can be used to describe a human being?
    a. brown eyes
    b. female
    c. red hair
    d. talk
    e. thin

34. A(n) _____ is a pattern or blueprint.
   a. attribute
   b. behavior
   c. class
   d. instance
   e. object

35. The object that you create from a class is called a(n) _____ .
   a. abstraction
   b. attribute
   c. instance
   d. procedure
   e. subclass

36. In the context of OOP, the combining of an object's attributes and behaviors into one package is called _____ .
   a. abstraction
   b. combining
   c. encapsulation
   d. exposition
   e. inheritance

37. In the context of OOP, the hiding of the internal details of an object from the user is called _____ .
   a. abstraction
   b. combining
   c. encapsulation
   d. exposition
   e. inheritance

38. Alcon Toys manufacturers several versions of a basic doll. Assume that the basic doll is called Model A and the versions are called Models B, C, and D. In the context of OOP, the Model A doll is called the _____ class; the other dolls are called the _____ class.
   a. base, derived
   b. base, inherited
   c. derived, base
   d. exposed, hidden
   e. inherited, derived

39. In the context of OOP, _____ refers to the fact that you can create one class from another class.
   a. abstraction
   b. combining
   c. encapsulation
   d. exposition
   e. inheritance

E X E R C I S E S

1. Briefly explain the history of programming languages as outlined in Lesson A.

2. Make a list of your computer system's input devices, output devices, and auxiliary storage devices. Which operating system is your computer using?

3. Appendix A in this book lists the ASCII codes for the letters, numerals, and special symbols included in a computer's character set. On a piece of paper, write down the ASCII codes for the ampersand (&), the letter S, and the letter s.

4. Explain the difference between top-down design and object-oriented design.

5. List and explain two advantages of using object-oriented languages.

Exercises 6 through 10 are Discovery exercises, which allow you both to "discover" the solutions to problems on your own and to experiment with material that is not covered in the tutorial.

discovery ▶ 6. Research the C++ programming language. Where did it originate? Who developed it? What is the meaning of the two plus signs in the C++ name? (You can use either the Internet or the library to do your research.) Write a one or two paragraph summary of your research.

discovery ▶ 7. Use Figure 1-9 to answer the following questions.
   a. What are the attributes (data) associated with a dog class?
   b. What are the behaviors associated with a dog class?
   c. How many instances (objects) of the dog class are shown in Figure 1-9?
   d. Use the information in Figure 1-9 to explain the term *encapsulation*.

Figure 1-9

discovery ▶ 8. Use Figure 1-10 to answer the following questions.
   a. What are the attributes and behaviors associated with a customer class?
   b. Recall that inheritance refers to the fact that you can create one class from another class. The original class is called the base class; the new class is called the derived class. In Figure 1-10, which is the base class and which are the derived classes?
   c. What are the attributes and behaviors of the savings account class? How do these differ from those of a customer class?
   d. Recall that abstraction is the hiding of the internal workings of an object from the user. In the customer class shown in Figure 1-10, what is hidden from the user? What is exposed?
   e. How many instances of the savings account class are shown in Figure 1-10?
   f. Use the information in Figure 1-10 to explain the term *encapsulation*.

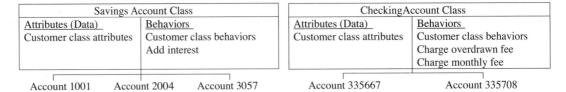

Figure 1-10

discovery ▶ 9. Lesson A's Figure 1-7 shows how you could define the attributes and behaviors for a date class, and also how you could create a date object named `payDay`. Using Figure 1-7 as a guide, define a time class that contains an hour, minute, and second. The time class should allow the user to both set and print the time. After defining the time class, create a time object called `appointmentTime`.

discovery ▶ 10. Research both the decimal number system and the binary number system. Explain how both systems work. For example, why do the digits 10100 represent a different number in each system? What number do those digits represent in each system? How can you convert a binary number to its decimal equivalent? How can you convert a decimal number to its binary equivalent? Write a one-page paper on your findings.

An Introduction to Control Structures

Defining Control Structures

All computer programs, no matter how simple or how complex, are written using one or more of three basic structures: sequence, selection, and repetition. These structures are called **control structures** or **logic structures** because they control the flow of a program's logic. You will use the sequence structure in every program you write. In most programs, you also will use both the selection and repetition structures.

This lesson will give you an introduction to the three control structures used in computer programs. It will also introduce you to a mechanical man named Rob, who will help illustrate the control structures. More detailed information about each structure, as well as how to implement these structures using the C++ language, is provided in subsequent tutorials. Begin by learning about the sequence structure.

The Sequence Structure

You are already familiar with the sequence structure as you use it each time you follow a set of directions, in order, from beginning to end. A cookie recipe, for example, is a good example of the sequence structure. To get to the finished product—edible cookies—you need to follow each instruction in order, beginning with the first instruction and ending with the last. Likewise, the **sequence structure** in a computer program directs the computer to process the instructions, one after another, in the order listed in the program. You will find the sequence structure in every program.

You can observe how the sequence structure works by programming a mechanical man named Rob. Like a computer, Rob has a limited instruction set—in other words, Rob can understand only a specific number of instructions, also called commands. Rob's instruction set includes the following three commands: `walk`, `turn`, and `sit`. When told to `walk`, Rob takes one complete step forward; in other words, Rob moves his right foot forward one step, then moves his left foot to meet his right foot. When told to `turn`, Rob turns 180 degrees, which is half of a full turn of 360 degrees. When told to `sit`, Rob simply sits down.

Assume that Rob is facing a chair that is two steps away from him. Your task is to write the instructions, using only the commands that Rob understands, that will direct Rob to sit in the chair. Figure 1-11 shows Rob, the chair, and the instructions that will get Rob seated in the chair.

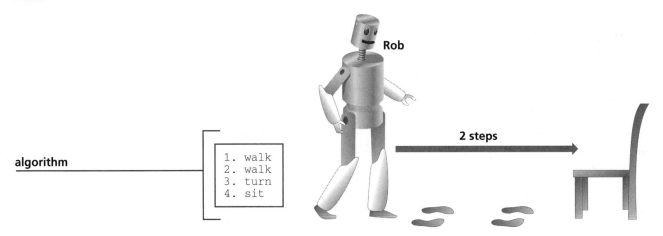

Figure 1-11: An example of the sequence structure

The four instructions shown in Figure 1-11 are called an algorithm. An **algorithm** is simply the step-by-step instructions that accomplish a task. Figure 1-11's algorithm, for example, contains the instructions that are necessary to get Rob seated in the chair. Notice that it is important that Rob follow the instructions in the list in order—in other words, in sequence. Rob must first walk two times, then turn, and then sit; he cannot turn first, then walk two times, and then sit.

Learn about the repetition structure next.

Mini-Quiz 3

1. The three basic control structures are _____ , _____ and _____ .

2. All programs contain the _____ structure.

3. When using the _____ structure, instructions are followed in the order that they appear in the program.

4. The step-by-step instructions that accomplish a task are called a(n) _____ .

The Repetition Structure

As with the sequence structure, you are already familiar with the repetition structure. For example, shampoo bottles typically include the repetition structure in the directions for washing your hair. Those directions usually tell you to repeat both the lathering and rinsing steps until your hair is clean. When used in a program, the **repetition structure** also directs the computer to repeat one or more instructions until some condition is met.

You can observe how the repetition structure works by programming Rob, the mechanical man. In this example, Rob is facing a chair that is 50 steps away from him. Your task is to write the algorithm that will sit Rob in the chair. If the only available control structure was the sequence structure, you would need to write the `walk` instruction 50 times, followed by `turn`, then `sit`. Although that algorithm would work, it is quite cumbersome to write. Imagine if Rob were 500 steps away from the chair! The best way to write the algorithm to get Rob seated in a chair that is 50 steps away from him is to use the repetition structure. To do

tip

▶ The repetition structure is also referred to as **iteration**.

so, however, you will need to add another instruction to Rob's instruction set: in addition to `walk`, `turn`, and `sit`, Rob can now understand the command `repeat x times`, where `x` is the number of times you want him to repeat something. The illustration of Rob and the chair, along with the correct algorithm, are shown in Figure 1-12.

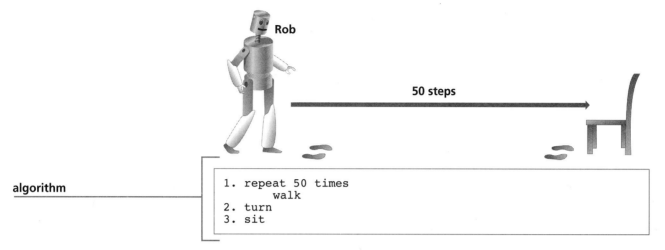

Figure 1-12: An example of the repetition structure

Rather than writing the `walk` instruction 50 times, this algorithm uses the `repeat x times` instruction to direct Rob to walk 50 times before he turns and then sits. Notice that this algorithm is both easier to write and much clearer than one containing 50 `walk` instructions. Also notice that the algorithm uses both the sequence and repetition structures.

Recall that the repetition structure repeats one or more instructions until some condition is met, at which time the repetition structure ends. In the example shown in Figure 1-12, the repetition structure ends after Rob walks 50 times. Rob is then free to continue on to the next instruction in the algorithm—in this case, `turn`, followed by `sit`. But what if you don't know precisely how many steps there are between Rob and the chair? In that case, you simply need to change the condition.

In this example, assume that Rob is facing a chair that is zero or more steps away from him. As before, your task is to write the algorithm that will get Rob seated in the chair. In order to accomplish this task, you will need to add another instruction to Rob's instruction set: Rob can now understand the instruction `repeat until you are directly in front of the chair`. The new algorithm is shown in Figure 1-13.

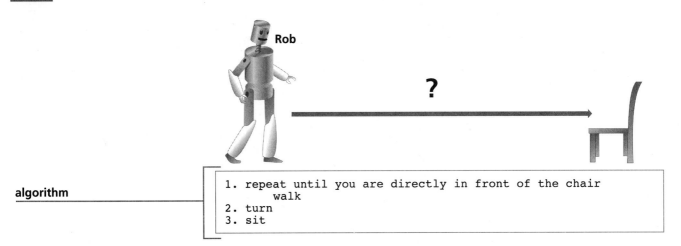

algorithm

```
1. repeat until you are directly in front of the chair
        walk
2. turn
3. sit
```

Figure 1-13: Another example of the repetition structure

The repetition structure shown in Figure 1-13's algorithm ends when Rob is standing directly in front of the chair. If Rob is ten steps away from the chair, the repetition structure directs him to walk ten times before he turns and then sits. If Rob is 500 steps away from the chair, the repetition structure directs him to walk 500 times before he turns and then sits. If Rob is directly in front of the chair, the repetition structure is bypassed, and Rob simply turns and then sits.

The last of the three control structures is the selection structure.

The Selection Structure

Like the sequence and repetition structures, you are already familiar with the **selection structure**, also called the **decision structure**. The selection structure makes a decision, and then takes an appropriate action based on that decision. You use the selection structure every time you drive your car and approach an intersection. Your decision, as well as the appropriate action, is based on whether the intersection has a stop sign. If the intersection has a stop sign, then you stop your car; otherwise, you proceed with caution through the intersection. When used in a computer program, the selection structure alerts the computer that a decision needs to be made. The selection structure also provides the appropriate action to take based on the result of that decision.

As before, Rob can demonstrate the selection structure, although you will need to add to his instruction set to do so. Assume that Rob is holding either a red or yellow balloon, and that he is facing two boxes. One of the boxes is colored yellow and the other is colored red. The two boxes are located 20 steps away from Rob. Your task is to have Rob drop the balloon into the appropriate box—a yellow balloon belongs in the yellow box, and a red balloon belongs in the red box. After Rob drops the balloon, you should then return him to his original position. To write an algorithm to accomplish the current task, you will need to add four more instructions to Rob's instruction set. The new instructions will allow Rob to make a decision about the color of the balloon he is holding, and then take the appropriate action based on that decision. Rob's new instruction set is shown in Figure 1-14.

```
walk
turn
sit
repeat x times
repeat until you are directly in front of the chair
if the balloon is red, do this:
otherwise, do this: (This instruction can be used only in combination with an if instruction)
drop the balloon in the red box
drop the balloon in the yellow box
```

four new instructions

Figure 1-14: Rob's new instruction set

Figure 1-15 shows an illustration of this example, along with the correct algorithm.

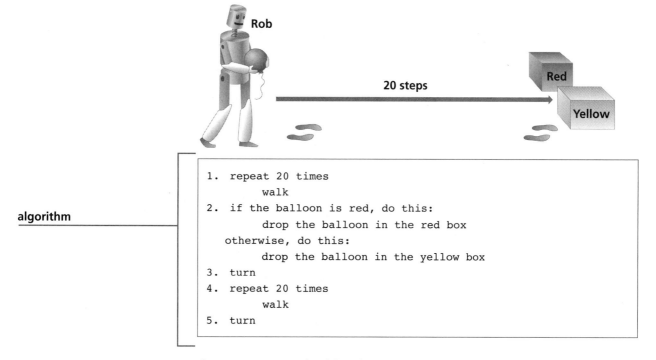

algorithm

```
1. repeat 20 times
       walk
2. if the balloon is red, do this:
       drop the balloon in the red box
   otherwise, do this:
       drop the balloon in the yellow box
3. turn
4. repeat 20 times
       walk
5. turn
```

Figure 1-15: An example of the selection structure

Notice that this algorithm contains all three control structures: sequence, selection, and repetition. The repetition structure, which directs Rob to walk 20 times, is processed first. After Rob walks the 20 steps, the repetition structure ends and Rob proceeds, sequentially, to the next instruction listed in the algorithm; that instruction involves a decision. If the balloon Rob is holding is red, then Rob should drop it into the red box; otherwise, he should drop it into the yellow box. Once the decision is made and the proper action is taken, the selection structure ends and Rob proceeds to the next instruction listed in the algorithm—turn. After turning 180 degrees, the second repetition structure, which directs Rob to walk 20 times, and the last instruction, which turns Rob around 180 degrees, returns Rob to his original position.

You have now completed Lesson B. You can either take a break or complete the end-of-lesson questions and exercises. The exercises at the end of this lesson will give you additional practice with the sequence, selection, and repetition structures.

Mini-Quiz 4

1. You use the _____ structure to repeat one or more instructions in a program.
2. The _____ structure ends when its condition has been met.
3. The _____ structure, also called the decision structure, instructs the computer to make a decision, and then take some action based on the result of the decision.

S U M M A R Y

The algorithms for all computer programs contain one or more of the following three control structures: sequence, selection, and repetition. An algorithm is the step-by-step instructions that solve a problem. The control structures, also called logic structures, are so named because they control the flow of a program's logic.

The sequence structure directs the computer to process the instructions, one after another, in the order listed in the program. The repetition structure directs the computer to repeat one or more instructions until some condition is met. The selection structure, also called the decision structure, directs the computer to make a decision, and then select an appropriate action to take based on that decision. The sequence structure is used in all programs. Most programs also contain both the selection and repetition structures.

A N S W E R S   T O   M I N I - Q U I Z Z E S

Mini-Quiz 3

1. sequence, selection, repetition **2.** sequence **3.** sequence **4.** algorithm

Mini-Quiz 4

1. repetition **2.** repetition **3.** selection

Q U E S T I O N S

1. Which of the following is not a programming control structure?
   a. repetition
   b. selection
   c. sequence
   d. sorting

2. Which of the following control structures is used in every program?
   a. repetition
   b. selection
   c. sequence
   d. switching

3. The set of instructions for how to tie a bow is an example of the _____ structure.
   a. control
   b. repetition
   c. selection
   d. sequence
   e. switching

4. The step-by-step instructions that solve a problem are called _____ .
   a. an algorithm
   b. a list
   c. a plan
   d. a sequential structure

5. The recipe instruction "Beat until smooth" is an example of the _____ structure.
   a. control
   b. repetition
   c. selection
   d. sequence
   e. switching

6. The instruction "If it's raining outside, then take an umbrella to work" is an example of the _____ structure.
   a. control
   b. repetition
   c. selection
   d. sequence
   e. switching

E X E R C I S E S

You will use Rob, the mechanical man, to do Exercises 1 through 7. Rob's instruction set is shown in Figure 1-16.

```
walk        (Rob moves his right foot forward one step, then moves his left foot to meet his right foot)
stand
sit
turn        (180-degree turn)
jump        (allows Rob to jump over anything in his path)
fly         (allows Rob to fly over anything in his path)
drop the toy in the box
pick up the flower with your right hand
pick up the flower with your left hand
pick up the ball
fix the chair
if the box is red, do this:
if the flower is red, do this:
if the chair is broken, do this:
if the box is not full, do this:
otherwise, do this:  (This instruction can be used only in combination with an if instruction)
repeat x times
repeat until you are directly in front of the chair
repeat until you are directly in front of the box
```

Figure 1-16

1. Rob is five steps away from a box, and the box is 10 steps away from a chair, as illustrated in Figure 1-17. Create an algorithm, using only the instructions shown in Figure 1-16, that will sit Rob in the chair. Assume that Rob must jump over the box before he can continue toward the chair.

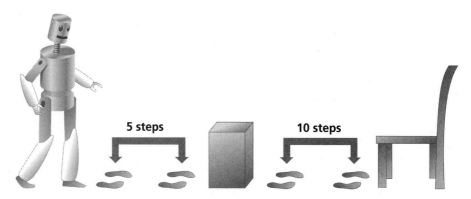

5 steps   **10 steps**

Figure 1-17

2. Rob is five steps away from a box, and the box is 10 steps away from a chair, as illustrated in Figure 1-17. Create an algorithm, using only the instructions shown in Figure 1-16, that will sit Rob in the chair. Assume that Rob will need to jump over the box if the box is red; otherwise he will need to fly over the box.

3. Rob is standing in front of a flowerbed that contains six flowers, as illustrated in Figure 1-18. Create an algorithm, using only the instructions shown in Figure 1-16, that will direct Rob to pick the flowers as he walks to the other side of the flower bed. Rob should pick all red flowers with his right hand; flowers that are not red should be picked with his left hand.

Rob should end up on the other side of the flower bed

Figure 1-18

4. Rob is seated in a chair and is four steps away from a table. A ball is resting on the top of the table, as illustrated in Figure 1-19. Create an algorithm, using only the instructions shown in Figure 1-16, that will direct Rob to pick up the ball, and then return him to his original position.

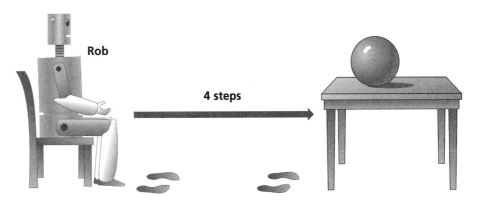

Rob

4 steps

Figure 1-19

5. Rob is facing a box that is located zero or more steps away from him. Rob is carrying a toy in his right hand. Create an algorithm, using only the instructions shown in Figure 1-16, that will direct Rob to drop the toy in the box.

6. Rob is facing a chair that is located zero or more steps away from him. Create an algorithm, using only the instructions shown in Figure 1-16, that will sit Rob in the chair, but only if the chair is not broken. If the chair is broken, the algorithm should instruct Rob to fix the chair before he sits down in it.

7. Rob, who is seated in a chair, is facing a box that is zero or more steps away from him. Rob is holding a toy in his left hand. Create an algorithm, using only the instructions

shown in Figure 1-16, that will direct Rob to drop the toy in the box—but only if the box is not full. The algorithm should also return Rob to his original position.

8. Using only the instructions shown in Figure 1-20, create an algorithm that shows the steps an instructor takes when grading a test that contains 25 questions.

```
if the student's answer is not the same as the correct answer, do this:
repeat 25 times
read the student's answer and the correct answer
mark the student's answer incorrect
```

Figure 1-20

9. You have just purchased a new microcomputer system. Before putting the system components together, you read the instruction booklet that came with the system. The booklet contains a list of the components that you should have received. The booklet advises you to verify that you received all of the components by matching those that you received with those on the list. If a component was received, you should cross its name off the list; otherwise, you should draw a circle around the component's name in the list. Using only the instructions shown in Figure 1-21, create an algorithm that shows the steps you should take to verify that a package contains the correct components.

```
cross the component name off the list
read the component name from the list
circle the component's name on the list
search the package for the component
if the component was received, do this:
otherwise, do this:   (This instruction can be used only in combination with an if instruction)
repeat for each component name on the list
```

Figure 1-21

discovery ▶ 10. Create an algorithm that shows the steps you take to eat a sandwich.

discovery ▶ 11. Create an algorithm that directs a payroll clerk how to calculate and print the net pay for five workers. If an employee works more than 40 hours, he or she should receive time and one-half for the hours over 40.

discovery ▶ 12. Create an algorithm that directs a payroll clerk how to calculate and print the commission for any number of sales people.

discovery ▶ 13. Create an algorithm that tells someone how to evaluate the following expression (the / operator means division and the * operator means multiplication):

12 / 2 + 3 * 2 – 3

discovery ▶ 14. Create an algorithm that tells someone how to evaluate the following expression (the / operator means division and the * operator means multiplication):

12 / 2 + 3 * (4 – 2) + 1

debugging 15. The algorithm shown in Figure 1-22 should evaluate the expression x + y / z * 3, but it is not working correctly. Correct the algorithm.

```
1.  add x to y
2.  divide the result of step 1 by z
3.  multiply the result from step 2 by 3
```

Figure 1-22

debugging 16. The algorithm shown in Figure 1-23 is not working correctly; it does not get Rob seated in the chair. Correct the algorithm.

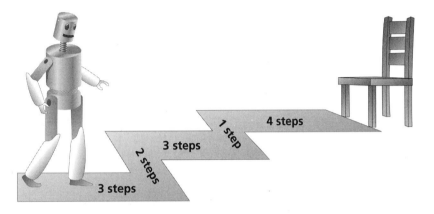

```
 1.  repeat 3 times
          walk
 2.  turn left 90 degrees
 3.  repeat 2 times
          walk
 4.  turn right 90 degrees
 5.  repeat 2 times
          walk
 6.  turn right 90 degrees
 7.  walk
 8.  turn right 90 degrees
 9.  repeat 4 times
          walk
10.  turn around 180 degrees
11.  sit
```

Figure 1-23

17. The algorithm shown in Figure 1-24 does not get Rob through the maze. Correct the algorithm.

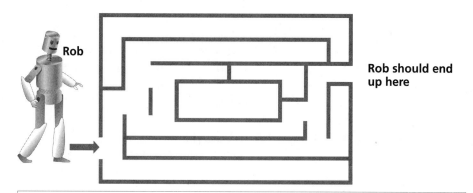

Rob

Rob should end
up here

```
  1.  walk into maze
  2.  turn left 90 degrees
  3.  repeat until you are directly in front of a wall
          walk
  4.  turn right 90 degrees
  5.  repeat until you are directly in front of a wall
          walk
  6.  turn right 90 degrees
  7.  repeat until you are directly in front of a wall
          walk
  8.  turn right 90 degrees
  9.  repeat until you are directly in front of a wall
          walk
 10.  turn right 90 degrees
 11.  repeat until you are directly in front of a wall
          walk
 12.  turn left 90 degrees
 13.  repeat until you are directly in front of a wall
          turn right 90 degrees
 14.  repeat until you are out of the maze
          walk
```

Figure 1-24

An Introduction to Problem Solving and the C++ Language

case ▶ Faye Chang is a programmer trainee at Quality Builders Incorporated. Her current project is to assist Jeff Jacobson, one of the full-time programmers, in writing some small C++ programs—such as one that calculates an employee's weekly raise and new weekly pay. Faye notices that Jeff can write programs much more quickly and accurately than she can, and she asks Jeff to share his secret with her. Jeff explains that he attributes his success to his Introduction to Programming course in college, where he learned a structured approach to solving problems. You will learn this approach in this tutorial. You will also be introduced to the C++ programming language.

LESSON A
objectives

In this lesson you will learn how to:

- Explain the six problem-solving steps used to create a computer program
- Complete an IPO chart
- Plan an algorithm using pseudocode and flowcharts
- Desk-check an algorithm

An Introduction to Problem Solving

Problem Solving

As you learned in this tutorial's opening case, Jeff Jacobson attributes his success in writing programs to the problem-solving process that he learned in his Introduction to Programming course. Although you may not realize it, you use a similar process to solve hundreds of small problems every day—such as how to get to school and what to do when you are hungry. Because most of these problems occur so often, however, you typically solve them almost mechanically, without giving much thought to the process your brain goes through to arrive at the solutions. Unfortunately, problems that are either complex or unfamiliar usually cannot be solved so easily; most require extensive thinking and planning. Understanding the thought process involved in solving simple and familiar problems will make solving complex or unfamiliar ones easier.

In this lesson, you will explore the thought process that you follow when solving common, daily problems. You will also learn how to use a similar process to create a computer solution to a problem—in other words, to create a computer program.

Solving Everyday Problems

If you are like most people, you typically do not give much thought to the process you follow when solving a familiar problem; that's because much of this process occurs quickly and seemingly effortlessly in your mind. You might be surprised to discover that you first analyze the problem; you then plan, review, implement, evaluate, and modify (if necessary) the solution. Consider, for example, how you solve the everyday problem of being hungry. First, your mind analyzes the problem to identify its important components. One very important component of any problem is the goal of solving the problem; in this case, the goal is to stop the hunger pangs. Other important components of a problem are the things that you can use to accomplish the goal. For example, you can use the lettuce, tomato, and cucumber that are in your refrigerator to relieve your hunger pangs.

After analyzing the problem, your mind plans an algorithm. Recall from Tutorial 1 that an algorithm is simply the step-by-step instructions that describe how to accomplish a task—in other words, an algorithm is a solution to a problem.

The hunger problem's algorithm, for example, describes how to use the lettuce, tomato, and cucumber to stop your hunger pangs. Figure 2-1 shows a summary of the analysis and planning steps for the hunger problem.

Result of analysis step

Items used to accomplish the goal	Algorithm	Goal
lettuce tomato cucumber	1. rinse the lettuce, tomato, and cucumber 2. cut up the lettuce, tomato, and cucumber 3. place the lettuce, tomato, and cucumber in a salad bowl 4. eat the lettuce, tomato, and cucumber	stop the hunger pangs

Result of planning step

Figure 2-1: Summary of the analysis and planning steps for the hunger problem

After planning the algorithm, you review it (in your mind) to verify that it will work as intended. When you are satisfied that the algorithm is correct, you implement the algorithm by following each of its instructions in the order indicated. In this case, for example, you rinse the lettuce, tomato, and cucumber, and then cut them up, place them in a salad bowl, and eat them.

Finally, you evaluate the algorithm (again, in your mind) and, if necessary, you modify it. In this case, if your hunger pangs are gone after eating the salad, then your algorithm is correct because it accomplishes its goal. If, on the other hand, you are still hungry, then you know that you need to modify the algorithm. An example of a modified algorithm for the hunger problem is shown in Figure 2-2.

Items used to accomplish the goal	Algorithm	Goal
lettuce tomato cucumber apple	1. rinse the lettuce, tomato, and cucumber 2. cut up the lettuce, tomato, and cucumber 3. place the lettuce, tomato, and cucumber in a salad bowl 4. eat the lettuce, tomato, and cucumber 5. rinse the apple 6. eat the apple	stop the hunger pangs

Modifications made to original algorithm

Figure 2-2: Modified algorithm for the hunger problem

In the next section, you will learn that you can use a similar thought process to create computer solutions to problems.

Creating Computer Solutions to Problems

In the previous section, you learned how you create a solution to a problem that occurs every day. You can use a similar problem-solving process to create a computer program. A computer program is also a solution, but one that is implemented with a computer. The problem-solving process that you should use when creating a computer program is shown in Figure 2-3.

1. Analyze the problem.

2. Plan the algorithm.

3. Desk-check the algorithm.

4. Code the algorithm into a program.

5. Desk-check the program.

6. Evaluate and modify (if necessary) the program.

Figure 2-3: The problem-solving process for creating a computer program

Like you, a computer programmer also first analyzes the problem. He or she then plans the algorithm—the steps that tell the computer how to solve the problem. Programmers use tools such as IPO (Input, Processing, Output) charts, pseudocode, and flowcharts to help them analyze problems and develop algorithms. You will learn about these tools in this lesson.

After the analysis and planning steps, the next step in the problem-solving process is to desk-check the algorithm. **Desk-checking**, also called **hand-tracing**, means that you use pencil and paper, along with sample data, to walk through each of the steps in the algorithm manually, just as if you were the computer. Programmers desk-check the algorithm to verify that it will work as intended. If any errors are found in the algorithm, the errors are corrected before the programmer continues to the next step in the problem-solving process. Any errors that are eliminated at this pencil and paper stage will make it much easier to produce a correct program in the later steps of the problem-solving process.

When the programmer is satisfied that the algorithm is correct, he or she then translates the algorithm into a language that the computer can understand. Programmers refer to this step as **coding** the algorithm. A coded algorithm is called a **program**. In this book, you will use the C++ programming language to code your algorithms.

After creating the program—the coded version of the algorithm—the programmer desk-checks the program to assure that he or she translated each of the algorithm's steps correctly. If any errors are found in the program, the errors are corrected before the programmer continues to the final step in the problem-solving process.

The final step in the problem-solving process is to evaluate and modify (if necessary) the program. A programmer evaluates a program by executing it, along with sample data, on the computer. If the program does not work as intended, then the programmer makes the necessary modifications until it does.

The term *desk-checking* refers to the fact that the programmer is seated at his or her desk, rather than in front of the computer, when reviewing the algorithm. The term *hand-tracing* refers to the fact that the programmer uses a pencil and paper to follow each of the steps in the algorithm by hand.

In the following sections, you will learn how to use the first three problem-solving steps to create a computer program; you will explore the last three steps in Lesson B. Begin with the first step in the problem-solving process, which is to analyze the problem.

Analyzing the Problem

You cannot solve a problem unless you understand the problem, and you cannot understand a problem unless you analyze it—in other words, unless you identify its important components. The purpose of analyzing a problem is to determine the goal of solving the problem, and the items that are needed to achieve that goal. Programmers refer to the goal as the **output**, and the items needed to reach the goal as the **input**. When analyzing a problem, you always search first for the output, and then for the input. Many times you will need to consult with the program's user—the person for whom you are creating the program—to determine the output and the input. This is especially true if the problem specification provided by the user is unclear or incomplete. Analyze the problem specification shown in Figure 2-4.

Sarah Martin works for Quality Builders. Sarah's current weekly pay is $250, but she is

scheduled to receive a 3 percent raise next week. Sarah wants you to write a program that

will display, on the computer screen, the amount of her new weekly pay.

Figure 2-4: Problem specification

When analyzing a problem, you always determine the output first. A helpful way to identify the output is to search the problem specification for an answer to the following question: *What does the user want to see either printed or displayed on the screen?* The answer to this question will typically be stated as nouns and adjectives in the problem specification. The problem specification shown in Figure 2-4, for instance, indicates that Sarah (the program's user) wants to see her new weekly pay displayed on the screen; the output, therefore, is the new weekly pay. Notice that the words *new* and *weekly* are adjectives, and that the word *pay* is a noun.

Programmers use an IPO (Input, Processing, Output) chart to organize and summarize the results of a problem analysis. A partially completed IPO chart is shown in Figure 2-5. Notice that you list the output items in the Output column of the IPO chart.

Input	Processing	Output
	Processing items:	new weekly pay
	Algorithm:	

Figure 2-5: Partially completed IPO chart showing the output

After determining the output, you then determine the input. A helpful way to identify the input is to search the problem specification for an answer to the following question: *What information will the computer need to know in order to either print or display the output items?* As with the output, the input is typically stated as nouns and adjectives in the problem specification. When determining the input, it helps to think about the information that you would need to use to solve the problem manually. The computer will need to know the same information. For example, to determine Sarah's new weekly pay, both you and the computer will need to know Sarah's current weekly pay, as well as her raise rate; both of these items, therefore, are the input. Here again, notice that *current*, *weekly*, and *raise* are adjectives; *pay* and *rate* are nouns. The partially completed IPO chart, which shows both the output and the input, is shown in Figure 2-6. Notice that you list the input items in the Input column of the IPO chart.

Input	Processing	Output
current weekly pay raise rate	Processing items: Algorithm:	new weekly pay

Figure 2-6: Partially completed IPO chart showing both the output and the input items

You have now completed the analysis step for the current problem. Keep in mind that analyzing real-world problems will not always be as easy as analyzing the ones found in a textbook. You will find that the analysis step is the most difficult of the problem-solving steps. This is primarily because most problem specifications contain either too much information or too little information.

A problem specification that contains too much information—more than is necessary to solve the problem—can be confusing to analyze. If you are not sure if an item of information is important, ask yourself this question: *If I didn't know this information, could I still solve the problem?* If your answer is "Yes," then the information is superfluous and you can simply ignore it. The current problem specification, for example, tells you that Sarah works for Quality Builders. Now ask yourself the following question: *If I didn't know that Sarah worked for Quality Builders, could I still solve the problem?* The answer is "Yes," so you can ignore this information.

When reading a problem specification, it helps to use a pencil to lightly cross out the information that you feel is unimportant to the solution, thereby reducing the amount of information you need to consider in your analysis. If you later find that the information is important, you can always erase the pencil line. In the current problem, for example, you can cross out the unimportant information as shown in Figure 2-7.

~~Sarah Martin works for Quality Builders.~~ Sarah's current weekly pay is $250, but she is scheduled to receive a 3 percent raise ~~next week. Sarah wants you to~~ write a program that will display, on the computer screen, the amount of her new weekly pay.

Figure 2-7: Problem specification with unimportant information crossed out

Even worse than having too much information in a problem specification is not having enough information to solve a problem. Consider, for example, the problem specification shown in Figure 2-8.

Jack Wade, one of the shipping clerks at Quality Builders, earns $7 per hour. Last week, Jack worked 40 hours. He wants you to write a program that will display his weekly net pay.

Figure 2-8: Problem specification that does not contain enough information

It is clear from reading the problem specification that the output is the weekly net pay. The input appears to be both the hourly pay and the number of hours worked during the week. However, is that the only information the computer needs to know in order to display Jack's net pay? Although you can display a person's gross pay if you know only the hours worked and the hourly pay, a net pay calculation typically involves deducting federal and state taxes, as well as insurance, from the gross pay. What taxes and insurance, if any, will you need to deduct from Jack's gross pay in order to calculate his net pay? You cannot tell because the problem specification does not contain enough information. Before you can solve this problem, you will need to ask Jack to be more specific about how his net pay is to be calculated.

As a programmer, it is important to distinguish between information that is missing in the problem specification, and information that is simply not explicitly stated in the problem specification—that is, information that is implied. For example, consider the problem specification shown in Figure 2-9.

Sharon Bartlett, who works for Quality Builders, needs a program that will display the area of any rectangle. The dimensions of the rectangle will be given in feet.

Figure 2-9: Problem specification in which the input is not explicitly stated

As you may remember from your math courses, you calculate the area of a rectangle by multiplying its length by its width. Therefore, the length and width are the input items for this problem. Notice, however, that the words *length* and *width* do not appear in the problem specification. Although both items are not stated explicitly in the problem, both are not considered missing information because the formula for calculating the area of a rectangle is common knowledge—or, at least, the formula can be found in any math book. With practice, you will be able to "fill in the gaps" in a problem specification also.

If you are having trouble analyzing a problem, try reading the problem specification several times, as it is easy to miss information during the first reading. If the problem is still not clear to you, do not be shy about asking the user for more information. Remember, the greater your understanding of a problem, the easier it will be for you to write a correct and efficient solution to the problem.

After analyzing a problem, you then plan its algorithm—its solution.

Mini-Quiz 1

For each problem specification that follows, identify the output and the input. Also identify what information, if any, is missing from the problem specification.

1. Paul Eisenstein lives in a state that charges a 3 percent state income tax on his yearly taxable wages. He wants you to write a program that will display the state income tax he would need to pay at the end of the year.

2. Deepa Charna belongs to a CD (compact disc) club. The club requires Deepa to purchase 10 CDs each year, at a reduced cost of $8 per CD. Deepa wants to know how much she saves each year by buying the CDs through the club rather than through a store.

3. Penny Long saves $1.25 per day. Penny would like to know the total amount she saved during the month of January.

4. Jerry Rides saves $1.45 per day. Jerry would like to know the amount of his annual savings.

Planning the Algorithm

The second step in the problem-solving process is to plan the algorithm—the step-by-step instructions that the computer needs to follow to transform the problem's input into its output. You record the algorithm in the Processing column of the IPO chart.

Most algorithms begin by entering the input items into the computer. The input items are the items listed in the Input column of the IPO chart. To determine Sarah Martin's weekly pay, for example, you will record the instruction, "enter the current weekly pay and raise rate," as the first step in the algorithm. You will record this instruction in the Processing column of the IPO chart, below the word "Algorithm."

After the instruction to enter the input items, you usually record instructions to process those items, typically by performing some calculations on them, to achieve the problem's required results. The required results are listed in the Output column of the IPO chart. In this problem, consider how you can use the input items (current weekly pay and raise rate) to achieve the output item (new weekly pay).

Before you can display the new weekly pay, you must compute it. To compute the new weekly pay, you first calculate the weekly raise amount by multiplying the current weekly pay by the raise rate; you then add that amount to the current weekly pay. You will record the instructions, "calculate the weekly raise amount by multiplying the current weekly pay by the raise rate" and "calculate the new weekly pay by adding the weekly raise amount to the current weekly pay," as steps 2 and 3 in the IPO chart. Notice that both calculation instructions state both *what* is to be calculated and *how* to calculate it.

Unlike the current weekly pay, raise rate, and new weekly pay, the weekly raise amount calculated within the algorithm is neither an input item nor an output item; rather, it is a special item, commonly referred to as a processing item. A **processing item** represents an intermediate value that the algorithm uses when processing the input into the output. In this case, the algorithm uses the two input items (current weekly pay and raise rate) to calculate the intermediate value—weekly raise amount—which the algorithm uses to compute the new weekly pay.

You list the processing items in the Processing column of the IPO chart, below the words "Processing items." You will enter "weekly raise amount" as a processing item used in the current algorithm.

Most algorithms end with an instruction either to print or display the output items—the ones listed in the Output column of the IPO chart. (*Display* refers to the screen; *print* refers to the printer.) In this case, you need simply to display Sarah's new weekly pay. Record the instruction, "display the new weekly pay," as the last step in the IPO chart. The completed IPO chart is shown in Figure 2-10. Notice that the algorithm begins by entering some data (the input items), then processing that data (the two calculations), and then displaying some data (the output item). Most algorithms will follow this same format.

Input	Processing	Output
current weekly pay raise rate	Processing items: weekly raise amount Algorithm: 1. enter the current weekly pay and raise rate 2. calculate the weekly raise amount by multiplying the current weekly pay by the raise rate 3. calculate the new weekly pay by adding the weekly raise amount to the current weekly pay 4. display the new weekly pay	new weekly pay

Figure 2-10: Completed IPO chart

You will notice that the algorithm shown in Figure 2-10 is composed of short statements. The statements represent the steps the computer needs to follow to display the new pay. In programming terms, the list of steps shown in Figure 2-10 is called pseudocode. **Pseudocode** is a tool programmers use to help them plan an algorithm. Pseudocode is not standardized—every programmer has his or her own version—but you will find some similarities among the various versions.

Although the word *pseudocode* might be unfamiliar to you, you have already written pseudocode without even realizing it. Think about the last time that you gave directions to someone. You wrote each direction down on paper, in your own words. These directions were a form of pseudocode. A programmer uses the pseudocode as a guide when coding the algorithm.

In addition to using pseudocode, programmers also use flowcharts to help them plan the algorithm for a problem. Unlike pseudocode, which consists of short, English-like statements, a **flowchart** uses standardized symbols to show the steps the computer needs to take to accomplish the program's goal. Figure 2-11 shows the current problem's algorithm in flowchart form.

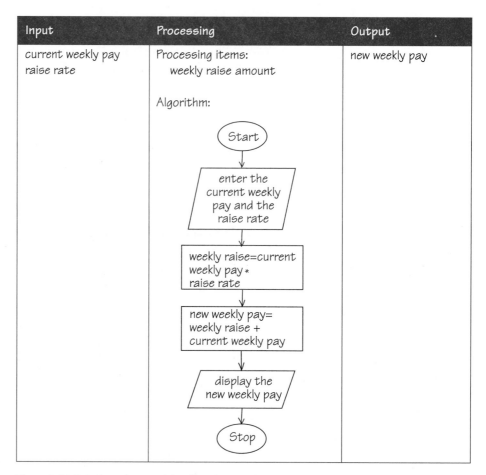

Input	Processing	Output
current weekly pay raise rate	Processing items: weekly raise amount Algorithm:	new weekly pay

Figure 2-11: IPO chart shown with a flowchart in the Processing column

Notice that the flowchart shown in Figure 2-11 contains three different symbols: an oval, a rectangle, and a parallelogram. The symbols are connected with lines, called **flowlines**. The oval symbol is called the **start/stop symbol**. The start oval indicates the beginning of the flowchart, and the stop oval indicates the end of the flowchart. Between the start and the stop ovals are two rectangles, called **process symbols**. You use the process symbol to represent tasks such as calculations.

The parallelogram is called the **input/output symbol** and is used to represent input tasks, such as getting information from the user, and output tasks, such as displaying or printing information. The first parallelogram shown in Figure 2-11 represents an input task. The last parallelogram represents an output task.

When planning the algorithm, you do not need to create both a flowchart and pseudocode; you need to use only one of these planning tools. Which tool you use is really a matter of personal preference. For simple algorithms, pseudocode works just fine. When an algorithm becomes more complex, however, the program's logic may be easier to see in a flowchart.

In the next section, you will learn some hints for writing algorithms.

Hints for Writing Algorithms

It is important to remember that you don't need to "reinvent the wheel" each time you create a solution to a problem. Before you write an algorithm, consider whether the problem you are solving is similar to one you've already solved. If it is, you can then

tip

Many programmers prefer flowcharts over pseudocode because, as the old adage goes, a picture is sometimes worth a thousand words.

use that problem's algorithm to solve the current problem, many times with very little modification. For example, consider the problem specification shown in Figure 2-12.

Quality Builders is increasing each of its prices by 3 percent. The owner of the company wants

you to write a program that will display the amount of the increase and the new price.

Figure 2-12: Problem specification similar to the one you worked with in this lesson

Although it may not be obvious at first glance, the problem shown in Figure 2-12 is almost identical to one that you solved in this lesson—only the terminology is different. (You may want to review the problem specification shown in Figure 2-4 to verify the similarity.) In a previous problem, you calculated both the increase in Sarah's pay and her new pay. That is no different than calculating an increase in an item's price and a new price, which Figure 2-12's problem requires you to do. The IPO chart for Figure 2-12's problem is shown in Figure 2-13. If you compare this IPO chart with the one shown in Figure 2-10, you will notice the similarity between both solutions.

Input	Processing	Output

current price
increase rate
	Processing items: none
	
	Algorithm:
	1. enter the current price and
	   increase rate
	2. calculate the increase amount
	   by multiplying the current
	   price by the increase rate
	3. calculate the new price
	   by adding the increase
	   amount to the current price
	4. display the increase amount
	   and new price
		increase amount
		new price

Figure 2-13: IPO chart for the problem specification shown in Figure 2-12

Even if the problem you are trying to solve is not identical to one that you have already solved, you may be able to use a portion of a previous solution to solve the current problem. Consider, for example, the problem specification shown in Figure 2-14.

At the end of every year, Quality Builders gives each of its employees a bonus. This year

the bonus rate is 6 percent of the employee's current yearly salary. Mary Vasko wants you to

write a program that will display her bonus.

Figure 2-14: Problem specification that contains a portion that is similar to the one you worked with in this lesson

Although this problem is not identical to any that you solved in this lesson, it does require you to use a part of a previous algorithm to solve it. Calculating a bonus is no different than calculating a raise; both require you to take an amount and multiply it by a percentage rate. Earlier, you multiplied Sarah's current weekly pay by her raise rate. Similarly, in Figure 2-14's problem, you need to multiply Mary's yearly salary by her bonus rate. The IPO chart for this problem is shown in Figure 2-15. If you compare this IPO chart with the one shown in Figure 2-10, you will notice how part of Figure 2-10's algorithm is used in Figure 2-15's algorithm.

Input	Processing	Output
current yearly salary bonus rate	Processing items: none Algorithm: 1. enter the current yearly salary and bonus rate 2. calculate the bonus by multiplying the current yearly salary by the bonus rate 3. display the bonus	bonus

Figure 2-15: IPO chart for the problem specification shown in Figure 2-14

If you have not solved a similar problem, and you cannot find a portion of an existing algorithm that you can use, try solving the problem manually, writing down on paper every step you take to do so. If you were to solve Figure 2-14's problem manually, for example, you would need first to read Mary's yearly salary and her bonus rate into your mind. You would then need to calculate her bonus by multiplying the bonus rate by the yearly salary. Lastly, you would write the bonus amount down on a piece of paper. You can use the steps that you wrote down as a guide when creating your algorithm.

Figure 2-16 summarizes what you learned in this section about planning algorithms.

1. Before writing an algorithm, consider whether you have already solved a similar problem. If you have, you can use the same solution, often with little modification, to solve the current problem.

2. If you have not solved a similar problem, consider whether you can use a portion of an existing algorithm to solve the current problem.

3. Solve the problem manually, noting each step you take to do so.

Figure 2-16: Hints for planning algorithms

After analyzing a problem and planning its algorithm, you then desk-check the algorithm, using either the flowchart or the pseudocode, along with sample data.

mini-quiz

Mini-Quiz 2

1. The input/output symbol in a flowchart is represented by a(n) _____ .

2. Calculation tasks are placed in a processing symbol, which is represented in a flowchart by a(n) _____ .

3. Paul Eisenstein lives in a state that charges a 3 percent state income tax on his yearly taxable wages. He wants you to create a program that will display the state income tax he would need to pay at the end of the year. The output is the annual state income tax; the input is the yearly taxable wages and the state income tax rate. Complete the Processing section of the IPO chart. (Use pseudocode to show the steps.)

4. Deepa Charna belongs to a CD (compact disc) club. The club requires Deepa to purchase 10 CDs each year, at a reduced cost of $8 per CD. Deepa wants to know how much she saves each year by buying the CDs through the club rather than through a store that charges $12 for each CD. The output is the annual savings. The input is the number of CDs purchased each year, the club's CD price, and the store's CD price. Complete the Processing section of the IPO chart. (Use pseudocode to show the steps.)

Desk-Checking the Algorithm

A programmer reviews an algorithm by desk-checking, or hand-tracing, it—in other words, by completing each step in the algorithm manually. You desk-check an algorithm to verify that it is not missing any steps, and that the existing steps are correct and in the proper order. Before you begin the desk-check, you first choose a set of sample data for the input values which you can use to manually compute the expected output values. For example, you will use input values of $250 and .03 (3 percent) as Sarah Martin's current weekly pay and raise rate, respectively. Sarah's new weekly pay should be $257.50, which is her current weekly pay of $250 plus her weekly raise of $7.50 (250 times .03); the 257.50 is the expected output value. You now use the sample input values (250 and .03) to desk-check the algorithm. If the algorithm produces the expected output value of 257.50, then the algorithm appears to be correct.

You can use a desk-check table to help you desk-check an algorithm. The table should contain one column for each input item shown in the IPO chart, as well as one column for each output item and one column for each processing item. Figure 2-17 shows a partially completed desk-check table for Sarah Martin's problem.

Current weekly pay	raise rate	weekly raise	new weekly pay

Figure 2-17: Desk-check table showing columns for the input, processing, and output items from the IPO chart

You can desk-check an algorithm using either its pseudocode or its flowchart. The pseudocode for Sarah Martin's problem is shown in Figure 2-10 and the flowchart is shown in Figure 2-11. In both figures, the first step is to enter the input values—in this case, the current weekly pay of 250 and the raise rate of .03. You record the results of this step by writing 250 and .03 in the current weekly pay and raise rate columns, respectively, in the desk-check table. See Figure 2-18.

current weekly pay	raise rate	weekly raise	new weekly pay
250	.03		

Figure 2-18: Desk-check table showing input values entered in appropriate columns

The second step in the algorithm is to calculate the weekly raise by multiplying the current weekly pay by the raise rate. The desk-check table shows that the current weekly pay is 250 and the raise rate is .03. Notice that you use the table to determine what the current weekly pay and raise rate values are. This helps to verify the accuracy of the algorithm. If, for example, the table did not show any amount in the raise rate column, you would know that your algorithm missed a step—in this case, it missed entering the raise rate.

Multiplying the current weekly pay of 250 by the raise rate of .03 results in a 7.50 raise. You would then write the number 7.50 in the weekly raise column, as shown in Figure 2-19.

current weekly pay	raise rate	weekly raise	new weekly pay
250	.03	7.50	

Figure 2-19: Weekly raise entry included in the desk-check table

The next step in the algorithm is to calculate the new weekly pay by adding the weekly raise to the current weekly pay. According to the desk-check table, the raise is 7.50 and the current weekly pay is 250. Added together, those amounts result in a new weekly pay of 257.50. You would then write 257.50 in the new weekly pay column, as shown in Figure 2-20.

current weekly pay	raise rate	weekly raise	new weekly pay
250	.03	7.50	257.50

Figure 2-20: New weekly pay entry included in the desk-check table

The last instruction in the algorithm is to display the new weekly pay—in this case, 257.50. This amount agrees with the manual calculation you performed prior to desk-checking the algorithm, so the algorithm appears to be correct. The only way to know for sure, however, is to test it a few more times with different input values. For example, you can test the algorithm with a current weekly pay of $100 and a raise rate of .10 (10 percent). The new weekly pay should be $110, which is the current weekly pay of $100 plus the weekly raise of $10 (100 times .10).

Recall that the first instruction in the algorithm is to enter the current weekly pay and the raise rate. Therefore, you would write 100 in the current weekly pay column and .10 in the raise rate column, as shown in Figure 2-21.

current weekly pay	raise rate	weekly raise	new weekly pay
~~250~~ 100	~~.03~~ .10	7.50	257.50

Figure 2-21: Desk-check table for second set of input values

Notice that you cross out the previous values of these two items in the table because each column should contain only one value at any time.

The next step is to calculate the weekly raise. Multiplying the current weekly pay, which is listed in the table as 100, by the raise rate, which is listed as .10, results in a weekly raise of 10. So you would then cross out the 7.50 that appears in the weekly raise column in the table and write 10 immediately below it.

The next step is to calculate the new weekly pay. Adding the raise, which is listed in the table as 10, to the current weekly pay, which is listed in the table as 100, results in a new weekly pay of 110. Therefore, you would cross out the 257.50 that appears in the new weekly pay column in the table and write 110 immediately below it. The completed desk-check table is shown in Figure 2-22.

current weekly pay	raise rate	weekly raise	new weekly pay
~~250~~ 100	~~.03~~ .10	~~7.50~~ 10	~~257.50~~ 110

Figure 2-22: Desk-check table showing results of a second desk-check

The last step in the algorithm is to display the new weekly pay—in this case, the algorithm will display 110. This amount agrees with the manual calculation you performed earlier, so the algorithm still appears to be correct. To be sure, however, you should desk-check it a few more times.

In later tutorials, you will learn that you should also use invalid data to desk-check the algorithm. **Invalid data** is data that the algorithm is not expecting. In this case, the algorithm is not expecting you to enter a negative value as the current weekly pay. A negative weekly pay is obviously an input error because an employee cannot earn a negative amount for the week. In later tutorials, you will learn how to create algorithms that correctly handle input errors. For now, however, you can assume that the user of the program will always input the correct values.

You have now completed the first three of the six steps required to create a computer program: analyze the problem, plan the algorithm, and desk-check the algorithm. You will complete the last three steps—code the algorithm into a program, desk-check the program, and evaluate and modify (if necessary) the program—in Lesson B. You can either take a break or complete the questions and exercises at the end of the lesson.

mini-quiz

Mini-Quiz 3

1. Desk-check the following algorithm. Use a yearly taxable wage of $20,000 and a 3 percent state income tax rate, and then use a yearly taxable wage of $10,000 and a 2 percent state income tax.

Input	Processing	Output
yearly taxable wages state income tax rate	Processing items: none	annual state income tax

Algorithm:
1. enter the yearly taxable wages and the state income tax rate
2. calculate the annual state income tax by multiplying the yearly taxable wages by the state income tax rate
3. display the annual state income tax

2. Desk-check the following algorithm. Use 5 and 7 as the first set of input values, then use 6 and 8 as the second set of input values.

Input	Processing	Output
first number second number	Processing items: 　sum	average

Algorithm:
1. enter first number and second number
2. calculate the sum by adding together the first number and the second number
3. calculate the average by dividing the sum by 2
4. display the average

S U M M A R Y

If you are like most people, you probably do not pay much attention to the problem-solving process that you use when solving everyday problems. This process typically involves analyzing the problem, and then planning, reviewing, implementing, evaluating, and modifying (if necessary) the solution. You can use a similar problem-solving process to create a computer program, which is also a solution to a problem.

Programmers use tools such as IPO (Input, Processing, Output) charts, pseudocode, and flowcharts to help them analyze problems and develop algorithms. During the analysis step, the programmer first determines the output, which is the goal or purpose of solving the problem. The programmer then determines the input, which is the information he or she needs to reach the goal. During the planning step, programmers write the steps that will transform the input into the output. Most algorithms begin by entering some data (the input items), then processing that data (usually by doing some calculations), and then displaying some data (the output items).

After the analysis and planning steps, a programmer then desk-checks the algorithm to see if it will work as intended. Desk-checking means that the programmer follows each of the steps in the algorithm by hand, just as if he or she were the computer. When the programmer is satisfied that the algorithm is correct, he or she then codes the algorithm. Coding refers to translating the algorithm into a language that the computer can understand. A coded algorithm is called a program. After coding the algorithm, the programmer then desk-checks the program to be sure that he or she translated each of the steps in the algorithm correctly. The programmer then evaluates and modifies (if necessary) the program by executing it, along with sample data, using the computer. If the program does not work as intended, then the programmer makes the necessary modifications until it does.

Before writing an algorithm, you should consider whether you have already solved an identical problem. If you have, you can use that solution, often with little modification, to solve the current problem. If you have not solved an identical problem, consider whether a portion of an existing algorithm is similar enough to use in the current problem. If no existing algorithms help, try solving the problem manually, being sure to write down every step you take to do so because the computer will need to follow the same steps.

ANSWERS TO MINI-QUIZZES

Mini-Quiz 1

1. Output: annual state income tax

   Input: yearly taxable wages, state income tax rate

   Missing information: none

2. Output: annual savings

   Input: number of CDs purchased each year, CD cost when purchased through the club, CD cost when purchased through the store

   Missing information: CD cost when purchased through the store

3. Output: total amount saved in January

   Input: amount saved per day, number of days in January

   Missing information: none (Although the number of days in January is not specified in the problem specification, that information can be found in any calendar.)

4. Output: total annual savings

   Input: amount saved per day, number of days in the year

   Missing information: number of days in the year (Because some years are leap years, you would need to know the number of days in the year.)

Mini-Quiz 2

1. parallelogram ⟋

2. rectangle ▭

3.

Input	Processing	Output
yearly taxable wages state income tax rate	Processing items: none	annual state income tax

Algorithm:

1. enter the yearly taxable wages and state income tax rate

2. calculate the annual state income tax by multiplying the yearly taxable wages by the state income tax rate

3. display the annual state income tax

4.

Input	Processing	Output
number of CDs purchased each year club's CD price store's CD price	Processing items: amount spent through the club amount spent at the store	annual savings

Algorithm:

1. enter the number of CDs purchased each year, the club's CD price, and the store's CD price

2. calculate the amount spent through the club by multiplying the number of CDs purchased each year by the club's CD price

3. calculate the amount spent at the store by multiplying the number of CDs purchased each year by the store's CD price

4. calculate the annual savings by subtracting the amount spent through the club from the amount spent at the store

5. display the annual savings

Mini-Quiz 3

1.

yearly taxable wages	state income tax rate	annual state income tax
~~20000~~	~~.03~~	~~600~~
10000	.02	200

2.

first number	second number	sum	average
~~5~~	~~7~~	~~12~~	~~6~~
6	8	14	7

Q U E S T I O N S

1. The first step in the problem-solving process is to _____ .
   a. plan the algorithm
   b. analyze the problem
   c. desk-check the algorithm
   d. evaluate and modify (if necessary) the program
   e. code the algorithm

2. Programmers refer to the goal of solving a problem as the _____ .
   a. input
   b. output
   c. processing
   d. purpose

3. Programmers refer to the items needed to reach a problem's goal as the _____ .
   a. input
   b. output
   c. processing
   d. purpose

4. A problem's _____ will answer the question, "What does the user want to see either printed or displayed on the screen?"
   a. input
   b. output
   c. processing
   d. purpose

5. Programmers use _____ to organize and summarize the results of their problem analysis.
   a. flowcharts
   b. input charts
   c. IPO charts
   d. output charts
   e. processing charts

6. A problem's _____ will answer the question, "What information will the computer need to know in order to either print or display the output items?"
   a. input
   b. output
   c. processing
   d. purpose

7. Most algorithms begin by _____ .
   a. displaying the input items
   b. displaying the output items
   c. entering the input items into the computer
   d. entering the output items into the computer
   e. processing the input items by doing some calculations on them

8. You record the algorithm in the _____ column of the IPO chart.
   a. Input
   b. Output
   c. Processing
   d. Purpose

9. The calculation instructions in an algorithm should state _____ .
   a. only *what* is to be calculated
   b. only *how* to calculate something
   c. both *what* is to be calculated and *how* to calculate it
   d. both *what* is to be calculated and *why* is it calculated

10. Most algorithms follow the format of _____ .
    a. entering the input items, then displaying the input items, and then processing the output items
    b. entering the input items, then processing the output items, and then displaying the output items
    c. entering the input items, then processing the input items, and then displaying the output items
    d. entering the output items, then displaying the output items, and then processing the output items
    e. entering the output items, then processing the output items, and then displaying the output items

11. The short statements that represent the steps the computer needs to follow to solve a problem are called _____ .
    a. flowcharts
    b. flow diagrams
    c. IPO charts
    d. pseudocharts
    e. pseudocode

12. _____ use standardized symbols to represent an algorithm.
    a. Flowcharts
    b. Flow diagrams
    c. IPO charts
    d. Pseudocharts
    e. Pseudocode

13. The _____ symbol is used in a flowchart to represent a calculation task.
    a. input
    b. output
    c. process
    d. start
    e. stop

14. The _____ symbol is used in a flowchart to represent a step that gets information from the user.
    a. input/output
    b. process
    c. selection/repetition
    d. start/stop

15. The process symbol in a flowchart is the _____ .
    a. ◇
    b. ⬭
    c. ▱
    d. ▭
    e. ☐

16. The input/output symbol in a flowchart is the _____ .
a. ◇
b. ⬭
c. ▱
d. ▭
e. ☐

17. The start/stop symbol, which marks both the beginning and ending of a flowchart, is a(n) _____ .
a. ◇
b. ⬭
c. ▱
d. ▭
e. ☐

18. After planning an algorithm, you should _____ to verify that it will work correctly.
a. analyze the algorithm
b. code the algorithm
c. desk-check the algorithm
d. evaluate and modify (if necessary) the program

19. A programmer reviews the accuracy of an algorithm by _____ it.
a. analyzing
b. coding
c. desk-checking
d. planning

20. When desk-checking an algorithm, you should set up a table that contains _____ .
a. one column for each input item
b. one column for each output item
c. one column for each processing item
d. both a and b
e. a, b, and c

E X E R C I S E S

1. Hai Chang needs a program that will calculate and display the square of a number. Complete and submit an IPO chart for this problem. Use pseudocode in the Processing column. Also complete and submit a desk-check table for your algorithm. Use 4 as the number for the first desk-check, then use the number 6.

2. Mingo Sales needs a program that the company can use to enter the sales made in each of two states. The program should display the total sales and the total commission, which is 5 percent of the sales. (In other words, if you have sales totaling $3,000, your commission is $150.) The commission rate may change in the future. Complete and submit an IPO chart for this problem. Use pseudocode in the Processing column. Also complete and submit a desk-check table for your algorithm. For the first desk-check, use 1000 and 2000 as the two state sales, and use .05 (the decimal equivalent of 5 percent) as the commission rate. Then use 3000 and 2500 as the two state sales, and use .06 as the commission rate.

3. Sarah Brimley is the accountant at Paper Products. The salespeople at Paper Products are paid a commission, which is a percentage of the sales they make. The current commission rate is 10 percent, but that rate may change in the future. (In other words, if you have sales totaling $2,000, your commission is $200.) Sarah wants you to create a program that will display the commission after she enters the salesperson's sales. Complete and submit an IPO chart for this problem. Use a flowchart in the Processing column. Also complete and submit a desk-check table for your algorithm. Use 2000 and .1 (the decimal equivalent of 10 percent) as the salesperson's sales amount and commission rate, respectively. Then use 5000 and .06.

4. RM Sales divides its sales territory into three regions: 1, 2, and 3. Robert Gonzales, the sales manager, wants an application in which he can enter the current year's sales for each region and the projected increase (expressed as a percentage) in sales for each region. He then wants the program to display the following year's projected sales for each region. (For example, if Robert enters 10000 as the current sales for region 1, and then enters a 10 percent projected increase, the program should display 11000 as next year's projected sales.) Complete and submit an IPO chart for this problem. Use a flowchart in the Processing column. Also complete and submit a desk-check table for your algorithm. Use the following information for the first desk-check:

Region	Sales	Increase rate
1	10000	.1 (the decimal equivalent of 10 percent)
2	3000	.09 (the decimal equivalent of 9 percent)
3	6000	.1 (the decimal equivalent of 10 percent)

   Use the following information for the second desk-check:

Region	Sales	Increase rate
1	5000	.02 (the decimal equivalent of 2 percent)
2	2000	.03 (the decimal equivalent of 3 percent)
3	1000	.02 (the decimal equivalent of 2 percent)

5. John Lee wants an application in which he can enter the following three pieces of information: his savings account balance at the beginning of the month, the amount of money he deposited during the month, and the amount of money he withdrew during the month. He wants the program to display his ending balance. Complete and submit an IPO chart for this problem. Use pseudocode in the Processing column. Also complete and submit a desk-check table for your algorithm. Use the following information for the first desk-check:

savings account balance at the beginning of the month:	2000
money deposited during the month:	775
money withdrawn during the month:	1200

   Use the following information for the second desk-check:

savings account balance at the beginning of the month:	500
money deposited during the month:	100
money withdrawn during the month:	610

6. Lana Jones wants an application that will display the average of any three numbers she enters. Complete and submit an IPO chart for this problem; use pseudocode in the Processing column. Also complete and submit a desk-check table for your algorithm. Use the following three numbers for the first desk-check: 25, 76, 33. Use the following three numbers for the second desk-check: 10, 15, 20.

7. Jackets Unlimited is having a sale on all of its merchandise. The store manager asks you to create a program that requires the clerk simply to enter the original price of a jacket and the discount rate. The program should then display both the sales discount and the new sales price. Complete and submit an IPO chart for this problem. Use pseudocode in the Processing column. Also complete and submit a desk-check table for your algorithm. For the first desk-check, use 100 as the jacket price and .25 (the decimal equivalent of 25 percent) as the discount rate. For the second desk-check, use 50 as the jacket price and .1 as the discount rate.

8. Typing Salon currently charges $.10 per typed envelope and $.25 per typed page, although those prices may change in the future. The company accountant wants a program that will help her prepare the customer bills. She will enter the number of typed envelopes and the number of typed pages, as well as the current charges per typed envelope and per typed page. The application should display the total amount due from the customer. Complete and submit an IPO chart for this problem. Use pseudocode in the Processing column. Complete and submit a desk-check table for your algorithm. Use the following information for the first desk-check:

charge per typed envelope:	.10
charge per typed page:	.25
number of typed envelopes:	100
number of typed pages:	100

Use the following information for the second desk-check:

charge per typed envelope:	.20
charge per typed page:	.30
number of typed envelopes:	10
number of typed pages:	15

9. Management USA, a small training center, plans to run two full-day seminars on December 1. (Because each seminar lasts the entire day, a person can register for only one of the two seminars at a time.) The current seminar price is $200, but that price could change in the future. Registration for the seminars will be taken by telephone. When a company calls to register its employees, the telephone representative will ask for the following two items of information: the number of employees registering for the first seminar and the number registering for the second seminar. Claire Jenkowski, the owner of Management USA, wants a program that will display the total number of employees the company is registering and the total cost. Complete and submit an IPO chart for this problem. You can use either pseudocode or a flowchart in the Processing column. Also complete and submit a desk-check table for your algorithm. Use the following information for the first desk-check:

seminar price:	200
number registering for the first seminar:	10
number registering for the second seminar:	10

Use the following information for the second desk-check:

seminar price:	100
number registering for the first seminar:	30
number registering for the second seminar:	10

10. Suman Gadhari, the payroll clerk at Sun Projects, wants a program that will compute an employee's net pay. Suman will enter the hours worked, the hourly rate of pay, the federal withholding tax (FWT) rate, the Social Security tax (FICA) rate, and the state income tax rate. For this program, you do not have to worry about overtime, as this company does not allow anyone to work more than 40 hours. Suman wants the program to display the employee's gross pay, FWT, FICA, state income tax, and net pay. Complete and submit an IPO chart for this problem. You can use either pseudocode or a flowchart in the Processing column. Also complete and submit a desk-check table for your algorithm. Use the following information for the first desk-check:

hours worked:	20
hourly pay rate:	6
FWT rate:	.2
FICA rate:	.08
state income tax rate:	.02

Use the following information for the second desk-check:

hours worked:	30
hourly pay rate:	10
FWT rate:	.2
FICA rate:	.08
state income tax rate:	.04

11. Perry Brown needs a program that will allow him to enter the length of four sides of a polygon. The program should display the perimeter of the polygon. Complete and submit an IPO chart for this problem. Use pseudocode in the Processing column. Also complete and submit a desk-check table. Desk-check the algorithm twice, using your own sample data.

12. Builders Inc. needs a program that will allow its sales clerks to enter both the diameter of a circle and the price of railing material per foot. The program should display the circumference of the circle and the total price of the railing material. (Use 3.14 as the value of pi.) Complete and submit an IPO chart for this problem. Use a flowchart in the Processing column. Also complete and submit a desk-check table for your algorithm. Desk-check the algorithm twice, using your own sample data.

13. Tile Limited wants a program that will allow its sales clerks to enter the length and width, in feet, of a rectangle, and the price of a square foot of tile. The program should display the area of the rectangle and the total price of the tile. Complete and submit an IPO chart for this problem. Use pseudocode in the Processing column. Also complete and submit a desk-check table for your algorithm. Desk-check the algorithm twice, using your own sample data.

14. Willow Pools wants a program that will allow its salespeople to enter the dimensions of a rectangle in feet. The program should display the volume of the rectangle. Complete and submit an IPO chart for this problem. Use pseudocode in the Processing column. Also complete and submit a desk-check table for your algorithm. Desk-check the algorithm twice, using your own sample data.

15. IMY Industries needs a program that its personnel clerks can use to display the new hourly pay, given both the current hourly pay for each of three job codes (1, 2, and 3) and the raise rate (entered as a decimal). The company also wants to display the message "Raise rate: XX" on the screen. The XX in the message should be replaced by the actual raise rate. Complete and submit an IPO chart for this problem. Use either pseudocode or a flowchart in the Processing column. Also complete and submit a desk-check table for your algorithm. Use the following information for the first desk-check:

current hourly pay for job code 1:	7.55
current hourly pay for job code 2:	10.00
current hourly pay for job code 3:	10.30
raise rate:	.02

    Use the following information for the second desk-check:

current hourly pay for job code 1:	8.00
current hourly pay for job code 2:	6.50
current hourly pay for job code 3:	7.25
raise rate:	.02

16. Sue Chen attends Jefferson University in Kentucky. Students attending Jefferson University are considered full-time students if they are registered for at least 15 semester hours. If the student is registered for less than 15 hours, the student is considered a part-time scholar. Sue would like you to create a program that will display her semester bill, including tuition and room and board, at Jefferson. Tuition is $100 per semester hour. Room and board is $3000. (Assume that all students live on campus and will have room and board charges.) Complete and submit an IPO chart for this problem. Use a flowchart in the Processing column. Also complete and submit a desk-check table for your algorithm. Desk-check the algorithm twice. Use 20 semester hours for the first desk-check, and use 14 hours for the second desk-check.

discovery ▶ 17. George Wang, the payroll clerk at Microstep Company, wants a program that will compute an employee's net pay. George will enter the hours worked, the hourly rate of pay, the federal withholding tax (FWT) rate, the Social Security tax (FICA) rate, and the state income tax rate. Employees working over 40 hours receive time and one-half on the hours over 40. George wants the program to display the employee's gross pay, FWT, FICA, state income tax, and net pay. Complete and submit an IPO chart for this problem.

Use pseudocode in the Processing column. Also complete and submit a desk-check table for your algorithm. Use the following information for the first desk-check:

hours worked:	20
hourly pay rate:	6
FWT rate:	.2
FICA rate:	.08
state income tax rate:	.02

Use the following information for the second desk-check:

hours worked:	43
hourly pay rate:	10
FWT rate:	.2
FICA rate:	.08
state income tax rate:	.02

debugging   18. Etola Systems wants you to write a program that will display the ending inventory amount, given the beginning inventory amount, the amount sold, and the amount returned. The algorithm shown in Figure 2-23 is supposed to solve this problem, but it is not working correctly. First calculate the expected results using a beginning inventory of 50, an amount sold of 10, and an amount returned of 2. Then use these values to desk-check the algorithm. Rewrite the algorithm correctly, then desk-check it again. Submit the desk-check of the incorrect algorithm, as well as the corrected algorithm and the desk-check of the corrected algorithm.

Input	Processing	Output
beginning inventory amount sold amount returned	Processing items: none Algorithm: 1. enter the beginning inventory, amount sold, and amount returned 2. calculate the ending inventory by adding the amount sold to the beginning inventory, then subtracting the amount returned 3. display the ending inventory	ending inventory

Figure 2-23

debugging   19. Jean Marie wants a program that will display the cube of a number. The algorithm shown in Figure 2-24 is supposed to solve this problem, but it is not working correctly. First calculate the expected result using the number 4. Then use this value to desk-check the algorithm. Rewrite the algorithm correctly, then desk-check it again. Submit the desk-check of the incorrect algorithm, as well as the corrected algorithm and the desk-check of the corrected algorithm.

Input	Processing	Output
number	Processing items: none Algorithm: 1. calculate the cube of the number by multiplying the number by itself three times	cube of the number

Figure 2-24

debugging

20. GeeBees Clothiers is having a sale. The manager of the store wants a program that will allow the clerk to enter the original price of an item and the discount rate. The program will then display the discount, as well as the sale price. The algorithm shown in Figure 2-25 is supposed to solve this problem, but it is not working correctly. First calculate the expected result using an original price of $100 and a discount rate of 25 percent. Then use this value to desk-check the algorithm. Rewrite the algorithm correctly, then desk-check it again. Submit the desk-check of the incorrect algorithm, as well as the corrected algorithm and the desk-check of the corrected algorithm.

Input	Processing	Output
original price discount rate	Processing items: none Algorithm: 1. enter the original price and the discount rate 2. calculate the sale price by subtracting the discount from the original price 3. display the discount and the sale price	discount sale price

Figure 2-25

In this lesson you will learn how to:

- Understand the origins of the C++ programming language
- Differentiate between source code and object code
- Open a C++ source file
- Code an algorithm
- Compile, build, and execute a C++ program
- Evaluate and modify a program

An Introduction to the C++ Language

Completing the Problem-Solving Process

In Lesson A you learned how to analyze a problem, as well as how to plan and desk-check an algorithm. Recall that analyzing, planning, and desk-checking are only the first three steps in the problem-solving process, which is shown in Figure 2-26.

1. Analyze the problem.

2. Plan the algorithm.

3. Desk-check the algorithm.

4. Code the algorithm into a program.

5. Desk-check the program.

6. Evaluate and modify (if necessary) the program.

Figure 2-26: The problem-solving process

To complete the problem-solving process, you need to learn how to code the algorithm into a program, as well as how to desk-check, evaluate, and modify the program. First, however, learn about the C++ programming language, which is the language that you will use to code your algorithms.

The C++ Programming Language

C++ evolved from the procedure-oriented C programming language, which was developed in 1972 at Bell Laboratories by Dennis Ritchie. In 1985, Bjarne Stroustrup, also of Bell Laboratories, added, among other things, object-oriented features to the C language. This enhanced version of the C language was named C++.

C++ is a superset of C, which means that, with few exceptions, everything available in C is also available in C++. That means that you can use C++ as a procedural, as well as an object-oriented, language. Before using the object-oriented features of C++, you will learn how to use C++ to create procedure-oriented programs. The techniques you learn from procedural programming will help you create object-oriented programs later.

To create and execute a C++ program, you need to have access to a text editor, often simply called an editor, and a C++ compiler. You use the editor to enter the C++ instructions, called the **source code**, into the computer. After entering the source code, you then use the C++ compiler to convert the source code into machine code—the 0s and 1s that the computer can understand. Machine code is most often called **object code**.

Many C++ systems, such as Microsoft Visual C++ and Borland C++ Builder, contain both the editor and the compiler in one integrated environment, referred to as an IDE (Integrated Development Environment). Other C++ systems, called command-line compilers, contain only the compiler and require you to use a general-purpose editor (such as Notepad and WordPad) to enter the program instructions into the computer. Keep in mind that the different C++ systems, such as Visual C++ and C++ Builder, are not different languages. Rather, they are different implementations of the C++ language. Although this book assumes that you are using Microsoft Visual C++ 5.0 to create your programs, you will be able to use the C++ instructions that you learn in most C++ systems.

Next, learn how to use the C++ programming language to code an algorithm.

Coding the Algorithm

After desk-checking an algorithm to verify that it is correct, the programmer then translates the algorithm into a language that the computer can understand—in other words, he or she codes the algorithm. As you may remember from Lesson A, a coded algorithm is called a program.

Before you can create a C++ program, you need to start C++. The instructions for starting C++ depend on the C++ system you are using. The following instructions show you how to start Microsoft Visual C++ 5.0. If you are using a different C++ system, you will need to ask your instructor or your technical support person for the appropriate instructions to start that system. Before you begin the following steps, you should have copied the C++ student data files for this book to your computer's hard disk, as specified in the Read This Before You Begin page found at the beginning of this book.

To start the Microsoft Visual C++ 5.0 program:

1 If necessary, start Windows, then hide the Windows 95 taskbar.

HELP? To hide the Windows 95 taskbar, click the Start button, point to Settings, and then click Taskbar to display the Taskbar Properties window. On the Taskbar Options tab, click the Auto hide check box. A check mark appears in the check box. Click the OK button to remove the Taskbar Properties window. The taskbar is now hidden from view; only a thin line appears in its place at the bottom of the screen. (Depending on how you have Windows 95 set up, your taskbar could be at the top, right, left, or bottom edge of the screen. The thin line will appear in the location of the taskbar. This book assumes that the taskbar is located at the bottom of the screen.)

tip

Recall from Tutorial 1 that a compiler translates the entire program into machine code before executing the program.

2 Display the hidden taskbar temporarily by moving the mouse to a location below the thin line that represents the taskbar. Click the **Start** button on the Windows 95 taskbar to display the Start menu, then point to **Programs**. The Programs menu appears to the right of the Start menu. Point to **Microsoft Visual C++ 5.0** on the Programs menu. The Visual C++ menu appears to the right of the Programs menu. Click **Microsoft Visual C++ 5.0** on the Visual C++ menu. The Microsoft Visual Studio 97 copyright screen appears momentarily, and then the Microsoft Developer Studio window appears. You may see one or more of the windows shown in Figure 2-27.

HELP? If a Tip of the Day dialog box appears, read the tip, and then click the Show tips at startup check box both to remove the check mark and deselect this option. Click the Close button to close the Tip of the Day dialog box.

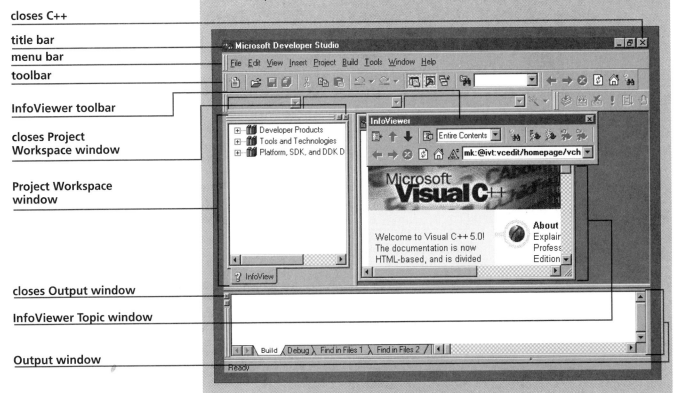

closes C++

title bar

menu bar

toolbar

InfoViewer toolbar

closes Project
Workspace window

Project Workspace
window

closes Output window

InfoViewer Topic window

Output window

Figure 2-27: Microsoft Visual C++ 5.0 Developer Studio window

Microsoft Visual C++ 5.0 provides an easy-to-use graphical user interface, referred to as a GUI (pronounced *gooey*), which you can use to create C++ applications. The Visual C++ GUI contains a title bar, a menu bar, and toolbars. It also contains a Project Workspace window, an Output window, and an InfoViewer Topic window.

3 If the Output window is open, click the **Close** button ⊠ on its title bar to close it.

4 If the InfoViewer toolbar is showing, click the **Close** button ⊠ on its title bar to close it.

5 If the InfoViewer Topic window is open, click the **Close** button ⊠ on its title bar to close it.

6 If the Project Workspace window is open, click the **Close** button ☒ on its title bar to close it.

Important note: In the future, you will be instructed simply to "start Visual C++."

The first algorithm that you will code is one that you created in Lesson A to display Sarah Martin's new weekly pay. The IPO chart that contains the pseudocode version of the algorithm is shown in Figure 2-28.

Input	Processing	Output
current weekly pay raise rate	Processing items: weekly raise amount Algorithm: 1. enter the current weekly pay and raise rate 2. calculate the weekly raise amount by multiplying the current weekly pay by the raise rate 3. calculate the new weekly pay by adding the weekly raise amount to the current weekly pay 4. display the new weekly pay	new weekly pay

Figure 2-28: Completed IPO chart

Programmers use the information in the IPO chart to code the algorithm—in other words, to create the program. The C++ program that corresponds to this algorithm has already been entered in a file for you. You will open that program file now.

To open an existing C++ program:

1 Click **File** on the menu bar, and then click **Open**. The Open dialog box appears. Locate the LbProg01.cpp file, which is stored in the Cpp\Tut02\LbProg01 folder on your computer's hard disk, then click **LbProg01.cpp** in the list of filenames. (The *LbProg01* in the filename stands for *Lesson B, Program1*; the *.cpp* stands for *C plus plus*.) Click the **Open** button to open the file. The LbProg01 program appears in the LbProg01.cpp window, as shown in Figure 2-29.

HELP? The instructions to copy the C++ student files for this book to the computer's hard disk can be found in the Read This Before You Begin page at the beginning of the book.

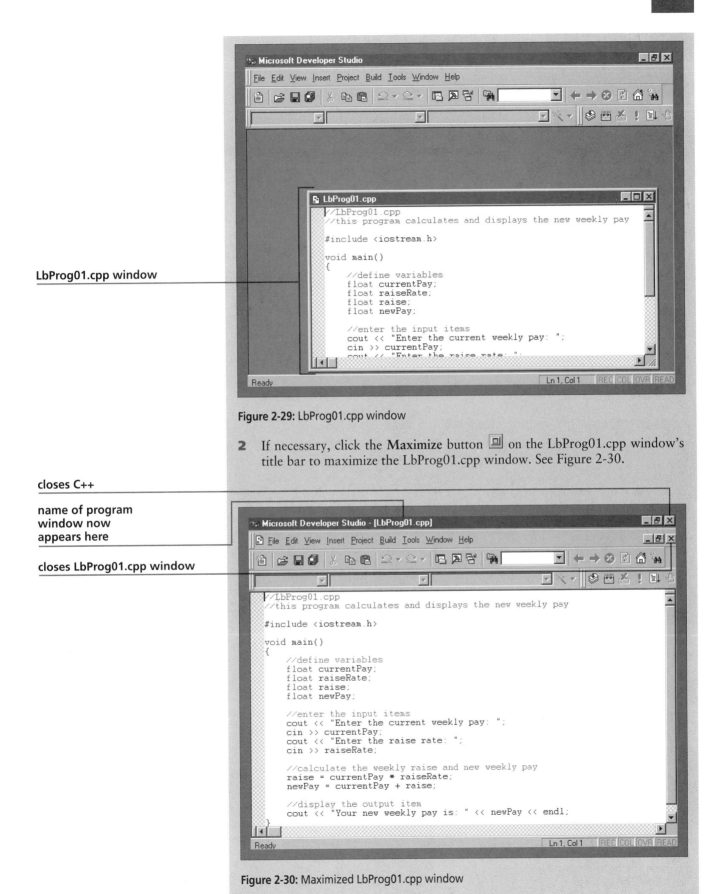

Figure 2-29: LbProg01.cpp window

2 If necessary, click the **Maximize** button 回 on the LbProg01.cpp window's title bar to maximize the LbProg01.cpp window. See Figure 2-30.

closes C++

name of program window now appears here

closes LbProg01.cpp window

Figure 2-30: Maximized LbProg01.cpp window

The LbProg01.cpp program instructions are shown in Figure 2-31.

```cpp
//LbProg01.cpp
//this program calculates and displays the new weekly pay

#include <iostream.h>

void main()
{
    //define variables
    float currentPay;
    float raiseRate;
    float raise;
    float newPay;

    //enter the input items
    cout << "Enter the current weekly pay: ";
    cin >> currentPay;
    cout << "Enter the raise rate: ";
    cin >> raiseRate;

    //calculate the weekly raise and new weekly pay
    raise = currentPay * raiseRate;
    newPay = currentPay + raise;

    //display the output item
    cout << "Your new weekly pay is: " << newPay << endl;
} //end of main function
```

Figure 2-31: C++ instructions contained in the LbProg01.cpp file

Like most programming languages, the C++ language follows a specific format, referred to as its syntax. The **syntax** of a language, whether it is C++ or English, is simply the rules that you must follow to use the language. The syntax of the C++ language, like the syntax of the English language, will take some time and effort to learn.

Do not be concerned if the program shown in Figure 2-31 looks confusing to you. Each program instruction is described in this lesson with a minimal amount of explanation. You will learn more detail about each instruction in the following tutorials. For now, however, you need simply to pay attention to the C++ syntax. You should also note how the instructions in this program correspond to Figure 2-28's algorithm. You will learn how to create your own C++ applications in Tutorial 3.

The first two lines in the program are `//LbProg01.cpp` and `//this program calculates and displays the new weekly pay`. When you see `//` (two forward slashes) in a C++ program, it tells you that what follows on that line is a **comment**, which is simply a message to the person reading the program. In this case, the `//LbProg01.cpp` comment reminds you that the program you are viewing is named LbProg01.cpp. The comment `//this program calculates and displays the new weekly pay` tells the viewer what the program does. Comments, which are referred to as **internal documentation**, make the program instructions more readable and easier to understand by anyone viewing the program. The C++ compiler ignores the comments when it translates the source code into object code.

tip

C++ saves the source code, which is the instructions that the programmer enters, in the .cpp file. When the compiler translates the source code into object code, it saves the object code in a file with the same name as the source code, but with an .obj extension. For example, the object code that corresponds to the LbProg01.cpp source code will be saved in a file named LbProg01.obj.

If you are using a color monitor, you will notice that comments appear in a different color than the rest of the code. Visual C++ displays comments in a different color to help you quickly identify them in the code.

The third line in the program, #include <iostream.h>, is called a directive. C++ programs typically include at least one directive and most include many directives. The **#include directive** is a special instruction for the C++ compiler that tells the compiler to include the contents of another file, in this case the iostream.h file, in the current program. The #include directive provides a convenient way to merge the source code from one file with the source code in another file, without having to retype the code. Notice that you place the name of the file—in this case, iostream.h —in angle brackets (< >). The angle brackets indicate that the file is located in C++'s *include* folder. The *include* folder, which contains the standard C++ header files, comes with the C++ system.

In C++, the iostream.h file contains the instructions (source code) needed to handle input and output operations, such as entering data from the keyboard and displaying information on the computer screen. If your program will perform either of those tasks, you will need to use the #include directive to include the iostream.h file in the program. Files that have an .h at the end of their names are called **header files**. *Header* refers to the fact that these files are included at the beginning (head) of a program.

If you are using a color monitor, you will notice that #include appears in a different color than the comments or the rest of the code. #include is one of the C++ keywords. A **keyword** is a word that has a special meaning in a programming language.

When you enter the C++ instructions, keep in mind that the C++ compiler is case sensitive. Typing #Include, rather than #include, will create a syntax error because the C++ compiler will not recognize the word Include. In other words, include is not the same as Include or INCLUDE.

The next program instruction is void main( ). main is the name of a function. A **function** is simply a block of code that performs a task. You can recognize a function in a C++ program by the parentheses immediately following the name. Some functions require you to enter information between the parentheses; others, like main, do not. The execution of a C++ program always begins with the main function; every C++ program must have a main function.

In Tutorial 4, you will learn that some functions return a value, while others, referred to as **void functions**, do not. The main function shown in Figure 2-31 is a void function; you can tell that because the word void appears before the function's name. The main function shown in Figure 2-31, therefore, does not return a value.

After the function's name, you enter the code that directs the function on how to perform its assigned task. In C++, you enclose a function's code within a set of braces ({ }). The braces mark the beginning and the end of the code block. In the current program, the opening brace ({) is immediately below the void main( ) instruction, and the closing brace (}) is at the end of the program. Everything between the opening and closing braces is included, in this case, in the main function.

Immediately below the opening brace is the //define variables comment, which describes the purpose of the next four program instructions. Those four instructions float currentPay;, float raiseRate;, float raise;, and float newPay;—declare, or create, four **variables**, which are simply memory locations that the program will use while it is running. You will need to create a variable for each input, processing, and output item that appears in the IPO chart. (One exception to this is a named constant, which will appear in your IPO chart, but will not need a variable. You will learn about named constants in Tutorial 3.)

tip

The #include **directive is one of many directives that you can use in a C++ program.**

You may want to look at this algorithm's IPO chart, which is shown in Figure 2-28, to verify that each input, processing, and output item in the chart corresponds to a variable in the program.

    `float`, which must be typed using lowercase letters, is a keyword in C++. When you precede a variable's name with `float`, it tells the C++ compiler that the variable (memory location) can store a number with a decimal point.

    A common convention for naming variables in a C++ program is to type the name in lowercase. If the variable name contains two words, however, you use an uppercase letter for the first letter in the second word, as shown in the variable names `currentPay`, `raiseRate`, and `newPay`. Keep in mind that this is just one convention for naming variables; many others are also used. The important thing is to select the method that makes the most sense to you, and then use that method consistently in all of your programs.

    Unlike the instructions you have seen so far, each of the variable declaration instructions ends in a semicolon (;). The instruction to declare a variable is considered a **statement**, which is simply a C++ instruction that can be executed, or processed, by the computer. All C++ statements must end with a semicolon. In the remaining tutorials, you will learn which instructions are statements and which are not.

    The line below the variable declaration statements, `//enter the input items`, is a comment that informs the reader that the purpose of the next set of instructions is to enter the input values into the computer. Entering the input values is the first step in the program's algorithm. (You can refer to Figure 2-28 to verify this.) You will have the user enter the input values at the keyboard. To do so, first you will prompt the user for the information you want him or her to enter; then you will pause the program to allow him or her to enter it.

    In C++, you use **streams**, which are just sequences of characters, to perform standard input and output operations. The standard output stream is called `cout` (pronounced *see out*), which refers to the computer screen. The standard input stream, on the other hand, is called `cin` (pronounced *see in*), which refers to the keyboard. To make the concept of streams easier to understand, it may help to think of the `cout` output stream as simply a sequence of characters being sent "out" to the user through the computer screen, and think of the `cin` input stream as a sequence of characters sent "in" to the computer through the keyboard.

    The `cout << "Enter the current weekly pay: ";` statement, which is the next instruction in the program, prompts the user to enter the current weekly pay by displaying an appropriate message on the computer screen. (You can tell that this line is a statement because it ends in a semicolon.) The `<<` that follows `cout` in the statement is called the **insertion operator**. It may help to think of the insertion operator as meaning "sends to." In this case, the insertion operator (`<<`) sends the "Enter the current weekly pay:" message to the computer screen. Keep in mind that this statement only displays the message on the screen. The statement does not pause the program to allow the user to actually enter the pay; you will need to use the standard input stream, `cin`, to do so.

    The next statement in the program, `cin >> currentPay;`, uses the `cin` stream to pause the program to allow the user to enter the current weekly pay. The `>>` that follows `cin` is called the **extraction operator**. It may help to think of the `>>` operator as meaning "gets from." In this case, the `cin >> currentPay;` statement gets the current weekly pay from the keyboard (`cin`), then stores that amount in the `currentPay` variable (the memory location).

    The next statement in the program, `cout << "Enter the raise rate: ";`, prompts the user to enter the raise rate. The `cin >> raiseRate;` statement then pauses the program to allow the user to enter the rate; the statement stores the user's response in the `raiseRate` variable.

The comment `//calculate the weekly raise and new weekly pay` describes the purpose of the two statements below it. You will notice that those statements correspond to the next two steps in the algorithm. The `raise = currentPay * raiseRate;` statement calculates the raise by multiplying the value in the `currentPay` variable by the value in the `raiseRate` variable. (Notice that a computer uses an asterisk to represent multiplication.) The `newPay = currentPay + raise;` statement calculates the new pay by adding the contents of the `currentPay` variable to the contents of the `raise` variable.

The `//display the output item` comment describes the statement immediately below it. The `cout << "Your new weekly pay is: " << newPay << endl;` statement, which corresponds to the last step in the algorithm, displays the "Your new weekly pay is: " message along with the new weekly pay. (Notice that you can use more than one insertion operator in a statement.) The `endl`, which stands for "end of line," is one of the C++ stream manipulators. A **stream manipulator** allows the program to manipulate, or manage, the input and output stream characters in some way. When outputting information to the screen, for example, you can use the `endl` stream manipulator to advance the cursor to the next line on the computer screen.

The last line in the program is the closing brace, }, that marks the end of the `main` function. You can include a comment—in this case, `//end of main function`—on the same line with any C++ instruction; but you must be sure to enter the comment after the instruction, and not before it. Any text appearing after the // is interpreted as a comment; text that appears before the //, however, is not interpreted as a comment.

After coding the algorithm, you then desk-check the resulting program.

mini-quiz

Mini-Quiz 4

1. The C++ compiler translates _____ code into _____ code.
2. Write a C++ instruction that you could use to enter the message "My first program" as a comment in a program.
3. Write a C++ statement that declares a float variable named `hoursWorked`.
4. Write a C++ statement that gets the number of hours worked from the user at the keyboard, and then stores the response in the `hoursWorked` variable.
5. Write a C++ statement that displays the message "Number of hours worked " on the screen, followed by the contents of the `hoursWorked` variable. The statement should then advance the cursor to the next line on the screen

Desk-checking the Program

After the programmer codes the program, he or she then desk-checks it to assure that each step in the algorithm was translated correctly. You can desk-check the program using the same sample data that you used to desk-check the algorithm. As you may remember from Lesson A, you desk-checked the algorithm using 250 as the current weekly pay and .03 as the raise rate.

The `main` function begins by defining four variables (memory locations). You would place the names of these variables in the desk-check table, as shown in Figure 2-32.

currentPay	raiseRate	raise	newPay

Figure 2-32: Variable names shown in the desk-check table

The cout << "Enter the current weekly pay: "; statement prompts the user to enter the current weekly pay. The cin >> currentPay; statement stores the user's response—in this case, 250—in the currentPay variable. In the desk-check table, you would record the number 250 in the currentPay column.

The cout << "Enter the raise rate: "; statement prompts the user to enter the raise rate. The cin >> raiseRate; statement stores the user's response—in this case, .03—in the raiseRate variable. In the desk-check table, you would record the number .03 in the raiseRate column.

The raise = currentPay * raiseRate; statement multiplies the contents of the currentPay variable (250) by the contents of the raiseRate variable (.03), and then stores the result (7.50) in the raise variable. In the desk-check table, you would record the number 7.50 in the raise column.

The newPay = currentPay + raise; statement adds the contents of the currentPay variable (250) to the contents of the raise variable (7.50), and then stores the result (257.50) in the newPay variable. In the desk-check table, you would record the number 257.50 in the newPay column.

The cout << "Your new weekly pay is: " << newPay << endl; displays the "Your new weekly pay is:" message, along with the contents of the newPay variable (257.50), on the screen. The endl stream manipulator then advances the cursor to the next line on the screen. The completed desk-check table is shown in Figure 2-33.

currentPay	raiseRate	raise	newPay
250	.03	7.50	257.50

Figure 2-33: Completed desk-check table after desk-checking the program

After desk-checking the program, the programmer then evaluates and modifies (if necessary) the program.

Evaluating and Modifying the Program

The final step in the problem-solving process is to evaluate and modify (if necessary) the program. Programmers refer to this as the "testing and debugging" step. You test a program by executing it and entering some sample data. You should use both valid and invalid test data. **Valid data** is data that the program is expecting—for example, the current program is expecting the user to enter a positive number as the current pay. **Invalid data**, on the other hand, is data that the application is not expecting. In this program, for example, the program is not expecting the user to enter a negative number for either the current pay or the raise rate. You should test the program as thoroughly as possible. You do not want to give the user a program that ends abruptly because invalid data was entered. (You will learn more about handling invalid data in later tutorials.)

Debugging refers to the process of locating and removing the errors in a program. Program errors, called **bugs**, can be either syntax errors or logic errors. When you enter an instruction incorrectly—for example, typing `ednl` instead of `endl`—you create a **syntax error**. The C++ compiler can detect syntax errors for you, as you will learn in this lesson. An example of a much more difficult type of error to find, and one that the C++ compiler cannot find for you, is a logic error. When you enter an instruction that will not give you the results for which you are looking, you create a **logic error**. The instruction `raise = currentPay + raiseRate;`, which is supposed to calculate the raise, is an example of a logic error. Although the instruction is syntactically correct, it is logically incorrect. The instruction to calculate the raise, written correctly, should be `raise = currentPay * raiseRate;`.

You evaluate a C++ program by executing it.

Executing a C++ Program

Before you can execute a C++ program, you need to compile it—in other words, you need to tell the C++ compiler to translate the source code into object code. The method of telling C++ to compile and execute a program varies with the different C++ systems. In the following steps, you will learn how to use Visual C++ to compile and execute a program. If you are using a different C++ system, you will need to ask your instructor or your technical support person for the appropriate instructions for that system.

tip

••••••••••••••

You should always save a program before compiling the program. That way, if a fatal error occurs in the program, you will not lose the instructions you entered; you can simply reopen the file. (In this case, the LbProg01.cpp file already exists on your disk. You are saving it simply to develop the habit of saving before compiling.)

To save, compile, and then execute a C++ program in Visual C++:

1 Click **File** on the menu bar. The File menu opens. You will notice that the File menu contains the Save and Save As options. You use the Save option to save a file under its current name. The Save As option is used to save a file under a different name.

2 Click **Save** to save the LbProg01.cpp file under its current name.

3 Click **Build** on the menu bar, then click **Compile LbProg01.cpp**. The Microsoft Developer Studio dialog box appears, as shown in Figure 2-34.

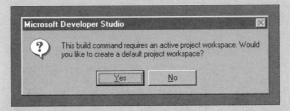

Figure 2-34: Microsoft Developer Studio dialog box

For Visual C++ to compile a program, the program must be in a project workspace. (You will learn about projects and workspaces in Tutorial 3.) Because you did not create a project workspace before opening the current program, Visual C++ asks if you would like to create a default workspace. You can simply click the Yes button to do so.

4   Click the **Yes** button to create a default project workspace for the current program.

The compiler translates the C++ instructions (the source code) into the 0s and 1s (the object code) that the computer can understand. The Output window appears as the compiler is working.

5   When the compiler is finished, scroll the Output window as shown in Figure 2-35.

you may need to scroll

source code file

object code file

indicates no problems found during compile process

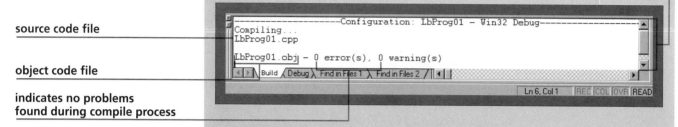

Figure 2-35: Output window at the end of the compile phase

The Output window indicates that the compiler translated the source code contained in the LbProg01.cpp file into object code, and stored that object code in the LbProg01.obj file. According to the Output window, the compiler found no errors or warnings during the compiling phase.

In many C++ systems, you could now simply execute the object code version of the program. In Visual C++, however, you need first to build an executable file.

6   Click **Build** on the menu bar, then click **Build LbProg01.exe**. When the build process is finished, the Output window appears as shown in Figure 2-36.

executable file

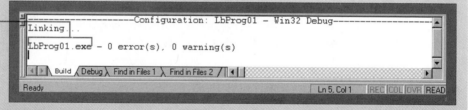

Figure 2-36: Output window at the end of the build phase

Visual C++ links the necessary files together into one executable file named LbProg01.exe. Your program is now ready to execute.

7   Click **Build** on the menu bar, then click **Execute LbProg01.exe**. The "Enter the current weekly pay: " prompt appears in a DOS window, as shown in Figure 2-37.

In this book, you use Microsoft Visual C++ 5.0 to create console applications, which are explained in Tutorial 3. The ouput from console applications appears in a DOS window.

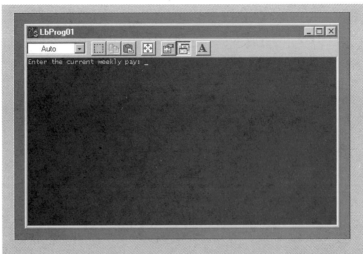

Figure 2-37: Prompt appears in a DOS window

8 Type 250 as the current weekly pay, and then press the **Enter** key. The prompt to enter the raise rate appears. Type .03 as the raise rate, and then press the **Enter** key. The new weekly pay (257.5) appears on the screen, along with the "Press any key to continue" message. Microsoft Visual C++ automatically displays the "Press any key to continue" message on the screen when your program ends. See Figure 2-38.

Figure 2-38: DOS window showing the new weekly pay and the "Press any key to continue" message

9 Press the **Enter** key to close the DOS window.

Next, you will introduce a syntax error into the current program. You will then learn how to locate and correct the error; in other words, you will learn how to debug and modify the program.

Locating and Correcting an Error in a Program

It is extremely easy to make a typing error when entering a C++ program. A typing error typically results in a C++ syntax error. Observe what happens when a C++ program contains a syntax error.

You can also use the Save command on the File menu to save the program under its current name.

If your program was not previously compiled, the Build command will simply say Build; you will not see the name of the .exe file in the command.

To introduce a syntax error, then locate and correct the error:

1 Close the Output window. Position the I at the end of the **cin >> currentPay;** statement in the LbProg01.cpp window, and then click at that location. The insertion point appears after the ; (semicolon) on that line. Press the **Backspace** key to delete the ; (semicolon) that appears at the end of the statement. The statement should now say **cin >> currentPay**. (Do not type the period.)

2 Click the **Save** button 🖫 on the Visual C++ Standard toolbar to save the program under its current name.

To execute a Visual C++ program, recall that you need to compile it, then build it, and then execute it. In the previous section, you ran the program by selecting three commands on the Build menu: Compile, Build, and Execute. Rather than using this three-step process, you can execute a Microsoft Visual C++ 5.0 program in two steps: by first selecting the Build command, and then selecting the Execute command. The Compile command is not necessary to select because, in Microsoft Visual C++ 5.0, the Build command compiles the program, if it has not been compiled, before it builds the executable file.

3 Click **Build** on the menu bar, then click **Build LbProg01.exe**.

4 Scroll the Output window as shown in Figure 2-39. (The drive letter and path in the instruction may differ from the one shown in the figure.)

your drive letter and path may differ

indicates an error was found in the program

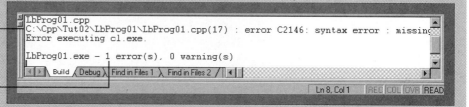

Figure 2-39: Output window showing an error

The Output window tells you that the compiler encountered a syntax error in the program. The syntax error was caused by a missing semicolon before **cout**. (You may need to scroll the Output window to see the full message.)

5 Double-click the error message in the Output window to select it, as shown in Figure 2-40.

location of error

**your drive letter and
path may differ**

description of error

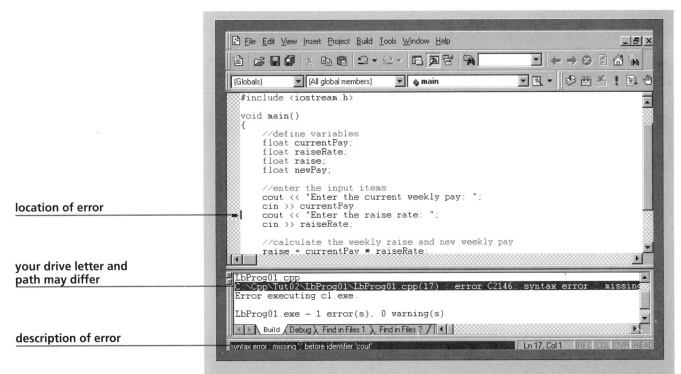

Figure 2-40: Screen showing the description and location of the error

You will notice that the "syntax error : missing ';' before identifier 'cout'" message appears below the Output window. In the LbProg01.cpp window, Visual C++ displays an arrow at the location where the error was encountered. In this case, the arrow is pointing to the `cout << "Enter the raise rate: ";` statement. Although that is the statement where the compiler discovered the error, that is not the statement that actually caused the error. Rather, the error was caused by the statement immediately above it—the `cin >> currentPay` instruction. You will notice that the semicolon is missing from that statement.

6   Close the Output window. Position the cursor at the end of the `cin >> currentPay` instruction in the LbProg01.cpp window, and then type ; (a semicolon).

Now save and execute the program to verify that it is working correctly.

7   Save the program under its current name. Click **Build** on the menu bar, then click **Build LbProg01.exe**. The Output window indicates that the compiler encountered no errors and no warnings. Click **Build** on the menu bar, then click **Execute LbProg01.exe**. C++ executes the LbProg01.exe file.

Important note: In the future, you will be instructed simply to "save, build, and execute the program."

8   Type **120** as the current weekly pay, and then press the **Enter** key. The prompt to enter the raise rate appears. Type **.02** as the raise rate, and then press the **Enter** key. The new weekly pay (122.4) appears on the screen. When the "Press any key to continue" message appears, press the **Enter** key to close the DOS window.

Although the program is not currently designed to handle invalid data correctly, you will test it with invalid data simply to see the results. You will use a negative number—for example, a –100—as the current weekly pay. Because you did not make any changes to the program since the last time it was compiled and built, you can simply execute the program; you do not need to compile and build it again.

9   Click **Build** on the menu bar, then click **Execute LbProg01.exe**. Type **–100** as the current weekly pay, and then press the **Enter** key. The prompt to enter the raise rate appears. Because the current weekly pay should not be a negative number, the program should respond at this point by prompting the user to enter a positive number, rather than by prompting the user to enter the raise rate; you will learn how to design a program that does so in a later tutorial. Type **.1** as the raise rate, and then press the **Enter** key. The new weekly pay (–110) appears on the screen. When the "Press any key to continue" message appears, press the **Enter** key to close the DOS window.

10 Close the Output window.

You have now completed the six-step process for creating a computer program. Recall that those steps are to analyze the problem, then plan, desk-check, and code the algorithm, and then desk-check, evaluate, and modify (if necessary) the program. After completing the process, you should place your planning tools (IPO chart, flowchart, or pseudocode) and a printout of the program in a safe place, so you can refer to them if you need to change the program in the future. The planning tools and printout are referred to as **external documentation**. You will learn how to print the program, as well as how to close the program, in the next section.

Printing and Closing a Program

The File menu on the Visual C++ menu bar contains a Print command, which you can use to print the program. The File menu also contains the Close Workspace command, which allows you to close the current program without exiting C++. You use the Close Workspace command when you are finished with one program and you want to begin another program. Print the current program, then close the current program's workspace.

To print the program, and then close the program's workspace and exit Microsoft Visual C++:

1   Click **File** on the menu bar, and then click **Print**. When the Print dialog box appears, click the **OK** button. The program prints on your printer.

2   Click **File** on the menu bar, and then click **Close Workspace**. The "Do you want to close all document windows?" message appears in the Microsoft Developer Studio dialog box. Click the **Yes** button. Visual C++ closes the current program. You can now open either a new or an existing program. (You will learn how to open a new program in Tutorial 3.)

3   Click **File** on the menu bar, and then click **Exit** to exit Microsoft Visual C++.

You have now completed Lesson B. You can either take a break or complete the questions and exercises at the end of the lesson.

mini-quiz

Mini-Quiz 5

1. _____ refers to the process of locating and removing the bugs in a program.

2. You should always test your program with both _____ data, which the program is expecting, and _____ data, which the program is not expecting.

3. External documentation includes _____ .

4. The C++ source code is contained in a file that has a(n) _____ extension on its filename.

5. When the compiler translates the source code into object code, the object code is stored in a file with a(n) _____ extension on its filename.

6. When you execute a file, C++ executes the file that has a(n) _____ extension on its filename.

S U M M A R Y

C++ is the object-oriented successor to the procedure-oriented C language. Almost everything available in the C language is also available in C++; that means that you can use C++ as a procedural, as well as an object-oriented, language.

To create and execute a C++ program, you need to have access to an editor and a C++ compiler. You use the editor to enter the source code (the C++ instructions) into the computer. You use the compiler to convert the source code into object code—the 0s and 1s the computer can understand. Many C++ systems contain both the editor and the compiler in one integrated environment, referred to as an IDE (Integrated Development Environment). Other C++ systems contain only the compiler; you need to use a general-purpose editor to enter the program instructions into the computer.

You code an algorithm, which is the fourth step in the problem-solving process, by translating it into a programming language—in other words, by creating a program. This process is called coding. The information in the problem's IPO chart is used as a guide when coding the algorithm.

Like most programming languages, the C++ language has a very precise syntax, which takes a lot of time and effort to learn. You can make a program easier to understand by including explanatory comments in the program code. To include a comment in a program, you simply begin the comment with //, which tells the C++ compiler to ignore what follows on that line. Comments are referred to as internal documentation.

Almost all C++ programs contain at least one directive and most will contain more than one. The #include directive is a special instruction that allows you to merge the source code from one file with the source code in another file, without having to retype the code. The iostream.h file, which handles input and output operations, is an example of a file that you may need to merge with another file. Files that have an .h at the end of their names are called header files because they are included at the beginning of a program.

In C++, program execution always begins with the main function, so every C++ program must contain a function named main. A function is simply a block of code that performs a task. You typically use the instruction void main() to declare the main function in a program. You use an opening brace ({) to mark the beginning of the function's block of code; you use a closing brace (}) to mark the end of the function. Keep in mind that the C++ compiler is case sensitive, which means that `main` is not the same as either `Main` or `MAIN`.

You must use C++ to declare variables, which are simply memory locations that the program will use while it is executing. You should have a variable declared for each input, processing, and output item in your IPO chart. One convention for naming the variables in a C++ program is to type the name using all lowercase letters. If the variable name contains two words, however, you use an uppercase letter for the first letter in the second word—for example, `currentPay`. In C++, you use the word `float` before a variable name to tell the C++ compiler that the variable will store a number that has a decimal point.

Some C++ instructions, such as variable declarations, are executable instructions, called statements. A statement in a C++ program must end in a semicolon (`;`).

In C++, you use streams to perform standard input and output operations. The standard output stream, called `cout`, refers to the computer screen. The standard input stream, called `cin`, refers to the keyboard. You use the `<<` (insertion operator) to send a stream of characters to `cout`. When sending information to `cout`, you can use the stream manipulator, `endl`, to tell C++ to advance the cursor to the next line on the screen. You use the `>>` (extraction operator) to get data from `cin`.

The fifth step in the problem-solving process is to desk-check the program to ensure that the algorithm was translated correctly. The final step in the problem-solving process is to evaluate and modify (if necessary) the algorithm. Programmers refer to this as the "testing and debugging" step. You test a program by executing it and entering some sample data. You should test the program using both valid and invalid test data. Debugging refers to the process of locating and removing the errors, called bugs, in a program.

Before you can execute a C++ program, you need to compile it. The method of telling C++ to compile and execute a program varies with the different C++ systems.

After completing the problem-solving process, you should assemble the external documentation and place it in a safe place, so you can refer to it if you need to modify the program in the future. The external documentation includes the IPO chart, flowchart or pseudocode, and printout of the program.

ANSWERS TO MINI-QUIZZES

Mini-Quiz 4

1. source, object
2. `//My first program`
3. `float hoursWorked;`
4. `cin >> hoursWorked;`
5. `cout << "Number of hours worked " << hoursWorked << endl;`

Mini-Quiz 5

1. Debugging **2.** valid, invalid **3.** the IPO chart, flowchart or pseudocode, and a printout of the program code **4.** .cpp **5.** .obj **6.** .exe

Q U E S T I O N S

1. Which of the following is the fourth problem-solving step?
    a. analyze the problem
    b. evaluate and modify (if necessary) the program
    c. code the algorithm
    d. plan the algorithm
    e. desk-check the program

2. You can use C++ as a procedural, as well as an object-oriented, language.
    a. True
    b. False

3. To create and execute a C++ program, you need to have access to _____ .
    a. a C++ compiler
    b. a C++ translator
    c. an object code editor
    d. a text editor
    e. both a and d

4. The instructions you enter into the computer are called the _____ .
    a. edited code
    b. machine code
    c. object code
    d. source code

5. The compiler converts your C++ instructions into _____ .
    a. edited code
    b. object code
    c. source code
    d. translated code

6. Machine code is _____ .
    a. edited code
    b. source code
    c. the 0s and 1s that the computer can understand
    d. both b and c

7. The rules of a programming language are called its _____ .
    a. code
    b. guidelines
    c. procedures
    d. regulations
    e. syntax

8. To enter a comment in a program, you begin the comment with _____ .
    a. **
    b. &&
    c. \\
    d. @
    e. //

9. Which of the following instructions tells C++ to merge the source code from the iostream.h file into the current file?
    a. `#Include <iostream.h>`
    b. `#include iostream.h`
    c. `/#include <iostream.h>`
    d. `#merge iostream.h`
    e. none of the above

10. The #include instruction is called a _____ .
  a. direction
  b. directive
  c. merge instruction
  d. statement

11. Files whose names end in .h are called _____ files.
  a. handy
  b. header
  c. helper
  d. helping

12. Which of the following can be used to declare the main function?
  a. void main
  b. void Main()
  c. void main()
  d. main
  e. either b or c can be used

13. The C++ keyword for declaring a variable that contains a decimal point is
_____ .
  a. dec
  b. decimal
  c. float
  d. floater
  e. none of the above

14. You mark the beginning of a function's block of code with the _____ .
  a. /
  b. *
  c. {
  d. }
  e. either c or d can be used

15. Which of the following statements declares a variable that can contain a decimal number?
  a. dec payRate;
  b. dec hourlyPay
  c. float payRate
  d. float hourlyPay;
  e. none of the above

16. A C++ statement must end in a _____ .
  a. : (colon)
  b. , (comma)
  c. . (period)
  d. ; (semicolon)

17. In C++, you use _____ to perform standard input and output operations.
  a. characters
  b. sequences
  c. streams
  d. tests

18. The standard output stream, which refers to the computer screen, is called

_____ .

a. `cin`
b. `cout`
c. `stin`
d. `stout`
e. none of the above

19. The standard input stream, which refers to the keyboard, is called _____ .
a. `cin`
b. `cout`
c. `stin`
d. `stout`
e. none of the above

20. Which of the following statements will display the word "Hello" on the computer screen?
a. `cin << "Hello";`
b. `cin >> "Hello";`
c. `cout << "Hello";`
d. `cout >> "Hello";`
e. none of the above

21. Which of the following is the extraction operator?
a. `>>`
b. `<<`
c. `//`
d. `/*`
e. both a and b

22. Which of the following statements allows the user to enter data at the keyboard?
a. `cin << currentPay;`
b. `cin >> currentPay;`
c. `cout << currentPay;`
d. `cout >> currentPay;`
e. none of the above

23. Which of the following is the insertion operator?
a. `>>`
b. `<<`
c. `//`
d. `/*`
e. both a and b

24. To execute a C++ program, you first need to translate the source code into object code. This process is called _____ .
a. coding
b. compiling
c. sourcing
d. translating

25. Which of the following stream manipulators advances the cursor to the next line on the computer screen?
a. `adln`
b. `advln`
c. `edlin`
d. `endl`
e. `lineadv`

26. The final step in the problem-solving process is to _____ .
   a. analyze the problem
   b. evaluate and modify (if necessary) the program
   c. code the algorithm
   d. plan the algorithm
   e. desk-check the program

27. _____ refers to the process of locating and removing the errors in a program.
   a. Analyzing
   b. Correcting
   c. Debugging
   d. Executing
   e. Tracking

28. Typing the function's name as `Main`, rather than `main`, is an example of _____ .
   a. an entry error
   b. a function error
   c. a logic error
   d. a syntax error

29. Typing the instruction `grossPay = hoursWorked — hourlyPay` is an example of _____ .
   a. an entry error
   b. a function error
   c. a logic error
   d. a syntax error

30. External documentation includes _____ .
   a. a printout of the program's code
   b. flowcharts
   c. IPO charts
   d. pseudocode
   e. all of the above

31. Errors in a program are called _____ .
   a. accidents
   b. annoyances
   c. bugs
   d. mistakes
   e. typing errors

E X E R C I S E S

1. In this exercise, you will complete an existing program.
   a. Open the T2e01.cpp file, which is located in the Cpp\Tut02\T2e01 folder on your computer's hard disk. This program calculates and displays the square of a number. Review the IPO chart that you created in Lesson A's Exercise 1. You will notice that two instructions are missing from the code: the instruction that prompts the user to enter a number, and the instruction that pauses the program to allow the user to enter the number. Enter the following two statements in the appropriate area of the program. (Be sure to enter the semicolon that appears at the end of each statement.)

```
cout << "Enter the number: ";
cin >> number;
```

    b. Desk-check the program twice, using the number 4 and the number 6.

    c. Save and then build the program. If necessary, correct any syntax errors, and then save and build the program again. Execute the program. Test the program twice, using the number 4 and the number 6. Compare your results to the desk-check table that you created in step b. When the program is working correctly, print the program code. On the code printout, underline the keywords and draw a circle around the comments. Also indicate the results of your two tests.

    d. Close the Output window, then use the File menu to close the workspace.

2. In this exercise, you will complete an existing program.

    a. Open the T2e02.cpp file, which is located in the Cpp\Tut02\T2e02 folder on your computer's hard disk. This program calculates and displays the total sales and the total commission for two states. Review the IPO chart that you created in Lesson A's Exercise 2. The programmer neglected to declare the variables for this program. Enter the following five statements in the appropriate area of the program. (Be sure to enter the semicolon that appears at the end of each statement.)

```
float state1Sales;
float state2Sales;
float commissionRate;
float totalSales;
float totalCommission;
```

    b. Desk-check the program twice, using the following data:

        1000 and 2000 as the sales, .05 as the commission rate

        3000 and 2500 as the sales, .06 as the commission rate

    c. Save and then build the program. If necessary, correct any syntax errors, and then save and build the program again. Execute the program. Test the program twice, using the data supplied in step b. Compare your results to the desk-check table that you created in step b. When the program is working correctly, print the program code. On the code printout, underline the keywords and draw a circle around the comments. Also indicate the results of your two tests.

    d. Close the Output window, then use the File menu to close the workspace.

3. In this exercise, you will complete an existing program.

    a. Open the T2e03.cpp file, which is located in the Cpp\Tut02\T2e03 folder on your computer's hard disk. This program calculates and displays a commission. Review the IPO chart that you created in Lesson A's Exercise 3. The programmer neglected to enter the instruction to display the commission. Enter an appropriate instruction that will display the message, "Your commission is $", followed by the commission. (Be sure to enter a semicolon at the end of the statement.)

    b. Desk-check the program twice: use 2000 as the sales and .10 as the commission rate, then use 5000 as the sales and .06 as the commission rate.

    c. Save and then build the program. If necessary, correct any syntax errors, and then save and build the program again. Execute the program. Test the program twice, using the data supplied in step b. Compare your results to the desk-check table that you created in step b. When the program is working correctly, print the program code. On the code printout, circle the statement that you entered and indicate the results of your two tests.

    d. Close the Output window, then use the File menu to close the workspace.

4. In this exercise, you will complete an existing program.

    a. Open the T2e04.cpp file, which is located in the Cpp\Tut02\T2e04 folder on your computer's hard disk. This program calculates and displays the projected sales for three regions. Review the IPO chart that you created in Lesson A's Exercise 4. The programmer neglected to calculate the projected sales in each region. Enter the three appropriate statements. (Be sure to enter a semicolon at the end of each statement.)

b. Desk-check the program twice, using the following data:

Region	Sales	Increase rate	Region	Sales	Increase rate
1	10000	.1	1	5000	.02
2	3000	.09	2	2000	.03
3	6000	.1	3	1000	.02

c. Save and then build the program. If necessary, correct any syntax errors, and then save and build the program again. Execute the program. Test the program twice, using the data supplied in step b. Compare your results to the desk-check table that you created in step b. When the program is working correctly, print the program code. On the code printout, circle the statements that you entered and indicate the results of your two tests.

d. Close the Output window, then use the File menu to close the workspace.

5. In this exercise, you will complete an existing program.
   a. Open the T2e05.cpp file, which is located in the Cpp\Tut02\T2e05 folder on your computer's hard disk. This program calculates and displays the ending balance. Review the IPO chart that you created in Lesson A's Exercise 5. The instructions to prompt the user to enter the beginning balance, the deposits, and the withdrawals are missing from the code. The instructions to pause the program to allow the user to enter these three amounts are also missing. Complete the program by entering the missing statements. (Be sure to enter a semicolon at the end of each statement.)
   b. Desk-check the program, using the following data:

beginning balance:	2000	beginning balance:	500
deposits:	775	deposits:	100
withdrawals:	1200	withdrawals:	610

   c. Save and then build the program. If necessary, correct any syntax errors, and then save and build the program again. Execute the program. Test the program twice, using the data supplied in step b. Compare your results to the desk-check table that you created in step b. When the program is working correctly, print the program code. On the code printout, circle the statements that you entered and indicate the results of your two tests.
   d. Close the Output window, then use the File menu to close the workspace.

6. In this exercise, you will complete an existing program.
   a. Open the T2e06.cpp file, which is located in the Cpp\Tut02\T2e06 folder on your computer's hard disk. This program calculates and displays the average of three numbers. Review the IPO chart that you created in Lesson A's Exercise 6. Complete the program by entering the instructions both to enter the input values (three numbers) and display the average number.
   b. Desk-check the program twice: use 25, 76, and 33 for the first set of numbers, then use 10, 15, and 20 for the second set of numbers.
   c. Save and then build the program. If necessary, correct any syntax errors, and then save and build the program again. Execute the program. Test the program twice, using the data supplied in step b. Compare your results to the desk-check table that you created in step b. When the program is working correctly, print the program code. On the code printout, circle the statements that you entered and indicate the results of your two tests.
   d. Close the Output window, then use the File menu to close the workspace.

7. In this exercise, you will complete an existing program.

   a. Open the T2e07.cpp file, which is located in the Cpp\Tut02\T2e07 folder on your computer's hard disk. This program calculates and displays the sales discount and the new sales price. Review the IPO chart that you created in Lesson A's Exercise 7. Complete the program by entering the instructions to enter the input values (original price and discount rate), calculate the discount and new price, and display the discount and new price.

   b. Desk-check the program twice: use 100 as the original price and .25 as the discount rate, then use 50 as the original price and .1 as the discount rate.

   c. Save and then build the program. If necessary, correct any syntax errors, and then save and build the program again. Execute the program. Test the program twice, using the data supplied in step b. Compare your results to the desk-check table that you created in step b. When the program is working correctly, print the program code. On the code printout, circle the statements that you entered and indicate the results of your two tests.

   d. Close the Output window, then use the File menu to close the workspace.

debugging 8. In this exercise, you will debug an existing program.

   a. Open the T2e08.cpp file, which is located in the Cpp\Tut02\T2e08 folder on your computer's hard disk. Review the IPO chart that you created in Lesson A's Exercise 8. This program is supposed to calculate and display the total amount due.

   b. Desk-check the program twice, using the following data:

charge per typed envelope:	.10	charge per typed envelope:	.20
charge per typed page:	.25	charge per typed page:	.30
number of typed envelopes:	100	number of typed envelopes:	10
number of typed pages:	100	number of typed pages:	15

   c. Modify the program, if necessary.

   d. Save and then build the program. If necessary, correct any syntax errors, and then save and build the program again. Execute the program. Test the program using the data supplied in step b. Modify the program, if necessary.

   e. When the program is working correctly, print the program code. On the code printout, circle any corrections you made to the program. Briefly explain what was wrong with the program. Also indicate the results of your two tests.

   f. Close the Output window, then use the File menu to close the workspace.

debugging 9. In this exercise, you will debug an existing program.

   a. Open the T2e09.cpp file, which is located in the Cpp\Tut02\T2e09 folder on your computer's hard disk. Review the IPO chart that you created in Lesson A's Exercise 9. This program is supposed to calculate and display the total number registered for two seminars and the total cost.

   b. Desk-check the program twice, using the following data:

seminar price:	200	seminar price:	100
number registering for first seminar:	10	number registering for first seminar:	30
number registering for second seminar:	10	number registering for second seminar:	10

   c. Modify the program, if necessary.

   d. Save and then build the program. Correct any syntax errors, if necessary, then save, build, and execute the program. Test the program using the data supplied in step b. Modify the program, if necessary.

e. When the program is working correctly, print the program code. On the code printout, circle any corrections you made to the program. Briefly explain what was wrong with the program. Also indicate the results of your two tests.

f. Close the Output window, then use the File menu to close the workspace.

debugging   **10.** In this exercise, you will debug an existing program.

a. Open the T2e10.cpp file, which is located in the Cpp\Tut02\T2e10 folder on your computer's hard disk. Review the IPO chart that you created in Lesson A's Exercise 10. This program is supposed to calculate and display the gross pay, FWT, FICA, state income tax, and net pay.

b. Desk-check the program twice, using the following data:

hours worked:	20	hours worked:	30
hourly pay rate:	6	hourly pay rate:	10
FWT rate:	.2	FWT rate:	.2
FICA rate:	.08	FICA rate:	.08
state income tax rate:	.02	state income tax rate:	.04

c. Modify the program, if necessary.

d. Save and then build the program. Correct any syntax errors, if necessary, then save, build, and execute the program. Modify the program, if necessary.

e. When the program is working correctly, print the program code. On the code printout, circle any corrections you made to the program. Briefly explain what was wrong with the program. Also indicate the results of your two tests.

f. Close the Output window, then use the File menu to close the workspace.

discovery ▶ **11.** In this exercise, you will complete an existing program.

a. Open the T2e11.cpp file, which is located in the Cpp\Tut02\T2e11 folder on your computer's hard disk. Review the IPO chart that you created in Lesson A's Exercise 11. This program should calculate and display the perimeter of a polygon. Complete the program appropriately.

b. Desk-check the program, using the following information: Each day Perry Brown rides his bicycle around a park that has side lengths of ½ mile, 1 mile, ½ mile, and 1 mile. How far does Perry ride his bicycle each day?

c. Complete the program.

d. Save and then build the program. Correct any syntax errors, if necessary, then save, build, and execute the program. Test the program using the information supplied in step b. When the program is working correctly, print the program code. On the code printout, indicate the results of your test.

e. Close the Output window, then use the File menu to close the workspace.

discovery ▶ **12.** In this exercise, you will practice with the cout stream.

a. Open the T2e12.cpp file, which is located in the Cpp\Tut02\T2e12 folder on your computer's hard disk. The program shows three different ways to display on the screen the message "C++ is a programming language."

b. Save, build, and execute the program. What difference, if any, do you see in the manner in which each of the three ways displays the message? What does that tell you about how the cout stream and the insertion operator handle the display of data on the screen?

c. Close the Output window, then use the File menu to close the workspace.

Variables, Constants, and Equations

case ▶ Jack Faye, the cashier at Jackson College in Alabama, wants a program that the clerks can use to display each student's name, the tuition, and the total amount the student owes for the semester, including tuition, insurance, and room and board. The tuition at Jackson is $100 per semester hour, and room and board is $1800 per semester. For students purchasing the school's insurance, the insurance fee is $12.50 per semester. In this tutorial, you will learn how to use variables, constants, and equations in a program. You will use this knowledge to create a C++ program that will calculate and display the tuition information for students enrolling at Jackson College.

In this lesson you will learn how to:

- Distinguish between a variable, a literal constant, and a named constant
- Select an appropriate name, data type, and initial value for a variable
- Create and initialize a variable
- Perform explicit type conversion
- Create a named constant
- Write an assignment statement
- Use the `cin` stream and the `>>` operator to enter data into a variable

Using Variables and Constants

Program Components

In Tutorial 2, you viewed and modified an existing program written in the C++ language. Most programs, like Tutorial 2's program, include the following components: variables, constants, arithmetic operators, and functions. You will learn about variables and two types of constants—named and literal—in this lesson; arithmetic operators, which are used in equations, are covered in Lesson B. The fourth component, functions, are covered in Tutorial 4. Begin by learning about variables.

Using Variables to Store Information

Recall from Tutorial 2 that a **variable** is simply a memory location (inside the computer) where you can temporarily store data. The data may be entered by the user at the keyboard, it may be read in from a file, or it may be the result of a calculation made by the computer. For example, in the program you worked with in Tutorial 2, you stored the current weekly pay and the raise rate, which were entered by the user, in the `currentPay` and `raiseRate` variables, respectively. You also stored the raise and the new weekly pay in the `raise` and `newPay` variables, respectively; both amounts were the result of calculations performed by the computer.

It may be helpful to picture a variable as a small box inside the computer. You can enter and store data in the box, but you cannot actually see the box. The reason these boxes (memory locations) are called "variables" is that their contents can change (vary) as the program is running.

Before learning how to create a variable in C++, you will learn how to select an appropriate name, data type, and value for it. You must assign both a name and a data type to each variable you create. It is also a good programming practice to assign an initial value to each newly created variable.

Selecting an Appropriate Name

You should use a descriptive name for each variable. The variable's name, also called its **identifier**, should help you remember the purpose of the variable. One popular naming convention for variables in a C++ program is to type the variable name using lowercase letters. If the variable name contains two or more words, however, you capitalize the first letter in the second and subsequent words, as in the names `currentPay`, `raiseRate`, and `newWeeklyPay`. Keep in mind that this is just one convention for naming variables; many others are also used. The important thing is to select the method that makes the most sense to you, and then use that method, consistently, in all of your programs.

In addition to being descriptive, the name (identifier) that a programmer assigns to a variable must follow several specific rules. These rules, along with examples of valid and invalid names, are listed in Figure 3-1. Figure 3-1 also lists the keywords—often referred to as **reserved words**—in C++. As you may remember from Tutorial 2, a **keyword** is a word that has a special meaning in a programming language. You cannot use a keyword—for example, the word `void`—as a name in a program, as indicated in the fourth rule shown in the figure.

Rules for names (identifiers) in a program

1. The name must begin with a letter.
2. The name must contain only letters, numbers, and the underscore. No punctuation characters or spaces are allowed in the name.
3. The C++ compiler you are using determines the maximum number of characters in a name. In Microsoft Visual C++ 5.0, a name cannot be longer than 247 characters.
4. The name cannot be a keyword, such as `private`, because a keyword has a special meaning in C++. The C++ keywords, also called reserved words, are listed below.
5. Names in C++ are case sensitive.

Valid names:	Invalid names:	
`deposit`	`98deposit`	(the name must begin with a letter)
`end_Balance`	`end Balance`	(the name cannot contain a space)
`withdrawal`	`withdrawal.amt`	(the name cannot contain punctuation)
`privateLocation`	`private`	(the name cannot be a keyword)

C++ keywords

`asm`	`continue`	`float`	`new`	`signed`	`try`
`auto`	`default`	`for`	`operator`	`sizeof`	`typedef`
`break`	`delete`	`friend`	`private`	`static`	`union`
`case`	`do`	`goto`	`protected`	`struct`	`unsigned`
`catch`	`double`	`if`	`public`	`switch`	`virtual`
`char`	`else`	`inline`	`register`	`template`	`void`
`class`	`enum`	`int`	`return`	`this`	`volatile`
`const`	`extern`	`long`	`short`	`throw`	`while`

Figure 3-1: Naming rules, examples of valid and invalid names, and C++ keywords

Pay particular attention to the last rule shown in Figure 3-1, "Names in C++ are case sensitive." This rule means that, in a C++ program, the names `currentPay`, `CurrentPay`, and `Currentpay` do not refer to the same variable (location in memory). It is important to use the exact capitalization of a name throughout the entire program; otherwise, the program will not work correctly.

In addition to selecting an appropriate name, you also must determine the appropriate data type for the variables you create.

Selecting an Appropriate Data Type

Each variable must be assigned a data type by the programmer. The data type determines the type of data the variable (memory location) can store. As you may remember from Tutorial 1, data is stored in the computer as a series of 0s and 1s. The letter X, for example, is typically stored as the series 01011000. (You can refer to Appendix A to verify this.) However, this is also the pattern of 0s and 1s used to store the number 88. The computer knows whether the 01011000 represents the letter X or the number 88 by the data type of the variable in which it is stored. If the 01011000 is stored in a Character variable, then the pattern represents the letter X. If the 01011000 is stored in a Short Integer variable, however, then it represents the number 88. In other words, the variable's data type is necessary for the computer to determine the value stored in the variable; this is why it is important for you to specify the data type when you create a variable.

Figure 3-2 describes the most commonly used data types in C++: Character, Short Integer, Integer, Long Integer, Float, and Double.

tip

· · · · · · · · · · · · · · ·
Microsoft Visual C++ 5.0 also includes the Boolean data type, which is not available in every C++ system. You assign the Boolean data type to variables that will store only the Boolean values—True and False. You can learn more about the Boolean data type in Lesson A's Discovery Exercise 16.

Data type	Stores	Bytes of memory required	Range of values
Character	one character	1	one character
Short Integer	integers	2	–32,768 to 32,767
Integer	integers	4	–2,147,483,648 to 2,147,483,647
Long Integer	integers	4	–2,147,483,648 to 2,147,483,647
Float	numbers with a decimal place and floating-point numbers	4	1.17549e–038 to 3.40282e+038, 0.0, –1.17549e–038 to –3.40282e+038
Double	numbers with a decimal place and floating-point numbers	8	2.22507e–308 to 1.79769e+308, 0.0, –2.22507e–308 to –1.79769e+308

Figure 3-2: Most commonly used C++ data types

Notice that Figure 3-2 shows the range of values that each data type can store and the amount of memory required to do so. For instance, variables assigned either the Short Integer, Integer, or Long Integer data type can store **integers**, which are whole numbers—numbers without any decimal places. The differences among the three data types are in the range of integers each type can store and the amount of memory each type needs to store the integer. The range of values and the amount of memory are machine-dependent, so your system may have different values. For example, on some systems, the Integer data type has the same range and memory requirement as the Short Integer data type, rather than the Long Integer data type, which is shown in Figure 3-2.

In Lesson A's Discovery Exercise 15, you will run a program that will tell you what values your system uses for the data types shown in Figure 3-2.

The size of the Integer data type varies among operating systems. In DOS and Windows 3.1, the size of an Integer is two bytes; in Windows 95, the size is four bytes. If your program will need to run on more than one operating system, it is best to use either the Short Integer or the Long Integer data type when creating variables that store integers.

You can also use an uppercase E in exponential notation—in other words, 3.2e6 is the same as 3.2E6.

The single quotes around a letter, number, or symbol tell C++ to treat the letter, number, or symbol as a character.

The memory requirement of a data type is an important consideration when coding an application. If you want to optimize an application's code, and thereby conserve system resources, you should use variables with smaller memory requirements wherever possible. For example, although a Long Integer variable can store numbers in the Short Integer range of –32,768 to 32,767, the Long Integer data type takes twice as much memory to do so. Therefore, it is more efficient to store a person's age in a Short Integer variable. Conversely, you need to use a Long Integer variable to store the population of a large city.

Figure 3-2 also shows that both Float and Double type variables can store numbers with a decimal place (such as 3.2), including floating-point numbers (such as 3.2e6). A **floating-point number** is a number that is expressed as a multiple of some power of 10. In C++, floating-point numbers are written in e (exponential) notation, which is similar to scientific notation. For example, the number 3,200,000 written in e (exponential) notation is 3.2e6; written in scientific notation it is $3.2 * 10^6$. Notice that exponential notation simply replaces $* 10^6$ with the letter e followed by the power number—in this case, 6.

Another way of viewing the 3.2e6 is that the positive number after the e indicates how many places to the right to move the decimal point. In this case, e6 says to move the decimal point six places to the right—so, 3.2e6 becomes 3,200,000. Moving the decimal point six places to the right is the same as multiplying the number by 10 to the sixth power.

Floating-point numbers can also have a negative number after the e. For example, 3.2e–6 means 3.2 divided by 10 to the sixth power, or .0000032. The negative number after the e tells you how many places to the left to move the decimal point. In this case, e–6 means to move the decimal point six places to the left.

Floating-point numbers are used to represent very large and very small numbers. For example, according to Figure 3-2, the minimum positive value you can store in a Double type variable is 2.22507e–308 (a very small number) and the maximum positive value is 1.79769e+308 (a very large number.)

The differences between the Float type and the Double type are in the range of numbers each type can store and the amount of memory each type needs to store the numbers. Although the Double type can store numbers in the Float type's range, the Double type takes twice as much memory to do so.

Also listed in Figure 3-2 is the Character data type. A variable assigned the Character data type can store precisely one character of data, which must be enclosed in single quotes—for example, the letter 'A', the number '3', or the dollar sign, '$'.

Assigning an appropriate data type to the variables in a program will make the program run more efficiently. Here are some guidelines to follow when assigning the data type:

- Assign the Short Integer, Integer, or Long Integer data type when you are sure that a variable will always contain whole numbers—numbers without decimal places. Which type you choose will depend on the size of the numbers you expect to store in the variable.
- Assign either the Float or the Double data type when you need to store numbers with a decimal fraction. Here again, the type you choose, Float or Double, will depend on the size of the numbers you expect to store in the variable.
- Assign the Character data type if the variable will always contain one character of data.

In addition to selecting an appropriate name and data type for each variable you create, recall that it is a good programming practice also to assign an initial, or beginning, value to the variable. The initial value that you assign will typically be a literal constant. You will learn about literal constants next.

Using Literal Constants

A **literal constant** is an item of data whose value does not change while the program is running. C++ has three types of literal constants: numeric, character, and string. A **numeric literal constant** is a number—for example, the number 2. Numeric literal constants can contain numbers, the plus sign (+), the minus sign (–), the decimal point (.), and the letter e in upper or lowercase (for exponential notation). Numeric literal constants cannot contain a space, a comma, or a special character, such as a dollar sign ($) or the percent sign (%).

A **character literal constant** is one character enclosed in single quotes. The letter 'X' is a character literal constant, and so is the dollar sign '$'. A **string literal constant**, on the other hand, is zero or more characters enclosed in double quotes, such as the word "Hello" and the message "Enter the weekly pay:". Figure 3-3 shows examples of numeric, character, and string literal constants.

Literal Constants		
Numeric	Character	String
2	`'X'`	`"Hello"`
45.98	`'$'`	`"Enter the weekly pay: "`
3.2e6	`'b'`	`"450"`
–2300	`'2'`	`"345AB"`
0	`' '` (a space between single quotes)	`"509-999-9999"`
Important Note:		
Notice that character literal constants are enclosed in single quotes, and string literal constants are enclosed in double quotes. Numeric literal constants, however, are not enclosed in any quotes.		

Figure 3-3: Examples of numeric, character, and string literal constants

Be aware that the character literal constant 'X' (the letter X enclosed in single quotes) is not equivalent to the string literal constant "X" (the letter X enclosed in double quotes). Character literal constants and string literal constants are stored differently inside the computer. A character literal constant, which is precisely one character enclosed in single quotes, is stored as that one character only. A string literal constant, on the other hand, is stored as one more than the number of characters contained within the double quotes. This is because C++ appends an additional character, referred to as the **null character**, to the end of a string literal constant when it is stored in memory. In other words, C++ stores the character literal constant 'X' as the one character X; however, it stores the string literal constant "X" as two characters—an X and the null character.

Now that you understand how to select an appropriate name and data type for a variable, as well as how to recognize a literal constant, you will use that knowledge to declare, or create, a variable in C++.

mini-quiz

Mini-Quiz 1

1. Which two of the following are invalid names for a variable? Why is each invalid?

   a. `class` b. `gallonsOfGas` c. `88TaxAmt` d. `yearTotal` e. `tuition`

2. The number 125.35 is a _____.

   a. character literal constant b. numeric literal constant c. string literal constant
   d. variable

3. The letter 'w' is a _____.

   a. character literal constant b. numeric literal constant c. string literal constant
   d. variable

4. "Jacob Motors" is a _____.

   a. character literal constant b. numeric literal constant c. string literal constant
   d. variable

5. `bonusAmt` is a _____.

   a. character literal constant b. numeric literal constant c. string literal constant
   d. variable

6. Assume that a variable will need to store only integers in the range of 1 through 20000. The most efficient data type for the variable is _____.

   a. Character b. Float c. Integer d. Long Integer e. Short Integer

Declaring a Variable

tip

Recall from Tutorial 2 that the execution of a C++ program always begins with the `main` function.

tip

Notice that a variable declaration is considered a statement in C++. As is true of all statements in C++, a variable declaration must end in a semicolon.

In C++, you must declare a variable before you can use it. You declare, or create, a variable by entering a C++ statement that specifies both the data type and the name of the variable, as well as its beginning, or initial, value. Most programmers place the variable declaration statements at the beginning of the program—in other words, as the first statements in the `main` function. An exception to this is a program that contains functions other than `main`; you will learn about this exception in Tutorial 4. For now, however, always declare the variables at the beginning of the `main` function.

To declare a variable in a C++ statement, you use the following syntax: *datatype variablename = initialvalue;*. In the syntax, *datatype* designates the type of data the variable will store, *variablename* is the name of the variable, and *initialvalue* is typically a literal constant that represents the beginning, or initial, value for the variable. Assigning a beginning value to a variable is called **initializing** the variable.

You use the C++ keywords shown in Figure 3-4 to designate the *datatype* in a variable declaration statement.

The *variablename* used in the variable declaration statement must follow the rules shown in Figure 3-1.

Data type	C++ keyword
Character	`char`
Short Integer	`short`
Integer	`int`
Long Integer	`long`
Float	`float`
Double	`double`

Figure 3-4: C++ keywords for declaring a variable's *datatype*

When you declare a variable, C++ sets aside a small section of the computer's internal memory to which C++ attaches both the name and data type specified in the statement declaration. C++ also stores the initial value included in the statement inside the memory location. The statement `short age = 0;`, for example, creates a variable (memory location) named `age` that can contain only values in the Short Integer range and it initializes the memory location to the numeric literal constant 0. When you want to refer to this section of memory—for example, to display the section's contents—you simply use the variable's name to do so. You could use the `cout << age;` statement, for instance, to display the contents of the `age` variable—in this case, a 0 would display.

It is important to initialize the variables that you create. If you do not supply an initial value for a variable, the variable will contain a meaningless value, referred to by programmers as **garbage**. The garbage is the remains of what was last stored at the memory location that the variable now occupies. You will observe this by running a program that displays the values stored in uninitialized variables.

OOP Concepts

When you declare a variable, you create an object, or an instance, of the *datatype's* class. For example, the `age` variable created by the `short age = 0;` statement is an instance of the Short Integer class.

To run a program that displays the values contained in uninitialized variables:

1 Start Visual C++. Click **File** on the menu bar, then click **Open**. In the Open dialog box, open the Cpp\Tut03\LaProg01 folder on your computer's hard disk, then click **LaProg01.cpp** in the list of filenames. Click the **Open** button to open the file. The LaProg01 program appears in the LaProg01.cpp window.

2 If the Project Workspace window is open, close it by clicking the **Close** button on its title bar. If necessary, click the LaProg01.cpp window's **Maximize** button to maximize the LaProg01.cpp window. The LaProg01 program instructions are shown in Figure 3-5.

The LaProg01 in the filename stands for Lesson A, program 1; the .cpp stands for C plus plus.

```
//LaProg01.cpp
//this program displays the values stored in the variables

#include <iostream.h>

void main()
{

    //declare variables
    char    response;
    short   hoursWkd;
    int     sales;
    long    city_Pop;
    double  salesAmt;
    float   taxRate;

    //display contents of variables
    cout << "Variable     " << "Value" << endl;
    cout << "----------   " << "--------------" << endl;
    cout << "response     " << response << endl;
    cout << "hoursWkd     " << hoursWkd << endl;
    cout << "sales        " << sales << endl;
    cout << "city_Pop     " << city_Pop << endl;
    cout << "salesAmt     " << salesAmt << endl;
    cout << "taxRate      " << taxRate << endl;
    cout << endl;

} //end of main function
```

Figure 3-5: LaProg01 program instructions

The `main` function begins by declaring six variables. Notice that each declaration specifies only the variable's data type and name; neither specifies an initial value. Also notice that each declaration statement ends with a semicolon. After declaring the variables, both the `cout` stream and the `<<` (insertion) operator, which you learned about in Tutorial 2, display the contents of the variables on the computer screen.

3 Click **Build** on the menu bar, then click **Build** on the Build menu. When you are asked if you would like to create a default project workspace, click the **Yes** button. After the build operation is complete, the Output window shows no errors or warnings.

4 Click **Build** on the menu bar, then click **Execute LaProg01.exe**. The names of the uninitialized variables, along with their current value, appear in a DOS window. See Figure 3-6.

tip

Recall from Tutorial 2 that cout (pronounced *see out*) and the << (insertion) operator send a sequence of characters—in other words, a stream—"out" to the user through the computer screen. Also recall that endl, which is one of C++'s stream manipulators, advances the cursor to the next line on the screen. You may remember that a stream manipulator allows the program to manipulate, or manage, the input and output stream characters in some way.

Figure 3-6: DOS window showing values in uninitialized variables

Don't be concerned if the values on your screen differ from the ones shown in Figure 3-6. The purpose of running this program is to show you that an uninitialized variable does have a value, but you can never be sure what that value is going to be. If you use a variable that contains garbage in an equation, either the program will give incorrect results or, worse yet, the program, and possibly the computer system, may crash (end with an error).

Close the current program before learning more about how to initialize a variable.

5 Press the **Enter** key to continue. The DOS window closes. Close the Output window by clicking its **Close** button ![x].

The only way to ensure that a variable does not contain garbage is to initialize it.

Initializing Variables

It is a good programming practice to initialize a variable in the statement that creates the variable. When you supply an initial value for a variable, that value overwrites (replaces) any garbage value stored at that memory location. You usually initialize a variable by assigning a literal constant to it. The literal constant must be the same data type as the variable that is being initialized. For example, you initialize a Character variable by assigning to it a character—typically a space, enclosed in single quotes. You initialize Short Integer, Integer, and Long Integer variables by assigning to them an integer—usually the number 0. Initialize the Character, Short Integer, Integer, and Long Integer variables in the current program.

tip

• • • • • • • • • • • • • •

Although numeric and character variables are typically initialized to 0 and a space, respectively, you can initialize them to other values. The initial values you select will depend on the program you are writing.

To initialize the first four variables in the program:

1 Position the insertion point I between the last e and the semicolon in the `char response;` statement, and then click at that location. The insertion point is now located between the e and the semicolon. Press the **spacebar**, and then type = (the equal sign) and press the **spacebar**. Type ' (a single quote), press the **spacebar**, and then type ' (a single quote). The statement should now say `char response = ' ';`. When the program is executed, this statement will initialize the `response` variable to a space.

Now initialize the `hoursWkd`, `sales`, and `city_Pop` variables to the number 0.

2 Change the next three statements in the program as shown in Figure 3-7. The statements you need to change are highlighted in the figure. Although C++ does not require you to align the equal signs (=) in a list of variable declaration statements, doing so helps to make the program easier to read.

```
//declare variables
char    response = '';
short   hoursWkd = 0;
int     sales    = 0;
long    city_Pop = 0;
double  salesAmt;
float   taxRate;
```

modify these statements

Figure 3-7: Initialization of `short`, `int`, and `long` variables in the program

The `salesAmt` variable is the next variable you will initialize in the program. In this case, you cannot use the number 0 to initialize the `salesAmt` variable because the number 0 is an integer and `salesAmt` is a Double type variable. As you know, the data type of the literal constant assigned to a variable must match the data type of the variable. Double type variables, you may remember from Figure 3-2, have decimal places. Therefore, the literal constant you assign to a Double variable must also contain a decimal place. Instead of using the integer 0, you initialize a Double variable by assigning 0.0 to it in the declaration statement. In C++, a numeric literal constant that has a decimal point is automatically treated as a Double data type. Initialize the Double `salesAmt` variable to 0.0.

3 Change the `double salesAmt;` statement to **double salesAmt = 0.0;**.

The last variable you need to initialize in the program is the `taxRate` variable, which has a Float data type. As with a Double variable, you cannot use the integer 0 to initialize a Float variable because the data types do not match. You also cannot use the number 0.0 to initialize a Float variable because, in C++, a number with a decimal point is automatically treated as a Double data type. To initialize a variable that has a Float data type, you will use a process called explicit type conversion. You will need to learn about explicit type conversion before you can initialize the `taxRate` variable.

Explicit Type Conversion

Explicit type conversion, also known as **type casting**, is the explicit conversion of data from one data type to another. You explicitly convert, or type cast, an item of data by preceding it with the C++ keyword that represents the desired data type; you enclose the keyword in parentheses. To explicitly convert a number—for example, the Double type number 0.0—to the Float data type, you would use the type cast `(float) 0.0`. The `(float)` before the 0.0 tells C++ to treat the 0.0 as a Float data type rather than as a Double data type. You will use the `(float) 0.0` type cast to initialize the `taxRate` variable in the current program. (You will learn more about type casting in Lesson B.)

To initialize the `taxRate` variable, then save, build, and execute the LaProg01 program:

1 Change the `float taxRate;` statement in the program to **float taxRate = (float) 0.0;**. Figure 3-8 shows the modified declaration statements in the program.

```
//declare variables
char    response = '';
short   hoursWkd = 0;
int     sales    = 0;
long    city_Pop = 0;
double  salesAmt = 0.0;
float   taxRate  = (float) 0.0;
```

modify this statement

Figure 3-8: Modified declaration statements in the LaProg01 program

2 Save and then build the program. After the build operation is complete, the Output window shows no errors or warnings.

3 Execute the LaProg01 program. The names of the initialized variables, along with their current value, appear in a DOS window. See Figure 3-9.

Figure 3-9: DOS window showing values in initialized variables

Although it is not apparent when viewing either the figure or your screen, the Character variable `response` contains one space. You will notice that the remaining variables, on the other hand, contain the number 0. Although the Double `salesAmt` variable and the Float `taxRate` variable actually contain 0.0, only the 0 displays on the screen.

4 Press the **Enter** key to continue. The DOS window closes. Click **File** on the menu bar, and then click **Close Workspace**. When you are asked if you want to close all document windows, click the **Yes** button.

5 Close the Output window.

In summary, a variable is a memory location in which you can temporarily store data. You must assign both a data type and a name to the variables you create. It is also a good programming practice to initialize each variable in its declaration statement. You typically initialize Short Integer, Integer, and Long Integer variables to the integer 0, and Double variables to the Double type number 0.0. Character variables are usually initialized to a space enclosed in single quotes. You use a type cast—typically `(float) 0.0`—to initialize a Float variable.

In addition to variables and literal constants, you will also find named constants in many programs. You will learn about named constants in the next section.

Named Constants

As discussed earlier, a literal constant is a specific value (such as 2) that does not change while a program is running. A **named constant**, on the other hand, is a *memory location* whose *contents* cannot change while the program is running. Named constants make your program more self-documenting and, therefore, easier to modify because they allow you to use meaningful words in place of values that may be less clear.

You create a named constant in C++ by using the keyword `const`, which stands for *constant*, in a statement that uses the following syntax: **const** *datatype constantname = expression;*. In the syntax, *datatype* is the type of data the constant will store, *constantname* is the name of the constant, and *expression* is the value you want assigned to the constant. The rules for naming a named constant are the same as for variables. (The rules are listed in Figure 3-1.) As with variables, the data type of the value assigned to the constant must match the data type of the constant. Figure 3-10 shows examples of how to create a named constant in C++.

Named constants	Explanation
`const short two = 2;`	Creates a Short Integer named constant called `two`, and assigns the numeric literal constant 2 (an integer) to it.
`const char yes = 'Y'`	Creates a Character named constant called `yes`, and assigns the character literal constant `'Y'` to it.
`const float pi = (float) 3.141593;`	Creates a Float named constant called `pi`, and assigns the numeric literal constant `3.141593`, treated as a Float data type, to it.

Important Note:
Notice that character literal constants are enclosed in single quotes, but numeric literal constants and the names of named constants are not. The type cast in the last example is necessary because C++ treats a number with a decimal point as a Double, rather than as a Float, data type.

Figure 3-10: Examples of creating named constants

After you create a named constant, you can then use its name, instead of its value, in another C++ statement. For example, you could use the `cout << pi;` statement to display the value of the `pi` constant, shown in Figure 3-10, on the screen; C++ would display 3.141593. You could also use the `pi` constant in an equation that calculates the area of a circle—for instance, `area = pi * radius * radius;`. C++ would use the value stored in the `pi` constant (3.141593) to calculate the area.

You cannot change the value of a named constant while the program is running. For example, you cannot use the `cin >> pi;` statement to input data into the `pi` constant; the statement would produce a syntax error when C++ attempted to compile it. You also cannot use a named constant on the left side of an equal sign in an equation. For example, the `pi = 2 * 3;` statement, which tells C++ to change the value in `pi` to 6, would also result in a syntax error during the compilation phase.

When distinguishing between a literal constant, a named constant, and a variable, it is helpful to remember that a literal constant is simply an item of data whose value does not change while the program is running. A named constant, on the other hand, is a memory location where you store items of data (literal constants). Unlike a variable, which is also a memory location that stores items of data (literal constants), the value stored in a named constant cannot change while the program is running.

In the next section, you will learn how to write an assignment statement, which you can use to change the contents of a variable. An assignment statement can contain, among other things, literal constants, named constants, and variables.

mini-quiz

Mini-Quiz 2

1. Write a statement that creates a Short Integer variable named `numItems` and initializes it to 0.
2. Write a statement that creates a Character variable named `letter` and initializes it to a space.
3. Write a statement that creates a Double variable named `population` and initializes it to 0.0.
4. Write a statement that creates a Float variable named `average` and initializes it to 0.0.
5. Write a statement that declares a Short Integer named constant called `daysInWeek` whose value is 7.
6. Write a statement that declares a Float named constant called `newPay` whose value is 10.45.

Using an Assignment Statement to Store Data in a Variable

The syntax of an assignment statement that stores data in a variable is *variable-name = expression*;, where *expression* can include items such as literal constants, named constants, variables, functions, and operators. When C++ encounters an assignment statement in a program, it assigns the value of the *expression* appearing on the right side of the equal sign to the variable whose *variablename* appears on the left side of the equal sign. The assignment statement `hoursWkd = 9;`, for example, stores the number 9, a numeric literal constant, in the variable named `hoursWkd`. The `overTime = hoursWkd - 40;` assignment statement first subtracts the number 40 from the contents of the `hoursWkd` variable, and then assigns the result to the `overTime` variable.

When using an assignment statement, keep in mind that the data type of the *expression* must match the data type of the variable to which it is assigned. For example, you should assign only values in the Short Integer range to Short Integer type variables; you should not assign a number with a decimal point to a Short Integer variable. If you assign an incorrect value type, C++ uses a process called **implicit type conversion** to convert the value to fit the variable's data type; however, it is not always possible to make the conversion. Implicit type conversion can lead to unexpected results in a program, so it is best to avoid this type of conversion. You can avoid implicit type conversion by using a type cast to convert a value explicitly to the appropriate data type. For example, when initializing a Float variable, recall that you use the `(float) 0.0` type cast to convert the Double type number 0.0 explicitly to a Float data type.

Figure 3-11 shows examples of assignment statements. In each assignment statement, notice that the data type of the elements appearing on the right side of the equal sign (the *expression*) matches the data type of the variable whose name appears on the left side of the equal sign.

tip

▶ It is easy to confuse a variable declaration statement with an assignment statement. You use a variable declaration statement, which must begin with a data type, to create and initialize a new variable. You use an assignment statement to change the value stored in an existing variable. An assignment statement does not create a variable in memory.

Assume that age, newNum, and oldNum are Short Integer variables, and that two is a Short Integer named constant, response is a Character variable, and newPrice is a Float variable.

Assignment statement	Result
age = 32;	Stores the numeric literal constant 32 in the age variable
newNum = oldNum * two;	Multiplies the contents of the oldNum variable by the contents of the named constant two, then stores the result in the newNum variable
newNum = newNum + 3;	Adds the contents of the newNum variable to the numeric literal constant 3, then stores the result in the newNum variable
response = 'Y';	Stores the character literal constant 'Y' (without the single quotes) in the response variable
newPrice = (float) 9.55;	Stores the numeric literal constant 9.55, treated as a Float data type, in the newPrice variable

Important Note:
Notice that character literal constants are enclosed in single quotes, but numeric literal constants and variable names are not. Also notice that a type cast is necessary to convert the 9.55, which C++ treats as a Double data type, to a Float data type.

Figure 3-11: Examples of assignment statements

It is important to remember that a variable can store only one item of data at any one time. When you use an assignment statement to assign another item to the variable, the new data replaces the existing data. For example, assume that a program contains the following statements and comments:

```
short age = 0;    //declare and initialize variable
age = 25;         //assign 25 to the variable
age = age + 1;    //increase the variable's value by 1
```

When you run this program, the three lines of code are processed as follows:

- The short age = 0; statement creates the Short Integer age variable in memory and initializes it to the integer 0. Here again, you may want to picture the age variable as a small box inside the computer. This statement tells C++ to place the number 0 inside the box.
- The age = 25; assignment statement removes the zero from the age variable and stores the number 25 there instead. The variable (box) now contains the number 25 only. Notice that the data type of the literal constant 25 matches the data type of the age variable.
- The age = age + 1; assignment statement first adds the contents of the age variable (25) to the number 1, giving 26. The assignment statement then removes the number 25 from the age variable and stores the number 26 there instead. Notice that C++ performs the calculation appearing on the right side of the equal sign before assigning the result to the variable whose name appears on the left side. (You will learn more about calculations in Lesson B.) Also notice that the data type of the elements on both sides of the equal sign is the same.

In addition to using an assignment statement, you can also use `cin` and the >> operator to change the value stored in a numeric or Character variable. As you may remember, you use `cin` and the >> operator to get data from the user while the program is running.

Mini-Quiz 3

1. Write an assignment statement that assigns the value 23.25 to a Float type variable named price.

2. Write an assignment statement that assigns the number 5 to a Short Integer variable named order.

3. Write an assignment statement that assigns the number 125.67 to a Double type variable named rate.

4. Write an assignment statement that assigns the letter T to a Character variable named insured.

5. Write an assignment statement that assigns the number 45 to a Float type variable named payRate.

Using cin and >> to Store Data in a Variable

As you learned in Tutorial 2, you can use the `cin` stream and the >> (extraction) operator to obtain input from the user. You store the entered data in a variable by including both the stream and the operator in a statement that uses the following syntax: `cin >> variablename;`. When C++ encounters a program statement using this syntax, it pauses the program and waits for the user to enter the information. After the user types the appropriate data and presses the Enter key, C++ stores the data in the variable named in the statement.

The >> (extraction) operator stops reading characters from the keyboard as soon as the user either presses the Enter key or types a character that is inappropriate for the variable's data type. A numeric variable, for instance, can contain only numbers, the plus sign (+), the minus sign (−), and, if it is either a Float or a Double variable, the decimal point (.) and the letter e (in upper or lowercase). Examples of an inappropriate character for a numeric variable are a letter, a space, a comma, and a special character (such as a dollar sign). If you try to enter the number 5,000 in a numeric variable, for example, C++ will store only the number 5 in the variable because the comma is not an appropriate character for a numeric variable. You will now run a program that shows how to use `cin` and the >> operator to enter data into a variable.

tip

....

Recall from Tutorial 2 that `cin` (pronounced *see in*) and the >> (extraction) operator get a sequence of characters—in other words, a stream—"in" to the computer through the keyboard.

To run a program that shows how to use `cin` and >> to enter data into a variable:

1 Use the File menu to open the **LaProg02.cpp** file, which is located in the Cpp\Tut03\LaProg02 folder on your computer's hard disk. The LaProg02 program instructions shown in Figure 3-12 appear in the LaProg02.cpp window.

```
//LaProg02.cpp
//this program shows how to use cin and >>
//to enter data into a variable

#include <iostream.h>

void main()
{
    //declare and initialize variable
    short number = 0;

    //enter input value
    cout << "Enter a number: ";
    cin  >> number;

    //display output value
    cout << "The value in the variable is: " << number << endl << endl;

} //end of main function
```

Figure 3-12: LaProg02 program instructions

The `main` function first creates and initializes a Short Integer variable named `number`, and then prompts the user to enter the appropriate information. The `cin` stream and the `>>` operator allow the user to enter the information, which is then stored in the `number` variable. The program then displays the contents of the `number` variable on the screen.

2 Build and execute the program.

First enter a value whose data type matches the data type of the `number` variable (Short Integer)—for example, enter the number 5.

3 When you are prompted to enter a number, type 5 and press the **Enter** key. The value stored in the `number` variable—5—correctly appears in the DOS window on the screen.

4 Press the **Enter** key to close the DOS window.

Now run the program again and type a number that contains an incorrect character—for example, type a number that includes a comma, such as 5,000. You have not made any changes to the program, so you can simply execute it; you do not have to build it again.

5 Execute the program again. When you are prompted for a number, type 5,000 and press the **Enter** key. The DOS window shows that the value stored in the `number` variable is 5, and not the 5,000 that you entered. In this case, the `cin >> number;` statement stopped reading characters into the `number` variable as soon as you typed the comma.

6 Press the **Enter** key to close the DOS window.

Now observe what happens when you enter a number that is not the same data type as the variable—for example, enter the number 5.9.

7 Execute the program again. When you are prompted to enter a number, type 5.9 and press the **Enter** key. The DOS window shows that the value in the `number` variable is 5, and not 5.9.

tip

· · · · · · · · · · · · · ·

In Lesson A's Exercise 10, you will learn more about how cin and the >> operator handle the input of values into various data types.

Because the Short Integer data type can store only whole numbers, the decimal point is considered an invalid character for this type. Therefore, the cin >> number; statement stopped reading characters into the number variable as soon as you typed the period.

8 Press the **Enter** key to close the DOS window.

You can now close the current workspace.

9 Click **File** on the menu bar, and then click **Close Workspace**. When prompted to close all open document windows, click the **Yes** button. Also close the Output window.

mini-quiz

Mini-Quiz 4

1. Write a C++ statement that allows the user to enter a value into a Double type variable named totalAmt.

2. Write a C++ statement that allows the user to enter a letter into a Character variable named initial.

3. Assume that a program uses cin and the >> operator to enter data into an Integer variable named quantity. If the user enters the number 9.2e6, C++ will store the number _____ in the variable.

You have now completed Lesson A. In this lesson, you learned about variables, literal constants, named constants, and assignment statements. You also learned how to enter data into a variable by using the cin stream along with the >> (extraction) operator. In Lesson B, you will learn about a special data type, called the String data type. You will also learn how to write equations in C++, as well as how to create your own C++ applications. Now you can either exit Visual C++ and take a break or complete the questions and exercises at the end of the lesson.

S U M M A R Y

Most programs include variables, constants, arithmetic operators (which are used in equations), and functions. (You will learn about arithmetic operators and equations in Lesson B; functions are covered in Tutorial 4.) A variable is simply a memory location inside the computer where you can temporarily store data. The contents of a variable can change as the program is running. You must assign both a name and a data type to each variable you create. You should also initialize—in other words, assign a beginning value to—each newly created variable. This ensures that a variable does not contain garbage.

The name you assign to a variable must follow several very specific rules. The name should also be descriptive to help you remember the purpose of the variable. The most commonly used data types for variables in C++ are Character, Short Integer, Integer, Long Integer, Float, and Double. Each data type has a specific memory requirement and range of values, which are machine-dependent. To optimize an application's code, and thereby conserve system resources, you should use variables with smaller memory requirements wherever possible.

You declare, or create, a variable by specifying its data type, name, and initial value in a statement, which must end in a semicolon. The syntax of a variable declaration statement is *datatype variablename = initialvalue;*. You typically initialize a variable by assigning a literal constant to it. The data type of the *initialvalue* must match the data type of the variable being declared.

A literal constant is an item of data whose value does not change while the program is running. C++ has three types of literal constants: numeric, character, and string. A numeric literal constant is simply a number. A character literal constant is one letter, number, or symbol enclosed in single quotes (' '). A string literal constant is zero or more characters enclosed in double quotes (""). C++ appends an additional character, called the null character, to the end of a string literal constant when it is stored in memory.

You usually initialize Short Integer, Integer, and Long Integer variables to the number (numeric literal constant) 0, and Double variables to the number 0.0. Character variables are typically initialized to a space enclosed in single quotes. You must use a type cast to initialize a Float variable. Float variables are usually initialized to `(float) 0.0`.

In addition to variables and literal constants, many programs also contain named constants. A named constant is a *memory location* whose *contents* cannot change while the program is running. Named constants make your program more self-documenting and, therefore, easier to modify because they allow you to use meaningful words in place of values that may be less clear. A statement that creates a named constant must conform to the following syntax: **const** *datatype constantname = expression;*.

You can use an assignment statement to store data in a variable; the statement must conform to the following syntax: *variablename = expression;*. The data type of the *expression* must match the data type of the variable. When C++ encounters an assignment statement in a program, it assigns the value of the *expression* appearing on the right side of the equal sign to the variable whose *variablename* appears on the left side of the equal sign. A variable can store only one item of data at any one time. When you assign another item to the variable, the new data replaces the existing data.

When assigning a value to a variable, it is important that the value fit the variable's data type. If you assign a value that does not match the data type of the variable, C++ tries to convert the value to fit the variable's data type. This process, called implicit type conversion, can lead to unexpected results in a program. It is best to convert a value explicitly to fit a variable's data type; you can do so by using a type cast.

You can also enter data into a variable by using the `cin` stream and the extraction operator (>>) in a statement that conforms to the following syntax: **cin >>** *variablename;*. When C++ encounters a program statement using this syntax, it waits for the user to enter the information. When the user presses the Enter key, the information is stored in the variable whose name appears in the statement. It's important to remember that the >> (extraction) operator stops reading characters from the keyboard as soon as the user either presses the Enter key or types a character that is inappropriate for the variable's data type.

ANSWERS TO MINI-QUIZZES

Mini-Quiz 1

1. a is invalid because `class` is a keyword, c is invalid because variable names must begin with a letter **2.** b **3.** a **4.** c **5.** d **6.** e

Mini-Quiz 2

1. `short numItems = 0;`
2. `char letter = ' ';`
3. `double population = 0.0;`
4. `float average = (float) 0.0;`
5. `const short daysInWeek = 7;`
6. `const float newPay = (float) 10.45;` (Recall that C++ treats a number with a decimal point as a Double type number.)

Mini-Quiz 3

1. `price = (float) 23.25;`
2. `order = 5;`
3. `rate = 125.67;`
4. `insured = 'T';`
5. `payRate = (float) 45;`

Mini-Quiz 4

1. `cin >> totalAmt;`
2. `cin >> initial;`
3. `9`

Q U E S T I O N S

1. A variable is _____ .
   a. an item of data
   b. a memory location whose value can change while the program is running
   c. a memory location whose value cannot change while the program is running

2. To create a variable, you must assign _____ to it.
   a. a data type
   b. a name
   c. both a data type and a name
   d. the word `var`

3. Which of the following declares and initializes an Integer variable named `numItems`?
   a. `int numItems = 0;`
   b. `int numItems = '0';`
   c. `integer numItems = 0;`
   d. `numItems int = 0;`
   e. `numItems integer = 0;`

4. Which of the following, if any, are valid names for variables?
   a. `amt.Sold`
   b. `amt   Sold`
   c. `amt_Sold`
   d. `98Sold`
   e. None of the above are valid names for variables.

5. Which of the following, if any, are valid names for variables?
   a. class
   b. friend
   c. #OnHand
   d. void
   e. None of the above are valid names for variables.

6. Which of the following, if any, are invalid names for a variable?
   a. bankAccountNumber
   b. first_Name
   c. doubleNumber
   d. operator
   e. All of the above are valid names for variables.

7. The variable names total, Total, and toTAL refer to _____.
   a. different locations in memory
   b. the same location in memory

8. The number 4.5e3 is a _____ constant.
   a. character literal
   b. named literal
   c. numeric literal
   d. string literal

9. '3' is a _____ constant.
   a. character literal
   b. named literal
   c. numeric literal
   d. string literal

10. "C++" is a _____ constant.
    a. character literal
    b. named literal
    c. numeric literal
    d. string literal

11. 6.5 is a _____ constant.
    a. character literal
    b. named literal
    c. numeric literal
    d. string literal

12. What does C++ append to the end of a string literal constant?
    a. a space
    b. a number sign (#)
    c. an asterisk (*)
    d. a null character

13. The most efficient data type for a variable that stores the number 20000 is the _____ data type.
    a. Character
    b. Double
    c. Float
    d. Long Integer
    e. Short Integer

14. The most efficient data type for a variable that stores the number 5.6e20 is the
    _____ data type.
    a. Character
    b. Double
    c. Float
    d. Long Integer
    e. Short Integer

15. The most efficient data type for a variable that stores the letter C is the
    _____ data type.
    a. Character
    b. Double
    c. Float
    d. Long Integer
    e. Short Integer

16. Which of the following will store the letter H in a Character variable named `initial`?
    a. `initial = 'H'`
    b. `initial = 'H';`
    c. `initial = "H"`
    d. `initial = "H";`

17. Which of the following will store the number 320000 as a Float number?
    a. `countryPop = (float) 3.2e5;`
    b. `countryPop = (float) 3.2e6;`
    c. `countryPop = (float) .32e5;`
    d. `countryPop = (float) .32e7;`
    e. `countryPop = (float) 3.2-e5;`

18. You typically initialize Short Integer, Integer, and Long Integer variables to
    _____ .
    a. a space enclosed in double quotes
    b. a space enclosed in single quotes
    c. the letter O
    d. the number 0
    e. the value `false`

19. You typically initialize Character variables to _____ .
    a. a space enclosed in double quotes
    b. a space enclosed in single quotes
    c. the letter O
    d. the number 0
    e. the value `false`

20. Which of the following statements shows the correct way to create and initialize the
    Double `population` variable to the number 0?
    a. `double population = 0.0;`
    b. `double population = float (0);`
    c. `double population = float (0.0);`
    d. `population = (double) 0;`
    e. `population = (double) 0.0;`

21. Which of the following statements shows the correct way to create and initialize the
    `rate` variable, which is a Float variable, to the number 0.0?
    a. `float rate = 0.0;`
    b. `float rate = float ('0.0');`
    c. `float rate = (float) 0.0;`
    d. `rate = (double) 0;`
    e. `rate = (double) 0.0;`

22. Which of the following is a string literal constant?
  a. "Visual C++"
  b. "123.45"
  c. "A"
  d. "2,345"
  e. all of the above

23. The character literal constant 'Y' is stored in memory in the same manner as the string literal constant "Y".
  a. True
  b. False

24. Which of the following are valid characters for a numeric literal constant?
  a. a decimal point
  b. the letter e
  c. a minus sign
  d. a plus sign
  e. all of the above

25. Which of the following are valid characters for a numeric literal constant?
  a. a comma
  b. a dollar sign ($)
  c. a percent sign (%)
  d. a space
  e. none of the above

26. Which of the following statements creates a named constant called `driverAge` whose value is 16?
  a. `const driverAge = 16;`
  b. `const short driverAge = 16;`
  c. `driverAge = 16;`
  d. `driverAge const = 16;`
  e. `namedconst driverAge = 16;`

27. Assume that the following instructions are part of a valid C++ program. What is the value contained in the `number` variable after the instructions are processed?
  ```
  short number = 0;
  number = 10;
  number = number + 5;
  ```
  a. 0
  b. 5
  c. 10
  d. 15
  e. none of the above

28. The >> (extraction) operator stops reading characters from the keyboard as soon as the user _____ .
  a. presses the Enter key
  b. types a character that is inappropriate for the variable's data type
  c. both a and b

29. Assume that you use `cin` and >> to enter the number 3.24 into an Integer variable. The >> operator will _____ .
  a. stop reading characters as soon as you type the 2
  b. store the number 3 in the Integer variable
  c. store the number 3.24 in the Integer variable
  d. both a and b

E X E R C I S E S

1. Assume your program needs to store an item's price. The item's price will range from $15.50 to $20. On a piece of paper:
    a. Write the appropriate declaration statement to create the necessary variable and initialize it to 0.0.
    b. Write an assignment statement that assigns the value $16.23 to the variable.
    c. Write a statement that stores in the variable the value entered by the user.

2. Assume your program needs to store an item's height and width. Both dimensions can contain decimal places. On a piece of paper:
    a. Write the appropriate declaration statements to create the necessary variables and initialize them to 0.0.
    b. Write an assignment statement that assigns the value 4.5 to the height variable.
    c. Write an assignment statement that assigns the value 6.9 to the width variable.
    d. Write a statement that stores in the height variable the value entered by the user.
    e. Write a statement that stores in the width variable the value entered by the user.

3. Assume your program needs to store the population of a city. (The population will never be more than 75000.) On a piece of paper:
    a. Write the appropriate declaration statement to create the necessary variable and initialize it to 0.
    b. Write an assignment statement that assigns the value 60000 to the variable.
    c. Write a statement that stores in the variable the value entered by the user.

4. Assume your program needs to store a letter of the alphabet. On a piece of paper:
    a. Write the appropriate declaration statement to create the necessary variable and initialize it to a space.
    b. Write an assignment statement that assigns the letter A to the variable.
    c. Write a statement that stores in the variable the value entered by the user.

5. Assume your program needs to store a person's age. On a piece of paper:
    a. Write the appropriate declaration statement to create the necessary variable and initialize it to 0.
    b. Write an assignment statement that assigns the number 45 to the variable.
    c. Write a statement that stores in the variable the value entered by the user.

6. Assume your program needs to store the first character of a person's first name, and the first character of a person's last name. On a piece of paper:
    a. Write the appropriate declaration statements to create the necessary variables and initialize them to a space.
    b. Write an assignment statement that assigns the letter C to the first name variable.
    c. Write an assignment statement that assigns the letter R to the last name variable.
    d. Write a statement that stores in the first name variable the value entered by the user.
    e. Write a statement that stores in the last name variable the value entered by the user.

7. Assume your program needs to store the part number of an item and its cost. The part number contains only whole numbers in the range of 5000 to 8000. The cost of an item ranges from $1200 to $3500; the cost can contain a decimal place. On a piece of paper:
    a. Write the appropriate declaration statements to create the necessary variables and initialize them to the appropriate value—either 0 or 0.0.
    b. Write an assignment statement that assigns the value 5123 to the part number variable.
    c. Write an assignment statement that assigns the value 2500.65 to the cost variable.
    d. Write a statement that stores in the part number variable the value entered by the user.
    e. Write a statement that stores in the cost variable the value entered by the user.

8. On a piece of paper, write a statement to declare a named constant called `taxRate` whose value is .15.

9. On a piece of paper, write a statement to declare a named constant called `age` whose value is 21.

10. In this exercise, you will observe how `cin` and the `>>` operator handle values entered into variables.

    a. Open the T3Ae10.cpp file, which is located in the Cpp\Tut03\T3Ae10 folder on your computer's hard disk. Notice that the program uses one variable: a Short Integer variable named `data`. Use the program to complete the following chart. You will need first to build and then to execute the T3Ae10.exe program. When you are prompted to enter a value, enter each of the values shown in the center column, one at a time. (You will need to execute the program three times—once for each value.)

Data type of the `data` variable	Value entered	Value displayed in the DOS window
Short	30000	
Short	40000	
Short	7.3e10	

    b. Change the `short data = 0;` statement to `long data = 0;`. Save, build, and then execute the T3Ae10.exe program. Use the program to complete the following chart.

Data type of the `data` variable	Value entered	Value displayed in the DOS window
Long	10.3	
Long	9.333	
Long	$4	

    c. Change the `long data = 0;` statement to `float data = (float) 0.0;`. Save, build, and then execute the T3Ae10.exe program. Use the program to complete the following chart.

Data type of the `data` variable	Value entered	Value displayed in the DOS window
Float	7	
Float	3.6	
Float	$4.67	

    d. Change the `float data = (float) 0.0;` statement to `double data = 0.0;`. Save, build, and then execute the T3Ae10.exe program. Use the program to complete the following chart.

Data type of the data variable	Value entered	Value displayed in the DOS window
Double	8.46e5	
Double	9.3e-2	
Double	6,000	

e. Change the `double data = 0.0;` statement to `char data = ' ';` (a space between two single quotes). Save, build, and then execute the T3Ae10.exe program. Use the program to complete the following chart.

Data type of the data variable	Value entered	Value displayed in the DOS window
Character	W	
Character	Hello	

f. Use the File menu to close the workspace. Also close the Output window. Submit the answers contained in the completed charts.

discovery ▶ 11. Assume your program needs to store the number of units in stock at the beginning of the current month, the number of units purchased during the current month, the number of units sold during the current month, and the number of units in stock at the end of the current month. (The number of units is always a whole number that will never be larger than 10000.) On a piece of paper:

a. Write the appropriate declaration statements to create the necessary variables and initialize them to 0.

b. Write three assignment statements that assign the following values to the appropriate variables:

number of units at the beginning of the current month: 5000
number of units purchased during the current month: 1000
number of units sold during the current month: 3500

c. Write an assignment statement that calculates the number of units in stock at the end of the current month.

discovery ▶ 12. Assume your program needs to calculate the square of a number. The number will always be an integer in the range of 1 through 100. On a piece of paper:

a. Write the appropriate declaration statements to create the necessary variables and initialize them to 0.

b. Write a statement that stores in the appropriate variable the value entered by the user.

c. Write an assignment statement that calculates the square of the number.

discovery ▶ 13. Assume your program needs to calculate a bonus. The bonus is 5 percent of the sales. On a piece of paper:

a. Write a statement to declare a named constant called `bonusRate` whose value is .05.

b. Write the appropriate declaration statements to create two Float variables named `sales` and `bonus`. Initialize the variables to 0.0.

c. Write a statement that stores in the `sales` variable the value entered by the user.

d. Write an assignment statement that calculates the `bonus`.

discovery ▶ 14. Assume your program needs to calculate the area of a circle, which is πr^2. On a piece of paper:

a. Write a statement to declare a named constant called `pi` whose value is 3.141593.

b. Write the appropriate declaration statements to create two Float variables named `area` and `radius`. Initialize the variables to 0.0.

c. Write a statement that stores in the `radius` variable the value entered by the user.

d. Write an assignment statement that calculates the `area`.

discovery ▶ 15. In this program, you will discover the memory requirements and range of values your system uses for the C++ data types shown in Lesson A's Figure 3-2. Although the memory requirements and range of values are machine-dependent, in C++, the size of a Character variable is always less than or equal to the size of a Short Integer variable. A Short Integer variable is always less than or equal to the size of an Integer variable, which is always less than or equal to the size of a Long Integer variable. In addition, the size of a Float variable is always less than or equal to the size of a Double variable.

a. Open the T3Ae15.cpp file, which is located in the Cpp\Tut03\T3Ae15 folder on your computer's hard disk. Build and execute the program. The memory requirements and range of values for each data type shown in Lesson A's Figure 3-2 appear in a DOS window on the screen. Close the DOS window.

In steps b through d, you will learn how to send the program's output to a file for printing. Then, in step e, you will use C++ to print the contents of the file.

b. Enter the following two statements in the blank line below the opening brace ({):

```
ofstream outFile;
outFile.open("T3Ae15.dat");
```

In the `ofstream outFile;` statement, `ofstream` is the name of a class and `outFile` is the name of an object. The `ofstream outFile;` statement tells C++ to create an `ofstream` object, called `outFile`, that represents an output file. An output file is a file in which you can store data. The `outFile.open("T3Ae15.dat");` statement uses C++'s `open` function both to open the output file and to give the file a name.

c. Rather than sending the output to the screen (`cout`), you will send it to the output file (`outFile`). Use the Edit menu's Replace command to replace all occurrences of `cout` with `outFile`. (Don't include the period after `outFile`.)

d. Save, build, and then execute the T3Ae15.exe program. The program sends the output to the output file (T3Ae15.dat) rather than to the DOS window. When the "Press any key to continue" message appears, press the Enter key to close the DOS window.

e. To print the T3Ae15.dat file, click File on the menu bar, then click Open. The Open dialog box appears. Click the Files of type list arrow. Scroll the Files of type list box, then click All Files (*.*) in the list. Click T3Ae15.dat in the list of filenames, then click the Open button. The T3Ae15.dat file appears in the T3Ae15.dat window. Click File on the menu bar, then click Print, and then click the OK button.

f. Use the File menu to close the workspace. Also close the Output window.

discovery ▶ 16. You will be able to complete this exercise only if you are using Microsoft Visual C++ version 5.0 or later.

Microsoft Visual C++ 5.0 also includes the Boolean data type, which is not available in every C++ system. A variable assigned the Boolean data type can store either the numbers 0 and 1 or the values `false` and `true`. In Microsoft Visual C++ 5.0, `false` and `true` are keywords that stand for the Boolean values False and True, respectively; the keywords must be typed in lowercase. As in many computer languages, the Boolean value False, as well as the C++ keyword `false`, is equivalent to the number 0. The Boolean value True, as well as the C++ keyword `true`, is equivalent to the number 1. (The Boolean values True and False are named after the English mathematician George Boole.) You assign the Boolean data type to a variable by using the keyword `bool`. You can initialize a Boolean variable by assigning either the value `false` or the value `true` to it; most times, you will assign the value `false`. You can also initialize a Boolean variable to either the number 0, which is the same as `false`, or the number 1, which is the same as `true`. The `false` and `true` values, however, make your program more self-documenting.

a. Open the T3Ae16.cpp file, which is located in the Cpp\Tut03\T3Ae16 folder on your computer's hard disk. The program initializes a Boolean variable named `insured` and then displays its value. Build and execute the program. On a piece of paper, indicate what displays in the DOS window. Close the DOS window.

b. Change the `bool insured = false;` statement to `bool insured = true;`. Save, build, and then execute the program. On a piece of paper, indicate what displays in the DOS window. Close the DOS window.

c. Use the File menu to close the workspace. Also close the Output window.

debugging 17. In this exercise, you will debug a program.

a. Open the T3Ae17.cpp file, which is located in the Cpp\Tut03\T3Ae17 folder on your computer's hard disk. The program simply gets a pay rate from the user and then displays the rate on the screen. Build the program. Correct any errors. Save, build, and then execute the program. When the program is working correctly, print the code. On the printout, indicate what was wrong with the program. Also circle the corrections you made.

b. Use the File menu to close the workspace. Also close the Output window.

debugging 18. In this exercise, you will debug a program.

a. Open the T3Ae18.cpp file, which is located in the Cpp\Tut03\T3Ae18 folder on your computer's hard disk. The program first initializes the `temp` variable. It then adds 1.5 to the `temp` variable before displaying its value. Build the program. Correct any errors. Save, build, and then execute the program. When the program is working correctly, print the code. On the printout, indicate what was wrong with the program. Also circle the corrections you made.

b. Use the File menu to close the workspace. Also close the Output window.

debugging 19. In this exercise, you will debug a program.

a. Open the T3Ae19.cpp file, which is located in the Cpp\Tut03\T3Ae19 folder on your computer's hard disk. The program initializes a Character variable and then prompts the user to enter a character, which the program stores in the Character variable. The program then displays the contents of the Character variable on the screen.

b. Build the program. Correct the errors in the program. (Do not be overwhelmed by the number of errors shown in the Output window. Begin by correcting the first error, then save and build the program again. Most times you will find that correcting one error corrects many of the errors that follow it.)

c. Save, build, and then execute the program. When the program is working correctly, print the code. On the printout, indicate what was wrong with the program. Also circle the corrections you made.

d. Use the File menu to close the workspace. Also close the Output window.

In this lesson you will learn how to:

- Implement the String data type
- Use the `getline` and `strcpy` functions
- Create C++ equations
- Perform explicit type conversions in equations
- Create a console application

Using the String Data Type and C++ Equations

The String Data Type

As you learned in Lesson A, C++ provides numeric data types (Short Integer, Integer, Long Integer, Float, and Double) for storing numbers, and a Character data type for storing one character only. However, unlike many other languages, C++ does not provide a built-in String data type for storing more than one character of data—in other words, for storing a string literal constant. Although the String data type is not built into the C++ language, you can implement it using C++'s Character data type.

The syntax for declaring a String variable is almost identical to the syntax for declaring a Character variable. Recall that you create and initialize a Character variable by using the **char** *variablename* = *initialvalue*; syntax, where *initialvalue* is one character, typically a space, enclosed in single quotes (' '). Similarly, you create and initialize a String variable by using the **char** *variablename*[*x*] = *initialvalue*; syntax; in this syntax, *initialvalue* is zero or more characters enclosed in double quotes (" ").

You will notice that the String variable's syntax includes [*x*] after the *variablename*. The *x*, which must be enclosed in square brackets ([ ]), is a number that is one more than the maximum number of characters you want to store in the variable. For example, to store 10 characters in a String variable, *x* must be 11; to store 99 characters, *x* must be 100. You learned the reason for this in Lesson A. Recall that C++ appends an additional character, referred to as the null character, to the end of a string literal constant when the constant is stored in memory.

The *x* in the syntax tells C++ how many one-byte memory locations to save for use by the String variable. The `char petName[10];` statement, for example, saves 10 memory locations—nine of them for the name and one for the null character.

Unlike Character variables, which you typically initialize to one space enclosed in single quotes, String variables are usually initialized to a zero-length string. A **zero-length string** is simply a set of double quotes with no space in between, like this: `""`. The `char empName[25] = "";` statement, for example, creates and initializes, to the zero-length string, a String variable named `empName` that can store a maximum of 24 characters plus the null character.

tip

"Desk" and "ABC Company" are two examples of string literal constants.

You can also use the Character data type to create a String named constant. As you learned in Lesson A, a named constant is a memory location whose contents cannot change while the program is running. Named constants make your program more self-documenting and, therefore, easier to modify because they allow you to use meaningful words in place of values that may be less clear. The syntax for creating a String named constant—**const char** *constantname*[*x*] = *expression*; — is similar to the syntax for creating a Character named constant—**const char** *constantname* = *expression*;. Figure 3-13 shows examples of creating and initializing String variables and String named constants.

`char empName[25]="";`	Creates and initializes, to a zero-length string, a String variable named `empName` that can store 24 characters plus the null character
`char partNo[5] = "";`	Creates and initializes, to a zero-length string, a String variable named `partNo` that can store four characters plus the null character
`char response[4] = "Yes";`	Creates and initializes, to the string `"Yes"`, a String variable named `response` that can store three characters plus the null character
`const char title[5] = "Z Co";`	Creates a String named constant called `title` whose value is `"Z Co"` (without the quotes) plus the null character

Figure 3-13: Examples of String variables and String named constants

In Lesson A, you learned that you can use the `cin` stream and the `>>` operator to obtain data from the user at the keyboard; to do so, you use the **cin >>** *variablename*; syntax. You can also use this same syntax to enter data into a String variable. As you learned in Lesson A, the `>>` operator stops reading characters from the keyboard as soon as the user either presses the Enter key or types a character that is inappropriate for the variable's data type. In the case of String variables, an inappropriate character is the space. Run a program that uses `cin` and `>>` to enter data into a String variable.

To use `cin` and `>>` to enter data into a String variable:

1   If necessary, start Visual C++. Use the File menu to open the **LbProg01.cpp** file, which is located in the Cpp\Tut03\LbProg01folder on your computer's hard disk. The program instructions are shown in Figure 3-14.

```
//LbProg01.cpp
//this program enters data into a String variable

#include <iostream.h>

void main()
{
    //create and initialize variable
    char petName[10] = "";  //initialized to a zero-length string

    //enter value into variable
    cout << "Enter your pet's name: ";
    cin >> petName;

    //display contents of variable
    cout << "Your pet's name is " << petName << endl;

} //end of main function
```

Figure 3-14: LbProg01 program instructions

The program creates and initializes a String variable named `petName`. The variable can contain 10 characters—nine for the name and one for the null character.

2 Build and then execute the program. When you are prompted to enter your pet's name, type **Budd** and press the **Enter** key. The message, "Your pet's name is Budd," appears in the DOS window. Press the **Enter** key to close the DOS window, then close the Output window.

One caution when using `cin` and the `>>` operator to enter information into a String variable: if the user enters more characters than the String variable can store, C++ stores the additional characters in memory locations adjacent to, but not reserved for, the variable. Storing the additional characters in these unreserved locations may write over some important information in memory, perhaps crashing either the program or your system. If you use `cin` and the `>>` operator to read information into a String variable, you must be careful to enter only the correct number of characters.

As you learned in Lesson A, the `>>` operator stops reading characters from the keyboard as soon as the user either presses the Enter key or types a character that is inappropriate for the variable's data type. In the case of String variables, an inappropriate character is the space. Execute the LbProg01 program and enter a name that contains a space.

tip
· · · · · · · · · · · · · ·
Later in this lesson, you will learn about the `getline` function, which is a much safer way to enter data into a String variable.

To observe how the LbProg01 program handles input that contains a space:

1 Execute the program. (Because you did not make any changes to the program, you do not need to rebuild it before executing it.) When prompted to enter your pet's name, type **Budd**, then press the **Spacebar**, and then type the letter **R**. Press the **Enter** key. The DOS window shows that only the four letters Budd are stored in the `petName` variable.

2 Press the **Enter** key to close the DOS window.

Because it is common for string literal constants to contain one or more spaces, the next section will show you a different way to enter data into a String variable—a way that will allow the data to contain spaces. You can use one of the `cin` stream's member functions—`getline`—to enter data that contains spaces into a String variable.

Entering Data That Contains Spaces into a String Variable

As you may remember from Tutorial 2, `cin` is an object that belongs to a class named `istream`, which is defined in the iostream.h header file. Included in the definition of the `istream` class are functions—referred to as **member functions** because they are members (parts) of the class. One of the `istream` member functions is called `getline`.

As you learned in Tutorial 2, a function is a block of code that performs a specific task. In this case, the `getline` function's task is to read an entire line of text, including the spaces. The syntax for using the `getline` member function is *object*.**getline**(*variablename, length of string*);. The period (.) between *object* and the name of the member function—in this case, `getline`—is called the **dot member selection operator**. In the syntax, *variablename* is the name of a String variable, and *object* is the `cin` stream (the keyboard). *Length of string* is the number of characters to store in the String variable, including the null character that C++ appends to the end of the string. The `cin.getline(petName, 10);` statement, for example, tells C++ to read up to nine characters from the keyboard; C++ will store the null character in the 10th memory location. Change the current program to use the `getline` function.

OOP
Concepts

The object `cin` is an instance of the `istream` class.

To use the `getline` function in the current program:

1 Change the **cin >> petName;** statement to **cin.getline(petName, 10);**.

2 Save the program.

3 Build and then execute the program. When you are prompted to enter your pet's name, type **Budd**, then press the **spacebar**, and then type the letter **R**. Press the **Enter** key. The DOS window shows that the value in the `petName` String variable is Budd R. Notice that, unlike the >> operator, the `getline` function reads the space as part of the name.

4 Press the **Enter** key to close the DOS window. Close the Output window.

Unlike other variables, a String variable cannot be assigned a new value from an assignment statement. Rather, you use C++'s `strcpy` (*string copy*) function to assign a new value to a String variable.

Assigning a Value to a String Variable

C++ has many useful functions for handling, or managing, strings. One such function is `strcpy`. You use the `strcpy` function, whose syntax is **strcpy**(*variablename, string*);, to assign a value to a String variable. In the syntax, *variablename* is the name of the String variable, and *string* can either be zero or more characters enclosed in double quotes, or the name of another string variable. To use the `strcpy` function, you must include the string.h header file in your program. You will use the string.h header file and the `strcpy` function in the LbProg01 program, which is currently open.

To use the string.h header file and the **strcpy** function in the open LbProg01 program:

1 Type **#include <string.h>** in the line below the **#include <iostream.h>** directive, and then press the **Enter** key.

2 Remove the **cout << "Enter your pet's name: ";** and the **cin.getline(petName, 10);** statements from the program. Replace these two statements with the following statement: **strcpy(petName, "Trigger");**. This statement will store the pet name, Trigger, in the **petName** variable.

3 Save the program.

4 Build and then execute the program. The DOS window indicates that the name Trigger is stored in the **petName** variable. Press the **Enter** key to close the DOS window.

You are finished with this program, so now close the workspace.

5 Use the File menu to close the workspace, then close the Output window.

As you learned in Lesson A, most programs include the following components: variables, constants, arithmetic operators, and functions. You already know about variables and constants—both literal and named. You will learn about arithmetic operators, which are used in C++ equations, in the remaining sections of this lesson. (Functions, you may remember, are covered in Tutorial 4.) You will use arithmetic operators and C++ equations to solve the Jackson College case problem outlined at the beginning of this tutorial.

mini-quiz

Mini-Quiz 5

1. Write a C++ statement to create and initialize, to a zero-length string, a String variable named **myName**. The **myName** variable should be able to store 25 characters plus the null character.

2. Write a C++ statement to create and initialize, to the word Chicago, a String constant named **cityName**.

3. Write a C++ statement that uses **cin** and the **>>** operator to enter data into a String variable named **myName**.

4. Write a C++ statement that uses the **getline** function to enter data into a String variable named **myName**. The variable can store a maximum of 26 characters, which includes the null character.

5. Write a C++ statement that uses the **strcpy** function to assign the string "Paris" to the **cityName** String variable.

Writing C++ Equations

Most programs require the computer to perform one or more calculations. You instruct the computer to perform a calculation by writing an arithmetic equation that conforms to the syntax *variablename = expression*. *Variablename* is the name of the variable that will store the result of the *expression*. *Expression* can contain variables, constants, functions, and relational, logical, and mathematical operators. You will learn about the mathematical operators in this lesson. Functions are covered in Tutorial 4; the relational and logical operators are covered in Tutorial 5.

The most common mathematical operators used in an arithmetic expression, along with their precedence numbers, are listed in Figure 3-15. The precedence numbers represent the order in which C++ performs the mathematical operations in an expression. You can, however, use parentheses to override the order of precedence. Operations within parentheses are always performed before operations outside of parentheses.

Operator	Operation	Precedence number
( )	override normal precedence rules	1
–	negation	2
*, /, %	multiplication, division, and modulus arithmetic	3
+, –	addition and subtraction	4

Figure 3-15: Mathematical operators and their order of precedence

When you create an arithmetic expression, keep in mind that C++ follows the same order of precedence as you do when solving expressions—that is, an operation with a precedence number of 1 is done before an operation with a precedence number of 2, and so on. If the expression contains more than one operator having the same priority, those operators are evaluated from left to right. For example, in the expression 3+9/3*5, the division (/) would be done first, then the multiplication (*), and then the addition (+). In other words, C++ would first divide 9 by 3, then multiply the result of the division (3) by 5, and then add 3 to the result of the multiplication (15). The expression evaluates to 18. You can use parentheses to change the order in which the operators are evaluated. For example, the expression (3+9)/3*5 (notice the parentheses around the 3+9) evaluates to 20, not 18. That is because the parentheses tell C++ to add 3 + 9 first, then divide by 3, and then multiply by 5.

One of the mathematical operators listed in Figure 3-15, the modulus arithmetic operator (%), might be less familiar to you. The **modulus arithmetic operator** is used to divide two integers, and results in the remainder of the division. For example, 211 % 4 (read 211 mod 4) equals 3, which is the remainder of 211 divided by 4. One use for the modulus operator is to determine if a year is a leap year—one that has 366 days rather than 365 days. As you may know, if a year is a leap year, then its year number is evenly divisible by the number 4—in other words, if you divide the year number by 4 and the remainder is 0 (zero), then the year is a leap year. You can determine if the year 2000 is a leap year by using the expression 2000 % 4. This expression evaluates to 0 (the remainder of 2000 divided by 4), so the year 2000 is a leap year. Similarly, you can determine if the year 2001 is a leap year by using the expression 2001 % 4. This expression evaluates to 1 (the remainder of 2001 divided by 4), so the year 2001 is not a leap year.

When entering a numeric literal constant in an expression, you do not enter the comma (,), the dollar sign ($), or the percent sign (%). If you want to enter a percentage, you must convert the percentage to its decimal equivalent—for example, you would need to convert 5 percent to .05, and 120 percent to 1.20.

As you learned in Lesson A, when you assign a value to a variable, the data type of both the value and the variable must be the same. In many cases, you will need to use explicit type conversion, or type casting, to force a value to match the variable's data type. You were introduced to type casting in Lesson A. Recall that you use the (float) 0.0 type cast to initialize a Float variable to 0.0.

First you will execute a program in which the value's data type does not match the variable's data type. The purpose of executing this program is to observe how C++ treats this error.

To execute the LbProg02 program:

1   Use the File menu to open the **LbProg02.cpp** file, which is located in the Cpp\Tut03\LbProg02 folder on your computer's hard disk. The program instructions are shown in Figure 3-16.

```
//LbProg02.cpp
//this program calculates and displays an average

#include <iostream.h>

void main()
{
    //declare and initialize variables
    short sum    = 0;
    short count  = 0;
    float average = (float) 0.0;

    //assign values to variables
    sum   = 30;
    count = 4;

    //calculate average
    average = sum / count;

    //display average
    cout << "The average is: " << average << endl;

} //end of main function
```

Figure 3-16: LbProg02 program instructions

The program creates and initializes two Short Integer variables (sum and count) and a Float variable (average). The integer 30 is then assigned to the sum variable, and the integer 4 is assigned to the count variable. The equation average = sum / count divides the contents of the sum variable by the contents of the count variable, then stores the result in the average variable. The program then displays the average on the screen.

2   Click **Build** on the menu bar, then click **Build**. When you are prompted to create a default project workspace, click the **Yes** button. The Output window displays one warning message: "warning C4244: '=' : conversion from 'int' to 'float', possible loss of data."

3   Double-click the warning message.

The arrow in the LbProg02.cpp window indicates that the warning message relates to the `average = sum / count;` statement.

Recall that both the `sum` and `count` variables are declared as Short Integer. In C++, when you divide an integer by another integer, the result is always an integer. In this case, dividing the integer stored in the `sum` variable (30) by the integer stored in the `count` variable (4) results in the integer 7; it does not result in the Float number 7.5, which is the correct average. The warning message advises you that, when C++ converts from an integer to a Float number, some loss of data may occur. This is because not every integer can be stored, precisely, as a Float number. You should always locate and correct the problem to which a warning message pertains before executing the program. In this case, however, you will execute the program simply to observe that C++ stores the number 7, rather than the number 7.5, in the `average` variable.

4   Click **Build** on the menu bar, and then click **Execute LbProg02.exe**. The message "The average is: 7" appears in the DOS window. Press the **Enter** key to close the DOS window.

To display the correct average of 7.5, you will need to use explicit type conversion—a type cast—in the equation that calculates the average.

Mini-Quiz 6

1. Solve the following expression: $5 + 6 / 3 * 3 - 2$
2. Solve the following expression: $-2 * 3 + 8 * 4 / 2$
3. Solve the following expression: $6 * (4 + 5) - 3 * 2$
4. Solve the following expression: $100 \% 25 * 3$
5. Solve the following expression: $100 \% (25 * 3)$
6. Solve the following expression: $(4 + 6) / 5 * 3 - 2$

Using Explicit Type Conversion in an Equation

As you learned in Lesson A, explicit type conversion, also called type casting, is the explicit conversion of data from one data type to another. You type cast an item of data by preceding it with the C++ keyword that represents the desired data type; you enclose the keyword in parentheses. To type cast a Short Integer variable named `count` to a Float type, for example, you would use the type cast `(float) count`. When you type cast a variable, C++ creates a temporary copy of that variable using the new data type. Type casting does not change either the data type or contents of the original variable. Figure 3-17 shows examples of type casts.

Type cast	Result
(float) count	Creates a temporary copy of the count variable. The copy is stored as a Float type.
(short) number	Creates a temporary copy of the number variable. The copy is stored as a Short Integer type.
(double) total	Creates a temporary copy of the total variable. The copy is stored as a Double type.

Figure 3-17: Examples of type casts

When an equation contains mixed data types, you should use type casts to make each item of data that appears on the right side of the equal sign the same data type as the variable that appears on the left side of the equal sign. Figure 3-18 shows two examples of using type casts in equations.

You cannot use a type cast on the left side of the equal sign in an equation.

Example 1:
```
//declare and initialize variables
short hoursWkd = 0;
float payRate  = (float) 0.0;
float grossPay = (float) 0.0;
//calculate gross pay
grossPay = (float) hoursWkd * payRate
```

Example 2:
```
//declare and initialize variables
int total   = 0;
float sales = (float) 0.0;
//calculate total
total = total + (int) sales;
```

Figure 3-18: Examples of using type casts in equations

Look closely at the equation in the first example: grossPay = (float) hoursWkd * payRate. The variable on the left side of the equal sign (grossPay) is a Float variable, so the items on the right side of the equal sign (hoursWkd and payRate) must also be of the Float data type. (Recall that you must use the same data type on both sides of the equal sign.) The payRate variable is already a Float variable, so no type cast is necessary for this variable. The hoursWkd variable, however, is declared as a Short Integer variable. You will notice that the equation uses a type cast to make the hoursWkd variable's data type match the grossPay variable's data type—Float. Recall that when you type cast a variable, C++ creates a temporary copy of that variable using the new data type. In this case, C++ will create a copy of the hoursWkd variable, using Float as its data type. C++ will use the contents of the Float hoursWkd variable, rather than the contents of the Short Integer hoursWkd variable, in the equation that calculates the gross pay.

tip

▶ Keep in mind that type casting does not change either the data type or contents of the original variable.

tip

▶ In Lesson B's Discovery Exercise 21, you will learn how to round a Float number to the nearest integer.

Now look at the equation in the second example: `total = total + (int) sales;`. The variable on the left side of the equation (`total`) is an Integer variable. The `sales` variable on the right side of the equation, however, is a Float variable. You will notice that the equation uses the `(int) sales` type cast to make the `sales` variable's data type match the `total` variable's data type. Be aware that when C++ converts the value in a Float variable to either the Short Integer, Integer, or Long Integer data type, it **truncates** (removes or drops) the decimal portion of the number. For example, if the `sales` variable contains the number 1500.56, the `(int) sales` type cast will store the number 1500, rather than the number 1500.56, in the temporary Integer `sales` variable.

In the LbProg02 program, the `average = sum / count;` equation contains mixed data types: Short Integer and Float. The proper way to write this equation is to use a type cast to convert the Short Integer variables (`sum` and `count`) to the Float data type to ensure their data type will agree with the data type of the `average` variable. When you divide a Float number by a Float number, the result is a Float number. In this case, the Float result of dividing the `sum` variable by the `count` variable will be stored, correctly, in the Float `average` variable.

Change the LbProg02 program so it uses type casts to convert the Short Integer variables in the average calculation to the Float data type.

To include type casts in the LbProg02 program:

1 The LbProg02 program should be open. Change the `average = sum / count;` equation to **average = (float) sum / (float) count;**. (Do not include the period.)

2 Save the program, then build and execute the program. The DOS window shows that the `average` variable contains the number 7.5, which is the correct result of dividing 30 by 4.

3 Press the **Enter** key to close the DOS window.

You are now finished with this program, so close the workspace and the Output window.

4 Use the File menu to close the workspace. Also close the Output window.

You will now combine what you know about variables, constants, arithmetic operators, and equations to solve the Jackson College case problem outlined at the beginning of the tutorial.

mini-quiz

Mini-Quiz 7

1. Write an equation that subtracts a Long Integer variable named `num1` from a Float variable named `num2`, and assigns the result to a Long Integer variable named `num3`.

2. Write a C++ statement that multiplies the contents of the `quantity` variable by the contents of the `price` variable. Assign the result to a Float variable named `total`. `quantity` is a Short Integer variable and `price` is a Float variable.

3. Write a C++ statement that increases the contents of the `temp` variable by 5. The `temp` variable is a Float variable.

4. Assume that a Float variable named `hourlyPay` contains the number 9.75. The `(short) hourlyPay` type cast would create a temporary Short Integer variable named `hourlyPay` and would store the number _____ in it.

Solving the Jackson College Problem

Recall that Jack Faye is the cashier at Jackson College in Alabama. Jack wants a program that the clerks can use to display the student's name and the total amount the student owes for the semester, including tuition, insurance, and room and board. Tuition at Jackson is $100 per semester hour, room and board is $1800 per semester, and insurance is $12.50 per semester. The IPO chart for this problem is shown in Figure 3-19.

Input	Processing	Output
name hours enrolled fee per semester hour room and board fee insurance fee	Processing items: none Algorithm: 1. enter the name, hours enrolled, fee per semester hour, room and board fee, and insurance fee 2. calculate the semester tuition by multiplying the hours enrolled by the fee per semester hour 3. calculate the total amount owed by adding together the semester tuition, room and board fee, and insurance fee 4. display the name, semester tuition, and total amount owed	name semester tuition total amount owed

Figure 3-19: IPO chart for the Jackson College problem

You will notice that the output for this problem is the student's name, the semester tuition, and the total amount owed for the semester. To display the output, the program needs to know the student's name, the number of hours the student is enrolled for the semester, the fee per semester hour, the room and board fee, and the insurance fee. The program will input these items, then calculate both the tuition and the total amount owed. It will then display the output items. You can use the following data to desk-check the algorithm:

Student's name:	Rachel Woods
Hours enrolled:	15
Fee per semester hour:	$100
Room and board fee:	$1800
Insurance fee:	$12.50

The desk-check is shown in Figure 3-20.

Name	Hours enrolled	Fee per semester hour	Room and board fee	Insurance fee	Semester Tuition	Total amount owed
Rachel Woods	15	100	1800	12.50	1500	3312.50

Figure 3-20: Desk-check table for the Jackson College algorithm

After writing the algorithm and desk-checking it, you are ready to translate the algorithm into a program. Up to this point, you have been opening existing programs. In the next section, you will learn how to use Visual C++ to create your own programs.

Creating a Console Application

Although you can create many different types of applications in Visual C++, in this book you will create console applications only. A **console application** is a program that runs in a DOS window under Windows 95 or Windows NT. Learn how to create a Visual C++ console application.

To create a Visual C++ console application:

1 Click **File** on the menu bar, and then click **New**. The New dialog box appears. Click the **Projects** tab, if necessary, then click **Win32 Console Application** in the list of project types. If necessary, click the **Create new workspace** option button to select it. See Figure 3-21.

this should display the location of the Tut03 folder on your computer's hard disk

your list may differ

select this project type

be sure this option is selected

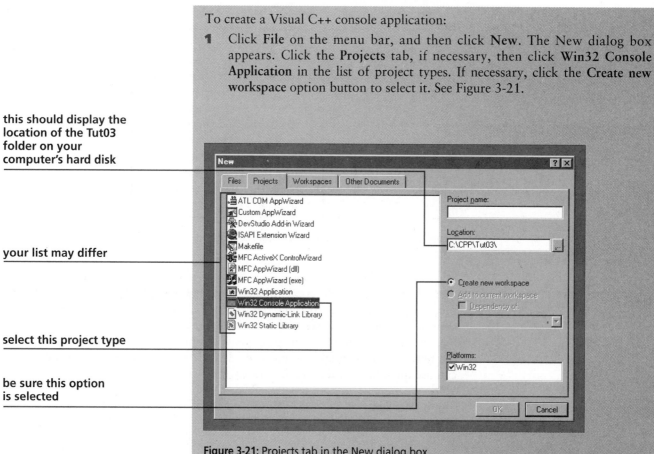

Figure 3-21: Projects tab in the New dialog box

HELP? If the Location text box does not display the location of the Tut03 folder on your computer's hard disk (the location will typically be C:\CPP\Tut03\), click the Location button. The Choose Directory dialog box appears. Use the Choose Directory dialog box to open the Tut03 folder on your computer's hard disk, then click the OK button.

2 Click the **Project name** text box, then type **LbProg03** in the Project name text box. See Figure 3-22.

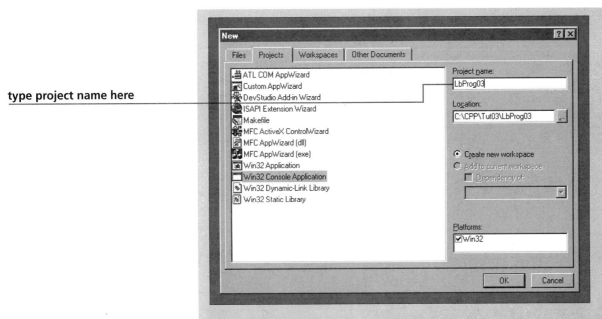

type project name here

Figure 3-22: Project name entered in the New dialog box

3 Click the **OK** button to close the New dialog box. The Microsoft Developer Studio window appears as shown in Figure 3-23.

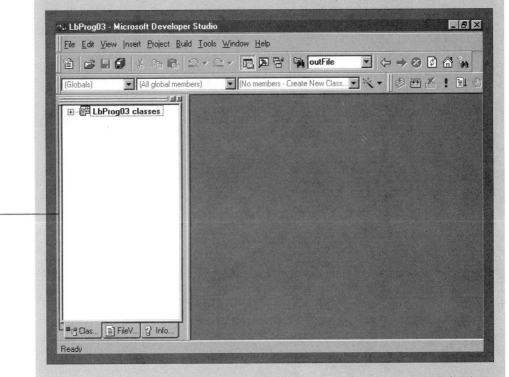

Project Workspace window

Figure 3-23: Microsoft Developer Studio window showing the LbProg03 console application

When you use the New dialog box to create a console application, C++ creates both a Visual C++ workspace and a Visual C++ project. A **workspace** is a container for one or more projects, and a **project** is a container for one or more files that contain source code, usually referred to as **source files**. (The current project does not contain any source files yet.) Although the idea of workspaces, projects, and source files may sound confusing, the concept of placing things in containers is nothing new to you. Think of a workspace as being similar to a drawer in a filing cabinet. A project is then similar to a file folder that you store in the drawer, and a file that contains source code is similar to a document that you store in the file folder. You can place many file folders in a filing cabinet drawer, just as you can place many projects in a workspace. You can also store many documents in a file folder, similar to the way you can store many source files in a C++ project. Figure 3-24 illustrates this analogy.

source file

project

workspace

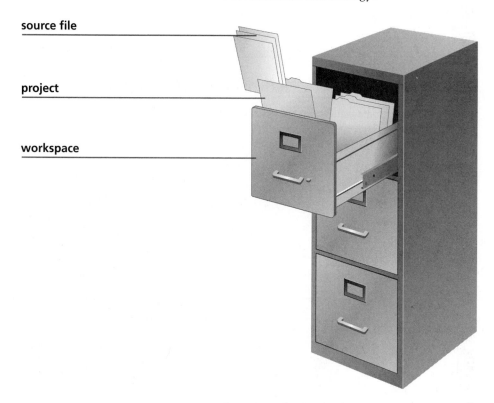

Figure 3-24: Illustration of a workspace, project, and source file

After you create the workspace and the project, you then add a source file to the project. You can add either a new source file or an existing source file. You will add a new source file to the project.

tip
. . . .
If a project contains only one file, most programmers give the file the same name as the project.

To add a new source file to the project:

1   Click **Project** on the menu bar, point to **Add To Project**, and then click **New**. The New dialog box appears. If necessary, click the **Files** tab. Click **C++ Source File** in the list of file types, then type **LbProg03** in the File name text box, as shown in Figure 3-25.

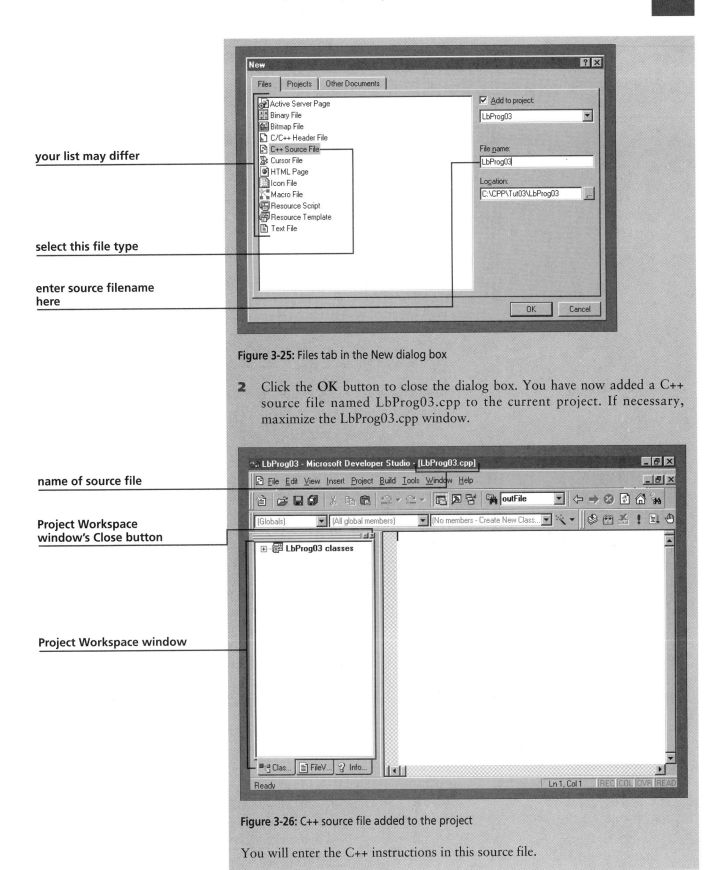

your list may differ

select this file type

enter source filename
here

Figure 3-25: Files tab in the New dialog box

2   Click the **OK** button to close the dialog box. You have now added a C++ source file named LbProg03.cpp to the current project. If necessary, maximize the LbProg03.cpp window.

name of source file

Project Workspace
window's Close button

Project Workspace window

Figure 3-26: C++ source file added to the project

You will enter the C++ instructions in this source file.

3 If necessary, close the Project Workspace window by clicking the **Close** button ▣ on its title bar.

Figure 3-27 shows the basic structure of a C++ program.

#include *directives*

void main( )
{

    [comments or one or more statements ending in a semicolon (;)]

} //end of main function

Items in square brackets ([ ]) in the structure are optional. Items in **bold**, on the other hand, are required. Items in *italics* represent places where the programmer must supply information relative to the program.

Figure 3-27: Basic structure of a C++ program

Before following this basic structure to enter the current program instructions, enter comments that identify the Jackson College program's name and purpose.

To begin entering the Jackson College program instructions:

1 Type **//LbProg03.cpp** and press the **Enter** key, then type **//this program displays the student's name, tuition, and total** and press the **Enter** key. Type **//amount owed for the semester** and press the **Enter** key twice.

According to the structure shown in Figure 3-27, you first enter the `#include` directives. As you may remember from Tutorial 2, a directive is a special instruction for the C++ compiler. The `#include` directive tells C++ to include the contents of another file, typically a header file that contains source code, in the current program. The LbProg03 program will need to include only the iostream.h header file, which contains the instructions (source code) needed for input and output operations. The name of the iostream.h header file must be enclosed in angle brackets (< >).

2 Type **#include <iostream.h>** and press the **Enter** key twice.

According to the structure, you can now enter the `main` function. Recall that every C++ program must have a `main` function; this is where program execution begins. Also recall that the `main` function is a `void` function, which means that it does not return a value.

3 Type **void main( )** and press the **Enter** key. (Do not type a space between the parentheses.)

A function's instructions must be enclosed in a set of braces. You will type the opening brace now, and the closing brace when you have completed the `main` function.

4 Type **{** (the opening brace) and press the **Enter** key.

tip

You may remember from Tutorial 2 that the angle brackets (<>) in the `#include` directive tell C++ that the header file is located in the C++ *include* folder.

Now enter the `main` function's instructions. You will begin by declaring and initializing the variables and constants. You need either a variable or a named constant for each input, processing, and output item in your IPO chart. (See Figure 3-19 for this problem's IPO chart.) After declaring the variables and constants, you will then translate the algorithm into C++ statements.

To give you experience in using variables and constants in a program, you will declare and initialize variables for the name, hours enrolled, insurance fee, semester tuition, and total amount owed. You will declare and initialize named constants for the fee per semester hour, as well as the room and board fee. The names and data types of the variables and named constants are shown in Figure 3-28.

Variables	/	Data type	Named constants	/	Data type	/	Value
name[20]		char	hrlyFee		short		100
hoursEnrolled		float	roomBoard		short		1800
totalOwed		float					
insurance		float					
tuition		float					

Figure 3-28: Names and data types of variables and named constants

Continue entering the program.

To declare and initialize variables and named constants in the Jackson College program:

1 Type the additional instructions highlighted in Figure 3-29. After typing the last instruction shown in the figure, press the **Enter** key twice.

enter these instructions

```
//LbProg03.cpp
//this program displays the student's name, tuition, and total
//amount owed for the semester

#include <iostream.h>

void main( )
{
    //declare and initialize the variables and constants
    char name[20] = "";
    float hoursEnrolled   = (float) 0.0;
    float totalOwed       = (float) 0.0;
    float insurance       = (float) 0.0;
    float tuition         = (float) 0.0;
    const short hrlyFee   = 100;
    const short roomBoard = 1800;
```

Figure 3-29: Instructions to declare and initialize the variables and constants

The first step in the algorithm shown in Figure 3-19 is to enter the name, hours enrolled, fee per semester hour, room and board fee, and insurance fee. The user will not need to enter either the fee per semester hour or the room and board fee because you have already created named constants for these items in the program. However, the user will need to enter the name, hours enrolled, and insurance fee.

2 The insertion point should be positioned two lines below the `const short roomBoard = 1800;` statement. Beginning in that blank line, type the additional instructions shown in Figure 3-30. After typing the last line, press the **Enter** key twice.

```
//enter the input items
cout << "Enter the student's name: ";
cin.getline(name, 20);
cout << "Enter the hours enrolled: ";
cin >> hoursEnrolled;
cout << "Enter the insurance amount: ";
cin >> insurance;
```

Figure 3-30: Instructions to enter the name, hours enrolled, and insurance fee

The next two steps in the algorithm are to calculate the semester tuition and the total amount owed. The semester tuition is calculated by multiplying the number of hours enrolled by the fee per semester hour. The total amount owed is calculated by adding together the semester tuition, the room and board fee, and the insurance fee. Because both calculations involve mixed data types, you will need to use a type cast in each equation. In the semester tuition calculation, you will type cast the `hrlyFee` constant from Short Integer to Float so that it agrees with the data type of both the `tuition` and `hoursEnrolled` variables. In the total amount owed calculation, you will type cast the `roomBoard` constant from Short Integer to Float so that it agrees with the `tuition`, `insurance`, and `totalOwed` variables.

3 The insertion point should be positioned two lines below the `cin >> insurance;` statement. Beginning in that blank line, type the instructions shown in Figure 3-31. After typing the last line, press the **Enter** key twice.

```
//calculate the tuition
tuition = hoursEnrolled * (float) hrlyFee;
//calculate the total amount owed
totalOwed = tuition + (float) roomBoard + insurance;
```

Figure 3-31: Calculation instructions

The last step in the algorithm is to display the name, semester tuition, and total amount owed. After entering the instructions to display these items, you can then complete the program by typing the `main` function's closing brace.

4   The insertion point should be positioned two lines below the `totalOwed` `= tuition + (float) roomBoard + insurance;` statement. Beginning in that blank line, type the instructions highlighted in Figure 3-32. Also, enter the `main` function's closing brace and the final comment. The additional instructions, as well as the closing brace and the final comment, are highlighted in the figure, which shows the completed LbProg03 program.

```cpp
//LbProg03.cpp
//this program displays the student's name, tuition, and total
//amount owed for the semester

#include <iostream.h>

void main( )
{
    //declare and initialize the variables and constants
    char name[20] = "";
    float hoursEnrolled  = (float) 0.0;
    float totalOwed      = (float) 0.0;
    float insurance       = (float) 0.0;
    float tuition         = (float) 0.0;
    const short hrlyFee   = 100;
    const short roomBoard = 1800;

    //enter the input items
    cout << "Enter the student's name: ";
    cin.getline(name, 20);
    cout << "Enter the hours enrolled: ";
    cin >> hoursEnrolled;
    cout << "Enter the insurance amount: ";
    cin >> insurance;

    //calculate the tuition
    tuition = hoursEnrolled * (float) hrlyFee;
    //calculate the total amount owed
    totalOwed = tuition + (float) roomBoard + insurance;

    //display the output items
    cout  << "The tuition is $" << tuition << endl;
    cout  << "The total amount owed for "
          << name << " is $" << totalOwed;
    cout  << endl;
} //end of main function
```

enter these instructions

Figure 3-32: Completed LbProg03 program for Jackson College

5   Save the program.

6   Build and execute the program. When you are prompted for the student's name, type **Rachel Woods** and press the **Enter** key. When you are prompted for the hours enrolled, type **15** and press the **Enter** key. When you are prompted for the insurance, type **12.50** and press the **Enter** key. The DOS window shows that the tuition is $1500, and the total amount owed is $3312.5. These values agree with the results of the desk-check table shown in Figure 3-20, so the program appears to be working correctly. You should, however, test it several more times with different data.

7   Press the **Enter** key to close the DOS window.

8   On your own, try running this program using other values for the name, hours enrolled, and insurance fee. When you are finished experimenting, use the File menu to close the workspace, then close the Output window.

tip

In Lesson B's Discovery Exercise 22, you will learn how to format your output. You will also learn more on formatting your output in Tutorial 4.

You have now completed Lesson B. You can either exit Visual C++ and take a break or complete the questions and exercises at the end of the lesson.

SUMMARY

C++ does not provide a built-in String data type that can store string literal constants. However, you can use C++'s Character data type to implement the String data type. You create and initialize a String variable with a statement that conforms to the following syntax: **char** *variablename*[*x*] = *initialvalue*;. In the syntax, *x*, which must be enclosed in square brackets ([ ]), is a number that is one more than the maximum number of characters you want to store in the variable. If you want to store 15 characters in a String variable, for example, then *x* must be 16 because C++ appends an additional character, referred to as the null character, to the end of a string literal constant when the constant is stored in memory. You typically initialize a String variable to a zero-length string, which is simply a set of double quotes with no space in between, like this: `""`. You can also use the Character data type to create a String named constant, which is a memory location whose contents cannot change while a program is running. The syntax for creating a String named constant is **const char** *constantname*[*x*] = *expression*;.

You can use `cin` and the >> operator to enter data into a String variable. However, you must be careful not to enter more characters than the String variable can store. If the number of characters you enter exceeds the number of characters reserved in memory for the String variable, C++ stores the additional characters in memory locations that are adjacent to, but not reserved for, the variable. The additional characters may write over some important information stored in memory, which could crash either the program or your system.

The >> operator stops reading characters from the keyboard as soon as the user either presses the Enter key or types a character that is inappropriate for the variable's data type. In the case of String variables, an inappropriate character is the space. If you want to enter into a String variable some data that contains a space, you can use the `cin` stream's `getline` member function to do so. The syntax for using the `getline` function is *object*.**getline**(*variablename*, *length of string*);. The period (.) between the *object* and the member function—in this case, `getline`—is called the dot member selection operator. In the syntax, *variablename* is the name of a String variable, and *object* is the `cin` stream (the keyboard). *Length of string* is the number of characters to store in the String variable, including the null character that C++ appends to the end of the string. It is safer to use the `getline` function, rather than the >> operator, to read data into a String variable.

You cannot use an assignment statement to assign a new value to a String variable. You can, however, use C++'s `strcpy` function, whose syntax is **strcpy**(*variablename*, *string*). In the syntax, *variablename* is the name of the String variable; *string* can either be zero or more characters enclosed in double quotes, or the name of another String variable. To use the `strcpy` function, you must include the string.h header file in your program.

Most programs require the computer to perform one or more calculations. You instruct the computer to perform a calculation by writing an arithmetic equation that conforms to the syntax *variablename* = *expression*;. *Variablename* is the name of the variable that will store the result of the *expression*. The *expression* can contain variables, constants, functions, and relational, logical, and mathematical operators. The data type of the expression must match the data type of the variable whose name appears on the left side of the equal sign.

The mathematical operators used in an expression have an order of precedence. However, you can use parentheses to override that order of precedence. Operations within parentheses are always performed before operations outside of parentheses.

Rather than allowing the C++ compiler to perform implicit type conversion, which can lead to unexpected results in a program, it is better to use a type cast (explicit type conversion) to convert data from one data type to another. You type cast an item of data by preceding it with the name of the desired data type. When you type cast a variable, C++ creates a temporary copy of that variable using the new data type. Type casting does not change either the data type or contents of the original variable. When an equation contains mixed data types, you should use type casts to make each item of data that appears on the right side of the equal sign the same data type as the variable that appears on the left side of the equal sign.

In this book, you will use Microsoft Visual C++ to create console applications, which are programs that run in a DOS window under Windows 95 or Windows NT. When you create a console application in Microsoft Visual C++, C++ creates both a Visual C++ workspace and a Visual C++ project. A workspace is a container for one or more projects, and a project is a container for one or more files that contain source code, usually referred to as source files.

ANSWERS TO MINI-QUIZZES

Mini-Quiz 5

1. `char myName[26] = "";`
2. `const char cityName[8] = "Chicago";`
3. `cin >> myName;`
4. `cin.getline(myName, 26);`
5. `strcpy(cityName, "Paris");`

Mini-Quiz 6

1. 9 **2.** 10 **3.** 48 **4.** 0 **5.** 25 **6.** 4

Mini-Quiz 7

1. `num3 = (long) num2 - num1;`
2. `total = (float) quantity * price;`
3. `temp = temp + (float) 5;`
4. 9

QUESTIONS

1. The String data type is an extension of the _____ data type.
   a. Character
   b. Double
   c. Letter
   d. Long
   e. Text

2. The syntax for declaring and initializing a String variable is **char** *variablename*[*x*] = *initialvalue*;. In the syntax, *x* is a number that is _____ the length of the string you want to store in the variable.
   a. one less than
   b. one more than
   c. the same as
   d. two more than

3. If you want to store a maximum of 15 characters in a String variable, you need to tell C++ to put aside _____ memory locations. (The 15 characters include the null character.)
   a. 14
   b. 15
   c. 16
   d. either a or b will work

4. You typically initialize a String variable to _____ .
   a. an asterisk
   b. a space enclosed in single quotes
   c. the number 0
   d. a zero-length string

5. Which of the following creates a String named constant called `partNo`, whose value is AB45?
   a. `const char[4] partNo = "AB45";`
   b. `const char[5] partNo = 'AB45';`
   c. `const char[5] partNo = "AB45";`
   d. `const char partNo[5] = 'AB45';`
   e. none of the above

6. Assume that a program contains the following three statements:
   ```
   char itemName[10] = "";
   cout << "Enter the item: ";
   cin >> itemName;
   ```
   If, after executing the program, the user enters the two words Red Coat, C++ will store _____ in the `itemName` variable.
   a. Coat
   b. Red
   c. Red Coat

7. Assume that a program contains the following three statements:
   ```
   char itemName[10] = "";
   cout << "Enter the item: ";
   cin.getline(itemName, 10);
   ```

If, after executing the program, the user enters the two words Red Coat, C++ will store _____ in the `itemName` variable.

a. Coat

b. Red

c. Red Coat

8. You can use the C++ _____ function to assign a value to a String variable.

a. `assign`

b. `copy`

c. `string`

d. `strcopy`

e. `strcpy`

9. To use the `strcpy` function, you must include the _____ header file in your program.

a. assign.h

b. copy.h

c. string.h

d. strcopy.h

e. strcpy.h

10. Complete the following chart by evaluating the expressions.

Expression	Result
3 + 6 * 2	
(3 + 6) / 2	
2 + 4 / 2 + 5 * 4 – 2	
(5 + 3) / 4 * 2	
3 + 4 / 2 * 3 + 3	
25 / 4	
25 % 4	

11. Which of the following type casts will convert an Integer variable named `amount` to a Double type?

a. `(double) amount`

b. `(int to double) amount`

c. `int to double(amount)`

d. `int (amount) to double`

12. Assume that a program declares a Long Integer type variable named `amtSold`, a Float variable named `bonus`, and a Float variable named `bonusRate`. Which of the following is the correct equation to use to calculate a salesperson's bonus?

a. `bonus = (float) amtSold * bonusRate;`

b. `(float) bonus = (float) amtSold * (float) bonusRate;`

c. `(long) bonus = amtSold * (long) bonusRate;`

d. `(long) bonus = (long) amtSold * (long) bonusRate;`

e. `bonus = amtSold * (float) bonusRate;`

13. A C++ _____ is a program that runs in a DOS window.

a. algorithm

b. cast application

c. console application

d. source application

14. In Microsoft Visual C++, a _____ is a container for one or more projects.
   a. console
   b. source file
   c. window
   d. workspace

15. In Microsoft Visual C++, a _____ is a container for one or more files that contain source code.
   a. console
   b. project
   c. window
   d. workspace

16. The code that you enter into a C++ program is called _____ .
   a. console code
   b. object code
   c. project code
   d. source code

17. The following chart shows the basic structure of a C++ program. Complete the chart by filling in the missing information.

```
#_____


void _____


___
     [ comments or one or more statements ending in a semicolon (;)]


___//end of main function
```

E X E R C I S E S

1. On a piece of paper, create and initialize, to a zero-length string, a String variable named `bookTitle` that can store up to 30 characters. The 30 characters includes the null character.

2. On a piece of paper, create and initialize, to the string "Alpha Works", a String variable named `company` that can store up to 15 characters. The 15 characters includes the null character.

3. On a piece of paper, create a String named constant called `country` whose value is "Mexico".

4. On a piece of paper, create a String named constant called `phone` whose value is "911".

5. On a piece of paper, write a statement that uses `cin` and the `>>` operator to store a value in a String variable named `bookTitle`. (The variable will not contain a space.)

6. On a piece of paper, write a statement that uses `cin` and the `>>` operator to store a value in a String variable named `company`. (The variable will not contain a space.)

7. On a piece of paper, write a statement that uses the cin stream's getline function to store a value in a String variable named bookTitle. The variable can store a maximum of 30 characters. The 30 characters includes the null character.

8. On a piece of paper, write a statement that uses the cin stream's getline function to store a value in a String variable named company. The variable can store a maximum of 15 characters. The 15 characters includes the null character.

9. On a piece of paper, write a statement that uses the strcpy function to store the value "Blooming Roses" in a String variable named bookTitle.

10. On a piece of paper, write a statement that uses the strcpy function to store the value "Rogers Heating" in a String variable named company.

11. On a piece of paper, write a statement that multiplies a Float variable named taxRate by an Integer variable named grossPay, and assigns that value to the Float variable named tax.

12. On a piece of paper, write a statement that multiplies a Short Integer variable named numItems by a Float variable named price, and assigns that value to the Float variable named totalPrice.

13. In this exercise, you will create a console application.

   Scenario: Builders Inc. needs an application that will allow the company's salesclerks to enter both the diameter of a circle (in feet) and the price of railing material per foot. (The diameter and the price may contain decimal places.) The program should display both the circumference of the circle and the total price of the railing material. Assign the value of pi to a named constant. (Use 3.14 as the value of pi.)

   a. Complete and submit an IPO chart for this problem.
   b. Complete and submit a desk-check table. Use 36.5 feet as the diameter, and $2 as the price per foot of railing material.
   c. Create a console application. Name the project workspace T3Be13. Add a new C++ source file to the project. Name the source file T3Be13.
   d. Use the information in both the IPO chart and the desk-check table to code the program.
   e. Save, build, and execute the program. Test the program using the data from your desk-check table.
   f. When the program is working correctly, print the code. On the code printout, indicate the results of your test from step e.
   g. Use the File menu to close the workspace. Also close the Output window.

14. In this exercise, you will create a console application.

   Scenario: Tile Limited wants a program that will allow the company's salesclerks to enter the length and width, in feet, of a rectangle, and the price of a square foot of tile. (The length, width, and price may contain decimal places.) The program should display the area of the rectangle and the total price of the tile.

   a. Complete and submit an IPO chart for this problem.
   b. Complete and submit a desk-check table. Use 12 feet as the length, 14 feet as the width, and $1.59 as the price per square foot of tile.
   c. Create a console application. Name the project workspace T3Be14. Add a new C++ source file to the project. Name the source file T3Be14.
   d. Use the information in both the IPO chart and the desk-check table to code the program.
   e. Save, build, and execute the program. Test the program using the data from your desk-check table.
   f. When the program is working correctly, print the code. On the code printout, indicate the results of your test from step e.
   g. Use the File menu to close the workspace. Also close the Output window.

15. In this exercise, you will create a console application.

Scenario: The swimming pool at Fitness Health Club is 100 feet long, 30.5 feet wide, and 4 feet deep. How many cubic feet of water will the pool contain? (*Hint*: Find the volume of the rectangle.)

a. Complete and submit an IPO chart for this problem.

b. Complete and submit a desk-check table.

c. Create a console application. Name the project workspace T3Be15. Add a new C++ source file to the project. Name the source file T3Be15.

d. Use the information in both the IPO chart and the desk-check table to code the program.

e. Save, build, and execute the program. Test the program using the data from your desk-check table.

f. When the program is working correctly, print the code. On the code printout, indicate the results of your test from step e.

g. Use the File menu to close the workspace. Also close the Output window.

16. In this exercise, you will create a console application.

Scenario: Temp Employers wants a program that will allow the company's clerks to enter an employee's name (allow a maximum of 20 characters, which includes the null character) and number of hours worked during the month. The program will display the name, number of weeks (assume a 40-hour week), days (assume an eight-hour day), and hours worked. For example, if the employee enters the number 70, the program will display the employee's name, then 1 week, 3 days, and 6 hours.

a. Complete and submit an IPO chart for this problem.

b. Complete and submit a desk-check table. Trace the program three times using the following data:

Test 1: Mary Claire, 88 hours worked

Test 2: Jackie Smith, 111 hours worked

Test 3: Sue Jones, 12 hours worked

c. Create a console application. Name the project workspace T3Be16. Add a new C++ source file to the project. Name the source file T3Be16.

d. Use the information in both the IPO chart and the desk-check table to code the program.

e. Save, build, and execute the program. Test the program using the data from your desk-check table.

f. When the program is working correctly, print the code. On the code printout, indicate the results of your test from step e.

g. Use the File menu to close the workspace. Also close the Output window.

17. In this exercise, you will create a console application.

Scenario: Colfax Industries needs a program that allows the shipping clerk to enter an item's name (allow a maximum of 15 characters, which includes the null character), the quantity of the item in inventory, and how many of the item can be packed in a box for shipping. The program should display the item's name, the number of full boxes that can be packed, and how many of the item are left over.

a. Complete and submit an IPO chart for this problem.

b. Complete and submit a desk-check table. Trace the program three times using the following data:

Test 1: Cleanser, 45 in inventory, six can be packed in a box

Test 2: Hair Spray, 100 in inventory, three can be packed in a box

Test 3: Comb, 78 in inventory, five can be packed in a box

c. Create a console application. Name the project workspace T3Be17. Add a new C++ source file to the project. Name the source file T3Be17.

d. Use the information in both the IPO chart and the desk-check table to code the program.

e. Save, build, and execute the program. Test the program using the data from your desk-check table.

f. When the program is working correctly, print the code. On the code printout, indicate the results of your test from step e.

g. Use the File menu to close the workspace. Also close the Output window.

18. In this exercise, you will create a console application.

Scenario: RM Sales wants a program that allows the clerk to enter the current sales for four sales regions (North, South, East, and West) and the projected sales percentages for those regions. The program should display the projected sales.

a. Complete and submit an IPO chart for this problem.

b. Complete and submit a desk-check table. Trace the program twice using the following data:

	Region	Sales	Projected Percentage
Test 1:	North:	2000	10
	South:	5000	5
	East:	4500	7
	West:	9000	10
Test 2:	North:	4000	3
	South:	5000	2
	East:	7500	4
	West:	4500	5

c. Create a console application. Name the project workspace T3Be18. Add a new C++ source file to the project. Name the source file T3Be18.

d. Use the information in both the IPO chart and the desk-check table to code the program.

e. Save, build, and execute the program. Test the program using the data from your desk-check table.

f. When the program is working correctly, print the code. On the code printout, indicate the results of your test from step e.

g. Use the File menu to close the workspace. Also close the Output window.

19. In this exercise, you will create a console application.

Scenario: Your friend Joe saves pennies in a jar, which he empties every month when he goes to the bank. You decide to create a program that allows him to enter the number of pennies, and then calculates the number of dollars, quarters, dimes, nickels, and pennies he will receive when he trades in the pennies at the bank.

a. Complete and submit an IPO chart for this problem.

b. Complete and submit a desk-check table. Trace the program twice using the following data: 2311 pennies and 7333 pennies.

c. Create a console application. Name the project workspace T3Be19. Add a new C++ source file to the project. Name the source file T3Be19.

d. Use the information in both the IPO chart and the desk-check table to code the program.

e. Save, build, and execute the program. Test the program using the data from your desk-check table.

f. When the program is working correctly, print the code. On the code printout, indicate the results of your test from step e.

g. Use the File menu to close the workspace. Also close the Output window.

20. In this exercise, you will create a console application.

Scenario: A math teacher at Hinsbrook School would like you to create a program that will help her students, who are in grades 1 through 6, learn how to make change. The program should allow the student to enter the amount the customer owes and the amount of money the customer paid. The program should calculate the amount of change, as well as how many dollars, quarters, dimes, nickels, and pennies to return to the customer. For now, you do not have to worry about the situation where the price is greater than what the customer pays. You can always assume that the customer paid either the exact amount or more than the exact amount.

a. Complete and submit an IPO chart for this problem.

b. Complete and submit a desk-check table. Trace the program three times using the following data:

Test 1: 75.33 as the amount due and 80.00 as the amount paid

Test 2: 39.67 as the amount due and 50.00 as the amount paid

Test 3: 45.55 as the amount due and 45.55 as the amount paid

c. Create a console application. Name the project workspace T3Be20. Add a new C++ source file to the project. Name the source file T3Be20.

d. Use the information in both the IPO chart and the desk-check table to code the program.

e. Save, build, and execute the program. Test the program using the data from your desk-check table.

f. When the program is working correctly, print the code. On the code printout, indicate the results of your test from step e.

g. Use the File menu to close the workspace. Also close the Output window.

discovery ▶ **21.** In this exercise, you will learn how to round a Float number to the nearest integer.

a. Open the T3Be21.cpp file, which is located in the Cpp\Tut03\T3Be21 folder on your computer's hard disk. This program is supposed to round the original sales value to the nearest integer, but it is not working properly. Verify that the T3Be21 program is not working correctly by building and executing the program. When you are prompted to enter a value, type the number 35.4 and press the Enter key. The DOS window shows that the value in the original sales variable is 35.4, and the value in the rounded sales variable is 35, which is correct. Execute the program again. This time type the number 35.7 and press the Enter key. The DOS window shows that the value in the original sales variable is 35.7, and the value in the rounded sales variable is 35, which is incorrect.

b. Change the `roundSales = (int) origSales;` statement to `roundSales = (int) (origSales + .5);`.

c. Save, build, and then execute the program. Test the program twice by entering the number 35.4 and the number 35.7.

d. Print the code. On the code printout, indicate the results of your test from step c. Also write a brief explanation of how the `roundSales = (int) (origSales + .5);` statement rounds a Float number to the nearest integer.

e. What happens to the program if you change the statement to `roundSales = (int) origSales + .5;`? First, change the statement in the program. Save and build the program. On the code printout from step d, indicate the warning message displayed in the Output window. Execute the program. Test the program twice by entering the number 35.4 and the number 35.7. Write an explanation of how the change to the statement affects the program's output.

f. Correct the statement by changing it to `roundSales = (int) (origSales + .5);`. Save the program.

g. Use the File menu to close the workspace. Also close the Output window.

discovery ▶ 22. In this exercise, you will discover the stream manipulators `setprecision()` and `setiosflags()`. These two manipulators allow you to format your output.

a. Open the LbProg03.cpp file that you created in Lesson B.

b. The two stream manipulators that you will use to format your output are defined in the iomanip.h header file. Enter the `#include <iomanip.h>` directive in the program.

c. Click at the end of the `//display the output items` comment, then press the Enter key to insert a blank line below the comment. Enter the following statement in the blank line:

`cout << setprecision(2) << setiosflags(ios::fixed | ios::showpoint);`. (The | is called the pipe symbol. It is usually on the same key as the \.)

The `setprecision(2)` stream manipulator tells C++ to display two decimal places in the output values. The `setiosflags` stream manipulator sets two flags, `ios::fixed` and `ios::showpoint`. The `ios::fixed` flag tells C++ to display a Float number in fixed-point notation rather than in e notation. The `ios::showpoint` flag tells C++ to display a decimal point in the output value. If the output value is a whole number—such as the number 5—the `ios::showpoint` flag will display the number with a decimal point and trailing zeros. In this case, for example, because `setprecision` is set to 2, `ios::showpoint` will display the number 5 as 5.00.

d. Save, build, and then execute the LbProg03 program. When prompted for the name, enter the name Mary. When prompted for the hours enrolled and the insurance, enter 15 and 12.5, respectively. The tuition displays as $1500.00 and the total amount owed displays as $3312.50. Press the Enter key to close the DOS window.

e. Print the code. Use the File menu to close the workspace. Also close the Output window.

debugging 23. In this exercise, you will debug a program.

a. Open the T3Be23.cpp file, which is located in the Cpp\Tut03\T3Be23 folder on your computer's hard disk.

b. Build and then execute the program. The average hours worked should be about 8.83, but the output shows that it is 8.

c. Correct the program so that it produces the proper output. Save, build, and then execute the program. When the program is running correctly, print the code. On the code printout, indicate what was wrong with the program. Also, circle any corrections on the code printout.

d. Use the File menu to close the workspace. Also close the Output window.

debugging 24. In this exercise, you will debug a program.

a. Open the T3Be24.cpp file, which is located in the Cpp\Tut03\T3Be24 folder on your computer's hard disk.

b. First build the program. You will notice that the program contains an error. Correct the program.

c. Save, build, and then execute the program. When you are prompted to enter a name, type the name George Washington and press the Enter key. You will notice that the DOS window does not display the full name. Correct the program.

d. When the program is running correctly, print the code. On the code printout, indicate what was wrong with the program. Also, circle any corrections on the code printout.

e. Use the File menu to close the workspace. Also close the Output window.

debugging   25. In this exercise, you will debug a program.

a. Open the T3Be25.cpp file, which is located in the Cpp\Tut03\T3Be25 folder on your computer's hard disk. This program is supposed to display the average employee pay, but it is not working correctly.

b. Correct the program. Save, build, and execute the program. When the program is running correctly, print the code. On the code printout, indicate what was wrong with the program. Also, circle any corrections on the code printout.

c. Use the File menu to close the workspace. Also close the Output window.

debugging   26. In this exercise, you will debug a program.

a. Open the T3Be26.cpp file, which is located in the Cpp\Tut03\T3Be26 folder on your computer's hard disk. This program is supposed to display the average employee pay (440.2), but it is not working correctly.

b. Correct the program. Save, build, and execute the program. When the program is running correctly, print the code. On the code printout, indicate what was wrong with the program. Also, circle any corrections on the code printout.

c. Use the File menu to close the workspace. Also close the Output window.

Built-in Functions and Programmer-defined Functions

case ▶ David Liu is in the market for a new car. Recently, David has noticed that many car manufacturers, in an effort to boost sales, are offering buyers either large cash rebates or drastically low financing rates, much lower than the 11 percent rate he would pay by financing through his local credit union. Because he is not sure whether to take the lower financing rate from the dealer, or take the dealer's rebate and then finance through the credit union, David visits Juan Menudo, the manager of the credit union, to ask his advice. Juan explains that it all depends on the amount of the loan, the amount of the rebate, the interest rates, and the term of the loan (the number of payments). Although the lower interest rate is appealing, Juan tells David that it is sometimes better to take the rebate instead. David asks you to create a program that will compute his monthly payment using each of the two options.

In this tutorial, you will learn how to use the C++ built-in functions, as well as how to create your own functions. You will use functions in the program that calculates David's monthly payments.

LESSON A
objectives

In this lesson you will learn how to:

- Use the C++ built-in mathematical functions
- Create and invoke a void function
- Pass information, by value, to a function
- Pass information, by reference, to a function
- Understand local variables

Mathematical Functions and Void Functions

Functions

As you may remember from Tutorial 3, most programs include variables, constants, and functions, as well as arithmetic operators, which are used in equations. You learned about variables, constants, arithmetic operators, and equations in Tutorial 3. You also learned about the C++ getline and strcpy functions. You will learn more about functions in this tutorial.

A **function** is simply a block of code that performs a specific task. The getline function, you may recall, accepts an entire line of text, including spaces, from the keyboard. The strcpy function, on the other hand, assigns a value to a String variable. Some functions, like getline and strcpy, are built into the C++ language; others, like the main function, are created by the programmer.

Functions serve three main purposes in a program. First, functions make problem-solving easier by allowing programmers to break large and complex problems into small and manageable tasks. Second, functions speed up program writing by allowing programmers to use existing code to perform common tasks, such as assigning a value to a String variable. Third, because functions can be used as many times as necessary in a program, the programmer does not have to duplicate the code in different parts of the program.

Before learning how to create your own functions, you will experiment with the C++ built-in mathematical functions.

Using the Mathematical Functions

tip

Appendix B in this book contains a listing of the mathematical functions typically available in the math.h header file.

The C++ language contains many mathematical functions that programmers can use to perform common calculations, such as finding the square root of a number or raising a number to a power. These functions are defined in the math.h header file. To use one of the mathematical functions, you need simply to enter the #include <math.h> directive in your program. You will now complete a program that uses two of the mathematical functions, pow and sqrt, to calculate both the square and the square root, respectively, of a number. The program will then display a report showing the results of both calculations. The IPO chart for the program is shown in Figure 4-1.

Input	Processing	Output
number	Processing items: none Algorithm: 1. enter the number 2. calculate the square of the number 3. calculate the square root of the number 4. display the square of the number and the square root of the number	square of the number square root of the number

Figure 4-1: IPO chart for a program that calculates the square and square root of a number

Now open a partially completed program that corresponds to the IPO chart shown in Figure 4-1.

To open the partially completed square and square root program:

1 Start Visual C++. Open the **LaProg01.cpp** file, which is located in the Cpp\Tut04\LaProg01 folder on your computer's hard disk. The square and square root program, which appears in the LaProg01.cpp window, is shown in Figure 4-2.

```cpp
//LaProg01.cpp
//this program uses the pow and sqrt mathematical functions
//to calculate the square and square root of a number

#include <iostream.h>

void main()
{
    //declare and initialize variables
    float numberInput = (float) 0.0;
    float square      = (float) 0.0;
    float sqRoot      = (float) 0.0;

    //enter input item
    cout << "Enter a number: ";
    cin >> numberInput;

    //calculate square and square root

    //display output items
    cout << "Square and Square Root Calculations" << endl;
    cout << "Square:      " << square << endl;
    cout << "Square Root: " << sqRoot << endl;
} //end of main function
```

Figure 4-2: Partially completed square and square root program

This partial program declares and initializes three float variables: `numberInput`, `square`, and `sqRoot`. The `numberInput` variable will store the number entered by the user, the `square` variable will store the square of the number, and the `sqRoot` variable will store the square root of the number.

After declaring and initializing the variables, the program prompts the user to enter a number, and then stores the user's response in the `numberInput` variable. According to the IPO chart, the program should then calculate both the square and the square root of the number before displaying those values on the screen. You will need to enter the instructions that calculate the square and square root as these instructions are currently missing from the program.

The `pow` and `sqrt` Mathematical Functions

As you may remember from your mathematics courses, the expression 10^2 indicates that the number 10 is being raised to the second power—in other words, the number 10 is being squared, or multiplied by itself two times. The number 10 in the expression is called the **base**, and the number 2 is called the **exponent**. Although the expression 10^2 is written correctly mathematically, it cannot be entered in that form in a program. You will need to use the C++ pow function (pow stands for *power*) to raise a number to a power.

The syntax of the pow function is **pow**(*base*, *exponent*). The items inside the parentheses—*base* and *exponent*—are called actual arguments. The **actual arguments** represent information that is passed, or sent, to a function. The function needs to know this information to perform its task. In this case, the pow function needs to know the base number and the exponent number. Both the *base* and the *exponent* can be values in the Float range. The pow function returns the result of raising the number (*base*) to the power (*exponent*). The value returned by the pow function is a number in the Double type range. Figure 4-3 shows some examples of using the pow function to raise a number to a power.

Examples	Result
`pow(10, 2)`	returns the Double type result of raising the number 10 to the second power
`(float) pow(3.5, 3)`	type casts, to Float, the Double type result of raising the number 3.5 to the third power
`(int) pow(9, 5)`	type casts, to Integer, the Double type result of raising the number 9 to the fifth power
`pow(num1, powNum)`	returns the Double type result of raising the contents of the `num1` variable to the power number contained in the `powNum` variable

Figure 4-3: Examples of using the pow function

You will notice that the second and third examples use a type cast to convert explicitly to another data type the Double type value returned by the pow function. You may need to use a type cast when including the pow function in an equation that contains mixed data types.

In the current program, you will use the pow function to calculate the square of the number entered by the user; that number is stored in the `numberInput` variable. You will use an assignment statement to assign the result of the pow function, a Double type value, to the `square` variable. Because the `square` variable is a Float variable, you will need to type cast the value returned by the pow function to a Float value in the assignment statement. The appropriate assignment statement to enter in the current program is `square = (float) pow(numberInput, 2);`.

When C++ processes the `square = (float) pow(numberInput, 2);` statement, it first evaluates the expression that appears on the right side of the equal sign. In this case, the `(float) pow(numberInput, 2)` expression **calls**, or invokes, the `pow` function, sending it two items of information (two actual arguments): the value stored in the `numberInput` variable and the numeric literal constant 2. Although the idea of calling something and providing it with information may sound confusing at first, the concept is really nothing new to you. When you register for classes at school, you typically call the registrar and provide him or her with your name, Social Security number, and list of classes you want to take. Like a function, you call the registrar to perform a task for you. The registrar's task is to register you for the next semester; the `pow` function's task is to raise a number to a power. Before either can perform the designated task, you must provide each with some very specific information. The `pow` function uses the information you provide—the actual arguments—to raise a number to a power, and the registrar uses the information you provide—your Social Security number, name, and so on—to register you for the next semester's classes.

After the `pow` function performs its task of raising the `numberInput` variable to the second power, the result is returned to the `square = (float) pow(numberInput, 2);` assignment statement that called the `pow` function. The assignment statement then type casts the `pow` function's result to a Float number and assigns that number to the `square` variable.

Recall that you also need to calculate the square root of the number stored in the `numberInput` variable; you can use the C++ `sqrt` (square root) function to do so. The syntax of the `sqrt` function is **sqrt(*number*)**, where the actual argument, *number*, is the value for which you want to find the square root. Like the `pow` function, the `sqrt` function returns a Double type number. Figure 4-4 shows examples of using the `sqrt` function.

As you learned in Tutorial 3, when C++ processes an assignment statement, it first evaluates the expression that appears on the right side of the equal sign, and then assigns that value to the variable whose name appears on the left side of the equal sign.

Examples	Result
`sqrt(4)`	returns the Double type result of calculating the square root of the number 4
`(float) sqrt(9.2)`	type casts, to Float, the Double type result of calculating the square root of the number 9.2
`(int) sqrt(num1)`	type casts, to Integer, the Double type result of calculating the square root of the number stored in the `num1` variable

Figure 4-4: Examples of using the `sqrt` function

Recall that both the `pow` and the `sqrt` functions are defined in the math.h header file, which you need to include in a program that uses these functions.

In the current program, you will use the `sqrt` function to find the square root of the number stored in the `numberInput` variable, and you will assign the result to the `sqRoot` variable. Here again, you will need to use a type cast in the statement that assigns the result of the `sqrt` function, a Double type number, to the Float `sqRoot` variable. The correct assignment statement to use in the current program is `sqRoot = (float) sqrt(numberInput);`. When C++ processes this statement in the program, it first calls the `sqrt` function, sending the function the value stored in the `numberInput` variable. After processing the instructions in the `sqrt` function, C++ type casts the Double type result to a Float value before assigning it to the `sqRoot` variable.

You can now complete the LaProg01 program by entering the instructions to calculate both the square and square root of the number entered by the user, as well as the instruction to include the math.h header file in the program.

To complete the square and square root program:

1 In the blank line below the #include <iostream.h> instruction, type **#include <math.h>** and press the **Enter** key.

2 In the blank line below the //calculate square and square root comment, type **square = (float) pow(numberInput, 2);** and press the **Enter** key, then type **sqRoot = (float) sqrt(numberInput);** and press the **Enter** key. The completed program is shown in Figure 4-5. The three instructions you entered are highlighted in the figure.

```
//LaProg01.cpp
//this program uses the pow and sqrt mathematical functions
//to calculate the square and square root of a number

#include <iostream.h>
#include <math.h>

void main()
{
    //declare and initialize variables
    float numberInput = (float) 0.0;
    float square       = (float) 0.0;
    float sqRoot       = (float) 0.0;

    //enter input item
    cout << "Enter a number: ";
    cin >> numberInput;

    //calculate square and square root
    square = (float) pow(numberInput, 2);
    sqRoot = (float) sqrt(numberInput);

    //display output items
    cout << "Square and Square Root Calculations" << endl;
    cout << "Square:      " << square << endl;
    cout << "Square Root: " << sqRoot << endl;
} //end of main function
```

enter this instruction

enter these instructions

Figure 4-5: Completed square and square root program

3 Save, build, and then execute the program. When prompted to enter a number, type 4 and press the **Enter** key. First the program displays the "Square and Square Root Calculations" message as the title of the report. It then displays the number 16 as the square of the number 4, and the number 2 as its square root, as shown in Figure 4-6.

Figure 4-6: Square and square root program's output

4 Press the **Enter** key to close the DOS window.

You have now completed this program, so you can close it.

5 Close the Output window, and then close the workspace.

In addition to using the C++ built-in functions, you can also create your own functions, referred to as programmer-defined functions, in C++.

Creating a Programmer-defined Function

The functions that a programmer creates in C++ are referred to as **programmer-defined functions**. A programmer-defined function can be either a value-returning function or a void function. A value-returning function is one that returns a value. The sqrt and pow functions are examples of value-returning functions; sqrt returns the square root of a number, and pow returns the result of raising a number to a power. A void function, on the other hand, is a function that does not return a value. The main function used in your programs is an example of a void function.

After creating a function, the programmer can then call, or invoke, it from one or more places in the program. You call a programmer-defined function in exactly the same way as you call a built-in function. As with the C++ built-in functions, you can also pass, or send, information to a programmer-defined function. In the remainder of this lesson, you will learn how to create and invoke a void function, as well as how to pass information to a programmer-defined function. You will learn how to create and invoke a value-returning function in Lesson B.

Creating a Void Function

In C++, a function that does not return a value is called a **void function**. You may want to use a void function in a program simply to display information, such as a title and column headings, at the top of each page in a report. Rather than repeat the necessary code several times, you would enter the code once, in a function, and then call the function whenever the program needed to display the information. You could also use a void function to calculate the federal and state taxes in a payroll program. Recall that one of the advantages of using a function is that it allows you to break a complex problem, such as a payroll problem, into small and more manageable tasks; one such task would be to calculate the payroll taxes. View a partially completed program that uses a void function to display a straight line on the screen.

To view a partially completed program that uses a programmer-defined void function:

1 Open the **LaProg02.cpp** file, which is located in the Cpp\Tut04\LaProg02 folder on your computer's hard disk. The partially completed LaProg02 program, which appears in the LaProg02.cpp window, is shown in Figure 4-7.

```cpp
//LaProg02.cpp
//this program uses a void function, with no arguments, to display
//a straight line

#include <iostream.h>
#include <math.h>

//function prototype

void main()
{
    //declare and initialize variables
    float numberInput = (float) 0.0;
    float square      = (float) 0.0;
    float sqRoot      = (float) 0.0;

    //enter input item
    cout << "Enter a number: ";
    cin >> numberInput;

    //calculate square and square root
    square = (float) pow(numberInput,2);
    sqRoot = (float) sqrt(numberInput);

    //display output items
    displayLine();
    cout << "Square and Square Root Calculations" << endl;
    cout << "Square:      " << square << endl;
    cout << "Square Root: " << sqRoot << endl;

} //end of main function

//*****programmer-defined function definitions*****

void displayLine()
{
    cout << "---------------------------------";
    cout << endl;
} //end of displayLine function
```

function call (label pointing to `displayLine();`)

function definition (label pointing to `void displayLine()` block)

Figure 4-7: Partially completed LaProg02 program

You can also enter a programmer-defined function definition above the `main` function in a program rather than below it. In this book, you will always place the function definitions below the `main` function.

You are already familiar with most of the code shown in Figure 4-7. This program is similar to the square and square root program that you just completed, except it uses a programmer-defined void function named `displayLine` to display a straight line, composed of a string of hyphens, above the "Square and Square Root Calculations" report title. As the figure indicates, the LaProg02 program includes a call to the `displayLine` function, as well as a function definition for the `displayLine` function. First, learn about the function definition, which appears in the programmer-defined section in the program.

Function Definition

You will usually enter the function definition, which defines the function's task, in the programmer-defined section in the program. Figure 4-8 shows the syntax you use to create, or define, a void function and gives an example of a void function that uses this syntax in the current program.

function header

beginning of function

end of function

Syntax:	**void** *functionname* (*[parameterlist]*) **{** *one or more statements ending in a semicolon* **}** [//end of *functionname* function]

Example:	```void displayLine()
	{
	    cout << "------------------------------------";
	    cout << endl;
	} //end of displayLine function```

Important note: In the syntax, items in **bold** are required. Items contained in square brackets, on the other hand, are optional. Items in *italics* indicate places where the programmer must supply information pertaining to the current program.	

Figure 4-8: Syntax and an example of a void function definition

To make the program easier to read, use a comment, such as `//*****programmer-defined function definitions*****`, to separate the section that contains the function definitions from the rest of the program.

The first line of the function definition—**void** *functionname([parameterlist])*—is called the **function header**. You will notice that the function header does not end in a semicolon because it is not considered a C++ statement. The function header for a void function begins with the keyword **void**, which tells the C++ compiler that the function does not return a value. You follow the **void** keyword with the name of the function. The rules for naming programmer-defined functions are the same as for naming variables. To make your programs more self-documenting and easier to understand, you should use meaningful function names that describe the task the function is to perform. In the current program, for example, the name of the function, `displayLine`, indicates that the function can be used to display a line.

You will notice that a set of parentheses and an optional *parameterlist* follow the function's name in the syntax. Like the C++ built-in functions, a programmer-defined function can also receive variables or constants that you send (pass) to it. Each item of information received by a function is called a **formal parameter** and each is listed in the *parameterlist*. If the *parameterlist* contains more than one parameter, a comma separates each parameter from another.

The rules for naming variables, which should also be followed for naming functions, are shown in Tutorial 3's Figure 3-1.

Rather than using an empty set of parentheses to indicate that a function does not receive any information, some programmers enter the word void within the parentheses.

You pass information to a function when you want the function to process the information in some way. For example, in the square and square root program you worked with earlier in the lesson and in the current program you are viewing, you pass the value stored in the numberInput variable to the sqrt function, which processes the value by finding its square root. You might also create a function that sorts a list of numbers. The information you pass would be the numbers themselves; the function would receive the numbers and then sort, and perhaps display, those numbers. You will learn more about passing information to a function later in this lesson.

Not every function requires information to be passed to it, so not every function will have parameters listed in its function header. The displayLine function in the current program is an example of a function that does not have a *parameterlist*. Functions that do not require a *parameterlist* will have an empty set of parentheses after the function's name.

As Figure 4-8 indicates, you enclose the statements that comprise the function in a set of braces. The opening brace ({) marks the beginning of the function and the closing brace (}) marks the end of the function. The displayLine function in the current program contains two statements: the first statement displays the row of hyphens, and the second advances the cursor to the next line.

Next, learn how to call a programmer-defined void function in a program.

Calling a Programmer-defined Void Function

You call, or invoke, a programmer-defined void function by using its name and actual arguments, if any, as a separate statement in the program. Figure 4-9 shows the syntax and an example of a statement that invokes a programmer-defined void function. The example shows how to invoke the current program's displayLine function.

Syntax	Example
functionname(*[argumentlist]*);	`displayLine();`
Important note: In the syntax, items in **bold** are required. Items contained in square brackets, on the other hand, are optional. Items in *italics* indicate places where the programmer must supply information pertaining to the current program.	

Figure 4-9: Syntax and an example of a statement that calls a programmer-defined void function

In the syntax, *functionname* is the name of the function you are calling, and *argumentlist*, which is optional, is one or more actual arguments. Recall that an actual argument is an item of information sent to a function. If the *argumentlist* contains more than one actual argument, a comma separates each argument from another.

The items listed in the function call are called **actual arguments**, whereas the items listed in the function header are called **formal parameters**.

As Figure 4-9 shows, you call the `displayLine` function, which requires no actual arguments, with the `displayLine();` statement. When C++ processes this statement in the current program, it temporarily leaves the `main` function in order to process the instructions in the `displayLine` function. C++ processes the statements within the `displayLine` function in the order in which they are entered in the function. In this case, the function's statements will display the row of hyphens first, and will then advance the cursor to the next line. When C++ encounters the `displayLine` function's closing brace (}), which marks the end of the function, C++ returns to the statement immediately following the one that called the function—in this case, for example, C++ returns to the `cout << "Square and Square Root Calculations" << endl;` statement in the `main` function. Figure 4-10 illustrates this concept.

temporarily leaves `main` **function to process** `displayLine` **function's instructions**

returns to `main` **function**

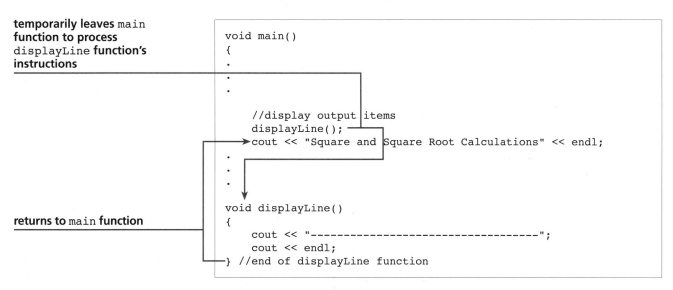

Figure 4-10: Illustration of a call to a function

Now that you know how to both define and call a void function, you will execute the current program.

To execute the LaProg02 program:

1   The LaProg02 program should still be open. Build the program. You will notice that two errors appear in the Output window. Scroll the Output window as shown in Figure 4-11, and then double-click the first error message.

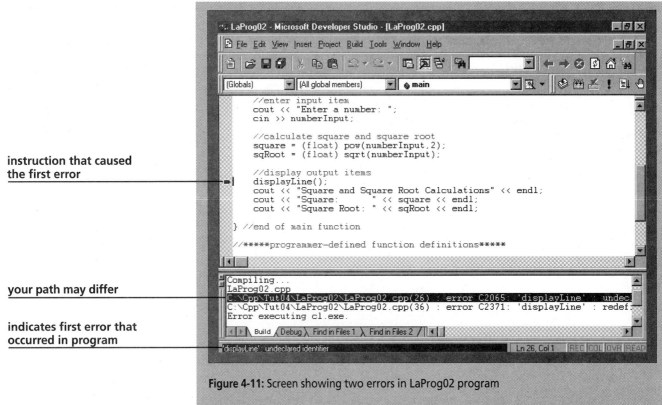

instruction that caused the first error

your path may differ

indicates first error that occurred in program

Figure 4-11: Screen showing two errors in LaProg02 program

According to the first error listed in the Output window, `displayLine` is an undeclared identifier. As you learned in Tutorial 3, an identifier is simply a name. In this case, both the error message and the arrow that appears in the LaProg02.cpp window tell you that C++ does not recognize the `displayLine` name used in the `displayLine();` statement. This type of error is referred to as a syntax error. As you may remember from Tutorial 2, a syntax error occurs when you use the C++ language incorrectly. Close the Output window before learning about this error.

2   Close the Output window, and then scroll the LaProg02.cpp window to view the beginning of the program.

tip

If the function definition appears above the `main` function in a program, then you do not need to include a function prototype for the function. The function prototype is necessary only when the function is defined after the `main` function.

Before you can call a function in C++, you must first either define it or declare it. You define a function with a function definition, and you declare it with a function prototype, which you will learn about in the next section. One way to fix the undeclared identifier problem in the current program is to move the function definition to a location above the `main` function so that it appears before the function call—the `displayLine();` statement. When you place a programmer-defined function above the `main` function, C++ does not process the statements within the function until the function is called; C++ merely remembers the function's name so that calling the function later in the program will not produce the undeclared identifier error.

Another way to fix the undeclared identifier problem in the current program is to leave the function definition in its current location, and then declare the function by entering a function prototype above the `main` function. A function prototype alerts C++ that the function will be defined later in the program. It may help to think of a program's function prototypes as being similar to a book's table of contents. Each prototype, like each entry in a table of contents, is simply a preview of what will be expanded on later in the program (or in the book). In the programs you will create in the tutorials in this book, you will use function prototypes to declare functions.

Using Function Prototypes

You declare a function by using a **function prototype**, which is a statement that tells C++ the function's name, the data type of its return value (either void or another data type), and the data type of each of its formal parameters. If the programmer-defined section is located after the `main` function in a program, the program will have one function prototype for each function defined in that section. You usually place the function prototypes at the beginning of the program, after the `#include` directives.

Figure 4-12 shows the syntax of a function prototype, as well as the function prototype for the current program's `displayLine` function.

notice that a function prototype ends in a semicolon

Syntax:	**void** *functionname* (*[parameterlist]*);
Example:	`void displayLine();`

Figure 4-12: Syntax and an example of a function prototype

. . . .
Some programmers also include the name of each formal parameter in the function prototype, but this is optional.

If you compare Figure 4-12 to Figure 4-8, you will notice that the syntax of both the function prototype and the function header is almost identical. The only difference is that the prototype ends in a semicolon, whereas the function header does not. Enter the function prototype for the `displayLine` function and then execute the current program to view its output.

To enter the function prototype and then view the current program's output:

1 The LaProg02 program should be open. In the blank line below the `//function prototype` comment, type **void displayLine();** and press the **Enter** key.

2 Save and build the program. This time the undeclared identifier error does not occur because the function prototype declares the `displayLine` function before the function is called in the program.

3 Execute the program. When prompted for a number, type **4** and press the **Enter** key. The output appears in a DOS window, as shown in Figure 4-13.

row of hyphens displayed by the `displayLine` function

Figure 4-13: LaProg02 program output

Notice the row of hyphens that the `displayLine` function displays above the "Square and Square Root Calculations" report title.

4 Press the **Enter** key to close the DOS window, then close the Output window.

The advantage of placing the code that displays the row of hyphens in a function is that you can now display the hyphens as many times as necessary in the program without having to duplicate the code. For example, in addition to displaying a line above the report title, you can also display a line below the entire report. Do that next.

5 In the blank line above the `}  //end of main function` line, type **displayLine( );** and press the **Enter** key.

6 Save, build, and then execute the program. When prompted to enter a number, type **16** and press the **Enter** key. The DOS window shows a row of hyphens both above and below the report.

7 Press the **Enter** key to close the DOS window.

You have now completed this program, so you can close it.

8 Close the Output window, and then close the workspace.

The `displayLine` function did not require any information to be passed to it. In most programs, however, you will need to pass information to a function in order for the function to perform its task. You already have some experience with passing information to a function. In both the LaProg01 and LaProg02 programs, for example, you passed the numeric literal constant 2 to the `pow` function, and you passed the contents of the `numberInput` variable to both the `pow` and `sqrt` functions. You can also pass information to the functions that you create.

mini-quiz

Mini-Quiz 1

1. To create and invoke a programmer-defined function, you need to include three items of information in the program. List those three items. (You can assume that the programmer-defined section is located below the `main` function in the program.)

2. Write a function definition for a void function named **displayState**. The function, which requires no formal parameters, should display Hawaii on one line, and a row of six asterisks (*) on the next line, and then advance the cursor to the next line on the screen.

3. Write a function prototype for the function defined in question 2.

4. Write a function call for the function defined in question 2.

Passing Information to a Programmer-defined Function

In most cases, the information that you pass to a function is either a literal constant, the contents of a variable, or the address of a variable in memory. You pass information by including one or more actual arguments in the function call's *argumentlist*. For example, the `displayGross(hoursWkd, payRate);` statement calls the `displayGross` function and passes to it the values stored in the `hoursWkd` and `payRate` variables.

You allow a function to receive information that is passed to it by including one or more formal parameters in the function header's *parameterlist*. Both the data type and name of the formal parameters must be explicitly stated in the function header. For example, the function header, `void displayGross(float hours, float hrlyPay)`, allows the `displayGross` function to receive two Float values; the function stores the values in the `hours` and `hrlyPay` formal parameters. The data type of each formal parameter listed in the function header must match the data type of its corresponding actual argument listed in the function call. The first actual argument is passed to the first formal parameter, the second actual argument is passed to the second formal parameter, and so on. Figure 4-14 illustrates the relationship between the actual arguments in the function call and the formal parameters in the function header.

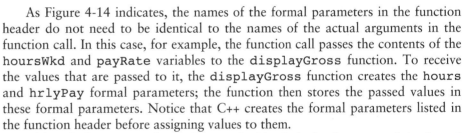

Figure 4-14: Relationship between the actual arguments and the formal parameters

tip

••••••••••••••

The function header must include both a data type and a name for each formal parameter in the *parameterlist*. The function call, however, includes only the name, and not the data type, of the actual arguments.

As Figure 4-14 indicates, the names of the formal parameters in the function header do not need to be identical to the names of the actual arguments in the function call. In this case, for example, the function call passes the contents of the `hoursWkd` and `payRate` variables to the `displayGross` function. To receive the values that are passed to it, the `displayGross` function creates the `hours` and `hrlyPay` formal parameters; the function then stores the passed values in these formal parameters. Notice that C++ creates the formal parameters listed in the function header before assigning values to them.

Although their names do not have to be identical, the data type of the formal parameters must match the data type of the actual arguments. Furthermore, the order in which the formal parameters are listed in the function header must match the order of the actual arguments listed in the function call. In other words, if the function call's *argumentlist* lists a Short Integer variable first and a Character variable second, then the function header's *parameterlist* must list a Short Integer formal parameter first and a Character formal parameter second.

In the next set of steps, you will view another version of the square and square root program; this version includes a void function, named `calcSquareSqRoot`, that calculates the square and square root of the number stored in the `numberInput` variable.

To view the LaProg03 program:

1 Open the **LaProg03.cpp** file, which is located in the Cpp\Tut04\LaProg03 folder on your computer's hard disk. The LaProg03 program, which appears in the LaProg03.cpp window, is shown in Figure 4-15.

function prototype

function call

function definition

```cpp
//LaProg03.cpp
//this program uses a void function to calculate the square
//and square root of a number, and a void function to display
//a straight line.

#include <iostream.h>
#include <math.h>

//function prototypes
void displayLine();
void calcSquareSqRoot();

void main()
{
    //declare and initialize variables
    float numberInput = (float) 0.0;
    float square      = (float) 0.0;
    float sqRoot      = (float) 0.0;

    //enter input item
    cout << "Enter a number: ";
    cin >> numberInput;

    //calculate square and square root
    calcSquareSqRoot();

    //display output items
    displayLine();
    cout << "Square and Square Root Calculations" << endl;
    cout << "Square:       " << square << endl;
    cout << "Square Root: " << sqRoot << endl;
    displayLine();
} //end of main function

//*****programmer-defined function definitions*****

void displayLine()
{
    cout << "--------------------------------";
    cout << endl;
} //end of displayLine function

void calcSquareSqRoot()
{
    square = (float) pow(numberInput, 2);
    sqRoot = (float) sqrt(numberInput);
} //end of calcSquareSqRoot function
```

Figure 4-15: LaProg03 program

As Figure 4-15 indicates, the program includes a function prototype, function call, and function definition for the calcSquareSqRoot function. The function call does not contain any actual arguments because it does not need to pass any information to the function. Because no information is being passed to the function, no information needs to be received by it; therefore, no formal parameters are listed in the function header.

2 Build the program. The C++ compiler locates three errors in the program. Scroll the Output window to view the error messages, then double-click the first error message. See Figure 4-16.

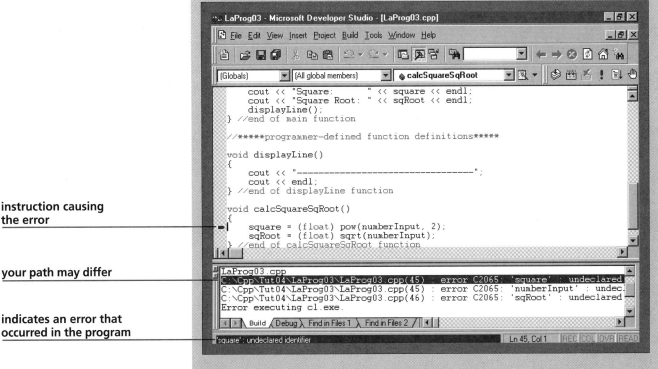

instruction causing the error

your path may differ

indicates an error that occurred in the program

Figure 4-16: Errors found in the LaProg03 program

The arrow in the LaProg03.cpp window shows that the `square = (float) pow(numberInput,2);` statement in the `calcSquareSqRoot` function is causing the first error. The error message in the Output window indicates that the function does not recognize the `square` identifier (name).

3 Double-click the second error message in the Output window. The arrow in the LaProg03.cpp window points to the same line in the `calcSquareSqRoot` function, but the error message indicates that the function also does not recognize the `numberInput` identifier.

4 Double-click the third error message in the Output window. The arrow in the LaProg03.cpp window points to the `sqRoot = (float) sqrt (numberInput);` statement in the `calcSquareSqRoot` function. The error message indicates that the function does not recognize the name `sqRoot`.

5 Close the Output window.

To understand why these errors occurred, you need to know about the scope and lifetime of a variable.

Local variables remain in memory until the function or statement block ends, which is typically when the closing brace (}) is encountered as the program is executing.

In Lesson A's Discovery Exercise 8, you will experiment with using a global variable in a program.

Global variables remain in memory until the program ends.

The Scope and Lifetime of a Variable

A variable's **scope** indicates which portions of the program can use the variable. A variable's **lifetime**, on the other hand, indicates how long the variable remains in the computer's memory. The scope, which can be either local or global, is determined by *where* you declare the variable in the program. **Local variables** are declared in a **statement block**, which is simply a group of instructions enclosed in braces. Exceptions to this rule are the formal parameters listed in a function header, which C++ also treats as local variables. Local variables are known only to the function or statement block in which they are declared.

Global variables, on the other hand, are declared outside of any function in the program. Unlike a local variable, which can be used only by the function or block in which it is declared, a global variable can be used by any statement that follows its declaration in the program. Declaring a variable as global rather than local allows unintentional errors to occur when a function that should not have access to the variable inadvertently changes its contents. You should avoid using global variables in your programs. If more than one function needs access to the same variable, it is better to create a local variable in one of the functions and then pass that variable only to the other functions that need it.

In the current program, the `square`, `numberInput`, and `sqRoot` variables are local to the `main` function because that is the statement block in which they are declared. Therefore, only the `main` function can use those variables. The `calcSquareSqRoot` function does not know about the `square`, `numberInput`, and `sqRoot` variables, so it treats them as undeclared identifiers. To allow the `calcSquareSqRoot` function to use the information stored in the three variables, you will need to pass the variables to the function.

Passing Variables by Value and by Reference

Variables can be passed either by value or by reference. When you pass a variable **by value**, C++ passes only the contents of the variable to the receiving function. The receiving function does not have access to the variable in memory, so it cannot change the variable's contents. You pass a variable by value when the receiving function needs to know only the value stored inside the variable, but the receiving function does not need to change the value stored in the variable. As you observed in the original square and square root program, where you passed the contents of the `numberInput` variable to both the `pow` and `sqrt` functions, you pass a variable by value simply by including the variable's name in the statement that calls the function. Unless specified otherwise, all variables in C++ are passed by value.

You can also pass a variable by reference. When you pass a variable **by reference**, C++ passes the variable's address—in other words, its location—in memory. As you learned in Tutorial 1, the internal memory of a computer is like a large post office, where each memory cell, like each post office box, has a unique address. Because the variable's address (location) is passed to the receiving function, the contents of the variable can be changed by the receiving function. To pass a variable by reference in C++, you must include an ampersand (&), called the **address-of operator**, before the corresponding formal parameter's name in the receiving function's *parameterlist*. The address-of operator tells the C++ compiler to pass the variable's address rather than its contents. You pass a variable by reference when the receiving function needs to change the contents of the variable.

Although the idea of passing information by value and by reference may sound confusing at first, it is a concept with which you are already familiar. To illustrate, assume that you have a savings account at a local bank. During a conversation with a friend, you mention the amount of money you have in the account. Telling someone the amount of money in your account is similar to passing information by value. Knowing the balance in your account doesn't give your friend access to your bank account; it merely gives your friend some information that he or she can use—perhaps to compare to the amount of money he or she has saved.

You can also use the savings account example to illustrate passing information by reference. To deposit money to or withdraw money from your account, you must provide the bank teller with your account number. The account number represents the location of your account and allows the teller to change the account balance. Giving the teller your bank account number is similar to passing a variable by reference. The account number allows the teller to change the contents of your bank account; the variable's address allows the receiving function to change the contents of the variable.

To allow the current program's `calcSquareSqRoot` function to use the information stored in the `numberInput`, `square`, and `sqRoot` variables, you will need to pass the three variables to the function. First, try passing all three variables by value, which is the default in C++. To pass the three variables, you will need to modify the function prototype, the function call, and the function definition. Begin with the function call.

tip

Some programmers also include the name of each formal parameter in the function prototype, but this is optional.

To modify the function call, function prototype, and function definition in the LaProg03 program:

1 The LaProg03 program should be open. Change the function call statement, which is located below the `//calculate square and square root` comment, from `calcSquareSqRoot();` to **calcSquareSqRoot(numberInput, square, sqRoot);**. The new statement tells C++ to call the `calcSquareSqRoot` function and pass it the values stored in the three variables.

Now modify the function definition appropriately. Because the function call passes three Float values, the function header will need to list three Float formal parameters in its *parameterlist*. As you may remember, the names of the formal parameters do not have to be identical to the names of the actual arguments. For convenience, however, you will use the same names in the function header as in the function call.

2 Change the function header, which is located in the programmer-defined section of the program, from `void calcSquareSqRoot()` to **void calcSquareSqRoot(float numberInput, float square, float sqRoot)**.

When you change the function header in the function definition, you must also make a similar change to the function prototype. Recall that the function prototype must include the function's name, the data type of its return value (either void or another data type), and the data type of each of its formal parameters. In this case, the `calcSquareSqRoot` function does not return a value, so its data type is `void`. The function will need to list three formal parameters, each of which is a Float variable.

3 Change the function prototype from `void calcSquareSqRoot();` to **void calcSquareSqRoot(float, float, float);**. Figure 4-17 shows the modified LaProg03 program.

modified function prototype

modified function call

modified function header

```cpp
//LaProg03.cpp
//this program uses a void function to calculate the square
//and square root of a number, and a void function to display
//a straight line.

#include <iostream.h>
#include <math.h>

//function prototypes
void displayLine();
void calcSquareSqRoot(float, float, float);

void main()
{
    //declare and initialize variables
    float numberInput = (float) 0.0;
    float square      = (float) 0.0;
    float sqRoot      = (float) 0.0;

    //enter input item
    cout << "Enter a number: ";
    cin >> numberInput;

    //calculate square and square root
    calcSquareSqRoot(numberInput, square, sqRoot);

    //display output items
    displayLine();
    cout << "Square and Square Root Calculations" << endl;
    cout << "Square:      " << square << endl;
    cout << "Square Root: " << sqRoot << endl;
    displayLine();
} //end of main function

//*****programmer-defined function definitions*****

void displayLine()
{
    cout << "---------------------------------";
    cout << endl;
} //end of displayLine function

void calcSquareSqRoot(float numberInput, float square, float sqRoot)
{
    square = (float) pow(numberInput, 2);
    sqRoot = (float) sqrt(numberInput);
} //end of calcSquareSqRoot function
```

Figure 4-17: Modified LaProg03 program

4   Save, build, and execute the program. When prompted to enter a number, type **25** and press the **Enter** key. The output shows that both the square and the square root of the number 25 are 0, which is incorrect. Press the **Enter** key to close the DOS window, then close the Output window.

Although the changes you made to the current program fixed the "undeclared identifier" errors, the program is still not working correctly. You will find that fixing one type of error in a program can sometimes introduce another type of error. To understand why the program is still giving incorrect results, you will need to desk-check it. Figure 4-18 shows a desk-check table for this program.

main function			calcSquareSqRoot function		
numberInput	square	sqRoot	numberInput	square	sqRoot

Figure 4-18: Desk-check table for the square and square root program

The desk-check table contains a column for each variable and formal parameter used in the program. You will notice that the table shows the variables created in the `main` function, as well as the formal parameters created in the `calcSquareSqRoot` function.

When you execute the LaProg03 program, the `main` function initializes its local `numberInput`, `square`, and `sqRoot` variables to 0. It then prompts the user to enter a number, which it stores in its `numberInput` variable. The `main` function calls the `calcSquareSqRoot` function, passing it the values stored in the `main` function's `numberInput`, `square`, and `sqRoot` variables. (Recall that, unless specified otherwise, C++ passes variables by value.) At this point, C++ leaves the `main` function to process the instructions in the `calcSquareSqRoot` function.

The first instruction processed in the `calcSquareSqRoot` function is the function header, which tells C++ to create three local formal parameters named `numberInput`, `square`, and `sqRoot`. Although these three formal parameters have the same names as the variables used in the `main` function, these three formal parameters are local to the `calcSquareSqRoot` function and, therefore, are recognized by that function only. The `calcSquareSqRoot` function stores the values passed by the `main` function in its three local formal parameters. The first value passed by the `main` function is stored in the first formal parameter listed in the function header, the second value is stored in the second formal parameter, and so on. Figure 4-19 shows the current status of the desk-check table, assuming the user entered the number 25 in response to the prompt to enter a number.

main function			calcSquareSqRoot function		
numberInput	square	sqRoot	numberInput	square	sqRoot
Ø 25	0	0	25	0	0

Figure 4-19: Current status of the desk-check table for the square and square root program

The `calcSquareSqRoot` function calculates both the square and square root of the number contained in its local `numberInput` formal parameter, and assigns the results to its local `square` and `sqRoot` formal parameters, respectively. Figure 4-20 shows the current status of the desk-check table.

main function			calcSquareSqRoot function		
numberInput	square	sqRoot	numberInput	square	sqRoot
Ø 25	0	0	25	Ø 625	Ø 5

Figure 4-20: Current status of the desk-check table for the square and square root program

When the `calcSquareSqRoot` function ends, C++ returns to the `main` function, which displays the report title, as well as the contents of the `main` function's `square` and `sqRoot` variables. As Figure 4-20 shows, the `main` function's `square` and `sqRoot` variables contain the number 0, which is why the program displays 0 as the square and square root of the number 25.

When a program displays incorrect output, it is many times a result of the programmer passing information to a function improperly. Recall that C++ allows you to pass variables both by value and by reference. In the current program, you pass the variables by value, which means that only the contents of the variables are passed to the `calcSquareSqRoot` function. The `calcSquareSqRoot` function stores the values passed to it—25, 0, 0—in its local `numberInput`, `square` and `sqRoot` formal parameters. The `calcSquareSqRoot` function then uses its local `square` and `sqRoot` formal parameters to store the results of the two calculations it performs—in this case, 625 and 5. In this program, however, you need the `calcSquareSqRoot` function to record the results of the calculations in the `main` function's `square` and `sqRoot` variables. (Recall that, when the `calcSquareSqRoot` function ends, the program displays the contents of the `main` function's `square` and `sqRoot` variables.) To give the `calcSquareSqRoot` function access to the `main` function's `square` and `sqRoot` variables, you will need to pass them by reference rather than by value. When you pass by reference, C++ passes the address of the variable in memory. Recall that you tell C++ to pass a variable by reference simply by including the address-of operator—an ampersand (&)—before the variable's name; you do so in both the function's prototype and in its function header, but not in the statement that calls the function. Include the address-of operator in the `calcSquareSqRoot` function's prototype and in its header.

The `calcSquareSqRoot` function does not need to change the value in the `main` function's `numberInput` variable, so you can pass that variable by value.

To modify the current program to pass the `square` and `sqRoot` variables by reference:

1 The LaProg03 program should be open. Make the appropriate changes to the `calcSquareSqRoot` function's prototype and header, as shown in Figure 4-21.

include the address-of operator in both places

```
//LaProg03.cpp
//this program uses a void function to calculate the square
//and square root of a number, and a void function to display
//a straight line.

#include <iostream.h>
#include <math.h>

//function prototypes
void displayLine();
void calcSquareSqRoot(float, float &, float &);

void main()
{
    //declare and initialize variables
    float numberInput = (float) 0.0;
    float square      = (float) 0.0;
    float sqRoot      = (float) 0.0;

    //enter input item
    cout << "Enter a number: ";
    cin >> numberInput;

    //calculate square and square root
    calcSquareSqRoot(numberInput, square, sqRoot);

    //display output items
    displayLine();
    cout << "Square and Square Root Calculations" << endl;
    cout << "Square:      " << square << endl;
    cout << "Square Root: " << sqRoot << endl;
    displayLine();
} //end of main function

//*****programmer-defined function definitions*****

void displayLine()
{
    cout << "---------------------------------";
    cout << endl;
} //end of displayLine function

void calcSquareSqRoot(float numberInput, float &square, float &sqRoot)
{
    square = (float) pow(numberInput, 2);
    sqRoot = (float) sqrt(numberInput);
} //end of calcSquareSqRoot function
```

you do not include the address-of operator in the function call

include the address-of operator before each of these formal parameters to pass by reference

passed by value

Figure 4-21: Completed LaProg03 program

tip

You will notice that the statement that calls a function does not indicate if an item is being passed by value or by reference. To determine whether an item is being passed by value or by reference, you need to examine either the function header or the function prototype.

2 Save, build, and then execute the LaProg03 program. When prompted to enter a number, type **25** and press the **Enter** key. The output in the DOS window correctly shows that the square and square root of the number 25 is 625 and 5, respectively. Press the **Enter** key to close the DOS window.

Desk-checking the completed program shown in Figure 4-21 can help you understand why it is working correctly. First, you will close the Output window and the workspace.

3   Close the Output window, and then close the workspace.

Figure 4-22 shows a desk-check table for the completed program shown in Figure 4-21.

main function			calcSquareSqRoot function
numberInput	square	sqRoot	numberInput

Figure 4-22: Desk-check table for the completed square and square root program

Although the `calcSquareSqRoot` function header lists three formal parameters in its *parameterlist*, only the one that is passed by value—`numberInput`—is listed in its section of the table. Because the `main` function's `square` and `sqRoot` variables are passed by reference, which means that their addresses are passed, the `calcSquareSqRoot` function will record the results of the square and square root calculations in the `main` function's variables.

When you execute the completed square and square root program, the `main` function initializes its local `numberInput`, `square`, and `sqRoot` variables to 0. It then prompts the user to enter a number (assume the user enters the number 25), which it stores in its `numberInput` variable. The `main` function calls the `calcSquareSqRoot` function, passing it the value stored in the `main` function's `numberInput` variable, and the memory addresses of the `square` and `sqRoot` variables. The `calcSquareSqRoot` function creates a formal parameter named `numberInput`, and stores the passed value (25) in that parameter. Figure 4-23 shows the current status of the desk-check table.

main function			calcSquareSqRoot function
numberInput	square	sqRoot	numberInput
$\emptyset$ 25	0	0	25

Figure 4-23: Current status of the desk-check table for the completed square and square root program

The `calcSquareSqRoot` function calculates both the square and square root of the number contained in its `numberInput` formal parameter, and assigns the results to the `main` function's `square` and `sqRoot` variables, respectively. Figure 4-24 shows the completed desk-check table.

main function			calcSquareSqRoot function
numberInput	square	sqRoot	numberInput
Ø 25	Ø 625	Ø 5	25

Figure 4-24: Completed desk-check table for the completed square and square root program

When the `calcSquareSqRoot` function ends, C++ returns to the `main` function, which displays the report title, as well as the contents of the `main` function's `square` and `sqRoot` variables. As Figure 4-24 shows, the `main` function's `square` and `sqRoot` variables contain the numbers 625 and 5, respectively.

mini-quiz

Mini-Quiz 2

1. The items listed in the function call are called the _____ .

2. Write the function header for a void function named `updateQuantity`. The function receives, by value, a Short Integer variable named `quantity`.

3. Write a function prototype for the function defined in question 2.

4. Write a function call for the function defined in question 2. The function call should pass a Short Integer variable named `inStock`.

5. Write the function header for a void function named `updateQuantity`. The function receives, by reference, a Short Integer variable named `quantity`.

6. Write a function prototype for the function defined in question 5.

7. Write a function call for the function defined in question 5. The function call should pass the address of a Short Integer variable named `inStock`.

You have now completed Lesson A. In this lesson, you learned about the C++ mathematical functions. You also learned how to create and invoke void functions, as well as how to pass information by value and by reference. You can either exit Visual C++ and take a break or complete the questions and exercises at the end of the lesson before continuing to Lesson B. In Lesson B, you will learn how to create and invoke functions that return a value.

S U M M A R Y

A function is a block of code that performs a specific task. The C++ language includes a variety of built-in functions. For example, the math.h header file contains the C++ mathematical functions. You can also create your own functions, called programmer-defined functions, in C++. Functions allow programmers to write programs quickly and easily.

Programmer-defined functions can be either value-returning functions or void functions. Void functions are functions that do not return a value. After creating a function, the programmer can then call (invoke) it from one or more places in the program.

You create and invoke a programmer-defined void function by including a function definition and one or more function calls in a program. If the function definition appears below the main function in the program, you will also need to include a function prototype in the program. You enter the function prototype above the main function. The function prototype, as well as the function definition's header, must begin with the keyword void. A call to a void function appears as a separate statement in a program.

Like the C++ built-in functions, programmer-defined functions can receive information that you send (pass) to it. In most cases, the information that you pass to a function is either a literal or named constant, the contents of a variable, or the address of a variable in memory. You pass information when you want the function to process the information in some way. Not all functions require information to be passed in order for the function to perform its designated task.

The items listed in the function call are called the actual arguments. The items listed in the function definition's header are called the formal parameters. The names of the formal parameters do not need to be identical to the names of the actual arguments, although you may choose to use the same names for convenience. However, the data type of the formal parameters must match the data type of the actual arguments. In addition, the order in which the formal parameters are listed in the function header must match the order of the actual arguments listed in the function call.

A variable's scope indicates which portions of the program can use the variable. A variable's lifetime, on the other hand, indicates how long the variable remains in the computer's memory. The scope, which can be either local or global, is determined by *where* you declare the variable in the program. A local variable is declared in a statement block. The formal parameters listed in the function header's *parameterlist* are also treated as local variables.

A local variable can be used only within the statement block or function in which it is declared. Such a variable remains in memory until the statement block or function ends. A global variable is declared outside of any function and can be used by any statement that follows its declaration in the program. A global variable remains in memory until the end of the program. You should avoid using global variables as it is safer to pass local variables from one function to another.

Variables can be passed either by value or by reference. When you pass a variable by value, C++ passes the contents of the variable to the receiving function. You pass a variable by value when the receiving function needs to know only the value stored inside the variable, but the receiving function does not need to change that variable's contents. Unless specified otherwise, all variables in C++ are passed by value.

When you pass a variable by reference, C++ passes the variable's address in memory. To pass a variable by reference in C++, you must include an ampersand (&), called the address-of operator, before the corresponding formal parameter's name in the receiving function's header. You also include the address-of operator in the function's prototype. You pass a variable by reference when the receiving function needs to change the contents of the variable.

ANSWERS TO MINI-QUIZZES

Mini-Quiz 1

1. a function prototype, one or more function calls, a function definition

2.  ```
    void displayState()
    {
        cout << "Hawaii" << endl;
        cout << "******" << endl;
    } //end of displayState function
    ```

3.  ```
    void displayState();
    ```

4.  ```
    displayState();
    ```

Mini-Quiz 2

1. actual arguments

2.  ```
    void updateQuantity(short quantity)
    ```

3.  ```
    void updateQuantity(short);
    ```

4.  ```
    updateQuantity(inStock);
    ```

5.  ```
    void updateQuantity(short &quantity)
    ```

6.  ```
    void updateQuantity(short &);
    ```

7.  ```
    updateQuantity(inStock);
    ```

QUESTIONS

1. Which of the following statements is false?
    a. A function is a block of code that performs a specific task.
    b. Functions allow programmers to break large and complex problems into small and manageable tasks.
    c. Functions allow programmers to use existing code to perform common tasks.
    d. Functions can be called, or invoked, only once in a program.
    e. Programmer-defined functions can be either value-returning or void.

2. To use one of the C++ built-in mathematical functions, you must include the _____ header file in your program.
    a. calculation.h
    b. compute.h
    c. expression.h
    d. math.h
    e. mathematical.h

3. Which of the following C++ expressions is equivalent to the mathematical expression 5^3?
    a. `5^3`
    b. `cube(5)`
    c. `pow(3, 5)`
    d. `pow(5, 3)`
    e. `sqrt(5, 3)`
    ```

4. Which of the following C++ expressions will find the square root of the number 16?
   a. pow(16, 2)
   b. root(16, 2)
   c. sqroot(16)
   d. sqrt(16, 2)
   e. sqrt(16)

5. The pow and sqrt functions return a(n) _____ type number.
   a. Double
   b. Float
   c. Integer
   d. Long
   e. Short

6. Programmer-defined functions can be _____.
   a. value-returning functions only
   b. void functions only
   c. either value-returning or void functions

7. The items listed in the function header are called _____.
   a. actual arguments
   b. formal parameters
   c. passed parameters
   d. sent arguments

8. You declare a function with a function _____, which is typically entered at the beginning of the program, below the #include directives.
   a. call
   b. declaration
   c. definition
   d. prototype

9. You invoke a function with a function _____.
   a. call
   b. declaration
   c. definition
   d. prototype

10. Which of the following is false?
    a. You enclose a function's statements in a set of braces.
    b. The function header is considered a C++ statement, so it must end in a semicolon.
    c. The keyword void tells the C++ compiler that the function does not return a value.
    d. A function can receive information that you send (pass) to it.
    e. An empty set of parentheses after the function's name in the function header tells you that the function does not receive any information.

11. Which of the following calls a function named displayName, passing it no actual arguments?
    a. call displayName;
    b. call displayName();
    c. displayName;
    d. displayName()
    e. displayName();

12. Assume a program contains a void function named displayName, which requires no formal parameters. Which of the following is a correct function prototype for this function?
    a. displayName;
    b. displayName();
    c. void displayName;
    d. void displayName();
    e. void displayName(none);

13. Assume that a program contains a programmer-defined void function. When C++ encounters the function's closing brace (}), C++ returns to the statement _____ .
    a. immediately above the statement that called the function
    b. that called the function
    c. immediately below the statement that called the function

14. A program will have one function prototype for each function defined in the programmer-defined section of the program. (Assume that the programmer-defined section is located below the main function.)
    a. true
    b. false

15. Variables that are known only to the function in which they are declared are called _____ variables.
    a. global
    b. local
    c. main
    d. separate
    e. void

16. When you pass a variable _____ , C++ passes only the contents of the variable to the receiving function.
    a. by reference
    b. by value
    c. globally
    d. locally

17. Which of the following is false?
    a. When you pass a variable by reference, the receiving function can change its contents.
    b. When you pass a variable by value, the receiving function creates a local formal parameter that it uses to store the passed value.
    c. Unless specified otherwise, all variables in C++ are passed by value.
    d. To pass a variable by reference in C++, you place an ampersand (&) before the variable's name in the statement that calls the function.

18. Assume a program contains a void function named calcNewPrice that receives two Float variables, oldPrice and newPrice. The function multiplies the contents of the oldPrice variable by 1.1, and then stores the result in the newPrice variable. Which of the following is the best function prototype for this function?
    a. void calcNewPrice(float, float);
    b. void calcNewPrice(float &, float);
    c. void calcNewPrice(float, float &);
    d. void calcNewPrice(float &, float &);
    e. void calcNewPrice(oldPrice, newPrice);

19. Which of the following can be used to call question 18's calcNewPrice function?
    a. calcNewPrice(float oldPrice, float newPrice);
    b. calcNewPrice(&oldPrice, newPrice);
    c. calcNewPrice(oldPrice, &newPrice);
    d. calcNewPrice(&oldPrice, &newPrice);
    e. calcNewPrice(oldPrice, newPrice);

20. Which of the following is false?
    a. The names of the formal parameters in the function header must be identical to the names of the actual arguments in the function call.
    b. When listing the formal parameters in a function header, you must include each parameter's data type and name.
    c. The formal parameters should be the same data type as the actual arguments.
    d. If a function call passes an Integer variable first and a Character variable second, the receiving function must receive an Integer variable first and a Character variable second.

21. A variable's _____ indicates which portions of the program can use the variable.
    a. area
    b. extent
    c. lifetime
    d. reach
    e. scope

22. A variable's _____ indicates how long the variable remains in the computer's memory.
    a. area
    b. extent
    c. lifetime
    d. reach
    e. scope

23. The variables declared in a statement block or listed in a function header's *parameterlist* are considered _____ variables.
    a. area
    b. global
    c. local
    d. reference
    e. value

24. _____ variables remain in memory until the program ends.
    a. Area
    b. Global
    c. Local
    d. Reference
    e. Value

25. _____ variables are declared outside of any statement block.
    a. Area
    b. Global
    c. Local
    d. Reference
    e. Value

26. A variable declared in a function is called a(n) _____ variable.
    a. area
    b. global
    c. local
    d. reference
    e. value

27. _____ variables remain in memory until the statement block ends.
    a. Area
    b. Global
    c. Local
    d. Reference
    e. Value

E X E R C I S E S

1. In this exercise, you will create a void function that requires no arguments.
   a. Open the T4Ae01.cpp file, which is located in the Cpp\Tut04\T4Ae01 folder on your computer's hard disk.
   b. Complete the program by adding a void function that will display a row of 15 asterisks (*). The program should call the function twice: once to display the row of asterisks above the company name, and once to display the row of asterisks below the company name. Be sure to enter the function prototype, the function calls, and the function definition.
   c. Save, build, and execute the program. When the program is working correctly, print the code. On the code printout, circle the function prototype, the function calls, and the function definition.
   d. Close both the Output window and the workspace.

2. In this exercise, you will create a void function that requires no arguments.
   a. Open the T4Ae02.cpp file, which is located in the Cpp\Tut04\T4Ae02 folder on your computer's hard disk.
   b. Complete the program by adding two void functions. The first function should display your name. The second function should display your address. Be sure to enter the function prototypes, the function calls, and the function definitions.
   c. Save, build, and execute the program. When the program is working correctly, print the code. On the code printout, circle the function prototypes, the function calls, and the function definitions.
   d. Close both the Output window and the workspace.

3. In this exercise, you will create a void function that requires one argument.
   a. Open the T4Ae03.cpp file, which is located in the Cpp\Tut04\T4Ae03 folder on your computer's hard disk.
   b. Complete the program by adding a void function that increases by one the contents of the `age` variable, which is passed to the function.
   c. Save, build, and execute the program. When the program is working correctly, print the code.
   d. Close both the Output window and the workspace.

4. In this exercise, you will create a void function that requires arguments.
   a. Open the T4Ae04.cpp file, which is located in the Cpp\Tut04\T4Ae04 folder on your computer's hard disk.
   b. Complete the program by adding a void function that calculates the amount remaining in inventory.
   c. Save, build, and execute the program. When the program is working correctly, print the code.
   d. Close both the Output window and the workspace.

5. In this exercise, you will add two void functions to Lesson A's square and square root program.
   a. Open the T4Ae05.cpp file, which is located in the Cpp\Tut04\T4Ae05 folder on your computer's hard disk.
   b. Modify the program by adding a void function to input the number from the user. (*Hint:* You will need to move the corresponding `cout` and `cin` statements from the `main` function to the new function.)
   c. Modify the program by adding a void function that will display the output items. (*Hint:* You will need to move the five statements that currently display the output from the `main` function to the new function.)
   d. Save, build, and execute the program. When the program is working correctly, print the code.
   e. Close both the Output window and the workspace.

discovery ▶ 6. In this exercise, you will create a program that calculates and displays the log (base 10) of a number. A log is the exponent of the power to which a number, referred to as the base, must be raised to give a required number. For example, using a base of 10, the log of 1000 is 3 because the base number 10 must be raised to the third power in order to result in the number 1000. The math.h header file in C++ contains a function, named log10, that you can use to calculate the log of a number using a base of 10. The syntax of the log10 function is **log10**(*number*), where *number* is a Float value for which you want to find the log.

    a. Create a console application named T4Ae06 in the Cpp\Tut04 folder on your computer's hard disk.

    b. Write a program that inputs a number, calculates the log of that number, and then displays the log on the screen. Use three void functions: one to input the number, another to calculate the log, and another to display the output.

    c. Save, build, and execute the program. Test the program by finding the log of the number 100000. When the program is working correctly, print the code.

    d. Close both the Output window and the workspace.

discovery ▶ 7. In this exercise, you will confirm that the names of the formal parameters do not have to be identical to the names of the actual arguments.

    a. Open the T4Ae07.cpp file, which is located in the Cpp\Tut04\T4Ae07 folder on your computer's hard disk.

    b. In the calcSquareSqRoot function's header, change numberInput to num1, &square to &num2, and &sqRoot to &num3. In the assignment statements that are located in the calcSquareSqRoot function definition, change numberInput to num1, square to num2, and sqRoot to num3. After making these changes, you will notice that the names of the formal parameters are not identical to the names of the actual arguments.

    c. Save, build, and then execute the program to see that the changes you made in step b have no effect on the program. Use the program to find the square and square root of the number 55.

    d. Print the code. On the code printout, mark down the square and square root of the number 55.

    e. Close both the Output window and the workspace.

discovery ▶ 8. In this exercise, you will experiment with the concept of scope.

    a. Open the T4Ae08.cpp file, which is located in the Cpp\Tut04\T4Ae08 folder on your computer's hard disk. Study the program. You will notice that both the main function and the getNumber function use a variable named number.

    b. Build the program. The C++ compiler locates an error in the program; the getNumber function does not recognize the number variable. This error occurs because the number variable is local to the main function. At this point, either you can use what you learned in Lesson A to pass the number variable to the getNumber function, or you can create a global variable named number. Although passing a variable is the preferred way of communicating between functions, you will create a global variable as this will give you an opportunity to see how global variables work in a program.

    c. Change the short number = 0; statement in the main function to a comment by preceding the statement with //. Recall that global variables are declared outside of any functions in the program. In the blank line above void main(), type short number = 0; and press the Enter key. Because the number variable is now a global variable, both the main and getNumber functions have access to it. You can verify that by running the program.

d. Save, build, and execute the program. When prompted for a number, type 5 and press the Enter key. The DOS window shows that doubling the number 5 results in the number 10.

e. Print the code.

f. Modify the program so that it passes the number variable to the getNumber function, rather than using a global variable. Save, build, and execute the program. When prompted for a number, type 5 and press the Enter key. The DOS window shows that the number 5 doubled equals 10.

g. Print the code. Close the Output window and the workspace.

debugging 9. In this exercise, you will debug a program that contains functions.

a. Open the T4Ae09.cpp file, which is located in the Cpp\Tut04\T4Ae09 folder on your computer's hard disk.

b. Build the program. (Do not be overwhelmed by the number of errors shown in the Output window. Begin by correcting the first error, then save and build the program again. Most times you will find that correcting one error corrects many of the errors that follow it.) Correct the errors, then save, build, and execute the program. When the program is working correctly, print the code. On the code printout, indicate what was wrong with the program. Also circle the corrections you made.

c. Close the Output window and the workspace.

debugging 10. In this exercise, you will debug a program that contains functions.

a. Open the T4Ae10.cpp file, which is located in the Cpp\Tut04\T4Ae10 folder on your computer's hard disk.

b. Build the program. (Do not be overwhelmed by the number of errors shown in the Output window. Begin by correcting the first error, then save and build the program again. Most times you will find that correcting one error corrects many of the errors that follow it.) Correct the errors, then save, build, and execute the program. When the program is working correctly, print the code. On the code printout, indicate what was wrong with the program. Also circle the corrections you made.

c. Close the Output window and the workspace.

In this lesson you will learn how to:

- Create a function that returns a value
- Format numeric output
- Send output to a file

Value-returning Functions

Value-returning Functions

In Lesson A, you learned how to create and invoke void functions, which are functions that do not return a value. You also learned how to use two of the C++ built-in mathematical functions, pow and sqrt. Both functions, you may remember, are value-returning functions. In this lesson, you will learn how to create and invoke your own value-returning functions.

Creating and invoking a value-returning function is very similar to creating and invoking a void function. You typically enter the same three items of information (a function prototype, one or more function calls, and a function definition) in the program. Figure 4-25 shows the syntax and an example of a function prototype and a function definition for a value-returning function.

Function prototype syntax	Function definition syntax

returndatatype functionname ([parametertlist]);	*returndatatype functionname ([parameterlist])*
	{
	    one or more statements ending in a semicolon
	    return *expression;*
	}

Function prototype example	**Function definition example**

`float calcSquare(float);`	`float calcSquare(float numberInput)`
	`{`
	`        float numSq = (float) 0.0;`
	`        numSq = (float) pow(numberInput, 2);`
	`        return numSq;`
	`}`

Figure 4-25: Syntax and example of a function prototype and a function definition for a value-returning function

The syntax for creating and declaring a value-returning function differs from the syntax for creating and declaring a void function in two ways. First, a value-returning function's syntax begins with a *returndatatype*, which indicates the type of data the function will return. Recall that a void function's syntax begins with the keyword `void`, which indicates that the function will not return a value. Second, the last statement in a value-returning function is always **return** *expression*;, where *expression* represents the *only* value the function will return. A void function does not contain a **return** *expression*; statement.

Unlike a void function call, a call to a value-returning function does not typically appear as a statement by itself; rather, it is usually a part of another statement. For example, although valid syntactically, the `sqrt(numberInput);` statement is not valid logically because `sqrt` is a value-returning function and the statement does not tell C++ what to do with the return value. However, the `sqRoot = (float) sqrt(numberInput);` statement is valid both logically and syntactically because it tells C++ to store the `sqrt` function's return value in the `sqRoot` variable. The `cout << sqrt(numberInput);` statement is also valid both logically and syntactically because it tells C++ to display the `sqrt` function's return value on the screen.

You will now view another version of the square and square root program. This version contains two value-returning functions.

In certain situations—for example, when a function has encountered an error while the program is running—you may need to use a `return` statement, without an *expression*, to leave a void function prematurely—in other words, before the function's closing brace is encountered.

To view the LbProg01 program:

1 If necessary, start Visual C++. Open the **LbProg01.cpp** file, which is located in the Cpp\Tut04\LbProg01 folder on your computer's hard disk. The LbProg01 program, which appears in the LbProg01.cpp window, is shown in Figure 4-26. Notice the instructions that pertain to the two value-returning functions, `calcSquare` and `calcSqRoot`.

function prototypes

function calls

```cpp
//LbProg01.cpp
//This program uses two value-returning functions to calculate
//the square and square root of a number that is passed to it.
//It also uses a void function, with no arguments, to display
//a straight line.

#include <iostream.h>
#include <math.h>

//function prototypes
void displayLine();
float calcSquare(float);
float calcSqRoot(float);

void main()
{
    //declare and initialize variables
    float numberInput = (float) 0.0;
    float square      = (float) 0.0;
    float sqRoot      = (float) 0.0;

    //enter input item
    cout << "Enter a number: ";
    cin >> numberInput;

    //calculate square and square root
    square = calcSquare(numberInput);
    sqRoot = calcSqRoot(numberInput);

    //display output items
    displayLine();
    cout << "Square and Square Root Calculations" << endl;
    cout << "Square:      " << square << endl;
    cout << "Square Root: " << sqRoot << endl;
    displayLine();
} //end of main function

//*****programmer-defined function definitions*****

void displayLine()
{
    cout << "-----------------------------------";
    cout << endl;
} //end of displayLine function
```

Figure 4-26: LbProg01 program

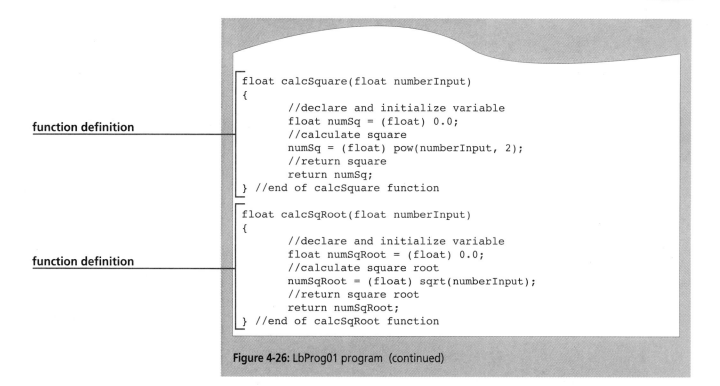

function definition

function definition

```
float calcSquare(float numberInput)
{
        //declare and initialize variable
        float numSq = (float) 0.0;
        //calculate square
        numSq = (float) pow(numberInput, 2);
        //return square
        return numSq;
} //end of calcSquare function

float calcSqRoot(float numberInput)
{
        //declare and initialize variable
        float numSqRoot = (float) 0.0;
        //calculate square root
        numSqRoot = (float) sqrt(numberInput);
        //return square root
        return numSqRoot;
} //end of calcSqRoot function
```

Figure 4-26: LbProg01 program (continued)

First, study the `calcSquare` and `calcSqRoot` function prototypes, which appear above the `main` function. The prototypes indicate that the `calcSquare` and `calcSqRoot` functions both receive and return a Float value. You can tell that the functions receive a Float value because the keyword `float` appears in their *parameterlist*. You can tell that both functions return a value because their prototypes begin with a data type—in this case, `float`—rather than the keyword `void`. The data type indicates that each function returns a Float value.

At this point, you may be wondering why the LbProg01 program uses two value-returning functions rather than one value-returning function. Recall that a value-returning function can return only one value. Therefore, to return two values—the square and the square root—you need to use two functions.

Next, study the function calls, which are located in the `main` function. You will notice that the value-returning `calcSquare` and `calcSqRoot` functions appear in assignment statements. Recall that when C++ processes an assignment statement, it first evaluates the expression appearing on the right side of the equal sign, and then assigns the result to the variable whose name appears on the left side of the equal sign. For example, when C++ processes the `square = calcSquare(numberInput);` statement, C++ calls the `calcSquare` function, passing it the value in the `main` function's `numberInput` variable. C++ temporarily leaves the `main` function to process the instructions in the `calcSquare` function. The `calcSquare` function creates a formal parameter named `numberInput`, in which it stores the passed value. (Recall that the formal parameters listed in a function's header are local to that function.) The first statement within the function definition creates and initializes a Float variable named `numSq`, which is also local to the `calcSquare` function. The second statement, `numSq = (float) pow(numberInput, 2);`, squares the number stored in the `numberInput` variable and assigns that value, type casted to Float, to the `numSq` variable. The last statement in the `calcSquare` function returns the Float value stored in the `numSq` variable to the `main` function, which stores the returned value in the `main` function's `square` variable. A similar process occurs when C++ encounters the `sqRoot = calcSqRoot(numberInput);` statement, which calls the `calcSqRoot` function.

Lastly, study the function definitions, which appear in the programmer-defined function section of the program. Like the function prototypes, the function header in both function definitions indicates that the functions both receive and return a Float value. The `return numSq;` statement in the `calcSquare` function returns the square of the number entered by the user. The `return numSqRoot;` statement in the `calcSqRoot` function returns the square root of the number entered by the user.

Run the LbProg01 program to view its output.

To view the LbProg01 program's output:

1 Build and execute the LbProg01 program. When you are prompted to enter a number, type **4** and press the **Enter** key. The output in the DOS window shows that the square of the number 4 is 16 and the square root is 2. Both results are correct.

2 Press the **Enter** key to close the DOS window.

You are now finished with this program, so you can close it.

3 Close the Output window, then close the workspace.

Now combine what you know about variables, constants, arithmetic operators, and functions to solve David Liu's problem, which is outlined in the case at the beginning of the tutorial.

Mini-Quiz 3

1. Write a value-returning function named `calcBonus`. The function will receive a Float variable by value. Use `sales` as the name of the formal parameter. The function declares and initializes a Float variable named `bonusAmt`, to which it assigns the bonus amount, which is calculated by multiplying the contents of the `sales` formal parameter by 3 percent. The function returns the bonus amount as a Float value.

2. Write a function prototype for the function defined in question 1.

3. Write a function call for the function defined in question 1. The function call should pass a Float variable named `mthlySales`.

Solving David Liu's Problem

Recall that David Liu is in the market for a new car. David is not sure whether to finance the car through the dealer, at a very low interest rate, or take the dealer's rebate and then finance through the credit union, which is charging a much higher rate. David wants you to create a program that will compute his monthly payment using each of the two options. He thinks he will need to borrow $12,000 for three years. The dealer is currently offering a choice of either a $3,000 rebate or a 5 percent interest rate. The credit union is charging an 11 percent interest rate on loans.

The expression to calculate a periodic payment on a loan is *principal* * (*rate* / (1 − (*rate* + 1)$^{-term}$), where *principal* is the amount of the loan, *rate* is the periodic interest rate, and *term* is the number of periodic payments. To calculate the monthly payments for David, you will need to convert the annual interest rates (5 and 11 percent) to monthly rates by dividing the annual rates by 12. You will also need to convert the term of the loan, which is stated in years, to months. You can make this conversion simply by multiplying the number of years by 12.

Most of the program that calculates the monthly car payments has already been entered for you. You will need to enter only one value-returning function and one void function. The value-returning function will calculate and return the monthly payment for each option. The void function will send the monthly payment information to a file, which can then be printed.

To complete the monthly payment program:

1 Open the **LbProg02.cpp** file, which is located in the Cpp\Tut04\LbProg02 folder on your computer's hard disk. The monthly payment program, which appears in the LbProg02.cpp window, is shown in Figure 4-27.

```
//LbProg02.cpp
//this program calculates and displays monthly car payments, and
//saves the program output to a file for printing

#include <iostream.h>
#include <math.h>

//function prototypes

void main()
{
    //declare and initialize variables
    short principal     = 0;
    short rebate        = 0;
    float creditRate    = (float) 0.0;
    float dealerRate    = (float) 0.0;
    short term          = 0;
    float creditFinanced = (float) 0.0;
    float dealerFinanced = (float) 0.0;

    //enter the input items
    cout << "Enter the principal: ";
    cin >> principal;
    cout << "Enter the rebate amount: ";
    cin >> rebate;
    cout << "Enter the credit union rate: ";
    cin >> creditRate;
    cout << "Enter the dealer rate: ";
    cin >> dealerRate;
    cout << "Enter the term: ";
    cin >> term;

    //calculate monthly payments

    //display monthly payments

    cout << "Rebate and credit union financing: "<< creditFinanced << endl;
    cout << "No rebate and dealer financing: " << dealerFinanced << endl;

    //save output in a file for printing

} //end of main function

//*****programmer-defined function definitions*****
```

Figure 4-27: The monthly payment program

First, study the existing code. The program includes two directives: `#include <iostream.h>` and `#include <math.h>`. The iostream.h file contains the instructions needed to perform input and output operations. The math.h file contains the pow mathematical function, which you will need to use in the monthly payment calculations.

You will notice that the program declares and initializes seven variables. The first five variables (`principal`, `rebate`, `creditRate`, `dealerRate`, and `term`) will store the values entered by the user. The `creditFinanced` variable will store David's monthly payment if he accepts the dealer's rebate and finances through the credit union. The `dealerFinanced` variable will store the monthly payment if David finances through the dealer at the lower interest rate.

After declaring and initializing the variables, the program prompts the user to enter the principal, rebate amount, credit union rate, dealer rate, and term. You will notice that the instructions to calculate the monthly payments, which should come next in the program, are missing; you will create and invoke a value-returning function named `calcMthlyPay` to make the calculations. After the monthly payments are calculated, the program displays the payments on the screen. You will create a void function named `saveToFile` that saves the program output in a file. You will then use C++ to print the contents of the file.

Begin completing the current program by entering the function definition and prototype for the `calcMthlyPay` function, which will calculate the monthly payments. The function will need to know the principal, the interest rate, and the term of the loan, as well as the dealer's rebate. Because a monthly payment may include decimal places, the function will return a Float value. Figure 4-28 shows two ways of writing the `calcMthlyPay` definition.

Version 1:

```
float calcMthlyPay(short principal, short rebate, float rate, short months)
{
    float tempPay = (float) 0.0;
    tempPay = (float) (principal — rebate) * rate / (1 — (float) pow(rate + 1, (float) —months));
    return tempPay;
} //end of calcMthlyPay function
```

Version 2:

```
float calcMthlyPay(short principal, short rebate, float rate, short months)
{
    return (float) (principal — rebate) * rate / (1 — (float) pow(rate + 1, (float) —months));
} //end of calcMthlyPay function
```

Figure 4-28: Two versions of the `calcMthlyPay` function

You will notice that the first version of the `calcMthlyPay` function declares a local variable named `tempPay`, which the function uses to store the result of the monthly payment calculation. The `return` statement in the first version returns the contents of the local `tempPay` variable to the `main` function. The second version of the function, on the other hand, uses the `return` statement both to calculate and return the monthly payment. Either version will work correctly. You will enter the first version.

To begin completing the monthly payment program:

1 Enter the `calcMthlyPay` function's prototype and definition, as shown in Figure 4-29. The instructions are highlighted in the figure.

```cpp
//LbProg02.cpp
//this program calculates and displays monthly car payments, and
//saves the program output to a file for printing

#include <iostream.h>
#include <math.h>

//function prototypes
float calcMthlyPay(short, short, float, short);

void main()
{
    //declare and initialize variables
    short principal      = 0;
    short rebate         = 0;
    float creditRate     = (float) 0.0;
    float dealerRate     = (float) 0.0;
    short term           = 0;
    float creditFinanced = (float) 0.0;
    float dealerFinanced = (float) 0.0;

    //enter the input items
    cout << "Enter the principal: ";
    cin >> principal;
    cout << "Enter the rebate amount: ";
    cin >> rebate;
    cout << "Enter the credit union rate: ";
    cin >> creditRate;
    cout << "Enter the dealer rate: ";
    cin >> dealerRate;
    cout << "Enter the term: ";
    cin >> term;

    //calculate monthly payments

    //display monthly payments

    cout << "Rebate and credit union financing: "<< creditFinanced << endl;
    cout << "No rebate and dealer financing: " << dealerFinanced << endl;

    //save output in a file for printing

} //end of main function

//*****programmer-defined function definitions*****

float calcMthlyPay(short principal, short rebate, float rate, short months)
{
    float tempPay = (float) 0.0;
    tempPay = (float) (principal - rebate) *
        rate / (1 - (float) pow(rate + 1, (float) - months));
    return tempPay;
} //end of calcMthlyPay function
```

enter this function prototype

enter this function definition

Figure 4-29: `calcMthlyPay` function prototype and definition entered in the program

Next, enter the instructions to call the `calcMthlyPay` function. First you will call the function to calculate David's monthly payment if he accepts the rebate and finances through the credit union. You will need to pass the `calcMthlyPay` function the contents of the `principal`, `rebate`, `creditRate`, and `term` variables. Recall that to calculate a monthly payment, you will need to divide the `creditRate` by 12 and to multiply the `term` by 12. You can make these calculations right in the function call's *argumentlist*. You will assign the result of the calculation to the `creditFinanced` variable.

2   In the blank line below the `//calculate monthly payments` comment, type **creditFinanced = calcMthlyPay(principal, rebate, creditRate/12, term * 12);** and press the Enter key.

Now call the `calcMthlyPay` function to calculate the monthly payment if David finances through the dealer. The actual arguments in this function call will be identical to the ones in the prior function call, except you will change the `creditRate/12` argument to `dealerRate/12`, and you will pass the numeric literal constant 0 as the rebate. (Recall that the dealer offers a choice of either the rebate or the lower interest rate. If David decides to finance through the dealer, he will not receive a rebate.)

3   Type **dealerFinanced = calcMthlyPay(principal, 0, dealerRate/12, term * 12);** and press the **Enter** key. The two statements you entered are shown in Figure 4-30.

verify that you entered these statements correctly

```
//calculate monthly payments
creditFinanced = calcMthlyPay(principal, rebate, creditRate/12, term * 12);
dealerFinanced = calcMthlyPay(principal, 0, dealerRate/12, term * 12);
```

Figure 4-30: Function calls entered in the program

4   Save, build, and execute the program. When prompted, enter the following data:

Principal:	**12000**
Rebate:	**3000**
Credit union rate:	**.11**
Dealer rate:	**.05**
Term:	**3**

The program calculates and displays the monthly payments, as shown in Figure 4-31.

```
Enter the principal: 12000
Enter the rebate amount: 3000
Enter the credit union rate: .11
Enter the dealer rate: .05
Enter the term: 3
Rebate and credit union financing: 294.648
No rebate and dealer financing: 359.651
Press any key to continue_
```

Figure 4-31: Monthly payment program output showing monthly payments

The output indicates that it would be better for David to accept the rebate from the dealer and finance at the higher interest rate offered through the credit union.

5 Press the **Enter** key to close the DOS window, then close the Output window.

You will notice that the monthly payment amounts shown in Figure 4-31 display with more than two decimal places; monetary amounts, however, are usually displayed as numbers with either no decimal places or two decimal places. You can use the C++ `setprecision()` and `setiosflags()` stream manipulators to format the output so that it displays with two decimal places.

Formatting the Output

You are already familiar with one of the C++ stream manipulators, `endl`, which advances the cursor to the next line on the screen. C++ has many other stream manipulators. For example, C++ has two stream manipulators, called `setprecision()` and `setiosflags()`, which you can use to format your program's output. Unlike the `endl` stream manipulator, which is defined in the iostream.h header file, the `setprecision()` and `setiosflags()` stream manipulators are defined in a header file named iomanip.h.

You use the `setprecision()` manipulator to specify the number of decimal places to display in the output's numbers. The syntax of the `setprecision()` manipulator is **setprecision**(*number*), where *number* represents the number of decimal places. `setprecision(2)`, for example, tells C++ to display two decimal places in the numbers. The `setprecision()` manipulator's setting remains in effect until the program encounters another `setprecision()` manipulator.

You can also format a program's numeric output with the `setiosflags()` manipulator, whose syntax is **setiosflags**(*formatflag*). The *formatflag* argument represents one or more C++ format options. For example, to display numbers in fixed notation, rather than e (exponential) notation, you use the *formatflag* `ios::fixed`. (Notice the two colons between `ios` and `fixed`.) To make sure that numbers display with a decimal point, you use the *formatflag* `ios::showpoint`.

You can include more than one *formatflag* in the `setiosflags` manipulator; you simply separate each *formatflag* with a pipe symbol (|). For example, `setiosflags(ios::fixed | ios::showpoint)` tells C++ to display the numeric output in fixed notation, and to include a decimal point in the display of whole numbers. Include both the `setprecision()` and `setiosflags()` manipulators in the current program. Set the precision to two decimal places.

To include the `setprecision()` and `setiosflags()` manipulators in the current program:

1 The LaProg02 program should be open. In the blank line below the `#include <math.h>` directive, type `#include <iomanip.h>` and press the **Enter** key.

2 In the blank line below the `//display monthly payments` comment, type **cout << setprecision(2) << setiosflags(ios::fixed | ios::showpoint);**.

3 Save, build, and execute the program. When prompted, enter the following information:

Principal: 12000

Rebate: 3000

Credit union rate: **.11**

Dealer rate: .05

Term: 3

The program calculates and displays the monthly payments as 294.65 and 359.65. Notice that C++ rounded the 294.648 to 294.65.

4 Press the **Enter** key to close the DOS window, then close the Output window.

All of the programs you have written so far have sent the output to the screen. Many times, however, you will need to print a program's output. You can print the output by first sending it to a file, and then using C++ to open and print the file.

Sending Output to a File

To send a program's output to a file, you must include the fstream.h header file in your program. This header file contains the definition of the ofstream (the *of* stands for *output file*) class. You can use the ofstream class to create an object that represents an output file. Modify the current program so that it sends the output to a file.

OOP
Concepts

As you may remember from Tutorial 1, a class is a pattern from which an object can be made. The output file object that you make will be an instance of the ofstream class.

tip
....
If the concept of classes and objects is confusing to you, think of the ofstream class as being similar to a data type, and the output file object as being similar to a variable.

To modify the current program:

1 In the blank line below the #include <iomanip.h> directive, type **#include <fstream.h>** and press the **Enter** key.

You will now create an ofstream object, which you will name outFile.

2 In the blank line below the float dealerFinanced = (float) 0.0; statement, type **ofstream outFile;** and press the **Enter** key.

In addition to including the fstream.h header file and creating an ofstream object, you also need to open the output file and give it a name. You will name the file LbProg02.dat.

3 In the blank line below the ofstream outFile; statement, type **outFile.open("LbProg02.dat");** and press the **Enter** key. This statement opens a file named LbProg02.dat for output.

The final step is to send the output to the file.

4 In the blank line below the //save output in a file for printing comment, type **outFile << setprecision(2) << setiosflags(ios::fixed | ios:: showpoint);** and press the **Enter** key. Then type **outFile << "Rebate and credit union financing: " << creditFinanced << endl;** and press the **Enter** key, and then type **outFile << "No rebate and dealer financing: " << dealerFinanced << endl;** and press the **Enter** key. Notice that these three statements are identical to the statements found below the //display monthly payments comment, except cout was replaced with outFile. cout tells C++ to send the output to the screen, and outFile tells C++ to send the output to the file object. The instructions that pertain to sending the program output to a file are highlighted in Figure 4-32, which shows the completed LbProg02 program.

```
//LbProg02.cpp
//this program calculates and displays monthly car payments, and
//saves the program output to a file for printing

#include <iostream.h>
#include <math.h>
#include <iomanip.h>
#include <fstream.h>

//function prototypes
float calcMthlyPay(short, short, float, short);

void main()
{
    //declare and initialize variables
    short principal      = 0;
    short rebate         = 0;
    float creditRate     = (float) 0.0;
    float dealerRate     = (float) 0.0;
    short term           = 0;
    float creditFinanced = (float) 0.0;
    float dealerFinanced = (float) 0.0;
    ofstream outFile;
    outFile.open("LbProg02.dat");

    //enter the input items
    cout << "Enter the principal: ";
    cin >> principal;
    cout << "Enter the rebate amount: ";
    cin >> rebate;
    cout << "Enter the credit union rate: ";
    cin >> creditRate;
    cout << "Enter the dealer rate: ";
    cin >> dealerRate;
    cout << "Enter the term: ";
    cin >> term;

    //calculate monthly payments
    creditFinanced = calcMthlyPay(principal, rebate, creditRate/12, term * 12);
    dealerFinanced = calcMthlyPay(principal, 0, dealerRate/12, term * 12);

    //display monthly payments
    cout << setprecision(2) << setiosflags(ios::fixed | ios::showpoint);
    cout << "Rebate and credit union financing: " << creditFinanced << endl;
    cout << "No rebate and dealer financing: " << dealerFinanced << endl;

    //save output in a file for printing
    outFile << setprecision(2) << setiosflags(ios::fixed | ios::showpoint);
    outFile << "Rebate and credit union financing: " << creditFinanced << endl;
    outFile << "No rebate and dealer financing: " << dealerFinanced << endl;

} //end of main function

//*****programmer-defined function definitions*****

float calcMthlyPay(short principal, short rebate, float rate, short months)
{
    float tempPay = (float) 0.0;
    tempPay = (float) (principal - rebate) *
        rate / (1 - (float) pow(rate + 1, (float) - months));
    return tempPay;
} //end of calcMthlyPay function
```

Figure 4-32: Completed monthly payment program showing instructions that send output to a file

5 Save, build, and execute the program. When prompted, enter the following information:

Principal: 12000

Rebate: 3000

Credit union rate: .11

Dealer rate: .05

Term: 3

6 Press the **Enter** key to close the DOS window, then close the Output window.

Now use C++ to print the LbProg02.dat output file.

7 Click **File** on the menu bar, then click **Open**. The Open dialog box appears. Click the **Files of type list arrow**, then click **All Files** (*.*) in the list of file types. Click **LbProg02.dat** in the list of filenames, then click the **Open** button. The LbProg02.dat file appears in the LbProg02.dat window, as shown in Figure 4-33.

data filename

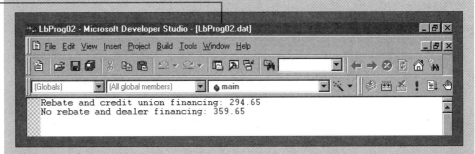

Figure 4-33: LbProg02.dat window showing the contents of the output file

8 Click **File** on the menu bar, then click **Print**, and then click the **OK** button. You have completed this program, so you can close it.

9 Close the workspace and the Output window.

mini-quiz

Mini-Quiz 4

1. Which of the following tells C++ to display numbers with zero decimal places?
   a. `setiosflags(0)`
   b. `setiosflags(zero)`
   c. `setprecision(0)`
   d. `setprecision(zero)`

2. Which of the following tells C++ to display numbers in fixed notation?
   a. `setiosflags(fixed)`
   b. `setiosflags(fixed::ios)`
   c. `setiosflags(ios, fixed)`
   d. `setiosflags(ios::fixed)`

3. You include more than one *formatflag* in the `setiosflags` manipulator by separating each with a(n) _____ .
   a. /
   b. \
   c. &
   d. :
   e. |

4. Which of the following statements opens a file named temp.dat for output?
   a. `outFile.open("temp.dat");`
   b. `fileOut.output("temp.dat");`
   c. `openFile.out("temp.dat");`
   d. `fileOpen.out("temp.dat");`
   e. `out.fileOpen("temp.dat");`

You have now completed Lesson B. You can either exit Visual C++ and take a break or complete the questions and exercises at the end of the lesson.

SUMMARY

You create and invoke a value-returning function in the same manner that you create and invoke a void function—by entering one or more function calls and a function definition in the program. If the function definition appears in the programmer-defined section, below the `main` function, you will also need to enter a function prototype. The function prototype, as well as the function definition's header, must begin with a data type, which indicates the type of data the function is to return. The function definition must end with a `return` statement that returns a value to the caller. Unlike a void function call, a call to a value-returning function usually does not appear as a statement by itself; rather, it is typically part of another statement.

You can use the C++ `setprecision()` and `setiosflags()` stream manipulators to format a program's numeric output; both manipulators are defined in the iomanip.h header file. The `setprecision()` manipulator allows you to specify the number of decimal places to display in the numbers. The **setiosflags** (*formatflags*) manipulator allows you to specify *formatflags* that control the format of the output. For example, the `ios::fixed` *formatflag* tells C++ to display the numbers in fixed notation, rather than e (exponential) notation. The `ios:: showpoint` *formatflag* tells C++ to display whole numbers with a decimal point. To include more than one *formatflag* in the `setiosflags` manipulator, you separate each *formatflag* with a pipe symbol (|).

To send output to a file, you need to include the fstream.h header file in your program. This allows you to create an `ofstream` object that represents the output file. After creating the output file object, you then open the file and give it a name. You send the output to the open file by using the object's name, along with the insertion operator, in a statement.

ANSWERS TO MINI-QUIZZES

Mini-Quiz 3

1.
```
float calcBonus(float sales)
{
    float bonusAmt = (float) 0.0;
    bonusAmt = sales * .03;
    return bonusAmt;
} //end of calcBonus function
```

2. `float calcBonus(float);`

3. `calcBonus(mthlySales);`

Mini-Quiz 4

1. c **2.** d **3.** e **4.** a

QUESTIONS

1. Which of the following are void functions?
   a. `main`
   b. `pow`
   c. `sqrt`
   d. all of the above

2. Which of the following is a function prototype for a value-returning function?
   a. `int quantity();`
   b. `int quantity(float);`
   c. `void quantity(float);`
   d. both a and b
   e. both b and c

3. The data type listed at the beginning of a value-returning function's header indicates the type of data the function will _____ .
   a. return
   b. pass
   c. receive

4. The last statement in a value-returning function is always _____ .

    a. `};`

    b. `result` *expression*;

    c. `return;`

    d. `return` *expression*;

5. Which of the following is false?

    a. A void function's header begins with the keyword **void**.

    b. A value-returning function's header begins with a data type, which represents the type of data the function will return.

    c. Assuming `displayAge` is the name of a void function, `displayAge();` is a both logically and syntactically valid C++ statement.

    d. Assuming `calcNewPrice` is the name of a value-returning function, `calcNewPrice();` is a both logically and syntactically valid C++ statement.

    e. Both void and value-returning functions can receive arguments.

6. Which of the following tells C++ to display numbers in fixed notation, and to include the decimal point when displaying whole numbers?

    a. `setiosflags(ios::fixed | ios::showpoint)`

    b. `setiosflags(ios::fixed , ios::showpoint)`

    c. `setprecision(ios::fixed | ios::showpoint)`

    d. `setprecision(ios::fixed , ios::showpoint)`

7. Which of the following tells C++ to display numbers with two decimal places?

    a. `setdecimal(2)`

    b. `setiosflags(2)`

    c. `setiosflags(2.00)`

    d. `setprecision(2)`

8. To send output to a file, you need to include the _____ header file in your program.

    a. file.h

    b. fstream.h

    c. iomanip.h

    d. iostream.h

    e. ofstream.h

E X E R C I S E S

1. In this exercise, you will create a program that uses both void and value-returning functions.

    a. Create a console application named T4Be01 in the Cpp\Tut04 folder on your computer's hard disk.

    b. Write a program that corresponds to the IPO chart shown in Figure 4-34. Use a value-returning function to calculate and return the cube of the number that is passed to the function. Use a void function to save the output to a file named T4Be01.dat for printing. Format the output to show two decimal places. The output should appear in a fixed format. Whole numbers should display and print with a decimal point. Use a descriptive message to display and print the output.

Input	Processing	Output
number	Processing items: none Algorithm: 1. enter the number 2. call a function to calculate the cube of the number 3. display the cube of the number 4. call a function to save the program output in a file	cube of the number

Figure 4-34

    c. Save, build, and execute the program. When prompted to enter a number, enter the number 3. The output should show that the cube of 3 is 27.

    d. Print the program code, then use C++ to open and print the T4Be01.dat file, which is located in the Cpp\Tut04\T4Be01 folder on your computer's hard disk.

    e. Close both the Output window and the workspace.

2. In this exercise, you will create a program that uses both void and value-returning functions.

    a. Create a console application named T4Be02 in the Cpp\Tut04 folder on your computer's hard disk.

    b. Write a program that corresponds to the IPO chart shown in Figure 4-35. Use a value-returning function to update the age by 1, then return the new age. Use a void function to save the output in a file named T4Be02.dat for printing. Use a descriptive message to display and print the output.

Input	Processing	Output
age	Processing items: none Algorithm: 1. enter the age 2. call a function to calculate the new age by adding 1 to the age 3. display the new age 4. call a function to save the program output in a file	new age

Figure 4-35

    c. Save, build, and execute the program. When prompted to enter a number, enter the number 23. The output should show that the new age is 24.

    d. Print the program code, then use C++ to print the T4Be02.dat file, which is located in the Cpp\Tut04\T4Be02 folder on your computer's hard disk.

    e. Close both the Output window and the workspace.

3. In this exercise, you will create a program that uses both void and value-returning functions.
   a. Create a console application named T4Be03 in the Cpp\Tut04 folder on your computer's hard disk.
   b. Write a program that corresponds to the IPO chart shown in Figure 4-36. Use a value-returning function to calculate and return the amount remaining in inventory. Use a void function to save the output to a file named T4Be03.dat for printing. Format the output to show two decimal places. The output should appear in a fixed format. Whole numbers should display and print with a decimal point. Use a descriptive message to display and print the output.

Input	Processing	Output
current inventory	Processing items: none	current inventory
purchases		purchases
sales	Algorithm:	sales
	1. enter the current inventory, purchases, and sales	new inventory
	2. call a function to calculate the new inventory	
	3. display the current inventory, purchases, sales, and new inventory	
	4. call a function to save the program output in a file	

Figure 4-36

   c. Save, build, and execute the program. To test the program, use 1200 as the current inventory, 300 as the purchases, and 500 as the sales.
   d. Print the program code, then use C++ to print the T4Be03.dat file, which is located in the Cpp\Tut04\T4Be03 folder on your computer's hard disk.
   e. Close both the Output window and the workspace.

4. In this exercise, you will create a program that uses void functions.
   a. Create a console application named T4Be04 in the Cpp\Tut04 folder on your computer's hard disk.
   b. Write a program that corresponds to the IPO chart shown in Figure 4-37. The program should contain three void functions. The first function should get the input values from the user. The second function should calculate both the raise and new salary. The third function should display the output on the screen, and save the output to a file named T4Be04.dat for printing. Format the output to show two decimal places. The output should appear in a fixed format. Whole numbers should display and print with a decimal point. Use a descriptive message to display and print the output.

Input	Processing	Output
current salary raise rate	Processing items: none Algorithm: 1. call a function to enter the current salary and raise rate 2. call a function to calculate the raise and the new salary 3. call a function both to display the current salary, raise rate, raise, and new salary and to save the program output in a file	current salary raise rate raise new salary

Figure 4-37

   c. Save, build, and execute the program. To test the program, use 30000 as the current salary and 4 percent as the raise rate.

   d. Print the program code, then use C++ to print the T4Be04.dat file, which is located in the Cpp\Tut04\T4Be04 folder on your computer's hard disk.

   e. Close both the Output window and the workspace.

5. In this exercise, you will create a program that uses both void and value-returning functions.

   a. Create a console application named T4Be05 in the Cpp\Tut04 folder on your computer's hard disk.

   b. Write a program that corresponds to the IPO chart shown in Figure 4-38. The program should contain two value-returning functions and two void functions. The first value-returning function should calculate and return the raise; the second should calculate and return the new salary. The first void function should get the input values from the user. The second void function should display the output on the screen, and save the output to a file named T4Be05.dat for printing. Format the output to show two decimal places. The output should appear in a fixed format. Whole numbers should display and print with a decimal point. Use a descriptive message to display and print the output.

Input	Processing	Output
current salary raise rate	Processing items: none Algorithm: 1. call a function to enter the current salary and raise rate 2. call a function to calculate the raise 3. call a function to calculate the new salary 4. call a function both to display the current salary, raise rate, raise, and new salary and save the program output in a file	current salary raise rate raise new salary

Figure 4-38

   c. Save, build, and execute the program. To test the program, use 25000 as the current salary and 3 percent as the raise rate.

   d. Print the program code, then use C++ to print the T4Be05.dat file, which is located in the Cpp\Tut04\T4Ae05 folder on your computer's hard disk.

   e. Close both the Output window and the workspace.

discovery ▶ **6.** In this exercise, you will modify Lesson A's Discovery Exercise 6 by changing two of the void functions to value-returning functions, and by including an additional void function.

   a. In Lesson A's Discovery Exercise 6, you learned about the C++ `log10` function, which you can use to calculate the log of a number using a base of 10. In that exercise, you created a program that used three void functions: one to input a number, another to calculate the log, and another to display the output.

   b. Open the T4Ae06.cpp file, which is located in the Cpp\Tut04\T4Ae06 folder on your computer's hard disk. Highlight all of the code, then use the Edit menu to copy the code to the clipboard. Use the File menu to close the file.

   c. Create a console application named T4Be06 in the Cpp\Tut04 folder on your computer's hard disk. Paste the code from the clipboard into the T4Be06.cpp window.

   d. Change the void function that inputs the number to a value-returning function. Also change the void function that calculates the log to a value-returning function.

   e. Add a void function to the program. The void function should save the output to a file for printing. Save the output in a file named T4Be06.dat. Format the output to show two decimal places. The output should display and print in a fixed format. Use a descriptive message to display and print the output.

   f. Save, build, and execute the program. When prompted to enter a number, enter the number 100.

   g. Print the program code, then use C++ to print the T4Be06.dat file, which is located in the T4Be06 folder on your computer's hard disk.

   h. Close both the Output window and the workspace.

discovery ▶ 7. In addition to using the C++ header files, such as iostream.h and math.h, you can also create your own header files. In this exercise, you will create a header file that contains a value-returning function.

   a. Open the file named T4Be07 in the Cpp\Tut04 folder on your computer's hard disk. Notice that this program prompts the user to input a Short Integer number in the range of 1 to 10, then calls a programmer-defined function named cube, passing it the number.

   b. Build the program. The Output window informs you that cube is an undeclared identifier; this is because the cube function is not defined in the program. Rather than defining it in the current program, you will define it in a header file so you will be able to use the cube function in any program that needs it.

   c. Use the Project menu to add a new C/C++ Header File to the project. Name the header file T4Be07. Enter the code shown in Figure 4-39 in the header file.

```
//T4Be07.h
//this header file defines a function that will return the cube of a
//number passed to it

short cube(short number)
{
    return number * number * number;
} //end of cube function
```

Figure 4-39

   d. Use the File menu to save the header file. Also use the File menu to print the header file's code.

   e. Use the Window menu to activate the T4Be07.cpp file. Recall that you use the #include directive to include a header file in a program. If the header file is located in the same folder as the program file, you enclose the header file's name in double quotes, rather than angle brackets, in the #include directive. (The angle brackets tell C++ to look in its include folder for the header file.) Below the #include <iostream.h> directive in the T4Be07.cpp file, type #include "T4Be07.h" and press the Enter key.

   f. Print the program's code. Save, build, and then execute the program. When prompted to enter a number, enter the number 2. The DOS window shows that the cube of the number 2 is 8. Press the Enter key to close the DOS window, then use the File menu to close the workspace. Also close the Output window.

   g. You can also include a programmer-defined header file in another program. Create a console application named T4Be07a in the Cpp\Tut04 folder on your computer's hard disk. Enter the code shown in Figure 4-40 in the T4Be07a.cpp window. Notice that this program allows the user to enter a number in the 1 to 20 range.

```
//T4Be07a.cpp
//this program uses a programmer-defined header file that is located in
//a different folder

#include <iostream.h>

void main()
{
    //declare and initialize variables
    short num = 0;
    short numCubed = 0;

    //enter input item
    cout << "Enter a number between 1 and 20: ";
    cin >> num;

    //call function to cube number
    numCubed = cube(num);

    //display output item
    cout << "The cube is " << numCubed << endl;
} //end of main function
```

Figure 4-40

    h. Recall that the cube function is defined in the T4Be07.h header file, which is located in the c:\Cpp\Tut04\T4Be07 folder. You can include the T4Be07.h header file in the current program by using the following directive: `#include "c:\Cpp\Tut04\T4Be07\T4Be07.h"`. Because the header file is located in a different folder from the program, you need to specify the header file's full path in the directive. In the line below the `#include <iostream.h>` directive in the current program, type `#include "c:\Cpp\Tut04\T4Be07\T4Be07.h"` and press the Enter key.

    i. Print the program's code. Save, build, and then execute the program. When prompted to enter a number, enter the number 13. Press the Enter key to close the DOS window, then close the workspace. Also close the Output window.

discovery ▶ 8. In this exercise, you will complete a program that uses a void function to display a name that is passed to it. The function will also save the output in a file for printing.

    a. Open the T4Be08.cpp file, which is located in the Cpp\Tut04\T4Be08 folder on your computer's hard disk.

    b. The instruction that allows the user to enter the name is missing from the program. Enter the missing instruction.

    c. Create a void function that displays the name on the screen, and also saves the output in a file named T4Be08.dat. Use a meaningful name for the function. Also use a meaningful message when displaying or saving the output—for example, use the message, "You entered the first name," followed by the name the user entered.

    d. Enter the appropriate function prototype and function call.

    e. Save, build, and execute the program. When prompted, type your name and press the Enter key.

    f. Print the code, then use C++ to print the T4Be08.dat file.

    g. Close both the Output window and the workspace.

discovery ▶ 9. In this exercise, you will complete a program that uses a value-returning function to get a name from the user, and then return that name to the main function. You will also need to create a function to save the output in a file for printing.

    a. Open the T4Be09.cpp file, which is located in the Cpp\Tut04\T4Be09 folder on your computer's hard disk.

    b. Notice that the name of the value-returning function is getName. The getName function's header and return statement are missing from the function definition. Enter the two missing instructions.

    c. The call to the getName function is missing. Enter the missing function call.

    d. Write the instructions to create and invoke a void function that saves the output in a file named T4Be09.dat. Use a meaningful name for the function.

    e. Save, build, and execute the program. When prompted, type your name and press the Enter key.

    f. Print the code, then use C++ to print the T4Be09.dat file.

    g. Close both the Output window and the workspace.

debugging 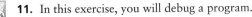 10. In this exercise, you will debug a program.

    a. Open the T4Be10.cpp file, which is located in the Cpp\Tut04\T4Be10 folder on your computer's hard disk.

    b. Print the code.

    c. Build and then execute the program. Enter the number 6 as the first number and the number 5 as the second number. You will notice that the program is not working correctly. Correct the errors. Save the program, then execute it. When the program is working correctly, print the code. On the code printout, indicate what was wrong with the program. Also circle the instructions that you corrected.

    d. Close both the Output window and the workspace.

debugging 11. In this exercise, you will debug a program.

    a. Open the T4Be11.cpp file, which is located in the Cpp\Tut04\T4Be11 folder on your computer's hard disk.

    b. Print the code.

    c. Build the program. Correct any errors. Save the program, then execute it. When the program is working correctly, print the code. On the code printout, indicate what was wrong with the program. Also circle the instructions that you corrected.

    d. Close both the Output window and the workspace.

debugging 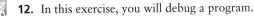 12. In this exercise, you will debug a program.

    a. Open the T4Be12.cpp file, which is located in the Cpp\Tut04\T4Be12 folder on your computer's hard disk.

    b. Print the code.

    c. Build the program. Correct any errors. Save the program, then execute it. When the program is working correctly, print the code. On the code printout, indicate what was wrong with the program. Also circle the instructions that you corrected.

    d. Close both the Output window and the workspace.

debugging 13. In this exercise, you will debug a program.

    a. Open the T4Be13.cpp file, which is located in the Cpp\Tut04\T4Be13 folder on your computer's hard disk.

    b. Print the code.

    c. Build the program. Correct any errors. Save the program, then execute it. When the program is working correctly, print the code. On the code printout, indicate what was wrong with the program. Also circle the instructions that you corrected.

    d. Close both the Output window and the workspace.

The Selection Structure

case Susan Chen, the principal of a local primary school, wants a program that the first and second grade students can use to practice both adding and subtracting numbers. The program should display either an addition or a subtraction problem on the screen, then allow the student to enter the answer, and then verify that the answer is correct. The problems displayed for the first grade students should use numbers from 1 through 10 only; the problems displayed for the second grade students should use numbers from 10 through 100. Because the first and second grade students have not learned about negative numbers yet, the subtraction problems should never ask them to subtract a larger number from a smaller number. Before you can begin coding the math program, you will need to learn about the selection structure. You will use the selection structure to determine whether the student answered the math problem correctly.

LESSON A
o b j e c t i v e s

In this lesson you will learn how to:

■ Write pseudocode for the selection structure

■ Create a flowchart for the selection structure

■ Code the `if` and `if/else` selection structure

■ Write code that uses relational operators and logical operators

■ Write a nested selection structure

■ Include character and string data in comparisons

tip

▶ As you may remember from Tutorial 1, the selection structure is one of the three programming structures. The other two are sequence, which was covered in the previous tutorials, and repetition, which will be covered in Tutorial 6.

condition

The `if` Statement

Using the Selection Structure

The programs you created in the previous four tutorials used the sequence programming structure only, where each of the program instructions was processed, one after another, in the order in which it appeared in the program. In many programs, however, the next instruction to be processed will depend on the result of a decision or a comparison that the program must make. For example, a payroll program might need to determine if an employee worked overtime. Assuming a 40-hour workweek, the program can make that determination by comparing the number of hours the employee worked to the number 40. Based on the result of that comparison, the program will then select either an instruction that computes regular pay or an instruction that computes overtime pay.

You use the **selection structure**, also called the **decision structure**, when you want a program to make a decision or comparison and then, based on the result of that decision or comparison, to select one of two paths. You will need to use the selection structure to complete the math program for Susan Chen.

Each day you probably make hundreds of decisions, some so minor that you might not even realize you've made them. For example, every morning you have to decide if you are hungry and, if you are, what you are going to eat. Figure 5-1 shows other decisions you might have to make today.

Example 1	Example 2
if (it is raining)	if (you have a test tomorrow)
wear a rain coat	study tonight
bring an umbrella	else
	watch a movie

Figure 5-1: Decisions you might need to make today

In the examples shown in Figure 5-1, the portion in parentheses, called the **condition**, specifies the decision you are making and is phrased so that it results in either a true or false answer only. For example, either it's raining (true) or it's not raining (false); either you have a test tomorrow (true) or you don't have a test tomorrow (false).

If the condition is true, you perform a specific set of tasks. If the condition is false, however, you might or might not need to perform a different set of tasks. For instance, look at the first example shown in Figure 5-1. If it is raining (a true condition), then you will wear a raincoat and bring an umbrella. Notice, however, that you do not have anything in particular to do if it is not raining (a false condition).

Compare this to the second example shown in Figure 5-1. If you have a test tomorrow (a true condition), then you will study tonight. If you do not have a test tomorrow (a false condition), however, then you will watch a movie.

Including the Selection Structure in Pseudocode

Like you, the computer can also evaluate a condition and then select the appropriate tasks to perform based on that evaluation. The programmer must be sure to phrase the condition so that it results in either a true or a false answer only. The programmer must also specify the tasks to be performed when the condition is true and, if necessary, the tasks to be performed when the condition is false. Programmers refer to this as the selection structure (or the decision structure). Most programming languages offer three forms of the selection structure: `if`, `if/else`, and `case`. You will learn about the `if` and `if/else` forms of the selection structure in this tutorial; the `case` form is covered in Appendix C. Figure 5-2 shows examples of both the `if` and the `if/else` selection structures written in pseudocode.

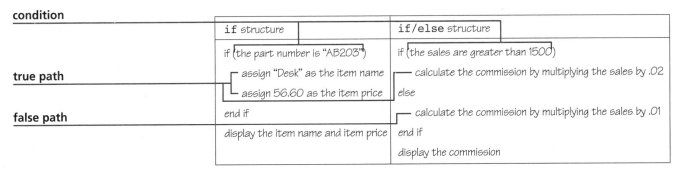

Figure 5-2: Examples of the `if` and `if/else` selection structures written in pseudocode

Although pseudocode is not standardized—every programmer has his or her own version—you will find some similarities among the various versions. For example, many programmers begin the selection structure with the word `if` and end the structure with the two words `end if`; they also use the word `else` to designate the instructions to be performed when the condition is false.

In the examples shown in Figure 5-2, the portion shown in parentheses indicates the condition to be evaluated. Notice that each condition results in either a true or a false answer only. Either the part number is "AB203" or it isn't; either the sales are greater than the number 1500 or they aren't.

When the condition is true, the set of instructions following the condition is selected for processing. The instructions following the condition are referred to as the true path—the path you follow when the condition is true. The true path ends when you come to the `else` or, if there is no `else`, when you come to the end of the selection structure (the `end if`). After the true path instructions are processed, the instruction following the `end if` is processed. In the examples shown in Figure 5-2, the display instructions would be processed after the instructions in the true path.

The instructions selected for processing when the condition is false—the false path—depend on whether the selection structure contains an `else`. When there is no `else`, as in the first example shown in Figure 5-2, the instruction following the `end if` is processed when the condition is false. In the first example, for instance, the "display the item name and item price" instruction is processed when the part number is not "AB203." In cases where the selection structure contains an `else`, as in the second example shown in Figure 5-2, the instructions between the `else` and the `end if` are processed before the instruction after the `end if` is processed. In the second example, the "calculate the commission by multiplying the sales by .01" instruction is processed first, followed by the "display the commission" instruction.

Besides using pseudocode, programmers also use flowcharts to help them plan algorithms. In the next section, you will learn how to show the selection structure in a flowchart.

Drawing a Flowchart of a Selection Structure

Unlike pseudocode, which consists of English-like statements, a flowchart uses standardized symbols to show the steps the computer needs to take to accomplish the program's goal. Figure 5-3 shows Figure 5-2's examples in flowchart form.

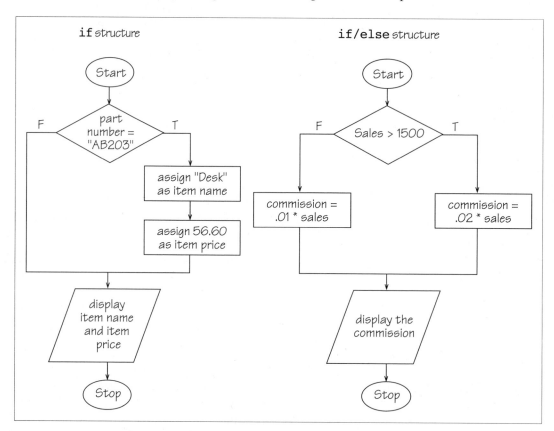

Figure 5-3: Examples of the `if` and `if/else` selection structure drawn in flowchart form

Recall from Tutorial 2 that the oval in the figure is the start/stop symbol, the rectangle is the process symbol, and the parallelogram is the input/output symbol. The new symbol in the flowchart, the diamond, is called the **selection/repetition symbol** because it is used to represent both selection and repetition. In Figure 5-3's flowcharts, the diamonds represent the selection structure. (You will learn how to

You can also mark the flowlines leading out of the diamond with a "Y" and an "N" (for yes and no).

Recall from Tutorial 2 that flowlines are the lines that connect the flowchart symbols.

use the diamond to represent repetition in Tutorial 6.) Notice that inside each diamond is a question that has a true or false answer only. Each diamond also has one flowline entering the symbol and two flowlines leaving the symbol. The two flowlines leading out of the diamond should be marked so that anyone reading the flowchart can distinguish the true path from the false path. You mark the flowline leading to the true path with a "T" (for true), and you mark the flowline leading to the false path with an "F" (for false).

Next, learn how to code both the if and if/else selection structures in C++.

Coding the if and if/else Selection Structures in C++

You use the if statement to code both the if and the if/else selection structures in C++. The syntax of the if statement is shown in Figure 5-4.

if (*condition*)

    one statement, or a block of statements enclosed in braces, to be processed
    when the condition is true

[**else**

    one statement, or a block of statements enclosed in braces, to be processed
    when the condition is false]

//end if

Important note: In the syntax, items in **bold** are required. Items contained in square brackets, on the other hand, are optional. Items in *italics* indicate places where the programmer must supply information pertaining to the current program.

Figure 5-4: Syntax of the if statement

The items in square brackets ([ ]) in the syntax are optional. For example, you do not need to include the else portion of the syntax (referred to as the else clause) in an if statement. Items in **bold**, however, are essential components of the if statement. The word if, for instance, must be included in the statement's if clause, and so must the parentheses that surround the *condition*. The word else must be included only if the statement uses the else clause.

Items in italics in the syntax indicate where the programmer must supply information pertaining to the current program. For instance, the programmer must supply the *condition* to be evaluated. The *condition* must be enclosed in a set of parentheses and it must be a Boolean expression, which is an expression that results in either a True or False value only. The True and False values are called logical, or **Boolean**, values.

In addition to supplying the *condition*, the programmer must also supply the statements to be processed when the *condition* is true and, optionally, when the *condition* is false. If more than one statement needs to be processed when the *condition* is either true or false, the statements must be entered as a statement block. You create a statement block by enclosing the statements in a set of braces ({ }).

The Boolean values *True* and *False* are named after the English mathematician George Boole (1815–1864), who invented Boolean algebra—an algebra that is based on only two numbers, 0 and 1. In Boolean algebra, 0 stands for False and 1 stands for True.

Recall from Tutorial 4 that a function is one example of a statement block—a group of statements enclosed in a set of braces.

Although it is not required in the `if` statement, it is a good programming practice to mark the end of the `if` statement with a comment, such as `//end if`. The comment will make your program easier to read and understand. It will also help you to keep track of the required `if` and `else` statements when you begin nesting `if` statements—in other words, including one `if` statement inside another `if` statement. You will learn how to nest `if` statements later in this lesson.

As mentioned earlier, the `if` statement's *condition* must be a Boolean expression, which is an expression that results in either a True or False value only. The Boolean expression can contain variables, constants, functions, mathematical operators, relational operators, and logical operators. You already know about variables, constants, functions, and the mathematical operators. You will learn about the relational operators and the logical operators in the following sections.

Relational Operators

Figure 5-5 lists the relational operators that you can use to make comparisons in a program. The figure also shows the order of precedence for the relational operators.

Entering a space between the symbols in a relational operator (for example, entering > =, < =, = =, or ! =) is a syntax error. Reversing the symbols in a relational operator (for example, entering =>, =<, or = !) is also a syntax error. Always use >=, <=, and !=.

Operator	Operation	Precedence number
<	less than	1
<=	less than or equal to	1
>	greater than	1
>=	greater than or equal to	1
==	equal to	2
!=	not equal to	2
Important note: Notice that four of the operators are composed of two symbols. When using these operators, do not include any spaces between the symbols. Also be sure you do not reverse the symbols—in other words, use >=, but don't use =>.		

Figure 5-5: Relational operators

In many programming languages other than C++, you use one equal sign (=) to test for equality and you use a less-than sign followed by a greater-than sign (<>) to test for inequality.

As Figure 5-5 shows, you test for equality in C++ by using two equal signs (==) rather than one equal sign (=). As you learned in Tutorial 3, you use one equal sign in C++ only to assign a value to a variable or a named constant. To test for inequality in C++, you use an exclamation point, which stands for *not*, followed by an equal sign (!=). Be careful when comparing two Float values. Because some Float values cannot be stored, precisely, in memory, you should never compare Float values for equality or inequality. Rather, test that the difference between the numbers you are comparing is less than some acceptable small value, such as .00001. You will learn how to do this in Lesson A's Discovery Exercise 24.

It is easy to confuse the equality operator (==) with the assignment operator (=). In C++, the num = 1; statement assigns the number 1 to the num variable. The num == 1; statement, on the other hand, tells C++ to compare the contents of the num variable to the number 1.

Figure 5-6 shows some examples of using the relational operators in an if statement's *condition*.

if statement's *condition*	Meaning
if (quantity < 50)	Compares the contents of the quantity variable to the number 50. The *condition* will evaluate to True if the quantity variable contains a number that is less than 50; otherwise, it will evaluate to False.
if (age >= 25)	Compares the contents of the age variable to the number 25. The *condition* will evaluate to True if the age variable contains a number that is greater than or equal to 25; otherwise, it will evaluate to False.
if (onhand == target)	Compares the contents of the onhand variable to the contents of the target variable. The *condition* will evaluate to True if the onhand variable contains a number that is equal to the number in the target variable; otherwise, it will evaluate to False.
if (quantity != 7500)	Compares the contents of the quantity variable to the number 7500. The *condition* will evaluate to True if the quantity variable contains a number that is not equal to 7500; otherwise, it will evaluate to False.

Figure 5-6: Examples of relational operators in an if statement's *condition*

You will notice that the expression contained in each *condition* evaluates to either the Boolean value True or the Boolean value False. All expressions containing a relational operator will result in either a True or False answer only.

As with the mathematical operators, if an expression contains more than one relational operator with the same precedence number, C++ evaluates the operators from left to right in the expression. Keep in mind, however, that relational operators are evaluated after any mathematical operators in the expression. In other words, in the expression $5 - 2 > 1 + 2$, the two mathematical operators (− and +) will be evaluated before the relational operator (>). The result of the expression is False, as shown in Figure 5-7.

Evaluation steps	Result
Original expression	5 – 2 > 1 + 2
5 – 2 is evaluated first	3 > 1 + 2
1 + 2 is evaluated second	3 > 3
3 > 3 is evaluated last	False

Figure 5-7: Evaluation steps for an expression containing mathematical and relational operators

When included in a C++ program, the expression shown in Figure 5-7 results in the number 0. In C++, the number 0 represents the Boolean value False.

In the next section, you will open a partially completed program that will allow you to experiment with relational operators in an `if` statement's *condition*.

Using Relational Operators in an `if` Statement

The LaProg01.cpp file, which is located in the Cpp\Tut05\LaProg01 folder on your computer's hard disk, will allow you to experiment with relational operators in an `if` statement's *condition*.

To open the partially completed LaProg01.cpp program:

1   Start Visual C++. Open the **LaProg01.cpp** file, which is located in the Cpp\Tut05\LaProg01 folder on your computer's hard disk. The LaProg01 program, which appears in the LaProg01.cpp window, is shown in Figure 5-8.

```cpp
//LaProg01.cpp
//this program demonstrates the if statement

#include <iostream.h>

void main()
{
    //declare and initialize variable
    short numberInput = 0;

    //enter input value
    cout << "Enter a number: ";
    cin >> numberInput;

    //display output

} //end of main function
```

Figure 5-8: Partially completed LaProg01 program

After declaring and initializing a Short Integer variable named `numberInput`, the program prompts the user to enter a number; it then stores the user's response in the `numberInput` variable.

Assume that you want the LaProg01 program to display the string "Negative number" if the number you enter is less than 0. Figure 5-9 shows the flowchart, pseudocode, and C++ code for the selection structure that will accomplish this.

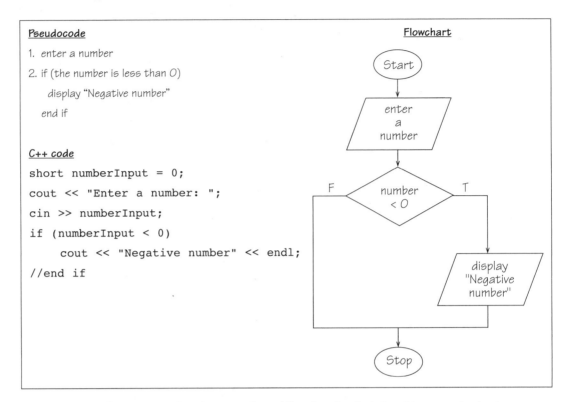

Pseudocode

1. enter a number
2. if (the number is less than 0)
    display "Negative number"
   end if

C++ code

```cpp
short numberInput = 0;
cout << "Enter a number: ";
cin >> numberInput;
if (numberInput < 0)
    cout << "Negative number" << endl;
//end if
```

Figure 5-9: Pseudocode, C++ code, and flowchart for the LaProg01 program's selection structure

The `(numberInput < 0)` *condition* in the C++ code shown in Figure 5-9 tells C++ to compare the contents of the `numberInput` variable to the number 0. If the *condition* is true, which means the number entered is less than 0, then the selection structure displays "Negative number" on the screen. If the *condition* is false, which means the number entered is not less than 0 (in other words, it's greater than or equal to 0), the `if` selection structure does not display anything on the screen. Enter the `if` selection structure in the LaProg01 program.

To enter the `if` selection structure in the LaProg01 program:

1   In the blank line below the `//display output` comment, type **if (numberInput < 0)** and press the **Enter** key. Be sure to type the number 0, and not the letter O. Notice that you do not put a semicolon after the **if** clause.

Now enter the true path instructions. Programmers usually indent these instructions to make them easier to read. You will notice that Visual C++ indents the instructions within the true path for you.

2   Type **cout << "Negative number" << endl;** and press the **Enter** key. Because the true path needs only one statement, you do not need to enclose the statement in braces.

3   To document the end of the selection structure, type **//end if** and press the **Enter** key. Compare the instructions you entered to the highlighted instructions shown in Figure 5-10.

```cpp
//LaProg01.cpp
//this program demonstrates the if statement

#include <iostream.h>

void main()
{
    //declare and initialize variable
    short numberInput = 0;

    //enter input value
    cout << "Enter a number: ";
    cin >> numberInput;

    //display output
    if (numberInput < 0)
        cout << "Negative number" << endl;
    //end if

} //end of main function
```

selection structure

Figure 5-10: `if` selection structure entered in the program

4   Save, build, and then execute the program.

5   When prompted to enter a number, type **–25** (be sure to type the minus sign) and press the **Enter** key. The string "Negative number" appears in the DOS window. In this case, because the number entered is less than zero—a true *condition*—C++ processes the true path statement before processing the main function's closing brace (**}**).

6   Press the **Enter** key to close the DOS window, then close the Output window.

Now observe how the program responds when you enter a positive, rather than a negative, number.

tip

C++ does not process the `//end if` comment that marks the end of the selection structure. As you may remember from Tutorial 2, the compiler ignores comments when it translates the source code into object code.

7 Execute the program again. Type **500** and press the **Enter** key. This time the program does not display "Negative number" on the screen. Notice that when the number you enter is not less than zero—a false *condition*—the instruction in the true path is not processed. Instead, C++ processes the instruction following the end of the selection structure; in this case, the **main** function's closing brace, which marks the end of the **main** function, is processed.

8 Press the **Enter** key to close the DOS window.

Modifying the `if` Selection Structure in a Program

Now assume that you want the LaProg01 program to display the string "Negative number" when the number entered by the user is less than zero, and the string "Positive number" when the number is greater than or equal to zero. Figure 5-11 shows both the flowchart and the pseudocode to accomplish this.

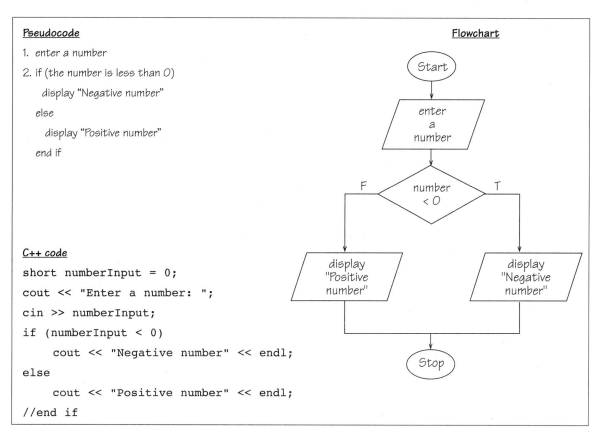

Pseudocode

1. enter a number
2. if (the number is less than 0)
   display "Negative number"
   else
   display "Positive number"
   end if

C++ code

```
short numberInput = 0;
cout << "Enter a number: ";
cin >> numberInput;
if (numberInput < 0)
    cout << "Negative number" << endl;
else
    cout << "Positive number" << endl;
//end if
```

Figure 5-11: Modified pseudocode, C++ code, and flowchart for the LaProg01 program

Now modify the current program to include an `else` clause (a false path) in the `if` statement.

To modify the LaProg01 program:

1 Enter the additional instructions highlighted in Figure 5-12.

```
//LaProg01.cpp
//this program demonstrates the if statement

#include <iostream.h>

void main()
{
    //declare and initialize variable
    short numberInput = 0;

    //enter input value
    cout << "Enter a number: ";
    cin >> numberInput;

    //display output
    if (numberInput < 0)
        cout  << "Negative number" << endl;
    else
        cout  << "Positive number" << endl;
    //end if

} //end of main function
```

enter these instructions

Figure 5-12: `else` clause entered in the `if` selection structure

2 Save, build, and then execute the program.

First enter a negative number.

3 When prompted to enter a number, type **–15** (be sure to type the minus sign) and press the **Enter** key. "Negative number" appears in the DOS window. Press the **Enter** key to close the DOS window.

Now see how the program responds when you enter a positive number.

4 Execute the program again. When prompted to enter a number, type **5** and press the **Enter** key. This time, "Positive number" appears in the DOS window. Press the **Enter** key to close the DOS window, then close the Output window.

Recall that you can also use logical operators to form the `if` statement's *condition*. You will learn about that next.

mini-quiz

Mini-Quiz 1

1. Assume that a program needs to determine if a student's score is less than or equal to 69. If it is, display the "Fail" message; otherwise, display the "Pass" message. Write the pseudocode for this selection structure.

2. Write an `if` statement that compares the contents of the `quantity` variable to the number 10. If the `quantity` variable contains a number that is greater than 10, display the string "Over 10"; otherwise, display the string "Not over 10".

3. Write a *condition* for an `if` statement that checks if the Short Integer `quantity` variable contains the number 100.

4. Which of the following assigns the number *5* to the `area` variable?

   a. `area != 5`   b. `area = 5`   c. `area == 5`   d. `area -> 5`
   e. `area <> 5`

5. Which of the following operators is the equality operator?

   a. `!=`   b. `=`   c. `==`   d. `->`   e. `<>`

6. Which of the following is the inequality operator?

   a. `!=`   b. `=`   c. `==`   d. `->`   e. `<>`

Logical Operators

tip

Logical operators are also referred to as Boolean operators.

In addition to using mathematical and relational operators, you can use logical operators to combine several *conditions* into one compound *condition*. The most commonly used logical operators are Not, And, and Or. C++ uses special symbols to represent these operators. The Not operator in C++ is an exclamation point (`!`), the And is two ampersands (`&&`), and the Or is two pipe symbols (`||`). Figure 5-13 shows the three logical operators, as well as their C++ symbol, meaning, and order of precedence.

Logical operator	C++ symbol	Meaning	Precedence
Not	`!`	Reverses the value of the *condition*; True becomes False, False becomes True	1
And	`&&`	All *conditions* connected by the And operator must be true for the compound *condition* to be true	2
Or	`||`	Only one of the *conditions* connected by the Or operator needs to be true for the compound *condition* to be true	3

Figure 5-13: Logical operators

The tables shown in Figure 5-14, called **truth tables**, summarize how C++ evaluates the logical operators in an expression.

Truth table for the ! (Not) operator	
Value of *condition*	Value of !*condition*
True	False
False	True

Truth table for the && (And) operator		
Value of *condition1*	Value of *condition2*	Value of *condition1* && *condition2*
True	True	True
True	False	False
False	True	False
False	False	False

Truth Table for the || (Or) operator		
Value of *condition1*	Value of *condition2*	Value of *condition1* || *condition2*
True	True	True
True	False	True
False	True	True
False	False	False

Figure 5-14: Truth tables for the Not, And, and Or logical operators

tip
. . . .

If you use the && **(And)** operator to combine two conditions, C++ does not evaluate
the second condition if the
first condition is False.
Because both conditions
combined with the &&
operator need to be True
for the compound condition
to be True, there is no need
to evaluate the second
condition if the first condition is False. If, on the other
hand, you use the \|\| **(Or)**
operator to combine two
conditions, C++ does not
evaluate the second condition if the first condition is
True. Because only one of
the conditions combined
with the \|\| operator needs
to be True for the com-
pound condition to be True,
there is no need to evaluate
the second condition if the
first condition is True.

As Figure 5-14 indicates, the Not (!) operator reverses the truth value of the *condition*. If the value of the *condition* is True, then the value of !*condition* is False. Likewise, if the value of the *condition* is False, then the value of !*condition* is True. As you can see, the ! operator can be confusing, so it is best to avoid using it if possible. However, you will need to use the ! operator to test for inequality; recall that the inequality operator is !=.

Now look at the truth tables for the And and Or logical operators. Notice that when you use the And (&&) operator to combine two conditions (*condition1* && *condition2*) the resulting compound condition is True only when both conditions are True. If either condition is False or if both conditions are False, then the compound condition is False. Compare that to the Or operator. When you combine conditions using the Or (\|\|) operator, as in *condition1* \|\| *condition2*, notice that the compound condition is False only when both conditions are False. If either condition is True or if both conditions are True, then the compound condition is True. Two examples might help to clarify the difference between the And and the Or operators.

Examples of the And and the Or Operators

Assume that you want to pay a bonus to the A-rated salespeople whose sales total more than $10,000. To receive a bonus, the salesperson must be rated A and he or she must sell more than $10,000 in product. Assuming the program uses the two variables `rate` and `sales`, you can phrase *condition1* as `rate == 'A'` and *condition2* as `sales > 10000`. Now the question is, should you use the And operator or the Or operator to combine both conditions into one compound condition? To answer this question, you will need to look at the truth tables, shown in Figure 5-14, for the And and the Or operators.

For a salesperson to receive a bonus, remember that both *condition1* (`rate == 'A'`) and *condition2* (`sales > 10000`) must be True at the same time. If either condition is False, or if both conditions are False, then the compound condition should be False, and the salesperson should not receive a bonus. According to the truth tables, both the And and the Or operators will evaluate the compound condition as True when both conditions are True. Only the And operator, however, will evaluate the compound condition as False when either one or both of the conditions are False. The Or operator, you will notice, evaluates the compound condition as False only when *both* conditions are False. Therefore, the correct compound condition to use here is (`rate == 'A' && sales > 10000`).

Now assume that you want to send a letter to all A-rated salespeople and all B-rated salespeople. Assuming the program uses the variable `rate`, you can phrase *condition1* as `rate == 'A'` and *condition2* as `rate == 'B'`. Now which operator do you use—And or Or?

At first it might appear that the And operator is the correct one to use. That is probably because the example says to send the letter to "all A-rated salespeople and all B-rated salespeople." In everyday conversations, you will find that people sometimes use the word *and* when what they really mean is *or*. Although both words do not mean the same thing, using *and* instead of *or* generally does not cause a problem because we are able to infer what another person means. Computers, however, cannot infer anything; they simply process the directions you give them, word for word. In this case, you actually want to send a letter to all salespeople with either an A or a B rating, so you will need to use the Or operator. The Or operator is the only operator that will evaluate the compound condition as True if either one of the conditions is True. The correct compound condition to use here is (`rate == 'A' || rate == 'B'`).

Like expressions containing relational operators, expressions containing logical operators always result in either a True or a False answer. The logical operators have an order of precedence as follows: the Not operator is evaluated first, then the And operator, and then the Or operator. Figure 5-15 shows the order of precedence for the mathematical, relational, and logical operators you have learned so far.

Operator	Operation	Precedence number
( )	Overrides all other normal precedence rules	1
! (Not)	Reverses the value of the *condition*; True becomes False, False becomes True	2
-	Performs negation	3
*, /, %	Performs multiplication, division, and modulus arithmetic	4
+, –	Performs addition and subtraction	5
<, <=, >, >=	Less than, less than or equal to, greater than, greater than or equal to	6
==, !=	Equal to, not equal to	7
&& (And)	All *conditions* connected by the And operator must be true for the compound *condition* to be true	8
|| (Or)	Only one of the *conditions* connected by the Or operator needs to be true for the compound *condition* to be true	9

Figure 5-15: Order of precedence for the mathematical, relational, and logical operators

You will notice that both the And and the Or logical operators are evaluated after any mathematical operators or relational operators in the expression. In other words, in the expression 12 > 0 && 12 < 10 * 2, the mathematical operator (*) is evaluated first, followed by the two relational operators (> and <), followed by the And logical operator (&&). The expression evaluates to True, as shown in Figure 5-16.

Evaluation steps:	Result:
Original Expression	12 > 0 && 12 < 10 * 2
10 * 2 is evaluated first	12 > 0 && 12 < 20
12 > 0 is evaluated second	True && 12 < 20
12 < 20 is evaluated third	True && True
True && True is evaluated last	True

Figure 5-16: Evaluation steps for an expression containing mathematical, relational, and logical operators

When included in a C++ program, the expression shown in Figure 5-16 results in the number 1. In C++, the number 1, as well as any nonzero number, represents the Boolean value True.

Now assume that you want the LaProg01 program, which is currently open, to display the string "In-range" when the number entered by the user is greater than or equal to 1500, but less than 3000. If the number does not fall in that range, then you want to display the string "Out-of-range." Figure 5-17 shows both the pseudocode and the flowchart to accomplish this.

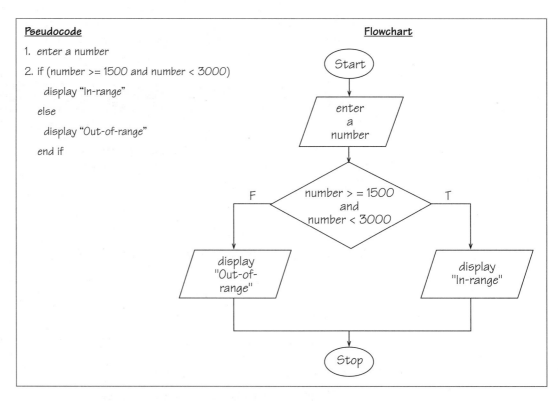

Figure 5-17: Pseudocode and flowchart for the revised LaProg01 program

To modify the selection structure to use relational and logical operators:

1 The LaProg01 program should be open. Modify the code in the current program's selection structure as highlighted in Figure 5-18.

relational operator

logical operator

relational operator

```
//LaProg01.cpp
//this program demonstrates the if statement

#include <iostream.h>

void main()
{
    //declare and initialize variable
    short numberInput = 0;

    //enter input value
    cout << "Enter a number: ";
    cin >> numberInput;

    //display output
    if (numberInput >= 1500 && numberInput < 3000)
        cout  <<  "In-range" << endl;
    else
        cout << "Out-of-range" << endl;
    //end if

} //end of main function
```

Figure 5-18: Selection structure showing relational and logical operators

2 Save, build, and then execute the program. When prompted to enter a number, type **2500** and press the **Enter** key. The string "In-range" appears in the DOS window because the number 2500 satisfies both of the conditions listed in the compound condition—it is greater than or equal to 1500 and it is less than 3000. Press the **Enter** key to close the DOS window. Now try a value that will return the "Out-of-range" message.

3 Execute the program again. When prompted to enter a number, type **6500** and press the **Enter** key. The string "Out-of-range" appears in the DOS window because the number 6500 does not satisfy both of the conditions listed in the compound condition. Although 6500 is greater than or equal to 1500, it is not less than 3000. Press the **Enter** key to close the DOS window, then close the Output window.

Now you will modify the code to see what happens when you use the Or operator, instead of the And operator, in the `if` statement.

To modify the code to use the Or operator:

1 Change the `&&` in the `if` statement's *condition* to ||. The *condition* should now say (`numberInput >= 1500 || numberInput < 3000`).

2 Save, build, and then execute the program. When prompted to enter a number, type **2500** and press the **Enter** key. The string "In-range" appears in the DOS window because the number 2500 satisfies both conditions listed in the compound condition. Press the **Enter** key to close the DOS window.

3 Execute the program again. When prompted to enter a number, type **6500** and press the **Enter** key. The string "In-range" appears in the DOS window because the number 6500 satisfies one of the conditions listed in the compound condition—specifically, the number 6500 is greater than or equal to the number 1500. Remember, when you use the Or operator, only one of the conditions needs to be true for the compound condition to be True. Press the **Enter** key to close the DOS window.

4 Execute the program again. When prompted to enter a number, type **3** and press the **Enter** key. The string "In-range" appears in the DOS window because the number 3 satisfies one of the conditions listed in the compound condition—specifically, the number 3 is less than the number 3000. Press the **Enter** key to close the DOS window.

By changing the And to an Or, the *condition* (`numberInput >= 1500 || numberInput < 3000`) will always evaluate as True; it will never evaluate as False because all numbers lie within this range.

5 Change the `||` back to `&&` in the `if` statement's condition, then save the program.

You are finished experimenting with this program, so you can close it.

6 Close the workspace and the Output window.

You can also use a character comparison in an `if` statement. You will try that next.

mini-quiz

Mini-Quiz 2

1. Use the truth tables shown in Figure 5-14 to help you evaluate the following compound condition: (`True || False`).

2. Use the truth tables shown in Figure 5-14 to help you evaluate the following compound condition: (`7 > 3 && 5 < 2`).

3. Use the truth tables shown in Figure 5-14 to help you evaluate the following compound condition: (`5 * 4 < 20 || False`).

4. Write a compound condition for an `if` statement that checks if the value in the `age` variable is between 30 and 40, including 30 and 40.

5. Write a compound condition for an `if` statement that checks if the value in the `age` variable is either less than 30 or greater than 50.

6. Evaluate the following expression: `4 * 3 < (6 + 7) && 7 < 6 + 9`.

Using a Character Comparison in an if Statement

Assume you want a program to display the word "Pass" if the user enters the letter P, and the word "Fail" if the user enters anything else. Open a character comparison program which already contains an `if` statement that will accomplish this.

To open the LaProg02 program:

1 Open the **LaProg02.cpp** file, which is located in the Cpp\Tut05\LaProg02 folder on your computer's hard disk. The character comparison program, which appears in the LaProg02.cpp window, is shown in Figure 5-19.

```
//LaProg02.cpp
//this program demonstrates how to compare characters

#include <iostream.h>

void main()
{
    //declare and initialize variable
    char letter = ' ';

    //enter input item
    cout << "Enter a letter: ";
    cin >> letter;

    //display output
    if (letter == 'P')
        cout << "Pass" << endl;
    else
        cout << "Fail" << endl;
    //end if

} //end of main function
```

Figure 5-19: LaProg02 program instructions

tip

As you learned in Tutorial 3, character literal constants—for example, the letter 'P'—are enclosed in single quotes. However, string literal constants—for example, the word "Pass"—are enclosed in double quotes.

You will notice that the program prompts the user to enter a letter. The user's response is stored in the `letter` variable. The selection structure then compares the contents of the `letter` variable to the uppercase letter P. If the `letter` variable contains the uppercase letter P, the program displays the string "Pass"; otherwise, it displays the string "Fail."

2 Build and execute the program. When prompted to enter a letter, type **P** (be sure to use an uppercase P) and press the **Enter** key. The string "Pass" appears in the DOS window. Press the **Enter** key to close the DOS window.

Next you will enter a letter other than the letter P.

3 Execute the program again. When prompted to enter a letter, type **K** and press the **Enter** key. The string "Fail" appears in the DOS window. Press the **Enter** key to close the DOS window.

Now enter a lowercase letter p.

4 Execute the program again. When prompted to enter a letter, type **p** (be sure to type a lowercase p) and press the **Enter** key. Although one might expect the word "Pass" to appear, the word "Fail" appears instead. You will learn how to fix this problem in the next section. Press the **Enter** key to close the DOS window, then close the Output window.

As is true in many programming languages, character comparisons in C++ are case sensitive. That means that the uppercase version of a letter is not the same as its lowercase counterpart. So, although a human recognizes P and p as being the same letter, a computer does not; to a computer, a P is different from a p. The `toupper` function can be used to address this problem.

The `toupper` Function

The `toupper` function works only on Character variables; it does not work on String variables. As you will learn later in this lesson, you use the C++ `stricmp` function to perform case-insensitive string comparisons.

As you observed in the LaProg02 program, a problem occurs when you need to include a character, entered by the user, in a comparison. The problem occurs because you cannot control the case in which the user enters the character. One way of handling the character comparison problem is to include the `toupper` (which stands for *to uppercase*) function in your character comparisons. The syntax of the `toupper` function, which is defined in the ctype.h header file, is **toupper**(*charactervariable*). The `toupper` function requires one actual argument: the name of a Character variable. Recall that a Character variable is a variable that can store precisely one character. The `toupper` function returns the uppercase equivalent of the character stored in the *charactervariable*. This function does not actually change the character in the variable to uppercase. Figure 5-20 shows some examples of the `toupper` function.

`toupper` **function**	**Result**
`if (toupper(letter) == 'P')`	Compares the uppercase version of the character entered in the `letter` variable to the character P
`if (toupper(code) > toupper(key))`	Compares the uppercase version of the character entered in the `code` variable to the uppercase version of the character entered in the `key` variable
`letter = toupper(code)`	Assigns the uppercase version of the character contained in the `code` variable to the `letter` variable
`code = toupper(code)`	Changes the contents of the `code` variable to uppercase

Figure 5-20: Examples of the `toupper` function

In the character comparison program, LaProg02.cpp, you will need to change the `if` statement's condition from (`letter == 'P'`) to (`toupper(letter) == 'P'`). Then when C++ processes the `if` statement, the `toupper` function will return the uppercase equivalent of the character stored in the `letter` variable. C++ will then compare the uppercase version of the character to the uppercase letter P. If both are equal, C++ will process the true path instructions; otherwise, it will process the false path instructions. Because the condition includes the `toupper` function, the user can enter the letter P in any case and have the "Pass" message appear.

C++ also has a `tolower` function that temporarily converts a character to lowercase. To produce the same results in the LaProg02 program, you could use the `tolower` function as follows: `(tolower(letter) == 'p')`.

When using the `toupper` function, be sure that everything you are comparing is in uppercase. In other words, `(toupper(letter) == 'p')` is incorrect because it tells C++ to compare the uppercase version of a character to the lowercase letter p; this condition would always evaluate as False.

To modify the character comparison program to include the `toupper` function:

1 Enter the `#include <ctype.h>` directive and the `toupper` function that are highlighted in Figure 5-21.

enter this directive

enter the `toupper` function

```
//LaProg02.cpp
//this program demonstrates how to compare characters

#include <iostream.h>
#include <ctype.h>

void main()
{
    //declare and initialize variable
    char letter = ' ';

    //enter input item
    cout << "Enter a letter: ";
    cin >> letter;

    //display output
    if (toupper(letter) == 'P')
        cout << "Pass" << endl;
    else
        cout << "Fail" << endl;
    //end if

} //end of main function
```

Figure 5-21: `#include <ctype.h>` directive and the `toupper` function entered in the program

2 Save, build, and then execute the program. When prompted to enter a letter, type **p** and press the **Enter** key. This time "Pass" appears in the DOS window. Press the **Enter** key to close the DOS window.

You are now finished experimenting with this program, so you can close it.

3 Close the workspace and the Output window.

You now know how to compare numeric and character data. You will learn how to compare strings in the next section. As with character comparisons, string comparisons are also case sensitive.

Comparing Strings

Assume you want a program to display the string "The Microsoft Network" if the user enters the letters MSN, and the string "Other Network" if the user enters anything else. Open a partially completed program that will allow you to use the appropriate `if` statement to compare strings.

To open the LaProg03 program:

1 Open the **LaProg03.cpp** file, which is located in the Cpp\Tut05\LaProg03 folder on your computer's hard disk. The string comparison program, which appears in the LaProg03.cpp window, is shown in Figure 5-22.

```
//LaProg03.cpp
//this program demonstrates how to compare strings

#include <iostream.h>

void main()
{
    //declare and initialize variable
    char id[4] = "";

    //enter input item
    cout << "Enter a three-character ID: ";
    cin.getline(id, 4);

    //display output

} //end of main function
```

Figure 5-22: Partially completed LaProg03 program

The program declares and initializes a string variable named `id` that can store four characters: three for the ID and one for the null character that C++ appends to the end of the string. The program then prompts the user to enter a three-character ID, and stores the response in the `id` variable. The `if` statement that compares the contents of the `id` variable to the string "MSN" and also displays the appropriate message is missing from the program. Before you can enter the appropriate code, you need to learn about the `strcmp` function and the `stricmp` function.

The `strcmp` and `stricmp` Functions

In Tutorial 3, you learned about the `strcpy` function, which you use to assign a value to a string variable. Recall that the `strcpy` function is defined in the string.h header file. The string.h file also contains a function named `strcmp` and a function named `stricmp`. You use the `strcmp` function, whose syntax is **strcmp**(*string1*, *string2*), to perform a case-sensitive comparison of two strings, *string1* and *string2*. (`strcmp` stands for *string compare*.) You use the `stricmp` function, whose syntax is **stricmp**(*string1*, *string2*), to perform a case-insensitive comparison of *string1* and *string2*. Think of `stricmp` as meaning *string, ignore case, compare*.

If *string1* is equal to *string2*, both functions return the number 0. If, however, *string1* is less than *string2*, the functions return the value –1. The `strcmp` (`"A"`, `"B"`) function, for example, will return a –1; `"A"` is considered to be less than `"B"` because `"A"` comes before `"B"` in the ASCII coding scheme. (You can refer to Appendix A to verify this.) If, on the other hand, *string1* is greater than *string2*, the functions return the number 1. For instance, `stricmp("Cat", "Ant")` will return a 1. Figure 5-23 shows examples of using the `strcmp` and `stricmp` functions.

The strcmp and stricmp functions return: 0 if *string1* is equal to *string2* 1 if *string1* is greater than *string2* –1 if *string1* is less than *string2*	
Example	**Result**
`strcmp("Kelly", "Kate")`	Returns 1 because the e in Kelly (*string1*) is greater than the a in Kate (*string2*)
`strcmp("Kelly", "Kelly")`	Returns 0 because both strings are equal
`strcmp("Kelly", "KELLY")`	Returns 1 because the e in Kelly (*string1*) is greater than the E in KELLY (*string2*)
`stricmp("Kelly", "KELLY")`	Returns 0 because, ignoring case, both strings are equal
`strcmp("Kelly", "KYLE")`	Returns 1 because the e in Kelly (*string1*) is greater than the Y in KYLE (*string2*)
`stricmp("Kelly", "KYLE")`	Returns –1 because, ignoring case, the e in Kelly (*string1*) is less than the Y in KYLE (*string2*)
Assume the `empName` variable contains Kelly, and the `fName` variable contains KELLY.	
`strcmp(empName, "KELLY")`	Returns 1 because the e in Kelly (*string1*) is greater than the E in KELLY (*string2*)
`strcmp(fName, empName)`	Returns –1 because the E in KELLY (*string1*) is less than the e in Kelly (*string2*)
`stricmp(fName, empName)`	Returns 0 because, ignoring case, both strings are equal
Important note: Notice that lowercase letters are considered greater than uppercase letters. This is because lowercase letters appear after the uppercase letters in the ASCII coding scheme. (You can refer to Appendix A to verify this fact.)	

Figure 5-23: Examples of the `strcmp` and `stricmp` functions

You will use the `stricmp` function to perform a case-insensitive comparison in the LaProg03 program. If the user enters MSN, in any case, the program will display "The Microsoft Network"; otherwise, it will display "Other Network."

To include the `stricmp` function in the string comparison program:

1   The LaProg03 program should be open. Enter the `#include <string.h>` directive and the `if` statement highlighted in Figure 5-24.

---

enter this directive

enter this `if` statement

```
//LaProg03.cpp
//this program demonstrates how to compare strings

#include <iostream.h>
#include <string.h>

void main()
{
    //declare and initialize variable
    char id[4] = "";

    //enter input item
    cout << "Enter a three-character ID: ";
    cin.getline(id, 4);

    //display output
    if (stricmp(id, "MSN") == 0)   //0 means they are equal
        cout << "The Microsoft Network" << endl;
    else
        cout << "Other Network" << endl;
    //end if

} //end of main function
```

Figure 5-24: `#include <string.h>` directive and `if` statement entered in the program

---

2   Save, build, and then execute the program. When prompted to enter the ID, type **msn** and press the **Enter** key. The string "The Microsoft Network" appears in the DOS window. Press the **Enter** key to close the DOS window.

3   On your own, execute the program three more times and try entering **MSN**, **abc**, and **x**. The program should display "The Microsoft Network," "Other Network," and "Other Network," respectively.

You have now completed this program, so you can close it.

4   Close the workspace and the Output window.

`if` statements can also be nested, which means you can place one `if` statement inside another `if` statement. You will try this in the next section.

mini-quiz

Mini-Quiz 3

1.   Write a condition for an `if` statement that checks if the value in the Character variable named `key` is the letter R (in any case).

2.   Write a condition for an `if` statement that checks if the value in the String variable named `status` is either "Cash" or "Charge" (in any case).

3.   Write a condition for an `if` statement that checks if the value in the String variable named `status` is "Cash." Perform a case-sensitive comparison.

Nested Selection Structures

A nested selection structure is one in which either the true path or the false path includes yet another selection structure. Figures 5-25 and 5-26 show two examples of writing a nested selection structure both in pseudocode and in a flowchart. Figure 5-25 shows a nested selection structure in the true path; Figure 5-26 shows a nested selection structure in the false path. (The lines connecting the `if`, `else`, and `end if` in the pseudocode are not necessary. They are included in the figures to help you see which clauses are related to each other.)

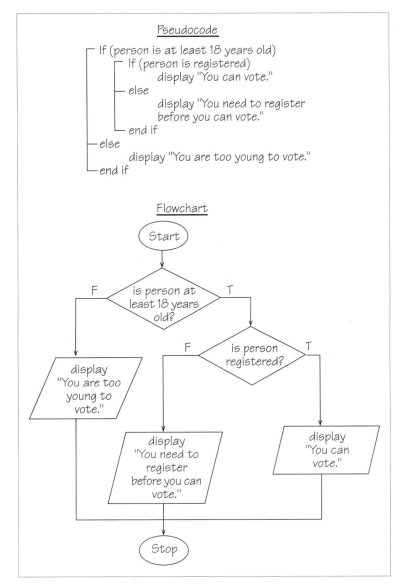

Figure 5-25: Pseudocode and flowchart showing a nested selection structure in the true path

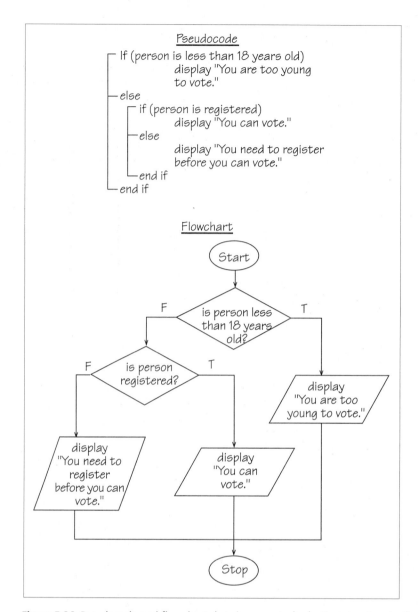

Figure 5-26: Pseudocode and flowchart showing a nested selection structure in the false path

You will notice that Figure 5-25 shows the nested `if` statement immediately after the first `if` clause, whereas Figure 5-26 shows the nested `if` statement immediately after the `else` clause. When writing a nested selection structure, keep in mind that any of the statements within either the true or false path of one `if` statement may, in turn, be another `if` statement. In other words, the nested `if` statement will not always come immediately after either the `if` clause or the `else` clause.

Figure 5-27 shows two examples of the nested selection structure written in C++. In the first example, the nested `if` statement is in the true path; in the second example, it is in the false path.

Nested **if** in the true path

if (*condition1*)
    one statement, or a block of statements enclosed in braces, to process when
    condition1 is true
    if (*condition2*)
        one statement, or a block of statements enclosed in braces, to process when both
        condition1 and condition2 are true
    [**else**
        one statement, or a block of statements enclosed in braces, to process when
        condition1 is true and condition2 is false]
    //end if (*condition2*)
[**else**
    one statement, or a block of statements enclosed in braces, to process when
    condition1 is false]
//end if (*condition1*)

Nested **if** in the false path

if (*condition1*)
    one statement, or a block of statements enclosed in braces, to process when
    condition1 is true
else
    if (*condition2*)
        one statement, or a block of statements enclosed in braces, to process when
        condition1 is false and condition2 is true
    [**else**
        one statement, or a block of statements enclosed in braces, to process when both
        condition1 and condition2 are false]
    //end if (*condition2*)
//end if (*condition1*)

Important note: In the syntax, items in **bold** are required. Items contained in square brackets, on the other hand, are optional. Items in *italics* indicate places where the programmer must supply information pertaining to the current program.

Figure 5-27: Syntax of the C++ nested selection structure

As the syntax indicates, when nesting `if` statements, it is a good programming practice to specify the *condition* in each `if` statement's corresponding `//end if` comment as this makes the nested `if` structure clearer and easier to understand.

Now open a program that uses a nested selection structure with the nested `if` in the false path and review how it works. This program allows a user to determine if a person is eligible to vote.

To open the voting eligibility program that contains a nested `if`:

1   Open the **LaProg04.cpp** file, which is located in the Cpp\Tut05\LaProg04 folder on your computer's hard disk. The voting eligibility program, which appears in the LaProg04.cpp window, is shown in Figure 5-28.

```
//LaProg04.cpp
//this program demonstrates a nested if selection structure

#include <iostream.h>
#include <ctype.h>

void main()
{
    //declare and initialize variables
    short age       = 0;
    char registered = ' ';

    //enter input item
    cout << "Enter your age: ";
    cin >> age;

    //display output
    if (age < 18)
        cout << "You are too young to vote." << endl;
    else
    {
        cout << "Are you registered to vote? ";
        cin >> registered;
        if (toupper(registered) == 'Y')
            cout << "You can vote." << endl;
        else
            cout << "You need to register before you can vote." << endl;
        //end if (toupper(registered) == 'Y')
    }
    //end if (age < 18)

} //end of main function
```

Figure 5-28: Voting eligibility program instructions

The program prompts the user to enter an age, which it stores in a Short Integer variable named age. The nested selection structure first compares the contents of the age variable to the number 18. If the number contained in the age variable is less than 18, then C++ processes the instruction in the true path, which displays the message, "You are too young to vote"; otherwise, C++ processes the instructions in the false path. Notice that the first instruction in the false path asks the user if he or she is registered to vote; the next instruction stores the user's response in the Character variable named registered. The false path also contains another if statement. This if statement compares the uppercase version of the user's response, which is stored in the registered variable, to the letter 'Y'. If the registered variable contains either 'Y' or 'y', then C++ processes the instruction in the nested if statement's true path, which displays the message, "You can vote"; otherwise, C++ processes the instruction in the false path, which displays the message, "You need to register before you can vote."

2 Build and then execute the program.

First you will enter the number 17. A person who is 17 years old is too young to vote.

3 When prompted to enter an age, type **17** and press the **Enter** key. The DOS window displays the message "You are too young to vote." Press the **Enter** key to close the DOS window.

Now you will enter the number 21. A person who is 21 years old can vote, but only if he or she is registered.

4   Execute the program again. When prompted to enter an age, type **21** and press the **Enter** key. The program displays the "Are you registered to vote?" prompt. Type **y** and press the **Enter** key. The DOS window displays the message "You can vote." Press the **Enter** key to close the DOS window.

Now try answering n to the "Are you registered to vote?" prompt.

5   Execute the program again. When prompted to enter an age, type **21** and press the **Enter** key. The program displays the "Are you registered to vote?" prompt. Type **n** and press the **Enter** key. The DOS window displays the message "You need to register before you can vote." Press the **Enter** key to close the DOS window.

You are now finished with this program, so you can close it.

6   Close the workspace and the Output window.

You have now completed Lesson A. In this lesson, you learned how to include the selection structure in both pseudocode and a flowchart, as well as how to code the selection structure in C++. In Lesson B, you will code the math program for Susan Chen. Before beginning Lesson B, you can either exit Visual C++ and take a break or complete the questions and exercises at the end of the lesson.

SUMMARY

As you learned in Tutorial 1, the selection structure, also called the decision structure, is one of the three programming structures. The other two are sequence and repetition. You use the selection structure when you want a program to make a decision or comparison and then, based on the result of that decision or comparison, to select one of two paths: either the true path or the false path. Most programming languages offer three forms of the selection structure: `if`, `if/else`, and `case`.

A diamond, called the selection/repetition symbol, is used in a flowchart to represent the selection structure. The diamond contains a question that has a true or false answer only. Each selection diamond has one flowline entering the symbol and two flowlines leaving the symbol. The two flowlines leading out of the diamond should be marked so it is clear to the reader which path is the true path and which is the false path.

You can use the C++ `if` statement to code both the `if` and `if/else` forms of the selection structure. If either the `if` statement's true path or false path contains more than one statement, you must enclose the statements in a pair of braces (`{}`). It is a good programming practice to include an `//end if` comment to identify the end of the `if` statement.

The *condition* in an `if` statement can contain variables, constants, functions, mathematical operators, relational operators, and logical operators. The relational operators are `<`, `<=`, `>`, `>=`, `==`, and `!=`. The logical operators—Not, And, and Or—are signified in C++ by the symbols `!`, `&&`, and `||`, respectively. If more than one operator with the same precedence number appears in an expression, C++ evaluates those operators from left to right in the expression. All expressions containing either a relational or logical operator will result in either a True or False answer only.

As is true in many programming languages, character comparisons in C++ are case sensitive. That means that the uppercase version of a letter is not the same as its lowercase counterpart. You should use the `toupper` function in comparisons involving a Character variable. String comparisons in C++ are also case sensitive. You use either the `strcmp` or `stricmp` function to compare strings. The `strcmp` function performs a case-sensitive comparison of two strings; the `stricmp` function performs a case-insensitive comparison.

You can also nest `if` statements. A nested `if` statement is one in which either the true path or the false path includes yet another `if` statement.

ANSWERS TO MINI-QUIZZES

Mini-Quiz 1

1. if (student's score <= 69)
     display "Fail"
   else
     display "Pass"
   end if

2. ```
   if (quantity > 10)
         cout << "Over 10" << endl;
   else
         cout << "Not over 10" << endl;
   //end if
   ```

3. `(quantity == 100)`
4. b
5. c
6. a

Mini-Quiz 2

1. True
2. False
3. False
4. `(age >= 30 && age <= 40)`
5. `(age < 30 || age > 50)`
6. True

Mini-Quiz 3

1. `(toupper(key) == 'R')`
2. `(stricmp(status, "Cash") || stricmp(status, "Charge"))`
3. `(strcmp(status, "Cash"))`
   ```

Q U E S T I O N S

1. Which of the following is a valid *condition* for an `if` statement? (The *condition* should be both syntactically and logically valid.)
   a. `(age) > 65`
   b. `(age > 0 and < 10)`
   c. `(sales > 500 && < 800)`
   d. `(sales > 100 && sales <= 1000)`
   e. `(sales > 100 || sales <= 1000)`

2. The _____ function returns the uppercase equivalent of a character.
   a. `caseupper`
   b. `charupper`
   c. `toupper`
   d. `uCase`
   e. `upper`

3. Assume you want to compare the character stored in the `initial` variable to the letter a. Which of the following *conditions* should you use in the `if` statement? (Be sure the *condition* will handle a or A.)
   a. `(initial = 'a' or 'A')`
   b. `(initial == 'a' or 'A')`
   c. `(toupper(initial) = 'A')`
   d. `(toupper(initial) == 'A')`
   e. `(toupper(initial) = "A")`

4. Assume you want to compare the contents of the `firstName` variable to the name Bob. Which of the following *conditions* should you use in the `if` statement? (Be sure the *condition* will handle Bob, BOB, and so on.)
   a. `(firstName = 'Bob' or 'BOB')`
   b. `(firstName == 'Bob' or 'BOB')`
   c. `(strcmp(firstName, "BOB") = 0)`
   d. `(stricmp(firstName, "BOB") == 0)`
   e. `(toupper(firstName) == "BOB")`

5. Which of the following will change the contents of the Character variable named `initial` to uppercase?
   a. `initial = stringupper(initial)`
   b. `initial == toupper(initial)`
   c. `initial = toupper(initial)`
   d. `toupper(initial) = initial`
   e. `toupper(initial) == initial`

6. Assuming the following three operators appear in an expression (without parentheses), which of the operators will be performed first?
   a. `&&`
   b. `!`
   c. `||`

7. Evaluate the following expression: `3 > 6 && 7 > 4`
   a. True   b. False

8. Evaluate the following expression: `4 > 6 || 10 < 2 * 6`
   a. True   b. False

9. Evaluate the following expression: `7 >= 3 + 4 || 6 < 4 && 2 < 5`
   a. True   b. False

Use the following information to answer questions 10–16.
X = 5, Y = 3, Z = 2, A = True, B = False

10. Evaluate the following expression: X - Y == Z
    a. True   b. False

11. Evaluate the following expression: X * Z > X * Y && A
    a. True   b. False

12. Evaluate the following expression: X * Z < X * Y || A
    a. True   b. False

13. Evaluate the following expression: A && B
    a. True   b. False

14. Evaluate the following expression: A || B
    a. True   b. False

15. Evaluate the following expression: X * Y > Y * Y
    a. True   b. False

16. Evaluate the following expression: X * Y > Y * Y && A || B
    a. True   b. False

Use the following selection structure to answer questions 17–19. You can assume that the number variable was declared as a Short Integer variable and was initialized to 0.

```
if (number <= 100)
    number = number * 2;
else
    if (number > 500)
        number = number * 3;
    //end if (number > 500)
//end if (number <= 100)
```

17. Assume the number variable contains the number 90. What value will be in the number variable after the preceding selection structure is processed?
    a. 0
    b. 90
    c. 180
    d. 270

18. Assume the number variable contains the number 1000. What value will be in the number variable after the preceding selection structure is processed?
    a. 0
    b. 1000
    c. 2000
    d. 3000

19. Assume the number variable contains the number 200. What value will be in the number variable after the preceding selection structure is processed?
    a. 0
    b. 200
    c. 400
    d. 600

20. Which of the following flowchart symbols represents the `if` selection structure?
    a. diamond
    b. hexagon
    c. oval
    d. parallelogram
    e. rectangle

21. The function `strcmp("Jose", "JOSE")` will return _____.
    a. −1
    b. 0
    c. 1

22. The function `stricmp("Jose", "JOSE")` will return _____.
    a. −1
    b. 0
    c. 1

E X E R C I S E S

1. On a piece of paper, write the C++ code that corresponds to the following flowchart.

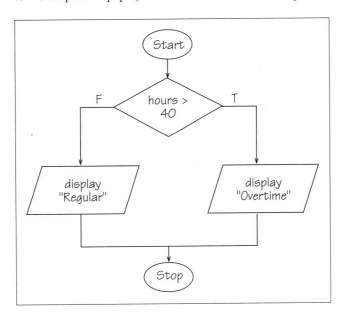

Figure 5-29

2. Open the T5Ae02.cpp file, which is located in the Cpp\Tut05\T5Ae02 folder on your computer's hard disk. Complete the program by writing an `if` statement that will display the string "Pontiac" if the user enters the string "Grand Am" (in any case) in the `carModel` variable. When the program is working correctly, print the code. Close the workspace and the Output window.

3. Open the T5Ae03.cpp file, which is located in the Cpp\Tut05\T5Ae03 folder on your computer's hard disk. Complete the program by writing an `if` statement that will display the string "Entry error" if the user enters a number that is less than 0; otherwise, display the string "Valid number". When the program is working correctly, print the code, then close the workspace and the Output window.

4. Open the T5Ae04.cpp file, which is located in the Cpp\Tut05\T5Ae04 folder on your computer's hard disk. Complete the program by writing an **if** statement that will display the string "Reorder" if the user enters a number that is less than 10; otherwise, display the string "OK". When the program is working correctly, print the code, then close the workspace and the Output window.

5. Open the T5Ae05.cpp file, which is located in the Cpp\Tut05\T5Ae05 folder on your computer's hard disk. Complete the program by writing an **if** statement that will assign the number 10 to the **bonus** variable if the user enters a sales amount that is less than or equal to $250; otherwise, assign the number 15. Display the bonus. When the program is working correctly, print the code, then close the workspace and the Output window.

6. Open the T5Ae06.cpp file, which is located in the Cpp\Tut05\T5Ae06 folder on your computer's hard disk. The program should prompt the user to enter a state, and then store the response in the **state** variable. If the **state** variable contains the string "Hawaii" (in any case), then the program should display the number 25; otherwise, it should display the number 50. Complete the program appropriately. When the program is working correctly, print the code, then close the workspace and the Output window.

7. Open the T5Ae07.cpp file, which is located in the Cpp\Tut05\T5Ae07 folder on your computer's hard disk. Assume you want to calculate a 3 percent sales tax if the **state** variable contains the string "Colorado" (in any case); otherwise, you want to calculate a 4 percent sales tax. Complete the program by entering an **if** statement that calculates the sales tax. When the program is working correctly, print the code, then close the workspace and the Output window.

8. Open the T5Ae08.cpp file, which is located in the Cpp\Tut05\T5Ae08 folder on your computer's hard disk. Assume you want to calculate an employee's gross pay. Employees working more than 40 hours should receive overtime pay (time and one-half) for the hours over 40. Complete the program by entering an **if** statement that calculates the gross pay, then display the gross pay. When the program is working correctly, print the code, then close the workspace and the Output window.

9. Open the T5Ae09.cpp file, which is located in the Cpp\Tut05\T5Ae09 folder on your computer's hard disk. The program should prompt the user to enter an animal ID; it should store the ID in a Character variable named **animal**. The program should display the string "Dog" if the **animal** variable contains the letter D (in any case); otherwise, it should display the string "Cat". Complete the program appropriately. When the program is working correctly, print the code, then close the workspace and the Output window.

10. Open the T5Ae10.cpp file, which is located in the Cpp\Tut05\T5Ae10 folder on your computer's hard disk. Complete the program by entering an **if** statement that calculates a 10 percent discount on desks sold to customers in Colorado, and an 8 percent discount on everything else. (Perform case-insensitive comparisons for the String variables.) When the program is working correctly, print the code, then close the workspace and the Output window.

11. Open the T5Ae11.cpp file, which is located in the Cpp\Tut05\T5Ae11 folder on your computer's hard disk. Complete the program by entering an **if** statement that calculates a 10 percent discount on sales made to customers in California and in Texas, and a 5 percent discount on all other sales. (Perform case-insensitive comparisons for the String variables.) When the program is working correctly, print the code, then close the workspace and the Output window.

12. Open the T5Ae12.cpp file, which is located in the Cpp\Tut05\T5Ae12 folder on your computer's hard disk. Complete the program by writing an **if** statement that displays the string "Valid entry" when the user enters either the number 1 or the number 2 in the **entry** variable; otherwise, display the string "Entry error". When the program is working correctly, print the code, then close the workspace and the Output window.

13. a. Open the T5Ae13.cpp file, which is located in the Cpp\Tut05\T5Ae13 folder on your computer's hard disk.

   b. Complete the program by writing an `if` statement that calculates a 2 percent price increase on all red shirts, but a 1 percent price increase on all other items. In addition to calculating the price increase, also calculate the new price. (Perform case-insensitive comparisons for the String variables.)

   c. Add the code to send the output to a file named T5Ae13.dat for printing. Format the output to show two decimal places and a decimal point.

   d. When the program is working correctly, print the code.

   e. Execute the program twice, using the following data: red, shirt, 100, and then red, blouse, 20. Use C++ to open and then print the T5Ae13.dat file after each execution.

   f. Close the workspace and the Output window.

14. a. Open the T5Ae14.cpp file, which is located in the Cpp\Tut05\T5Ae14 folder on your computer's hard disk.

   b. Complete the program by writing an `if` statement that displays the string "Dog" if the `animal` variable contains the number 1. Display the string "Cat" if the `animal` variable contains the number 2. Display the string "Bird" if the `animal` variable contains anything other than the number 1 or the number 2. When the program is working correctly, print the code, then close the workspace and the Output window.

15. Scenario: Assume you offer programming seminars to companies. Your price per person depends on the number of people the company registers, as shown in the following table. (For example, if the company registers seven people, then the total amount owed by the company is $560.) Your task is to create a program that will prompt the user to enter the number of people registered, and will then calculate the total amount owed.

Number of registrants	Charge
1–4	$100 per person
5–10	$ 80 per person
11 or more	$ 60 per person

   a. Complete and submit an IPO chart for this problem.

   b. Complete and submit a desk-check table. Use 3 as the number of people registered.

   c. Create a console application named T5Ae15 in the Cpp\Tut05 folder on your computer's hard disk. Write a program that corresponds to the IPO chart you created in step a.

   d. In addition to displaying the output, the program should also save the program information (number of people registered and total amount owed) to a file for printing. Name the file T5Ae15.dat.

   e. When the program is working correctly, print the code. Execute the program twice using the following as the number of people registered: 3 and 12. Use C++ to open and then print the T5Ae15.dat file after each execution.

   f. Close the workspace and the Output window.

16. Scenario: Assume a company charges for shipping based on the state in which the customer lives, as shown in the following table. (The user can type the state in any case.)

State	Shipping charge ($)
Hawaii	25
Oregon	30

Any other state should result in an "Incorrect state" message.

   a. Create a console application named T5Ae16 in the Cpp\Tut05 folder on your computer's hard disk. Create a program that prompts the user to enter the state and then displays the shipping charge.

   b. In addition to displaying the output, the program should also save the program information (the state and either the shipping charge or the message) to a file for printing. Name the file T5Ae16.dat.

   c. Close the workspace and the Output window.

17. Scenario: Assume you want to calculate a 10 percent discount on sales made to customers in California and in Texas, a 7 percent discount on sales made to customers in Oregon and New Mexico, and a 6 percent discount on sales made to customers in all other states. Your task is to create a program that prompts the user to enter the state and the sales. The program should then calculate and display the amount of the discount, as well as the new sales amount. (The new sales amount is calculated by subtracting the discount from the original sales amount. Use Float variables for the numeric data.)

a. Complete and submit an IPO chart for this problem.

b. Complete and submit a desk-check table. Use Texas as the state and 2000 as the sales.

c. Create a console application named T5Ae17 in the Cpp\Tut05 folder on your computer's hard disk. Write a program that corresponds to the IPO chart you created in step a.

d. In addition to displaying the output, the program should also save the program information (state, sales amount, discount rate, discount amount, and new sales amount) to a file for printing. Name the file T5Ae17.dat.

e. When the program is working correctly, print the code. Execute the program three times using the following information:

State	Sales ($)
Texas	2000
Oregon	5000
South Dakota	3000

f. Use C++ to open and then print the T5Ae17.dat file after each execution.

g. Close the workspace and the Output window.

discovery ▶ 18. Scenario: Assume that the price of a concert ticket depends on the seat location, as shown in the following table. (The user can enter the seat location in any case.)

Seat location	Concert ticket price ($)
Box	75
Pavilion	30
Lawn	21

Any other seat location should result in an "Incorrect seat location" message.

a. Create a console application named T5Ae18 in the Cpp\Tut05 folder on your computer's hard disk. Write a program that prompts the user to enter the seat location. The program should then display the ticket price.

b. In addition to displaying the output, the program should also save the program information (seat location and ticket price) to a file for printing. Name the file T5Ae18.dat.

c. When the program is working correctly, print the code. Execute the program twice using the following seat locations: Lawn and Box. Use C++ to open and then print the T5Ae18.dat file after each execution.

d. Close the workspace and the Output window.

discovery ▶ 19. Scenario: Assume that the amount of vacation an employee receives from his or her employer depends on the number of years the employee has been with the company, as shown in the following table.

Years with the company	Weeks of vacation
0	0
1 to 5	1
6 to 10	2
11 and over	3

a. Create a console application named T5Ae19 in the Cpp\Tut05 folder on your computer's hard disk. Write a program that prompts the user to enter the number of years the employee has been with the company. Use a Short Integer variable. The program should then display the appropriate number of vacation weeks.

b. In addition to displaying the output, the program should also save the program information (the number of years with the company and the number of vacation weeks) to a file for printing. Name the file T5Ae19.dat.

c. When the program is working correctly, print the code. Execute the program three times using the following years: 0, 5, and 11. Use C++ to open and then print the T5Ae19.dat file after each execution.

d. Close the workspace and the Output window.

discovery ▶   **20.** Scenario: XYZ Corporation pays its salespeople a commission based on the amount of their sales, as shown in the following table.

Sales ($)	Commission rate (%)
10,000.01 and over	10.0
5,000.01–10,000	7.5
0–5,000	5.0

If the sales are less than 0, then display a "Data error" message.

a. Create a console application named T5Ae20 in the Cpp\Tut05 folder on your computer's hard disk. Write a program that prompts the user to enter the sales. The program should then calculate and display the appropriate commission.

b. In addition to displaying the output, the program should also save the program information (sales, commission rate, and commission) to a file for printing. Name the file T5Ae20.dat.

c. When the program is working correctly, print the code. Execute the program three times using the following sales: 5000.25, 45.67, and 12000. Use C++ to open and then print the T5Ae20.dat file after each execution.

d. Close the workspace and the Output window.

discovery ▶   **21.** Scenario: Recall that character comparisons in C++ are case sensitive, which means that a 'P' is different from a 'p'. In Lesson A's LaProg02 program, you learned how to use the `toupper` function to handle the character comparison problem. Recall that the code in that program is as follows:

```
if (toupper(letter) == 'P')
    cout << "Pass" << endl;
else
    cout << "Fail" << endl;
//end if
```

As you may also remember, one of the tips in Lesson A showed you how to use the C++ `tolower` function to perform a character comparison.

a. Not all languages have a `toupper` or a `tolower` function. Just for practice, assume that C++ does not have either function. Without using either the `toupper` or `tolower` functions, rewrite the `if` statement's *condition* so that it displays the "Pass" message when the user enters the letter 'P' in either lowercase or uppercase.

discovery ▶   **22.** In this exercise, you will learn about the `strupr` and `strlwr` functions, which are defined in the string.h header file. You use the `strupr` (*string to uppercase*) function to convert a string to uppercase using the syntax **strupr(***string***)**. You use the `strlwr` (*string to lowercase*) function to convert a string to lowercase using the syntax **strlwr(***string***)**.

a. Open the T5Ae22.cpp file, which is located in the Cpp\Tut05\T5Ae22 folder on your computer's hard disk. The program uses the `strupr` function to convert the contents of the `firstName` variable to uppercase. Study the code. Build and execute the program. When prompted to enter a name, type your first name (up to 14 characters) in lowercase letters and press the Enter key. You will notice that the `strupr` function converts your first name to uppercase. Close the DOS window and the Output window.

b. Modify the code so that it converts a name, entered in uppercase letters, to lowercase. Save, build, and then execute the program. When prompted to enter a name, type your first name (up to 14 characters) in uppercase letters (or a combination of uppercase and lowercase letters) and press the Enter key. You will notice that the `strlwr` function converts your first name to lowercase.

c. Close the DOS window, then print the code.

d. Close the workspace and the Output window.

discovery ▶ 23. In this exercise, you will learn about the `strlen` function, which is defined in the string.h header file. You use the `strlen` (*string length*) function to determine the length of a string. The syntax is **strlen**(*string*). When calculating the length of the string, the `strlen` function ignores the null character.

a. Open the T5Ae23.cpp file, which is located in the Cpp\Tut05\T5Ae23 folder on your computer's hard disk. This partially completed program prompts the user to enter a four-character password, then stores the password in the `password` variable.

b. Enter a statement that assigns the length of the `password` variable to the `numCharacters` variable.

c. You will notice that the output section of the program contains two display messages. Complete the program by entering an `if` statement that displays the first message if the user enters less than the required four characters; otherwise, display the second message.

d. Save, build, and then execute the program. When prompted to enter a password, type any two letters and press the Enter key. The program should display the message informing you that the password is incorrect. Close the DOS window.

e. Execute the program again. When prompted to enter a password, type any four characters and press the Enter key. The program should display the message informing you that the password is correct.

f. Close the DOS window, then print the code.

g. Close the workspace and the Output window.

discovery ▶ 24. Recall that you must be careful when comparing two Float values. Because some Float values cannot be stored, precisely, in memory, you should never compare Float values for equality or inequality. Rather, you should test that the difference between the numbers you are comparing is less than some acceptable small value, such as .00001.

a. Open the T5Ae24.cpp file, which is located in the Cpp\Tut05\T5Ae24 folder on your computer's hard disk. After declaring and initializing a Float variable named num, the program divides the number 10 by the number 3, and assigns the quotient to the num variable. (Notice that both the 10 and the 3 are typecast to Float values to agree with the data type of the num variable.) The program then displays the contents of the num variable—the quotient. An `if` statement is used to compare the contents of the num variable to the number 3.33333. The `if` statement then displays an appropriate message, indicating whether the numbers are or are not equal.

b. Build and execute the program. Although the DOS window shows that the quotient is 3.33333, the `if` statement, which compares the quotient to the number 3.33333, displays the message "No, they are not equal." Press the Enter key to close the DOS window.

The proper procedure for comparing two Float values is first to find the difference between the values, and then compare the absolute value of that difference to a small number, such as .00001. You can use the C++ `fabs` function, which is defined in the math.h header file, to find the absolute value of a Float number. (`fabs` stands for *Float absolute value*.) The absolute value of a number is a positive number that represents how far the number is from 0. The absolute value of 5 is 5; the absolute value of −5 is also 5.

c. Enter the `#include <math.h>` directive below the `#include <iostream.h>` directive.

d. Change the `if` clause to `if (fabs(num - 3.33333) < .00001)`.

e. Save, build, and execute the program. The DOS window displays the quotient (3.33333) and the message "Yes, they are equal." Press the Enter key to close the DOS window.

f. Close the workspace and the Output window.

debugging 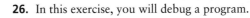   **25.** In this exercise, you will debug a program.

a. Open the T5Ae25.cpp file, which is located in the Cpp\Tut05\T5Ae25 folder on your computer's hard disk. This program is not working correctly.

b. Print the code. Debug the code.

c. When the program is working correctly, print the code. On the corrected code printout, indicate what was wrong with the program. Also, circle the corrections you made to the program.

d. Close the workspace and the Output window.

debugging 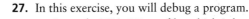   **26.** In this exercise, you will debug a program.

a. Open the T5Ae26.cpp file, which is located in the Cpp\Tut05\T5Ae26 folder on your computer's hard disk. This program is not working correctly.

b. Print the code. Debug the code.

c. When the program is working correctly, print the code. On the corrected code printout, indicate what was wrong with the program. Also, circle the corrections you made to the program.

d. Close the workspace and the Output window.

debugging 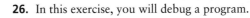   **27.** In this exercise, you will debug a program.

a. Open the T5Ae27.cpp file, which is located in the Cpp\Tut05\T5Ae27 folder on your computer's hard disk. This program is not working correctly.

b. Print the code. Debug the code.

c. When the program is working correctly, print the code. On the corrected code printout, indicate what was wrong with the program. Also, circle the corrections you made to the program.

d. Close the workspace and the Output window.

LESSON B
objectives

In this lesson you will learn how to:

■ Write function stubs for testing programs

■ Generate random numbers using the `srand`, `rand`, and `time` functions

■ Swap the values in variables

Coding the Math Program

The Math Program

Recall that Susan Chen, the principal of a local primary school, wants a program that the first and second grade students can use to practice both adding and subtracting numbers. The program should display the addition or subtraction problem on the screen, then allow the student to enter the answer, and then verify that the answer is correct. If the student's answer is not correct, the program should display the correct answer for the student.

The problems displayed for the first grade students should use numbers from one through 10 only; the problems for the second grade students should use numbers from 10 through 100. Because the first and second grade students have not learned about negative numbers yet, the subtraction problems should never ask them to subtract a larger number from a smaller one. The IPO chart for the math program's `main` function is shown in Figure 5-30.

Input	Processing	Output

grade level (1 or 2) operation (a or s) user's answer	Processing items: none
	
	Algorithm:
	
	1. enter grade level and operation
	
	2. generate two random numbers (`getRandomNumbers` function)
	
	3. display a math problem for the user (`displayProblem` function)
	
	4. enter the user's answer to the math problem
	
	5. calculate the correct answer (`calcCorrectAnswer` function)
	
	6. if (user's answer equals the correct answer) display "You are correct" message
	else
	    display "Sorry, the correct answer is" message and the correct answer
	end if
		math problem message

Figure 5-30: IPO chart for the math program's `main` function

According to the IPO chart, the program should prompt the user to enter the grade level (either 1 or 2) and the operation (either a for addition or s for subtraction). It should then invoke two functions: `getRandomNumbers`, which will generate two random numbers, and `displayProblem`, which will display the numbers in a math problem on the screen. After the user enters his or her answer to the math problem, the program should invoke a function named `calcCorrectAnswer` to calculate the correct answer to the math problem. The program should then compare the user's answer to the correct answer, and display an appropriate message indicating if the user's answer is correct or incorrect.

You should also create an IPO chart for each of the programmer-defined functions in the program—in this case, the `getRandomNumbers`, `calcCorrectAnswer`, and `displayProblem` functions. You will view these IPO charts when you create the functions later in this lesson.

Much of the code for the math program is already entered in a file for you. You will now open the file and begin completing the program.

To open the math program and finish coding the `main` function:

1 If necessary, start Visual C++. Open the **LbProg01.cpp** file, which is located in the Cpp\Tut05\LbProg01 folder on your computer's hard disk. The partially completed math program, which appears in the LbProg01.cpp window, is shown in Figure 5-31.

```
//LbProg01.cpp
//math program

#include <iostream.h>
#include <ctype.h>

//function prototypes

void main()
{
    //declare and initialize variables
    short gradeLevel    = 0;
    char  operation     = ' ';
    short num1          = 0;
    short num2          = 0;
    short correctAnswer = 0;
    short userAnswer    = 0;

    //enter input
    cout << "Enter grade level (1 or 2): ";
    cin >> gradeLevel;
    cout << "Enter operation (a or s): ";
    cin >> operation;
    operation = toupper(operation);

    //get two random numbers

    //display math problem

    //get user's answer
    cin >> userAnswer;

    //calculate correct answer

    //display appropriate message

} //end of main function

//*****programmer-defined function definitions*****
```

Figure 5-31: Partially completed math program

To begin completing the LbProg01 program, you will first use the IPO chart shown in Figure 5-30 to enter the code that is missing from the program's main function. After completing the main function, you will then enter the missing code from the programmer-defined function definitions section of the program.

You will notice that the main function declares six local variables. The gradeLevel variable will store the student's grade level, either 1 or 2. The operation variable will store either the letter a for addition or the letter s for subtraction. The num1 and num2 variables will store two random numbers. The correctAnswer variable and the userAnswer variable will store the correct answer and the user's answer to the math problem, respectively.

After declaring the variables, the `main` function prompts the user to enter the grade level and the operation, then stores the responses in the appropriate variables. It then uses the `toupper` function to convert the operation entry, either a or s, to uppercase. According to the IPO chart shown in Figure 5-30, the `main` function should now call the `getRandomNumbers` function both to generate and return two random numbers. Because you want the function to return two values, you will need to declare it as a void function. (Recall that a value-returning function can return one value only.) For now, you don't need to decide what information, if any, should be passed to the `getRandomNumbers` function. You will determine that when you enter the function's definition in the programmer-defined section of the program.

2   In the blank line below the `//get two random numbers` comment, type **getRandomNumbers( );** and press the **Enter** key. (Recall that a call to a void function typically appears as a statement by itself.)

The next step in the IPO chart is to call the `displayProblem` function to display a math problem for the user. The `displayProblem` function will not need to return a value, so you will define it as a void function. For now, don't be concerned about what information, if any, needs to be passed to the `displayProblem` function.

3   In the blank line below the `//display math problem` comment, type **displayProblem( );** and press the **Enter** key.

According to the IPO chart, the program should now get the user's answer to the math problem. The answer should be stored in the `userAnswer` variable. The instruction to accomplish this, `cin >> userAnswer;`, is already entered below the `//get user's answer` comment in the program.

The next step in the IPO chart is to call the `calcCorrectAnswer` function, which will both calculate and return the correct answer to the math problem that appears on the screen. Because the `calcCorrectAnswer` function will need to return one value only, you will define it as a value-returning function. As you may remember from Tutorial 4, a call to a value-returning function does not typically appear as a statement by itself; rather, it is usually a part of another statement. In the math program, you will use the `calcCorrectAnswer` function in an assignment statement that assigns the function's return value to the `correctAnswer` variable. For now, do not be concerned about what information needs to be passed to the `calcCorrectAnswer` function.

4   In the blank line below the `//calculate correct answer` comment, type **correctAnswer = calcCorrectAnswer( );** and press the **Enter** key.

According to the IPO chart, the program should now compare the user's answer to the correct answer, and then display an appropriate message that indicates if the user's answer is correct or incorrect.

5   Enter the selection structure highlighted in Figure 5-32. Also verify that you entered the instructions from steps 2, 3, and 4 correctly.

```
//LbProg01.cpp
//math program

#include <iostream.h>
#include <ctype.h>

//function prototypes

void main()
{
    //declare and initialize variables
    short gradeLevel    = 0;
    char  operation     = ' ';
    short num1          = 0;
    short num2          = 0;
    short correctAnswer = 0;
    short userAnswer    = 0;

    //enter input
    cout << "Enter grade level (1 or 2): ";
    cin >> gradeLevel;
    cout << "Enter operation (a or s): ";
    cin >> operation;
    operation = toupper(operation);

    //get two random numbers
    getRandomNumbers();

    //display math problem
    displayProblem();

    //get user's answer
    cin >> userAnswer;

    //calculate correct answer
    correctAnswer = calcCorrectAnswer();

    //display appropriate message
    if (userAnswer == correctAnswer)
        cout << "You are correct." << endl;
    else
        cout << "Sorry, the correct answer is "
             << correctAnswer << "." << endl;
    // end if

} //end of main function

//*****programmer-defined function definitions*****
```

verify that you entered
these statements correctly

enter this selection
structure

Figure 5-32: Selection structure entered in the math program

6 Save the program.

tip

As you learned earlier in this lesson, when either the true or false path in a selection structure contains only one statement, that statement does not need to be enclosed in braces. In Figure 5-32's selection structure, for example, you will notice that the `cout` statement shown in the true path is not enclosed in braces. The `cout` statement shown in the false path is also not enclosed in braces because it is simply one statement that appears on two lines in the program.

You have now finished coding the `main` function, with the exception of entering the actual arguments in each function call's *argumentlist*. After completing the code for one function, it is a good programming practice to test the code before writing the code for another function. This way, if there is an error in the program, you know which function is causing the error. In the math program, you will need to enter both a function prototype and a function definition for each of the three programmer-defined functions— `getRandomNumbers`, `displayProblem`, and `calcCorrectAnswer`—before you can test the `main` function's code. Recall that a program cannot refer to a function unless the function first has been declared and defined. However, how do you define a function without writing its code? You do so by using a function stub.

Using Function Stubs in a Program

A **function stub** is simply a skeleton of a function. The stub contains the function header, the required braces, and, if it's a value-returning function, a `return` statement. Within the function braces, programmers usually include a statement that displays a message indicating whether the function was called at the appropriate time—for example, a statement such as `cout << "Function <functionname> called" << endl;` could be used. To test the `main` function in the current program, you will need to enter three stubs and three function prototypes. First enter the prototypes. Recall that both the `getRandomNumbers` and `displayProblem` functions are void functions, and that the `calcCorrectAnswer` function is a value-returning function.

To enter the prototypes into the math program:

1 In the blank line below the `//function prototypes` comment, type **void getRandomNumbers();** and press the **Enter** key, then type **void displayProblem();** and press the **Enter** key.

Unlike the `getRandomNumbers` and `displayProblem` functions, the `calcCorrectAnswer` function is a value-returning function, which means that its prototype must begin with a data type. Recall from Tutorial 4 that the data type indicates the type of data the function will return. In this case, because the program assigns the function's return value to a Short Integer variable (`correctAnswer`), the function's data type should also be Short Integer.

2 Type **short calcCorrectAnswer();** and press the **Enter** key.

Now enter a function stub for each of the three programmer-defined functions. Because `calcCorrectAnswer` is a value-returning function, recall that its stub must contain a `return` statement. You can return any value, but 0 (zero) is typically used.

3 Enter the function stubs highlighted in Figure 5-33. Also verify that you entered the prototypes from steps 1 and 2 correctly.

verify that you entered
these prototypes
correctly

```cpp
//LbProg01.cpp
//math program

#include <iostream.h>
#include <ctype.h>

//function prototypes
void getRandomNumbers();
void displayProblem();
short calcCorrectAnswer();

void main()
{
    //declare and initialize variables
    short gradeLevel    = 0;
    char  operation     = ' ';
    short num1          = 0;
    short num2          = 0;
    short correctAnswer = 0;
    short userAnswer    = 0;

    //enter input
    cout << "Enter grade level (1 or 2): ";
    cin >> gradeLevel;
    cout << "Enter operation (a or s): ";
    cin >> operation;
    operation = toupper(operation);

    //get two random numbers
    getRandomNumbers();

    //display math problem
    displayProblem();

    //get user's answer
    cin >> userAnswer;

    //calculate correct answer
    correctAnswer = calcCorrectAnswer();

    //display appropriate message
    if (userAnswer == correctAnswer)
        cout << "You are correct." << endl;
    else
        cout << "Sorry, the correct answer is "
             << correctAnswer << "." << endl;
    // end if

} //end of main function
```

Figure 5-33: Function prototypes and stubs entered in the program

```
//*****programmer-defined function definitions*****
void getRandomNumbers()
{
    cout << "Function getRandomNumbers called" << endl;
} //end of getRandomNumbers function

void displayProblem()
{
    cout << "Function displayProblem called" << endl;
} //end of displayProblem function

short calcCorrectAnswer()
{
    cout << "Function calcCorrectAnswer called" << endl;
    return 0;
} //end of calcCorrectAnswer function
```

enter these
function stubs

Figure 5-33: Function prototypes and stubs entered in the program (continued)

4 Save, build, and then execute the program. When prompted to enter the grade level, type **1** and press the **Enter** key. When prompted to enter the operation, type **a** and press the **Enter** key.

The `getRandomNumbers();` statement in the `main` function calls the `getRandomNumbers` function, whose function stub displays "Function getRandomNumbers called" in the DOS window, indicating that the function was called correctly. The `main` function's `displayProblem();` statement then calls the `displayProblem` function, whose function stub displays "Function displayProblem called" in the DOS window, indicating that this function was also called correctly. The `main` function's `cin >> userAnswer;` statement then allows the user to enter an answer to the math problem.

5 Type **0** (the number 0) and press the **Enter** key. C++ stores the number 0 in the `userAnswer` variable.

The `main` function's `correctAnswer = calcCorrectAnswer();` statement calls the value-returning `calcCorrectAnswer` function, whose function stub displays the "Function calcCorrectAnswer called" message in the DOS window, and also returns the number 0, which is stored in the `correctAnswer` variable. At this point, both the `userAnswer` and `correctAnswer` variables contain the number 0. The `if (userAnswer == correctAnswer)` clause in the `main` function's selection structure compares both variables to determine if their contents are equal. In this case, the contents of both variables are equal, so the selection structure displays in the DOS window the message "You are correct."

6 Press the **Enter** key to close the DOS window, then close the Output window.

After testing the main function, you can begin writing the code for each of the programmer-defined functions. The first function you will code is the getRandomNumbers function.

Coding the getRandomNumbers Function

The getRandomNumbers function is responsible for generating two random numbers, which should be stored in the num1 and num2 variables. If the user's grade level is 1, the random numbers should be in the range of 1 through 10; otherwise, the numbers should be in the range of 10 through 100. Figure 5-34 shows the IPO chart for the getRandomNumbers function.

Input	Processing	Output

grade level
address of num1
address of num2
	Processing items: first random number
	                         second random number
	Algorithm:
	1. if (the grade level is 1)
	    generate first random number
	    between 1 and 10
	    generate second random number
	    between 1 and 10
	  else
	    generate first random number
	    between 10 and 100
	    generate second random number
	    between 10 and 100
	  end if
		first random number
		second random number

Figure 5-34: IPO chart for the getRandomNumbers function

tip

As you learned in Tutorial 4, when you pass a variable by value, C++ passes only the contents of the variable to the receiving function. Unless specified otherwise, all variables in C++ are passed by value. When you pass a variable by reference, C++ passes the variable's address—in other words, its location—in memory. This allows the receiving function to change the contents of the variable.

tip

As you may remember from Tutorial 4, the names of the formal parameters listed in the function header do not need to be identical to the names of the actual arguments listed in the function call. The data type of the formal parameters, however, must match the data type of the actual arguments. Furthermore, the order in which the formal parameters are listed in the function header must match the order of the actual arguments listed in the function call.

According to the IPO chart, the getRandomNumbers function needs to know the grade level, as well as the addresses of the num1 and num2 variables; the main function will need to pass this information to the getRandomNumbers function. The grade level, which is stored in the gradeLevel variable, is necessary for the function to determine the range of random numbers. The gradeLevel variable will be passed by value because the getRandomNumbers function needs to know only the value stored in the variable, but the function does not need to change the contents of the variable. The num1 and num2 variables, however, will be passed by reference—in other words, their addresses in memory will be passed—because the getRandomNumbers function will need to store random numbers in those variables.

To include the getRandomNumbers function in the math program:
1 Modify the getRandomNumbers function prototype, function call, and function header highlighted in Figure 5-35.

modify this prototype

modify this function call

modify this function header

```cpp
//LbProg01.cpp
//math program

#include <iostream.h>
#include <ctype.h>

//function prototypes
void getRandomNumbers(short, short &, short &);
void displayProblem();
short calcCorrectAnswer();

void main()
{
    //declare and initialize variables
    short  gradeLevel    = 0;
    char   operation     = ' ';
    short  num1          = 0;
    short  num2          = 0;
    short  correctAnswer = 0;
    short  userAnswer    = 0;

    //enter input
    cout << "Enter grade level (1 or 2): ";
    cin >> gradeLevel;
    cout << "Enter operation (a or s): ";
    cin >> operation;
    operation = toupper(operation);

    //get two random numbers
    getRandomNumbers(gradeLevel, num1, num2);

    //display math problem
    displayProblem();

    //get user's answer
    cin >> userAnswer;

    //calculate correct answer
    correctAnswer = calcCorrectAnswer();

    //display appropriate message
    if (userAnswer == correctAnswer)
        cout << "You are correct." << endl;
    else
        cout << "Sorry, the correct answer is "
                << correctAnswer << "." << endl;
    // end if

} //end of main function

//*****programmer-defined function definitions*****
void getRandomNumbers(short level, short &firstNum, short &secondNum)
{
    cout << "Function getRandomNumbers called" << endl;
}
```

Figure 5-35: Modified function prototype, function call, and function header

Before you can complete the getRandomNumbers function, you will need to learn how to generate random numbers in C++.

Generating Random Numbers

In C++, you use both the rand and srand functions, which are defined in the stdlib.h header file, when generating random numbers. Of the two functions, the rand function, also referred to as the **random number generator**, is the one that actually produces the random numbers. The srand function, on the other hand, allows you to set the starting point for (or initialize) the random number generator. If the program does not use the srand function before using the rand function, the rand function will generate the same set of random numbers each time the program is executed.

The syntax of the srand function is **srand(*seed*)**, where *seed* is a number that represents the starting point for the random number generator. When generating random numbers in a program, most programmers use the C++ time function as the *seed*. The time function, which is defined in the time.h header file, returns the number of seconds that have elapsed since midnight of January 1, 1970, according to your computer system's clock. The syntax for using the time function as the *seed* for the srand function is **time(NULL)**. NULL, which is a symbolic constant defined in both the stdlib.h and time.h header files, has a value of 0 (zero).

The rand function, whose syntax is **rand()**, produces integers that are greater than or equal to 0, but less than or equal to the value of RAND_MAX—a symbolic constant defined in the stdlib.h header file. Although the value of RAND_MAX varies with different systems, its value is always at least 32767.

You can use the modulus arithmetic operator (%) to control the range of integers produced by the rand function using the formula *lowerbound* + **rand()** % (*upperbound* - *lowerbound* + 1). In the formula, *lowerbound* is the lowest number in the range, and *upperbound* is the highest number in the range. To generate numbers from 1 through 10, for example, use the formula 1 + rand() % (10 − 1 + 1). Likewise, to generate numbers from 10 through 100, use the formula 10 + rand() % (100 − 10 + 1). Use the srand, time, and rand functions to generate the random numbers in the math program's getRandomNumbers function.

tip

If you want to view the value of RAND_MAX on your computer system, do Lesson B's Discovery Exercise 10.

tip

As you may remember from Tutorial 3, the modulus arithmetic operator divides two numbers and results in the remainder of the division.

To continue coding the getRandomNumbers function in the math program:

1 Below the #include <ctype.h> instruction, type **#include <stdlib.h>** and press the **Enter** key, then type **#include <time.h>** and press the **Enter** key.

2 Remove the cout << "Function getRandomNumbers called" << endl; statement from the getRandomNumbers function, then enter the code highlighted in Figure 5-36.

```
//*****programmer-defined function definitions*****
void getRandomNumbers(short level, short &firstNum, short &secondNum)
{
    //this function generates two random numbers
    srand (time(NULL));          //initialize random number generator
    if(level == 1)
    {
        //generate numbers from 1 - 10
        firstNum = 1 + rand() % (10 - 1 + 1);
        secondNum = 1 + rand() % (10 - 1 + 1);
    }
    else
    {
        //generate numbers from 10 - 100
        firstNum = 10 + rand() % (100 - 10 + 1);
        secondNum = 10 + rand() % (100 - 10 + 1);
    }
    //end if
}//end of getRandomNumbers function
```

enter this code

Figure 5-36: Code entered in the `getRandomNumbers` function

You will notice that, because both the true and false path contain more than one statement, you must enclose the statements in a set of braces ({}). As you may remember from Tutorial 4, a group of statements enclosed in a set of braces is called a statement block.

To verify that the `getRandomNumbers` function is working correctly, you will enter a temporary `cout` statement below the `getRandomNumbers (gradeLevel, num1, num2);` function call in the `main` function. The `cout` statement will display the values in the `num1` and `num2` variables after the `getRandomNumbers` function has assigned values to them.

3   In the blank line below the `getRandomNumbers(gradeLevel, num1, num2);` statement in the `main` function, type **cout << num1 << " " << num2 << endl;** and press the **Enter** key, as shown in Figure 5-37.

```
//get two random numbers
getRandomNumbers(gradeLevel, num1, num2);
cout << num1 << "  " << num2 << endl;

//display math problem
displayProblem();
```

enter this temporary statement

Figure 5-37: Temporary `cout` statement entered in the `main` function

4   Save, build, and execute the program. When prompted for the level, type **1** and press the **Enter** key. When prompted for the operation, type **a** and press the **Enter** key.

The getRandomNumbers(gradeLevel, num1, num2); statement in the main function calls the getRandomNumbers function, passing it the value in the gradeLevel variable, as well as the address of the num1 and num2 variables. The getRandomNumbers function generates two random numbers, which are stored in the num1 and num2 variables. After the getRandomNumbers function completes its task, the temporary cout << num1 << "   " num2 << endl; statement that you entered in the main function then displays the random numbers on the screen.

After displaying the random numbers stored in the num1 and num2 variables, the main function calls the displayProblem function, whose function stub displays "Function displayProblem called" in the DOS window. Then the program waits for the user to enter an answer to the math problem.

5   Type 0 (the number 0) and press the **Enter** key. The program stores the 0 in the userAnswer variable.

The main function calls the calcCorrectAnswer() function, whose function stub displays "Function calcCorrectAnswer called" in the DOS window, and also returns the number 0, which is stored in the correctAnswer variable. The selection structure in the main function then compares the userAnswer and correctAnswer variables to determine if their contents are equal. As before, both variables contain the number 0, so the selection structure displays in the DOS window the message "You are correct." See Figure 5-38.

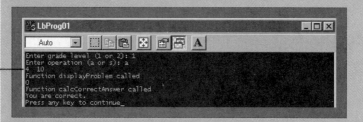

Figure 5-38: DOS window showing random numbers and messages

6   Press the **Enter** key to close the DOS window, then close the Output window.

Now that you know that the getRandomNumbers function is working correctly, you can delete the temporary cout << num1 << "   " << num2 << endl; statement from the main function.

7   Highlight the cout << num1 << "   " << num2 << endl; statement in the main function, then press the **Delete** key. If two blank lines appear between the getRandomNumbers(gradeLevel, num1, num2); statement and the //display math problem comment, press the **Delete** key again to remove one of the blank lines.

8   Save the program.

The next function you will code is the displayProblem function.

tip

Recall that you cannot determine from looking at the function call whether a variable is being passed by value or by reference. You must look in either the function prototype or the function header.

your random numbers may differ

Mini-Quiz 4

1. Name the four pieces of information typically included in a function stub for a value-returning function.

2. Write the statement that uses the computer's clock to initialize the random number generator.

3. Assuming the random number generator has been initialized, write the statement that assigns a random integer, in the range of 5 to 10, to a variable named **number**.

Coding the `displayProblem` Function

The `displayProblem` function is responsible for displaying the math problem on the screen. If the operation is addition, then the function needs simply to display a plus sign (+) between the two random numbers in the problem. If the operation is not addition, however, the `displayProblem` function may need to reverse the two random numbers before displaying them, separated with a minus sign (−), on the screen. Recall that, because the first and second grade students have not learned about negative numbers yet, the subtraction problems should never ask them to subtract a larger number from a smaller one. Figure 5-39 shows the IPO chart for the `displayProblem` function.

Input	Processing	Output

operation
address of num1
 	
address of num2
	Processing items: first random number
	                       second random number
	Algorithm:
	
	1. if (operation is addition)
	       display first random number + second random
	       number math problem
	   else
	       if (first random number < second random number)
	          swap both random numbers
	       end if (first random number < second random number)
	       display first random number − second random
	       number math problem
	   end if (operation is addition)
		math
		problem

Figure 5-39: IPO chart for the `displayProblem` function

According to the IPO chart, the `displayProblem` function needs to know the operation, as well as the addresses of the num1 and num2 variables; the `main` function will need to pass this information to the `displayProblem` function. The operation, which is stored in the `operation` variable, is necessary for the function to determine whether the math problem is one of addition or subtraction. The `operation` variable will be passed by value. The addresses of the num1 and num2 variables are necessary for the function to reverse, if necessary, the random numbers stored in these variables. Therefore, the num1 and num2 variables will be passed by reference. Enter the `displayProblem` function's code.

To enter the code for the `displayProblem` function:

1 Change the `displayProblem` function's prototype from void `displayProblem( );` to void **displayProblem(char, short &, short &);**.

2 Change the function call from `displayProblem( );` to **displayProblem (operation, num1, num2);**.

3 Change the function header from void `displayProblem( )` to void **displayProblem(char operation, short &firstNum, short &secondNum)**.

4 Delete the `cout << "Function displayProblem called" << endl;` statement from the `displayProblem` function, then enter the appropriate code in the `displayProblem` function highlighted in Figure 5-40.

enter this code

```
void displayProblem(char operation, short &firstNum, short &secondNum)
{
    //this function displays a math problem
    if (operation == 'A')
        cout << firstNum << " + " << secondNum << " = ";
    else
    {
        if (firstNum < secondNum)
        {
            short temp = 0;
            temp = firstNum;
            firstNum = secondNum;
            secondNum = temp;
        }
        //end if (firstNum < secondNum)
        cout << firstNum << " - " << secondNum << " = ";
    }
    //end if (operation == 'A')
} //end of displayProblem function
```

Figure 5-40: Code entered in the `displayProblem` function

Look closely at the code shown in Figure 5-40. If the operation is addition, the statement in the true path (`cout << firstNum << " + " << secondNum << " = ";`) simply displays an addition problem on the screen. If, however, the operation is not addition, the nested `if` clause checks to see if the value stored in the `firstNum` variable is less than the value stored in the `secondNum` variable. If the value in `firstNum` is not less than the value in `secondNum`, the `cout << firstNum << " - " << secondNum << " = ";` statement displays a subtraction problem on the screen. If, on the other hand, the value in `firstNum` is less than the value in `secondNum`, then the nested `if` statement's true path swaps the numbers contained in those variables.

The four statements that accomplish the swap are `short temp = 0;`, `temp = firstNum;`, `firstNum = secondNum;`, and `secondNum = temp;`. The `short temp = 0;` statement creates and initializes a local variable named `temp`. The `temp` variable is local only to the statement block in which it is defined—in this case, it is local only to the nested `if` statement's true path. The `temp = firstNum;` statement assigns the value in the `firstNum` variable to the `temp` variable. Next, the `firstNum = secondNum;` statement assigns the value in the `secondNum` variable to the `firstNum` variable. Lastly, the `secondNum = temp;` statement assigns the value in the `temp` variable to the `secondNum` variable. The `temp` variable is necessary to store the contents of the `firstNum` variable temporarily so that the swap can be made. If you did not store the `firstNum` value in the `temp` variable, the `secondNum` value would write over the value in the `firstNum` variable, and the value in the `firstNum` variable would be lost. Figure 5-41 illustrates the concept of swapping.

	firstNum	temp	secondNum
Original values stored in the variables	4		8
Result of the `temp = firstNum;` statement	4	4	8
Result of the `firstNum = secondNum;` statement	8	4	8
Result of the `secondNum = temp;` statement	8	4	4

Figure 5-41: Illustration of the swapping concept

5 Save, build, and execute the program. When prompted for the level, type **1** and press the **Enter** key. When prompted for the operation, type **a** and press the **Enter** key. A math problem involving addition appears in the DOS window, then the program waits for the user to enter his or her answer to the problem. Type **0** and press the **Enter** key. The message "Function calcCorrectAnswer called" appears in the DOS window, and then the message "You are correct" appears, as shown in Figure 5-42.

the numbers in your math problem may differ

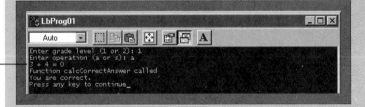

Figure 5-42: DOS window showing the math problem

6 Press the **Enter** key to close the DOS window, and then close the Output window.

Lastly, code the `calcCorrectAnswer` function.

Coding the `calcCorrectAnswer` Function

The `calcCorrectAnswer` function is responsible for calculating the correct answer to the math problem that appears on the screen. If the operation is addition, then the function needs simply to add the values stored in the `num1` and `num2` variables; otherwise, it needs to subtract the value in `num2` from the value in `num1`. Figure 5-43 shows the IPO chart for the `calcCorrectAnswer` function.

Input	Processing	Output

operation
num1
num2
	Processing items: first number
	                       second number
	Algorithm:
	1. if (operation is addition)
	      calculate correct answer by adding first number
	      to second number
	   else
	      calculate correct answer by subtracting second
	      number from first number
	   end if
	2. return correct answer
		correct
		answer

Figure 5-43: IPO chart for the `calcCorrectAnswer` function

According to the IPO chart, the `calcCorrectAnswer` function will need to know the values stored in the `operation`, `num1`, and `num2` variables. Notice that only the values of the three variables, and not their addresses, will be passed. The `calcCorrectAnswer` function will not need to make any changes to the values stored in these variables, so you should pass the variables by value rather than by reference.

Unlike the `getRandomNumbers` and `displayProblem` functions, the `calcCorrectAnswer` function will return a value—the correct answer. Complete the math program by entering the code for the `calcCorrectAnswer` function.

To complete the math program by entering the `calcCorrectAnswer` function:

1 Change the `calcCorrectAnswer` function prototype from **short calcCorrectAnswer();** to **short calcCorrectAnswer(char, short, short);**.

2 Change the `calcCorrectAnswer` function call from **correctAnswer = calcCorrectAnswer();** to **correctAnswer = calcCorrectAnswer(operation, num1, num2);**.

3 Change the `calcCorrectAnswer` function header from **short calcCorrectAnswer()** to **short calcCorrectAnswer(char operation, short firstNum, short secondNum)**.

4 Remove the **cout << "Function calcCorrectAnswer called" << endl;** and **return 0;** statements from the `calcCorrectAnswer` function's code, then enter the `calcCorrectAnswer` function's code highlighted in Figure 5-44.

```
short calcCorrectAnswer(char operation, short firstNum, short secondNum)
{
    //this function calculates the correct answer to a math problem
    short answer = 0;
    if (operation == 'A')
        answer = firstNum + secondNum;
    else
        answer = firstNum - secondNum;
    //end if
    return answer;
} //end of calcCorrectAnswer function
```

enter this code

Figure 5-44: `calcCorrectAnswer` function's code

5 Save, build, and execute the program. When prompted for the level, type **1** and press the **Enter** key. When prompted for the operation, type **a** and press the **Enter** key. A math problem involving addition appears in the DOS window. The program then waits for the user to enter his or her answer to the problem.

6 Type the correct answer to the math problem, and then press the **Enter** key. The DOS window displays the message, "You are correct." Press the **Enter** key to close the DOS window.

7 Execute the program again. When prompted for the level, type **2** and press the **Enter** key. When prompted for the operation, type **s** and press the **Enter** key. A math problem involving subtraction appears in the DOS window, then the program waits for the user to enter his or her answer to the problem.

8 Type an incorrect answer to the math problem, and then press the **Enter** key. The "Sorry, the correct answer is" message and the correct answer appear in the DOS window. Press the **Enter** key to close the DOS window.

9 On your own, execute the program several more times to be sure it is working correctly. When you are finished testing the program, close the workspace and the Output window.

You have now completed Lesson B. You can either exit Visual C++ and take a break or complete the questions and exercises at the end of the lesson.

S U M M A R Y

You can use function stubs to test a program, function by function. A function stub is merely a skeleton of a function. The skeleton contains the function header, braces, and, if it's a value-returning function, a return statement. Programmers also typically include a display message in the stub indicating whether the function was called at the appropriate time.

In C++, you use both the `srand` and `rand` functions, which are defined in the stdlib.h header file, to generate random numbers. The `srand` function initializes the random number generator. Programmers typically use the C++ `time` function as the *seed* for the `srand` function. The `time` function returns the number of seconds that have elapsed since midnight of January 1, 1970, according to your computer system's clock. The syntax for using the `time` function as the *seed* for the `srand` function is **time(NULL)**. **NULL**, which is a symbolic constant defined in both the stdlib.h and time.h header, has the value 0 (zero).

The `rand` function generates integers from 0 through **RAND_MAX**. You can use the following formula to control the range of integers produced by the `rand` function: *lowerbound* **+ rand( )** % (*upperbound - lowerbound* **+ 1**). In the syntax, *lowerbound* is the lowest value in the range, and *upperbound* is the highest value.

ANSWERS TO MINI-QUIZZES

Mini-Quiz 4

1. a function header, braces, a `return` statement, and a display message
2. `srand(time(NULL));`
3. `number = 5 + rand() % (10 − 5 + 1);`

QUESTIONS

1. A function stub typically contains _____ .
    a. the function header
    b. the function braces
    c. the return statement, if it's a value-returning function
    d. a display message
    e. all of the above

2. The C++ _____ function generates random numbers.
    a. `generate()`
    b. `genRand`
    c. `rand`
    d. `randGen`
    e. `srand`

3. The `srand` function is defined in the _____ header file.
    a. rand.h
    b. srand.h
    c. stdlib.h
    d. time.h

4. Which of the following formulas can be used to generate random integers between 1 and 10?
    a. `1 + rand() % (10 − 1 + 1)`
    b. `1 + (10 − 1 + 1) % rand()`
    c. `10 + rand() % (10 − 1 + 1)`
    d. `10 + rand() % (10 + 1)`

5. Which of the following statements uses the computer's clock to initialize the random number generator?

a. `srand(time);`

b. `srand(time(NULL));`

c. `time(srand);`

d. `time(srand(NULL));`

Use the following nested `if` structure to answer questions 6 through 9. `id` is a Short Integer variable.

```
if (id == 1)
    cout << "Janet" << endl;
else
   if (id == 2 || id == 3)
       cout << "Paul" << endl;
   else
       if (id == 4)
           cout << "Jerry" << endl;
       else
           cout << "Sue" << endl;
       //end if (id == 4)
   //end if (id == 2 || id == 3)
//end if (id == 1)
```

6. What will the `if` structure display if the `id` variable contains the number 2?

a. Janet

b. Jerry

c. Paul

d. Sue

e. nothing

7. What will the `if` structure display if the `id` variable contains the number 4?

a. Janet

b. Jerry

c. Paul

d. Sue

e. nothing

8. What will the `if` structure display if the `id` variable contains the number 3?

a. Janet

b. Jerry

c. Paul

d. Sue

e. nothing

9. What will the `if` structure display if the `id` variable contains the number 8?

a. Janet

b. Jerry

c. Paul

d. Sue

e. nothing

E X E R C I S E S

1. Scenario: Jacques Cousard has been playing the lotto for four years and has yet to win any money. He wants a program that will select the six lotto numbers for him. Each lotto number can range from 1 to 54 only. (An example of six lotto numbers is 4, 8, 35, 15, 20, 3. For this program, it is all right if each of the six lotto numbers is not unique. In Tutorial 8, which covers variable arrays, you will learn how to create a program that displays six unique random numbers.)

   a. Create an IPO chart or charts for the problem.

   b. Create a console application named T5Be01 in the Cpp\Tut05 folder on your computer's hard disk. Enter the code to display the lotto numbers. Use the `srand`, `rand`, and `time` functions to generate the random numbers. Also send the lotto numbers to a file for printing. Name the file T5Be01.dat.

   c. Save, build, and execute the program. When the program is working correctly, print the code. Use C++ to open and print the contents of the T5Be01.dat file.

2. Scenario: Ferris Seminars runs computer seminars. The owner of the company wants a program that the registration clerks can use to calculate the registration fee for each customer. Many of Ferris' customers are companies that register more than one person for a seminar. The registration clerk will need to enter the number registered for the seminar, the seminar ID (either 1 or 2), and whether the customer is entitled to a 10 percent discount (y or n). (The customer will register for only one seminar at a time.) The program should calculate and display the total due. Seminar 1 is $100 per person, and Seminar 2 is $120 per person.

   a. Create an IPO chart or charts for the program. (Use a value-returning function to calculate and return the total due.)

   b. Create a console application named T5Be02 in the Cpp\Tut05 folder on your computer's hard disk. First code the program using a stub for a value-returning function that will calculate and return the total due. Save, build, and execute the program. When the program is working correctly, print the code.

   c. Now code the value-returning function so that it calculates and returns the total due. (Perform a case-insensitive character comparison.) Save, build, and execute the program.

   d. Add the code to send the program information (the number registered, the seminar ID, whether the customer gets a discount, and the total due) to a file for printing. Name the file T5Be02.dat. Include a decimal point and two decimal places in the discount and the total due. Save, build, and execute the program.

   e. When the program is working correctly, execute it twice, using the following data. Use C++ to open and print the T5Be02.dat file after each execution.

	First execution	Second execution
Number registered	3	5
Seminar ID	2	1
Discount	n	y

   f. Print the code.

3. Scenario: Jacob Heaters, Inc. wants a program that the clerks can use to calculate and display the total amount due on an order. The clerk will need to enter the number of units ordered. The program should calculate the total amount due by multiplying the number of units by the price per unit. The price per unit depends on how many units are ordered, as follows:

Number of units	Price per unit ($)
1 – 4	10
5 – 10	9
11 and over	7

   a. Create an IPO chart or charts for the program. (Use a value-returning function to calculate and return the total due.)

b. Create a console application named T5Be03 in the Cpp\Tut05 folder on your computer's hard disk. First code the program using a stub for a value-returning function that will calculate and return the total due. Save, build, and execute the program. When the program is working correctly, print the code.

c. Now code the value-returning function so that it calculates and returns the total due. Save, build, and execute the program.

d. Add the code to send the program information (the number of units and the total due) to a file for printing. Name the file T5Be03.dat. Include a decimal point and two decimal places in the total due. Save, build, and execute the program.

e. When the program is working correctly, execute it twice, using the following data for the number of units: 10 and 15. Use C++ to open and print the T5Be03.dat file after each execution.

f. Print the code.

4. Scenario: Flowers Forever wants a program that the clerks can use to calculate and display each salesperson's annual bonus. The clerk will need to enter the salesperson's name and sales. The application should calculate the bonus based on the amount of sales, as follows:

Amount of sales	Bonus ($)
0 – 3000.99	0
3001 – 5000.99	50
5001 – 9999.99	100
10000 and over	250

a. Create an IPO chart or charts for the program. (Use a value-returning function to calculate and return the bonus.)

b. Create a console application named T5Be04 in the Cpp\Tut05 folder on your computer's hard disk. First code the program using a stub for a value-returning function that will calculate and return the bonus. Save, build, and execute the program. When the program is working correctly, print the code.

c. Now code the value-returning function so that it calculates and returns the bonus. Save, build, and execute the program.

d. Add the code to send the program information (the salesperson's name, sales, and bonus) to a file for printing. Name the file T5Be04.dat. Include a decimal point and two decimal places in the sales and bonus. Save, build, and execute the program.

e. When the program is working correctly, execute it twice, using the following data. Use C++ to open and print the T5Be04.dat file after each execution.

	First execution	Second execution
Salesperson's name	John Smith	Paula Gonzales
Sales	3001	5001.67

f. Print the code.

5. Scenario: Western Veterinarians wants a program that its receptionist can use to look up the veterinarian's fee for performing a specific medical procedure. The receptionist will need to enter a two-letter code that represents the procedure. The program should then display the procedure and the veterinarian's fee. The two-letter codes, as well as the corresponding procedure and fee, are as follows:

Code	Procedure	Fee ($)
TC	Teeth cleaning	50
RV	Rabies vaccination	15
OS	Other shots	5
HW	Heartworm test	15
FC	Fecal check	5
OV	Office visit	15

For any other codes, display an "Invalid entry" message.

a. Create an IPO chart or charts for the program. (Use a void function to display the procedure and the fee.)

b. Create a console application named T5Be05 in the Cpp\Tut05 folder on your computer's hard disk. First code the program using a stub for a void function that will display the procedure and the fee. Save, build, and execute the program. When the program is working correctly, print the code.

c. Now code the void function so that it displays both the procedure and fee that correspond to the two-letter code entered by the user. Perform a case-insensitive string comparison. (*Hint*: Notice that some of the procedures have the same fee.) Save, build, and execute the program.

d. Add the code to send the program information (the code, procedure, and fee) to a file for printing. Name the file T5Be05.dat. Include a decimal point and two decimal places in the fee. Save, build, and execute the program.

e. When the program is working correctly, execute it three times, using the following data for the two-letter code: TC, OS, and RR. Use C++ to open and print the T5Be05.dat file after each execution.

f. Print the code.

6. Scenario: Willow Health Club needs a program that it can use to calculate and display each member's monthly dues. The basic monthly fee is $80. Depending on the membership type, additional charges may need to be added to the basic fee. For example, if a person's membership includes tennis, you will need to add $30 to his or her monthly fee. If the membership includes golf, add $25 to the monthly fee; if it includes racquetball, add $20. Every member is charged the basic fee, but it is possible for a member to have zero or more additional charges.

a. Create an IPO chart or charts for the program.

b. Create a console application named T5Be06 in the Cpp\Tut05 folder on your computer's hard disk.

c. Write a program that calculates and displays a member's monthly dues. Save, build, and execute the program.

d. Add the code to send the program information (the basic monthly fee, any additional charges, and the total monthly dues) to a file for printing. Name the file T5Be06.dat. Include a decimal point and two decimal places in the numeric output. Save, build, and execute the program.

e. When the program is working correctly, execute it three times. The first membership includes golf, the second membership has only the basic fee, and the third membership has racquetball and tennis. Use C++ to open and print the T5Be06.dat file after each execution.

f. Print the code.

7. Scenario: Marine Packing Company wants a program that the order department can use to calculate and display the price of an order. The order clerks will need to enter the number of units ordered, and whether the customer is a retailer or a wholesaler. The price per unit depends on both the customer type (wholesaler or retailer) and the number of units ordered, as follows:

Wholesaler		Retailer	
Number of units	Price per unit ($)	Number of units	Price per unit ($)
1 – 4	10	1 – 3	15
5 and over	9	4 – 8	14
		9 and over	12

a. Create an IPO chart or charts for the program.

b. Create a console application named T5Be07 in the Cpp\Tut05 folder on your computer's hard disk.

c. Write a program that calculates and displays the total price of the order. Save, build, and execute the program.

d. Add the code to send the program information (the customer type, the number of units ordered, and the total price) to a file for printing. Name the file T5Be07.dat. Include a decimal point and two decimal places in the total price. Save, build, and execute the program.

e. When the program is working correctly, execute it four times. First, calculate the total price for a retailer ordering 10 units. Second, calculate the total price for a retailer ordering two units. Third, calculate the total price for a wholesaler ordering 10 units. Fourth, calculate the total price for a wholesaler ordering two units. Use C++ to open and print the T5Be07.dat file after each execution.

f. Print the code.

8. Scenario: Your brother is currently taking a geometry class. He would like you to create a program that he can use to verify his calculations. Specifically, he wants the program to calculate the area of a square, rectangle, parallelogram, circle, and triangle.

a. Create an IPO chart or charts for the program.

b. Create a console application named T5Be08 in the Cpp\Tut05 folder on your computer's hard disk.

c. Write a program that enters a numeric code that represents the type of area calculation to perform. A code of 1 represents a square, 2 is a rectangle, 3 is a parallelogram, 4 is a circle, and 5 is a triangle. The program will also need to enter the dimensions of the shape. The program should calculate the area of the shape. It should also display the name of the shape (Square, Rectangle, and so on) and the area.

d. Save, build, and execute the program. Test the program using your own data.

e. Add the code to send the program information (the shape name and area) to a file for printing. Name the file T5Be08.dat. Save, build, and execute the program.

f. When the program is working correctly, execute it five times, using the following data: a square side measurement of 4, a rectangle length of 5 and width of 3, a parallelogram base of 3 and height of 4, a circle radius of 2, a triangle base of 4 and height of 3. Use C++ to open and print the T5Be08.dat file after each execution.

g. Print the code.

9. Scenario: Your friend George wants a program that his young son can use to learn the concepts of "greater than," "less than," and "equal to." The game will simulate the rolling of two dice. As you know, a die has six sides; each side contains a number of dots, from 1 through 6. George wants the game to roll two dice and then display the number of dots appearing on each die. The program should then ask his son to select from the following three choices: the numbers on the dice are equal, the number on the first die is greater than the number on the second die, or the number on the first die is less than the number on the second die. The program should display an appropriate message that indicates whether his son's choice is correct or incorrect.

a. Create an IPO chart or charts for the program.

b. Create a console application named T5Be09 in the Cpp\Tut05 folder on your computer's hard disk.

c. Write a program that solves the problem outlined in the scenario.

d. Save, build, and execute the program.

e. When the program is working correctly, print the code.

discovery ▶ 10. In this exercise, you will display your system's value of RAND_MAX.

a. Open the T5Be10.cpp file, which is located in the Cpp\Tut05\T5Be10 folder on your computer's hard disk.

b. Study the code in the program. Build and execute the program.

c. Print the code. On the code printout, indicate the value of the RAND_MAX symbolic constant on your system.

debugging

11. In this exercise, you will debug a program.
   a. Open the T5Be11.cpp file, which is located in the Cpp\Tut05\T5Be11 folder on your computer's hard disk.
   b. Print the code.
   c. The program should display a random number from 1 through 25 on the screen. Debug the program.
   d. When the program is working correctly, print the code. On the code printout, indicate what was wrong with the program and circle the corrections you made.

debugging

12. In this exercise, you will debug a program.
   a. Open the T5Be12.cpp file, which is located in the Cpp\Tut05\T5Be12 folder on your computer's hard disk.
   b. Print the code. The program should display $45,000 if the user enters the number 1 as the code, $33,000 if the user enters either a 2 or a 5, and $25,000 if the user enters either a 3 or a 4.
   c. Build and then execute the program several times. You will notice that the program is not working correctly. Debug the program.
   d. When the program is working correctly, print the code. On the code printout, indicate what was wrong with the program and circle the corrections you made.

The Repetition Structure (Looping)

case ▶ Next Monday is career day at your alma mater. Professor Carver, one of your computer programming instructors, has asked you to be a guest speaker in his Introduction to Programming class. You gladly accept this speaking engagement and begin planning your presentation. You decide to show the students how to create a program that will calculate their grades in Professor Carver's class. Before you can begin coding the grade program, you will need to learn about the repetition structure. The grade program will use the repetition structure to enter the students' project and test scores.

LESSON A
objectives

In this lesson you will learn how to:

■ Write pseudocode for the `while` repetition structure

■ Create a flowchart for the `while` repetition structure

■ Code the `while` repetition structure

■ Initialize and update counters and accumulators

The while Loop

The Repetition Structure

As you may remember from Tutorial 1, the three control structures used in programs are sequence, selection, and repetition. The programs you created in Tutorials 2 through 4 used the sequence programming structure only, where each of the program instructions was processed, one after another, in the order in which it appeared in the program. In Tutorial 5, you learned how to include both the sequence and selection structures in a program. Recall that the selection structure allows the program to make a decision and then select the appropriate action to take based on the result of that decision. In addition to using the sequence and selection structures, most programs also use the repetition structure. As you learned in Tutorial 1, the repetition structure directs the computer to repeat one or more instructions until a condition is met.

As with the sequence and selection structures, you are already familiar with the repetition structure. Figure 6-1 shows examples of repetition structures that you may have encountered today. Example 1's instructions are similar to those found on a shampoo bottle. Example 2's instructions, which indicate how to make a glass of chocolate milk, are similar to those found on a can of chocolate syrup.

Example 1	Example 2

repeat (until hair is clean)
    apply shampoo to wet hair
    lather
    rinse
	pour eight ounces of milk into a glass
	pour two teaspoons of chocolate syrup into the glass
	repeat (until milk and syrup are mixed thoroughly)
	    stir

Figure 6-1: Examples of the repetition structure

You will notice that both examples direct the user to repeat one or more instructions until a specified condition is met. The repetition structure shown in Example 1, for instance, directs the user to repeat the "apply shampoo to wet hair," "lather," and "rinse" instructions until his or her hair is clean. In Example 2, the repetition structure directs the user to repeat the "stir" instruction until the milk and syrup are mixed thoroughly.

Programmers use the **repetition structure**, also called **looping** or **iteration**, to tell the computer to repeat one or more program instructions either a specified number of times or until some condition, referred to as the loop condition, is met. The two forms of the repetition structure are `while` and `do-while`. You will learn about the `while` loop in this lesson; the `do-while` loop is covered in Lesson B. First learn how to represent the `while` loop in pseudocode.

Representing the `while` Loop in Pseudocode

Figure 6-2 shows two examples of the `while` loop written in pseudocode. The first example allows a user to continue entering a letter until he or she enters the letter X. The second example uses the `while` loop simply to display the numbers 1 through 3 on the screen.

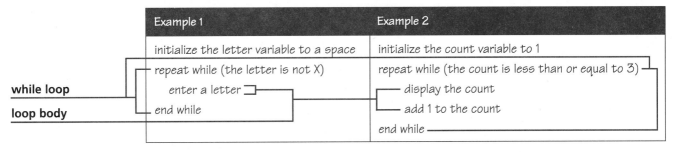

Example 1	Example 2
initialize the letter variable to a space	initialize the count variable to 1
repeat while (the letter is not X)	repeat while (the count is less than or equal to 3)
enter a letter	display the count
end while	add 1 to the count
	end while

while loop

loop body

Figure 6-2: Pseudocode for the `while` loop

As mentioned in Tutorial 5, pseudocode is not standardized—every programmer has his or her own version—but you will find some similarities among the various versions. For example, many programmers begin the `while` repetition structure with the two words `repeat while` and end the structure with the two words `end while`, as shown in Figure 6-2. The one or more instructions between the `repeat while` and the `end while` are called the body of the loop—or, simply, the **loop body**.

In the examples shown in Figure 6-2, the portion shown in parentheses indicates the loop condition that the `while` loop must evaluate. Notice that each loop condition results in either a True or a False answer only. Either the `letter` variable contains the letter X, or it doesn't; either the value in the `count` variable is less than or equal to 3, or it isn't. When the loop condition evaluates to True, the one or more instructions listed in the body of the loop are processed; otherwise, these instructions are skipped over. Because the `while` loop evaluates the loop condition before processing any of the statements within the loop, it is referred to as a **pretest loop**, or **top-driven loop**.

After each processing of the loop body instructions, the loop condition is reevaluated to determine if the instructions should be processed again. The loop's instructions will be processed and its loop condition evaluated until it evaluates to False, at which time the loop will end and processing will continue with the instruction immediately following the `end while`.

Recall that programmers, in addition to using pseudocode, also use flowcharts to help them plan algorithms. In the next section, you will learn how to illustrate the `while` loop in a flowchart.

Including the `while` loop in a Flowchart

Recall that a flowchart uses standardized symbols to show the steps the computer needs to take to accomplish a program's goal. Figure 6-3 shows Figure 6-2's examples in flowchart form.

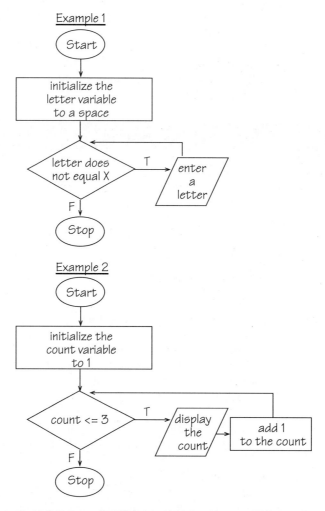

Figure 6-3: Examples of the `while` loop drawn in flowchart form

Recall that the oval in the figure is the start/stop symbol, the rectangle is the process symbol, the parallelogram is the input/output symbol, and the diamond is the selection/repetition symbol. In Figure 6-3's flowcharts, the diamonds indicate the beginning of a `while` repetition structure. As with the selection structure diamond, which you learned about in Tutorial 5, the repetition structure diamond contains a question that has a true or false answer only. The question represents the loop condition that the repetition structure must evaluate.

Like the selection diamond, the repetition diamond has two flowlines leaving the symbol. The flowline marked with a "T" (for true) leads to the body of the loop—the instructions to process when the loop condition evaluates to True. The flowline marked with an "F" (for false) leads to the instructions that will be processed once the loop condition evaluates to False.

Unlike the selection diamond, the repetition diamond has two flowlines leading into the diamond, rather than one flowline. One of the flowlines comes from the symbol located immediately above the diamond. In the examples shown in Figure 6-3, the symbols immediately above the repetition diamond are the rectangles that contain the instructions to initialize the `letter` and `count` variables. You will notice that each of those rectangles has a flowline that flows into the repetition diamond.

tip

....

The symbol located immediately above the repetition diamond represents the instruction that will be processed immediately before the loop condition is evaluated.

The second flowline leading into the repetition diamond flows from the repetition structure's true path, which contains the loop body instructions. In the first example shown in Figure 6-3, the flowline leading out of the "enter a letter" input parallelogram, which is the only symbol in the true path, flows back up to the repetition diamond. In the second example shown in Figure 6-3, the flowline leading out of the "add 1 to the count" process rectangle—the last symbol in the true path—flows back up to the repetition diamond. You will notice that the two flowlines leading into the repetition diamond, as well as the symbols and flowlines within the true path, form a circle or loop. It is this loop that distinguishes the repetition structure from the selection structure in a flowchart.

Study each symbol in the first flowchart shown in Figure 6-3. After the letter variable is initialized to a space, the loop condition in the repetition diamond compares the contents of the letter variable to the letter X. If the letter variable does not contain the letter X, then the instruction in the loop body will allow the user to enter a letter. After the user enters a letter, the letter he or she entered is compared to the letter X to determine if the loop instruction should be processed again. The repetition structure continues to allow the user to enter a letter until he or she enters the letter X, at which time the loop stops.

Now study the symbols in the second flowchart shown in Figure 6-3. After the count variable is initialized to the number 1, the loop condition in the repetition diamond compares the contents of the count variable to the number 3. If the count variable contains a number that is less than or equal to 3, then the instructions in the loop body will display the value contained in the count variable and will also increment the count variable by 1. The repetition structure continues to both display and increment the value in the count variable while that value is less than or equal to 3. When the value in the count variable is greater than 3, the loop stops.

Next, learn how to code the while loop in C++.

Coding the while Loop in C++

Recall that you can use the while loop to repeat one or more statements either a specified number of times, or as long as—or while—a loop condition is True. You use the C++ while statement to code the while loop. Figure 6-4 shows the syntax and two examples of the while statement. The two examples correspond to the pseudocode and flowchart examples shown in Figures 6-2 and 6-3, respectively. Example 1 shows how you can use the while statement to input one or more characters. Example 2 shows how you can use the while statement to display the numbers 1 through 3.

while **clause (does not end in a semicolon)**

loop body

Syntax

while (*loop condition*)
   one statement, or a block of statements enclosed in braces, that you want
   the loop to repeat
//end while

Example 1	Example 2
```char letter = ' ';```	```short count = 1;```
```while (toupper(letter) != 'X')```	```while(count <= 3)```
``` cin >> letter;```	```{```
```//end while```	``` cout << count << endl;```
	``` count = count + 1;```
	```}//end while```

Figure 6-4: Syntax and examples of the while statement

As the syntax in Figure 6-4 indicates, the while statement begins with the while clause—the keyword while followed by a *loop condition*. (Notice that the while clause does not end with a semicolon, because only C++ statements, and not clauses, end with a semicolon. Like the *condition* in the selection structure, which you learned about in Tutorial 5, the *loop condition* must be enclosed in parentheses.)

The while clause is followed by the body of the loop, which contains the one or more statements that you want the loop to repeat. If the loop body contains only one statement, as shown in Example 1, then the while loop ends when it encounters the semicolon at the end of that one statement. If, on the other hand, the loop body contains a group of statements enclosed in braces (a statement block), as shown in Example 2, then the while loop ends when it encounters the statement block's closing brace. As you did with the selection structure, you can use a comment, such as //end while, to mark the end of the while loop, as shown in Figure 6-4.

The *loop condition* in the while clause determines whether the statements listed in the body of the while loop are processed. Like the *condition* in the selection structure, the *loop condition* must be a Boolean expression, which is an expression that evaluates to either the Boolean value True or the Boolean value False. The *loop condition* can contain variables, constants, functions, mathematical operators, relational operators, and logical operators.

Recall that the while loop is a pretest or top-driven loop. This simply means that the loop evaluates the *loop condition* before processing any of the instructions within the loop. If the *loop condition* evaluates to True, then the loop instructions are processed until the *loop condition* evaluates to False, at which time C++ stops processing the loop instructions. Processing then continues with the statement immediately following the end of the loop.

Depending on the *loop condition*, the instructions in a while loop may not be processed at all. For example, if the *loop condition* evaluates initially to False, C++ skips the instructions within the loop and processing then continues with the first statement following the end of the loop.

Take a closer look at the instructions in Figure 6-4's Example 1. The instructions begin by declaring a Character variable named letter and initializing it to a space. The while (toupper(letter) != 'X') clause tells C++ to compare the contents of the letter variable, in uppercase, to the letter X. As long as—in other words, while—the letter variable does not contain either the letter X or the letter x, the cin >> letter; statement will get a character from the user at the keyboard and will store that character in the letter variable. Each time the user enters a character, the while clause compares the uppercase equivalent of that character to the letter X. When the user enters either the letter X or the letter x, C++ stops processing the loop. Processing then continues with the line immediately below the end of the loop—in Example 1, processing would continue with the statement located immediately below the //end while comment.

Next, study the instructions in Figure 6-4's Example 2, which displays the numbers 1 through 3 on the screen. The instructions begin by declaring a Short Integer variable named count and initializing it to 1. The while clause then evaluates the *loop condition*, (count <= 3), to determine whether the loop instructions should be processed. If the count variable contains a number that is

---

tip

Rarely will you use while loops that contain only one statement. Most will contain a statement block, which is a group of statements enclosed in braces. Even if a loop contains only one statement, as in Figure 6-4's Example 1, you can enclose the statement in braces, but that is not required by the C++ syntax. Including the braces in a loop that contains only one statement has the following advantage: you will not need to remember to enter the braces if additional statements are added to the loop in the future. Forgetting to enter the braces around a statement block is a common error made by programmers.

less than or equal to 3, the loop instructions, which display the value of count on the screen and also add 1 to count, are processed. After the body of the loop is processed, C++ returns to the beginning of the loop (the while clause), where the *loop condition* is tested again. If the value in count is still less than or equal to 3, the loop instructions are processed again, and so on.

If count does not contain a number that is less than or equal to 3 (in other words, if count is greater than 3), then the loop stops and the instructions within the loop are not processed. Processing then continues with the first statement following the end of the loop. In Figure 6-4's Example 2, the processing would continue with the statement located immediately below the }//end while line.

In the next section, you will open a program that allows you to observe how the while statement works in a program.

mini-quiz

Mini-Quiz 1

1. Write a while clause that processes the loop instructions as long as the value in the quantity variable is greater than the number 0.

2. Write a while clause that stops the loop when the value in the quantity variable is less than the number 0.

3. Write a while clause that processes the loop instructions as long as the value in the onHand variable is greater than the value in the reorder variable.

4. Assume that a program declares a Short Integer variable named evenNum and initializes it to 2. Write a while loop that uses the evenNum variable to display the even integers between 1 and 9.

Using a while Statement in a Program

The LaProg01.cpp file, which is located in the Cpp\Tut06\LaProg01 folder on your computer's hard disk, demonstrates how the while statement works in a program. The demo program contains a while statement that displays the numbers 1 through 3 on the screen.

To open the while statement demo program:

1 Start Visual C++. Open the **LaProg01.cpp** file, which is located in the Cpp\Tut06\LaProg01 folder on your computer's hard disk. The while statement demo program, which appears in the LaProg01.cpp window, is shown in Figure 6-5.

```
//LaProg01.cpp
//this program demonstrates the while loop

#include <iostream.h>

void main()
{
    //declare and initialize variable
    short count = 1;

    //display numbers 1 through 3
    while (count <= 3)
    {
      cout << count << endl;
      count = count + 1;
    } //end while

    cout << "End of the while loop" << endl;

} //end of main function
```

while **statement**

Figure 6-5: while statement demo program

Observe how the demo program displays the numbers 1 through 3 on the screen.

2   Build and execute the program. C++ processes the instructions as shown in Figure 6-6, and the numbers 1, 2, and 3, as well as the "End of the while loop" message, appear in the DOS window.`

1. count variable is created and initialized to the number 1.

2. while clause checks if the value in count is less than or equal to 3. It is.

3. First loop instruction displays 1 (the contents of count) on the screen.

4. Second loop instruction adds 1 to count, giving 2.

5. C++ returns to the beginning of the loop (the while clause).

6. while clause checks if the value in count is less than or equal to 3. It is.

7. First loop instruction displays 2 (the contents of count) on the screen.

8. Second loop instruction adds 1 to count, giving 3.

9. C++ returns to the beginning of the loop (the while clause).

10. while clause checks if the value in count is less than or equal to 3. It is.

11. First loop instruction displays 3 (the contents of count) on the screen.

12. Second loop instruction adds 1 to count, giving 4.

13. C++ returns to the beginning of the loop (the while clause).

14. while clause checks if the value in count is less than or equal to 3. It's not.

15. Loop stops. C++ processes the first statement following the end of the loop—in this case, C++ displays the "End of the while loop" message.

Figure 6-6: Processing steps for the while statement demo program

3 Press the **Enter** key to close the DOS window, then close the Output window.

Next, observe how the `while` statement works when the *loop condition* initially evaluates to False.

To observe how the `while` statement works when the *loop condition* initially evaluates to False:

1 Change the `short count = 1;` statement to **short count = 10;**.

By setting the initial value of `count` to 10, the *loop condition* (`count <= 3`) evaluates to False, so C++ will skip the loop instructions. See if that is, in fact, what happens.

2 Save, build, and execute the program. As expected, the numbers 1 through 3 do not appear on the screen. Instead, only the "End of the while loop" message appears. Because the *loop condition* (`count <= 3`) evaluated to False, the instructions within the loop body were not processed. Figure 6-7 shows how C++ processed the modified demo program's statements.

---

1. `count` variable is created and initialized to the number 10.

2. `while` clause checks if the value in `count` is less than or equal to 3. It's not.

3. Loop stops. C++ processes the first statement following the end of the loop—

    in this case, C++ displays the "End of the while loop" message.

Figure 6-7: Processing steps for the modified `while` statement demo program

3 Press the **Enter** key to close the DOS window, then close the Output window.

4 To return the file to its original state, change the `short count = 10;` statement back to **short count = 1;**.

5 Save, build, and execute the file to verify that it is working properly, then press the **Enter** key to close the DOS window.

You are finished with this program, so you can close it.

6 Close the workspace and the Output window.

You will now look at another program that uses the `while` loop.

Using the `while` Loop in a Game

In the next program, you will use the `while` loop to code a game that races two players against each other. The game program will include the three control structures: sequence, selection, and repetition.

To open the game program:

1 Open the **LaProg02.cpp** file, which is located in the Cpp\Tut06\LaProg02 folder on your computer's hard disk. The game program, which appears in the LaProg02.cpp window, is shown in Figure 6-8.

tip

You also could have written the two instructions that generate the random numbers as `player1 = 1 + rand() % 40;` and `player2 = 1 + rand() % 40;`. However, the two instructions shown in the game program are more self-documenting because they remind you that the formula for generating a random number is *lowerbound* + **rand**() % (*upperbound - lowerbound* + **1**).

selection structure

```cpp
//LaProg02.cpp
//this program simulates a game that races two players
//against each other

#include <iostream.h>
#include <stdlib.h>
#include <time.h>

//function prototypes
void displayAsterisks(short);

void main()
{
    //declare and initialize variables
    short player1 = 0;
    short player2 = 0;

    //seed random number generator
    srand(time(NULL));

    //generate two random numbers
    player1 = 1 + rand() % (40 - 1 + 1);
    player2 = 1 + rand() % (40 - 1 + 1);

    //call function to display asterisks
    displayAsterisks(player1);
    displayAsterisks(player2);

    //display appropriate message
    if (player1 > player2)
            cout << endl << "Player 1 wins!" << endl << endl;
    else
    {
            if (player1 < player2)
                    cout << endl << "Player 2 wins!"  << endl << endl;
            else
                    cout << endl << "It's a tie!" << endl << endl;
            //end if (player1 < player2)
    } //end if (player1 > player2)
} //end of main function
```

Figure 6-8: Game program

```
//*****programmer-defined function definitions*****
void displayAsterisks(short number)
{
    //this function displays a row of asterisks
    //the number of asterisks displayed depends on the value
    //stored in the number formal parameter

    //declare and initialize variable
    short count = 1;

    while (count <= number)
    {
        cout << '*';
        count = count + 1;
    } //end while
    cout << endl;
} //end of displayAsterisks function
```

repetition structure

Figure 6-8: Game program (continued)

After declaring and initializing two Short Integer variables, player1 and player2, the main function calls the srand function to initialize the C++ random number generator. Two random numbers from 1 through 40 are then generated and assigned to the player1 and player2 variables. The main function then calls the displayAsterisks function twice, first passing it the random number in the player1 variable and then passing it the random number in the player2 variable. The displayAsterisks function is a programmer-defined void function whose task is to display a row of asterisks on the screen. The number of asterisks to display depends on the random number sent to the function. If, for example, the number 5 is passed to the displayAsterisks function, then the function will display five asterisks.

After the appropriate number of asterisks is displayed for each player, the selection structure in the main function compares the contents of the player1 variable to the contents of the player2 variable and displays the appropriate message—either "Player 1 wins," "Player 2 wins," or "It's a tie."

Now look at the code in the displayAsterisks function. You will notice that the function creates a Short Integer formal parameter named number. The displayAsterisks function will use its formal parameter to store the values passed to it by the function calls in the main function. As you learned in Tutorial 4, the number formal parameter is local to the displayAsterisks function, which means that only the displayAsterisks function has access to that formal parameter.

The displayAsterisks function also declares a Short Integer variable named count and initializes it to 1. Like the number formal parameter, the count variable is local to the displayAsterisks function. After initializing the count variable, the function uses the while loop to display the appropriate number of asterisks. Each time an asterisk is displayed, the value in the count variable increases by 1. The while loop will continue displaying asterisks while the value in the count variable is less than or equal to the value in the number formal parameter. It will stop when the value in count is greater than the value in number. When the displayAsterisks function ends, C++ removes the count variable and the number formal parameter from memory.

▶ In addition to the main function, programmer-defined functions also can display information on the screen.

▶ You also could have initialized the count variable to 0, but then the while statement's *loop condition* would need to be (count < number).

Now run the game program to see how it works.

> **To run the game program:**
>
> **1** The LaProg02.cpp file should be open. Build and execute the program. Two rows of asterisks, each row representing a player, appear in the DOS window, along with either the "It's a tie!," "Player 1 wins!," or "Player 2 wins!" message.
>
> **2** Press the **Enter** key to close the DOS window.
>
> You are finished with this program, so you can close it.
>
> **3** Close the workspace and the Output window.

Now that you know how to use the `while` repetition structure, you can learn about counters and accumulators. You will often find either a counter or an accumulator, or both, within a repetition structure.

Using Counters and Accumulators

Counters and accumulators are used within a repetition structure to calculate subtotals, totals, and averages. A **counter** is a numeric variable used for counting something—such as the number of employees paid in a week. An **accumulator** is a numeric variable used for accumulating (adding together) something—such as the total dollar amount of a week's payroll.

Two tasks are associated with counters and accumulators: initializing and updating. **Initializing** means to assign a beginning value to the counter or accumulator. Although that beginning value is usually zero, counters and accumulators can be initialized to any number. The initialization task is typically done outside of the repetition structure.

Updating, also called incrementing, means adding a number to the value stored in the counter or the accumulator. A counter is always incremented by a constant value—typically the number 1—whereas an accumulator is incremented by a value that varies. The assignment statement that updates a counter or an accumulator is placed within the repetition structure.

You will use both a counter and an accumulator in the Sales Express Inc. program, which you will view next.

The Sales Express Inc. Program

Assume that Sales Express Inc. wants a program that the sales manager can use to calculate and display the average amount sold during the prior year. The sales manager will enter the amount of each salesperson's sales. The program will use both a counter and an accumulator to calculate the average sales, which will then be displayed on the screen. Figure 6-9 shows the IPO chart for this program. (The Processing column shows both the flowchart and the pseudocode for this problem. Recall, however, that you need to use only one of these two planning tools. Both tools are shown for your information only.)

tip

▶ Counters are used to answer the question, "How many?"—for example, "How many salespeople live in Virginia?" Accumulators are used to answer the question, "How much?"—for example, "How much did the salespeople sell this quarter?"

Input	Processing	Output
sales amounts	Processing items: a counter to count the number of sales amounts entered an accumulator to total the sales amounts entered Algorithm: 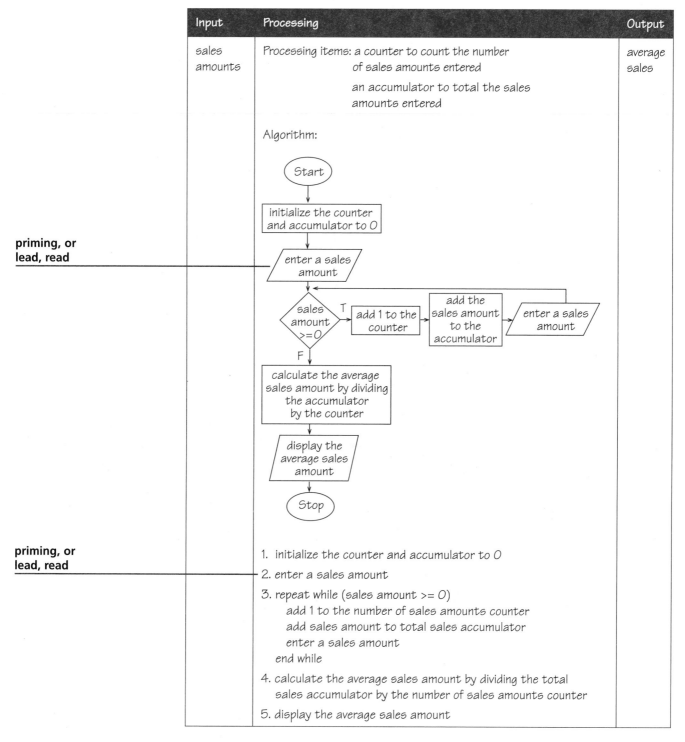	average sales

priming, or lead, read

priming, or lead, read

1. initialize the counter and accumulator to 0
2. enter a sales amount
3. repeat while (sales amount >= 0)
   add 1 to the number of sales amounts counter
   add sales amount to total sales accumulator
   enter a sales amount
   end while
4. calculate the average sales amount by dividing the total sales accumulator by the number of sales amounts counter
5. display the average sales amount

Figure 6-9: IPO chart for the Sales Express Inc. program

According to Figure 6-9, the program begins by initializing both a counter and an accumulator to 0. The program will use the counter to keep track of the number of sales amounts entered, using the accumulator to total those amounts. After initializing the counter and accumulator, the program will get a sales amount from the user. The `while` loop will then evaluate the *loop condition*—in this case, the loop will determine if the sales amount entered by the user is greater than or equal to zero. If it is, the loop instructions will increment the counter by one, then increment the accumulator by the sales amount, and then get another sales amount from the user. The program will then return to the beginning of the loop where the *loop condition* will be evaluated again. When the user enters a sales amount that is not greater than or equal to zero, the loop will stop and the average sales amount will be calculated and displayed.

You will notice that the flowchart shown in Figure 6-9 contains two input parallelograms that say "enter a sales amount." One of the input parallelograms is located above the repetition structure's diamond, and the other is the last symbol in the repetition structure's true path. You may be wondering why both input parallelograms are necessary in the flowchart. Recall that the `while` repetition structure begins with the repetition diamond, and that the flowlines leading into the diamond, along with the symbols and flowlines in the repetition structure's true path, form a circle or loop. Notice two things about the first input parallelogram in Figure 6-9's flowchart. First, it appears above the repetition diamond, and second, it is not one of the symbols included in the loop. The input parallelogram located above the repetition diamond represents what programmers refer to as the **priming read**, or the **lead read**. In this case, the priming read parallelogram will get only the first sales amount from the user. The second input parallelogram, the one located within the loop, will get each of the remaining sales amounts, if any, from the user.

You will notice that the pseudocode for this problem also contains two "enter a sales amount" instructions. Here again, the first "enter a sales amount" instruction is the priming read and it will get the first sales amount only. The "enter a sales amount" instruction that appears as the last instruction in the loop body will get the remaining sales amounts.

Open the Sales Express Inc. program, which contains the code that corresponds to the flowchart and pseudocode shown in Figure 6-9.

To open the Sales Express Inc. program:

1   Open the **LaProg03.cpp** file, which is located in the Cpp\Tut06\LaProg03 folder on your computer's hard disk. The Sales Express Inc. program, which appears in the LaProg03.cpp window, is shown in Figure 6-10.

```
//LaProg03.cpp
//this program displays the average sales amount

#include <iostream.h>

void main()
{
    //declare and initialize variables
    float   sales    = (float) 0.0;
    float   sumSales = (float) 0.0;        //accumulator
    float   avgSales = (float) 0.0;
    short   numSales = 0;                  //counter

    //enter first sales amount
    cout << "Type a sales amount and press Enter" << endl;
    cout << "Enter a negative number when finished: ";
    cin >> sales;

    //update counter and accumulator, enter remaining sales amounts
    while (sales >= 0)
    {
        numSales = numSales + 1;
        sumSales = sumSales + sales;
        cout << "Type a sales amount and press Enter" << endl;
        cout << "Enter a negative number when finished: ";
        cin >> sales;
    } //end while

    //calculate average sales
    avgSales = sumSales / (float) numSales;

    //display output
    cout << endl << "Average sales: " << avgSales << endl;
} //end of main function
```

Figure 6-10: Sales Express program

tip

Recall that counters and accumulators should be initialized with a beginning value. In this case, you initialized each of the variables when you declared them. Although most counters and accumulators are initialized to zero, you can initialize them to any value that the algorithm demands.

The main function begins by declaring and initializing four variables: sales, sumSales, avgSales, and numSales. Three of the variables (sales, sumSales, and avgSales) are declared as Float variables. One variable, the numSales variable, is declared as a Short Integer. The sales variable will store the sales amounts entered by the user. You will use the sumSales variable to accumulate the sales amounts, and the numSales variable to count the number of sales amounts the user entered. The avgSales variable will store the average sales amount after it is calculated by the program.

After declaring and initializing the variables, the program prompts the user to enter a sales amount, then stores the sales amount in the sales variable. Notice that the prompt tells the user to enter a negative number when he or she is finished entering the sales amounts. Values that are used to end loops are referred to as **sentinel values**, **trip values**, or **trailer values**. In the current program, the sentinel value is any negative number. The sentinel value should be one that is easily distinguishable from the valid data recognized by the program. In the current program, for example, a negative number is used as the sentinel value because a sales amount cannot be less than zero. You would not want to use a value such as 25000 as the current program's sentinel value because 25000 is a valid value for a sales amount.

The while clause evaluates the *loop condition*, (sales >= 0), to determine whether the loop instructions should be processed. If the value in the sales variable is greater than or equal to 0, the loop instructions are processed. If, however, the value in the sales variable is not greater than or equal to 0 (in other words, if it is less than 0), the loop instructions are not processed.

Now take a closer look at the instructions within the loop. The `numSales = numSales + 1;` statement updates the counter variable by a constant value of 1. Notice that the counter variable, `numSales`, appears on both sides of the assignment statement. The statement tells C++ to add 1 to the contents of the `numSales` variable, then place the result back in the `numSales` variable. `numSales` will be incremented by 1 each time the loop is processed.

The `sumSales = sumSales + sales;` statement updates the accumulator variable. Notice that the accumulator variable, `sumSales`, also appears on both sides of the assignment statement. The statement tells C++ to add the contents of the `sales` variable to the contents of the `sumSales` variable, then place the result back in the `sumSales` variable. `sumSales` will be incremented by a sales amount, which will vary, each time the loop is processed.

After the counter and accumulator are updated, the program prompts the user to enter another sales amount, and then stores that amount in the `sales` variable. Following the logic shown in the flowchart and pseudocode, the following statements get the sales amount from the user:

```
cout << "Type a sales amount and press Enter" << endl;
cout << "Enter a negative number when finished: ";
cin >> sales;
```

These instructions appear twice in the code: before the `while` loop and within the `while` loop. Recall that, after the `while` loop instructions are processed, the program returns to the beginning of the loop—the `while` clause. Because the first `cout` and `cin` instructions are located before the `while` clause, the program will never return to those instructions once the loop begins. In other words, the `cout` and `cin` instructions located above the loop get only the first sales amount from the user. The `cout` and `cin` instructions located within the loop get each of the remaining sales amounts, if any, from the user. If you forget to enter the second set of input instructions, the user will not be able to enter either another sales amount or, more importantly, the sentinel value that stops the loop. Until the sentinel value is entered, the loop will continue processing its instructions indefinitely. This type of loop is referred to as an **endless loop**. On most systems, you can stop a program that is in an endless loop by pressing Ctrl + c (press and hold down the Ctrl key as you press the letter c.) You can also use the DOS window's Close button to stop a program that is in an endless loop.

After the user enters another sales amount, the program returns to the `while` clause where the *loop condition* is evaluated again. If the *loop condition* evaluates to True, then the loop instructions are processed again. If the *loop condition* evaluates to False—in this case, if the user enters a sales amount that is less than zero—the loop stops and C++ processes the statement after the end of the loop. That statement calculates the average sales amount by dividing the contents of the accumulator variable (`sumSales`) by the contents of the counter variable (`numSales`). The last statement in the `main` function displays the average sales amount on the screen.

tip

You will practice stopping a program that contains an endless loop in Lesson A's Discovery Exercise 22.

To test the Sales Express program:

1 Build and execute the program. When prompted to enter a sales amount, type **3000** and press the **Enter** key. Because the sales amount is not less than zero, the loop instructions are processed. Those instructions add 1 to the numSales variable, giving 1, and also add 3000 to the sumSales variable, giving 3000. The user is then prompted for another sales amount.

2 Type **4000** and press the **Enter** key. Because the sales amount is not less than zero, the loop instructions are processed again. Those instructions add one to the numSales variable, giving 2, and also add 4000 to the sumSales variable, giving 7000.

Now stop the loop. Recall that you stop the loop by entering a negative sales amount.

3 Type **–1** and press the **Enter** key. Because the sales amount is less than zero, the loop stops. The average sales amount, 3500, is calculated and displayed on the screen.

4 Press the **Enter** key to close the DOS window, then close the Output window.

Now observe what happens if the user enters a negative value as the first sales amount.

5 Execute the program again. When prompted for a sales amount, type **–1** and press the **Enter** key. The DOS window shows that the average sales are –1.#IND, which is obviously an error. Press the **Enter** key to close the DOS window.

When you enter a negative number as the first sales amount, the loop instructions are never processed. This means that the numSales variable is not updated from its initial value of zero. Because division by zero is not allowed, C++ displays strange results—in this case, –1.#IND. (Recall that numSales is used as the divisor in the average sales calculation.)

You can use a selection structure to determine if the program will encounter the division by zero problem, and then take the appropriate action to avoid displaying the –1.#IND result. Before calculating the average sales amount, the selection structure will first determine if the value in numSales is greater than zero. If it is, the selection structure will calculate and display the average sales amount; otherwise, the selection structure will display a 0.

To enter the selection structure to determine if a division by zero error will occur:

1 Enter the selection structure highlighted in Figure 6-11.

enter this selection
structure

```
//LaProg03.cpp
//this program displays the average sales amount

#include <iostream.h>

void main()
{
    //declare and initialize variables
    float   sales    = (float) 0.0;
    float   sumSales = (float) 0.0;        //accumulator
    float   avgSales = (float) 0.0;
    short   numSales = 0;                  //counter

    //enter first sales amount
    cout << "Type a sales amount and press Enter" << endl;
    cout << "Enter a negative number when finished: ";
    cin >> sales;

    //update counter and accumulator, enter remaining sales amounts
    while (sales >= 0)
    {
        numSales = numSales + 1;
        sumSales = sumSales + sales;
        cout << "Type a sales amount and press Enter" << endl;
        cout << "Enter a negative number when finished: ";
        cin >> sales;
    } //end while

    //calculate average sales
    if (numSales > 0)
        avgSales = sumSales / (float) numSales;
    else
        avgSales = 0;
    //end if

    //display output
    cout << endl << "Average sales: " << avgSales << endl;
} //end of main function
```

Figure 6-11: Selection structure entered in the Sales Express program

2 Save, build, and then execute the program. When prompted to enter a sales amount, type **–1** and press the **Enter** key. This time the DOS window shows that the average sales amount is 0. Press the **Enter** key to close the DOS window.

You are now finished with this program, so you can close it.

3 Close the workspace and the Output window.

As the Sales Express program showed, if a program contains an instruction that divides two numbers, you should always verify that the divisor is a value other than zero before allowing the computer to perform the calculation.

Like the selection structure, the repetition structure also can be nested, which means you can place one repetition structure (loop) inside another repetition structure (loop). You will try this in the next section.

Nested Repetition Structures

In a nested repetition structure, one loop, referred to as the **inner loop**, is placed entirely within another loop, called the **outer loop**. Although the idea of nested loops may sound confusing, you are already familiar with the concept. A clock, for instance, uses nested loops to keep track of the time. For simplicity, consider a clock's second and minute hands only. You can think of the second hand as being the inner loop and the minute hand as being the outer loop. As you know, the second hand on a clock moves one position, clockwise, for every second that has elapsed. Only after the second hand completes its processing—in this case, only after it moves 60 positions (because there are 60 seconds in a minute)—does the minute hand move one position, clockwise; the second hand then begins its journey around the clock again. The logic used by a clock's second and minute hands is illustrated in Figure 6-12.

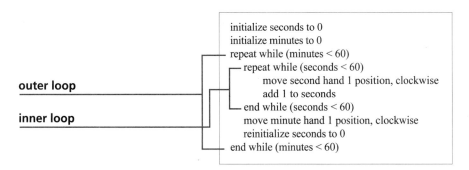

outer loop

inner loop

Figure 6-12: Nested loops used by a clock

You will use a nested `while` loop in the next program.

Using a Nested `while` Loop in a Program

Assume that Max Supplies has two regions: region 1 and region 2. The company's sales manager wants a program in which he can enter each region's sales amounts. The program should use this information to calculate and display the total amount sold in each region. The program will need to use a nested `while` loop, as well as an accumulator, to calculate and display the appropriate amounts. Figure 6-13 shows the IPO chart for this program.

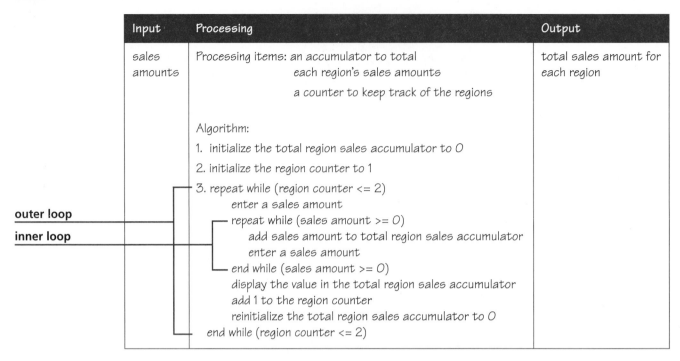

Input	Processing	Output
sales amounts	Processing items: an accumulator to total each region's sales amounts a counter to keep track of the regions Algorithm: 1. initialize the total region sales accumulator to 0 2. initialize the region counter to 1 3. repeat while (region counter <= 2) enter a sales amount repeat while (sales amount >= 0) add sales amount to total region sales accumulator enter a sales amount end while (sales amount >= 0) display the value in the total region sales accumulator add 1 to the region counter reinitialize the total region sales accumulator to 0 end while (region counter <= 2)	total sales amount for each region

outer loop

inner loop

Figure 6-13: IPO chart for the Max Supplies program

According to Figure 6-13, the program will first initialize both an accumulator and a counter to 0. The program will use the accumulator to total the amounts sold in each region, and it will use the counter to keep track of the two regions. After initializing the accumulator and counter, the program will use a nested `while` loop to calculate and display the total amount sold in each of the two regions. As indicated in Figure 6-13, the outer loop, which corresponds to a clock's minute hand, begins with the "repeat while (region counter <= 2)" instruction and ends with the "end while (region counter <= 2)" instruction. The inner loop, which corresponds to a clock's second hand, begins with the "repeat while (sales amount >= 0)" instruction and ends with the "end while (sales amount >= 0)" instruction. Notice that the entire inner loop is contained within the outer loop, which must be true for the loops to be nested and to work correctly.

The "repeat while (region counter <= 2)" instruction indicates that the outer loop's instructions should be processed while the `region` counter's value is less than or equal to 2. You will notice that the first instruction in the outer loop is to enter a sales amount. After the sales amount is entered, the inner *loop condition*, "(sales amount >= 0)," is evaluated. If the *loop condition* evaluates to True, the inner loop's instructions, which first add the sales amount to the accumulator and then allow the user to enter another sales amount, are processed. The program will then return to the beginning of the inner loop where the *loop condition* will be evaluated again. The program will continue processing the inner loop's instructions and evaluating the inner *loop condition* as long as the sales amount entered by the user is greater than or equal to zero. The program will stop processing the inner loop's instructions only when the user enters a sales amount that is less than zero. At that point, the remaining instructions in the outer loop will be processed.

> When loops are nested, the outer loop will typically need to reinitialize the inner loop's counters and accumulators.

In Figure 6-13's algorithm, for example, those instructions first display the region's total sales, which are stored in the sales accumulator, then add 1 to the region counter, and then reinitialize the sales accumulator to 0. You need to reinitialize the accumulator to 0 so that the sales from the first region are not included in the sales for the second region. The outer *loop condition*, "repeat while (region counter <= 2)," is then evaluated to see if the outer loop's instructions should be processed again.

Open and run a program that contains the code that corresponds to the algorithm shown in Figure 6-13.

To open and run the Max Supplies program:

1 Open the **LaProg04.cpp** file, which is located in the Cpp\Tut06\LaProg04 folder on your computer's hard disk. The Max Supplies program, which appears in the LaProg04.cpp window, is shown in Figure 6-14.

```cpp
//LaProg04.cpp
//this program displays the average amount sold
//in each of two regions

#include <iostream.h>

void main()
{
    //declare and initialize variables
    float   sales    = (float) 0.0;
    float   sumSales = (float) 0.0;      //accumulator
    short   region   = 1;                //counter

    while (region <= 2)
    {
        //enter first sales amount
        cout << "Type a sales amount for region "
             << region << " and press Enter" << endl;
        cout << "Enter a negative number when finished: ";
        cin >> sales;

        //update accumulator, enter remaining sales amounts
        while (sales >= 0)
        {
            sumSales = sumSales + sales;
            cout << "Type a sales amount for region "
                 << region << " and press Enter" << endl;
            cout << "Enter a negative number when finished: ";
            cin >> sales;
        } //end while (sales >= 0)


        //display output
        cout << endl << "Total sales for region "
             << region << ": " << sumSales << endl << endl;

        //update region counter
        region = region + 1;

        //reinitialize accumulator variable
        sumSales = (float) 0.0;
    } //end while (region <= 2)

} //end of main function
```

inner loop

outer loop

Figure 6-14: Max Supplies program

Following the logic shown in the Processing column of the IPO chart, the Max Supplies program uses nested `while` loops to calculate and display the total amount sold in each of the company's two regions. The outer loop begins with the `while (region <= 2)` line and ends with the `} //end while (region <= 2)` line. The instructions between those two lines constitute the body of the outer loop. The inner loop, which is contained wholly within the outer loop, begins with the `while (sales >= 0)` line and ends with the `} //end while (sales >= 0)` line. Run the program to observe how it works.

2 Build and execute the program. When prompted to enter a sales amount for region 1, type **3000** and press the **Enter** key, then type **2000** and press the **Enter** key. Type **–1** and press the **Enter** key to stop entering sales amounts for the first region. The DOS window shows that the total sales for region 1 are 5000.

You can now enter the sales amounts for region 2.

3 When prompted to enter a sales amount for region 2, type **500** and press the **Enter** key, then type **1300** and press the **Enter** key, and then type **4000** and press the **Enter** key. Type **–1** and press the **Enter** key to stop entering sales amounts for the second region. The DOS window shows that the total sales for region 2 are 5800. See Figure 6-15.

total of region 1 sales

total of region 2 sales

Figure 6-15: DOS window showing the results of the Max Supplies program

4 Press the **Enter** key to close the DOS window.

You are now finished with this program, so you can close it.

5 Close the Output window and the workspace.

tip

Desk-checking the Max Supplies program shown in Figure 6-14 will help you to understand nested loops better.

Mini-Quiz 2

1. A(n) _____ is updated by an amount that varies.

2. Write an assignment statement that updates a counter variable, named `quantity`, by 2.

3. Write an assignment statement that updates an accumulator variable, named `totalPurchases`, by the value in the `purchases` variable.

4. Which of the following is a good sentinel value for a program that inputs the number of hours each employee worked this week?
   a. –999   b. 32   c. 45.3   d. 0   e. a and d

5. Which of the following is a good sentinel value for a program that inputs a person's name?
   a. Abby   b. Barb   c. Done   d. Evelyn   e. Frank

6. Assume that a program has declared and initialized two Short Integer variables named `firstLoop` and `secondLoop`. Both variables are initialized to the number 1. Write a nested `while` loop that uses these variables to display the numbers 1 through 3 on four lines, as follows.
   ```
   1       2       3
   1       2       3
   1       2       3
   1       2       3
   ```

You have now completed Lesson A. In this lesson, you learned how to use the `while` form of the repetition structure, and how to use the C++ `while` statement to implement the `while` loop. You also learned how to use counters and accumulators, as well as how to use nested loops. In Lesson B, you will learn how to use the C++ `for` statement, which also can be used to implement the `while` loop. You will also learn about the `do-while` form of the repetition structure. Before beginning Lesson B, you can either exit Visual C++ and take a break or complete the questions and exercises at the end of the lesson.

S U M M A R Y

The repetition structure, also called looping, allows a programmer to repeat one or more program instructions either a specified number of times or until some condition, referred to as the *loop condition*, is met. The two forms of the repetition structure are `while` and `do-while`.

The `while` is called a pretest, or top-driven, loop because it evaluates the *loop condition* before processing any of the statements within the loop. The *loop condition* in a `while` loop is represented in a flowchart by a diamond. Like the diamond used in the selection structure, the repetition diamond should contain a question that has a true or false answer only. Also like the selection diamond, the repetition diamond should have two flowlines leading out of the diamond. Unlike the selection diamond, however, the repetition diamond has two flowlines, rather than one flowline, leading into the symbol.

Counters and accumulators are used within a repetition structure to calculate subtotals, totals, and averages. A counter is a numeric variable used for counting something, and an accumulator is a numeric variable used for accumulating (adding together) something. Counters and accumulators should be initialized, usually to 0, and updated. The initialization task is typically done outside of the repetition structure and the updating task is done inside the repetition structure.

Values that are used to end loops are referred to as sentinel values, trip values, or trailer values. A sentinel value should be one that is easily distinguishable from the valid data used by the program.

Like the selection structure, the repetition structure also can be nested, which means you can place one repetition structure, referred to as the inner loop, inside another repetition structure, referred to as the outer loop.

ANSWERS TO MINI-QUIZZES

Mini-Quiz 1

1. `while (quantity > 0)`

2. `while (quantity >= 0)`

3. `while (onHand > reorder)`

4.
```
while (evenNum < 9)
{
    cout << evenNum << endl;
    evenNum = evenNum + 2;
} //end while
```

Mini-Quiz 2

1. accumulator

2. `quantity = quantity + 2;`

3. `totalPurchases = totalPurchases + purchases;`

4. a

5. c

6.
```
while (firstNum <= 4)
{
    while (secondNum <= 3)
    {
        cout << secondNum << " ";
        secondNum = secondNum + 1;
    } //end while (secondNum <= 3)
    cout << endl;
    firstNum = firstNum + 1;
    secondNum = 1;
} //end while (firstNum <= 4)
```

Q U E S T I O N S

1. The `while` loop is referred to as a(n) _____ loop because the *loop condition* is tested at the beginning of the loop.
   a. beginning
   b. initial
   c. pretest
   d. priming

2. The *loop condition* in a flowchart is represented by a(n) _____ .
   a. diamond
   b. oval
   c. parallelogram
   d. rectangle

3. A(n) _____ is a numeric variable used for counting something.
   a. accumulator
   b. adder
   c. constant
   d. counter
   e. integer

4. Counters and accumulators must be _____ and _____ .
   a. added
   b. counted
   c. displayed
   d. initialized
   e. updated

5. A(n) _____ is always incremented by a constant amount, whereas a(n) _____ is incremented by an amount that varies.
   a. accumulator, counter
   b. counter, accumulator

6. Which of the following will correctly update the counter variable named `numEmployees`?
   a. `numEmployees = 0;`
   b. `numEmployees = 1;`
   c. `numEmployees = numEmployees + numEmployees;`
   d. `numEmployees = numEmployees + sumSalary;`
   e. `numEmployees = numEmployees + 1;`

7. Which of the following will correctly update the accumulator variable named `total`?
   a. `total = 0;`
   b. `total = 1;`
   c. `total = total + total;`
   d. `total = total + sales;`
   e. `total = total + 1;`

8. Which of the following would be a good sentinel value for a program that inputs a person's age?
   a. −4
   b. 350
   c. 999
   d. all of the above

9. Which of the following `while` clauses will stop the loop when the value in the `age` variable is less than the number 0?

    a. `while age < 0`
    b. `while (age < 0)`
    c. `while age >= 0;`
    d. `while (age >= 0);`
    e. `while (age >= 0)`

Refer to Figure 6-16 to answer questions 10 through 13.

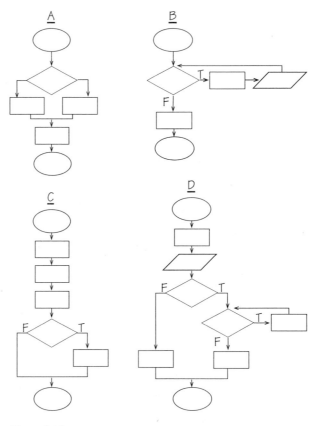

Figure 6-16

10. Which of the following control structures are used in Figure 6-16's flowchart A? (Select all that apply.)

    a. sequence
    b. selection
    c. repetition

11. Which of the following control structures are used in Figure 6-16's flowchart B? (Select all that apply.)

    a. sequence
    b. selection
    c. repetition

12. Which of the following control structures are used in Figure 6-16's flowchart C? (Select all that apply.)

    a. sequence
    b. selection
    c. repetition

13. Which of the following control structures are used in Figure 6-16's flowchart D? (Select all that apply.)
   a. sequence
   b. selection
   c. repetition

14. Values that are used to end loops are referred to as _____ values.
   a. end
   b. finish
   c. sentinel
   d. stop

15. Assume that a program allows the user to enter one or more numbers. The first input instruction, referred to as the _____ , will get the first number only.
   a. beginner
   b. entering read
   c. initializer
   d. priming read
   e. starter

E X E R C I S E S

1. Create a console application named T6Ae01 in the Cpp\Tut06 folder on your computer's hard disk. Write the C++ code that corresponds to the flowchart shown in Figure 6-17. Test and then print the code. Close the Output window and the workspace.

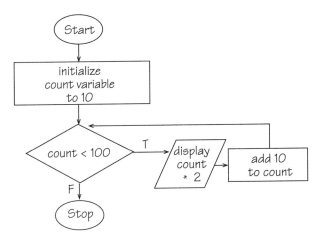

Figure 6-17

2. Create a console application named T6Ae02 in the Cpp\Tut06 folder on your computer's hard disk. Use the `while` loop to display the word "Hello" on the screen 10 times. Print the code. Close the Output window and the workspace.

3. On a piece of paper, write the `while` clause that tells C++ to stop the loop when the value in the `quantity` variable is less than 0. Then open the T6Ae03.cpp file, which is located in the Cpp\Tut06\T6Ae03 folder on your computer's hard disk. Use the T6Ae03.cpp file to test your `while` clause. Print the code. Close the Output window and the workspace.

4. On a piece of paper, write the `while` clause that tells C++ to stop the loop when the user enters the letter N in the Character variable named `more`. (Perform a case-insensitive comparison.) Then open the T6Ae04.cpp file, which is located in the Cpp\Tut06\T6Ae04 folder on your computer's hard disk. Use the T6Ae04.cpp file to test your `while` clause. Print the code. Close the Output window and the workspace.

5. On a piece of paper, write the `while` clause that tells C++ to stop the loop when the user enters the word "Done" in the `name` String variable. (Perform a case-insensitive comparison.) Then open the T6Ae05.cpp file, which is located in the Cpp\Tut06\T6Ae05 folder on your computer's hard disk. Use the T6Ae05.cpp file to test your `while` clause. Print the code. Close the Output window and the workspace.

6. What will display when the following code is processed? What is the value in `temp` when the loop stops? Complete and submit a desk-check table for this code.

```
short temp = 0;
while (temp < 5)
{
      cout << temp << endl;
      temp = temp + 1;
} //end while
```

7. The following code should display the numbers 1, 2, 3, and 4. An instruction is missing from the code. What is the missing instruction and where does it belong in the code?

```
short num = 1;
while (num < 5)
{
      cout << num;
} //end while
```

8. The following code should print the commission (`sales * .1`) for each sales amount that is entered. The code is not working properly because an instruction is missing. What is the missing instruction and where does it belong in the code?

```
float sales = (float) 0.0;
cout << "Enter a sales amount: ";
cin >> sales;
while (sales > 0)
{
      cout << sales * (float) .1;
}//end while
```

9. Write an assignment statement that updates a counter variable, named `numStudents`, by 1.

10. Write an assignment statement that updates a counter variable, named `quantity`, by 5.

11. Write an assignment statement that updates an accumulator variable, named `total`, by the value in the `sales` variable.

12. Write an assignment statement that updates an accumulator variable, named `total`, by the value in the `gross` variable.

13. What will display when the following code is processed?

```
short totEmp = 0;
while (totEmp <= 5)
{
      cout << totEmp << endl;
      totEmp = totEmp + 2;
}//end while
```

14. Scenario: Colfax Industries wants a program that it can use to display the sum of the sales made in four regions: North, South, East, and West. The four sales amounts will be entered by the user.
    a. Create an IPO chart for this program. Use a `while` loop to enter each sales amount, one at a time.
    b. Create a console application named T6Ae14 in the Cpp\Tut06 folder on your computer's hard disk.
    c. Write a program that corresponds to the IPO chart created in step a.
    d. In addition to displaying the output, the program should also save the program information (North sales, South sales, East sales, West sales, and total sales) to a file for printing. Name the file T6Ae14.dat.
    e. When the program is working correctly, print the code.
    f. Execute the program using the following as the North, South, East, and West sales, respectively: 10000, 25000, 30000, and 15000. Use C++ to open and print the T6Ae14.dat file. Close the data file, the Output window, and the workspace.

15. Scenario: Boots Inc. wants a program that displays an employee's name when the employee's ID is entered at the keyboard.
    a. Create an IPO chart for this problem. Use the `while` loop to allow the clerk to input as many IDs as desired. The program should display the employee's name that corresponds to the entered ID.
    b. Create a console application named T6Ae15 in the Cpp\Tut06 folder on your computer's hard disk.
    c. Write a program that corresponds to the IPO chart created in step a. The ID entered by the user will consist of four digits—for example, 1345. The program should display the employee's name that corresponds to the entered ID. The names and IDs are as follows:

ID	Name
1234	Sue Harter
1345	Janice Better
3456	Allen Jenkins

    Any other ID should result in an "Incorrect ID – Please try again" message.
    d. In addition to displaying the output, the program should also save the program information (ID and name) to a file for printing. Name the file T6Ae15.dat.
    e. When the program is working correctly, print the code.
    f. Execute the program using the following IDs: 1345 and 9999. Use C++ to open and print the T6Ae15.dat file. Close the data file, the Output window, and the workspace.

16. Scenario: Software Workshop offers programming seminars to companies. The price per person depends on the number of people a company registers. (For example, if a company registers four people, then the amount owed by that company is $400.) The following table shows the charges per registrant.

Number of registrants	Charge per person ($)
1–3	150
4–9	100
10 or more	90

    a. Create an IPO chart for this program. The program should prompt the user to enter the number of people registered. The program should allow the user to enter the registration for as many companies as desired. Use the `while` loop. The program should display the total number of people registered, the total charge, and the average charge per registrant. (For example, if one company registers four people and a second company registers two people, then the total number of people registered is six, the total charge is $700, and the average charge per registrant is $116.67.)

b. Create a console application named T6Ae16 in the Cpp\Tut06 folder on your computer's hard disk.

c. Write a program that corresponds to the IPO chart created in step a.

d. In addition to displaying the output, the program should also save the program information (total number of people registered, total charge, and average charge) to a file for printing. Name the file T6Ae16.dat.

e. When the program is working correctly, print the code. Execute the program using the following as the number of people registered: 3, 12, and 9. Use C++ to open and print the T6Ae16.dat file. Close the data file, the Output window, and the workspace.

17. Scenario: Collett Company charges a shipping charge based on the state in which the customer lives, as shown in the following table. (The state abbreviation could be typed by the user in any case.)

State	Shipping charge ($)
ME	25.00
TX	30.00
NJ	32.50

Any other state should result in an "Incorrect state—Please try again" message.

a. Create an IPO chart for this program. The program should prompt the user to enter the state abbreviation. The program should allow the user to enter as many state abbreviations as desired. Use the `while` loop. The program should then display the total number of times ME was entered, the total number of times TX was entered, the total number of times NJ was entered, and the total number of times an incorrect state abbreviation was entered. The program should also display the total shipping charge for the ME entries, the total shipping charge for the TX entries, and the total shipping charge for the NJ entries.

b. Create a console application named T6Ae17 in the Cpp\Tut06 folder on your computer's hard disk.

c. Write a program that corresponds to the IPO chart created in step a.

d. In addition to displaying the output, the program should also save the program information (the total number of times each state abbreviation was entered and each state's total shipping charge) to a file for printing. Name the file T6Ae17.dat.

e. When the program is working correctly, print the code. Execute the program using the following states: TX, ME, TN, me, tx, nj, NJ, MA, and IL. Use C++ to open and print the T6Ae17.dat file. Close the data file, the Output window, and the workspace.

18. In this exercise, you will modify an existing program. To complete this exercise, you must have completed Exercise 18 in Tutorial 5's Lesson A.

a. Use Windows to copy the T5Ae18.cpp file, which is located in the Cpp\Tut05\T5Ae18 folder on your computer's hard disk, to the Cpp\Tut06\T6Ae18 folder on your computer's hard disk. Rename the T5Ae18.cpp file as T6Ae18.cpp.

b. Open the T6Ae18.cpp file. The program prompts the user to enter a seat location; it then displays the ticket price. Change the name of the data file from T5Ae18.dat to T6Ae18.dat. Add a `while` loop to the program. The `while` loop should allow the user to enter as many seat locations as desired.

c. When the program is working correctly, print the code. Execute the program using the following seat locations: Lawn, Box, Pavilion, Lawn, and Pavilion. Use C++ to open and print the T6Ae18.dat file. Close the data file, the Output window, and the workspace.

19. In this exercise, you will modify an existing program. To complete this exercise, you must have completed Exercise 19 in Tutorial 5's Lesson A.

　　a. Use Windows to copy the T5Ae19.cpp file, which is located in the Cpp\Tut05\T5Ae19 folder on your computer's hard disk, to the T6Ae19 folder on your computer's hard disk. Rename the T5Ae19.cpp file as T6Ae19.cpp.

　　b. The program prompts the user to enter the number of years an employee has been with the company; it then displays the appropriate number of vacation weeks. Change the name of the data file from T5Ae19.dat to T6Ae19.dat. Add a `while` loop to the program. The `while` loop should allow the user to enter the number of years for as many employees as desired. Also add the appropriate code to display the total number of employees entered, their total number of vacation weeks, and the average weeks of vacation for these employees. Include the total number of employees entered, total number of vacation weeks, and average weeks of vacation in the T6Ae19.dat file.

　　c. When the program is working correctly, print the code. Execute the program using the following years: 0, 4, 7, and 20. Use C++ to open and print the T6Ae19.dat file. Close the data file, the Output window, and the workspace.

20. In this exercise, you will modify an existing program. To complete this exercise, you must have completed Exercise 4 in Tutorial 5's Lesson B.

　　a. Use Windows to copy the T5Be04.cpp file, which is located in the Cpp\Tut05\T5Be04 folder on your computer's hard disk, to the T6Ae20 folder on your computer's hard disk. Rename the T5Be04.cpp file as T6Ae20.cpp.

　　b. The program prompts the user to enter the salesperson's name and sales; it then displays the salesperson's bonus. Change the name of the data file from T5Be04.dat to T6Ae20.dat. Add a `while` loop to the program. The `while` loop should allow the user to enter as many names and sales as desired. Also add the appropriate code to display the total number of salespeople entered, their total sales amount, their total bonus amount, and the average bonus amount. Include the total number of salespeople entered, their total sales amount, their total bonus amount, and the average bonus amount in the T6Ae20.dat file.

　　c. When the program is working correctly, print the code. Execute the program using the following names and sales: John Smith, 1200; Paula Gonzales, 5001.67; Jackie Williams, 3000.50; and Jim Smith, 25000. Use C++ to open and print the T6Ae20.dat file. Close the data file, the Output window, and the workspace.

21. In this exercise, you will modify an existing program. To complete this exercise, you must have completed Exercise 9 in Tutorial 5's Lesson B.

　　a. Use Windows to copy the T5Be09.cpp file, which is located in the Cpp\Tut05\T5Be09 folder on your computer's hard disk, to the T6Ae21 folder on your computer's hard disk. Rename the T5Be09.cpp file as T6Ae21.cpp.

　　b. The program displays two numbers on the screen. It then asks the user to select from the following three choices: the numbers on the dice are equal, the number on the first die is greater than the number on the second die, or the number on the first die is less than the number on the second die. The program displays an appropriate message that indicates whether the user's choice is correct or incorrect. Add a `while` loop to the program. The `while` loop should allow the user to play the game for as long as he or she wants.

　　c. When the program is working correctly, print the code. Close the Output window and the workspace.

discovery ▶ 22. In this exercise, you will learn two ways to stop a program that is in an endless loop.

a. Open the T6Ae22.cpp file, which is located in the Cpp\Tut06\T6Ae22 folder on your computer's hard disk.

b. Build and execute the program. Notice that the program results in an endless loop.

c. On most systems, you can stop a program that is in an endless loop by pressing Ctrl + c (press and hold down the Ctrl key as you press the letter c.) Use the Ctrl + c key combination to stop the program. The DOS window closes.

d. Execute the program again. You can also use the DOS window's Close button to stop a program that is in an endless loop. Click the DOS window's Close button. A dialog box appears. The dialog box asks, "Do you wish to terminate this program now and lose any unsaved information in the program?" Click the Yes button in the dialog box. The DOS window closes.

e. Fix the program so that it does not result in an endless loop. Save, build, and then execute the program. When the program is working correctly, print the code. On the code printout, circle the changes you made to the program. Close the Output window and the workspace.

debugging 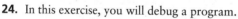 23. In this exercise, you will debug a program.

a. Open the T6Ae23.cpp file, which is located in the Cpp\Tut06\T6Ae23 folder on your computer's hard disk. This program should display the squares of the numbers from 1 through 5—in other words, the numbers 1, 4, 9, 16, and 25.

b. Build and execute the program. Notice that the program results in an endless loop. Stop the program. (Refer to Discovery Exercise 22 for how to stop a program that is in an endless loop.) What was causing the problem in the program?

c. Debug the program. Save, build, and then execute the program. Correct any logic errors. When the program is working correctly, print the code. On the code printout, circle the changes you made to the program. Close the Output window and the workspace.

debugging 24. In this exercise, you will debug a program.

a. Open the T6Ae24.cpp file, which is located in the Cpp\Tut06\T6Ae24 folder on your computer's hard disk.

b. Build and execute the program. Notice that the program results in an endless loop. Stop the program. (Refer to Discovery Exercise 22 for how to stop a program that is in an endless loop.) What was causing the problem in the program?

c. Debug the program. Save, build, and then execute the program. Correct any logic errors. When the program is working correctly, print the code. On the code printout, circle the changes you made to the program. Close the Output window and the workspace.

LESSON B

objectives

In this lesson you will learn how to:

- Use the C++ `for` statement to implement a counter-controlled `while` loop
- Write the pseudocode for the `do-while` loop
- Create a flowchart for the `do-while` loop
- Code the `do-while` loop

The for Statement and the do-while Loop

Using the for Statement to Implement a Counter-controlled while Loop

In Lesson A you learned how to use the `while` statement to implement the `while` loop. One of the examples you viewed in the lesson simply displayed the numbers 1 through 3 on the screen. The C++ code used in that example is shown in Figure 6-18.

```
short count = 1;                    //initialize counter
while(count <= 3)                   //test counter
{
    cout << count << endl;
    count = count + 1;              //update counter
}//end while
```

Figure 6-18: C++ code that uses a `while` statement to display the numbers 1 through 3

You will notice that the code begins by creating a variable named `count` and initializing it to the number 1. The *loop condition* in the `while` loop then tests to see if the `count` variable's value is less than or equal to 3. If it is, the loop instructions first display the value stored in the `count` variable, and then update the variable's value by adding 1 to it. The *loop condition* is then reevaluated to determine if the loop instructions should be processed again.

The loop shown in Figure 6-18 is commonly referred to as a **counter-controlled loop** because it uses a counter—in this case, the `count` variable—to control the number of times the loop is processed. (The loop in Figure 6-18 will be processed three times.) As you learned in Lesson A, counters need to be initialized (given a beginning value) and updated. In Figure 6-18's code, for example, the `short count = 1;` statement initializes the counter variable to the number 1. The `count = count + 1;` statement inside the loop updates the counter variable by adding the number 1 to it each time the loop instructions are processed. A counter-controlled loop uses the value in the counter variable to determine if the required number of loop repetitions have been performed. In Figure 6-18's code, for example, the loop's `while (count <= 3)` clause compares the value in the counter variable to the number 3—the number of times the loop needs to be processed.

Although you can use the `while` statement to implement a counter-controlled `while` loop, C++ provides another statement—the `for` statement—that allows you to code the loop in a more convenient and compact manner. Figure 6-19 shows both the syntax and two examples of the C++ `for` statement. In both examples, the `for` statement implements a counter-controlled `while` loop that simply displays the numbers 1 through 3 on the screen. When a programmer uses the `for` statement to code a `while` loop, he or she typically refers to the loop as a `for` loop rather than as a `while` loop. This naming convention helps the programmer distinguish between a `while` loop that is coded with the `while` statement and one that is coded with the `for` statement.

`for` clause does not end in a semicolon

> **tip**
>
> A common error is to separate the three items of information in the `for` clause with two commas rather than two semicolons.

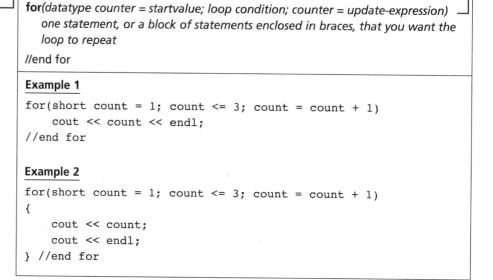

Syntax of the `for` statement used to code a counter-controlled `while` loop

for(*datatype counter = startvalue; loop condition; counter = update-expression*)
    one statement, or a block of statements enclosed in braces, that you want the loop to repeat
//end for

Example 1
```
for(short count = 1; count <= 3; count = count + 1)
    cout << count << endl;
//end for
```

Example 2
```
for(short count = 1; count <= 3; count = count + 1)
{
    cout << count;
    cout << endl;
} //end for
```

Figure 6-19: Syntax and two examples of the `for` statement used to code a counter-controlled `while` loop

> **tip**
>
> Although the most common use for the `for` statement is to code counter-controlled `while` loops, you can use the C++ `for` statement to code any `while` loop.

The syntax of the `for` statement begins with the `for` clause, followed by the body of the loop, which contains the one or more statements that you want the loop to repeat. If the loop body contains only one statement, as shown in Example 1, then the `for` loop ends when it encounters the semicolon at the end of that one statement. If, on the other hand, the loop body contains a group of statements enclosed in braces (a statement block), as shown in Example 2, then the `for` loop ends when it encounters the statement block's closing brace. As you did with the `while` statement, you should use a comment, such as `//end for`, to document the end of the `for` statement.

You will notice that the `for` clause used to code a counter-controlled loop requires three items of information, enclosed in parentheses and separated by two semicolons: (*datatype counter = startvalue; loop condition; counter = update-expression*). The first item, *datatype counter = startvalue*, specifies the data type, name, and initial value of the counter variable—the variable that the `for` loop will use to keep track of the number of times the loop instructions are processed. *datatype* must be one of the C++ numeric data types (Short Integer, Integer, Long Integer, Float, and Double). The *startvalue* can be a number that is either positive or negative, integer or noninteger. The *datatype counter = startvalue* portion of the `for` clause first creates the counter variable in memory, and then initializes it to the *startvalue*.

The information in the `for` clause controls how many times the `for` loop will process its instructions. The *startvalue* tells the loop where to begin counting. In Figure 6-19's examples, the loop begins counting with the number 1. The *loop condition* in the `for` clause specifies a requirement that the counter variable must meet before the loop instructions are processed. In Figure 6-19's examples, the `count <= 3` *loop condition* tells the `for` loop to process its instructions as long as the value in the `count` variable is less than or equal to 3. When the value in `count` is greater than 3, the `for` loop stops. The *update-expression* tells the loop how much to add to (or subtract from) the counter variable each time the loop is processed. In Figure 6-19's examples, the number 1 is added to the value in the `count` variable after each processing of the loop. The `for` clause shown in Figure 6-19's examples tells the loop simply to start counting at 1 and, adding 1 each time the loop is processed, continue counting through the number 3—in other words, count 1, 2, and then 3.

To summarize, the `for` statement performs the following three tasks:

1. The *datatype counter = startvalue* item first creates the numeric counter variable and then initializes it to the *startvalue*. This is done only once, at the beginning of the loop.
2. The `for` statement evaluates its *loop condition*. If the *loop condition* evaluates to True, the loop instructions are processed and the next task, task 3, is performed; otherwise, the loop stops.
3. The *counter = update-expression* item updates the value in the counter variable. The loop then repeats tasks 2 and 3 until the *loop condition* evaluates to False.

As step 2 indicates, the `for` statement evaluates the *loop condition* before processing any of the instructions within the loop. If the *loop condition* evaluates to True, then the loop instructions are processed; otherwise, they are not processed.

Open a program that will allow you to observe how the `for` statement works.

tip

You can also use the C++ increment (++) and decrement (−−) operators in the *update-expression*. You will learn about these operators in Lesson B's Discovery Exercise 17.

tip

If you compare the while statement code shown in Figure 6-18 to the for statement code shown in Figure 6-19's Example 1, you will notice that the for statement provides a more convenient and compact way of coding a counter-controlled while loop.

To open the demonstration program for the `for` statement:

1   If necessary, start Visual C++. Open the **LbProg01.cpp** file, which is located in the Cpp\Tut06\LbProg01 folder on your computer's hard disk. The `for` statement demo program, which appears in the LbProg01.cpp window, is shown in Figure 6-20.

```
//LbProg01.cpp
//this program uses the for loop to display the numbers 1 through 3

#include <iostream.h>

void main()
{
    //display numbers
    for(short count = 1; count <= 3; count = count + 1)
        cout << count << endl;
    //end for

    cout << "End of for loop" << endl;
} //end of main function
```

Figure 6-20: for statement demo program

The main function uses a for statement to print the numbers 1 through 3 on the screen.

2 Build and execute the program. C++ processes the for loop as shown in Figure 6-21, and the numbers 1, 2, and 3 appear in the DOS window.

1. Loop creates the Short Integer counter variable (count) and initializes it to 1 (*startvalue*).
2. Loop checks if value in count is less than or equal to 3 (*loop condition*). It is.
3. C++ prints 1 (the contents of count) on the screen.
4. Loop adds 1 to count (*update-expression*), giving 2.
5. Loop checks if value in count is less than or equal to 3 (*loop condition*). It is.
6. C++ prints 2 (the contents of count) on the screen.
7. Loop adds 1 to count (*update-expression*), giving 3.
8. Loop checks if the value in count is less than or equal to 3 (*loop condition*). It is.
9. C++ prints 3 (the contents of count) on the screen.
10. Loop adds 1 to count (*update-expression*), giving 4.
11. Loop checks if the value in count is less than or equal to 3 (*loop condition*). It's not.
12. Loop stops. C++ processes the instruction following the end of the loop.

Figure 6-21: Processing steps for the for loop

3 Press the **Enter** key to close the DOS window.

You are now finished with this program, so you can close it.

4 Close the workspace and the Output window.

When the for loop ends, notice that the value in the count variable is 4, not 3. This is because the loop stops with the first value that is greater than 3.

Now look at another example of the for statement. In this example, you will use the for statement in a game that races two players against each other.

Using a for Statement in a Game

In Lesson A, you learned how to use the while statement to code a game that races two players against each other. As you may remember, the while statement was used in the displayAsterisks programmer-defined function. You will now use a for statement, rather than a while statement, to code the function's repetition structure.

To use the for statement in the game program's displayAsterisks function:

1 Open the **LbProg02.cpp** file, which is located in the Cpp\Tut06\LbProg02 folder on your computer's hard disk. The game program appears in the LbProg02.cpp window.

2 Remove the //declare and initialize variable comment, the short count = 1; statement, and the while loop from the displayAsterisks function, which is located in the programmer-defined function section of the program. Replace the while statement with the for statement that is highlighted in Figure 6-22.

```
//*****programmer-defined function definitions*****
void displayAsterisks(short number)
{
    //this function displays a row of asterisks
    //the number of asterisks displayed depends on the value
    //stored in the number formal parameter

    for(short count = 1; count <= number; count = count + 1)
        cout << '*';
    //end for

    cout << endl;
} //end of displayAsterisks function
```

replace while **statement with this** for **statement**

Figure 6-22: for statement in the displayAsterisks function

3   Save, build, and then execute the program. Two rows of asterisks, each row representing a player, appear in the DOS window, along with either the "It's a tie!," "Player 1 wins!," or "Player 2 wins!" message.

4   Press the **Enter** key to close the DOS window.

You are finished with this program, so you can close it.

5   Close the workspace and the Output window.

Next, you will learn about the second form of the repetition structure—the do-while loop.

mini-quiz

Mini-Quiz 3

1.   Write a for clause that processes the loop instructions as long as the value in the counter variable, named quantity, is less than or equal to the number 10. Declare the counter variable as a Short Integer variable and initialize it to 0. Update the counter variable by 2.

2.   What is the value of the counter variable when the loop in question 1 ends?

3.   Write a for clause that processes the loop instructions as long as the value in the counter variable, named onHand, is not less than the number 5. Declare the counter variable as a Short Integer variable and initialize it to 25. Update the counter variable by −5.

4.   Write a for loop that displays the even integers between 1 and 9. Use number as the name of the counter variable.

The do-while Loop

tip

● ● ● ● ● ● ● ● ● ● ● ● ● ● ● ●

▶ Recall that the while loop is a pretest, or top-driven, loop.

As with the while loop, you can use the do-while loop to repeat one or more statements either a specified number of times or while some *loop condition* is True. However, unlike the while loop, which evaluates the *loop condition* before processing the loop instructions, the do-while loop evaluates the *loop condition* after first processing the loop instructions. Therefore, the do-while loop is called a **posttest** loop, or **bottom-driven loop**.

Figure 6-23 shows an example of the do-while loop written in pseudocode and drawn in a flowchart. The example simply displays the numbers 1 through 3 on the screen.

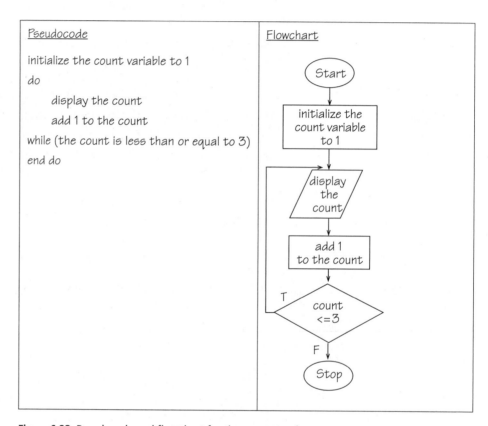

Figure 6-23: Pseudocode and flowchart for the do-while loop

As Figure 6-23 indicates, programmers typically use the word **do** to mark the beginning of the do-while loop in pseudocode, and the two words **end do** to mark its end. In the flowchart, you will notice that the repetition diamond appears at the bottom of the loop, rather than at the top of the loop as in the while loop flowchart. (The while loop flowchart for this example is shown in Figure 6-3.)

You use the C++ do statement to code the do-while loop.

The do Statement

Figure 6-24 shows the syntax and an example of the do-while loop. The example shows how you could use the do-while loop to display the numbers 1 through 3.

Syntax	Example

do
    one statement, or a block of
    statements enclosed in braces, that
    you want the loop to repeat
while (*loop condition*);
//end do
	```short count = 1;```
	```do```
	```{```
	``` cout << count << endl;```
	``` count = count + 1;```
	```}while (count <= 3);```
	```//end do```

notice that the do statement ends in a semicolon

Figure 6-24: Syntax and an example of the do-while loop

The do-while loop begins with the word do, followed by the body of the loop, which contains the one or more statements you want the loop to repeat. The do-while loop ends with the while (*loop condition*); instruction. You can use the //end do comment to document the end of the do-while loop.

You will notice that the *loop condition* is located at the bottom of the do-while loop, rather than at the top as in the while loop. As with the while *loop condition*, the do-while *loop condition* must be enclosed in parentheses and it must result in either the Boolean value True or False. The *loop condition* determines whether the instructions in the body of the loop are processed. Like the *loop condition* used in the while statement, the do-while *loop condition* can contain variables, constants, functions, mathematical operators, relational operators, and logical operators.

The do-while loop, which is a posttest loop, evaluates the *loop condition* after first processing the instructions within the loop. The do-while loop always processes the loop instructions at least once. After the first time, however, the do-while loop instructions will be processed only when the *loop condition* evaluates to True.

Take a closer look at Figure 6-24's do-while example, which displays the numbers 1 through 3. The short count = 1; statement declares a Short Integer variable named count and initializes it to 1. The do clause, which simply marks the beginning of the loop, is processed next. C++ then processes the loop instructions, which display the value of count on the screen and also add 1 to count. The while clause then evaluates the *loop condition*, (count <= 3), to determine whether the loop instructions should be processed again. Notice that the *loop condition* is not evaluated until after the loop instructions are processed the first time. If the count variable contains a number that is less than or equal to 3, the loop instructions are processed again. If, however, count contains a number that is not less than or equal to 3, the loop stops and processing then continues with the first statement following the while clause.

Open a program that demonstrates how the do-while loop works.

To open and run a program that demonstrates the do-while loop:

1   Open the **LbProg03.cpp** file, which is located in the Cpp\Tut06\LbProg03 folder on your computer's hard disk. The do-while demo program, which appears in the LbProg03.cpp window, is shown in Figure 6-25.

```
//LbProg03.cpp
//this program demonstrates the do-while loop

#include <iostream.h>

void main()
{
    //declare and initialize variable
    short count = 1;

    //display numbers 1 through 3
    do
    {
      cout << count << endl;
      count = count + 1;
    }while (count <= 3);
    //end do

    cout << "End of the do-while loop" << endl;

} //end of main function
```

Figure 6-25: do-while demo program

2   Build and execute the program. C++ processes the instructions as shown in Figure 6-26, and the numbers 1, 2, and 3 appear in the DOS window.

1. count variable is created and initialized to the number 1.
2. do clause marks the beginning of the loop.
3. First loop instruction displays 1 (the contents of count) on the screen.
4. Second loop instruction adds 1 to count, giving 2.
5. while clause checks if the value in count is less than or equal to 3. It is.
6. C++ returns to the beginning of the loop (the do clause).
7. First loop instruction displays 2 (the contents of count) on the screen.
8. Second loop instruction adds 1 to count, giving 3.
9. while clause checks if the value in count is less than or equal to 3. It is.
10. C++ returns to the beginning of the loop (the do clause).
11. First loop instruction displays 3 (the contents of count) on the screen.
12. Second loop instruction adds 1 to count, giving 4.
13. while clause checks if the value in count is less than or equal to 3. It's not.
14. Loop stops. C++ processes the first statement following the end of the loop.

Figure 6-26: Processing steps for the do-while loop

3   Press the **Enter** key to close the DOS window.
        You are now finished with this program, so you can close it.

4   Close the Output window and the workspace.

To summarize, you can use the while and do-while loops to repeat one or more statements either a specified number of times or while a *loop condition*, specified in the while clause, evaluates to True. When the *loop condition* evaluates to False, the loop stops. The difference between the while and the do-while loop is that the while loop evaluates the *loop condition* before processing the loop instructions, whereas the do-while loop evaluates the *loop condition* after first processing the loop instructions. The instructions in a while loop may never be processed; a do-while loop's instructions, however, are always processed at least once.

mini-quiz

Mini-Quiz 4

1. Write the C++ code that will display five asterisks, like this: *****. Use a do-while loop. Be sure to declare a counter variable named num and initialize it to 1.
2. What is the value of the num variable when the do-while loop in question 1 stops?

Now that you know how to use the repetition structure, you can complete the program for Professor Carver's class. You will use the while and for statements to code the program.

The Grade Program

Recall that Professor Carver, one of your computer programming instructors, has asked you to be a guest speaker in his Introduction to Programming class. You decide to show the students how to use the while and for statements in a program that will calculate and display their grade in the programming class. Professor Carver assigns five projects, worth 50 points each, and four tests, worth 100 points each. The IPO chart for this problem is shown in Figure 6-27.

Input	Processing	Output
project scores	Processing items: none	grade
number of tests		
test scores	Algorithm:	
	1. get the project scores (enterProjectScores function)	
	2. get the number of tests and the test scores (enterTestScores function)	
	3. assign the grade (assignGrade function)	
	4. display the grade	

Figure 6-27: IPO chart for the grade program

According to the IPO chart, the program will use three programmer-defined functions: `enterProjectScores`, `enterTestScores`, and `assignGrade`. The `enterProjectScores` function will get the project scores from the student, and the `enterTestScores` function will get the number of tests and the test scores. The `assignGrade` function will calculate the student's grade.

Most of the code that corresponds to this IPO chart is already entered in a file for you. You will need to complete only the `enterProjectScores` and the `enterTestScores` functions. In both functions you will need to use a repetition structure to allow the student to enter his or her scores. So that you can practice with both the `while` and `for` statements, you will use the `while` statement in the `enterProjectScores` function and the `for` statement in the `enterTestScores` function. Open the file and begin completing the program.

To open the partially completed grade program:

1   Open the **LbProg04.cpp** file, which is located in the Cpp\Tut06\LbProg04 folder on your computer's hard disk. The grade program, which appears in the LbProg04.cpp window, is shown in Figure 6-28.

```cpp
//LbProg04.cpp
//this program displays the grade earned in Professor Carver's class

#include <iostream.h>

//function prototypes
void enterProjectScores(short &, short &);
void enterTestScores(short &, short &);
char assignGrade(short, short);

void main()
{
    //declare and initialize variables
    short earnedAccum   = 0;
    short possibleAccum = 0;
    char  grade         = ' ';

    //enter project scores
    enterProjectScores(earnedAccum, possibleAccum);

    //enter test scores
    enterTestScores(earnedAccum, possibleAccum);

    //assign grade
    grade = assignGrade(earnedAccum, possibleAccum);

    //display grade
    cout << endl << "Your grade is " << grade << endl;
} //end of main function
```

Figure 6-28: Partially completed grade program

```
//*****programmer-defined function definitions*****
void enterProjectScores(short &earned, short &possible)
{
      //this function gets the project scores
      //it also accumulates the earned scores and the possible scores

} //end of enterProjectScores function

void enterTestScores(short &earned, short &possible)
{
      //this function gets the number of tests and the test scores
      //it also accumulates the earned scores and the possible scores

}//end of enterTestScores function

char assignGrade(short earned, short possible)
{
      //this function assigns the appropriate grade
      float ratio      = (float) 0.0;
      char letterGrade = ' ';
      if (possible > 0)
            //calculate ratio
            ratio = (float) earned / (float) possible;
      else
            ratio = 0;
      //end if

      //assign letterGrade
      if (ratio >= .9)
            letterGrade = 'A';
      else
            if (ratio >= .8)
                  letterGrade = 'B';
            else
                  if (ratio >= .7)
                        letterGrade = 'C';
                  else
                        if (ratio >= .6)
                              letterGrade = 'D';
                        else
                              letterGrade = 'F';
                        //end if (ratio >= .6)
                  //end if (ratio >= .7)
            //end if (ratio >= .8)
      //end if (ratio >= .9)

      return letterGrade;
}//end of assignGrade function
```

Figure 6-28: Partially completed grade program (continued)

First you will enter the code for the `enterProjectScores` function. The IPO chart for the `enterProjectScores` function is shown in Figure 6-29.

Input	Processing	Output

project scores
 	
earned score accumulator
 	
possible score accumulator
	Processing items: none
	
	Algorithm:
	1. get a project score from the user
	2. repeat while (project score is >= 0)
	    add the project score to the earned score accumulator
	    add 50 to the possible score accumulator
	    get a project score from the user
	end while
		accumulated earned scores
		accumulated possible scores

Figure 6-29: IPO chart for the `enterProjectScores` function

As the algorithm indicates, the `enterProjectScores` function will continue to get project scores from the user as long as the project score entered is greater than or equal to 0. Each time a project score is entered, it is added to the earned score accumulator. The number 50, which is the number of points each project is worth in Professor Carver's class, is then added to the possible score accumulator. After the last project score is entered, the earned score accumulator will contain the total number of points earned on the projects submitted by the student. The possible score accumulator will contain the total number of points that the student could have earned on those projects.

You can now complete the `enterProjectScores` function definition, which is located in the programmer-defined section of the program.

2 Enter the `enterProjectScores` function's code that is highlighted in Figure 6-30.

function name

```
//*****programmer-defined function definitions*****
void enterProjectScores(short &earned, short &possible)
{
    //this function gets the project scores
    //it also accumulates the earned scores and the possible scores

    short projScore = 0;

    cout << "Enter a project score (negative number to end): ";
    cin >> projScore;
    while (projScore >= 0)
    {
        earned = earned + projScore;
        possible = possible + 50;
        cout << "Enter a project score (negative number to end): ";
        cin >> projScore;
    } //end while
} //end of enterProjectScores function
```

enter these instructions

Figure 6-30: `enterProjectScores` code entered in the grade program

Now you will enter the code for the `enterTestScores` function. The IPO chart for the `enterTestScores` function is shown in Figure 6-31.

Input	Processing	Output

number of tests
test scores
earned score accumulator
possible score accumulator
	Processing items: counter
	
	Algorithm:
	1. get the number of tests from the user
	2. initialize counter to 1
	3. repeat while (counter <= number of tests)
	    get a test score from the user
	    add the test score to the earned
	    score accumulator
	    add 100 to the possible score
	    accumulator
	    add 1 to counter
	  end while
		accumulated earned scores
		accumulated possible scores

Figure 6-31: IPO chart for the `enterTestScores` function

As the algorithm indicates, the `enterTestScores` function will ask the user to enter the number of tests he or she has taken. The function will use a counter-controlled loop to get the appropriate number of test scores from the user. Each time a test score is entered, it is added to the earned score accumulator. Also, the number 100, which is the number of points each test is worth in the class, is added to the possible score accumulator. When the `enterTestScores` function completes its processing, the earned score accumulator will contain the total number of points earned on the student's projects and tests. The possible score accumulator will contain the total number of points that the student could have earned on the projects and tests.

You can now complete the `enterTestScores` function definition, which is located in the programmer-defined section of the program.

3 Enter the `enterTestScores` function's code highlighted in Figure 6-32.

```
void enterTestScores(short &earned, short &possible)
{
    //this function gets the number of tests and the test scores
    //it also accumulates the earned scores and the possible scores

    short testScore = 0;
    short numTests  = 0;

    cout << endl << "How many tests have you taken? ";
    cin >> numTests;

    for (short count = 1; count <= numTests; count = count + 1)
    {
        cout << "Enter a test score: ";
        cin >> testScore;
        earned = earned + testScore;
        possible = possible + 100;
    }//end for
}//end of enterTestScores function
```

enter these instructions

Figure 6-32: `enterTestScores` code entered in the grade program

4 Save, build, and then execute the program. Use the following data to test the program:

Project 1 score: 45

Project 2 score: 40

Stop the loop by entering a -1

Number of tests: 2

Test 1:   85

Test 2:   90

Your grade should be a B.

5 Press the **Enter** key to close the DOS window.

6 On your own, try other project and test scores. When you are finished testing the program, close the workspace and the Output window.

Figure 6-33 shows the completed grade program.

```cpp
//LbProg04.cpp
//this program displays the grade earned in Professor Carver's class

#include <iostream.h>

//function prototypes
void enterProjectScores(short &, short &);
void enterTestScores(short &, short &);
char assignGrade(short, short);

void main()
{
    //declare and initialize variables
    short earnedAccum   = 0;
    short possibleAccum = 0;
    char  grade         = ' ';

    //enter project scores
    enterProjectScores(earnedAccum, possibleAccum);

    //enter test scores
    enterTestScores(earnedAccum, possibleAccum);

    //assign grade
    grade = assignGrade(earnedAccum, possibleAccum);

    //display grade
    cout << endl << "Your grade is " << grade << endl;
} //end of main function



//*****programmer-defined function definitions*****
void enterProjectScores(short &earned, short &possible)
{
    //this function gets the project scores
    //it also accumulates the earned scores and the possible scores

    short projScore = 0;

    cout << "Enter a project score (negative number to end): ";
    cin >> projScore;
    while (projScore >= 0)
    {
        earned = earned + projScore;
        possible = possible + 50;
        cout << "Enter a project score (negative number to end): ";
        cin >> projScore;
    } //end while
} //end of enterProjectScores function
```

Figure 6-33: The completed grade program (continues on next page)

```cpp
void enterTestScores(short &earned, short &possible)
{
    //this function gets the number of tests and the test scores
    //it also accumulates the earned scores and the possible scores

    short testScore = 0;
    short numTests  = 0;

    cout << endl << "How many tests have you taken? ";
    cin >> numTests;

    for (short count = 1; count <= numTests; count = count + 1)
    {
        cout << "Enter a test score: ";
        cin >> testScore;
        earned = earned + testScore;
        possible = possible + 100;
    }//end for
}//end of enterTestScores function

char assignGrade(short earned, short possible)
{
    //this function assigns the appropriate grade
    float ratio      = (float) 0.0;
    char letterGrade = ' ';

    if (possible > 0)
        //calculate ratio
        ratio = (float) earned / (float) possible;
    else
        ratio = 0;
    //end if

    //assign letterGrade
    if (ratio >= .9)
        letterGrade = 'A';
    else
        if (ratio >= .8)
            letterGrade = 'B';
        else
            if (ratio >= .7)
                letterGrade = 'C';
            else
                if (ratio >= .6)
                    letterGrade = 'D';
                else
                    letterGrade = 'F';
                //end if (ratio >= .6)
            //end if (ratio >= .7)
        //end if (ratio >= .8)
    //end if (ratio >= .9)

    return letterGrade;
}//end of assignGrade function
```

Figure 6-33: The completed grade program (continued)

You have now completed Lesson B. You can either exit Visual C++ and take a break or complete the questions and exercises at the end of the lesson.

S U M M A R Y

The two forms of the repetition structure are the `while` and `do-while` loops. You can use either loop to repeat one or more instructions either a specified number of times or until some condition is met. Loops that repeat their instructions a specified number of times are commonly referred to as counter-controlled loops. The C++ `for` statement provides a convenient and compact way to code a counter-controlled `while` loop.

The `for` statement in C++ performs three tasks. First, it creates and initializes a numeric variable, referred to as the *counter* variable, to a beginning value. This is done only once, at the beginning of the loop. The loop then evaluates a *loop condition* to determine if the loop instructions should be processed. If the *loop condition* evaluates to True, the loop instructions are processed and the third task is performed; otherwise, the loop stops. The third task performed by the `for` statement is to update the value in the *counter* variable. Like the `while` statement, the `for` statement is also a pretest loop.

As with the `while` loop, you can use the `do-while` loop to repeat one or more statements either a specified number of times or while some *loop condition* is True. However, unlike the `while` loop, which evaluates the *loop condition* before processing the loop instructions, the `do-while` loop evaluates the *loop condition* after first processing the loop instructions. Therefore, the `do-while` loop is called a posttest, or bottom-driven, loop. You use the C++ `do` statement to code the `do-while` loop.

A N S W E R S   T O   M I N I - Q U I Z Z E S

Mini-Quiz 3

1. `for(short quantity = 0; quantity <= 10; quantity = quantity + 2)`
2. 12
3. `for(short onHand = 25; onHand >= 5; onHand = onHand - 5)`
4.
```
for (short number = 2; number < 9; number = number + 2)
     cout << number;
//end for
```

Mini-Quiz 4

1.
```
short num = 1;
do
{
   cout << '*';
   num = num + 1;
}while (num <= 5);
```
2. 6

QUESTIONS

1. How many times will the `cout << count << endl;` statement in the following loop be processed?
   ```
   for(short count = 1; count < 6; count = count + 1)
       cout << count << endl;
   //end for
   ```
   a. 0
   b. 1
   c. 5
   d. 6
   e. 7

2. What is the value of `count` when the loop in question 1 stops?
   a. 1
   b. 5
   c. 6
   d. 7
   e. 8

3. How many times will the `cout < count << endl;` statement in the following loop be processed?
   ```
   for(short count = 4; count <= 10; count = count + 2)
       cout << count << endl;
   //end for
   ```
   a. 0
   b. 3
   c. 4
   d. 5
   e. 12

4. What is the value of `count` when the loop in question 3 stops?
   a. 4
   b. 6
   c. 10
   d. 11
   e. 12

5. The `for` statement performs the following three tasks. Put these tasks in their proper order by placing the numbers 1 through 3 on the line to the left of the task.
   _____ Updates the *counter*
   _____ Initializes the *counter* to the *startvalue*
   _____ Evaluates the *loop condition*

6. The `do-while` loop is referred to as a _____ loop because the *loop condition* is tested after the loop instructions are processed the first time.
   a. beginning
   b. following
   c. posttest
   d. pretest
   e. priming

7. Which loop always processes its instructions at least once? (Select all that apply.)
   a. `do-while`
   b. `for`
   c. `while`

8. Depending on the *loop condition*, which loop may not process its instructions at all? (Select all that apply.)
    a. `do-while`
    b. `for`
    c. `while`

9. What will display when the following code is processed?
    ```cpp
    short x = 1;
    do
    {
         cout << x << endl;
         x = x + 1;
    } while (x < 5);
    //end do
    ```
    a. 0, 1, 2, 3, 4
    b. 0, 1, 2, 3, 4, 5
    c. 1, 2, 3, 4
    d. 1, 2, 3, 4, 5

10. What will display when the following code is processed?
    ```cpp
    short x = 20;
    do
    {
         cout << x;
         x = x - 4;
    } while (x > 10);
    //end do
    ```
    a. 16, 12, 8
    b. 16, 12
    c. 20, 16, 12, 8
    d. 20, 16, 12, 8, 4
    e. 20, 16, 12

11. What is the value of x when the loop in question 10 stops?
    a. 0
    b. 8
    c. 10
    d. 12

12. What will display when the following code is processed?
    ```cpp
    short total = 1;
    do
    {
         cout << total << endl;
         total = total + 2;
    } while (total >= 3);
    //end do
    ```
    a. 1
    b. 1, 3
    c. 1, 3, 5
    d. 0, 1, 3

E X E R C I S E S

1. Create a console application named T6Be01 in the Cpp\Tut06 folder on your computer's hard disk.
   a. Write a program that displays the product of the odd integers from 1 through 13 (in other words, 1 * 3 * 5 and so on). Use the **for** statement.
   b. Print the code. Indicate the answer on the code printout. Close the Output window and the workspace.

2. Create a console application named T6Be02 in the Cpp\Tut06 folder on your computer's hard disk.
   a. Write a program that displays the numbers 0 through 117, in increments of 9. Use the **while** statement. What value will be in the counter variable when the loop stops? Print the code. Indicate your answer on the code printout.
   b. Change the **while** statement to a **for** statement. What value will be in the counter variable when the loop stops? Print the code. Indicate your answer on the code printout. Close the Output window and the workspace.

3. Create a console application named T6Be03 in the Cpp\Tut06 folder on your computer's hard disk.
   a. Write a program that displays the squares of the even numbers from 10 through 25. Use the **while** statement. Print the code. Indicate the squares on the code printout.
   b. Change the **while** statement to a **for** statement. Print the code. Indicate the squares on the code printout. Close the Output window and the workspace.

4. Create a console application named T6Be04 in the Cpp\Tut06 folder on your computer's hard disk.
   a. Use the **for** statement to display the first 10 Fibonacci numbers (1, 1, 2, 3, 5, 8, 13, 21, 34, and 55) on the screen. (*Hint*: Notice that, beginning with the third number in the series, each Fibonacci number is the sum of the prior two numbers. In other words, 2 is the sum of 1 plus 1, 3 is the sum of 1 plus 2, 5 is the sum of 2 plus 3, and so on.)
   b. Save the first 10 Fibonacci numbers in a file named T6Be04.dat. Use C++ to open and print the T6Be04.dat file. Also print the code. Close the data file, the Output window, and the workspace.

5. Create a console application named T6Be05 in the Cpp\Tut06 folder on your computer's hard disk.
   a. Write a program that uses the **for** statement to display the following pattern of asterisks. Print the code.
      ```
      **
      ****
      ******
      ********
      **********
      ************
      ```
   b. Change the **for** statement to a **while** statement. Print the code.
   c. Change the **while** statement to a **do-while** statement. Print the code. Close the Output window and the workspace.

6. Create a console application named T6Be06 in the Cpp\Tut06 folder on your computer's hard disk.

a. Write a program that uses the `for` statement to display the following pattern of plus signs. Print the code.

```
+++++++++
++++++++
+++++++
++++++
+++++
++++
+++
++
+
```

b. Change the `for` statement to a `while` statement. Print the code.

c. Change the `while` statement to a `do-while` statement. Print the code. Close the Output window and the workspace.

7. What will display when the following code is processed? On a piece of paper, complete a desk-check table for the code. Record your answer on the paper.

```cpp
short temp = 0;
do
{
    cout << temp << endl;
    temp = temp + 1;
} while (temp < 5);
//end do
```

8. The following code should display the numbers 40, 30, 20, and 10. An instruction is missing from the code. On a piece of paper, complete a desk-check table for the code to help you determine which instruction is missing. What is the missing instruction and where does it belong in the code? Complete a desk-check table after entering the missing instruction. Record the missing instruction and its location on the paper that contains the desk-check tables.

```cpp
short num = 40;
do
{
    cout << num;
} while (num > 0);
//end do
```

9. What will display when the following code is processed? On a piece of paper, complete a desk-check table for the code. Record your answer on the paper.

```cpp
short totEmp = 1;
do
{
    cout << totEmp << endl;
    totEmp = totEmp + 2;
} while (totEmp >= 3);
//end do
```

10. In this exercise, you will modify an existing program. Before you can complete this exercise, you will need to have completed Lesson A's Exercise 2.

    a. Open the T6Ae02.cpp file, which you completed in Lesson A. The file is located in the Cpp\Tut06\T6Ae02 folder on your computer's hard disk.

    b. Modify the program so that it uses the `for` loop, rather than the `while` loop, to display the word "Hello" on the screen 10 times. Save the program using its original name. When the program is working correctly, print the code.

    c. Modify the code so that it uses the `do-while` loop, rather than the `for` loop, to display the word "Hello" on the screen 10 times. Save the program using its original name. When the program is working correctly, print the code. Close the Output window and the workspace.

11. In this exercise, you will modify an existing program. Before you can complete this exercise, you will need to have completed Lesson A's Exercise 3.

    a. Open the T6Ae03.cpp file, which you completed in Lesson A. The file is located in the Cpp\Tut06\T6Ae03 folder on your computer's hard disk.

    b. Modify the code so that it uses the `do-while` loop, rather than the `while` loop, to stop the loop when the `quantity` variable is less than 0. Save the program using its original name. When the program is working correctly, print the code. Close the Output window and the workspace.

12. In this exercise, you will modify an existing program. Before you can complete this exercise, you will need to have completed Lesson A's Exercise 4.

    a. Open the T6Ae04.cpp file, which you completed in Lesson A. The file is located in the Cpp\Tut06\T6Ae04 folder on your computer's hard disk.

    b. Modify the code so that it uses the `do-while` loop, rather than the `while` loop, to stop the loop when the user enters the letter N in the Character variable named `more`. (Perform a case-insensitive comparison.) Save the program using its original name. When the program is working correctly, print the code. Close the Output window and the workspace.

13. In this exercise, you will modify an existing program. Before you can complete this exercise, you will need to have completed Lesson A's Exercise 5.

    a. Open the T6Ae05.cpp file, which you completed in Lesson A. The file is located in the Cpp\Tut06\T6Ae05 folder on your computer's hard disk.

    b. Modify the code so that it uses the `do-while` loop, rather than the `while` loop, to stop the loop when the user enters the word "Done" in the `name` String variable. (Perform a case-insensitive comparison.) Save the program using its original name. When the program is working correctly, print the code. Close the Output window and the workspace.

14. In this exercise, you will modify an existing program. Before you can complete this exercise, you will need to have completed Lesson A's Exercise 14.

    a. Open the T6Ae14.cpp file, which you completed in Lesson A. The file is located in the Cpp\Tut06\T6Ae14 folder on your computer's hard disk.

    b. Modify the code so that it uses the `for` loop, rather than the `while` loop, to enter the four sales amounts. Send the program output to a file named T6Be14.dat. Save the program using its original name. When the program is working,correctly, print the code.

    c. Execute the program using the following as the North, South, East, and West sales, respectively: 23000, 10000, 4000, and 2000. Use C++ to open and print the T6Be14.dat file. Close the data file, the Output window, and the workspace.

15. In this exercise, you will modify an existing program. Before you can complete this exercise, you will need to have completed Lesson A's Exercise 15.

    a. Open the T6Ae15.cpp file, which you completed in Lesson A. The file is located in the Cpp\Tut06\T6Ae15 folder on your computer's hard disk.

    b. Modify the code so that it uses the **do-while** loop, rather than the **while** loop, to input the IDs. Send the program output to a file named T6Be15.dat. Save the program using its original name. When the program is working correctly, print the code.

    c. Execute the program using the following IDs: 1234, 3456, and 8888. Use C++ to open and print the T6Be15.dat file. Close the data file, the Output window, and the workspace.

discovery ▶ **16.** Although the **while** and **do-while** loops will produce the same results in most programs, that will not always be the case, as you will see in this exercise.

    a. Create a console application named T6Be16 in the Cpp\Tut06 folder on your computer's hard disk.

    b. Enter the following code:

```
#include <iostream.h>
void main()
{
      short number = 0;
      cout << "Enter a number: ";
      cin >> number;
      while (number > 0)
      {
            cout << "You entered " << number << endl;
            cout << "Enter a number: ";
            cin >> number;
      }//end while
      cout << "End of program" << endl;
}//end of main function
```

    c. Save, build, and execute the program. When prompted to enter a number, type 5 and press the Enter key, then type –1 and press the Enter key. The "You entered 5" and "End of program" messages appear in the DOS window. Press the Enter key to close the DOS window.

    d. Execute the program again. This time, enter –9 when prompted to enter a number. Only the "End of program" message appears. Press the Enter key to close the DOS window. On a piece of paper, explain why only this message appears.

    e. Modify the program so that it uses the **do-while** loop rather than the **while** loop.

    f. Save, build, and execute the program. When prompted to enter a number, type 5 and press the Enter key, then type –1 and press the Enter key. The "You entered 5" and "End of program" messages appear in the DOS window. Press the Enter key to close the DOS window.

    g. Execute the program again. When prompted to enter a number, type –9 and press the Enter key, then type –1 and press the Enter key. What does the program display in the DOS window? Press the Enter key to close the DOS window. On a piece of paper, explain why the program displayed the messages. Close the Output window and the workspace.

discovery ▶

17. In this exercise, you will learn about the C++ increment and decrement operators.

a. Open the T6Be17.cpp file, which is located in the Cpp\Tut06\T6Be17 folder on your computer's hard disk. The program uses the `for` loop to get five test scores from the user. A student must earn at least 70 points to pass the test. If the test score is greater than or equal to 70, a counter variable named `totalPass` is incremented by 1. The program then displays the total number of students passing the test.

C++ provides a more convenient way of writing an assignment statement that increments and decrements a variable by a value of 1. Rather than using the `totalPass = totalPass + 1;` statement to update the `totalPass` variable by 1, you can use the `totalPass++;` statement. The ++ (two plus signs with no spaces between) after the variable name is called the increment operator. In this case, the increment operator tells C++ to add 1 to the `totalPass` variable and then store the result in the `totalPass` variable.

b. Change the `totalPass = totalPass + 1;` statement to `totalPass++;`.

c. Save, build, and execute the program. Enter the following five scores: 78, 65, 43, 89, and 100. The DOS window shows that three students passed the test. Press the Enter key to close the DOS window.

d. You can also use the increment operator (++) to update the `for` loop's counter variable by 1. On your own, change the *update-expression* in the `for` clause so that it uses the increment operator to add 1 to the `x` variable.

e. Save, build, and execute the program. Enter the following five scores: 78, 65, 43, 89, and 100. The DOS window shows that three students passed the test. Press the Enter key to close the DOS window.

f. C++ also has a decrement operator, which is two minus signs (or hyphens) with no space between, like this: --. The decrement operator tells C++ to subtract 1 from a variable, and then store the result in the variable. The `temp--` statement, for example, tells C++ to subtract 1 from the `temp` variable, and then store the result in the `temp` variable. Modify the `for` clause so that the loop starts at 5, stops at 1, and uses the decrement operator to subtract 1 from the counter variable—in other words, to update the counter variable by –1.

g. Save, build, and execute the program. Enter the following five scores: 88, 85, 73, 89, and 54. The DOS window shows that four students passed the test. Press the Enter key to close the DOS window.

h. Print the code. Close the Output window and the workspace.

debugging

18. In this exercise, you will debug a program.

a. Open the T6Be18.cpp file, which is located in the Cpp\Tut06\T6Be18 folder on your computer's hard disk.

b. Debug the program. Save, build, and then execute the program. Summarize any problems you found and fix them. When the program is working correctly, print the code. On the code printout, circle the corrections you made to the program. Close the Output window and the workspace.

Sequential Access Files and Structs

case ▶ During July and August of each year, the Political Awareness Organization (PAO) sends a questionnaire to the voters in the organization's district. The questionnaire asks the voter to provide his or her name, age, and political party (Democrat, Republican, or Independent). The organization's secretary needs you to write two programs: one program will save the information from the returned questionnaires in a sequential access file, and the other program will use the information stored in the file to calculate the number of Democrats, Republicans, and Independents in the district. In this tutorial, you will learn how to create, open, and close a sequential access file, as well as write records to and read records from a sequential access file.

In this lesson you will learn how to:

- Open a sequential access data file
- Write information to a sequential access data file
- Close a sequential access data file
- Read information from a sequential access data file
- Test for the end of an input file

Creating and Manipulating Sequential Access Files

Data Files

In previous tutorials, you saved the program instructions in a file, called a **program file**, on your computer's hard disk. You also learned how to send the program output to a file whose contents you then printed. Although you saved the program instructions and the program output, recall that the input data required by the program—for example, the student's scores in Tutorial 6's grade program—was not saved, which means the user will need to enter the data (the student's scores) each time the program is run. In this lesson, you will learn how to save the input data in a file, called a **data file**, on your computer's hard disk. You will also learn how to access the saved information.

The information in a data file is typically organized into fields and records. A **field** is a single item of information about a person, place, or thing—for example, a Social Security number, a city, or a price. A **record** is one or more related fields that contain all of the necessary data about a specific person, place, or thing. For example, the college you are attending keeps a student record on you. Your student record might contain the following fields: your Social Security number, name, address, phone number, credits earned, grades earned, grade point average, and so on. The place where you are employed also keeps a record on you. Your employee record might contain your Social Security number, name, address, phone number, starting date, salary or hourly wage, and so on. A collection of related records is called a **data file**. The collection of records for each of the students in your class forms the class data file; the collection of employee records forms the employee data file. Figure 7-1 illustrates the concept of a field, a record, and a data file.

tip

Files whose contents are merely printed are often referred to as print files. However, a file can be both a print file and a data file. It is considered a print file when its contents are printed, and a data file when its contents are used as input in the same or another program.

data file

	Social Security number field	Name field	Phone number field
First record	100-00-0000	Joe Jacobs	555-9999
Second record	100-00-0001	Paul Smith	555-8888
Third record	100-00-0002	Sue Blass	555-7777

Figure 7-1: Illustration of fields and records in a data file

In most programming languages, you can create three different types of data files: sequential, random, and binary. The data file type refers to how the data is accessed. For example, the data in a sequential access file is always accessed sequentially—in other words, in consecutive order. The data in a random access file, on the other hand, can be accessed either in consecutive order or in random order. The data in a binary access file can be accessed by its byte location in the file. You will learn about sequential access files in this tutorial. Random and binary access files are beyond the scope of this book.

Sequential Access Data Files

Sequential access files are similar to cassette tapes in that each record in the file, like each song on a cassette tape, is both stored and retrieved in consecutive order (sequentially). Sequential access files have the advantage of being very easy to create. The drawback of this file type is the same drawback encountered with cassette tapes: the records in a sequential access file, like the songs on a cassette tape, can be processed only in the order in which they are stored. In other words, if you want to listen to the third song on a cassette tape, you must play (or fast-forward through) the first two songs. Likewise, if you want to read the third record in a sequential access file, you must first read the two records that precede it. Sequential access files work best when you want to process either a small file—one that contains less than 100 records—or a large file whose records are always processed in consecutive order.

The first program you will code in this lesson is one that saves a student's test scores, which are entered at the keyboard, in a sequential access file. Each record in the file will contain one field—a test score. (You will learn how to save records that contain more than one field in Lesson B.) The IPO chart for this program is shown in Figure 7-2.

Input	Processing	Output

test scores	Processing items: none
	
	Algorithm:
	1. open an output file
	2. if (open is successful)
	    enter first test score
	    repeat while (test score is greater than or equal to 0)
	      write test score to the output file
	      enter another test score
	    end while
	    close the output file
	  else
	    display message indicating that open
	    was not successful
	  end if
		output file containing the test scores

Figure 7-2: IPO chart for the test score program

As indicated in Figure 7-2's algorithm, the program will begin by opening an output file, which is a file to which information can be written. The program will then verify that C++ opened the file successfully. If the file was not opened successfully, perhaps because the disk on which the information is to be written is full, the program will display an appropriate message.

If the file was opened successfully, on the other hand, the program will prompt the user to enter the first test score, and will then evaluate the *loop condition*, which determines if the test score is greater than or equal to zero. If the *loop condition* evaluates to True, the instructions within the loop will be processed. You will notice that the loop instructions write the test score to the sequential file and then prompt the user to enter another test score. The loop instructions will be processed as long as—or while—the test score entered by the user is greater than or equal to zero. When the user enters a test score that is not greater than or equal to zero, the loop stops and the sequential file is closed before the program ends.

Before you can code this program, you will need to learn how to open a sequential access data file.

Opening a Sequential Access Data File

As you learned in Tutorial 2, you use stream objects to perform standard input and output operations in C++. The standard input stream object, `cin`, refers to the keyboard, and the standard output stream object, `cout`, refers to the computer screen. To use the standard input and output stream objects, recall that you must include the iostream.h header file in the program. The iostream.h header file contains the definitions of the `istream` and `ostream` classes, from which the `cin` and `cout` objects, respectively, are created. Recall that you do not have to create the `cin` and `cout` objects, as C++ creates these objects in the iostream.h header file for you.

In addition to getting information from the keyboard and sending output to the monitor, you can also get information from and send information to a file. Getting information from a file is referred to as "reading the file," and sending information to a file is referred to as "writing to the file." Data files to which information is written are called **output data files** because these files store the data output by a program. The test score program, for example, will store the test scores in an output data file. Data files that are read are called **input data files** because the program uses the data in these files as input. The information contained in the test score data file, for example, will be used later in this lesson in a program that calculates the student's average test score.

As with standard input and output operations, you use objects to perform file input and output operations. Unlike the standard cin and cout objects, which C++ creates for you, the input and output file objects must be created in your program. To create a file object, you must include the fstream.h header file in the program. The header file contains the definitions of the ifstream (*input file stream*) and ofstream (*output file stream*) classes that allow you to create input and output file objects, respectively. Figure 7-3 shows examples of statements that use the ifstream and ofstream classes to create input and output file objects.

<table>
<tr><th>Syntax</th><th>Examples</th><th>Result</th></tr>
<tr><td>ifstream object;</td><td>ifstream inFile;

ifstream inEmploy;</td><td>creates an input file object named inFile
creates an input file object named inEmploy</td></tr>
<tr><td>ofstream object;</td><td>ofstream outFile;

ofstream outSales;</td><td>creates an output file object named outFile
creates an output file object named outSales</td></tr>
</table>

Figure 7-3: Examples of using the ifstream and ofstream classes to create file objects

As Figure 7-3 shows, the syntax for creating an input file object is **ifstream** *object*; and the syntax for creating an output file object is **ofstream** *object*;. In both versions, *object* is the name of the file object you want to create. You will notice that the names of the input file objects (inFile and inEmploy) in the figure begin with the two letters in, and the names of the output file objects (outFile and outSales) begin with the three letters out. Although C++ does not require you to begin file object names with either in or out, using this naming convention helps to distinguish a program's input file objects from its output file objects.

You use the input and output file objects, along with the C++ open function, to open actual files on your computer's disk. The open function is a member function defined in both the ifstream and ofstream classes. The syntax of the open function is *object*.**open**(*filename*, [*mode*]);. In the syntax, *object* is the name of either an ifstream or an ofstream file object. *filename*, which must be enclosed in quotation marks, is the name of the file you want to open on the computer's disk. If the file you want to open is not in the same location as the program file, you will need to enter the file's full path in the *filename* argument. For example, to open the scores.dat file that is located in the Data folder on the A drive, you would use "a:\Data\scores.dat" as the *filename* in the open function. The open function associates the opened file with the file object whose name is specified in the syntax as *object*.

The *mode* argument, which is optional in the open function's syntax, tells C++ how the file is to be opened. Figure 7-4 lists the most commonly used *modes* and describes their meaning. Only one of the *modes* in the list—ios::in—is used when opening input files whereas the ios::out and ios::app *modes* are used when opening output files.

input file *modes*	Description
ios::in	Opens the file for input, which allows the program to read the file's contents. This is the default *mode* for input files.

output file *modes*	Description
ios::app	Opens the file for append, which allows the program to write new data to the end of the existing data in the file. If the file does not exist, the file is created before data is written to it.
ios::out	Opens the file for output, which creates a new, empty file to which data can be written. If the file already exists, its contents are erased before the new data is written. This is the default *mode* for output files.

Figure 7-4: Most commonly used open function *modes*

OOP
Concepts

As you learned in Tutorial 1, a base class is simply a class from which another class, referred to as the derived class, is created.

You will notice that ios:: appears in each *mode* shown in Figure 7-4. The two colons (::), called the **scope resolution operator**, tell C++ that the in, out, and app keywords are defined in the ios class, which is the base class that defines all input/output operations in C++.

The ios::in *mode* tells C++ to open the file for input, which allows the program to read the data stored in the file. You can use the ios::in *mode* in open functions that open input files only. You can use either the ios::app *mode* or the ios::out *mode*, on the other hand, in open functions that open output files only. Both of these modes allow the program to write data to the files. You use the ios::app (app stands for *append*) *mode* when you want to add data to the end of an existing file. If the file does not exist, C++ creates the file for you. You use the ios::out *mode* to open a new, empty file for output. If the file already exists, C++ erases the contents of the file before writing any data to it. Figure 7-5 shows examples of the open function used to open input and output files.

Important note: In the following examples, assume that the `ifstream` object, which represents the input file, is named `inFile`, and that the `ofstream` object, which represents the output file, is named `outFile`. All but the last example also assume that the file being opened is in the same location as the program file.

`open` function used to open input and output files	Result
`inFile.open ("sales.dat", ios::in);`	opens a file named sales.dat for input
`inFile.open ("sales.dat");`	opens a file named sales.dat for input
`outFile.open("payroll.dat", ios::out);`	opens a file named payroll.dat for output
`outFile.open("payroll.dat");`	opens a file named payroll.dat for output
`outFile.open("employ.dat", ios::app);`	opens a file named employ.dat for append
`outFile.open("a:\employ.dat", ios::app);`	opens a file named employ.dat, which is located on the A drive, for append

Figure 7-5: Examples of the `open` function used to open input and output files

In Lesson A's Discovery Exercise 6, you will learn about other `open` function *mode*s, as well as how to include more than one *mode* in an `open` function.

You should assign meaningful names to the files you create. For example, a meaningful name for a data file that contains test scores is scores.dat. Programmers typically use a .dat filename extension to indicate that a file is a data file.

As Figure 7-5 indicates, you can use either the `inFile.open ("sales.dat", ios::in);` statement or the `inFile.open ("sales.dat");` statement to open the sales.dat file for input. In C++, all files associated with an `ifstream` file object are opened for input automatically. Therefore, if you do not specify a *mode* when opening an input file, C++ uses the default *mode* of `ios::in`.

Files associated with an `ofstream` file object, on the other hand, are opened for output automatically—in other words, `ios::out` is the default *mode*. This explains why you can use either the `outFile.open("payroll.dat", ios::out);` statement or the `outFile.open("payroll.dat");` statement to open the payroll.dat file for output. In cases where the program needs to add data to the data already stored in an output file, you will need to specify the `ios::app` *mode* in the `open` function. You would use the `outFile.open ("employ.dat", ios::app);` statement, for example, to tell C++ to open the employ.dat file, which is located in the same location as the program file, for append. Notice, however, that you would need to use the `outFile.open ("a:\employ.dat", ios::app);` statement to open the employ.dat file located on the A drive for append. For most data files, you will want to append new information to the end of the existing information, rather than erase the existing information, so in most cases you will use the `ios::app` *mode* when opening output data files.

C++ uses a **record indicator** to keep track of the next record either to read or write in a data file. When you open a file for input, C++ positions the record indicator at the beginning of the file, immediately before the first record. When you open a file for output, C++ also positions the record indicator at the beginning of the file, but recall that the file is empty. (As you may remember, opening a file for output tells C++ to create a new, empty file or erase the contents of an existing file.) However, when you use the `ios::app` *mode* to open a file for append, C++ positions the record indicator immediately after the last record in the file. Figure 7-6 illustrates the positioning of the record indicator when files are opened for input, output, and append.

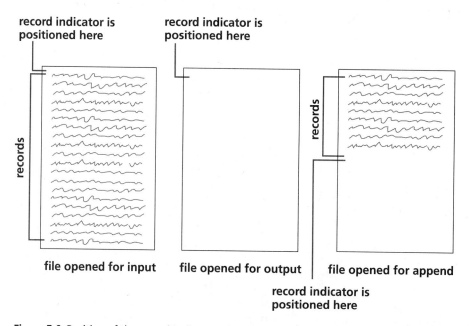

record indicator is positioned here

record indicator is positioned here

records

records

file opened for input   file opened for output   file opened for append

record indicator is positioned here

Figure 7-6: Position of the record indicator when files are opened for input, output, and append

Now that you know how to open a file, you can begin coding the test score program.

To begin coding the test score program:

1 Start Visual C++. Open the **LaProg01.cpp** file, which is located in the Cpp\Tut07\LaProg01 folder on your computer's hard disk. The partially completed test score program appears in the LaProg01.cpp window, as shown in Figure 7-7.

```
//LaProg01.cpp
//this program demonstrates how to write records to
//a sequential access file

#include <iostream.h>

void main()
{
    //declare and initialize variable
    short score = 0;

    //open output file

    //verify that open was successful

        //enter and write test scores

        //close file

} //end of main function
```

will store each test score

Figure 7-7: Partially completed test score program

Notice that the partially completed test score program creates a Short Integer variable named `score` and initializes it to 0. The program will use this variable to store each test score entered by the user.

According to the IPO chart shown in Figure 7-2, the program needs to open a sequential access output file. Before the program can open a file, recall that you first must enter the `#include <fstream.h>` directive in the program.

2   In the blank line below the `#include <iostream.h>` directive, type **#include <fstream.h>** and press the **Enter** key.

You can now use the `ofstream` class, which is defined in the fstream.h header file, to create an output file object named `outFile`. You are creating an output file object because the program will need to write information to, rather than read information from, the file.

3   In the blank line below the `//open output file` comment, type **ofstream outFile;** and press the **Enter** key.

Recall that you use the program's output file object, along with the C++ open function, to open an actual data file on your computer's disk. You will name the data file scores.dat and open it for append, which will allow you to add new test scores to the file each time the program is executed.

4   In the blank line below the `ofstream outFile;` statement, type **outFile.open("scores.dat", ios::app);** and press the **Enter** key.

tip

If you want the program to create the scores.dat file in a location other than the folder in which the program resides, you will need to include the file's full path in the *filename* argument.

Before attempting either to read data from or write data to a file, you should always verify that the file was opened successfully.

mini-quiz

Mini-Quiz 1

1. A collection of related records is called a(n) _____.

2. To use either an input or output file, the program must include the _____ header file.

   a. filestream.h b. fstream.h c. instream.h d. inoutstream.h e. iostream.h

3. The _____ mode tells C++ to open a file for input.

   a. `add::ios` b. `in::file` c. `ios::app` d. `ios::in` e. `ios::out`

4. Which of the following statements creates an output file object named `outName`?

   a. `filestream outName;` b. `ofstream outName;` c. `outFile outName;` d. `output outName;` e. `outstream outName;`

5. Which of the following statements uses the `outName` file object created in question 4 to open an output file named items.dat? New information should be written following the current information in the file.

   a. `outName.open("items.dat", ios::in);`
   b. `outName.open("items.dat", ios::out);`
   c. `outName.open("items.dat", ios::app);`
   d. `outName.open("items.dat", ios::add);`

Testing If a File Was Opened Successfully

It is possible for the `open` function to fail when attempting to open a file. For example, the `open` function will not be able to create an output file on a disk that is either full or write-protected. Before attempting either to read from or write to a file, you should use the C++ `fail` function to test if the file was opened successfully. The syntax of the `fail` function is *object*.**fail**(), where *object* is the name of either an input or output file object in the program. The `fail` function, which is defined in both the `ifstream` and `ofstream` classes, returns the number 1 if the open failed. If, on the other hand, the open did not fail—in other words, if the file was opened successfully—the `fail` function returns the number 0. In C++, as well as in most computer languages, the number 1 represents the Boolean value True, and the number 0 represents the Boolean value False.

You typically use the `fail` function in an `if` statement to test the file immediately after opening it. The `if` statement's *condition* can be phrased using either of the examples shown in Figure 7-8.

`if` statement's *condition*	

`(outFile.fail() == 1)`
or
`(outFile.fail())`
	you can use either of these to test if the open function failed

`(outFile.fail() == 0)`
or
`(!outFile.fail())`
	you can use either of these to test if the open function succeeded—in other words, to test if it did not fail

Figure 7-8: Examples of `if` statement *condition*s for testing the open function

As Figure 7-8 indicates, you can use either the (outFile.fail() == 1) *condition* or the (outFile.fail()) *condition* to test if the open failed. The (outFile.fail() == 1) *condition* compares the fail function's return value to the number 1, which represents the Boolean value True. If the fail function returns the value 1 (for True), then the open function failed to open the file. You can also evaluate the results of the fail function by using the (outFile.fail()) *condition* (you can think of this *condition* as meaning "the open function failed").

Figure 7-8 also indicates that you can use either the (outFile.fail() == 0) *condition* or the (!outFile.fail()) *condition* to test if the open succeeded—in other words, to test if the open did not fail. The (outFile.fail() == 0) *condition* compares the fail function's return value to the number 0, which represents the Boolean value False. If the fail function returns the number 0 (for False), then the open function did not fail; rather, it successfully opened the file. You can also determine if the open function was successful by using the (!outFile.fail()) *condition*. Recall that the ! is the Not logical operator, which you learned about in Tutorial 5. (You can think of the (!outFile.fail()) condition as meaning "the open function did not fail.") Most programmers use the (!outFile.fail()) *condition* in the if statement that determines the result of the open function.

According to the IPO chart shown in Figure 7-2, if the open function was successful, the test score program should get the test scores from the user and then write the scores to the file, before closing the file. However, if the open function was not successful, the program should display a message indicating that fact. You will use a selection structure, along with the fail function and the ! (Not) logical operator, to determine if the open function was successful and then take the appropriate action. You will begin entering the selection structure in the next set of steps.

To begin entering the selection structure that tests if the open function was successful:

1 In the blank line below the //verify that open was successful comment, type **if (!outFile.fail())** and press the **Tab** key, then type **//if open did not fail** and press the **Enter** key. The if clause will determine if the file associated with the outFile object—in this program, the scores.dat file—was opened successfully.

Because the algorithm shown in Figure 7-2 indicates that the selection structure's true path will contain more than one statement, you will need to enclose the statements in a set of braces.

2 Type **{** (the opening brace) to begin the statement block for the selection structure's true path.

According to the algorithm, if the open function is successful, the program should allow the user to enter the first test score. You will use the cout stream and the insertion operator (<<) to prompt the user to enter the appropriate response. You will then use the cin stream and the extraction operator (>>) to store the user's response in the score variable.

3 In the blank line below the //enter and write test scores comment, type **cout << "Enter a test score (enter a negative number to stop): ";** and press the **Enter** key, then type **cin >> score;** and press the **Enter** key.

The algorithm indicates that the program will now use a while loop whose instructions should be processed as long as—or while—the score variable contains a number that is greater than or equal to zero. First enter the while clause.

tip

As you learned in Tutorial 6, the input statement that appears above the repetition structure—in this case, the cin >> score; statement—is called the priming, or lead, read. As such, it will get only the first test score from the user.

4 Type **while (score >= 0)** and press the **Enter** key.

Because the `while` loop will contain more than one statement, you will need to enclose its statements in a set of braces.

5 Type **{** (the opening brace) and press the **Enter** key.

According to the algorithm, the first instruction in the loop writes the test score to the file. Before you can continue coding the program, you will need to learn how to write data to a file. First, however, save the statements you entered in the program thus far.

6 Save the program.

Next, learn how to write records to a sequential access data file.

Writing Records to a Sequential Access Data File

tip

In C++, the newline character is designated by '\n' (the backslash and the letter n enclosed in single quotes). When you open a data file, however, you will not see this character because the `endl` stream manipulator writes an invisible newline character at the end of each record in the file. You will learn more about the newline character in Lesson B.

The syntax for writing a record to a sequential access data file is similar to the syntax for displaying information on the monitor. Recall that the syntax for displaying information is **cout << data << endl;**, where *data* is one or more variables or constants. The `cout << score << endl;` statement, for example, would display the contents of the `score` variable and then advance the cursor to the next line on the screen.

Similarly, the syntax for writing a record to a file is *object << data << endl;*, where *object* is the name of the program's `ofstream` object, and *data* is the one or more fields included in each record. In this lesson, you will learn how to write records that contain one field only. You will learn how to write records that contain more than one field in Lesson B.

To distinguish one record from another in the data file, programmers typically write each record on a separate line in the file. The `endl` stream manipulator included at the end of the syntax accomplishes this by writing an invisible character—referred to as the **newline character**—at the end of each record. The newline character advances the cursor to the next line in the file immediately after a record is written. For example, assuming that a program's `ofstream` object is named `outFile`, the statement `outFile << score << endl;` would write both the contents of the `score` variable and the newline character on one line in the scores.dat file. The cursor would then be positioned on the next line in the file.

You can now continue to code the test score program by entering the statement that will write the contents of the `score` variable to the data file.

To continue coding the test score program:

1 The LaProg01 program should still be open. In the blank line below the `while` loop's opening brace (**{**), type **outFile << score << endl;** and press the **Enter** key. This statement will write the test score to the file associated with the `outFile` object—in other words, it will write the score to the scores.dat file.

After writing the test score to the file, the `while` loop should allow the user to enter another test score. You will need to enter the appropriate `cout` and `cin` instructions to do so.

As you learned in Tutorial 6, the `cout` and `cin` statements that appear above the `while` clause in the program will get only the first test score from the user. The `cout` and `cin` statements within the loop will get the remaining test scores.

Because it is so easy to forget to close the files used in a program, you should enter the statement to close the file as soon as possible after entering the one that opens it. Forgetting to close an open file can result in a loss of data.

2 Type **cout << "Enter a test score (enter a negative number to stop): ";** and press the **Enter** key, then type **cin >> score;** and press the **Enter** key.

According to the algorithm, you can now end the `while` loop, which you will do by typing a closing brace and a comment.

3 Type **}** (the closing brace) and press the **Spacebar**, then type **//end while** and press the **Enter** key.

4 Save the program.

As the algorithm indicates, after the `while` loop has completed its processing, you need to close the data file.

Closing a File

Both the `ifstream` and `ofstream` classes contain a member function named `close` that closes an open file. The syntax of the `close` function is *object*.**close( );**, where *object* is the name of the program's input or output file object. You will notice that the `close` function does not require a filename. This is because C++ automatically closes the file whose name is associated with the file object specified in *object*. As you may remember, the `open` function associates the filename with the file object when the file is opened. Use the `close` function to close the scores.dat file in the current program. You can then complete the selection structure and the program.

To include the `close` function in the current program and then complete the selection structure and the program:

1 In the blank line below the **//close file** comment, type **outFile.close( );** and press the **Enter** key. This statement will close the file associated with the `outFile` object—in this case, it will close the scores.dat file.

As the algorithm indicates, you have now completed the statement block in the selection structure's true path.

2 Type **}** (the closing brace) and press the **Enter** key to end the true path's statement block.

The selection structure's false path should display a message indicating that an error occurred when the program attempted to open the file.

3 Type **else** and press the **Tab** key, then type **//open failed** and press the **Enter** key to begin the false path. Type **cout << "Error opening file." << endl;** and press the **Enter** key, then type **//end if** and press the **Enter** key.

The completed test score program is shown in Figure 7-9.

```
//LaProg01.cpp
//this program demonstrates how to write records to
//a sequential access file

#include <iostream.h>
#include <fstream.h>

void main()
{
    //declare and initialize variable
    short score = 0;

    //open output file
    ofstream outFile;
    outFile.open("scores.dat", ios::app);

    //verify that open was successful
    if (!outFile.fail())        //if open did not fail
    {
        //enter and write test scores
        cout << "Enter a test score (enter a negative number to stop): ";
        cin >> score;
        while (score >= 0)
        {
            outFile << score << endl;
            cout << "Enter a test score (enter a negative number to stop): ";
            cin >> score;
        } //end while

        //close file
        outFile.close();
    }
    else        //open failed
        cout << "Error opening file." << endl;
    //end if

} //end of main function
```

opens file for append

determines if open was successful

writes score to file

closes file

displays message if open failed

Figure 7-9: Completed test score program

4 Save and build the program to verify that it does not contain any errors or warnings. If any errors or warnings appear in the Output window, compare your code with the code shown in Figure 7-9, then make any necessary corrections.

5 Execute the program.

Recall that the program opens the scores.dat file for append. Because the file does not exist, C++ first creates and then opens the file on your computer's hard disk.

6 When prompted to enter a test score, type **50** and press the **Enter** key. The program writes the test score—in this case, the number 50—as well as the invisible newline character to the scores.dat file. You are now prompted to enter another test score.

7 Type **85** and press the **Enter** key. The program writes the number 85 and the invisible newline character to the scores.dat file.

8 On your own, enter the following five test scores: **78, 56, 90, 95,** and **83**.

Now exit the program. Recall that you can do so by entering a number that is less than zero.

9 Type –1 and press the **Enter** key to exit the program. Then press the **Enter** key again to close the DOS window.

You can verify that the records were written correctly to the data file by opening the file in C++. Open the scores.dat file and view its contents.

To view the contents of the scores.dat file:

1 Use C++ to open the scores.dat file, which is located in the Cpp\Tut07\LaProg01 folder on your computer's hard disk. Figure 7-10 shows the contents of the file.

```
50
85
78
56
90
95
83
```

Figure 7-10: Contents of the scores.dat file

2 Close the scores.dat file.

You have now completed this program, so you can close it.

3 Close the Output window and the workspace.

The next program you will complete will use the test scores stored in the scores.dat file to calculate the average test score.

mini-quiz

Mini-Quiz 2

1. The `fail` function returns the number _____ if the open failed.

2. Which of the following statements will write the contents of the `quantity` variable to the inventory.dat file, whose file object is named `outInv`?

   a. `inventory.dat << quantity << endl;`
   b. `ofstream << quantity << endl;`
   c. `outInv << quantity << endl;`
   d. `outInv >> quantity << endl;`

3. Write the statement that will close the inventory.dat file, whose file object is named `outInv`.

The Average Score Program

The test score program, which you finished coding in the last set of steps, saved the student's test scores in the scores.dat file. In the test score program, the scores.dat file was considered an output file because it stored the output from the program. The average score program, which you will code next, will read the scores stored in the scores.dat file and use them to calculate the average score. In the average test score program, the scores.dat file is considered an input file because it provides data to the program. The IPO chart for the average score program is shown in Figure 7-11.

Input	Processing	Output

test scores stored in input file	Processing items: counter and accumulator
	
	Algorithm:
	1. open an input file
	2. if (open is successful)
	       read first test score
	       repeat while (it is not end of file)
	            add 1 to counter
	            add test score to the accumulator
	            enter another test score
	       end while
	       close input file
	       calculate average test score by dividing the accumulator by the counter
	       display average test score
	  else
	       display message indicating that open was not successful
	  end if
		average test score

Figure 7-11: IPO chart for the average score program

According to the algorithm, the program will open an input file—in this case, the program will open the scores.dat file. If the open fails, the program will display an appropriate message. If, on the other hand, the open does not fail, the program will read the first test score from the file. It will then use a `while` loop to count the number of test scores in the file and accumulate those test scores. To calculate the average test score, the program will need to know the number of test scores, as well as the total of the test scores, stored in the scores.dat file. The last instruction in the loop will read another test score from the file. The loop instructions will be processed as long as the end of the file has not been reached. When there are no more test scores to read, the program will close the file, and then calculate and display the average test score.

You already know how to code most of this algorithm—for example, you know how to open a file for input, as well as how to test the open and close the file. In the remaining sections of this lesson, you will learn how to read a record from a file and how to determine when the record indicator is at the end of the file. First view the existing code in the partially completed average score program.

To view the code in the partially completed average score program:

1 Open the **LaProg02.cpp** file, which is located in the Cpp\Tut07\LaProg02 folder on your computer's hard disk. The partially completed average score program, which appears in the LaProg02.cpp window, is shown in Figure 7-12.

```
//LaProg02.cpp
//this program demonstrates how to read records from
//a sequential access file

#include <iostream.h>
#include <fstream.h>

void main()
{
    //declare and initialize variable
    short score        = 0;
    short numScores    = 0;     //counter
    short totalScores = 0;     //accumulator
    float average      = (float) 0.0;

    //open input file
    ifstream inFile;
    inFile.open("scores.dat", ios::in);

    //verify that open was successful
    if (!inFile.fail()) //if open did not fail
    {
        //read test score

            //update counter and accumulator
            numScores = numScores + 1;
            totalScores = totalScores + score;

        //close file
        inFile.close();

        //calculate and display average test score
        average = (float) totalScores / (float) numScores;
        cout << "Average test score: " << average << endl;
    }
    else //open failed
        cout << "Error opening file." << endl;
    //end if

} //end of main function
```

opens file

determines if open was successful

the instruction to read the first record is missing

displays message if open failed

Figure 7-12: Partially completed average score program

Study the code shown in Figure 7-12. You will notice that the program declares and initializes four variables: score, numScores (the counter variable), totalScores (the accumulator variable), and average. The ifstream inFile; and inFile.open("scores.dat", ios::in); statements create the input file object and then open the scores.dat file for input. The if (!inFile.fail()) clause tests to see if the open failed. If the open failed, the selection structure's false path displays an appropriate message. If the open did not fail, the first instruction in the selection structure's true path should read the first test score from the file. The instruction to read the test score is missing from the program. You will learn how to code a program to read records from a file in the next section.

Reading Records from a Sequential Access File

The syntax for reading records from a file is similar to the syntax for getting information from the keyboard. Recall that the syntax for getting information from the keyboard is **cin >>** *variable;*. You could use the `cin >> score;` statement, for example, to get a test score from the user at the keyboard and then store the number in the `score` variable. The syntax for reading numeric and character information from a file is *object >> variable*, where *object* is the name of the program's `ifstream` object, and *variable* is the name of either a numeric or character variable included in each record. (You will learn how to read strings into String variables in Lesson B.) If a program's `ifstream` object is named `inFile`, as it is in the current program, the `inFile >> score;` statement would read a test score from the scores.dat file and store the score in the `score` variable.

Recall that Figure 7-10 shows the contents of the scores.dat file, which you created in the Cpp\Tut07\LaProg01 folder on your computer's hard disk. A copy of this file is stored in the Cpp\Tut07\LaProg02 folder on your computer's hard disk.

To enter the code that will read the first record in the scores.dat input file:

1   In the blank line below the `//read test score` comment, type **inFile >> score;** and press the **Enter** key.

According to the algorithm shown in Figure 7-11, the next step is to enter a `while` loop that tells C++ to continue processing the loop instructions until the end of the input file is reached. You will need to use the C++ `eof` function to determine that the loop has reached the end of the input file.

The `eof` Function

Recall that C++ uses a record indicator to keep track of which record it is looking at in the file. When you first open a sequential access file for input, C++ sets the record indicator before the first record in the file. Each time you read a record, the record indicator moves to the next record in the file. (Recall that sequential access files are read sequentially—one record after another in the order in which they appear in the file.) After reading the last record, C++ positions the record indicator after that last record in the file.

You can use the `ifstream` class's `eof` function, which stands for *end of file*, to test for the end of file—in other words, to determine whether the record indicator is located after the last record in the file. The syntax of the `eof` function is *object*.**eof**(), where *object* is the name of an input file object in the program. If the record indicator is located after the last record in the input file, the `eof` function will return the number 1 (for True) when the program attempts to read the next record; otherwise, it will return the number 0 (for False). You can use the `eof` function, along with the ! (Not) logical operator, to tell a `while` loop to process its instructions as long as—or while—the record indicator is not at the end of the file. The correct `while` clause to use to accomplish this is `while (!inFile.eof())`.

To complete the average score program, then execute it:

1   In the blank line below the `inFile >> score;` statement, type **while (!inFile.eof())** and press the **Enter** key.

The algorithm shown in Figure 7-11 indicates that the loop will contain more than one instruction, so you will need to enclose the instructions in a set of braces.

2   Type { (the opening brace).

According to the algorithm, the first two loop instructions should add 1 to the counter and add the test score to the accumulator. The statements to accomplish this are already entered in the program. However, the last loop instruction—the one to read another test score from the file—is missing from the program. Enter the missing instruction next.

3 In the blank line below the `totalScores = totalScores + score;` statement, type **inFile >> score;** and press the **Enter** key. Type the } (the closing brace) and press the **Spacebar**, then type **//end while** and press the **Enter** key to end the loop.

You will notice that the instructions to close the file and calculate and display the average are already entered in the program. The completed program is shown in Figure 7-13.

```cpp
//LaProg02.cpp
//this program demonstrates how to read records from
//a sequential access file

#include <iostream.h>
#include <fstream.h>

void main()
{
    //declare and initialize variable
    short score       = 0;
    short numScores   = 0;    //counter
    short totalScores = 0;    //accumulator
    float average     = (float) 0.0;

    //open input file
    ifstream inFile;
    inFile.open("scores.dat", ios::in);

    //verify that open was successful
    if (!inFile.fail())  //if open did not fail
    {
        //read test score
        inFile >> score;
        while (!inFile.eof())
        {
            //update counter and accumulator
            numScores = numScores + 1;
            totalScores = totalScores + score;
            inFile >> score;
        } //end while

        //close file
        inFile.close();

        //calculate and display average test score
        average = (float) totalScores / (float) numScores;
        cout << "Average test score: " << average << endl;
    }
    else    //open failed
        cout << "Error opening file." << endl;
    //end if

} //end of main function
```

verify that you entered these lines correctly

closes the file

calculates and displays the average

Figure 7-13: Completed average score program

> **4** Save, build, and execute the program. The DOS window shows that the average is 76.7143. Press the **Enter** key to close the DOS window.
>
> You have now completed this program, so you can close it.
>
> **5** Close the Output window and the workspace.

mini-quiz

Mini-Quiz 3

1. Which of the following statements will read the contents of the `quantity` variable from the inventory.dat file, whose file object is named `inInv`?

   a. `ifstream >> quantity;`   b. `inventory.dat >> quantity;`
   c. `inInv << quantity;`   d. `inInv >> quantity;`

2. Which of the following `while` clauses tells C++ to read each record in the inventory.dat file while the record indicator is not at the end of the file? The file object is named `inInv`.

   a. `while (inventory.dat.end())`   b. `while (inInv.end())`
   c. `while (!inInv.eof())`   d. `while (!inventory.dat.eof())`

3. If the record indicator is not at the end of the file, the `eof` function returns the number _____.

You have now completed Lesson A. In this lesson, you learned how to open and close a sequential access data file, as well as how to write records to and read records from a sequential file. In Lesson B, you will learn how to write records containing more than one field to a sequential file, as well as how to read those records. Now you can either exit Visual C++ and take a break or complete the questions and exercises at the end of the lesson.

SUMMARY

In addition to saving the C++ program instructions in a file, called a program file, you can also save input data in a file, called a data file. The information in a data file is typically organized into fields and records. A field is a single item of information about a person, place, or thing. A record is a group of related fields that contain all of the necessary data about a specific person, place, or thing. A data file is a collection of related records.

In most programming languages, you can create three different types of data files: sequential, random, and binary. The data file type refers to how the data is accessed. The data in a sequential access file is always accessed sequentially—in other words, in consecutive order. The data in a random access file, on the other hand, can be accessed either in consecutive order or in random order. The data in a binary access file can be accessed by its byte location in the file. This book covers sequential access data files only.

Sequential access data files can be either input data files or output data files. Input data files are those whose contents are read by a program, and output data files are those to which a program writes data.

For a program to use a sequential access file, you must include the fstream.h header file in the program. You then use the `ifstream` and `ofstream` classes, which are defined in the fstream.h header file, to create input or output file objects, respectively; these file objects are used to represent the actual files stored on your computer's disk. After creating the file object, you then use the C++ `open` function to open the file for either input, output, or append.

Before attempting either to read data from or write to a data file, you should always verify that the data file was opened successfully. You can use the C++ `fail` function, which is defined in both the `ifstream` and `ofstream` classes, to test if the file was opened successfully. The `fail` function returns the value 1 (for True) if the open failed, or it returns the value 0 (for False) if the open did not fail. You typically test the file immediately after opening it.

When a program is finished with a data file, you should use the `close` function, which is defined in both the `ifstream` and `ofstream` classes, to close it. Not closing an open data file can result in the loss of data.

To distinguish one record from another in a file, programmers usually write each record on a separate line in the file. You can do so by including the `endl` stream manipulator at the end of the statement that writes the record to the file.

When reading records from a data file, you use the C++ `eof` function to determine if the record indicator is at the end of the file. If a program attempts to read past the end of the file, the `eof` function returns 1 (for True); otherwise, it returns 0 (for False).

ANSWERS TO MINI-QUIZZES

Mini-Quiz 1

1. data file **2.** b **3.** d **4.** b **5.** c

Mini-Quiz 2

1. 1 **2.** c **3.** `outInv.close();`

Mini-Quiz 3

1. d **2.** c **3.** 0

QUESTIONS

1. A _____ is a single item of information about a person, place, or thing.
   a. data file
   b. field
   c. program file
   d. record

2. A group of related fields that contain all of the data about a specific person, place, or thing is called a _____ .
   a. data file
   b. field file
   c. program file
   d. record

3. A collection of related records is called a _____ .
   a. data file
   b. field
   c. program file
   d. record collection

4. A Social Security number is an example of a _____ .
   a. data record
   b. field
   c. program record
   d. record

5. The records in a(n) _____ file can be accessed only in consecutive order.
   a. consecutive access
   b. order access
   c. sequential access
   d. sorted access

6. To create a sequential access output file, you must include the _____ header file in your program.
   a. file.h
   b. fstream.h
   c. outFile.h
   d. sequential.h

7. The _____ class allows you to create an output file object.
   a. `cout`
   b. `fstream`
   c. `ofstream`
   d. `outstream`

8. Which of the following statements will create an object, named `outPayroll`, that represents an output file in the program?
   a. `fstream outPayroll;`
   b. `ofstream outPayroll;`
   c. `outPayroll as ofstream;`
   d. `outPayroll as outstream;`

9. Which of following statements will open the payroll.dat file for output?
   a. `outPayroll.open("payroll.dat");`
   b. `outPayroll.open("payroll.dat", ios::out);`
   c. `outPayroll.open("payroll.dat", ios::output);`
   d. both a and b

10. You use the _____ *mode* in the `open` function when you want to add records to the end of an existing output file.
    a. `add`
    b. `ios::add`
    c. `ios::app`
    d. `ios::out`

11. You use the _____ function to close a data file.
    a. `close()`
    b. `end()`
    c. `exit()`
    d. `finish()`

12. The `ofstream`'s `fail()` function returns the value _____ if the **open** function opened the file successfully.
    a. −1
    b. 0
    c. 1
    d. 2

13. Which of the following will write the `salary` variable to an output file named managers.dat?
    a. `managers.dat << salary << endl;`
    b. `ofstream << salary << endl;`
    c. `outFile << salary << endl;`
    d. `outFile >> salary >> endl;`

14. Which of the following will read the `salary` variable from an input file named managers.dat?
    a. `managers.dat >> salary;`
    b. `ifstream >> salary;`
    c. `inFile >> salary;`
    d. `inFile << salary;`

15. When used in a statement that writes a record to a file, the _____ writes an invisible newline character at the end of each record.
    a. `endl` stream manipulator
    b. `newline` stream manipulator
    c. `ofstream` class
    d. output file object

16. Which of the following `while` clauses tells C++ to read the records in a data file until the end of the file is reached?
    a. `while(inFile.eof())`
    b. `while(!ifstream.eof())`
    c. `while(!inFile.eof())`
    d. `while(!ifstream.fail())`

17. To open a sequential access file for input, you must include the _____ header file in your program.
    a. file.h
    b. fstream.h
    c. inFile.h
    d. sequential.h

18. The _____ class allows you to create an input file object.
    a. `cin`
    b. `fstream`
    c. `ifstream`
    d. `instream`

19. Which of the following statements will create an object, named inPayroll, that represents an input file in the program?
    a. `fstream inPayroll;`
    b. `ifstream inPayroll;`
    c. `inPayroll as ifstream;`
    d. `inPayroll as ifstream;`

20. Which of following statements will open the payroll.dat file for input?
    a. `inFile.open("payroll.dat", ios::app);`
    b. `inFile.open("payroll.dat");`
    c. `inFile.open("payroll.dat", ios::in);`
    d. both b and c

E X E R C I S E S

1. In this exercise, you will write records that contain one field to a sequential access file.

   Scenario: Mary Conrad wants a program that will allow her to save each letter of the alphabet in a sequential access file. She will enter the letters from the keyboard.
   a. Create an IPO chart for this program.
   b. Create a console application named T7Ae01 in the Cpp\Tut07 folder on your computer's hard disk.
   c. Use the IPO chart you created in step a to code the program. Name the sequential access data file T7Ae01.dat and open it for output.
   d. Save, build, and then execute the program. Enter the 26 letters of the alphabet.
   e. Stop the program, then print the code.
   f. Use C++ to open and then print the T7Ae01.dat file. The file should contain 26 letters. Each letter should appear on a separate line in the file.
   g. Close the data file, the Output window, and the workspace.

2. In this exercise, you will write records that contain one field to a sequential access file.

   Scenario: Cheryl Perry wants a program that will save the squares of the numbers from 1 through 25 in a sequential access file.
   a. Create an IPO chart for this program.
   b. Create a console application named T7Ae02 in the Cpp\Tut07 folder on your computer's hard disk.
   c. Use the IPO chart you created in step a to code the program. Name the sequential access data file T7Ae02.dat and open it for output.
   d. Save, build, and then execute the program.
   e. Stop the program, then print the code.
   f. Use C++ to open and then print the T7Ae02.dat file. The file should contain 25 numbers. Each number should appear on a separate line in the file.
   g. Close the data file, the Output window, and the workspace.

3. In this exercise, you will write records that contain one field to a sequential access file.

   Scenario: The manager of Checks Inc. wants a program that she can use to save each week's total payroll amount in a sequential access file.
   a. Create an IPO chart for this program.
   b. Create a console application named T7Ae03 in the Cpp\Tut07\T7Ae03 folder on your computer's hard disk.
   c. Use the IPO chart you created in step a to code the program. Name the sequential access data file T7Ae03.dat and open it for append.
   d. Save, build, and then execute the program. Enter the following two payroll amounts: 25000.89 and 35600.50.
   e. Stop the program, then execute it again. Enter the following two payroll amounts: 45678.99 and 67000.56.
   f. Stop the program, then print the code.
   g. Use C++ to open and then print the T7Ae03.dat file. The file should contain the four amounts listed in steps d and e. Each amount should appear on a separate line in the file.
   h. Close the data file, the Output window, and the workspace.

4. In this exercise, you will write records that contain one field to a sequential access file.

   Scenario: The manager of Boggs Inc. wants a program that he can use to save the price of each inventory item in a sequential access file.
   a. Create an IPO chart for this program.
   b. Create a console application named T7Ae04 in the Cpp\Tut07\T7Ae04 folder on your computer's hard disk.

c. Use the IPO chart you created in step a to code the program. Name the sequential access file T7Ae04.dat and open it for append.

d. Save, build, and then execute the program. Enter the following two prices: 10.50 and 15.99.

e. Stop the program, then execute it again. Enter the following three prices: 20.00, 76.54, and 17.34.

f. Stop the program, then print the code.

g. Use C++ to open and print the T7Ae04.dat file. The file should contain the five amounts listed in steps d and e. Each amount should appear on a separate line in the file.

h. Close the data file, the Output window, and the workspace.

5. In this exercise, you will read the records stored in a sequential access file. To complete this exercise, you will need to have completed Exercise 1 in this lesson.

   Scenario: Mary Conrad wants a program that will allow her to count the number of letters stored in the T7Ae01.dat file, which is located in the Cpp\Tut07\T7Ae01 folder on your computer's hard disk.

   a. Create an IPO chart for this program.

   b. Create a console application named T7Ae05 in the Cpp\Tut07\T7Ae05 folder on your computer's hard disk.

   c. Copy the T7Ae01.dat file, which is located in the Cpp\Tut07\T7Ae01 folder on your computer's hard disk, to the T7Ae05 folder. Rename the file T7Ae05.dat.

   d. Use the IPO chart you created in step a to code the program.

   e. Save, build, and then execute the program.

   f. Stop the program, then print the code. On the code printout, indicate the number of letters stored in the file.

   g. Close the Output window and the workspace.

6. In this exercise, you will read the records stored in a sequential access file. To complete this exercise, you will need to have completed Exercise 2 in this lesson.

   Scenario: Cheryl Perry wants a program that will display the sum of the numbers stored in the T7Ae02.dat file, which is located in the Cpp\Tut07\T7Ae02 folder on your computer's hard disk. (You created this data file in Exercise 2. Recall that the file contains the squares of the numbers from 1 through 25.)

   a. Create an IPO chart for this program.

   b. Create a console application named T7Ae06 in the Cpp\Tut07\T7Ae06 folder on your computer's hard disk.

   c. Copy the T7Ae02.dat file, which is located in the Cpp\Tut07\T7Ae02 folder on your computer's hard disk, to the T7Ae06 folder. Rename the file T7Ae06.dat.

   d. Use the IPO chart you created in step a to code the program.

   e. Save, build, and then execute the program.

   f. Stop the program, then print the code. On the code printout, indicate the sum.

   g. Close the Output window and the workspace.

7. In this exercise, you will read the records stored in a sequential access file. To complete this exercise, you will need to have completed Exercise 3 in this lesson.

   Scenario: The manager of Checks Inc. wants a program that she can use to calculate and display the total of the weekly payroll amounts stored in the T7Ae03.dat file, which is located in the Cpp\Tut07\T7Ae03 folder on your computer's hard disk. (You created this data file in Exercise 3.)

   a. Create an IPO chart for this program.

   b. Create a console application named T7Ae07 in the Cpp\Tut07\T7Ae07 folder on your computer's hard disk.

   c. Copy the T7Ae03.dat file, which is located in the Cpp\Tut07\T7Ae03 folder on your computer's hard disk, to the T7Ae07 folder. Rename the file T7Ae07.dat.

   d. Use the IPO chart you created in step a to code the program.

   e. Save, build, and then execute the program.

f. Stop the program, then print the code. On the code printout, indicate the total weekly payroll amount.

g. Close the Output window and the workspace.

8. In this exercise, you will read the records stored in a sequential access file. To complete this exercise, you will need to have completed Exercise 4 in this lesson.

Scenario: The manager of Boggs Inc. wants a program that he can use to calculate and display the average price of the company's inventory items. The price of each inventory item is stored in the T7Ae04.dat file, which is located in the Cpp\Tut07\T7Ae04 folder on your computer's hard disk. (You created this data file in Exercise 4.)

a. Create an IPO chart for this program.

b. Create a console application named T7Ae08 in the Cpp\Tut07\T7Ae08 folder on your computer's hard disk.

c. Copy the T7Ae04.dat file, which is located in the Cpp\Tut07\T7Ae04 folder on your computer's hard disk, to the T7Ae08 folder. Rename the file T7Ae08.dat.

d. Use the IPO chart you created in step a to code the program.

e. Save, build, and then execute the program.

f. Stop the program, then print the code. On the code printout, indicate the average price of the items in inventory.

g. Close the Output window and the workspace.

discovery ▶ **9.** In this exercise, you will discover two additional modes for the `ofstream` class's `open` function. You will also learn how to include more than one mode in an `open` function.

a. Open the T7Ae09.cpp file, which is located in the Cpp\Tut07\T7Ae09 folder on your computer's hard disk. In Lesson A, you learned about the `ios::out` and the `ios::app` *mode*s for the `ofstream` class's `open` function. You will notice that the `open` function in the T7Ae09 program uses the `ios::app` *mode* to open the T7Ae09.dat file for append.

In addition to the `ios::out` and `ios::app` *mode*s that you learned in Lesson A, the `ofstream` class's `open` function also has an `ios::nocreate` *mode* and an `ios::noreplace` *mode*. When the `ios::nocreate` *mode* is used in the `open` function, the function will fail if the output file does not already exist. You would use this *mode* in situations where the program expects the file to be available on the disk, and the program does not want C++ to create a new file if the output file does not already exist.

When the `ios::noreplace` *mode* is used in the `open` function, the function will fail if the file already exists. You would use this *mode* in situations where you do not want the program replacing the contents of an existing output file.

You can include more than one mode in an `open` function by using the bitwise OR (|) operator. For example, to tell the `open` function to open a file for append only if the file already exists on the disk, you would use the `outFile.open("T7Ae09.dat", ios::app | ios::nocreate);` statement.

b. Currently, the T7Ae09.dat file does not exist on the disk.
(If you have previously completed this exercise, use Windows to delete the T7Ae09.dat file from the Cpp\Tut07\T7Ae09 folder on your computer's hard disk.) Change the `outFile.open("T7Ae09.dat", ios::app);` statement to `outFile.open("T7Ae09.dat", ios::app | ios::nocreate);`.

c. Save, build, and then execute the program. The message in the DOS window tells you that the open was not successful. Press the Enter key to close the program.

d. Change the `outFile.open("T7Ae09.dat", ios::app | ios::nocreate);` statement to `outFile.open("T7Ae09.dat", ios::app);`.

e. Save, build, and then execute the program. The message in the DOS window tells you that the open was successful. Type the number 4 and then press the Enter key. Press the Enter key again to close the program.

      f. When you executed the program in step e, C++ created the T7Ae09.dat file on your computer's hard disk and stored the number 4 in the data file. How would you now tell C++ to open the T7Ae09.dat file for output (not append) only if the file does not already exist? Change the **open** function appropriately. Save, build, and then execute the program. The message in the DOS window should tell you that the **open** function was not successful. Print the program's code.

      g. Close the Output window and the workspace.

discovery ▶ 10. In this exercise, you will prompt the user to enter the filename, and then store the name in a String variable. You will then use the String variable, rather than the actual filename, in the **ofstream** class's **open** function.

      a. Open the T7Ae10.cpp file, which is located in the Cpp\Tut07\T7Ae10 folder on your computer's hard disk. Complete the program by declaring and initializing a String variable named `fileName`. The variable should allow the user to enter a filename that has a maximum of 15 characters, which does not include the null character that C++ appends to the end of a string. Also include the **open** function that will open the file whose name appears in the `fileName` variable for output.

      b. Save, build, and then execute the file. When prompted to enter the filename, type T7Ae10.dat and press the Enter key. Then enter the following two letters: a and b.

      c. After entering the records, type x to stop the program. Print the program's code. Also use C++ to open and then print the T7Ae10.dat file.

      d. Close the data file, the Output window, and the workspace.

debugging 11. In this exercise, you will debug a program.

      a. Open the T7Ae11.cpp file, which is located in the Cpp\Tut07\T7Ae11 folder on your computer's hard disk.

      b. Build the program. Correct the bugs in the program.

      c. When the program is working correctly, print the code. On the code printout, indicate what was wrong with the program.

      d. Close the Output window and the workspace.

LESSON B
objectives

In this lesson you will learn how to:

- Define a record structure with the struct statement
- Enter String data using the get function
- Consume characters using the ignore function
- Write records that contain more than one field to a sequential file
- Read records that contain more than one field from a sequential file

Structs

Using a Struct to Define a Record Structure

As you learned in Lesson A, the information in a data file is typically organized into fields and records. A field is a single item of information about a person, place, or thing—for example, a name, a zip code, or a salary. A record is a group of related fields that contain all of the necessary data about a specific person, place, or thing. The school you are attending keeps a record about you, as does the Internal Revenue Service. Recall that a collection of related records is called a data file.

In Lesson A, you learned how to write records that contain one field to a data file, as well as how to read those records. You will learn how to write records containing more than one field, as well as how to read those records, in this lesson. You will use this knowledge to complete the PAO (Political Awareness Organization) programs outlined in the case study at the beginning of this tutorial. As you may remember, one of the PAO programs will allow the secretary to save information in a sequential file and the other will allow her to use that information to calculate the number of Democrats, Republicans, and Independents in the district. Begin with the PAO entry program.

Coding the PAO Entry Program

Recall that each year the PAO sends a questionnaire to the voters in its district. The questionnaire asks the voter to provide his or her name, age, and political party (Democrat, Republican, or Independent). A sample questionnaire is shown in Figure 7-14.

PAO Questionnaire

Circle your political party affiliation:

        Democrat   Republican   Independent☐

Print your full name: _____

Please specify your age: _____

Thank you for taking the time to complete this questionnaire.

Figure 7-14: Sample PAO questionnaire

The first program you will create for the PAO is one that allows the secretary to save the information from the returned questionnaires in a sequential access data file. Each record in the data file will need to contain three fields (political party, name, and age), each corresponding to an item of information on the questionnaire. The IPO chart for the PAO entry program is shown in Figure 7-15.

Input	Processing	Output

party (d, r, i, or x)
name
age
	Processing items: none
	
	Algorithm:
	1. open voter.dat output file for append
	2. if (open is successful)
	　　get party
	　　repeat while (party is not x)
	　　　get name
	　　　get age
	　　　write record (party, name, and age) to output file
	　　　get party
	　　end while
	　　close output file
	　else
	　　display message indicating that open was not successful
	　end if
		output file containing party, name, and age

Figure 7-15: IPO chart for the PAO entry program

According to the algorithm shown in the IPO chart, the program will first open the voter.dat output file for append. This will allow the secretary to add records to the file each time the program is executed. If the open fails, the program will display an appropriate message. However, if the open succeeds, the program will get the party affiliation—d for Democrat, r for Republican, i for Independent, or x to exit the program—from the user. The program will then evaluate the loop condition to determine if the loop instructions should be processed. If the user enters the letter x, the loop will stop and the output file will be closed before the program ends; otherwise, the instructions within the loop will be processed. You will notice that the loop instructions first get the name and age from the user, and then write the political party, name, and age to the output file. The user is then asked to enter another party affiliation, after which the loop condition is evaluated again. Open a partially completed PAO entry program that corresponds to the algorithm shown in Figure 7-15.

To open the partially completed PAO entry program:

1　If necessary, start Visual C++. Open the **LbProg01.cpp** file, which is located in the Cpp\Tut07\LbProg01 folder on your computer's hard disk. The partially completed PAO entry program is shown in Figure 7-16.

```
//LbProg01.cpp
//this program saves records in a sequential access file

#include <iostream.h>
#include <ctype.h>
#include <fstream.h>

//define record structure

void main()
{
    //declare and initialize record variable

    //create and open output file
    ofstream outFile;
    outFile.open("voter.dat", ios::app);

    //determine if open was successful
    if (!outFile.fail()) //open was successful
    {
        //enter and write records
        cout << "Enter party (d, r, i, or x to exit): ";

        while ()
        {
            cout << "Enter name: ";

            cout << "Enter age: ";

            cout << "Enter party (d, r, i, or x to exit): ";

        } //end while

        //close file
        outFile.close();
    }
    else    //open was not successful
        cout << "Error in opening file." << endl;
    //end if
} //end of main function
```

Figure 7-16: Partially completed PAO entry program

Recall that each record in the PAO data file will contain three fields (political party, name, and age), each corresponding to an item of information on the questionnaire. Programmers typically use a record structure to group together the fields in a record. You will learn how to create a record structure in the next section.

Creating a Record Structure

Because a record structure in C++ is defined with the `struct` statement, it is often referred to simply as a struct.

You can use the C++ `struct` statement to group related fields together into one unit, called a **record structure**. In the PAO program, for example, you will use the `struct` statement to group the political party, name, and age fields into a record structure. Figure 7-17 shows the syntax of the `struct` statement, as well as an example of how to create a record structure for the PAO records.

Syntax	Example

struct *structurename*
 {
    datatype fieldname1;
    datatype fieldname2;
    datatype fieldnameN;
 };
	`struct voterInfo`
	 `{`
	    `char party;`
	    `char name[25];`
	    `short age;`
	 `};`

Important note: Items in **bold** are required. Items in *italics* denote areas where the programmer must supply information relative to the program.	

notice that the statement ends in a semicolon

Figure 7-17: Syntax and an example of using `struct` to create a record structure

Similar to the way that a class is a pattern for creating an object, a record structure is a pattern for creating a record variable.

As Figure 7-17 shows, the `struct` statement's syntax begins with the keyword `struct`, followed by the name of the structure. In the example shown in Figure 7-17, the name of the record structure is `voterInfo`. The data types and names of the fields you want to include in the record structure are enclosed in braces (`{}`), while the `struct` statement ends with a semicolon. The fields included in the structure are referred to as **members of the structure**. The `voterInfo` structure shown in Figure 7-17 contains three members: a Character field named `party`, a String field named `name`, and a Short Integer field named `age`. Notice that each member (field) in the `voterInfo` structure corresponds to a field in the PAO record. Programmers usually enter the record structure definitions after the `#include` directives in the program.

The record structure itself actually becomes a data type, referred to as a **programmer-defined data type**, that is separate and distinct from the standard C++ data types, such as Short Integer and Character. As with the standard C++ data types, you can use programmer-defined data types to create variables. The variables created with a programmer-defined data type that represents a record structure are often called **record variables**.

> **tip**
> ....
> ▶ Recall that programmers usually initialize Character, String, and Short Integer variables to a space, a zero-length string, and 0, respectively. Notice that these are the same values used to initialize the fields in a record variable.

The syntax for creating and initializing a record variable is *datatype variablename* = {*initialvalues*};, where *datatype* is a programmer-defined data type—in other words, the name of a record structure—and *variablename* is the name of the record variable you want to create. *initialvalues* in the syntax is a list of the beginning values you want assigned to each field in the record variable. The values in the list must be separated by commas and the entire list must be enclosed in braces ({}). You must provide a beginning value for each field in the structure. The order of the values in the *initialvalues* list must correspond to the order of the fields in the structure. For example, if the structure declares a Character field followed by a Short Integer field, then the first value in the *initialvalues* list must be a character and the second must be a number. To use the `voterInfo` record structure to declare and initialize a record variable named `voter`, you would use the `voterInfo voter = {' ', "", 0);` statement. This statement tells C++ to create a record variable named `voter`, which has three fields. The first field, a Character field, should be initialized to a space. The second field, a String field, should be initialized to a zero-length string. The third field, a Short Integer field, should be initialized to 0. Figure 7-18 illustrates the `voter` record variable in memory.

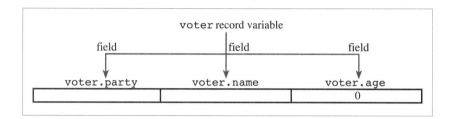

Figure 7-18: Illustration of a record variable in memory

As Figure 7-18 indicates, you refer to a field in the record variable by the record variable's name followed by a period and the field's name. To refer to the `age` field in the `voter` record variable, for example, you use `voter.age`. As you may remember from Tutorial 3, the period that appears between both names is called the dot member selection operator. `voter.age` tells C++ that the `age` field is a member of the `voter` record.

Now that you know how to create a record structure, as well as how to use the record structure to create and initialize a record variable, you can begin coding the PAO entry program. First you will define a record structure named `voterInfo` that contains three fields: a Character field named `party`, a String field named `name`, and a Short Integer field named `age`. You will then use the `voterInfo` record structure to declare and initialize a record variable named `voter`. You will initialize the `party` field in the `voter` record variable to a space, the `name` field to a zero-length string, and the `age` field to 0.

To enter the PAO record structure and record variable declaration:

1   The LbProg01.cpp file should be open. Type the record structure and the record variable declaration shown in Figure 7-19. (Be sure to enter a space between the single quotes, but do not enter any space between the double quotes. Also be sure to enter the number 0 and not the letter O.)

```
//LbProg01.cpp
//this program saves records in a sequential access file

#include <iostream.h>
#include <ctype.h>
#include <fstream.h>

//define record structure
struct voterInfo
{
    char party;
    char name[25];
    short age;
};

void main()
{
    //declare and initialize record variable
    voterInfo voter = {' ', "", 0};

    //create and open output file
    ofstream outFile;
    outFile.open("voter.dat", ios::app);

    //determine if open was successful
    if (!outFile.fail()) //open was successful
    {
        //enter and write records
        cout << "Enter party (d, r, i, or x to exit): ";

        while ()
        {
            cout << "Enter name: ";

            cout << "Enter age: ";

            cout << "Enter party (d, r, i, or x to exit): ";

        } //end while

        //close file
        outFile.close();
    }
    else    //open was not successful
        cout << "Error in opening file." << endl;
    //end if
} //end of main function
```

enter this structure

enter this declaration

opens output
file for append

determines if
open was successful

displays message
if open failed

Figure 7-19: Record structure and record variable declaration entered in the program

Now that you have defined the record structure and also created and initialized the record variable, you can begin coding the algorithm shown in Figure 7-15. According to the algorithm, the program begins by opening an output file for append. The code to open an output file named voter.dat for append is already included in the program. Notice that the program also includes the selection structure that verifies if the open was successful, which is the next step in the algorithm, and displays an appropriate message if the file cannot be opened. You will notice, however, that you still need to complete the true path of the selection structure. The first instruction in the true path is to get the political party information from the user. You will learn how to enter information into a record variable in the next section.

Entering Information into a Record Variable

The cout << "Enter party (d, r, i, or x to exit): "; statement that is located below the //enter and write records comment in the PAO entry program will prompt the user to enter the political party information. You will need to enter a statement that uses the cin stream and the extraction operator (>>) to store the user's response in the record variable's party field. To refer to a field in a record variable, recall that you must use the record variable's name, the dot member selection operator, and the field's name. The correct cin statement to use in the current program is cin >> voter.party;.

When referring to a field in a record variable, you must be sure to precede the field's name with the record variable's name and the dot member selection operator. If you neglect to include the record variable's name and the dot member selection operator, C++ will not be able to locate the field in the record. For example, if you use the cin >> party; statement rather than the cin >> voter.party; statement in the current program, C++ will attempt to store the user's response in a variable named party, rather than the party field in the voter record variable. Because the current program does not declare a party variable, only a party field within a record variable, the program will result in an error when you try to compile it because C++ won't recognize the variable name, party. However, if your program does declare a variable named party, in addition to a field named party, C++ will store the user's response in the party variable, which may or may not have been your intention.

As you may remember from Tutorial 5, the toupper function is defined in the ctype.h header file, which was already included in the program for you.

To store the political party information in the voter record variable's party field:

1   In the blank line above the while( )line, type cin >> voter.party; and press the Enter key. This statement will store the user's response in the voter record's party field.

According to the algorithm shown in Figure 7-15, the while loop should process its instructions as long as—or while—the party field does not contain the letter x. You will use the toupper function in the while clause to compare the uppercase equivalent of the user's response, which is stored in the party field, to the character literal constant 'X'. This will allow the user to stop the program by entering either x or X.

2   Change the while( ) clause in the program to while (toupper(voter.party) != 'X'). This clause tells C++ to process the loop instructions while the party field does not contain the letter X, entered in either upper or lowercase.

3   Save the program.

According to Figure 7-15's algorithm, the first step in the while loop is to get the respondent's name from the user. The cout << "Enter name: "; statement, which prompts the user to enter the name, is already entered in the body of the while loop. You will need to enter the appropriate statement to get the name from the user, and then store the name in the record variable's name field. In previous tutorials, you used the getline function to store string data entered at the keyboard in a String variable. In this lesson, you will learn another function that allows you to get and store string data—the get function.

Mini-Quiz 4

1. Write a `struct` statement that defines a record structure named `itemInfo`. The `itemInfo` structure should contain three fields: a 10-character String field named `itemName`, a Short Integer field named `quantity`, and a Short Integer field named `price`.

2. Use the `itemInfo` structure defined in question 1 to create and initialize a record variable named `item`.

3. Use your answers to questions 1 and 2 to write an assignment statement that multiplies the contents of the `quantity` field by the contents of the `price` field, and stores the result in a Short Integer variable named `totalValue`.

4. When referring to a field in a record variable, you must precede the field's name with the _____ and the _____ .

The `get` Function

> **tip**
> ●●●●●●●●●●●●●●●
> Recall that the last character in a String variable is reserved for the null character.

In addition to the `getline` function, which you learned about in Tutorial 3, you can also use the `get` function to enter string data into a String variable. Like the `getline` function, the `get` function's task is to read an entire line of text, including the spaces, from either the keyboard or an input file. The syntax of the `get` function is *object*.get(*variablename*, *length of string*, [*delimCharacter*]);, where *object* is either the `cin` stream, if the function is reading characters from the keyboard, or the name of an `ifstream` object, if the function is reading characters from an input file. *variablename* is the name of the String variable in which the characters will be stored. *length of string* is the maximum number of characters you want to store in the String variable, including the null character that C++ appends to the end of the string. The optional *delimCharacter* (short for *delimiter character*) argument is one character that, when encountered in the input stream, stops the `get` function from reading any more characters.

The `get` function stops reading characters either when it reads one character less than the number specified in *length of string* or when it encounters the *delimCharacter*, whichever comes first. The `cin.get(voter.name, 25, '#');` statement, for example, tells C++ to read characters from the keyboard either until a maximum of 24 characters is read or until the user types the # sign. The `inFile.get(voter.name, 25, '#')`, on the other hand, tells C++ to read characters from an input file either until a maximum of 24 characters is read or until the # sign is encountered in the file.

A common delimiter character used in `get` functions that get data from the keyboard is the newline character. Recall from Lesson A that C++ generates an invisible newline character when you use the `endl` stream manipulator in a statement that outputs information to either the screen or a file. C++ also generates an invisible newline character each time the user presses the Enter key when entering data. In C++, the newline character is represented as `'\n'` (the backslash and the letter n enclosed in single quotes). The `cin.get(voter.name, 25, '\n');` statement, for example, tells the `get` function to stop reading characters at the keyboard when either a maximum of 24 characters is read or when the user presses the Enter key, whichever comes first. If you omit the *delimCharacter* argument in the `get` function, the function uses the newline character as the default delimiter character. In other words, both the `cin.get(voter.name, 25, '\n');` and the `cin.get(voter.name, 25);`

statements will produce the same results. Figure 7-20 shows some examples of using the get function to read string data from the keyboard and from an input file.

Example	Result
`cin.get(city, 15, '&');`	Reads characters from the keyboard until a maximum of 14 characters have been read or until the user types the & character. The characters are stored in the `city` variable.
`cin.get(part.id, 5, '\n');`	Reads characters from the keyboard until a maximum of four characters have been read or until the user presses the Enter key. The characters are stored in the `part` record's `id` field.
`cin.get(part.id, 5);`	Reads characters from the keyboard until a maximum of four characters have been read or until the user presses the Enter key. The characters are stored in the `part` record's `id` field.
`inFile.get(partName, 11, '#');`	Reads characters from an input file until a maximum of 10 characters have been read or until the # character is encountered. The characters are stored in the `partName` variable.
`inPay.get(emp.name, 25);`	Reads characters from an input file until a maximum of 24 characters have been read or until the newline character is encountered. The characters are stored in the `emp` record's `name` field.

Figure 7-20: Examples of using the get function

The newline character is also the default *delimCharacter* in the `getline` function. The difference between the `get` and `getline` functions is in the manner that each handles the delimiter character. The `getline` function reads and then discards the delimiter character. C++ programmers refer to this as "consuming" the character. The `get` function, however, does not consume the delimiter character. Rather, the character remains in the input stream where it can either be read into another variable or ignored. In most cases, you will want to ignore the delimiter character that remains in the input stream after using the `get` function. You do this by using the C++ `ignore` function, which is discussed in the next section.

The ignore Function

You use the C++ `ignore` function to disregard, or skip, characters entered at the keyboard or read from an input file. The function actually reads and then discards the characters—in other words, the function consumes the characters. The syntax of the `ignore` function is **cin.ignore([*nCount*] [, *delimCharacter*]);**. You will notice that the `ignore` function has two arguments (*nCount* and *delimCharacter*), both of which are optional. *nCount* is an integer that represents the maximum number of characters you want the `ignore` function to consume. The `cin.ignore(100);` statement, for example, tells C++ to read and discard the next 100 characters. Although any number can be used for *nCount*, many programmers use a large number, such as 100, in situations where they are not sure of the number of characters to consume. The default value for *nCount* is 1.

The `ignore` function's *delimCharacter* (short for *delimiter character*) argument is a character that, when consumed, stops the `ignore` function from reading and discarding any additional characters. The `ignore` function stops reading and discarding characters either when it consumes *nCount* characters or when it consumes the *delimCharacter*, whichever occurs first. For example, the statement `cin.ignore(100, 'A');` tells the `ignore` function either to consume the next 100 characters or read and discard characters until it consumes the letter A. Unlike the `get` function, which leaves its *delimCharacter* in the input stream, the `ignore` function consumes its *delimCharacter*.

The most common delimiter character found in `ignore` functions that read and discard characters entered at the keyboard is the newline character—`'\n'` (the backslash and the letter n enclosed in single quotes). The `cin.ignore (100, '\n');` statement, for example, tells the `ignore` function either to consume the next 100 characters or read and discard characters until the user presses the Enter key, whichever occurs first. The `ignore` function will consume the newline character generated by the user pressing the Enter key. The default delimiter character for the `ignore` function is EOF, which tells the function to consume characters from the location of the record indicator in an input file through the end of the file. Figure 7-21 shows examples of using the `ignore` function to read and discard characters entered at the keyboard and read from a file.

OOP
Concepts

The `ignore` function is a member of the `istream` class.

Example	Result
`cin.ignore(100, '\n');`	Stops reading and discarding characters from the keyboard either after consuming the next 100 characters or after consuming the newline character, whichever occurs first.
`cin.ignore(25, '#');`	Stops reading and discarding characters from the keyboard either after consuming the next 25 characters or after consuming the # character, whichever occurs first.
`inFile.ignore(10, '#')`	Stops reading and discarding characters from an input file either after consuming the next 10 characters or after consuming the # character, whichever occurs first.
`inPay.ignore(1)`	Stops reading and discarding characters from an input file either after consuming the next character or after encountering the end of the file, whichever comes first.

Figure 7-21: Examples of the `ignore` function

tip

Recall that the newline character is the default *delimCharacter* in the `get` function. Therefore, you could have entered the `get` function as `cin.get(voter.name, 25);`. However, including the `'\n'` in the *delimCharacter* argument makes the program more self-documenting.

Now that you know how to use the `get` and `ignore` functions, you can continue coding the PAO entry program. You will use the `cin.get (voter.name, 25, '\n');` statement to get the voter's name from the user, and the `cin.ignore(100, '\n');` statement to read and discard the newline character that the `get` function leaves in the input stream.

To enter the get and ignore functions in the PAO entry program:

1 Enter the get and ignore functions in the body of the while loop, as highlighted in Figure 7-22.

```cpp
//LbProg01.cpp
//this program saves records in a sequential access file

#include <iostream.h>
#include <ctype.h>
#include <fstream.h>

//define record structure
struct voterInfo
{
    char party;
    char name[25];
    short age;
};

void main()
{
    //declare and initialize record variable
    voterInfo voter = {' ', "", 0};

    //create and open output file
    ofstream outFile;
    outFile.open("voter.dat", ios::app);

    //determine if open was successful
    if (!outFile.fail()) //open was successful
    {
        //enter and write records
        cout << "Enter party (d, r, i, or x to exit): ";
        cin >> voter.party;

        while (toupper(voter.party) != 'X')
        {
            cout << "Enter name: ";
            cin.get(voter.name, 25, '\n');
            cin.ignore(100, '\n');

            cout << "Enter age: ";

            cout << "Enter party (d, r, i, or x to exit): ";

        } //end while

        //close file
        outFile.close();
    }
    else    //open was not successful
        cout << "Error in opening file." << endl;
    //end if
} //end of main function
```

enter these two statements

Figure 7-22: get and ignore functions entered in the PAO entry program

> The next instruction in the loop should get the age from the user. The statement that prompts the user to enter the age—cout << "Enter age: ";—is already entered in the program; you need only to enter the cin >> voter.age; statement that will store the user's response in the voter record's age field.
>
> **2** In the blank line below the cout << "Enter age: "; statement, type **cin >> voter.age;** and press the **Enter** key.
>
> **3** Save the program.

The next step shown in Figure 7-15's algorithm is to write the respondent's political party, name, and age to the open output file. You will learn how to write records to a file in the next section.

mini-quiz

Mini-Quiz 5

1. Write a statement that allows the user to enter data into a 20-character String field named name. The String field is a member of the item record variable. Use the get function to enter the data. Stop the get function either when the appropriate number of characters have been entered or when the user presses the Enter key.

2. Write a statement that reads a 20-character String field named name from an input file. The name of the file object is inItems. The String field is a member of the item record variable. Use the get function to read the data. Stop the get function either when the appropriate number of characters have been entered or when the # sign is encountered in the file.

3. Write the ignore function that will either read and discard the next 200 characters read at the keyboard, or will read and discard characters until the Enter key is encountered, whichever comes first.

Writing Multifield Records to a Sequential Access File

As you learned in Lesson A, the syntax for writing information to a file is *object << data << endl;*, where *object* is the name of the program's ofstream object, and *data* is the one or more fields included in each record. Recall that programmers typically write each record on a separate line in the file. The endl stream manipulator accomplishes this by writing an invisible newline character at the end of each record. For example, assuming that a program's ofstream object is named outFile, as it is in the PAO entry program, the statement outFile << voter.party << endl; would write the contents of the party field to the voter.dat file.

To write a record that contains more than one field to a file, you need to separate each field with a character. A # sign is most commonly used. In the current program, for example, to write the contents of the `voter` record's `party`, `name`, and `age` fields, you would use the `outFile << voter.party << '#' << voter.name << '#' << voter.age << endl;` statement. This statement tells C++ to write each field, separated by # signs, to the open output file. The `endl` stream manipulator at the end of the statement will ensure that each record appears on a separate line in the file.

To enter the code that writes the PAO records to the output file:

1   In the blank line below the `cin >> voter.age;` statement, type **outFile << voter.party << '#'** and press the **Enter** key. Press the **Tab** key, then type **<< voter.name << '#' << voter.age << endl;** and press the **Enter** key. This statement tells C++ to write to the ouput file the contents of the `party` field, a # sign, the contents of the `name` field, a # sign, the contents of the `age` field, and the invisible newline character.

    The next step shown in Figure 7-15's algorithm is to get the political party information from the user. The program already includes the statement that will prompt the user to enter the appropriate response. You will need to enter the `cin >> voter.party;` statement that will store the user's response in the `voter.party` field.

2   In the blank line below the `cout << "Enter party (d, r, i, or x to exit): ";` statement within the while loop, type **cin >> voter.party;** and press the **Enter** key.

    According to Figure 7-15's algorithm, you have finished coding the `while` loop. You will notice that the program already contains the `while` loop's closing brace (`}`) and the `//end while` comment. After the `while` loop completes its processing, the output file should be closed. The statement to do so—`outFile.close();`—is already entered in the program. The current status of the PAO entry program is shown in Figure 7-23.

```
//LbProg01.cpp
//this program saves records in a sequential access file

#include <iostream.h>
#include <ctype.h>
#include <fstream.h>

//define record structure
struct voterInfo
{
    char party;
    char name[25];
    short age;
};

void main()
{
    //declare and initialize record variable
    voterInfo voter = {' ', "", 0};

    //create and open output file
    ofstream outFile;
    outFile.open("voter.dat", ios::app);

    //determine if open was successful
    if (!outFile.fail()) //open was successful
    {
        //enter and write records
        cout << "Enter party (d, r, i, or x to exit): ";
        cin >> voter.party;

        while (toupper(voter.party) != 'X')
        {
            cout << "Enter name: ";
            cin.get(voter.name, 25, '\n');
            cin.ignore(100, '\n');

            cout << "Enter age: ";
            cin >> voter.age;
            outFile << voter.party << '#'
                    << voter.name << '#' << voter.age << endl;

            cout << "Enter party (d, r, i, or x to exit): ";
            cin >> voter.party;

        } //end while

        //close file
        outFile.close();
    }
    else    //open was not successful
        cout << "Error in opening file." << endl;
    //end if
} //end of main function
```

gets party — cin >> voter.party;

gets name — cin.get(voter.name, 25, '\n'); cin.ignore(100, '\n');

gets age — cin >> voter.age;

gets party — cin >> voter.party;

closes file — outFile.close();

Figure 7-23: Current status of the PAO entry program

tip

· · · · · · · · · · · · · · · ·

You can also use Ctrl + c to both stop the program and close the DOS window.

3 Compare your code with the code shown in Figure 7-23 and make any needed corrections.

4 Save, build, and then execute the program. C++ creates and then opens a file named voter.dat for append on your computer's hard disk.

5 When prompted to enter either d, r, i, or x, type **d** and press the **Enter** key. The program displays the "Enter name: " prompt, followed immediately by the "Enter age: " prompt, as shown in Figure 7-24.

program does not allow you to enter the name

Figure 7-24: DOS window showing the prompts displayed by the program

6 Click the **Close** button in the DOS window's title bar and then click the **Yes** button to both stop the program and close the DOS window.

Because the `party` field is declared as the Character data type, it can store only one character at a time. Keep in mind that pressing the Enter key, which generated the newline character in the previous set of steps, counts as entering a character. The `cin >> voter.party;` statement could not store the newline character in the `party` field because it had already stored the letter d in that field. Therefore, the newline character remained in the input stream, waiting for the next input statement to be executed. In the current program, the next input statement is the `cin.get(voter.name, 25, '\n');` statement. Recall that this statement tells C++ to read characters from the keyboard until the newline character is encountered. Because the `get` function encountered the newline character in the input stream immediately, C++ stored the newline character in the `voter.name` field, and then proceeded to the next statement in the loop. You can use the C++ `ignore` function to fix this problem. After entering the party information, you will tell C++ to ignore all characters, including the newline character, entered after the first one. You will enter the `cin.ignore(100, '\n');` statement in two places in the program: above the loop and within the loop.

To consume the newline character after the party information is entered:

1 Enter the `cin.ignore(100, '\n');` statement in two places in the program, as highlighted in Figure 7-25.

```
//LbProg01.cpp
//this program saves records in a sequential access file

#include <iostream.h>
#include <ctype.h>
#include <fstream.h>

//define record structure
struct voterInfo
{
    char party;
    char name[25];
    short age;
};

void main()
{
    //declare and initialize record variable
    voterInfo voter = {' ', "", 0};

    //create and open output file
    ofstream outFile;
    outFile.open("voter.dat", ios::app);

    //determine if open was successful
    if (!outFile.fail()) //open was successful
    {
        //enter and write records
        cout << "Enter party (d, r, i, or x to exit): ";
        cin >> voter.party;
        cin.ignore(100, '\n');

        while (toupper(voter.party) != 'X')
        {
            cout << "Enter name: ";
            cin.get(voter.name, 25, '\n');
            cin.ignore(100, '\n');

            cout << "Enter age: ";
            cin >> voter.age;
            outFile << voter.party << '#'
                    << voter.name << '#' << voter.age << endl;

            cout << "Enter party (d, r, i, or x to exit): ";
            cin >> voter.party;
            cin.ignore(100, '\n');

        } //end while

        //close file
        outFile.close();
    }
    else        //open was not successful
        cout << "Error in opening file." << endl;
    //end if
} //end of main function
```

enter these two
statements

Figure 7-25: Additional `ignore` function statements entered in the program

2 Save, build, and execute the program. When prompted to enter the party information, type **d** and press the **Enter** key. The `cin >> voter.party;` statement stores the letter d in the `party` field, and the `cin.ignore(100, '\n');` statement consumes the newline character that was generated when the user pressed the Enter key. The program now correctly prompts you for a name.

3 When prompted to enter the name, type **Paul Smith** and then press the **Enter** key. The `cin.get >> (voter.name, 25, '\n');` statement stores the name Paul Smith in the `name` field. The `cin.ignore (100, '\n');` statement then reads and discards the newline character, which is generated when the user presses the Enter key.

4 When prompted to enter the age, type **34** and press the **Enter** key. The program writes the letter d, a # sign, the name Paul Smith, a # sign, the number 34, and the invisible newline character to the voter.dat file. You are now prompted to enter the party information.

5 Type **r** as the political party and press the **Enter** key. When prompted to enter the name, type **Jerry Sellser** and press the **Enter** key. The program now prompts you to enter the age.

This time, make an entry error when entering the age. For example, type a number followed by a letter.

6 Type **65b** as the age and press the **Enter** key. The program displays the political party prompt, followed immediately by the name prompt, as shown in Figure 7-26.

program does not allow you to enter the political party

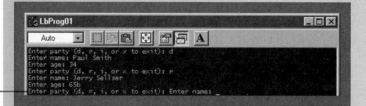

Figure 7-26: DOS window showing prompts

You will notice that the program did not give you an opportunity to enter the political party information. Stop the program before discussing why this happened.

7 Click the **Close** button in the DOS window's title bar and then click the **Yes** button to both stop the program and close the DOS window.

Because the Short Integer `age` field can store only numbers, only the numeric part of your 65b entry—in this case, the number 65—was stored in the `age` field. The letter b remained in the input stream, waiting for the next input statement. In the PAO entry program, the next input statement encountered was the `cin >> voter.party;` statement. The program used the letter b to answer that prompt, and then went on to the next prompt—the one that asks for the name. You can use the `cin.ignore(100, '\n');` statement to fix this problem also.

To complete the program and then execute it:

1 Enter the `cin.ignore(100, '\n');` statement as highlighted in Figure 7-27.

```cpp
//LbProg01.cpp
//this program saves records in a sequential access file

#include <iostream.h>
#include <ctype.h>
#include <fstream.h>

//define record structure
struct voterInfo
{
    char party;
    char name[25];
    short age;
};

void main()
{
    //declare and initialize record variable
    voterInfo voter = {' ', "", 0};

    //create and open output file
    ofstream outFile;
    outFile.open("voter.dat", ios::app);

    //determine if open was successful
    if (!outFile.fail()) //open was successful
    {
        //enter and write records
        cout << "Enter party (d, r, i, or x to exit): ";
        cin >> voter.party;
        cin.ignore(100, '\n');

        while (toupper(voter.party) != 'X')
        {
            cout << "Enter name: ";
            cin.get(voter.name, 25, '\n');
            cin.ignore(100, '\n');

            cout << "Enter age: ";
            cin >> voter.age;
            cin.ignore(100, '\n');

            outFile << voter.party << '#'
                    << voter.name << '#' << voter.age << endl;

            cout << "Enter party (d, r, i, or x to exit): ";
            cin >> voter.party;
            cin.ignore(100, '\n');

        } //end while

        //close file
        outFile.close();
    }
    else   //open was not successful
        cout << "Error in opening file." << endl;
    //end if
} //end of main function
```

enter this statement ──────────────── `cin.ignore(100, '\n');`

Figure 7-27: Completed PAO entry program

You must be sure to begin the age entry with a number. If you begin the entry with a letter, the program will enter an endless loop.

2   Save, build, and execute the program. When prompted to enter the political party, type **r** and press the **Enter** key. When prompted to enter the name, type **Rukshad Rakesh** and press the **Enter** key.

Now make an error when entering the age.

3   When prompted to enter the age, type **32e** and press the **Enter** key. The `cin >> voter.age;` statement stores the number 32 in the `age` field, and the `cin.ignore(100, '\n');` statement consumes the letter e and the newline character. You are now prompted to enter the political party information.

4   Use the program to enter the following records:

party	name	age
i	Josh Rover	23
d	Roger Perry	42
r	Jake Jaworski	56

Now exit the program.

5   When prompted to enter the political party, type **x** and press the **Enter** key to exit the program. Press the **Enter** key again to close the DOS window.

6   Use C++ to open the voter.dat file, which is located in the Cpp\Tut07\LbProg01 folder on your computer's hard disk. Figure 7-28 shows the contents of the file.

```
d#Paul Smith#34
r#Jerry Sellser#65
r#Rukshad Rakesh#32
i#Josh Rover#23
d#Roger Perry#42
r#Jake Jaworski#56
```

Figure 7-28: Contents of the voter.dat file

7   Close the voter.dat file.

You have completed the PAO entry program, so you can close it.

8   Close the Output window and the workspace.

In addition to requiring the entry program, which allows the PAO secretary to save the information from the returned questionnaires in a sequential access file, recall that the PAO also needs a program that will use the information stored in the file to calculate the number of Democrats, Republicans, and Independents in the district. The IPO chart for the counter program is shown in Figure 7-29.

Input	Processing	Output

record (party, name, and age)	Processing items: Democrat counter
	Republican counter
	Independent counter
	
	Algorithm:
	1. open voter.dat input file
	2. if (open is successful)
	    read first record (party, name, and age) from input file
	    repeat while (it is not end of file)
	      if (party is Democrat)
	        add 1 to Democrat counter
	      else
	        if (party is Republican)
	          add 1 to Republican counter
	        else
	          add 1 to Independent counter
	        end if (party is Republican)
	      end if (party is Democrat)
	      read another record (party, name, and age) from input file
	    end while
	    close input file
	    display values in Democrat counter, Republican counter, and Independent counter
	  else
	    display message indicating that open was not successful
	end if
		number of Democrats, Republicans, and Independents

Figure 7-29: IPO chart for the PAO counter program

According to the algorithm shown in Figure 7-29, the PAO counter program will open an input file. If the open is not successful, then an appropriate message will be displayed. If the open is successful, on the other hand, the program will read the first record from the input file. While the record indicator is not at the end of the file, the `while` loop instructions will update the appropriate counter (Democrat, Republican, or Independent) before reading another record from the file. The `while` loop will continue processing its instructions until all of the records in the file are read. At that point, the input file will be closed and the values in the three counters will be displayed. The LbProg02 folder on your computer's hard disk contains a partially completed PAO counter program file that corresponds to Figure 7-29's algorithm. Open that file now.

To open the partially completed PAO counter program:

1 Open the **LbProg02.cpp** file, which is located in the Cpp\Tut07\LbProg02 folder on your computer's hard disk. The PAO counter program, which appears in the LbProg02.cpp window, is shown in Figure 7-30.

```cpp
//LbProg02.cpp
//this program reads records from a sequential access file.

#include <iostream.h>
#include <ctype.h>
#include <fstream.h>

//define record structure
struct voterInfo
{
    char party;
    char name[25];
    short age;
};

void main()
{
    //declare and initialize variables
    short demCounter = 0;
    short repCounter = 0;
    short indCounter = 0;

    //declare and initialize record variable
    voterInfo voter = {' ', "", 0};

    //open input file
    ifstream inFile;
    inFile.open("voter.dat", ios::in);

    //determine if open was successful
    if (!inFile.fail())                    //open was successful
    {
        //read and count records

        while (!inFile.eof())   //repeat while not end of file
        {
            voter.party = toupper(voter.party);

            if (voter.party == 'D')
                demCounter = demCounter + 1;
            else
                if (voter.party == 'R')
                    repCounter = repCounter + 1;
                else
                    indCounter = indCounter + 1;
                //end if (voter.party == 'R')
            //end if (voter.party == 'D')
```

opens the input file

determines if the open was successful

Figure 7-30: Partially completed PAO counter program

```
                    } //end while

                    //close file
                    inFile.close();

                    //display values stored in counter variables
                    cout << "Number of Democrats    : " << demCounter << endl;
                    cout << "Number of Republicans : " << repCounter << endl;
                    cout << "Number of Independents: " << indCounter << endl;
                }
            else          //open was not successful
                    cout << "Error in opening file." << endl;
            //end if
        } //end of main function
```

displays a message
if the open failed

Figure 7-30: Partially completed PAO counter program (continued)

You will notice that the program defines a record structure named `voterInfo`, which contains three fields: a Character field named `party`, a String field named `name`, and a Short Integer field named `age`. The three fields in the structure correspond to the three fields in the PAO records. Recall that the entry program saved these records in the voter.dat data file. A copy of the voter.dat file is included in the LbProg02 folder on your computer's hard disk.

According to the algorithm shown in Figure 7-29, the program should open the voter.dat input file. The statements to open the input file are already included in the program. Notice that the program also includes the selection structure that determines if the open was successful, which is the next step in the algorithm, and displays an appropriate message if the file could not be opened. You will notice, however, that you still need to complete the true path of the selection structure. The first instruction in the true path is to read the first record from the input file. You will learn how to read information from a sequential file in the next section.

Reading Multifield Records from a Sequential Access File

As you learned in Lesson A, the syntax for reading numeric and character information from a file is *object >> variable*, where *object* is the name of the program's `ifstream` object, and *variable* is the name of either a numeric or character variable included in each record. If a program's `ifstream` object is named `inFile`, as it is in the PAO counter program, the `inFile >> voter.party;` statement would read the party information from the voter.dat file and store it in the `voter.party` field.

To read a string from a file, however, you use the syntax *object*.**get**(*variablename, length of string, delimCharacter*); where *object* is the name of the program's `ifstream` object, *variablename* is the name of a String variable, and *length of string* is an integer that represents the number of characters, including the null character, that you want the `get` function to read. Recall that *delimCharacter* is a character that, when read, stops the `get` function from reading any more characters. The `get` function stops reading characters either when the number of characters read is one less than the number specified in the *length of string* argument, or when the function reads the *delimCharacter* character, whichever comes first. To read the contents of the name variable in the current program, you would use the `inFile.get(voter.name, 25, '#');` statement.

Figure 7-31 shows the contents of the voter.dat sequential file, which is located in the Cpp\Tut07\LbProg02 folder on your computer's hard disk.

```
d#Paul Smith#34
r#Jerry Sellser#65
r#Rukshad Rakesh#32
i#Josh Rover#23
d#Roger Perry#42
r#Jake Jaworski#56
```

Figure 7-31: Contents of the voter.dat file

You will notice that a # sign separates the party information from the name, and the name from the age. (Recall that the PAO entry program, which is shown in Figure 7-27, uses the # sign to separate the fields when it writes the records to the file.) Therefore, you will need to tell the program to ignore the # sign after it reads the party information, and also after it reads the name information. You will also need to tell the program to ignore the invisible newline character that is at the end of each record.

To enter the code that will read the first record in the input file:

1 Enter the additional statements in the blank line below the //read and count records comment, as highlighted in Figure 7-32.

```cpp
//LbProg02.cpp
//this program reads records from a sequential access file

#include <iostream.h>
#include <ctype.h>
#include <fstream.h>

//define record structure
struct voterInfo
{
    char party;
    char name[25];
    short age;
};

void main()
{
    //declare and initialize variables
    short demCounter = 0;
    short repCounter = 0;
    short indCounter = 0;

    //declare and initialize record variable
    voterInfo voter = {' ', "", 0};
```

Figure 7-32: Statements to read the first record from the voter.dat input file

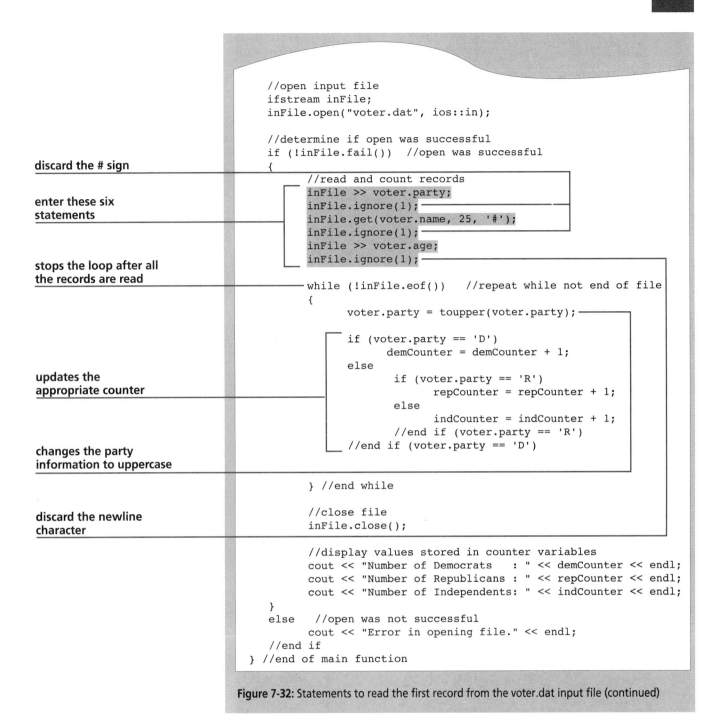

discard the # sign

enter these six statements

stops the loop after all the records are read

updates the appropriate counter

changes the party information to uppercase

discard the newline character

```
                     //open input file
                     ifstream inFile;
                     inFile.open("voter.dat", ios::in);

                     //determine if open was successful
                     if (!inFile.fail())  //open was successful
                     {
                         //read and count records
                         inFile >> voter.party;
                         inFile.ignore(1);
                         inFile.get(voter.name, 25, '#');
                         inFile.ignore(1);
                         inFile >> voter.age;
                         inFile.ignore(1);

                         while (!inFile.eof())  //repeat while not end of file
                         {
                             voter.party = toupper(voter.party);

                             if (voter.party == 'D')
                                 demCounter = demCounter + 1;
                             else
                                 if (voter.party == 'R')
                                     repCounter = repCounter + 1;
                                 else
                                     indCounter = indCounter + 1;
                                 //end if (voter.party == 'R')
                             //end if (voter.party == 'D')

                         } //end while

                         //close file
                         inFile.close();

                         //display values stored in counter variables
                         cout << "Number of Democrats    : " << demCounter << endl;
                         cout << "Number of Republicans : " << repCounter << endl;
                         cout << "Number of Independents: " << indCounter << endl;
                     }
                     else   //open was not successful
                         cout << "Error in opening file." << endl;
                     //end if
                 } //end of main function
```

Figure 7-32: Statements to read the first record from the voter.dat input file (continued)

According to the algorithm shown in Figure 7-29, the next step is to use a while loop that stops processing its instructions when the end of the input file is reached—in other words, after all of the records have been read. The while (!inFile.eof()) clause, which is already included in the program, will accomplish this for you.

The next step in the algorithm is to update the appropriate counter based on the information in the party field. You will notice that the selection structure to do this is already included in the program.

The next step in the algorithm is to read the remaining records from the input file. The instructions to accomplish this are missing from the program. You will enter them next.

To enter the instructions to read the remaining records from the input file:

1 Select the six `inFile` statements that appear above the `while` loop, then copy the six statements to the clipboard. Position the insertion point above the `}  //end while` line, and then paste the six `inFile` statements in the program, as shown in Figure 7-33.

```cpp
//LbProg02.cpp
//this program reads records from a sequential access file

#include <iostream.h>
#include <ctype.h>
#include <fstream.h>

//define record structure
struct voterInfo
{
    char party;
    char name[25];
    short age;
};

void main()
{
    //declare and initialize variables
    short demCounter = 0;
    short repCounter = 0;
    short indCounter = 0;

    //declare and initialize record variable
    voterInfo voter = {' ', "", 0};

    //open input file
    ifstream inFile;
    inFile.open("voter.dat", ios::in);

    //determine if open was successful
    if (!inFile.fail())     //open was successful
    {
```

Figure 7-33: Six statements that read a record entered in the loop body

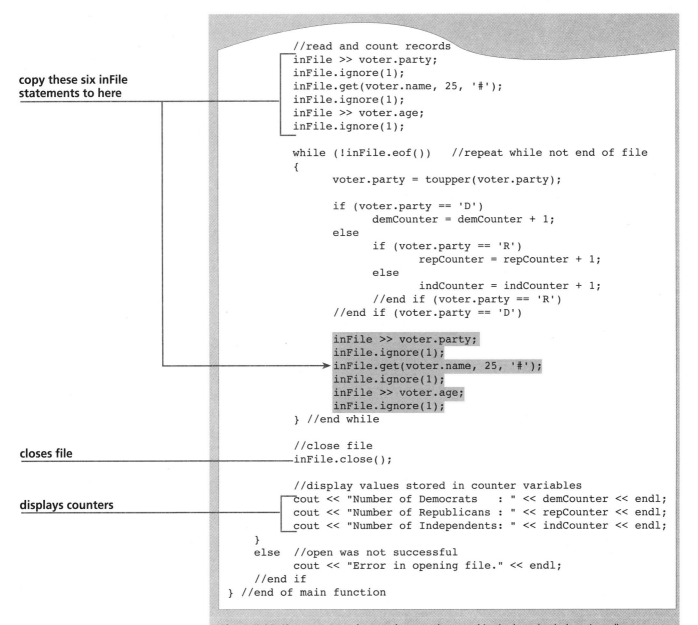

copy these six inFile
statements to here

```
                      //read and count records
                      inFile >> voter.party;
                      inFile.ignore(1);
                      inFile.get(voter.name, 25, '#');
                      inFile.ignore(1);
                      inFile >> voter.age;
                      inFile.ignore(1);

                      while (!inFile.eof())   //repeat while not end of file
                      {
                            voter.party = toupper(voter.party);

                            if (voter.party == 'D')
                                  demCounter = demCounter + 1;
                            else
                                  if (voter.party == 'R')
                                        repCounter = repCounter + 1;
                                  else
                                        indCounter = indCounter + 1;
                                  //end if (voter.party == 'R')
                            //end if (voter.party == 'D')

                            inFile >> voter.party;
                            inFile.ignore(1);
                            inFile.get(voter.name, 25, '#');
                            inFile.ignore(1);
                            inFile >> voter.age;
                            inFile.ignore(1);
                      } //end while

                      //close file
                      inFile.close();

                      //display values stored in counter variables
                      cout << "Number of Democrats   : " << demCounter << endl;
                      cout << "Number of Republicans : " << repCounter << endl;
                      cout << "Number of Independents: " << indCounter << endl;
                }
            else  //open was not successful
                  cout << "Error in opening file." << endl;
            //end if
} //end of main function
```

closes file

displays counters

Figure 7-33: Six statements that read a record entered in the loop body (continued)

According to the algorithm, when the while loop completes its processing, the input file should be closed, and the values in the three counters should be displayed. You will notice that the instructions to complete both of these tasks are already included in the program.

The program is now complete, so you can save, build, and execute it.

2   Save, build, and then execute the program. The results of the program appear in the DOS window, as shown in Figure 7-34.

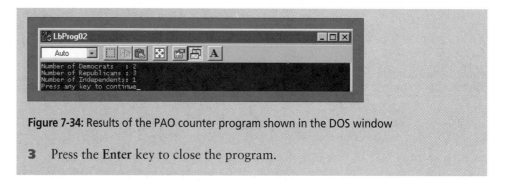

Figure 7-34: Results of the PAO counter program shown in the DOS window

3 Press the **Enter** key to close the program.

Mini-Quiz 6

Use the following record structure and record variable declaration to answer questions 1 through 3.

```
struct itemInfo
{
    char name[20];
    short quantity;
    short price;
};

itemInfo item = {"", 0, 0};
```

1. Write a statement that will write the **item** records to a file. The name of the output file object is **outItems**. Separate each field with a # sign, and be sure that each record appears on a separate line.

2. Write a statement that will read the **item** records that you wrote in question 1. The name of the input file object is **inItems**.

3. Write the **while** clause that tells C++ to process the loop instructions until there are no more records in the input file. The name of the input file object is **inItems**.

You have now completed Lesson B. You can either exit Visual C++ and take a break or complete the questions and exercises at the end of the lesson.

SUMMARY

The information in a data file is typically organized into fields and records. A field is a single item of information about a person, place, or thing. A record is a group of related fields that contain all of the necessary data about a specific person, place, or thing. A data file is simply a collection of related records.

When a record contains more than one field, programmers typically use a record structure to group the fields together. You can use the **struct** statement to create a record structure in C++. The fields included in the structure are referred to as members of the structure. The record structure itself actually becomes a data type, referred to as a programmer-defined data type, that is separate and distinct from the standard C++ data types. You can use a data type created with the **struct** statement to create and initialize record variables.

You refer to a field in a record variable by the record variable's name followed by a period and the field's name. The period that appears between both names is called the dot member selection operator.

In addition to using the `getline` function, you can also use the `get` function to enter string data into a String variable. Like the `getline` function, the `get` function has the task of reading an entire line of text, including the spaces, from either the keyboard or an input file. The `get` function stops reading characters either when it reads one character less than the length of the string or when it encounters the delimiter character specified in the function, whichever comes first. A common delimiter character used in `get` functions that get data from the keyboard is the newline character, which is represented in C++ by `'\n'` (the backslash and the letter n enclosed in single quotes). Unlike the `getline` function, the `get` function does not consume the delimiter character; rather, the character remains in the input stream, where it can either be read into another variable or ignored. In most cases, you will want to ignore the delimiter character that remains in the input stream after using the `get` function; you can do so by using the C++ `ignore` function. The `ignore` function actually reads and then discards the characters—in other words, the function consumes the characters.

When writing records that contain more than one field to a file, programmers typically separate each field with a character, such as the # sign. The programmer will also use the `endl` stream manipulator to write each record on a separate line in the file. When reading the records from the file, you must be sure to use the `ignore` function to skip the # sign and the newline character that is generated by the `endl` manipulator.

ANSWERS TO MINI-QUIZZES

Mini-Quiz 4

1. ```
   struct itemInfo
   {
        char itemName[10];
        short quantity;
        short price;
   };
   ```

2. `itemInfo item = {"", 0, 0};`

3. `totalValue = item.quantity * item.price;`

4. record variable's name, dot member selection operator (.)

Mini-Quiz 5

1. `cin.get(item.name, 20, '\n');`

2. `inItems.get(item.name, 20, '#');`

3. `cin.ignore(200, '\n');`

Mini-Quiz 6

1. ```
   outItems << item.name << '#' << item.quantity
            << '#' << item.price << endl;
   ```

2. ```
   inItems.get(item.name, 20, '#');
   inItems.ignore(1);
   inItems >> item.quantity;
   inItems.ignore(1);
   inItems >> item.price;
   inItems.ignore(1);
   ```

3. `while(!inItems.eof())`
   ```

Q U E S T I O N S

Use the following record structure to answer questions 1 through 11.

```
struct payInfo
{
    char empName[25];
    char code;
    short salary;
};
```

1. Which of the following will create and initialize a `payInfo` record variable named `payroll`?

   a. `payInfo payroll = "", ' ', 0;`

   b. `payInfo payroll = {"", ' ', 0};`

   c. `payRecord payroll = {"", "", 0};`

   d. `payInfo as payroll = {' ', ' ', 0};`

2. Which of the following will read the code information from a sequential access file and then store the information in the `code` member? (Assume that the record variable is named `payroll`.)

   a. `inFile >> code;`

   b. `inFile >> code.payroll;`

   c. `inFile >> payInfo.code;`

   d. `inFile >> payroll.code;`

3. Which of the following will read the employee name information from a sequential access file and then store the information in the `empName` member? (The fields in the sequential file are separated by a # sign. Assume that the record variable is named `payroll`.)

   a. `inFile >> {empName, 25, '#'};`

   b. `inFile >> payroll.empName;`

   c. `inFile.get(payInfo.empName, 25, '#');`

   d. `inFile.get(payroll.empName, 25, '#');`

4. Which of the following is the correct way to read the entire record from the input file? (Assume the fields are separated by a # sign, and each record appears on a separate line in the file. Also assume that the record variable is named `payroll`.)

   a.
   ```
   inFile.get(payInfo.empName, 25, '#');
   inFile.ignore(1);
   inFile << payInfo.code;
   inFile.ignore(1);
   inFile << payInfo.salary;
   inFile.ignore(1);
   ```

   b.
   ```
   inFile.get(payroll.empName, 25, '#');
   inFile.ignore(1);
   inFile >> payroll.code;
   inFile.ignore(1);
   inFile >> payroll.salary;
   inFile.ignore(1);
   ```

```
c. inFile >> payroll.empName;
   inFile.ignore(1);
   inFile << payroll.code;
   inFile.ignore(1);
   inFile << payroll.salary;
   inFile.ignore(1);
d. inFile >> payInfo.empName;
   inFile.ignore(1);
   inFile >> payInfo.code;
   inFile.ignore(1);
   inFile >> payInfo.salary;
   inFile.ignore(1);
```

5. Which of the following tells the program to stop reading characters from a sequential access file when it either reads 24 characters or when the # sign is encountered?

    a. `inFile.get(payroll.empName, 25, '#');`
    b. `inFile.get(payroll.empName, '#', 25);`
    c. `inFile.ignore(payroll.empName, 25, '#');`
    d. `inFile.skip(payroll.empName, '25', '#');`

6. The `eof` function returns the Boolean value _____ when the program attempts to read beyond the end of the file.

    a. False
    b. True

7. Which of the following statements tells C++ to continue processing the loop instructions until there are no more records in the file?

    a. `while (!inFile.eof())`
    b. `while (inFile.eof())`
    c. `while (inFile.end())`
    d. `while (!inFile.end())`

E X E R C I S E S

1. In this exercise, you will create a sequential access file that contains more than one field.

Scenario: The manager of Stellar Company wants a program that will allow him to save the company's payroll codes and corresponding salaries in a sequential access file.

    a. Create a console application named T7Be01 in the Cpp\Tut07 folder on your computer's hard disk.

    b. Write the code that corresponds to the algorithm shown in Figure 7-35. Use `payrollInfo` as the name of the record structure. The structure should contain two members: a Character member named `code`, and a Short Integer member named `salary`. Use `payroll` as the name of the record variable, which you should initialize appropriately. Save the payroll records in a data file named T7Be01.dat file.

Input	Processing	Output

payroll codes
 	
salaries
	Processing items: none
	
	Algorithm:
	1. open file for append
	2. if (open is successful)
	    get payroll code from user
	    repeat while (payroll code is not an X)
	        get salary from user
	        write payroll code and salary to file
	        get payroll code from user
	   end while
	   close file
	  else
	    display "File error" message
	  end if
		sequential access
		file containing
		payroll codes
		and salaries

Figure 7-35

    c. Save, build, and then execute the program. Enter the following codes and salaries:

Code	Salary
A	27200
B	15000
C	23000
D	12000
E	25500

    d. Stop the program, then print the code. Use C++ to open and print the T7Be01.dat file. Close the data file, the Output window, and the workspace.

2. Scenario: The manager of Boggs Inc. wants a program that she can use to record, in a sequential access file, the inventory number, quantity, and price of the items in inventory.

    a. Create a console application named T7Be02 in the Cpp\Tut07 folder on your computer's hard disk.

    b. Write the code that corresponds to the algorithm shown in Figure 7-36. Use `inventoryInfo` as the name of the record structure. The structure should contain three Short Integer members: `invNum`, `quantity`, and price. Use `inventory` as the name of the record variable, which you should initialize appropriately. Save the inventory records in a data file named T7Be02.dat file.

Input	Processing	Output
number	Processing items: none	sequential access file containing number, quantity, and price
quantity	Algorithm: 1. open file for append	

price	2. if (open is successful)
	　　get number from user
	　　repeat while (number is greater than 0)
	　　　　get quantity and price from user
	　　　　write number, quantity, and price to file
	　　　　get number from user
	　　end while
	　　close file
	else
	　　display "File error" message
	end if	

Figure 7-36

　　c. Save, build, and then execute the program. Enter the following inventory numbers, quantities, and prices:

Inventory number	Quantity	Price
20	400	5
30	550	9
45	600	20

　　d. Stop the program, then print the code. Use C++ to open and print the T7Be02.dat file. Close the data file, the Output window, and the workspace.

3. In this exercise, you will read a sequential access file that contains more than one field. To complete this exercise, you will need to have completed Lesson B's Exercise 1.

Scenario: In Lesson B's Exercise 1, you created a program for Stellar Company. The program wrote the company's payroll codes and corresponding salaries in a sequential access file. The manager of Stellar Company now wants a program that he can use to display the codes and salaries.

　　a. Copy the T7Be01.dat file, which is located in the Cpp\Tut07\T7Be01 folder on your computer's hard disk, to the Cpp\Tut07\T7Be03 folder. Rename the T7Be01.dat file as T7Be03.dat.

　　b. Open the T7Be03.cpp file, which is located in the Cpp\Tut07\T7Be03 folder on your computer's hard disk.

　　c. Write the code that corresponds to the algorithm shown in Figure 7-37.

Input	Processing	Output

sequential file containing payroll codes and salaries	Processing items: none
	
	Algorithm:
	1. open file for input
	2. if (open is successful)
	    read payroll code and salary from file
	    repeat while (not end of file)
	        display payroll code and salary
	        read payroll code and salary
	        from file
	    end while
	    close file
	  else
	    display "File error" message
	  end if
		payroll codes
		
		salaries

Figure 7-37

    d. Save, build, and then execute the program. Stop the program, then print the code. Close the Output window and the workspace.

4. In this exercise, you will read a sequential file that contains more than one field. To complete this exercise, you will need to have completed Lesson B's Exercise 2.

    Scenario: In Lesson B's Exercise 2, you created a program for Boggs Inc. The program wrote, to a sequential access file, the inventory numbers, quantities, and prices of the company's inventory items. The manager of Boggs Inc. now wants a program that she can use to display the inventory numbers, quantities, and prices on the screen.

    a. Copy the T7Be02.dat file, which is located in the Cpp\Tut07\T7Be02 folder on your computer's hard disk, to the Cpp\Tut07\T7Be04 folder. Rename the T7Be02.dat file as T7Be04.dat.

    b. Open the T7Be04.cpp file, which is located in the Cpp\Tut07\T7Be04 folder on your computer's hard disk.

    c. Write the code that corresponds to the algorithm shown in Figure 7-38.

Input	Processing	Output

sequential file containing numbers, quantities, and prices	Processing items: none
	
	Algorithm:
	1. open file for input
	2. if (open is successful)
	    read number, quantity, and price from file
	    repeat while (not end of file)
	        display number, quantity, and price
	        read number, quantity, and price
	        from file
	    end while
	    close file
	  else
	    display "File error" message
	  end if
		numbers, quantities, and prices

Figure 7-38

    d. Save, build, and then execute the program. Stop the program, then print the code. Close the Output window and the workspace.

5. In this exercise, you will read a sequential file that contains more than one field. To complete this exercise, you will need to have completed Lesson B's Exercise 2.

    Scenario: In Lesson B's Exercise 2, you created a program for Boggs Inc. The program wrote, to a sequential access file, the inventory numbers, quantities, and prices of the company's inventory items. The manager of Boggs Inc. now wants a program that she can use to calculate and display the total value of the company's inventory.

    a. Copy the T7Be02.dat file, which is located in the Cpp\Tut07\T7Be02 folder on your computer's hard disk, to the Cpp\Tut07\T7Be05 folder. Rename the T7Be02.dat file as T7Be05.dat.

    b. Create an IPO chart for this program.

    c. Open the T7Be05.cpp file, which is located in the Cpp\Tut07\T7Be05 folder on your computer's hard disk. Write a program that reads the information in the T7Be05.dat sequential data file and calculates and displays the total value of the company's inventory.

    d. Save, build, and then execute the program. Stop the program, then print the code. Close the Output window and the workspace.

discovery ▶   6.   In this exercise, you will read a sequential access file that contains more than one field. To complete this exercise, you will need to have completed Lesson B's Exercise 1.

Scenario: In Lesson B's Exercise 1, you created a program for Stellar Company. The program wrote the company's payroll codes and corresponding salaries in a sequential access file. The manager of Stellar Company now wants a program that he can use to display the salary corresponding to the code entered by the user.

a. Copy the T7Be01.dat file, which is located in the Cpp\Tut07\T7Be01 folder on your computer's hard disk, to the Cpp\Tut07\T7Be06 folder. Rename the T7Be01.dat file as T7Be06.dat.

b. Open the T7Be06.cpp file, which is located in the Cpp\Tut07\T7Be06 folder on your computer's hard disk.

c. Write the code that corresponds to the algorithm shown in Figure 7-39.

Input	Processing		Output
code	Processing items: flag variable		payroll codes

sequential file containing payroll codes and salaries	Algorithm:
	 1. get code from user
	 2. repeat while (code is not X)
	     open file for input
	     if (open is successful)
	         set flag variable to 'N'
	         read payroll code and salary from file
	         repeat while (not end of file and flag variable equals 'N')
	             if (payroll code is the same as code)
	                 display salary
	                 set flag variable to 'Y'
	             else
	                 read payroll code and salary from file
	             end if (payroll code is the same as code)
	         end while (not end of file and flag variable equals 'N')
	         close the file
	         get code from user
	     else
	         display "File error" message
	     end if (open is successful)
	 end while (code is not X)
			salaries

Figure 7-39

d. Save, build, and then execute the program. Stop the program, then print the code. Close the Output window and the workspace.

discovery ▶ 7. In this exercise, you will write records to and read records from a sequential access file.

Scenario: Consolidated Advertising wants a program that its managers can use to record various cities and their corresponding zip codes in a sequential access file. The program should also allow managers to look up a zip code in the file and display its corresponding city.

a. Create an IPO chart for this program. Use two programmer-defined functions named `enterInfo` and `lookupInfo`. The `enterInfo` function should allow the user to enter the cities and zip codes in a sequential access file. The `lookupInfo` function should allow the user to enter a zip code; it should then search the sequential file for the zip code and display its corresponding city. Allow the user to select which task he or she wants to perform: entry or lookup.

b. Create a console application named T7Be07 in the Cpp\Tut07 folder on your computer's hard disk.

c. Create a program that corresponds to the IPO chart you created in step a. Save the cities and zip codes in a sequential access file named T7Be07.dat in the Cpp\Tut07\T7Be07 folder on your computer's hard disk. The program will use the T7Be07.dat file to search for the zip code entered by the user and then display its corresponding city.

d. Save, build, and then execute the program. Test the `enterInfo` function by entering the following zip codes and cities, then stop the program.

Zip code	City
60561	Darien
60544	Hinsdale
60137	Glen Ellyn
60135	Downers Grove
60136	Burr Ridge

e. Execute the program again. Test the `lookupInfo` function by entering the 60135 zip code. The function should display Downers Grove.

f. Stop the program, then print the code. Use C++ to open and print the T7Be07.dat file. Close the data file, the Output window, and the workspace.

discovery ▶ 8. In this exercise, you will write records to and read records from a sequential access file.

Scenario: Pamela Orno wants a program she can use to record the names and telephone extensions of her friends at work. She also wants the program to allow her to display the corresponding telephone extension when she enters a friend's name.

a. Create an IPO chart for this program. Use two programmer-defined functions named `enterInfo` and `lookupInfo`. The `enterInfo` function should allow the user to enter the names and telephone extensions in a sequential access file. The `lookupInfo` function should allow the user to enter a name, then search the sequential file for the name and display the corresponding telephone extension. Allow the user to select which task he or she wants to perform: entry or lookup.

b. Create a console application named T7Be08 in the Cpp\Tut07 folder on your computer's hard disk.

c. Create a program that corresponds to the IPO chart you created in step a. Save the names and telephone extensions in a sequential access file named T7Be08.dat in the Cpp\Tut07\T7Be08 folder on your computer's hard disk. The program will use the T7Be08.dat file to search for the zip code entered by the user and then display its corresponding city.

d. Save, build, and then execute the program. Test the `enterInfo` function by entering the following names and extensions, then stop the program.

Name	Extension
Joe Smith	3388
Mary Jones	3356
Joel Adkari	2487
Sue Lin	1111
Vicky Li	2222

e. Execute the program again. Test the `lookupInfo` function by entering Sue Lin. The function should display 1111.

f. Stop the program, then print the code. Use C++ to open and print the T7Be08.dat file. Close the data file, the Output window, and the workspace.

discovery ▶ 9. In this exercise, you will read a sequential access file that contains more than one field.

Scenario: Each salesperson at BobCat Motors is assigned a code that consists of two characters. The first character is either the letter F for full-time employee, or the letter P for part-time employee. The second character is either a 1, indicating the salesperson sells new cars, or a 2, indicating the salesperson sells used cars.

a. Use C++ to open and print the T7Be09.dat file, which is located in the Cpp\Tut07\T7Be09 folder on your computer's hard disk.

b. Open the T7Be09.cpp file, which is located in the Cpp\Tut07\T7Be09 folder on your computer's hard disk.

c. The names of BobCat's salespeople, along with their codes, are contained in the T7Be09.dat sequential file. Create a program that prompts the user to enter the code—either F1, F2, P1, or P2. The program should search the T7Be09.dat file for that code, and should display only the names of the salespeople assigned that code.

d. Save, build, and then execute the program. Test the program by entering the F2 code. The program should display three records: Mary Jones, Joel Adkari, and Janice Paulo.

e. Stop the program, then print the code.

discovery ▶ 10. In this exercise, you will update a sequential access file.

a. Use C++ to open and print the T7Be10.dat file, which is located in the Cpp\Tut07\T7Be10 folder on your computer's hard disk. The sequential file contains one numeric field.

b. Open the T7Be10.cpp file, which is located in the Cpp\Tut07\T7Be10 folder on your computer's hard disk.

c. Create a program that reads the numbers from the T7Be10.dat file. The program should add the number 1 to each number, and then write the new value to another sequential file. Name the updated sequential file updated10.dat.

d. Save, build, and then execute the program.

e. Stop the program, then print the code. Also use C++ to open and print the updated10.dat file.

discovery ▶ 11. In this exercise, you will update a sequential access file.

a. Use C++ to open and print the T7Be11.dat file, which is located in the Cpp\Tut07\T7Be11 folder on your computer's hard disk. The sequential file contains one numeric field.

b. Open the T7Be11.cpp file, which is located in the Cpp\Tut07\T7Be11 folder on your computer's hard disk.

c. Create a program that reads the numbers from the T7Be11.dat file. The program should write only the even numbers to a new sequential file named updated11.dat. *Hint:* Use the % (modulus arithmetic) operator, which you learned about in Tutorial 3.

d. Save, build, and then execute the program.

e. Stop the program, then print the code. Also use C++ to open and then print the updated11.dat file.

debugging   12. In this exercise, you will debug a program.

a. Use C++ to open and print the T7Be12.dat file, which is located in the Cpp\Tut07\T7Be12 folder on your computer's hard disk. The sequential file contains a String field and two Short Integer fields.

b. Open the T7Be12.cpp file, which is located in the Cpp\Tut07\T7Be12 folder on your computer's hard disk. The program should simply display the records on the screen.

c. Save, build, and execute the program. The program results in an endless loop. Click the Close button in the DOS window, then click the Yes button both to stop the program and close the DOS window. (You can also press Ctrl + c.)

d. Debug the program. When the program is working correctly, print the code. On the code printout, indicate what was wrong with the program. Also circle the changes you made to the program.

debugging

13. In this exercise, you will debug a program.

a. Use C++ to open and print the T7Be13.dat file, which is located in the Cpp\Tut07\T7Be13 folder on your computer's hard disk. The sequential file contains a String field and two Short Integer fields.

b. Open the T7Be13.cpp file, which is located in the Cpp\Tut07\T7Be13 folder on your computer's hard disk. The program should display the name of each item in the file, along with each item's total value in inventory. (The total value of each item is calculated by multiplying its quantity by its price.)

c. Save, build, and execute the program. You will notice that the program is not working correctly.

d. Debug the program. When the program is working correctly, print the code. On the code printout, indicate what was wrong with the program. Also circle the changes you made to the program.

TUTORIAL 8

Arrays

case ▶ Colfax Industries, a large manufacturing company, employs over 1500 workers. About 200 of the employees are managers who are paid an annual salary, the amount of which depends on the manager's job code. Warehouse managers, for example, have a job code of 408, which pays an annual salary of $35,000. The manager of the Personnel department, Mr. Hendrickson, wants a program that he can use both to search for and display the salary assigned to a job code. In this tutorial, you will learn how to create and manipulate an array, which is simply a collection of variables that are related in some way. You will use arrays to store the Colfax Industries job codes and salaries.

LESSON A

objectives

In this lesson you will learn how to:

- Create a one-dimensional array
- Enter data into a one-dimensional array
- Compute the average of a one-dimensional array's contents
- Find the highest entry in a one-dimensional array
- Update the contents of a one-dimensional array

One-dimensional Arrays

Arrays

An **array** is a group of variables that have the same name and data type and are related in some way. For example, each variable in the array may contain an inventory quantity, an employee record (name, Social Security number, pay rate, and so on), or a character that, when grouped together with other letters, forms the name of a state. It may be helpful to picture an array as a group of small boxes inside the computer's memory. You can write information to the boxes and you can read information from the boxes; you just cannot *see* the boxes.

You actually have been using arrays since Tutorial 3, where you learned how to use the C++ built-in Character data type to create a String variable. A String variable, which stores a string literal constant, is simply an array of Character variables. Each variable in the array stores precisely one character. When you view all of the characters together—say, for example, the characters I, d, a, h, and o—the characters form a string—in this case, the word Idaho.

Although C++ does not place any restriction on the number of dimensions an array can have, the most commonly used arrays in business applications are one-dimensional and two-dimensional. Figure 8-1 illustrates both a one-dimensional and a two-dimensional array.

One-dimensional array

8.55
1.65
7.53
5.45
1.24

Two-dimensional array

8.55	1.65	7.53	5.45	1.24
3.46	1.89	8.76	2.34	7.89
9.87	4.56	7.32	1.34	5.78

Figure 8-1: Illustrations of both a one-dimensional and a two-dimensional array

As Figure 8-1 shows, a **one-dimensional** array is simply a column of variables. A **two-dimensional** array, on the other hand, resembles a table in that it has rows and columns. You will learn about one-dimensional arrays in this tutorial, and about two-dimensional arrays in Tutorial 9. (Arrays having more than two dimensions, which are used in scientific and engineering programs, are beyond the scope of this book.)

Programmers use arrays to store related data in the internal memory of the computer. By doing so, programmers can increase the efficiency of a program because data stored inside the computer can be both written and read much faster than data stored in a file on a disk. The following analogy may help illustrate this point. Think of the computer's internal memory as being comparable to the memory cells in your brain. Now assume that someone asks you to name the first U.S. president. Because that information is already stored in your brain, you can respond almost immediately with George Washington. Similarly, the computer has almost immediate access to the information stored in internal memory—the memory cells in *its* brain.

Now assume that someone asks you to name the eighth U.S. president. If that information is not stored in your memory cells, you will need to open a history book, find the page containing the listing of presidents, and then read the eighth name—a much more time-consuming process. Similarly, accessing information that is not stored in the computer's internal memory, but rather in a disk file, takes the computer much longer. The computer must wait for the disk drive to locate the needed information and then read that information into memory.

In addition to speedier access of information, another advantage of using an array is that data can be entered into an array once, usually at the beginning of the program, and can then be used by the program as many times as desired. For example, assume that you are creating a payroll program. To compute the net pay for an employee, the program will need to calculate his or her federal withholding tax. By storing the federal withholding tax table in an array at the beginning of the program, the program can use that stored information to calculate each employee's federal withholding tax.

Next, learn how to create and initialize one-dimensional arrays.

Creating and Initializing a One-dimensional Array

As with variables, you must create, or declare, an array before you can use it. The syntax for declaring a one-dimensional array is *datatype arrayname*[*nElements*] = {*initialValues*};. The *datatype* in the syntax is the type of data the array variables, referred to as **elements**, will store. Recall that each of the elements (variables) in an array has the same data type. You can use any of the C++ built-in data types (such as Character, Short Integer, Float, and so on) to create an array. You can also declare an array using a programmer-defined data type. (Recall that you learned how to use the C++ **struct** statement to create a programmer-defined data type in Tutorial 7.)

In the syntax for declaring an array, *arrayname* is the name of the array. The name must follow the same rules as for variables. *nElements* in the syntax is an integer that represents the number of elements you want in the array. For example, if you want 10 elements in the array, then you enter the number 10 as *nElements*. You will notice that *nElements*, which follows the name of the array, must be enclosed in a set of square brackets ([ ]).

In addition to initializing variables, it is also a good programming practice to initialize the elements in an array to ensure that the elements will not contain

You must list at least one value in the *initialValues* section. In other words, you cannot use an empty set of braces ({}) to initialize an array.

tip

As you may remember from Tutorial 3, garbage found in variables and array elements that are not initialized consists of the remains of what was last stored at the memory location that the variable or array element now occupies.

garbage. As the syntax for declaring an array indicates, you can initialize the array elements at the same time you create the array simply by entering one or more values, separated by commas, in the *initialValues* section of the syntax. You will notice that the syntax requires you to enclose the *initialValues* in a set of braces ({}). The only exception to this requirement is in a statement that declares a Character array that stores a string, where the braces are optional.

You usually initialize the elements in Short Integer, Integer, and Long Integer arrays to the number 0, and the elements in a Double array to 0.0. You typically use the (float) 0.0 type cast to initialize the elements in a Float array. Character arrays that will store strings are usually initialized to the empty string (""). Figure 8-2 shows some examples of creating and initializing arrays.

Example 1
`char item[5] = "";`
or
`char item[5] = {""};`
	You can use either of these statements to create and initialize, to the empty string, a Character array named `item` that can store a maximum of four characters and the null character.

Example 2
`char item[5] = "Desk";`
or
`char item[5] = {'D', 'e', 's', 'k', '\0'};`
	You can use either of these statements to create and initialize a Character array named `item` that can store a maximum of four characters and the null character. The first four array elements are initialized to the letters D, e, s, and k, respectively. The last element is initialized to the null character.

Example 3
`short num[3] = {0, 0, 0};`
or
`short num[3] = {0};`
	You can use either of these statements to create and initialize, to 0, a Short Integer array named num that can store a maximum of three numbers.

Example 4 `short num[3] = {1, 4, 9};`	Creates and initializes a Short Integer array named num that can store a maximum of three numbers. The three array elements are initialized to 1, 4, and 9, respectively.
Example 5 `float price[10] = {(float) 5.2};`	Creates and initializes a Float array named price that can store a maximum of ten numbers. The first array element is initialized to 5.2. C++ initializes the remaining elements to 0.

Figure 8-2: Examples of creating and initializing one-dimensional arrays

tip

You will learn more about array initialization in Lesson A's Discovery Exercise 12.

Carefully study the examples shown in Figure 8-2. The first example shows that you can use either the `char item[5] = "";` statement or the `char item[5] = {""};` statement to create and initialize, to the empty string, a five-element Character array named `item`. When declaring a Character array that will store a string, recall that the braces surrounding the values in the *initialValues* section are optional.

The second example in Figure 8-2 shows that both the `char item[5] = "Desk";` and the `char item[5] = {'D', 'e', 's', 'k', '\0'};` statements also create and initialize a five-element Character array named `item`. The `char item[5] = "Desk";` statement initializes the `item` array by assigning the string

As you learned in Tutorial 3, string literal constants are enclosed in double quotes (" "), whereas character literal constants are enclosed in single quotes (' '). The double quotes tell C++ to append the null character to the end of the string when the string is stored in memory.

tip

Although Visual C++ version 5.0 automatically initializes the uninitialized values in a numeric array, not all C++ systems do. To determine whether your C++ system performs the automatic initialization, do Lesson A's Discovery Exercise 12. If your C++ system does not automatically initialize the uninitialized elements, you will need to provide an initial value for each element when you declare the array. Optionally, you can omit the *initialValues* section from the array declaration statement and then use a counter-controlled loop to assign an initial value to each element.

tip

If you provide more values in the *initialValues* section than the number of array elements, Visual C++ version 5.0 will display a syntax error message when you attempt to compile the program. However, not all C++ systems will display a message when this error occurs; some systems will simply store the extra values in memory loca-tions adjacent to, but not reserved for, the array. To determine if your C++ system displays the syntax error message, do Lesson A's Discovery Exercise 12.

literal constant "Desk" to it. When this statement is processed, C++ will store the letter D in the first element of the `item` array, the letter e in the second element, the letter s in the third element, the letter k in the fourth element, and the null character in the fifth element. (Recall that C++ automatically appends the null character to the end of a string literal constant when the constant is stored in memory.)

Like the `char item[5] = "Desk";` statement, the `char item[5] = {'D', 'e', 's', 'k', '\0'};` statement also initializes the `item` array to the word *Desk*. However, rather than using a string literal constant (`"Desk"`), the latter statement uses character literal constants (`'D'`, `'e'`, `'s'`, `'k'`, and `'\0'`) to initialize the array, character by character. You will notice that when you use character literal constants to initialize the `item` array to the word *Desk*, you must be sure to assign the null character to the last element in the array. The null character, which is represented in C++ by `'\0'` (a backslash and the number 0 enclosed in single quotes), tells C++ that the array contains a string.

Example 3 in Figure 8-2 shows that you can use either the `short num[3] = {0, 0, 0};` statement or the `short num[3] = {0};` statement to declare and initialize, to 0, a three-element Short Integer array named num. You will notice that the `short num[3] = {0, 0, 0};` statement provides an initial value for each of the three elements in the array, but the `short num[3] = {0};` statement provides only one value. When you do not provide an initial value for each of the variables in a numeric array, C++ stores the number 0 in the uninitialized elements. One word of caution, however: C++ will initialize the uninitialized array elements only if you provide at least one value in the *initialValues* section of the statement that declares the array. If you omit the *initialValues* section from the declaration statement—for example, if you use the `short num[3];` statement to declare an array—C++ does not automatically initialize the elements, so the array elements will contain garbage. Although you can use both statements shown in Example 3 to declare and initialize the num array, for convenience, many programmers will use the `short num[3] = {0};` statement.

Examples 4 and 5 in Figure 8-2 show how you can use values other than zero to initialize one or more elements in a numeric array. The `short num[3] = {1, 4, 9};` statement, for example, initializes the three elements in the num array to the values 1, 4, and 9, respectively. The `float price[10] = {(float) 5.2};` statement initializes the first element in the `price` array to the number 5.2, and C++ initializes the remaining elements to the number 0. Recall that when you don't provide an initial value for each of the variables in a numeric array, C++ stores the number 0 in the uninitialized elements; however, this will occur only if you provide at least one value in the *initialValues* section of the statement.

Now that you know how to create and initialize arrays, you will learn how you can access each element in an array.

Accessing the Elements in an Array

Similar to the way each house on a street is identified by a unique address, each element in an array is identified by a unique number, called a **subscript**. C++ assigns the subscript to each of the array elements when you create the array. The first element in a one-dimensional array is always assigned a subscript of 0, the next element in the array is assigned a subscript of 1, and so on. You refer to each element in the array by the array's name and the element's subscript, which is specified in a set of square brackets (`[ ]`) immediately following the name. For example, `state[0]`—read "state sub zero"—refers to the first element in a one-dimensional array named `state`, while `pay[2]`—read "pay sub two"—refers to the third element in the `pay` array. Figure 8-3 illustrates this naming convention using both a one-dimensional Character array named `state` and a one-dimensional Short Integer array named `quantity`.

Created and initialized: `char state[6] = "Idaho";`

state[0]	I
state[1]	d
state[2]	a
state[3]	h
state[4]	o
state[5]	\0

Created and initialized: `short quantity[3] = {8, 10, 7};`

quantity[0]	8
quantity[1]	10
quantity[2]	7

Figure 8-3: Names of the elements in two one-dimensional arrays

As Figure 8-3 shows, a six-element array will have subscripts of 0 through 5, and a three-element array will have subscripts of 0 through 2. Notice that the last subscript in an array is always one number less than the number of elements. This is because the first array subscript is 0.

After you create and initialize an array, you can then store data in it.

mini-quiz

Mini-Quiz 1

1. Write a statement that declares and initializes, to 0, a 20-element Short Integer array named `number`.

2. Write a statement that declares and initializes, to the empty string, a 10-element Character array named `firstName`.

3. The first subscript in a 25-element array is the number _____.

4. The last subscript in a 25-element array is the number _____.

5. `quantity[7]` is read _____.

Storing Data in a One-dimensional Array

You can enter data into a one-dimensional array in a variety of ways. The examples shown in Figure 8-4, for instance, can be used to enter data into various one-dimensional arrays.

Example 1 – declared and initialized: `char item[4] = "";`

```
strcpy(item, "Pen");        or                 item[0] = 'P';
                                               item[1] = 'e';
                                               item[2] = 'n';
                                               item[3] = '\0';
```

Example 2 – declared and initialized: `float raiseRate[5] = {(float) 0.0};`

```
for(short x = 0; x <= 4; x = x + 1)
    cin >> raiseRate[x];
//end for
```

Example 3 – declared and initialized: `short squareNum[4] = {0};`

```
for(short x = 1; x <= 4; x = x + 1)
    squareNum[x — 1] = x * x;
//end for
```

Example 4 – declared and initialized: `short num[10] = {0};`

```
short x = 0;
while (x < 10)
{
    inFile >> num[x];
    x = x + 1;
} //end while
```

Figure 8-4: Examples of entering data into a one-dimensional array

Example 1 in Figure 8-4 shows two ways of storing the word *Pen* in a four-element Character array named `item`. You will notice that you can either use the `strcpy` function to assign the string literal constant "Pen" to the `item` array, or you can use four assignment statements to assign four character literal constants (`'P'`, `'e'`, `'n'`, and `'\0'`) to the array. When you assign a string literal constant to a Character array, C++ automatically appends the null character to the end of the string when it is stored in the array. However, when you assign character literal constants to a Character array, you must be sure to assign the null character to the array, as C++ does not handle this for you.

Example 2 in Figure 8-4 uses a `for` loop, along with the `cin >> raiseRate[x];` statement, to enter the user's keyboard input into a five-element, Float array named `raiseRate`. Notice that the `for` loop's *counter* variable, x, is initialized to 0, and its ending value is 4. These values correspond to the five subscripts (0, 1, 2, 3, and 4) in the `raiseRate` array.

Example 3 in Figure 8-4 uses a `for` loop, along with the `squareNum[x — 1] = x * x;` assignment statement, to fill the `squareNum` array, element by element, with the squares of the numbers from 1 through 4. You may be wondering why the `squareNum[x — 1] = x * x;` assignment statement first multiplies the value in x by itself and then stores the result in the `squareNum[x — 1]` rather than the `squareNum[x]` array element. In this example, the `for` loop's *counter* variable, x, is initialized to 1, and its ending value is 4; the array subscripts, however, are 0 through 3. To store the four squares in the array, you will need to store the square of the number 1 in the `squareNum[0]` element, the square of the number 2 in the `squareNum[1]` element, the square of the number 3 in the `squareNum[2]` element, and the square of the number 4 in the `squareNum[3]` element. You will notice that

Recall that it is the double quotes surrounding a string literal constant that tell C++ to append the null character to the end of the string when it is saved in memory.

You learned about the `strcpy` (*string copy*) function in Tutorial 3.

the value in x (the number to be squared) is always one number greater than the subscript of the array element where the square of x is to be stored. The squareNum[x − 1] = x * x; assignment statement compensates for this by subtracting the number 1 from x before storing the square in the array element. For example, when x is 1, squareNum[1 − 1] = 1 * 1; will store the square of 1 in the squareNum[0] element. When x is 2, squareNum[2 − 1] = 2 * 2; will store the square of 2 in the squareNum[1] element, and so on.

Example 4 in Figure 8-4 uses a counter-controlled loop, along with the inFile >> num[x]; statement, to read the data from a sequential access file and then store the data in the 10-element Short Integer num array.

In the remaining sections of Lesson A, you will view several programs that use a one-dimensional array. Begin with a program that uses a one-dimensional Character array.

Using a Character Array in a Program

On your computer's hard disk is a program that will allow you to observe how a one-dimensional Character array works. When you run the program, you will be prompted to enter a word. The program will store the word in a one-dimensional Character array. The program will then allow you to form a new word by changing a letter in the Character array. The purpose of this program is simply to allow you to practice accessing the elements in an array. The IPO chart for the program is shown in Figure 8-5.

Input	Processing	Output
word array subscript of the letter to change new letter	Processing items: five-element Character array Algorithm: 1. get a word and store in Character array 2. display the word (the contents of the array) 3. get the array subscript of the letter to change 4. repeat while (array subscript is valid) 　　get new letter and enter it into the array, forming a new word 　　display new word (the contents of the array) 　　get the array subscript of the letter to change end while	new word

Figure 8-5: IPO chart for the Character array demo program

According to the algorithm shown in Figure 8-5, the program will begin by getting a word from the user and storing the word in a five-element Character array. After displaying the word on the screen, the program will then get the array subscript that corresponds to the letter the user wants to change in the word. For example, if the user wants to change the first letter in the word, he or she will enter the number 0 as the array subscript because that is the location of the first letter in the array. If the user enters a valid subscript—one that exists in the array—then the while loop's instructions will be processed; otherwise, the program will end.

As the algorithm indicates, the while loop's instructions will get a new letter from the user and will enter the new letter into the array, forming a new word. The program will then display the contents of the array—the new word—before asking the user to enter the subscript of another letter to change. The `while` loop will continue to process its instructions as long as—or while—the user enters a valid subscript for the array.

Now open a C++ program that corresponds to this IPO chart.

To open the program:

1 Start Visual C++. Open the **LaProg01.cpp** file, which is located in the Cpp\Tut08\LaProg01 folder on your computer's hard disk. The LaProg01 program, which appears in the LaProg01.cpp window, is shown in Figure 8-6.

```cpp
//LaProg01.cpp
//this program demonstrates how to access the elements
//in a one-dimensional array

#include <iostream.h>

void main()
{
    //declare and initialize variable
    short arraySubscript = 0;

    //declare and initialize one-dimensional Character array
    char word[5] = "";

    //get a word
    cout << "Enter a word (maximum of 4 letters): ";
    cin.get(word, 5, '\n');
    cin.ignore(100, '\n');

    //display the word
    cout << "The word is: " << word << endl << endl;

    //get the subscript of the letter to change
    cout << "Enter the subscript of the letter" << endl;
    cout << "you want to change (0, 1, 2, 3, or -1 to stop): ";
    cin >> arraySubscript;
    cin.ignore(100, '\n');

    //process loop while subscript is valid
    while (arraySubscript >= 0 && arraySubscript < 4)
    {
        //get the new letter
        cout << "Enter the new letter: ";
        cin  >> word[arraySubscript];
        cin.ignore(100, '\n');

        //display the new word
        cout << "The new word is " << word << endl << endl;

        //get the subscript of the letter to change
        cout << "Enter the subscript of the letter" << endl;
        cout << "you want to change (0, 1, 2, 3, or -1 to stop): ";
        cin  >> arraySubscript;
        cin.ignore(100,'\n');
    }//end while

} //end of main function
```

Figure 8-6: Character array demo program

The program begins by declaring and initializing a Short Integer variable named `arraySubscript` to 0. The program will use this variable to store the array position of the letter that the user wants to change in the word. The program then declares and initializes a Character array named `word` to the empty string. The `word` array will store a maximum of four characters and the null character that C++ appends to the end of a string when it saves the string in memory.

The `cout << "Enter a word (maximum of 4 letters): ";` statement prompts the user to enter a word. The `cin.get(word, 5, '\n');` statement stores the user's response in the `word` array. As you learned in Tutorial 7, the `get` function stops reading characters when it either reads one less than the number specified in the function's second parameter, or when it encounters the delimiter character specified in the function's third parameter. In this case, the `get` function will stop either when it reads four characters from the keyboard or when the user presses the Enter key, whichever comes first. If the user types more than four characters before pressing the Enter key, the `cin.ignore(100, '\n');` statement tells C++ to ignore those additional characters. (Recall that you learned about the `ignore` function in Tutorial 7.)

The next statement in the program, `cout << "The word is " << word << endl  << endl;`, displays the contents of the `word` array on the screen. Notice that you can simply use a Character array's name—in this case, `word`—to refer to the entire array.

As you learned in Tutorial 7, `'\n'` represents the new-line character, which C++ generates when the user presses the Enter key.

The next four statements in the program first prompt the user to enter the array subscript of the letter he or she wants to change, and then store the response in the `arraySubscript` variable. Before changing the corresponding letter in the `word` array, the `while` statement's *loop condition* verifies that the number in the `arraySubscript` variable represents a valid subscript for the array. The valid subscripts for a five-element array are the numbers 0 through 4. It may seem inconsistent that the last part of the *loop condition* contains `arraySubscript < 4` rather than `arraySubscript <= 4`. However, because the `word` array stores a string, the last element in the array contains the null character that C++ appends to the end of the string when the string is saved in memory. Therefore, you should allow the user to change the letters only in elements 0 through 3 of the `word` array. The `word[4]` element should not be changed because it contains the null character.

If the `while` statement's *loop condition* determines that the value in the `arraySubscript` variable is invalid—in this case, the subscript is not either 0, 1, 2, or 3—then the program ends. Otherwise, the statements within the loop are processed. The first statement inside the loop, `cout << "Enter the new letter: ";`, prompts the user to enter a letter. The next statement, `cin >> word[arraySubscript];`, stores the letter in the proper location in the `word` array, replacing the current contents of that array element. If the user inadvertently enters more than one letter, the `cin.ignore(100, '\n');` statement tells C++ to ignore the excess characters. The `cout << "The new word is " << word << endl << endl;` statement then displays the current contents of the `word` array—in other words, the new word. The remaining statements within the loop first prompt the user to enter the subscript of another letter to change, and then store the user's response in the `arraySubscript` variable. The `while` statement's *loop condition* is then tested to see if the loop instructions should be processed again. Execute the program to observe how it works.

tip

Although you recognize the letter n to be the third letter in the word *bin*, computers consider it to be in position 2 of the word. This is because computers begin counting with the number 0 rather than with the number 1.

To execute the Character array demo program:

1   Build and execute the program. When prompted to enter a word, type **bin** and press the **Enter** key. The program displays the original word, *bin*, in the DOS window. First, change *bin* to *bit*. You can do so by replacing the letter n, which is stored in the `word[2]` element, with the letter t.

2   When prompted to enter the subscript of a letter to change, type **2** and press the **Enter** key. When prompted to enter the new letter, type **t** and press the **Enter** key. The program replaces the letter that was originally stored in the `word[2]` element (the letter n) with the letter t. The DOS window shows that the `word` array now contains the new word, *bit*. The program prompts you to enter the subscript of a letter to change. Change the empty string stored in `word[3]` to the letter e.

3   When prompted to enter the subscript of a letter to change, type **3** and press the **Enter** key. When prompted to enter the new letter, type **e** and press the **Enter** key. The program replaces the empty string stored in `word[3]` with the letter e. The DOS window shows that the new word is *bite*. The program prompts you to enter the subscript of a letter to change.

Change the first letter in the `word` array to the letter c.

4   When prompted to enter the subscript of a letter to change, type **0** and press the **Enter** key. When prompted to enter the new letter, type **c** and press the **Enter** key. The program replaces the letter b stored in `word[0]` with the letter c. The DOS window shows that the new word is *cite*. The program prompts you to enter the subscript of a letter to change, as shown in Figure 8-7.

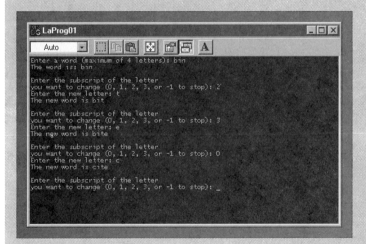

Figure 8-7: Results of the Character array demo program shown in the DOS window

Stop the program by typing a –1.

5 Type **–1** and press the **Enter** key to stop the program, then press the **Enter** key to close the DOS window.

6 Execute the program again. When you are prompted to enter a word, type **dog** and press the **Enter** key. On your own, change *dog* to **don**, then change *don* to **done**, then change *done* to **dine**, and then change *dine* to **fine**. When you are finished, type **–1** in response to the prompt to enter a subscript and press the **Enter** key to stop the program, then press the **Enter** key to close the DOS window.

You are finished with this program, so you can close it.

7 Close the workspace and the Output window.

In the next example, you will use a numeric array to store the student test scores contained in a sequential access file. You will use the information in the array to calculate the average and highest test score.

Using a Numeric Array in a Program

Mr. Gonzales teaches an advanced math course at a local high school. This semester his class contains eight students. After every test, Mr. Gonzales saves the students' scores in a sequential access file. For example, the eight scores earned on the first test are stored in the test.dat file, which is located in the Cpp\Tut08\ LaProg02 folder on your computer's hard disk. Mr. Gonzales would like you to create a program that allows him to calculate the average and highest score earned on a test.

After analyzing Mr. Gonzales' problem, you decide to use three programmer-defined functions in the program. You will use one of the functions—the `getMenuChoice` function—to display a menu that offers Mr. Gonzales three choices: display the average score, display the highest score, and exit the program. In addition to displaying the menu, the `getMenuChoice` function will need to return Mr. Gonzales' menu selection, so you will make it a value-returning function.

The other two programmer-defined functions—`displayAverage` and `displayHighest`—will be void functions. You will use the `displayAverage` function to display the average of the eight test scores, and the `displayHighest` function to display the highest test score. Because both functions need to use the scores stored in the test.dat file, you will enter the scores into an array at the beginning of the program and then pass the array to both functions. By storing the test scores in an array, you ensure that both functions will have much faster access to the test scores, because the computer can access the data stored in an array much faster than it can access the data stored in a file on a disk. The IPO chart for the test score program's `main` function is shown in Figure 8-8.

Input	Processing	Output
test scores stored in test.dat file	Processing items: eight-element Short Integer array named **score** counter	average test score

menu choice	Algorithm:
	1. open the test.dat file for input
	
	2. if (open is successful)
	   initialize counter to 0
	   repeat while (counter is less than 8)
	     read a test score from the file and store it in the array
	     add 1 to counter
	   end while (counter is less than 8)
	   close the test.dat file
	   display menu and get a menu choice (**getMenuChoice** function)
	   repeat while (menu choice is either 1 or 2)
	     if (menu choice is 1)
	       display average test score (**displayAverage** function)
	     else
	       display highest test score (**displayHighest** function)
	     end if (menu choice is 1)
	     display menu and get a menu choice (**getMenuChoice** function)
	   end while (menu choice is either 1 or 2)
	 else
	   display "Error opening file" message
	end if (open is successful)
		highest test score

reads scores from file and stores in array (label pointing to the read loop section)

determines which function to call (label pointing to the selection section)

Figure 8-8: IPO chart for the test score program's **main** function

As Figure 8-8's algorithm indicates, the test score program's **main** function will open the test.dat file for input. If the program encounters a problem when opening the file, the program will display an appropriate message. Otherwise, a counter-controlled loop will be used to read the contents of the test.dat file into an array.

After the counter-controlled loop finishes entering the scores into the array, the input file will be closed and the program will call the **getMenuChoice** function both to display the menu and get the user's menu choice. A **while** loop will then determine if the user selected either choice 1 or choice 2 from the menu. If the user selects neither of those choices, then the program will end; otherwise, the instructions in the **while** loop will be processed.

You will notice that the **while** loop contains a selection structure that calls either the **displayAverage** function or the **displayHighest** function. The appropriate function to call depends on the user's menu choice. If the user selected menu choice 1, then the selection structure calls the **displayAverage** function. Otherwise, it calls the **displayHighest** function. After the appropriate function completes its task, the **while** loop then calls the **getMenuChoice** function both to display the menu again and to get another choice from the user. The program will continue displaying the menu, getting the user's selection, and calling the appropriate function until the user enters a menu selection other than 1 or 2.

On your computer's hard disk is a partially completed program that corresponds to Figure 8-8's algorithm. Open that program now.

To open the partially completed test score program:

1 Open the **LaProg02.cpp** file, which is located in the Cpp\Tut08\LaProg02 folder on your computer's hard disk. The LaProg02 program appears in the LaProg02.cpp window. The partially completed main function is shown in Figure 8-9.

function prototypes

opens file

determines if open was successful

the code to enter the test scores is missing

displays message if open failed

```
//LaProg02.cpp
//this program allows the user to calculate the average and
//highest score stored in a numeric array

#include <iostream.h>
#include <fstream.h>

//function prototypes
char getMenuChoice();
void displayAverage();
void displayHighest();

void main()
{
    //declare and initialize variable
    char menuChoice = ' ';

    //declare and initialize numeric array

    //open file for input
    ifstream inFile;
    inFile.open("test.dat", ios::in);

    //verify that open was successful
    if (!inFile.fail())//open was successful
    {
        //enter test scores into the array

        //close file
        inFile.close();

        //display menu and get menu choice

        while (menuChoice == '1' || menuChoice == '2')
        {
            if (menuChoice == '1')        //display average score

            else                          //display highest score

            //end if

            //display menu and get menu choice

        }//end while
    }
    else                           //open was not successful
        cout << "Error opening file." << endl;
    //end if (!inFile.fail())
} //end of main function
```

Figure 8-9: Partially completed main function in the test score program

You will notice that the program includes the prototypes for the three programmer-defined functions: getMenuChoice, displayAverage, and displayHighest. Only one of the programmer-defined functions, getMenuChoice, is a value-returning function; it will return a character literal constant that represents the user's selection from the menu. The other two functions, displayAverage and displayHighest, are void functions.

The main function begins by declaring and initializing a Character variable named menuChoice. The main function will use the menuChoice variable to store the character literal constant returned by the getMenuChoice function. Missing from the main function is the statement that declares and initializes a numeric array that will store the test scores saved in the test.dat file. The array will need to contain eight elements—one for each test score in the file. Because the test scores are small integer values in the range of 0 through 100, you will use the Short Integer data type to declare the array. You will name the array score and initialize its elements to 0. Enter the missing declaration statement in the program.

To enter the missing array declaration statement in the program:

1 In the blank line below the //declare and initialize numeric array, type **short score[8] = {0};** and press the **Enter** key. (Be sure to type braces around the number 0.) When the program is executed, this statement will create the **score** array and initialize each of its eight elements to 0.

> Recall that not all C++ systems automatically initialize the uninitalized values in a numeric array. If your C++ system does not automatically initialize the array elements, you should enter eight zeros, separated by commas, in the *initialValues* section of the statement that declares the score array.

According to the algorithm shown in Figure 8-8, the main function should open the test.dat file for input and then determine if the file was opened successfully. Note that the code to accomplish this is already included in the program. If the open is not successful, then an appropriate message should be displayed. The cout << "Error opening file." << endl; statement in the if statement's false path handles this for you. If, on the other hand, the file is opened successfully, then the main function should use a counter-controlled loop to read the eight test scores from the test.dat file and enter each into the score array. You will notice that the code to accomplish this task is missing from the program.

When filling a numeric array with data, you must enter each value, one at a time, into the array. You can use a counter-controlled loop to do so. Recall that you use a counter-controlled loop when you know precisely how many times you want the loop to process its instructions. In the test scores program, for example, you want the loop to process its instruction—read a test score from the file and store it in the array—exactly eight times. As you learned in Tutorial 6, you can code a counter-controlled loop with either the while statement or the for statement. You will use the for statement in the test score program simply because it is a much more compact way of writing a counter-controlled loop.

To enter the for loop into the test score program's main function:

1 Enter the for loop highlighted in Figure 8-10.

```
//LaProg02.cpp
//this program allows the user to calculate the average and
//highest score stored in a numeric array

#include <iostream.h>
#include <fstream.h>

//function prototypes
char getMenuChoice();
void displayAverage();
void displayHighest();

void main()
{
    //declare and initialize variable
    char menuChoice = ' ';

    //declare and initialize numeric array
    short score[8] = {0};

    //open file for input
    ifstream inFile;
    inFile.open("test.dat", ios::in);

    //verify that open was successful
    if (!inFile.fail())              //open was successful
    {
        //enter test scores into the array
        for (short x = 0; x <= 7; x = x + 1)
            inFile >> score[x];
        //end for

        //close file
        inFile.close();

        //display menu and get menu choice

        while (menuChoice == '1' || menuChoice == '2')
        {
            if (menuChoice == '1')            //display average score

            else                             //display highest score

            //end if

            //display menu and get menu choice

        }//end while
    }
    else                                 //open was not successful
        cout << "Error opening file." << endl;
    //end if (!inFile.fail())
} //end of main function
```

enter this loop

closes the file

determines if the
program should continue

Figure 8-10: for loop entered in the main function

You could also write the for
clause as for (short x =
0; x < 8; x = x + 1).

The for loop's inFile >> score[x]; statement, which tells C++ to read a test score from the test.dat file and store it in the next element in the score array, will be processed eight times. You will notice that the for loop's counter variable (x), which will take on values of 0 through 7 as the loop is processed, is used as the array subscript in the inFile >> score[x]; statement.

The x variable keeps track of where in the array the next score should be stored. The first score in the file will be stored in score[0] and the last score in the file will be stored in score[7].

tip

. . . .

You can tell that the for **loop shown in Figure 8-10 will be processed eight times because the loop's** *counter* **variable,** x, **begins counting at 0, ends counting at 7, and is incremented by 1 each time the loop is processed. In other words, the loop instructions will be processed when the** x **variable contains the following eight values: 0, 1, 2, 3, 4, 5, 6, and 7. The loop will stop when the value in** x **is 8.**

According to the algorithm shown in Figure 8-8, the main function should now close the file. The appropriate statement to do this, inFile.close();, is already entered in the program. After closing the file, the main function should display a menu of choices and get the user's selection. Recall that you will use the value-returning getMenuChoice function to do both tasks. You will assign the value returned by the getMenuChoice function to the main function's menuChoice variable. Enter the appropriate statement that will call the getMenuChoice function and assign its return value to the menuChoice variable.

To call the getMenuChoice function and assign its return value to the menuChoice variable:

1 In the blank line above the while (menuChoice == '1' || menuChoice == '2') clause, type **menuChoice = getMenuChoice();** and press the **Enter** key. (Be sure to enter the assignment statement in the line above, and not below, the while clause.)

2 Save the program.

According to the algorithm, the while loop in the main function must now determine if the value in the menuChoice variable, which represents the user's menu selection, is either the character literal constant '1' or the character literal constant '2'. The appropriate while clause to do so, while (menuChoice == '1' || menuChoice == '2'), is already entered in the program. If the menuChoice variable does not contain either of these two character literal constants, then the program should end. If, however, the menuChoice variable contains the character literal constant '1', then the main function should call the displayAverage function to display the average test score. Otherwise, it should call the displayHighest function to display the highest test score. The statements to call both functions are missing from the program.

Before entering the missing function call statements, consider what information, if any, the main function will need to pass to the displayAverage and displayHighest functions. To calculate the average test score, the displayAverage function will need to use the scores stored in the main function's score array. To display the highest test score, the displayHighest function will also need access to the score array. Because the score array was declared in the main function, it can be used by that function only. To allow the displayAverage and displayHighest functions to use the score array, you will need to pass the array, as well as its size (the number of elements in the array), to both functions. You will enter the missing function call statements in the next set of steps.

According to the algorithm, the last instruction in the while loop should call the getMenuChoice function both to display the menu and get a menu selection from the user. Here again, you will assign the getMenuChoice function's return value to the menuChoice variable. After you enter the menuChoice = getMenuChoice(); statement and the two missing function call statements in the next set of steps, the main function's code will be complete.

To complete the main function:

1 Enter the three statements highlighted in Figure 8-11.

```cpp
//LaProg02.cpp
//this program allows the user to calculate the average and
//highest score stored in a numeric array

#include <iostream.h>
#include <fstream.h>

//function prototypes
char getMenuChoice();
void displayAverage();
void displayHighest();

void main()
{
    //declare and initialize variable
    char menuChoice = ' ';

    //declare and initialize numeric array
    short score[8] = {0};

    //open file for input
    ifstream inFile;
    inFile.open("test.dat", ios::in);

    //verify that open was successful
    if (!inFile.fail())             //open was successful
    {
        //enter test scores into the array
        for (short x = 0; x <= 7; x = x + 1)
            inFile >> score[x];
        //end for

        //close file
        inFile.close();

        //display menu and get menu choice
        menuChoice = getMenuChoice();

        while (menuChoice == '1' || menuChoice == '2')
        {
            if (menuChoice == '1')          //display average score
                displayAverage(score, 8);
            else                            //display highest score
                displayHighest(score, 8);
            //end if

            //display menu and get menu choice
            menuChoice = getMenuChoice();
        }//end while
    }
    else                            //open was not successful
        cout << "Error opening file." << endl;
    //end if (!inFile.fail())
} //end of main function
```

enter these statements

Figure 8-11: Completed main function in the test score program

> **2** Save the program.

Next, view the IPO chart and the code for the `getMenuChoice` function.

The `getMenuChoice` Function

Both the IPO chart and the code for the `getMenuChoice` function are shown in Figure 8-12.

Input	Processing	Output
none	Processing items: none Algorithm: 1. display menu 2. get user's menu choice 3. return user's menu choice	user's menu choice

```
char getMenuChoice()
{
    //this function displays a menu and gets the user's choice

    char choice = ' ';

    //display menu
    cout << endl;
    cout << "Menu                    " << endl;
    cout << "1 Display average score" << endl;
    cout << "2 Display highest score" << endl;
    cout << "3 Exit program         " << endl;
    cout << "Enter your choice: ";

    //get user's menu choice
    cin >> choice;
    cin.ignore(100, '\n');

    return choice;
} //end of getMenuChoice function
```

display menu — points to the display menu block

get user's choice — points to the cin >> choice block

return choice to `main` function — points to the return choice line

Figure 8-12: IPO chart and code for the `getMenuChoice` function

First, examine the `getMenuChoice` function's IPO chart. According to this chart, the function's tasks are simply to display a menu, get the user's menu choice, and then return the user's menu choice to the `main` function.

Next, look at the `getMenuChoice` function's code shown in Figure 8-12. After declaring and initializing a local Character variable named `choice`, the `getMenuChoice` function displays a menu on the screen and then prompts the user to enter his or her choice. The `cin >> choice;` statement stores the user's response in the function's local `choice` variable. If the user mistakenly enters more than one character in response to the "Enter your choice: " prompt, the `cin.ignore(100, '\n');` statement tells C++ to ignore the additional characters. After the user enters his or her menu selection, the `getMenuChoice` function returns the value in the choice variable to the main function. As you may remember, the main function stores the return value—a character literal constant—in its local menuChoice variable. The main function uses the value in the menuChoice variable to determine whether it should call the displayAverage or displayHighest function, or simply end the program.

Next, view the IPO chart and the code for the displayAverage function.

The displayAverage Function

The displayAverage function will calculate and display the average test score earned by the eight students. Figure 8-13 shows both the IPO chart and the partially completed code for the displayAverage function.

Input	Processing	Output
score array and array size from the main function	Processing items: accumulator counter Algorithm: 1. initialize accumulator to 0 2. initialize counter to 0 3. repeat while (counter < array size) add the test score in the array to the accumulator add 1 to counter end while 4. calculate average test score by dividing the accumulator by the counter 5. display average test score	average test score

function header

missing the for-mal parameters

```
void displayAverage()
{
        //this function displays the average test score
        short sum     = 0;
        float average = (float) 0.0;

        //accumulate scores
        for(short x = 0; x < size; x = x + 1)
            sum = sum + testScore[x];
        //end for

        //calculate average
        average = (float) sum / (float) x;

        //display average
        cout << endl << "The average test score is: "
            << average << endl;
} //end of displayAverage function
```

Figure 8-13: IPO chart and partially completed code for the displayAverage function

First, look at the algorithm in the IPO chart. The `displayAverage` function begins by initializing both a counter and an accumulator. A counter-controlled loop is then used to add each of the eight test scores to the accumulator. After the eight test scores are accumulated, the average test score is both calculated and displayed.

Notice that the Input column of the IPO chart indicates that the `displayAverage` function's input is the `score` array, as well as the array size, passed to it by the `main` function. In the `displayAverage` function, both the function's header and its prototype will need to provide formal parameters to receive both items. You will need to enter the appropriate formal parameters in the `displayAverage` function's header and in its prototype.

As you learned in Tutorial 4, before entering a formal parameter in the receiving function's header, you first must decide if the information being sent to the function is being passed by value or by reference. You may recall that the information stored in variables is automatically passed by value in C++. If you want to pass a variable by reference, you need to include the address-of (&) operator before the formal parameter's name in the receiving function's header, and you also need to include the & operator in the function's prototype.

C++ does not give you a choice of passing array information by value or by reference, as it does when passing variables. Arrays in C++ can be passed only by reference. When you pass an array, C++ passes the address of only the first array element to the receiving function. Because array elements are stored in contiguous locations in memory, the receiving function needs to know only where the first element is located in memory. From there, the function can easily locate the other elements.

Because arrays in C++ are always passed automatically by reference, you do not include the address-of (&) operator before the formal parameter's name in the receiving function's header, as you do when passing variables by reference. You also do not include the & in the function prototype.

To pass the `score` array to the `displayAverage function`, you need to enter the data type and name of the formal parameter, followed by an empty set of brackets, in the function's header. Then enter the data type and an empty set of brackets in the function's prototype. You will use `testScore` as the name of the formal parameter, and `short` as its data type. You will pass the array size—the numeric literal constant 8—to a Short Integer formal parameter named `size`.

To complete the `displayAverage` function:

1 Modify the `displayAverage` function's prototype and header as highlighted in Figure 8-14.

tip

Recall that the receiving function determines if the information passed to it is passed by value or by reference.

tip

Passing an array by reference is more efficient than passing it by value. Because many arrays are large, passing by value would consume a great deal of memory and time since C++ would need to duplicate the array in the receiving function's formal parameter.

tip

Recall from Tutorial 4 that the name of a formal parameter in the function header—in this case, `testScore`—does not have to match the name of the actual argument in the function call—in this case, `score`.

enter the array's data type
and [ ] in the prototype

main function's code
is not shown

getMenuChoice
function's code
is not shown

enter array's data
type, name, and [ ]
in the header

size of array

```cpp
//LaProg02.cpp
//this program allows the user to calculate the average and
//highest score stored in a numeric array

#include <iostream.h>
#include <fstream.h>

//function prototypes
char getMenuChoice();
void displayAverage(short [], short);
void displayHighest();

        .
        .
        .


//*****programmer-defined function definitions*****

        .
        .
        .

void displayAverage(short testScore[], short size)
{
    //this function displays the average test score
    short sum     = 0;
    float average = (float) 0.0;

    //accumulate scores
    for(short x = 0; x < size; x = x + 1)
        sum = sum + testScore[x];
    //end for

    //calculate average
    average = (float) sum / (float) x;

    //display average
    cout << endl << "The average test score is: "
        << average << endl;
} //end of displayAverage function
```

Figure 8-14: Completed displayAverage function

2   Save the program.

You will notice that the displayAverage function declares and initializes two local variables named sum and average. The sum = sum + testScore[x]; statement in the for loop then adds the eight test scores stored in the array, one at a time, to the sum variable. After the test scores are accumulated, the average score is calculated and then displayed. Figure 8-15 shows an illustration of the array, as well as a desk-check table for the displayAverage function.

Assume that the array contains these scores.

85
87
70
76
100
30
78
88

desk-check table

sum	average	x	size
~~0~~	~~0.0~~	~~0~~	8
85	76.75	~~1~~	
~~172~~		2	
~~242~~		3	
~~318~~		4	
418		5	
448		6	
526		7	
614		8	

Figure 8-15: Illustration of the array and a desk-check table for the displayAverage function

To understand the displayAverage function's code better:

1 Desk-check the displayAverage function's code shown in Figure 8-14. Use the array values shown in Figure 8-15 to perform the desk-check. When you have completed the desk-check, compare the values in your desk-check table to the values shown in Figure 8-15's desk-check table.

Lastly, view the IPO chart and the code for the displayHighest function.

The displayHighest Function

The displayHighest function will display the highest test score earned by the eight students. The function's IPO chart and partially completed code are shown in Figure 8-16.

Input	Processing	Output

score array and array size from the **main** function	Processing items: counter
	
	Algorithm:
	1. assign first array element's value as the highest test score
	2. initialize counter to 1
	3. repeat while (counter < array size)
	    if (value in array element is greater than the highest test score)
	        assign value in array element as the highest test score
	    end if
	    add 1 to counter
	  end while
	4. display highest test score
		highest test score

function header →
missing the formal parameters →

```
void displayHighest()
{
    //this function displays the highest test score
    short highest = 0;

    //search for highest score
    highest = testScore[0];
    for(short x = 1; x < size; x = x + 1)
        if (testScore[x] > highest)
            highest = testScore[x];
        //end if
    //end for

    //display highest score
    cout << endl << "The highest test score is: "
        << highest << endl;
} //end of displayHighest function
```

Figure 8-16: IPO chart and partially completed code for the `displayHighest` function

Like the `displayAverage` function, the `displayHighest` function will also receive the `score` array, as well as the array's size, from the `main` function. Therefore, both the function's header and its prototype will need to provide formal parameters to receive both items. (Recall that only the address of the first element in the `score` array will actually be passed to the `displayHighest` function.) You will notice that the function header shown in Figure 8-16 does not list any formal parameters in its *parameterlist*. To complete the `displayHighest` function, you need only to enter two formal parameters: one to receive the array, and the other to receive the array's size. You will use `short testScore` as the data type and name of the formal parameter that will receive the array, and `short size` as the data type and name of the formal parameter that will receive the array's size. You will need to enter the appropriate information in the function's header and its prototype.

To complete the `displayHighest` function:

1 Modify the `displayHighest` function's prototype and header as highlighted in Figure 8-17.

enter the array's data type and [ ] in the prototype

```
//LaProg02.cpp
//this program allows the user to calculate the average and
//highest score stored in a numeric array

#include <iostream.h>
#include <fstream.h>

//function prototypes
char getMenuChoice();
void displayAverage(short [], short);
void displayHighest(short [], short);
```

main **function's code is not shown**

getMenuChoice **and** displayAverage **functions' code is not shown**

```
//*****programmer-defined function definitions*****



void displayHighest(short testScore[], short size)
{
    //this function displays the highest test score
    short highest = 0;

    //search for highest score
    highest = testScore[0];
    for(short x = 1; x < size; x = x + 1)
        if (testScore[x] > highest)
            highest = testScore[x];
        //end if
    //end for

    //display highest score
    cout << endl << "The highest test score is: "
        << highest << endl;
} //end of displayHighest function
```

array

array size

Figure 8-17: Completed `displayHighest` function

You will notice that the `displayHighest` function declares a local Short Integer variable named `highest`. It then assigns the test score stored in the first array element (`testScore[0]`) to the `highest` variable. The `for` loop compares the contents of each of the remaining elements in the array—the elements with subscripts of 1 through 7—to the contents of the `highest` variable. If the test score contained in an array element is greater than the test score contained in the `highest` variable, then the array element's test score is assigned to `highest`. For example, if `highest` contains the number 85 and the array element contains the number 90, then the latter is assigned to `highest`. The remaining elements in the array are then compared to the number 90, the current value of `highest`. When the `for` loop completes its processing, the `highest` variable will contain the highest test score stored in the array. The highest test score is then displayed along with an appropriate message. Figure 8-18 shows an illustration of the array, as well as a desk-check table for the `displayHighest` function.

Assume that the array contains these scores.

85
87
70
76
100
30
78
88

highest	x	size
0	~~0~~	8
~~85~~	~~1~~	
~~87~~	~~2~~	
100	~~3~~	
	4	
	5	
	6	
	7	
	8	

Figure 8-18: Illustration of the array and a desk-check table for the `displayHighest` function

To understand the `displayHighest` function's code better:

1 Desk-check the `displayHighest` function's code shown in Figure 8-17. Use the array values shown in Figure 8-18 to perform the desk-check, then compare the values in your desk-check table to the values shown in Figure 8-18's desk-check table.

For your reference, the completed test score program is shown in Figure 8-19, and the contents of the test.dat file, which stores the eight student test scores, are shown in Figure 8-20.

```
//LaProg02.cpp
//this program allows the user to calculate the average and
//highest score stored in a numeric array

#include <iostream.h>
#include <fstream.h>

//function prototypes
char getMenuChoice();
void displayAverage(short [], short);
void displayHighest(short [], short);

void main()
{
    //declare and initialize variable
    char menuChoice = ' ';

    //declare and initialize numeric array
    short score[8] = {0};
```

main **function**

Figure 8-19: Completed test score program

```
        //open file for input
        ifstream inFile;
        inFile.open("test.dat", ios::in);

        //verify that open was successful
        if (!inFile.fail())          //open was successful
        {
            //enter test scores into the array
            for (short x = 0; x <= 7; x = x + 1)
                inFile >> score[x];
            //end for

            //close file
            inFile.close();

            //display menu and get menu choice
            menuChoice = getMenuChoice();

            while (menuChoice == '1' || menuChoice == '2')
            {
                if (menuChoice == '1')      //display average score
                    displayAverage(score, 8);
                else                        //display highest score
                    displayHighest(score, 8);
                //end if

                //display menu and get menu choice
                menuChoice = getMenuChoice();
            }//end while
        }
        else                        //open was not successful
            cout << "Error opening file." << endl;
        //end if (!inFile.fail())
} //end of main function

//*****programmer-defined function definitions*****
char getMenuChoice()
{
    //this function displays a menu and gets the user's choice

    char choice = ' ';

    //display menu
    cout << endl;
    cout << "Menu                    " << endl;
    cout << "1 Display average score" << endl;
    cout << "2 Display highest score" << endl;
    cout << "3 Exit program          " << endl;
    cout << "Enter your choice: ";

    //get user's menu choice
    cin >> choice;
    cin.ignore(100, '\n');

    return choice;
} //end of getMenuChoice function
```

main **function**

get MenuChoice **function**

Figure 8-19: Completed test score program (continues on next page)

array size

array

displayAverage function

displayHighest function

```
void displayAverage(short testScore[], short size)
{
    //this function displays the average test score
    short sum     = 0;
    float average = (float) 0.0;

    //accumulate scores
    for(short x = 0; x < size; x = x + 1)
        sum = sum + testScore[x];
    //end for

    //calculate average
    average = (float) sum / (float) x;

    //display average
    cout << endl << "The average test score is: "
        << average << endl;
} //end of displayAverage function

void displayHighest(short testScore[], short size)
{
    //this function displays the highest test score
    short highest = 0;

    //search for highest score
    highest = testScore[0];
    for(short x = 1; x < size; x = x + 1)
        if (testScore[x] > highest)
            highest = testScore[x];
        //end if
    //end for

    //display highest score
    cout << endl << "The highest test score is: "
        << highest << endl;
} //end of displayHighest function
```

Figure 8-19: Completed test score program (continued)

```
85
87
70
76
100
30
78
88
```

Figure 8-20: Contents of the test.dat file

Build and execute the test score program to observe how it works.

To observe how the test score program works:

1   Build and execute the LaProg02 program. The `main` function opens the test.dat file for input. It then reads the scores from the file into the `score` array. The `getMenuChoice` function in the program displays a menu along with the "Enter your choice: " prompt.

    Use the program to display the average score contained in the `score` array.

2   Type 1 and press the **Enter** key. The `displayAverage` function accumulates the eight scores stored in the array, and then calculates and displays the average score of 76.75. The menu and "Enter your choice: " prompt reappear.

    Now use the program to display the highest score stored in the array.

3   Type 2 and press the **Enter** key. The `displayHighest` function searches the array, element by element, for the highest test score and then displays that score—100—on the screen. The menu and "Enter your choice: " prompt appear on the screen again, as shown in Figure 8-21.

average test score

highest test score

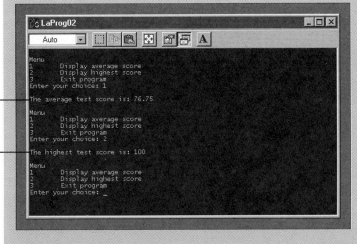

Figure 8-21: Average and highest test scores shown in the DOS window

    You can now exit the program.

4   Type 3 and press the **Enter** key to exit the program, then press the **Enter** key to close the DOS window.

    You are now finished with the test score program, so you can close it.

5   Close the workspace and the Output window.

The final program you will view in this lesson is one that updates the numbers stored in an array.

Updating the Elements in a Numeric Array

Assume that the Jillian Company has asked you to create a program that its sales manager can use either to increase or decrease the price of each item the company sells. The program should also display both the old and new prices. In addition to using the `main` function, you will use two programmer-defined functions named `displayPrices` and `updatePrices` in this program. The `displayPrices` function will display the old and new prices, and the `updatePrices` function will increase or decrease the price of each item. The IPO charts for the three functions in the price update program—main, displayPrices, and updatePrices—are shown in Figure 8-22.

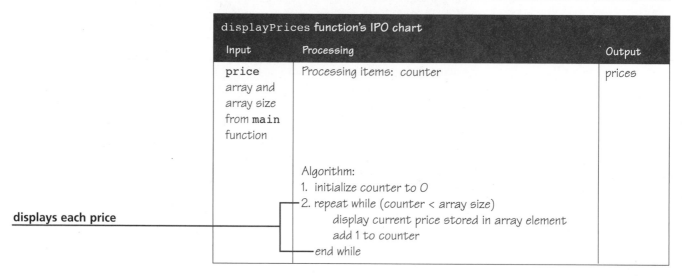

reads prices from file and stores in array

main function's IPO chart		
Input	Processing	Output

old prices stored in price.dat file	Processing items:
	      10-element Short Integer array named **price**
	      counter
	
	Algorithm:
	1. open price.dat file for input
	2. if (open is successful)
	    initialize counter to 0
	    repeat while (counter <= 9)
	       read a price from the file and store it in the array
	       add 1 to counter
	    end while (counter <= 9)
	    close file
	    display old prices (**displayPrices** function)
	    calculate new prices (**updatePrices** function)
	    display new prices (**displayPrices** function)
	else
	    display "Error opening file" message
	end if (open is successful)
		new prices

displays each price

displayPrices function's IPO chart		
Input	Processing	Output

price array and array size from **main** function	Processing items: counter
	
	Algorithm:
	1. initialize counter to 0
	2. repeat while (counter < array size)
	    display current price stored in array element
	    add 1 to counter
	end while
		prices

Figure 8-22: IPO charts for the main, displayPrices, and updatePrices functions in the price update program

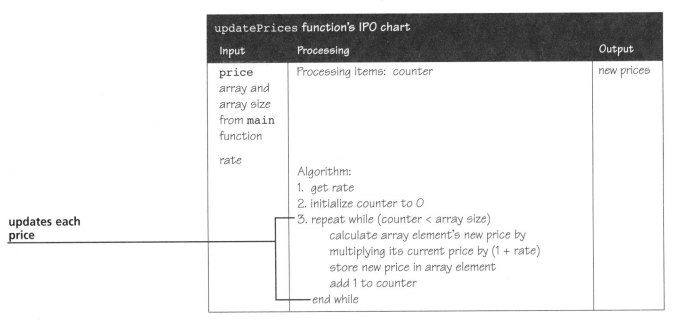

updates each price

Figure 8-22: IPO charts for the `main`, `displayPrices`, and `updatePrices` functions in the price update program (continued)

You will notice that the `main` function begins by opening the price.dat file, which contains the prices of the 10 items sold by Jillian Company. If the open is not successful, then an appropriate message is displayed. However, if the open is successful, then a counter-controlled loop is used to read each price from the price.dat file and store each price in the 10-element Short Integer `price` array.

After the 10 prices are stored in the array, the price.dat file is closed. The `main` function then calls the `displayPrices` function to display the current prices. You will notice that the algorithm in the `displayPrices` IPO chart indicates that the `displayPrices` function receives both the `price` array and the array's size from the `main` function and then uses a counter-controlled loop to display each price.

After the `displayPrices` function completes its task, the `main` function then calls the `updatePrices` function. If you review the algorithm in the `updatePrices` function's IPO chart, you will notice that the `updatePrices` function also receives both the `price` array and the array's size from the `main` function. The function then asks the user to enter the rate by which each item is to be increased or decreased. It then uses a counter-controlled loop to calculate the new price for each of the 10 items. When the `updatePrices` function completes its task, the `main` function calls the `displayPrices` function to display the new prices, after which the program ends.

On your computer's hard disk is a program that corresponds to the IPO charts shown in Figure 8-22. Open that program now.

To view the price update program:

1 Open the **LaProg03.cpp** file, which is located in the Cpp\Tut08\LaProg03 folder on your computer's hard disk. The LaProg03 program, which appears in the LaProg03.cpp window, is shown in Figure 8-23.

```cpp
//LaProg03.cpp
//this program updates the numbers stored in a numeric array

#include <iostream.h>
#include <fstream.h>
#include <iomanip.h>

//function prototypes
void displayPrices(float [], short);
void updatePrices (float [], short);

void main()
{
    //declare and initialize numeric array
    float price[10] = {(float) 0.0};

    //open file for input
    ifstream inFile;
    inFile.open("price.dat", ios::in);

    //verify that open was successful
    if (!inFile.fail())                 //open was successful
    {
        //enter prices into the array
        for(short x = 0; x <= 9; x = x + 1)
            inFile >> price[x];
        //end for

        //close file
        inFile.close();

        //display the old prices
        cout << endl << "Old prices" << endl;
        displayPrices(price, 10);

        //update the prices
        updatePrices(price, 10);

        //display new prices
        cout << endl << "New prices" << endl;
        displayPrices(price, 10);
    }
    else
        cout << "Error opening file." << endl;
    //end if
} //end of main function
```

reads prices and enters into array — (points to the for loop reading prices)

function calls — (points to the displayPrices and updatePrices calls)

Figure 8-23: Update price program

```
//*****programmer-defined function definitions*****
void displayPrices(float currentPrice[], short size)
{
    //this function displays the contents of the array
    cout << setprecision(2)
         << setiosflags(ios::fixed | ios::showpoint);

    for(short x = 0; x < size; x = x + 1)
        cout << currentPrice[x] << "  ";
    //end for
    cout << endl << endl;
} //end of displayPrices function

void updatePrices(float itemPrice[], short size)
{
    //this function updates the numbers stored in the array

    float rate = (float) 0.0;

    //get rate
    cout << endl << "Enter rate in decimal form: ";
    cin >> rate;
    cin.ignore(100, '\n');

    //update each price
    for(short x = 0; x < size; x = x + 1)
        itemPrice[x] = itemPrice[x] * ((float) 1 + rate);
    //end for
} //end of updatePrices function
```

displayPrices **function**

updatePrices **function**

Figure 8-23: Update price program (continued)

2 Build and execute the program.

The main function opens the price.dat file, which is also located in the Cpp\Tut08\LaProg03 folder on your computer's hard disk. The for loop within the main function reads each price from the price.dat file, one by one, and stores each in an element in the price array. After storing the prices in the array, the main function closes the price.dat file and calls the displayPrices function, passing it the price array and the array's size. (Recall that when you pass an array, C++ passes the address of its first element.) The displayPrices function displays the prices.

After the displayPrices function completes its task, the main function calls the updatePrices function, passing it the price array and the array's size. The updatePrices function asks you to enter a rate. Increase each price by 10 percent.

tip

You learned about the setprecision and setiosflags stream manipulators, as well as the iomanip.h header file, in Tutorial 4.

3 Enter **.1** as the rate and press the **Enter** key. The `updatePrices` function calculates the new price of each item.

When the `updatePrices` function completes its task, the `main` function calls the `displayPrices` function to display the new prices, as shown in Figure 8-24.

old prices

new prices are 10% higher than old prices

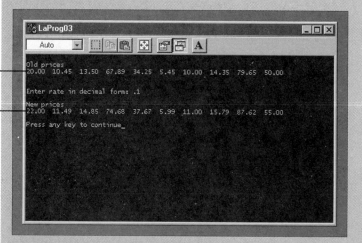

Figure 8-24: Old and new prices displayed in the DOS window

You will notice that each new price is 10 percent higher than its corresponding old price—for example, 22.00 is 10 percent (2.00) more than 20.00.

4 Press the **Enter** key to close the DOS window.

You are now finished with this program, so you can close it.

5 Close the workspace and the Output window.

mini-quiz

Mini-Quiz 2

When answering the following questions, assume that the program uses the `short quantity[5] = {0};` statement to declare and initialize a five-element array named `quantity`. The program also contains the `short totQuantity = 0;` and `short position = 0;` statements, which declare and initialize the `totQuantity` and `position` variables.

1. Write a `while` *condition* that verifies whether the `position` variable contains a valid subscript for the `quantity` array.

2. Write a statement that stores the number 5 in the first element of the `quantity` array.

3. Write a `for` loop that sums the values stored in the `quantity` array. Use x as the counter variable for the `for` loop, and use `totQuantity` as the accumulator variable.

4. Write a statement that reads a number from an input file and stores the number in element 5 of the `quantity` array. The name of the program's input file object is `inFile`.

5. Write a `while` loop that increases, by 2, each number stored in the `quantity` array. Use x as the counter variable for the `while` loop.

You have now completed Lesson A. In this lesson, you learned how to create and initialize a one-dimensional array, as well as how to enter data into the array and compute the average value stored in the array. You also learned how to find the highest value stored in an array, as well as how to update each element in the array. In Lesson B, you will learn about parallel arrays, which are simply two or more arrays whose elements are related in some way. You will also learn how to store a record in an array. For now, you can either take a break or complete the end-of-lesson questions and exercises.

SUMMARY

An array is a group of variables that have the same name and data type and are related in some way. You have used arrays previously in the tutorials. For example, the String variables that you learned how to create in Tutorial 3 are Character arrays.

The most commonly used arrays in business applications are one-dimensional and two-dimensional. A one-dimensional array is simply a column of variables. A two-dimensional array, on the other hand, resembles a table in that it has rows and columns. Programmers use arrays to store related data in the internal memory of the computer. By doing so, a programmer can increase the efficiency of a program because data stored inside the computer can be both written and read much faster than data stored in a file on a disk. Another advantage of using an array is that data can be entered into an array once, usually at the beginning of the program, and can then be used by the program as many times as desired.

You must create, or declare, an array before you can use it. You can use any C++ built-in data type to create an array. You can also use a programmer-defined data type to declare an array. It is a good programming practice to initialize the elements in an array. You can then use a variety of ways to enter data into the array. For example, you can enter data from the keyboard or from a file.

C++ assigns a unique number, called a subscript, to each of the array elements when you create the array. The first element in a one-dimensional array is always assigned a subscript of 0, the next element in the array is assigned a subscript of 1, and so on. Because the first array subscript is 0, the last subscript in an array is always one less than the number of elements. You refer to each element in the array by the array's name and the element's subscript, which is specified in a set of square brackets ([ ]) immediately following the name.

Unlike variables, arrays are always passed by reference rather than by value. When you pass an array, the address of only the first array element is passed to the receiving function. Because array elements are stored in contiguous locations in memory, the receiving function can use this address to locate the other elements.

ANSWERS TO MINI-QUIZZES

Mini-Quiz 1

1. `short number[20] = {0};`
2. `char firstName[10] = "";`   or   `char firstName[10] = {""};`
3. 0
4. 24
5. quantity sub 7

Mini-Quiz 2

1. ```
   while (position >= 0 && position < 5)  or
   while (position >= 0 && position <= 4)
   ```

2. ```
   quantity[0] = 5;
   ```

3. ```
   for(short x = 0; x < 5; x = x + 1)
       totQuantity = totQuantity + quantity[x];
   //end for
   ```

4. ```
   inFile >> quantity[5];
   ```

5. ```
   while (x <= 4)      or      while (x < 5)
   {
     quantity[x] = quantity[x] + 2;
     x = x + 1;
   }//end while
   ```

QUESTIONS

1. Which of the following is false?
   a. The elements in an array are related in some way.
   b. C++ automatically passes arrays by reference.
   c. All of the elements in an array have the same data type.
   d. All of the elements in an array have the same subscript.
   e. All of the elements in an array have the same name.

2. Elements in an array are identified by a unique _____ .
   a. data type
   b. order
   c. subscript
   d. symbol

3. `stock[2]` is read _____ .
   a. stock 2
   b. stock array 2
   c. stock bracket 2
   d. stock sub 2
   e. 2 sub stock

4. Which of the following is false?
   a. Data stored in an array can be accessed faster than data stored in a disk file.
   b. Data stored in an array needs to be entered only once, typically at the beginning of the program.
   c. Arrays allow the programmer to store information in the computer's internal memory.
   d. When using arrays, you will have fewer variable names to remember.
   e. None of the preceding statements are false.

5. Which of the following statements declares a one-dimensional Character array named `item` that consists of five elements?
   a. `char item[0 to 4] = "";`
   b. `char item[0 to 5] = "";`
   c. `char item[4] = "";`
   d. `char item[5] = "";`
   e. `string item[5] = ' ';`
   ```

Use the following array, named `empName`, to answer questions 6 through 8. The array was created with the following statement: `char empName[5] = "Mary";`.

M	a	r	y	\0

6. The `cout << empName[1]` statement will display _____ .
   a. M
   b. a
   c. r
   d. y
   e. the null character

7. The `empName[3] ='k';` statement will _____ .
   a. replace the letter r with the letter k
   b. replace the letter y with the letter k
   c. replace the letter k with the letter r
   d. replace the letter k with the letter y
   e. have no effect on the array

8. The `empName[0] = empName[2];` statement will _____ .
   a. replace the letter M with the letter r
   b. replace the letter r with the letter M
   c. replace the letter M with the letters Mr
   d. result in an error

Use the following array, named `sales`, to answer questions 9 through 13. The array was created with the following statement: `short sales[5] = {10000, 12000, 900, 500, 20000};`.

10000	12000	900	500	20000

9. The `sales[3] = sales[3] + 10;` statement will _____ .
   a. replace the 500 amount with 10
   b. replace the 500 amount with 510
   c. replace the 900 amount with 910
   d. result in an error
   e. none of the above

10. The `sales[4] = sales[4 − 2];` statement will _____ .
   a. replace the 20000 amount with 900
   b. replace the 20000 amount with 19998
   c. replace the 500 amount with 12000
   d. result in an error

11. The `cout << sales[0] + sales[1];` statement will _____ .
   a. display 22000
   b. display 10000 + 12000
   c. display `sales[0] + sales[1]`
   d. result in an error

12. Which of the following `if` clauses can be used to verify that the array subscript, called x, is valid for the `sales` array?

```
a. if (sales[x] >= 0 && sales[x] < 4)
b. if (sales[x] >= 0 && sales[x] <= 4)
c. if (sales[x] >= 0 && sales[x] >= 4)
d. if (x >= 0 && x < 4)
e. if (x >= 0 && x <= 4)
```

13. Which of the following will correctly add 100 to each variable in the `sales` array?

```
a. for (short x = 0; x <= 4; x = x + 1)
        x = x + 100;
   //end for
b. for (short x = 0; x <= 4; x = x + 1)
        sales = sales + 100;
   //end for
c. for (short sales = 0; sales <= 4; sales = sales + 100)
        x = x + 1;
   //end for
d. for (short x = 0; x < 4; x = x + 1)
        sales[x] = sales[x] + 100;
   //end for
```

Use the following array, named num, to answer questions 14 through 19. The array was created with the following statement: `short num[4] = {10, 5, 7, 2};`. Assume that total variable is declared as a Short Integer variable and that it is initialized to 0. Assume that the avg variable is declared as a Float variable and is initialized to 0.

14. Which of the following will correctly calculate and display the average of the num elements?

```
a. for (short x = 0; x < 4; x = x + 1)
        num[x] = total + total;
   //end for
   avg = (float) total / (float) x;
   cout << avg << endl;
b. for (short x = 0; x < 4; x = x + 1)
        total = total + num[x];
   //end for
   avg = (float) total / (float) x;
   cout << avg << endl;
c. for (short x = 0; x < 4; x = x + 1)
        num[x] = num[x] + total;
   //end for
   avg = (float) total / (float) x;
   cout << avg << endl;
d. for (short x = 0; x < 4; x = x + 1)
        total = total + num[x];
   //end for
   avg = (float) total / (float) x - (float) 1;
   cout << avg << endl;
e. for (short x = 0; x < 4; x = x + 1)
        total = total + num[x];
   //end for
   avg = (float) total / ((float) x - (float) 1);
   cout << avg << endl;
```

Only one of the five groups of code shown in question 14 will display the average of the num elements. What will the other groups of code display? Record your answers in questions 15 through 19.

15. The code in question 14's answer a will display _____ .
   a. 0
   b. 5
   c. 6
   d. 8

16. The code in question 14's answer b will display _____ .
   a. 0
   b. 5
   c. 6
   d. 8

17. The code in question 14's answer c will display _____ .
   a. 0
   b. 5
   c. 6
   d. 8

18. The code in question 14's answer d will display _____ .
   a. 0
   b. 5
   c. 6
   d. 8

19. The code in question 14's answer e will display _____ .
   a. 0
   b. 5
   c. 6
   d. 8

E X E R C I S E S

1. Write the statement to declare and initialize, to the empty string, a one-dimensional Character array named `partNumber`. The array should be able to store three characters and the null character.

2. Write the statement to declare a one-dimensional, 10-element Long Integer array named `population`. The statement should initialize each array element to 0.

3. a. Write the statement to declare and initialize, to the empty string, a one-dimensional Character array named `firstName`. The array should be able to store five characters and the null character.
   b. Write the assignment statement that will store the name Kevin in the array.
   c. Draw the one-dimensional `firstName` array. (*Hint*: Refer to Figure 8-1 in the tutorial.) Include each element's name and its contents in the drawing.
   d. Write the assignment statement that will store the name Susan, character by character, in the array.

4. a. Write the statement to declare a four-element, one-dimensional Float array named `sales`. The statement should initialize each array element to 0.
   b. Write the assignment statements that will assign the following four numbers to the array: 10000, 40000, 20000, and 5000.
   c. Draw the array. (*Hint*: Refer to Figure 8-1.) Include each element's name and its contents in the drawing.

5. a. Write the statement to declare a 10-element, one-dimensional Short Integer array named `quantity`. The statement should initialize each array element to 0.
    b. Write a programmer-defined function named `fillArray` that receives the `quantity` array, as well as the array's size, from the `main` function. The `fillArray` function should open a sequential access file named quantity.dat that contains 10 numbers. The function should fill the `quantity` array with the data contained in the file and then close the file.

6. In this exercise, you will modify an existing program so that it displays the lowest number contained in a one-dimensional array.
    a. Use C++ to open the test.dat file, which is located in the Cpp\Tut08\T8Ae06 folder on your computer's hard disk. Print the contents of the file, and then close the file.
    b. Open the T8Ae06.cpp file, which is located in the Cpp\Tut08\T8Ae06 folder on your computer's hard disk. This program is identical to the test score program that you viewed in Lesson A, except it handles 20 test scores rather than eight. Study the code.
    c. Change the "Exit program" option in the menu from option 3 to option 4. Be sure to modify the `while` loop so the program will stop when the user selects any option other than 1, 2, or 3.
    d. Add the following menu choice to the program: 3 Display lowest score.
    e. Create a function named `displayLowest` that will display the lowest score in the array.
    f. Save, build, and execute the program. Verify that each menu option works correctly. When the program is working correctly, print the code. On the code printout, circle all of the changes you made to the program, including those in steps c, d, and e. Also indicate the lowest score in the array.
    g. Close the Output window and the workspace.

7. In this exercise, you will modify an existing program so that it updates only specific elements in a one-dimensional array.
    a. Use C++ to open the price.dat file, which is located in the Cpp\Tut08\T8Ae07 folder on your computer's hard disk. Print the contents of the file, and then close the file.
    b. Open the T8Ae07.cpp file, which is located in the Cpp\Tut08\T8Ae07 folder on your computer's hard disk. This program is identical to the price update program that you viewed in Lesson A. Study the code.
    c. Assume that each of the 10 items is numbered 1 through 10. Modify the `updatePrices` function so that it asks the user which item number he or she wants to update before requesting the rate. For example, if the user wants to update item 1's price, which is stored in the first element of the array, the user will enter the number 1. (Remember, however, that the first element in an array has a subscript of 0.) Include a loop that will allow the user to modify as many prices as he or she desires.
    d. Save, build, and execute the program. Increase item 1's price by 20 percent, then increase item 3's price by 25 percent, and then decrease item 10's price by 15 percent. (*Hint:* To decrease a price, enter a negative rate.)
    e. When the program is working correctly, print the code. On the code printout, circle all of the changes you made to the program. Also indicate the new prices for items 1, 3, and 10.
    f. Close the Output window and the workspace.

8. In this exercise, you will modify an existing program so that it writes the contents of an updated array to a sequential access file.
    a. Use C++ to open the price.dat file, which is located in the Cpp\Tut08\T8Ae08 folder on your computer's hard disk. Print the contents of the file, and then close the file.
    b. Use C++ to open the T8Ae08.cpp file, which is located in the Cpp\Tut08\T8Ae08 folder on your computer's hard disk. This program is identical to the price update program that you viewed in Lesson A.

    c. Create a function named `writeUpdatedPrices`. The `main` function should call the `writeUpdatedPrices` function immediately after the `updatePrices` function. The `writeUpdatedPrices` function should write the contents of the updated array to the upprice.dat file.

    d. Save, build, and execute the program. Update the prices in the array by 15 percent.

    e. Print the code. On the code printout, circle all of the changes you made to the program.

    f. Use C++ to open and print the upprice.dat file, which is located in the Cpp\Tut08\T8Ae08 folder on your computer's hard disk. The prices on this printout should be 15 percent higher than the prices shown in the printout of the price.dat file from step a.

    g. Close the Output window and the workspace.

9. In this exercise, you will modify an existing program so that it displays the number of students earning a specific score.

    a. Use C++ open the scores.dat file, which is located in the Cpp\Tut08\T8Ae09 folder on your computer's hard disk. Print the contents of the file, and then close the file.

    b. Use C++ to open the T8Ae09.cpp file, which is located in the Cpp\Tut08\T8Ae09 folder on your computer's hard disk.

    c. Write a program that stores the contents of the scores.dat file in a Short Integer array. After filling the array with data, the program will allow the user to enter a score. The program will then display the number of students that earned that score. For example, if the user enters the number 100, the program will display the number 2 because two students earned that score.

    d. Save, build, and execute the program. Use the program to answer the following questions. (Use step a's printout of the scores.dat file to verify your answers.)

    How many students earned 72?

    How many students earned 88?

    How many students earned 20?

    How many students earned 99?

    e. When the program is working correctly, print the code. On the code printout, indicate the answers to the questions from step d.

    f. Close the Output window and the workspace.

10. In this exercise, you will modify an existing program so that it displays the number of students earning a score in a specific range.

    a. Use C++ to open the scores.dat file, which is located in the Cpp\Tut08\T8Ae10 folder on your computer's hard disk. Print the contents of the file, and then close the file.

    b. Use C++ to open the T8Ae10.cpp file, which is located in the Cpp\Tut08\T8Ae10 folder on your computer's hard disk.

    c. Write a program that stores the contents of the scores.dat file in a Short Integer array. After filling the array with data, the program will allow the user to enter a minimum score and a maximum score. The program will then display the number of students that earned a score within that range. For example, if the user enters a minimum score of 95 and a maximum score of 100, the program will display the number 4 because four students have scores within that range.

    d. Save, build, and execute the program. Use the program to answer the following questions. (Use step a's printout of the scores.dat file to verify your answers.)

    How many students earned scores between 70 and 79, including 70 and 79?

    How many students earned scores between 65 and 85, including 65 and 85?

    How many students earned scores between 0 and 50, including 0 and 50?

    e. When the program is working correctly, print the code. On the code printout, indicate the answers to the questions from step d.

    f. Close the Output window and the workspace.

discovery ▶ 11. In this exercise, you will display the contents of a Character array, character by character. You will also learn about the **strlen** function.

    a. Create a console application named T8Ae11 in the Cpp\Tut08 folder on your computer's hard disk.

    b. The string.h header file contains the **strlen** function. You use the **strlen** ("string length") function to determine the length of a string; its syntax is **strlen**(*string*). When calculating the length of the string, the **strlen** function ignores the null character. Write a program that prompts the user to enter a word, and then displays the word with each character on a separate line. For example, if the user enters the word *dog*, the program will display the letter d on one line, the letter o on the next line, and so forth. The word the user enters can be a maximum of nine characters long. (When declaring the string, be sure to include an additional array element for the null character.) You will need to use the **strlen** function to determine how many characters the user entered. Include a loop in the program that allows the user to enter as many words as desired. When the user enters the three letters XXX (in any case), the program should stop.

    c. Save, build, and execute the program. Test the program by entering the following words, one at a time: happy, computer, and hello.

    d. When the program is working correctly, print the code.

    e. Close the Output window and the workspace.

discovery ▶ 12. In this exercise, you will observe how arrays are initialized. This exercise will allow you to determine if your C++ system automatically initializes the uninitialized values in a numeric array. The program will also allow you to determine if your C++ system produces an error message when you list more values in the *initialValues* section than there are elements in the array.

    a. Open the T8Ae12.cpp file, which is located in the Cpp\Tut08\T8Ae12 folder on your computer's hard disk.

    b. Print the code, then study the code. You will notice that the *initialValues* section in each array declaration contains fewer values than there are elements in the array. To determine if your C++ system automatically initializes the uninitialized array elements, build and execute the program. The DOS window displays the contents of each array. Press the Enter key to close the DOS window. On a piece of paper, explain how your C++ system initializes numeric arrays.

    c. To determine if your C++ system produces an error message when you list more values in the *initialValues* section than there are elements in the array, change the `short num3[5] = {1, 2, 3};` statement in the program to `short num3[5] = {1, 2, 3, 4, 5, 6};`. Save and build the program. On a piece of paper, explain how your C++ system handles this error.

    d. Return the program to its original state by changing the `short num3[5] = {1, 2, 3, 4, 5, 6};` statement back to `short num3[5] = {1, 2, 3};`. Save the program.

    e. Close the Output window and the workspace.

debugging 13. In this exercise, you will debug a program.

    a. Use C++ to open the quantity.dat file, which is located in the Cpp\Tut08\T8Ae13 folder on your computer's hard disk. Print the contents of the file, and then close the file.

    b. Open the T8Ae13.cpp file, which is located in the Cpp\Tut08\T8Ae13 folder on your computer's hard disk. The program should display the quantities stored in the quantity.dat file. It should then prompt the user to enter the amount by which each quantity is to be increased or decreased.

    c. Build and execute the program. When prompted to enter a number, type 5 and press the Enter key. The DOS window shows both the old and new quantities. You will notice that the program is not working correctly.

d. Debug the program. When the program is working correctly, print the code. On the code printout, indicate what was wrong with the program. Also circle the corrections you needed to make to the program.

e. Close the Output window and the workspace.

debugging **14.** In this exercise, you will debug a program.

a. Use C++ to open the quantity.dat file, which is located in the Cpp\Tut08\T8Ae14 folder on your computer's hard disk. Print the contents of the file, and then close the file.

b. Open the T8Ae14.cpp file, which is located in the Cpp\Tut08\T8Ae14 folder on your computer's hard disk. The program should display the quantities stored in the quantity.dat file.

c. Build the program. Debug the program. When the program is working correctly, print the code. On the code printout, indicate what was wrong with the program. Also circle the corrections you needed to make to the program.

d. Close the Output window and the workspace.

LESSON B
objectives

In this lesson you will learn how to:

■ Manipulate parallel arrays

■ Search an array

■ Store records in an array

More on One-dimensional Arrays

Parallel Arrays

Parallel arrays are two or more arrays whose elements are related by their position—in other words, by their subscript—in the arrays. For example, you may have one array that stores employee job codes, and another array that stores the annual salaries that correspond to the codes, as shown in Figure 8-25.

code[0]	201	←→	25000	salary[0]
code[1]	212	←→	15000	salary[1]
code[2]	213	←→	23000	salary[2]
code[3]	315	←→	12000	salary[3]
code[4]	408	←→	35000	salary[4]

Figure 8-25: Illustration of parallel arrays

The arrays shown in Figure 8-25 are parallel because each element in the code array corresponds to the element located in the same position of the salary array. For example, the first element in the code array corresponds to the first element in the salary array—in other words, employees who have a job code of 201 (code[0]) earn $25000 (salary[0]) per year. Likewise, the second elements in both arrays—the elements with a subscript of 1—are also related; employees who have a job code of 212 earn an annual salary of $15000. The same relationship is true for the remaining elements in both arrays. If you want to know an employee's salary, locate the employee code in the code array and then view its corresponding element in the salary array. You will use parallel arrays to code the Colfax Industries program.

Using Parallel Arrays to Code the Colfax Industries Program

As you may remember from the case at the beginning of this tutorial, all Colfax Industries managers have a job code that determines their annual salary. Mr. Hendrickson, the personnel manager, wants a program that he can use to verify the salary assigned to a job code. You will use two parallel arrays to code this program. The first array, which you will name code, will store the job codes whereas the second array, which you will name salary, will store the salaries that correspond to the job codes.

You will also use two programmer-defined functions named `fillArray` and `searchAndDisplay` in the Colfax program. The `fillArray` function will read the job codes and salaries from the codes.dat file, which is located in the Cpp\Tut08\LbProg01 folder on your computer's hard disk, and store them in the `job` and `salary` arrays, respectively. The `searchAndDisplay` function will search the `code` array to see if it contains the job code whose salary the user wants to display. If the job code is in the `code` array, then the `searchAndDisplay` function will display its corresponding salary from the `salary` array. Otherwise, it will display a message indicating that the salary is not available. The IPO chart for the Colfax program's `main` function is shown in Figure 8-26.

Input	Processing	Output

codes and salaries stored in codes.dat file
 	
search code
	Processing items:
	    one 10-element Short Integer array named **code**
	    one 10-element Long Integer array named **salary**
	
	Algorithm:
	1. open codes.dat file for input
	2. if (open is successful)
	    read code and salary from file and store in arrays (**fillArray** function)
	    close file
	    get search code
	    repeat while (search code is not the number 0)
	        search **code** array and display salary or message (**searchAndDisplay** function)
	        get another search code
	    end while (search code is not the number 0)
	    else
	        display "Error opening file" message
	    end if (open is successful)
		salary or message

Figure 8-26: IPO chart for the Colfax program's `main` function

As Figure 8-26 indicates, the `main` function will open a file named codes.dat for input. The employee codes and salaries stored in the codes.dat file are shown in Figure 8-27. (Recall that the codes.dat file is located in the Cpp\Tut08\ LbProg01 folder on your computer's hard disk.)

```
201#25000
212#15000
213#23000
315#12000
408#35000
203#42500
406#14000
324#15000
234#11300
111#56000
```

Figure 8-27: Employee job codes and salaries stored in the codes.dat file

You will notice that the file contains 10 records, and that each record in the file has two fields, separated by the # symbol. The first field in each record is the code field, and the second field is the salary field. As you may remember from Tutorial 7, each record in the sequential access file ends with an invisible newline character.

According to the algorithm shown in Figure 8-26, if the codes.dat file is not opened successfully, then an appropriate message will be displayed. Otherwise, the main function will call the fillArray function both to read the data from the file and store the data in the code and salary arrays. When the fillArray function completes its task, the main function will close the codes.dat file before getting the search code from the user (the search code is simply the job code whose salary the user wants to display). If the user enters a search code of 0, then the program will stop. Otherwise, the instructions in the while loop will be processed.

As indicated in the algorithm, the first instruction in the while loop calls the searchAndDisplay function. Recall that the searchAndDisplay function's task is both to search the code array for the search code and display either its corresponding salary (if the code is in the array) or an appropriate message (if the code is not in the array). When the searchAndDisplay function completes its task, the main function will get another code from the user. The while loop will continue to process its instructions until the user enters the number 0 as the search code.

Your computer's hard disk contains a partially completed program that corresponds to the algorithm shown in Figure 8-26. Open that program now.

To open the partially completed Colfax Industries program:

1 Start Visual C++. Open the **LbProg01.cpp** file, which is located in the Cpp\Tut08\LbProg01 folder on your computer's hard disk. The Colfax Industries program appears in the LbProg01.cpp window. The program's partially completed main function is shown in Figure 8-28.

```
//LbProg01.cpp
//this program uses parallel arrays

#include <iostream.h>
#include <fstream.h>

//function prototypes
void fillArray();
void searchAndDisplay();

void main()
{
    //declare and initialize variable
    short searchCode = 0;

    //declare and initialize arrays

    //open file for input
    ifstream inFile;
    inFile.open("codes.dat", ios::in);
```

missing declaration statements

opens file

Figure 8-28: Partially completed main function in the Colfax Industries program

determines if open
was successful

closes file

gets search code

stops program

gets search code

displays message if
open failed

```
                    //verify that open was successful
                    if (!inFile.fail())          //open was successful
                    {
                        //fill arrays with data
                        fillArray();

                        //close file
                        inFile.close();

                        //get a code
                        cout << "Enter the code (0 to stop): ";
                        cin >> searchCode;
                        cin.ignore(100, '\n');

                        while (searchCode != 0)
                        {
                            //search the array for the code, display the salary
                            searchAndDisplay();

                            //get another code
                            cout << "Enter the code (0 to stop): ";
                            cin >> searchCode;
                            cin.ignore(100, '\n');
                        } //end while (searchCode != 0)
                    }
                    else                            //open was not successful
                        cout << "Error opening file." << endl;
                    //end if (!inFile.fail())
                } //end of main function
```

Figure 8-28: Partially completed `main` function in the Colfax Industries program (continued)

You will notice that the program includes the function prototypes for the two programmer-defined functions: `fillArray` and `searchAndDisplay`. Both of these functions are void functions.

The `main` function begins by declaring and initializing a Short Integer variable named `searchCode`, which the `main` function will use to store the job code whose salary the user wants to display. The `main` function should then declare and initialize the `code` and `salary` arrays. The code to accomplish this is missing from the program. The `code` array will need to store 10 numbers (job codes) in the Short Integer range and the `salary` array will need to store 10 numbers (salaries) in the Long Integer range. Enter the statements to declare the two arrays and initialize their elements to 0.

To begin completing the Colfax Industries program:

1   In the blank line below the `//declare and initialize arrays` comment, type **short code[10] = {0};** and press the **Enter** key, and then type **long salary[10] = {0};** and press the **Enter** key.

According to the algorithm shown in Figure 8-26, the `main` function should open the codes.dat file for input and then verify that the file was opened successfully. You will notice that the code to accomplish both tasks is already included in the program. If the open is not successful, then an appropriate message should be displayed. The `cout << "Error opening file." << endl;` statement in the `if` statement's false path handles this for you.

If the file is opened successfully, the `main` function should call the `fillArray` function to read the codes and salaries from the codes.dat file and store them in the `code` and `salary` arrays, respectively. For the `fillArray` function to read the information from the codes.dat file, the `main` function will need to pass the program's input file object (`inFile`), as well as the `code` and `salary` arrays and their size. You will need to complete the call to the `fillArray` function by entering its actual arguments.

To enter the actual arguments in the `fillArray` function call:

1 In the line below the `//fill arrays with data` comment, change `fillArray();` to **fillArray(inFile, code, salary, 10);**.

According to the algorithm, the main function should now close the file. The appropriate statement to do this, `inFile.close();`, is already entered in the program. After closing the file, the `main` function should get the search code—the code whose salary the user wants to display—and store the code in the `searchCode` variable. Note that the appropriate code is already entered in the program.

You will notice that the `while` loop's *condition* (`searchCode != 0`), which is already entered in the program, determines if the `searchCode` variable contains the number 0. If the user enters the number 0 as the search code, it means that the user wants to stop the program. If the `searchCode` variable does not contain the number 0, then the instructions in the `while` loop are processed.

According to the algorithm shown in Figure 8-26, the first instruction in the `while` loop is to call the `searchAndDisplay` function. Recall that the `searchAndDisplay` function will search the `code` array for the code stored in the `searchCode` variable and will then display either the corresponding salary or a message indicating that the salary is not available. For the `searchAndDisplay` function to perform its tasks, the `main` function will need to pass it the `searchCode` variable, as well as the `code` and `salary` arrays and their size. You will need to complete the call to the `searchAndDisplay` function by entering its actual arguments.

To enter the actual arguments in the `searchAndDisplay` function call:

1 In the line below the `//search the array for the code, display the salary` comment, change `searchAndDisplay();` to **searchAndDisplay (searchCode, code, salary, 10);**.

According to the algorithm shown in Figure 8-26, the last instruction in the `while` loop is to get another search code from the user. The code to do so is already entered in the program. The completed `main` function is shown in Figure 8-29.

```
//LbProg01.cpp
//this program uses parallel arrays

#include <iostream.h>
#include <fstream.h>

//function prototypes
void fillArray();
void searchAndDisplay();

void main()
{
    //declare and initialize variable
    short searchCode = 0;

    //declare and initialize arrays
    short code[10] = {0};
    long salary[10] = {0};

    //open file for input
    ifstream inFile;
    inFile.open("codes.dat", ios::in);

    //verify that open was successful
    if (!inFile.fail())             //open was successful
    {
        //fill arrays with data
        fillArray(inFile, code, salary, 10);

        //close file
        inFile.close();

        //get a code
        cout << "Enter the code (0 to stop): ";
        cin >> searchCode;
        cin.ignore(100, '\n');

        while (searchCode != 0)
        {
            //search the array for the code, display the salary
            searchAndDisplay(searchCode, code, salary, 10);

            //get another code
            cout << "Enter the code (0 to stop): ";
            cin >> searchCode;
            cin.ignore(100, '\n');
        } //end while (searchCode != 0)
    }
    else                            //open was not successful
        cout << "Error opening file." << endl;
    //end if (!inFile.fail())
} //end of main function
```

declares and
initializes arrays

opens file

calls function to fill
arrays with data

gets search code

calls function to
search the array

gets another search code

Figure 8-29: Completed main function in the Colfax program

Next, view the IPO chart for the fillArray function.

The `fillArray` Function

The IPO chart for the `fillArray` function is shown in Figure 8-30.

Input	Processing	Output

input file object named **inFile**, **code** array, **salary** array, and size of arrays from the **main** function	Processing items: counter
	
	Algorithm:
	1. initialize counter to 0
	2. repeat while (counter < array size)
	    read code and salary from file
	    store code in **code** array
	    store salary in **salary** array
	    add 1 to counter
	  end while
		codes and salaries stored in arrays

Figure 8-30: IPO chart for the `fillArray` function

According to the algorithm shown in Figure 8-30's IPO chart, the `fillArray` function will use a counter-controlled loop both to read the codes and salaries from the codes.dat file and store the codes and salaries in the appropriate array. You will notice that the Input column of the IPO chart indicates that the `fillArray` function will receive four items from the **main** function: the **main** function's input file object, which is named `inFile`, as well as its `code` and `salary` arrays and their size. When you code this function, you will need to provide a formal parameter for each of these four items. The formal parameter information for the `fillArray` function is currently missing from the program.

To complete the `fillArray` function, you will need to enter the formal parameter information in the function's header and in its prototype. You will use `inEmp` as the name of the formal parameter that represents the input file object. Because `inEmp` will receive an input file object—in this case, `inFile`—its data type will need to be `ifstream`. You will use `empCode` and `empSalary` as the names of the formal parameters that will receive the `code` and `salary` arrays and `size` as the name of the formal parameter that will receive the array size. To receive the Short Integer `code` array, the data type of the `empCode` formal parameter will need to be Short Integer. Likewise, the data type of the `empSalary` formal parameter will need to be Long Integer to receive the Long Integer `salary` array. To receive the array size—the numeric literal constant 10—the data type of the `size` formal parameter will be Short Integer. Complete the `fillArray` function by entering the missing formal parameter information in both the function's header and prototype.

To complete the `fillArray` function:

1 Modify the `fillArray` function's prototype and header as highlighted in Figure 8-31.

enter data types and [ ]
in the prototype

enter data type, name,
and [ ] in the header

pass the size
of the arrays

```
//LbProg01.cpp
//this program uses parallel arrays

#include <iostream.h>
#include <fstream.h>

//function prototypes
void fillArray(ifstream, short [], long [], short);
void searchAndDisplay();

    .
    .
    .
//*****programmer-defined function definitions*****
void fillArray(ifstream inEmp, short empCode[],
               long empSalary[], short size)
{
    //this function fills the arrays with data from a file
    for (short x = 0; x < size; x = x + 1)
    {
        //enter data from file into arrays
        inEmp >> empCode[x];
        inEmp.ignore(1);
        inEmp >> empSalary[x];
        inEmp.ignore(1);
    } //end for
} //end of fillArray function
```

Figure 8-31: Completed `fillArray` function

2   Save the program.

You will notice that the `fillArray` function uses a `for` loop to read the codes and salaries from the codes.dat file and store them in the arrays, element by element. The first time the loop is processed, the loop's counter variable, `x`, has a value of 0, and the `inEmp >> empCode[x];` statement within the loop reads the first code from the file and stores it in the `empCode[0]` element. The `inEmp.ignore(1);` statement that follows tells C++ to ignore the # symbol that separates the code from the salary in each record in the file. The `inEmp >> empSalary[x];` statement then reads a salary from the file and stores it in the appropriate element in the `empSalary` array. When x has a value of 0, the salary is stored in the `empSalary[0]` element. The `inFile.ignore(1);` statement that follows tells C++ to ignore the newline character that is located at the end of each record in the file. The `for` loop will continue processing its instructions until the 10 records are read from the codes.dat file and stored in the appropriate elements in the arrays.

Lastly, view the IPO chart for the `searchAndDisplay` function.

Recall that the valid subscripts for a 10-element array are the numbers 0 through 9.

The `searchAndDisplay` Function

The `searchAndDisplay` function will search the `code` array for the search code entered by the user and will display either the code's corresponding salary from the `salary` array or a message indicating that the salary is not available. The function's IPO chart is shown in Figure 8-32.

Input	Processing	Output

searchCode, code array, salary array, and size of arrays from the main function	Processing items:
	    counter
	      found variable
	
	Algorithm:
	1. initialize counter to 0
	2. initialize found variable to 'F'
	3. repeat while (counter < array size and found equals 'F')
	     if (array element's code equals the search code)
	        display salary
	        set found variable to 'T'
	     else
	        add 1 to counter
	     end if (array element's code equals the search code)
	   end while
	4. if (found variable equals 'F')
	    display the message "The salary is not available."
	   end if (found variable equals 'F')
		salary or message

Figure 8-32: IPO chart for the searchAndDisplay function

According to the algorithm, the function begins by initializing a counter to 0 and a variable named found to 'F' (which stands for *false*). The function will use the found variable to keep track of whether the search code is in the code array. When the function begins, the found variable is set to 'F' to indicate that, at this point, the code has not been located in the array.

The algorithm then uses a loop to search for the search code in the code array. You will notice that the loop will continue its processing as long as—or while—the counter is less than the size of the array and the found variable equals 'F'. In other words, it will continue processing its instructions while there are still array elements to search and the search code has not been found.

You will notice that the first instruction in the while loop compares the search code to the job code stored in the current array element. If both codes are the same, the code's corresponding salary is displayed and the found variable is set to 'T' to indicate that the code was found in the array. If the search code does not match the current array element's code, the counter is updated by the number 1 so that the search can continue in the next array element. The while loop will continue to process its instructions until either the found variable contains the value 'T' or the loop's counter variable contains the number 10.

When the while loop completes its processing, the program will use a selection structure to determine if the search code was found in the array, and display the appropriate message—in this case, "The salary is not available."—if it was not.

As the Input column of the IPO chart indicates, the searchAndDisplay function will need to receive the contents of the searchCode variable, as well as the code and salary arrays and their size, from the main function. When coding this function, you need to enter a formal parameter for each of these four items in the function's header and in its prototype. You will use inputCode as the name of the formal parameter that will receive the contents of the searchCode variable; its data type will be Short Integer. You will use empCode and empSalary as the names of the formal parameters that will receive the two arrays. Their data types will be Short Integer and Long Integer, respectively. You will use `size` as the name of the formal parameter that will receive the array size, and Short Integer as its data type. Before reviewing its code, you will complete the `searchAndDisplay` function by entering the missing formal parameter information in the function's header and prototype.

To complete the `searchAndDisplay` function:

1 Modify the `searchAndDisplay` function's prototype and header as highlighted in Figure 8-33.

```
//LbProg01.cpp
//this program uses parallel arrays

#include <iostream.h>
#include <fstream.h>

//function prototypes
void fillArray(ifstream, short [], long [], short);
void searchAndDisplay(short, short [], long [], short);

    .
    .
    .

//*****programmer-defined function definitions*****
    .
    .
    .
void searchAndDisplay(short inputCode,
                      short empCode[],
                      long empSalary[],
                      short size)
{
    //this function searches for the code in the empCode array
    //if the code is in the array, the salary is displayed
    //if the code is not in the array, a message is displayed

    short x = 0;
    char found = 'F';

    while(x < size && found == 'F')
    {
        if(empCode[x] == inputCode) //code is in the array
        {
            cout << "Salary: " << empSalary[x] << endl << endl;
            found = 'T';
        }
        else
            //add 1 to counter variable
            x = x + 1;
        //end if
    } //end while

    if(found == 'F') //code is not in the array
        cout << "The salary is not available." << endl << endl;
    //end if
} //end of searchAndDisplay function
```

Figure 8-33: Completed `searchAndDisplay` function

Following the algorithm shown in Figure 8-32, the `searchAndDisplay` function initializes a counter variable named x and a variable named `found` to 0 and 'F', respectively. The `while(x < size && found == 'F')` clause tells C++ to process the loop instructions as long as the counter variable, `x`, contains a value that is less than the array size (10) and the `found` variable contains the value 'F'. The selection structure within the loop compares the code stored in the current array element to the search code, which is stored in the `inputCode` formal parameter. If both codes match, the selection structure's true path displays the salary and assigns the value 'T' to the `found` variable to indicate that the code was found in the array. The next time the `while` loop's *condition* is evaluated, the `found` variable will contain 'T' and the loop will stop. If the code is already located in the array, there is no need to continue searching the `code` array.

However, if the code in the current array element does not match the search code, then the selection structure's false path updates the counter variable, `x`, by adding the number 1 to it. The search will then continue in the next array element.

The `while` loop will stop processing its instructions either when the entire array has been searched (`x` has a value of 10) or when the search code is located in the array (`found` has a value of 'T'). If, after searching the entire array, the search code was not found, then the selection structure below the `while` loop in the `searchAndDisplay` function displays an appropriate message. Execute the program to observe how it works.

To observe how the Colfax Industries program works:

1 Save, build, and execute the program. The program opens the codes.dat file for input, reads the codes and salaries from the file, stores them in the appropriate arrays, and then closes the file. You are now prompted to enter a code.

First enter a code that is in the `code` array—job code 408, for example.

2 Type **408** and press the **Enter** key. The DOS window shows that the salary for job code 408 is 35000. You are again prompted to enter a code.

Now enter a code that is not in the code array—job code 113, for example.

3 Type **113** and press the **Enter** key. The DOS window displays the message, "The salary is not available." You are again prompted to enter a code.

Stop the program by entering the number 0.

4 Type **0** and press the **Enter** key to stop the program, then press the **Enter** key to close the DOS window.

You have now completed this program, so you can close it.

5 Close the Output window and the workspace.

In the remaining sections of this lesson, you will learn how to use a record structure to code the Colfax Industries program. Recall that you learned how to use the C++ `struct` statement to create a record structure in Tutorial 7.

mini-quiz

Mini-Quiz 3

1. Assume that the socSecNum and empNum arrays are parallel. If an employee's Social Security number is stored in the socSecNum[3] element, where is his or her employee number located?

2. Assume that the socSecNum and empNum arrays are five-element, parallel arrays. The socSecNum array contains Social Security numbers, and the empNum array contains the employee numbers that correspond to the Social Security numbers. Write a while loop that will display the contents of both arrays. (Display a Social Security number, two spaces, and the corresponding employee number on each line.) You can use a counter variable named x.

Using a Record Structure in the Colfax Industries Program

As you learned in Lesson A, the values stored in the elements of an array must have the same data type. The data type can be either one of C++'s standard data types, or it can be a programmer-defined data type. You will use C++'s **struct** statement to create a programmer-defined data type that represents a Colfax Industries record—a job code and salary. You will then store each record in an array.

To modify the Colfax Industries program so that it uses a record structure:

1 Open the **LbProg02.cpp** file, which is located in the Cpp\Tut08\LbProg02 folder on your computer's hard disk. The Colfax Industries program appears in the LbProg02.cpp window. The program is identical to the LbProg01 program that you completed in the prior sections of this lesson, except the first comment refers to LbProg02.cpp, rather than LbProg01.cpp, and the second comment refers to a record structure rather than parallel arrays.

First you will define a record structure named jobInfo that will contain two fields: a Short Integer field named **code** and a Long Integer field named **salary**.

2 Enter the jobInfo record structure highlighted in Figure 8-34. (Be sure to enter the semicolon after the **struct** statement's closing brace.)

```
//LbProg02.cpp
//this program uses a record structure

#include <iostream.h>
#include <fstream.h>

struct jobInfo
{
        short code;
        long salary;
};

//function prototypes
void fillArray(ifstream, short [], long [], short);
void searchAndDisplay(short, short [], long [], short);

void main()
```

fields

be sure to enter the semicolon

Figure 8-34: jobInfo record structure entered in the Colfax Industries program

You won't need the `code` and `salary` arrays any more, so you can remove the `short code [10] = {0};` and `long salary[10] = {0};` statements from the `main` function. You will, however, need to declare and initialize an array of the `jobInfo` type. Each element in the array will be capable of storing a `jobInfo` record—a code and a salary. You will name the array `job`, and you will initialize the fields in each record in the array to 0.

3 Delete the `short code [10] = {0};` and `long salary[10] = {0};` statements, which appear below the `//declare and initialize arrays` comment in the `main` function.

4 Change the `//declare and initialize arrays` comment to **//declare and initialize the array**.

5 In the blank line below the `//declare and initialize the array` comment, type **jobInfo job [10] = {0, 0};** and press the **Enter** key. This statement creates a `jobInfo` array named `job` and also initializes the two fields in each record in the array to the number 0. (Recall from Tutorial 7 that braces are required in the syntax for initializing the fields in a record). See Figure 8-35.

```
//LbProg02.cpp
//this program uses a record structure

#include <iostream.h>
#include <fstream.h>

struct jobInfo
{
    short code;
    long salary;
};

//function prototypes
void fillArray(ifstream, short [], long [], short);
void searchAndDisplay(short, short [], long [], short);

void main()
{
    //declare and initialize variable
    short searchCode = 0;

    //declare and initialize the array
    jobInfo job[10] = {0, 0};

    //open file for input
    ifstream inFile;
    inFile.open("codes.dat", ios::in);

        .
        .
        .

} //end of main function
```

this statement replaces the two array declaration statements

initializes the code field

initializes the salary field

Figure 8-35: Array declared and initialized in the `main` function

6 Save the program.

Both the function prototypes and the function headers for the `fillArray` and `searchAndDisplay` functions also need to be modified. You will now need to pass the `job` array, rather than the individual arrays, to those two functions. You will also need to pass the size of the `job` array.

To pass the `job` array to the `fillArray` and `searchAndDisplay` functions appropriately:

1 Modify the `fillArray` and `searchAndDisplay` function prototypes and headers as highlighted in Figure 8-36.

```
//LbProg02.cpp
//this program uses a record structure

#include <iostream.h>
#include <fstream.h>

struct jobInfo
{
    short code;
    long salary;
};

//function prototypes
void fillArray(ifstream, jobInfo [], short);
void searchAndDisplay(short, jobInfo [], short);

    .
    .
    .

//*****programmer-defined function definitions*****
void fillArray(ifstream inEmp, jobInfo employ[], short size)
{
    .
    .
    .
} //end of fillArray function

void searchAndDisplay(short inputCode,
                      jobInfo employ[], short size)
{
    .
    .
    .
} //end of searchAndDisplay function
```

change the prototypes as shown

main **function's** code is not shown

change the headers as shown

Figure 8-36: Modified function prototypes and headers

You will also need to change the two statements that call the `fillArray` and `searchAndDisplay` functions so the statements pass the `job` array and its size rather than the `code` and `salary` arrays and their size.

2 Modify the two statements that call the `fillArray` and `searchAndDisplay` functions, highlighted in Figure 8-37.

```
//LbProg02.cpp
//this program uses a record structure

#include <iostream.h>
#include <fstream.h>

struct jobInfo
{
    short code;
    long salary;
};

//function prototypes
void fillArray(ifstream, jobInfo [], short);
void searchAndDisplay(short, jobInfo [], short);

void main()
{
    //declare and initialize variable
    short searchCode = 0;

    //declare and initialize the array
    jobInfo job[10] = {0, 0};

    //open file for input
    ifstream inFile;
    inFile.open("codes.dat", ios::in);

    //verify that open was successful
    if (!inFile.fail())            //open was successful
    {
        //fill arrays with data
        fillArray(inFile, job, 10);

        //close file
        inFile.close();

        //get a code
        cout << "Enter the code (0 to stop): ";
        cin >> searchCode;
        cin.ignore(100, '\n');

        while (searchCode != 0)
        {
            //search the array for the code, display the salary
            searchAndDisplay(searchCode, job, 10);

            //get another code
            cout << "Enter the code (0 to stop): ";
            cin >> searchCode;
            cin.ignore(100, '\n');
        } //end while (searchCode != 0)
    }
    else                           //open was not successful
        cout << "Error opening file." << endl;
    //end if (!inFile.fail())
} //end of main function
```

modify the function
call as shown

modify the function
call as shown

Figure 8-37: main function showing modified function call statements

3   Save the program.

To complete the modifications to the Colfax Industries program, only two minor changes need to be made to the `fillArray` and the `searchAndDisplay` functions. These changes will reflect the fact that the code and salary values are now fields in a record that is stored in an array.

To complete the modifications to the Colfax Industries program, then execute it:

1 Modify the `fillArray` and `searchAndDisplay` functions, making the changes highlighted in Figure 8-38.

```
//*****programmer-defined function definitions*****
void fillArray(ifstream inEmp, jobInfo employ[], short size)
{
    //this function fills the arrays with data from a file
    for (short x = 0; x < size; x = x + 1)
    {
        //enter data from file into arrays
        inEmp >> employ[x].code;
        inEmp.ignore(1);
        inEmp >> employ[x].salary;
        inEmp.ignore(1);
    } //end for
} //end of fillArray function

void searchAndDisplay(short inputCode,
                      jobInfo employ[], short size)
{
    //this function searches for the code in the array
    //if the code is in the array, the salary is displayed
    //if the code is not in the array, a message is displayed

    short x = 0;
    char found = 'F';

    while(x < size && found == 'F')
    {
        if(employ[x].code == inputCode) //code is in the array
        {
            cout << "Salary: " << employ[x].salary << endl << endl;
            found = 'T';
        }
        else
            //add 1 to counter variable
            x = x + 1;
        //end if
    } //end while

    if(found == 'F') //code is not in the array
        cout << "The salary is not available." << endl << endl;
    //end if
} //end of searchAndDisplay function
```

make these modifications

make this modification

make this modification

Figure 8-38: Modified `fillArray` and `searchAndDisplay` functions

The completed program is shown in Figure 8-39. All of the changes you made to the original program to accommodate the record structure are highlighted in the figure. (Recall, however, that you also removed the `short code[10] = {0};` and `long salary[10] = {0};` statements from below the `//declare and initialize the array` comment.)

```
//LbProg02.cpp
//this program uses a record structure

#include <iostream.h>
#include <fstream.h>

struct jobInfo
{
    short code;
    long salary;
};

//function prototypes
void fillArray(ifstream, jobInfo [], short);
void searchAndDisplay(short, jobInfo [], short);

void main()
{
    //declare and initialize variable
    short searchCode = 0;

    //declare and initialize the array
    jobInfo job[10] = {0, 0};

    //open file for input
    ifstream inFile;
    inFile.open("codes.dat", ios::in);

    //verify that open was successful
    if (!inFile.fail())      //open was successful
    {
        //fill arrays with data
        fillArray(inFile, job, 10);

        //close file
        inFile.close();

        //get a code
        cout << "Enter the code (0 to stop): ";
        cin >> searchCode;
        cin.ignore(100, '\n');

        while (searchCode != 0)
        {
            //search the array for the code, display the salary
            searchAndDisplay(searchCode, job, 10);

            //get another code
            cout << "Enter the code (0 to stop): ";
            cin >> searchCode;
            cin.ignore(100, '\n');
        } //end while (searchCode != 0)
    }
    else                              //open was not successful
        cout << "Error opening file." << endl;
    //end if (!inFile.fail())
} //end of main function
```

Figure 8-39: Completed Colfax Industries program with changes highlighted

```
//*****programmer-defined function definitions*****
void fillArray(ifstream inEmp, jobInfo employ[], short size)
{
    //this function fills the arrays with data from a file
    for (short x = 0; x < size; x = x + 1)
    {
        //enter data from file into arrays
        inEmp >> employ[x].code;
        inEmp.ignore(1);
        inEmp >> employ[x].salary;
        inEmp.ignore(1);
    } //end for
} //end of fillArray function

void searchAndDisplay(short inputCode,
                      jobInfo employ[], short size)
{
    //this function searches for the code in the array
    //if the code is in the array, the salary is displayed
    //if the code is not in the array, a message is displayed

    short x = 0;
    char found = 'F';

    while(x < size && found == 'F')
    {
        if(employ[x].code == inputCode) //code is in the array
        {
            cout << "Salary: " << employ[x].salary << endl << endl;
            found = 'T';
        }
        else
            //add 1 to counter variable
            x = x + 1;
        //end if
    } //end while

    if(found == 'F') //code is not in the array
        cout << "The salary is not available." << endl << endl;
    //end if
} //end of searchAndDisplay function
```

Figure 8-39: Completed Colfax Industries program with changes highlighted (continued)

2 Save, build, and execute the program.

Now try entering some job codes.

3 Enter a job code of **408**. The DOS window displays a salary of $35000 for this job code. Next, enter code **113**, which is not in the array. The DOS window displays the message, "The salary is not available." Type **0** as the job code and press the **Enter** key to stop the program.

4 Press the **Enter** key to close the DOS window. Close the Output window and the workspace.

mini-quiz

Mini-Quiz 4

1. Assume that `socSecNum` and `empNum` are fields defined in a record structure named `empInfo`. If the program declares an `empInfo` array named `employee`, then the employee number that corresponds to the Social Security number stored in the `employee[0].socSecNum` element of the array is located in the _____ element.

2. Assume that `socSecNum` and `empNum` are fields defined in a record structure named `empInfo`. Also assume that the program declares a five-element `empInfo` array named `employee`, and that the program fills the array with data from a file. Write a `while` loop that will display the contents of the array. (Display a Social Security number, two spaces, and the corresponding employee number on each line.) You can use a counter variable named `x`, which you can assume has already been declared and initialized to 0.

You have now completed Lesson B. You can either take a break or complete the end-of-lesson questions and exercises.

SUMMARY

Parallel arrays are two or more arrays whose elements are related by their position—in other words, by their subscript—in the arrays. For example, you may have a `partNum` array that contains the part numbers of the items you have in inventory, and a second array, named `quantity`, that contains the quantity on hand for each part number. If the two arrays are parallel, the part number stored in each element of the `partNum` array corresponds directly to the quantity stored in the same element of the `quantity` array.

After defining a record structure—a programmer-defined data type—you can then create an array of that type in the program. Each element in the array can then store a record.

ANSWERS TO MINI-QUIZZES

Mini-Quiz 3

1. `empNum[3]`

2.
```
while(x < 5)
{
    cout << socSecNum[x] << "  " << empNum[x] << endl;
    x = x + 1;
}//end while
```

Mini-Quiz 4

1. `employee[0].empNum`

2.
```
while(x <= 4)
{
    cout << employee[x].socSecNum
        << " " << employee[x].empNum << endl;
    x = x + 1;
}//end while
```

Q U E S T I O N S

1. Two or more arrays whose elements are related by their position (subscript) in the arrays are called _____ arrays.
   a. horizontal
   b. paired
   c. parallel
   d. related
   e. vertical

2. If the `code` and `fee` arrays are parallel, the fee that corresponds to the code stored in the `code[3]` element is located in the _____ element.
   a. `code[2]`
   b. `code[3]`
   c. `fee[2]`
   d. `fee[3]`
   e. The location is unknown given the information supplied in the question.

3. Assume that the `custNum` and `custDue` arrays are parallel numeric arrays and both have 10 elements. Which of the following can be used to display the amount due for customer number 34? (You can assume that the `x` and `found` variables have already been declared and initialized to 0 and 'F', respectively.)

```
a. while(x <= 9 and found == 'F')
       if(custNum[x] == 34)
           cout << custDue[x] << endl;
       else
           x = x + 1;
       //end if
   //end while
b. while(x <= 9 and found == 'F')
       if (custNum[x] == 34)
       {
           cout << custDue[x] << endl;
           found = 'T';
       }
       else
           x = x + 1;
       //end if
   //end while
```

```
c. while(x <= 9 and found == 'F')
        if (custNum[x] == 34)
        {
            cout << custDue[x] << endl;
            found = 'T';
        else
            x = x + 1;
        }//end if
    //end while
d. while(x <= 9 and found == 'F')
        if (custNum == 34)
        {
            cout << custDue << endl;
            found = 'T';
        else
        }
            x = x + 1;
        //end if
    //end while
```

Use the following record structure to answer questions 4 through 6.

```
struct feeInfo
{
    short code;
    short amount;
};
```

4. Which of the following statements will create and initialize a `feeInfo` array named `fee`?
   a. `fee feeInfo = {{0}, {0}};`
   b. `fee as feeInfo = 0, 0;`
   c. `feeInfo fee = 0, 0;`
   d. `feeInfo fee = [{0}, {0}];`
   e. `feeInfo fee = {0, 0};`

5. Which of the following will increase the value stored in the first element of the `fee` array by 2?
   a. `amount[0] = amount[0] + 2;`
   b. `amount.fee[0] = amount.fee[0] + 2;`
   c. `feeInfo.amount[0] = feeInfo.amount[0] + 2;`
   d. `fee[0].amount = fee[0].amount + 2;`
   e. `fee.amount[0] = fee.amount[0] + 2;`

6. Which of the following will display the fee amount associated with code 12, which is stored in the `fee[3].code` element?
   a. `cout << fee.code[3];`
   b. `cout << fee.amount[3];`
   c. `cout << fee[3].amount;`
   d. `cout << feeInfo[3].amount;`
   e. `cout << feeInfo.code[3];`

7. To pass an array by reference, you _____ .
   a. must include the address-of (&) operator before the array's name
   b. must include the number symbol (#) before the array's name
   c. do not have to do anything because arrays are automatically passed by reference

E X E R C I S E S

1. In this exercise, you will use two parallel arrays.

    Scenario: Ms. Jenkins uses the following grade table for her Introduction to Computers course.

Minimum points	Maximum points	Grade
0	299	F
300	349	D
350	399	C
400	449	B
450	500	A

   a. Create a console application named T8Be01 in the Cpp\Tut08 folder on your computer's hard disk.
   b. Store the minimum points in a one-dimensional array named `minPoints`. Store the grade in a parallel, one-dimensional array named `grade`. (*Hint*: You can initialize the arrays to the appropriate values when you create the arrays.) The program should display the appropriate grade after Ms. Jenkins enters the number of points earned by a student. The program should allow Ms. Jenkins to enter as many values as desired.
   c. Save, build, and execute the program. Test the program by entering the following amounts: 455, 210, 400, and 349.
   d. When the program is working correctly, print the code. Also indicate the grades displayed by the program in step c.
   e. Close the Output window and the workspace.

2. In this exercise, you will use a record structure and an array.
   a. Create a console application named T8Be02 in the Cpp\Tut08 folder on your computer's hard disk.
   b. Read and do Lesson B's Exercise 1, except use a structure to store both the minimum points and the grade.
   c. Save, build, and execute the program. Test the program by entering the following amounts: 455, 210, 400, and 349.
   d. When the program is working correctly, print the code. Also indicate the grades displayed by the program in step c.
   e. Close the Output window and the workspace.

3. In this exercise, you will modify an existing program. To complete this exercise, you will need to have completed either Lesson B's Exercise 1 or Exercise 2.
   a. Use Windows to copy either the T8Be01.cpp file (located in the Cpp\Tut08\T8Be01 folder) or the T8Be02.cpp file (located in the Cpp\Tut08\T8Be02 folder) to the Cpp\Tut08\T8Be03 folder on your computer's hard disk. Use Windows to rename the file as T8Be03.cpp.
   b. Open the T8Be03.cpp file. Modify the program so that it allows the instructor to enter the total number of points a student can earn in the course; the program should use this value to store the appropriate number of minimum points for each grade. Use the following table to determine the appropriate points to enter as the minimum number for each grade.

Minimum points	Grade
Less than 60% of total points	F
60% of total points	D
70% of total points	C
80% of total points	B
90% of total points	A

For example, if the instructor enters the number 500 as the total number of points a student can earn, the program should enter 450 (90 percent of 500) as the minimum number of points for an A. If the instructor enters the number 300, the program should enter 270 as the minimum number of points for an A.

c. Save, build, and execute the program. Test the program by entering 300 as the total number of points possible, then enter the following amounts: 185 and 159.

d. Execute the program again. This time enter 500 as the total number of points possible, then enter 363.

e. When the program is working correctly, print the code. Also indicate the grades displayed by the program in steps c and d.

f. Close the Output window and the workspace.

4. In this exercise, you will use three parallel numeric arrays. You will search one of the arrays and then display its corresponding values from the other two arrays.

a. Create a console application named T8Be04 in the Cpp\Tut08\T8Be04 folder on your computer's hard disk.

b. Write a program that uses three numeric arrays. Store the even numbers from 2 through 10 in the first array. Store the square of the even numbers from 2 through 10 in the second array using the pow function that you learned about in Tutorial 4. Store the square root of the even numbers from 2 through 10 in the third array using the sqrt function that you learned about in Tutorial 4.

After filling the arrays, the program should prompt the user to enter a number. The program should then search for the number in the first array, and then use the second and third arrays to display both the square and the square root of the number. Allow the user to display the square and square root for as many numbers as desired without having to execute the program again.

c. Save, build, and execute the program. Test the program by entering the following numbers, one at a time: 5, 10, 8, and 7.

d. When the program is working correctly, print the code. Also indicate the square and square roots displayed by the program in step c.

e. Close the Output window and the workspace.

5. In this exercise, you will use a record structure and an array. You will search one of the fields in the record and then display its corresponding values from the other two fields.

a. Create a console application named T8Be05. Read and do Lesson B's Exercise 4, except use a record structure to store the three numbers.

b. Save, build, and execute the program. Test the program by entering the following numbers, one at a time: 4, 9, 6, and 2.

c. When the program is working correctly, print the code. Also indicate the square and square roots displayed by the program in step b.

d. Close the Output window and the workspace.

6. In this exercise, you will count how many times a letter appears in a word.

a. Create a console application named T8Be06 in the Cpp\Tut08 folder on your computer's hard disk.

b. Write a program that prompts the user to enter a word. Store the word in a one-dimensional Character array that can store a maximum of 10 characters and the null character. After storing the word in the array, the program should then prompt the user to enter a letter. The program should count how many times the letter appears in the word, then display the value on the screen. The program should include a loop that allows the user to enter as many words as desired. It should also include a loop that allows the user to enter as many letters as desired. For example, if the user enters the word *ball*, the program should allow the user to count how many times the letter a appears in the word, how many times the letter x appears in the word, and so on. When the user is finished with one word, the program should allow him or her to enter another word.

c. Save, build, and execute the program. Test the program by entering the word *chalkboard*, then enter the letter k. The program should tell the user that the letter k appears once in the word. Now enter the letter a. The program should tell the user that the letter a appears twice in the word. Now enter the letter x. The program should tell the user that the letter x does not appear in the word. Stop the loop that allows the user to enter the letters.

d. Now enter the word *banana*, then enter the letter a. The program should tell the user that the letter a appears three times in the word. Stop the loop that enters the letters, and also stop the loop that enters the words.

e. When the program is working correctly, print the code.

f. Close the Output window and the workspace.

7. In this exercise, you will modify an existing program by adding a menu to it. (An example of a menu can be found in Lesson A's LaProg02.cpp file, which is located in the Cpp\Tut08\LaProg02 folder on your computer's hard disk.) To complete this exercise, you must have completed either Lesson B's Exercise 4 or Exercise 5.

a. Use Windows to copy either the T8Be04.cpp file (located in the Cpp\Tut08\T8Be04 folder) or the T8Be05.cpp file (located in the Cpp\Tut08\T8Be05 folder) to the Cpp\Tut08\T8Be07 folder on your computer's hard disk. Use Windows to rename the file as T8Be07.cpp.

b. Open the T8Be07.cpp file. Add a programmer-defined function that displays a menu with the following three choices: Display the square, Display the square root, and Exit the program. The function should also get the user's menu selection.

c. Save, build, and execute the program. Use the program to find the squares of the following numbers: 5 and 3. Use the program to find the square root of the following numbers: 8 and 5.

d. When the program is working correctly, print the code. Also indicate the square and square roots displayed by the program in step c.

e. Close the Output window and the workspace.

discovery ▶ 8. In this exercise, you will use a one-dimensional numeric array to store lotto numbers.

Scenario: Jacques Cousard has been playing the lotto for four years and has yet to win any money. He wants a program that will select the six lotto numbers for him. Each lotto number can range from 1 to 54 only. (An example of six lotto numbers is: 4, 8, 35, 15, 20, 3.)

a. Create a console application named T8Be08 in the Cpp\Tut08 folder on your computer's hard disk. Write a program that uses the `srand`, `rand`, and `time` functions, which you learned about in Tutorial 5, to generate 50 groups of six random lotto numbers—in other words, the six numbers 4, 8, 35, 15, 20, and 3 would be considered one group, and the six numbers 3, 54, 78, 21, 3, and 1 would be considered another group. Store the random numbers in a Short Integer array. Also send the 50 groups of random numbers to a file named T8Be08.dat. The program should prevent a number from appearing more than once in the same group—in other words, each number in the same group should be unique.

b. Save, build, and execute the program. When the program is working correctly, print the code. Also use C++ to open and print the contents of the T8Be08.dat file.

c. Close the Output window and the workspace.

discovery ▶ 9. In this exercise, you will search and update the contents of a numeric array. You will also create a menu. (An example of a menu can be found in Lesson A's LaProg02.cpp file, which is located in the Cpp\Tut08\LaProg02 folder on your computer's hard disk.)

Scenario: Jacob Wynn, the inventory manager at Parklane Inc., wants an application that he can use to keep track of each inventory item's quantity on hand. The program should display a menu that allows Mr. Wynn to do the following:

- record the purchase of an item (increase an item's quantity on hand)
- record the sale of an item (decrease an item's quantity on hand)
- display an item's quantity on hand
- write the updated information to the invent.dat file
- quit the program

a. Use C++ to open and print the invent.dat file, which is located in the Cpp\Tut08\T8Be09 folder on your computer's hard disk. This file contains the beginning inventory amount for the 10 items in Parklane's inventory. Each record contains two fields: the first field is the item's code, and the second is the beginning inventory amount for that item.

b. Use C++ to open the T8Be09.cpp file, which is located in the Cpp\Tut08\T8Be09 folder on your computer's hard disk. The program should use two arrays: one array will store the item codes, and the other will store the beginning inventory amounts.

c. Write the program according to the scenario outlined at the beginning of the exercise. *Hint:* While you are testing the program, write the updated information to a file other than the invent.dat file. This way, the invent.dat file will remain intact during the testing phase. When the program is working correctly, change the code to write the updated information to the invent.dat file. (If you want to return the invent.dat file to its original condition, use Windows to copy the invent.bak file to invent.dat.)

d. Save, build, and execute the program.

e. Use the program to record the following purchases:

Item code	Quantity purchased
11	50
78	100
22	50

f. Use the program to record the following sales:

Item code	Quantity sold
78	10
99	1
14	100

g. Use the program to display item 99's quantity on hand, then display item 78's quantity on hand.

h. Select the option that saves the updated information to the invent.dat file, then end the program.

i. Print the code, then use C++ to open and print the invent.dat file.

j. Close the Output window and the workspace.

discovery ▶ **10.** In this exercise, you will use parallel arrays to code the hangman game.

Scenario: On days when the weather is bad and the students cannot go outside to play, Mr. Mitchell, who teaches second grade at Hinsbrook School, spends recess time playing the hangman game with his class. Mr. Mitchell feels that the game is both fun—the students love playing it—and educational—the game allows the students to observe how letters are used to form words. Mr. Mitchell has asked you to write a program that the students can use to play the hangman game on the computer.

The hangman game requires at least two people to play. Currently, Mr. Mitchell thinks of a word that has a maximum of five letters. He then draws one dash (–) on the chalkboard for each letter in the word—for example, if the word is *baby*, he draws four dashes (––––) on the chalkboard. The student is then allowed to guess the word, letter by letter. If the student guesses a correct letter, Mr. Mitchell replaces the appropriate dash or dashes with the letter—for example, if the student guesses the letter b, Mr. Mitchell changes the four dashes on the chalkboard to b–b–. The student can continue to guess letters until he or she has made six incorrect guesses, at which time the game ends and Mr. Mitchell tells the student the word.

You will use two parallel arrays to code the hangman program. The first array, which you will name **word**, will store the word that the student needs to guess. The second array, which you will name **guesses**, will store a corresponding dash (hyphen) for each letter in the **word** array; as the student guesses correct letters, the program will replace the dashes in the **guesses** array with the correct letters. Both the **word** and **guesses** array will need to be six-element Character arrays. The IPO chart for the program's **main** function is shown in Figure 8-40.

Input	Processing	Output

word
 	
letter guess
	Processing items:
	    two six-element Character arrays
	    number of incorrect guesses counter
	
	1. get a word from the user, store word in the **word** array, store dashes in the guesses array (**getWord** function)
	2. repeat while (user has not exceeded six incorrect guesses and user has not guessed the word)
	    display contents of the **guesses** array
	    display number of guesses remaining
	    get a letter guess from the user (**getLetterGuess** function)
	    search **word** array for letter, replace dash with correct letter (**searchWord** function)
	  end while
	3. if (user guessed word)
	    display "Congratulations" message and contents of **word** array
	  else
	    display "Sorry" message and contents of **word** array
	  end if
		message
		
		number of incorrect guesses
		
		guesses
		
		word

Figure 8-40

As Figure 8-40 indicates, the main function will use a programmer-defined function named getWord to get a word from the user. The function will store the word in the word array; it will also store the appropriate number of dashes (–) in the guesses array. A while loop will then determine whether the user either has exceeded the maximum number of incorrect guesses (six) or has guessed the word. If the user has not exceeded the maximum number of guesses and he or she has not guessed the word, then the instructions within the while loop are processed. Those instructions first display both the contents of the guesses array and the number of guesses remaining. The loop instructions then call two programmer-defined functions, getLetterGuess and searchWord. The getLetterGuess function will simply get a letter from the user, and the searchWord function will search for the letter in the word array. If the letter is found in the word array, the searchWord function will replace the corresponding dash or dashes in the guesses array with the letter.

When the while loop ends, which is when the user has either exceeded the maximum number of incorrect guesses (six) or has guessed the word, a selection structure displays the appropriate message ("Congratulations" or "Sorry") along with the contents of the word array.

a. Create a console application named T8Be10 in the Cpp\Tut08 folder on your computer's hard disk.

b. Write a program that simulates the hangman game on the computer. You can either use the algorithm shown in Figure 8-40 or you can create and use your own algorithm.

c. Save, build, execute, and test the program. When the program is working correctly, print the code.

d. Close the Output window and the workspace.

discovery ▶ 11. In this exercise, you will use a record structure to store two parallel arrays.

a. Create a console application named T8Be11 in the Cpp\Tut08 folder on your computer's hard disk. Read and do Lesson B's Exercise 10, except use a record structure to store the word and guesses arrays.

b. Save, build, execute, and test the program. When the program is working correctly, print the code.

c. Close the Output window and the workspace.

debugging   12. In this exercise, you will debug a program.

a. Use C++ to open the numbers.dat file, which is located in the Cpp\Tut08\T8Be12 folder on your computer's hard disk. Print the contents of the file, and then close the file.

b. Use C++ to open the T8Be12.cpp file, which is located in the Cpp\Tut08\T8Be12 folder on your computer's hard disk. When the user enters a number from 1 through 9, the program should display the corresponding quantity. (Refer to the printout of the numbers.dat file from step a.)

c. Build and execute the program. When prompted to enter a number, type 3 and press the Enter key. You will notice that the program is not working correctly. Close the DOS window, then debug the program. Save, build, and execute the program again. When prompted to enter a number, type the number 3 and press the Enter key. The program should display the number 335; if it does not, you will need to continue debugging the program.

d. When the program is working correctly, print the code. On the code printout, summarize what was wrong with the program. Also circle the corrections you needed to make to the program.

e. Close the Output window and the workspace.

TUTORIAL

9

Two-dimensional Arrays

case ▶ Each year, Janet Hertel prepares the federal individual income tax returns for many of her friends and relatives. To make her job easier, Janet would like a program that she can use to display the amount of federal tax an individual owes. The amount of tax is based on the individual's taxable net income and his or her filing status—either single, married filing jointly, married filing separately, or head of household. Before you can create this program, you will need to learn how to declare and manipulate a two-dimensional array, which you will use to store the federal income tax table.

In this lesson you will learn how to:

- Create a two-dimensional array
- Enter data into a two-dimensional array
- Compute the average of a column in a two-dimensional array
- Find the highest entry in a column of a two-dimensional array

Two-dimensional Arrays

Arrays

As you learned in Tutorial 8, an array is a group of related variables. Each variable (element) in the array has the same data type and name; only the variables' subscripts differ. The most commonly used arrays in business applications are one-dimensional and two-dimensional arrays. Recall that a one-dimensional array is simply a column of elements, whereas a two-dimensional array, which you will learn about in this tutorial, resembles a table in that the elements are in rows and columns. Arrays having more than two dimensions, which are used in scientific and engineering programs, are beyond the scope of this book. Figure 9-1 illustrates both a one-dimensional and a two-dimensional array.

One-dimensional array

5
10
7
87
2

Two-dimensional array

8.55	1.65	7.53	5.45	1.24
3.46	1.89	8.76	2.34	7.89
9.87	4.56	7.32	1.34	5.78

Figure 9-1: Illustrations of a one-dimensional and a two-dimensional array

Creating and Initializing a Two-dimensional Array

As with one-dimensional arrays, you must create, or declare, a two-dimensional array before you can use it. Figure 9-2 compares the syntax for creating and initializing a one-dimensional array to the syntax for creating and initializing a two-dimensional array. The additional information required to create and initialize a two-dimensional array is highlighted in the figure.

One-dimensional array syntax:
datatype arrayname[*nElements*] = {*initialValues*};

Two-dimensional array syntax:
datatype arrayname[*nElements*] **[*nElements*]** = {{*initialValues*}, **{*initialValues*}, ...{*initialValues*}**};

Figure 9-2: Comparison of the syntax to create and initialize one-dimensional and two-dimensional arrays

Recall that you learned how to use the C++ `struct` statement to create a programmer-defined data type in Tutorial 7.

In both the one-dimensional and two-dimensional array syntax, *datatype* is the type of data the array elements will store. The *datatype* can be any of the C++ built-in data types or it can be a programmer-defined data type. In the syntax, *arrayname* is the name of the array and must follow the same rules as for variables.

You will notice that the two-dimensional array syntax includes an additional *nElements* enclosed in square brackets ([ ]) after the array's name. Recall that *nElements* in the one-dimensional array syntax represents the number of elements in the array. For example, an *nElements* value of [3] after the array name creates a three-element, one-dimensional array. When you create a two-dimensional array, however, the first *nElements* after the array name represents the number of rows in the array, and the second *nElements* represents the number of columns. To create an array that has three rows and four columns, for example, you would enter [3][4] after the array name. The number of rows in the syntax is listed first, followed by the number of columns. You can calculate the size of a two-dimensional array—in other words, the total number of elements in the array—by multiplying the number of rows by the number of columns. For example, a two-dimensional array created with [3][4] as the *nElements* values would contain a total of 12 (3 times 4) elements.

As discussed in Tutorial 8, you should always initialize the elements in an array. Recall that you can initialize the elements in a one-dimensional array at the same time you create the array simply by entering one or more values, separated by commas, in the *initialValues* section of the syntax. You can also initialize the elements in a two-dimensional array at the same time you create the array by entering a separate *initialValues* section, enclosed in braces, for each row in the array. For example, if the array has two rows, then the statement that declares and initializes the array can have a maximum of two *initialValues* sections. If the array has five rows, then the declaration statement will have a maximum of five *initialValues* sections.

Within the individual *initialValues* sections, you enter one or more values separated by commas. The maximum number of values you enter corresponds to the maximum number of columns in the array. For example, if the array contains 10 columns, then you can include up to 10 values in each *initialValues* section.

When declaring and initializing a two-dimensional array in Visual C++ version 5.0, you must include at least one initial value within a set of braces.

In addition to the set of braces that surrounds each individual *initialValues* section, you will notice in the syntax that a set of braces also surrounds all of the *initialValues* sections. Figure 9-3 shows some examples of creating and initializing two-dimensional arrays.

Example 1:

```
short num[2][4] = {{0},{0}};
```
or
```
short num[2][4] = {{0,0,0,0},{0,0,0,0}};
```

0	0	0	0
0	0	0	0

Example 2:

```
float price[2][4];
for(short row = 0; row < 2; row = row + 1)
   for(short col = 0; col < 4; col = col + 1)
      price[row][col] = (float) 0.0;
   //end for col
//end for row
```

0.0	0.0	0.0	0.0
0.0	0.0	0.0	0.0

Example 3:

```
short num[2][3] = {{1, 4, 9}, {2, 5, 8}};
```

1	4	9
2	5	8

Example 4:

```
short num[2][3] = {{1}, {4, 3}};
```

1	0	0
4	3	0

Example 5:

```
char name[4][6] = {{"Pat"}, {"Jean"}, {"Paul"}, {"Wanda"}};
```

P	a	t	\0		
J	e	a	n	\0	
P	a	u	l	\0	
W	a	n	d	a	\0

Example 6:

```
char grade[3][2] = {{'A', 'A'}, {'B', 'C'}, {'D', 'B'}};
```

A	A
B	C
D	B

Figure 9-3: Examples of creating and initializing two-dimensional arrays

tip

You will learn more about initializing two-dimensional arrays in Lesson A's Discovery Exercise 11.

Study carefully the examples shown in Figure 9-3. The first example shows that you can use either the `short num[2][4] = {{0}, {0}};` statement or the `short num[2][4] = {{0, 0, 0, 0}, {0, 0, 0, 0}};` statement to create and initialize a two-dimensional Short Integer array named num to 0. Notice that the latter statement provides an initial value for each of the eight elements in the array, whereas the former statement provides only one value for each row in the array. As you may remember from Tutorial 8, when you don't provide an initial value for each of the elements in a numeric array, C++ stores the number 0 in the uninitialized elements.

tip

As mentioned in Tutorial 8, although Visual C++ version 5.0 automatically initializes the uninitialized values in a numeric array, not all C++ systems do. If your C++ system does not automatically initialize the uninitialized elements, you will need to provide an initial value for each element when you declare the array. Optionally, you can omit the *initialValues* section in the statement that declares the array and then use a nested counter-controlled loop to assign the number 0 to each element in the array, as shown in Example 2 in Figure 9-3.

tip

If you provide more values in the *initialValues* section than the number of columns in the array, or if you provide more *initialValues* sections than there are rows in the array, Visual C++ version 5.0 will display a syntax error message when you attempt to compile the program. However, not all C++ systems will display this type of error message. Some systems will simply store the extra values in memory locations adjacent to, but not reserved for, the array.

tip

Recall that the double quotes around a string literal constant tell C++ to append the null character to the end of the string when it is stored in memory. A two-dimensional Character array that stores string literal constants is often referred to as a String array.

The second example in Figure 9-3 shows how you can first declare an array and then use a nested repetition structure—in this case, two `for` loops—to initialize each element in the array to 0. The third and fourth examples show how you can use values other than zero to initialize one or more elements in a numeric array. The `short num[2][3] = {{1, 4, 9}, {2, 5, 8}};` statement, for example, initializes the first row of array elements to the values 1, 4, and 9 and it initializes the second row to the values 2, 5, and 8. Notice that the statement contains an *initialValues* section for each of the two rows in the array, and that each *initialValues* section contains three values—one for each column in the array. C++ uses the values in the first *initialValues* section to initialize the first row in the array, and it uses the values in the second *initialValues* section to initialize the second row in the array.

The `short num[2][3] = {{1}, {4, 3}};` statement shown in Figure 9-3's Example 4 initializes the first element in the first row of the num array to the number 1, and it initializes the first and second elements in the second row of the array to the numbers 4 and 3, respectively. C++ initializes the remaining array elements to 0.

As you learned in Tutorial 8, C++ stores a string literal constant—for example, a person's name—in a one-dimensional Character array. However, if you wanted to store multiple items in an array, such as the names of all of your friends, you would need to use a two-dimensional Character array. Example 5 in Figure 9-3 shows how you can use the `char name[4][6] = {{"Pat"}, {"Jean"}, {"Paul"}, {"Wanda"}};` statement to create and initialize a two-dimensional Character array named name. The name array contains four rows and six columns. When initializing the name array, C++ stores the first string literal constant (in this case—the word "Pat" and the null character) in the first row of the array, and the second, third, and fourth string literal constants in the second, third, and fourth rows, respectively.

Two-dimensional Character arrays are used not only to store string literal constants, but character literal constants as well. The `char grade[3][2] = {{'A', 'A'}, {'B', 'C'}, {'D', 'B'}};` statement in Figure 9-3's Example 6, for instance, shows how you can use a two-dimensional Character array to store the midterm and final grades—each a character literal constant—earned by three students. The statement includes three *initialValues* sections—one for each row in the array. Within each *initialValues* section are two values—one for each column in the array. Unlike string literal constants, the character literal constants stored in an array do not end with the null character.

Now that you know how to create and initialize two-dimensional arrays, you will learn how you can refer to an element in a two-dimensional array.

Referring to an Element in a Two-dimensional Array

Recall that a unique number, called a subscript, identifies each element in a one-dimensional array. However, each element in a two-dimensional array is identified by a unique combination of two subscripts. The first subscript represents the element's row location in the array, and the second represents its column location. C++ assigns the subscripts to the elements when you create the array. The first row in a two-dimensional array is row 0, and the first column is column 0. You refer to each element in the array by the array's name and the element's subscripts. Each subscript is specified in its own set of square brackets (`[ ]`) immediately following the name. For example, `num[0][0]`—read "num sub zero zero"—refers to the first element in a two-dimensional array named num; the element is located in row 0, column 0 in the array. `grade[2][1]`—read "grade sub two one"—refers to the element located in row 2, column 1 of the grade array. Figure 9-4 illustrates this naming convention using both a two-dimensional Short Integer array named num and a two-dimensional Character array named grade.

tip

When initializing a two-dimensional Character array, you must enclose the *initialValues* section in a set of braces. Recall that the braces are optional when initializing a one-dimensional Character array.

Created and initialized:

```
short num[2][4] = {{0, 0, 0, 0}, {0, 0, 0, 0}};
```

num[0][0]	num[0][1]	num[0][2]	num[0][3]
0	0	0	0
0	0	0	0
num[1][0]	num[1][1]	num[1][2]	num[1][3]

Created and initialized:

```
char grade[3][2] = {{'A', 'A'}, {'B', 'C'}, {'D', 'B'}};
```

	grade[0][0]	grade[0][1]	
	A	A	
grade[1][0]	B	C	grade[1][1]
	D	B	
	grade[2][0]	grade[2][1]	

Figure 9-4: Names and subscripts of the elements in two two-dimensional arrays

As Figure 9-4 shows, each element in a two-dimensional array is identified by two subscripts: a row number and a column number. The row number is given first, then the column number is given. Notice that the last row subscript in a two-dimensional array is always one number less than the number of rows, and the last column subscript is always one number less than the number of columns. This is because the first row and column subscript in a two-dimensional array is 0.

After you create and initialize an array, you then can store data in it.

mini-quiz

Mini-Quiz 1

1. Write a statement that declares a four-row, two-column Short Integer array named `quantity`. The statement should initialize each element in the array to 0.

2. Write a statement that declares an eight-row, four-column Character array named `notes`. The statement should initialize the elements to the string literal constants "do", "re", "mi", "fa", "sol", "la", "ti", and "do".

3. Write a statement that declares a three-row, four-column Character array named `letters`. The statement should initialize the first row of elements to the character literal constants A, B, C, and D; the second row to E, F, G, and H; and the third row to I, J, K, and L.

4. A five-row, four-column array has a total of _____ elements.

5. `quantity[1][7]` is read _____.

6. A six-row, three-column array will have row subscripts of _____ through _____.

7. A six-row, three-column array will have column subscripts of _____ through _____.

Storing Data in a Two-dimensional Array

You can enter data into a two-dimensional array in a variety of ways. The examples shown in Figure 9-5, for instance, can be used to enter data into various two-dimensional arrays.

Example 1: Assume that the `item` array is a Character array that contains two rows and six columns.

```
strcpy(item[0], "Pen");
strcpy(item[1], "Chalk");
```

item array

P	e	n	\0		
C	h	a	l	k	\0

or

```
item[0][0] = 'P';
item[0][1] = 'e';
item[0][2] = 'n';
item[0][3] = '\0'
item[1][0] = 'C';
item[1][1] = 'h';
item[1][2] = 'a';
item[1][3] = 'l';
item[1][4] = 'k';
item[1][5] = '\0';
```

Example 2: Assume that the `grade` array is a Character array that contains three rows and two columns.

```
grade[0][0] = 'A';
grade[0][1] = 'B';
grade[1][0] = 'D';
grade[1][1] = 'C';
grade[2][0] = 'B';
grade[2][1] = 'A';
```

grade array

A	B
D	C
B	A

Example 3: Assume that the `num` array is a Short Integer array that contains three rows and three columns, and that the input file contains the numbers 1 through 9.

```
for(short row = 0; row < 3; row = row + 1)
   for(short col = 0; col < 3; col = col + 1)
        inFile >> num[row][col];
   //end for col
//end for row
```

num array

1	2	3
4	5	6
7	8	9

Example 4: Assume that the `num` array is a Short Integer array that contains three rows and three columns, and that the input file contains the numbers 1 through 9.

```
for(short col = 0; col < 3; column = col + 1)
   for(short row = 0; row < 3; row = row + 1)
        inFile >> num[row][col];
   //end for row
//end for column
```

num array

1	4	7
2	5	8
3	6	9

Figure 9-5: Examples of entering data into a two-dimensional array

The first example in Figure 9-5 shows two ways of assigning values to a two-dimensional Character array. You will notice that you can use the `strcpy` function, which you learned about in Tutorial 3, to assign a string literal constant to each row in the array. The `strcpy(item[0], "Pen");` statement, for example, will assign the word "Pen", followed by the null character, to the four elements located in the first row of the `item` array. The `strcpy(item[1], "Chalk");` statement will assign the word "Chalk" and the null character to the six elements located in the second row of the `item` array. Notice that you can refer to a row in a Character array simply by using the array name followed by the row subscript—in this case, `item[0]` and `item[1]`.

Example 1 also shows how you can enter a value, character by character, into a Character array. Like the `strcpy(item[0], "Pen");` statement, the four statements—`item[0][0] = 'P';`, `item[0][1] = 'e';`, `item[0][2] = 'n';`, and `item[0][3] = '\0';`—also assign the word "Pen" and the null character to the `item` array. Notice that it would take six assignment statements to assign the string literal constant "Chalk", character by character, to the second row in the `item` array.

Example 2 in Figure 9-5 shows how you can assign the character literal constants 'A', 'B', D', 'C', 'B', and 'A' to the elements in a two-dimensional Character array named `grade`. Unlike the string literal constants shown in Example 1, character literal constants do not end with the null character.

Examples 3 and 4 in Figure 9-5 use a nested repetition structure—in this case, two `for` loops—to read the numbers 1 through 9 from a file and enter the numbers in the `num` array. As you may recall from Tutorial 6, in a nested repetition structure, one loop, referred to as the inner loop, is placed entirely within another loop, called the outer loop. In Example 3, the `col` variable, which represents the column subscripts in the array, controls the processing of the inner loop, and the `row` variable, which represents the row subscripts in the array, controls the outer loop. In Example 4, this situation is reversed. The inner loop is controlled by the `row` variable, and the outer loop is controlled by the `col` variable.

The nested `for` loops shown in Figure 9-5's Example 3 enter the numbers into the array, row by row. **Row by row** means that the loops enter a value in each of the elements in one row before entering values in the next row. Therefore, row 0 is filled with values before row 1 is. The nested loop structure shown in Example 3, for instance, first initializes the `row` variable, which controls the outer loop, to 0. Because the `row` variable contains a value that is less than 3, the instructions in the outer loop are processed. The first instruction in the outer loop initializes the `col` variable, which controls the inner loop, to 0. Because the `col` variable contains a value that is less than 3, the instructions in the inner loop are processed. The first instruction in the inner loop—`inFile >> num[row][col];`—reads the first number from the input file and stores the number in the `num[0][0]` element in the array. This is because both the `row` and `col` variables currently contain the number 0.

After storing the first number in the array, the inner loop increments the `col` variable by 1, giving 1. The `col` variable still contains a value that is less than 3, so the `inFile >> num[row][col];` statement reads the second number from the input file and stores the number in the `num[0][1]` element. This is because the `row` variable currently contains the number 0, whereas the `col` variable contains the number 1.

After storing the second number in the array, the inner loop increments the `col` variable by 1, giving 2. The `col` variable still contains a value that is less than 3, so the statement `inFile >> num[row][col];` reads the third number from the input file and stores the number in the `num[0][2]` element in the array. This is because the row variable currently contains the number 0, whereas the column variable contains the number 2.

tip

Recall that the double quotes around a string literal constant tell C++ to append the null character to the end of the string when the string is stored in memory.

tip

You can tell if a nested repetition structure is entering the data row by row, or column by column, simply by looking at the outer loop. If the number of rows in the array controls the outer loop, then the data is being entered row by row. However, if the number of columns in the array controls the outer loop, then the data is being entered column by column.

After storing the third number in the array, the inner loop increments the `col` variable by 1, giving 3. Because the value in the `col` variable is not less than 3, the inner loop ends. At this point, the outer loop increments the `row` variable by 1, giving 1. The `row` variable's value is less than 3, so the outer loop instructions are processed again. Those instructions initialize the `col` variable to 0, and then read the next three numbers from the input file and store them in the `num[1][0]`, `num[1][1]`, and `num[1][2]` elements in the array. Figure 9-6 shows the values stored in the `row` and `col` variables and the `num` array after the inner loop completes each of its three processes. (The `num` array was initialized to 0 when it was created.)

Contents of `row`, `col`, and the `num` array after the inner loop is processed the first time

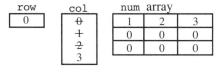

Contents of `row`, `col`, and the `num` array after the inner loop is processed the second time

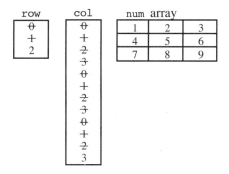

Contents of `row`, `col`, and the `num` array after the inner loop is processed the third time

Figure 9-6: Illustration of the row-by-row entry of data into an array

The nested `for` loops shown in Figure 9-5's Example 4 enter the numbers into the array column by column rather than row by row. **Column by column** means that the loops enter a value in each of the elements in one column before entering values in the next column. So column 0 is filled with values before column 1 is. The nested loop structure shown in Example 4, for instance, first initializes the `col` variable, which controls the outer loop, to 0. Because the `col` variable contains a value that is less than 3, the instructions in the outer loop are processed. The first instruction in the outer loop initializes the `row` variable, which controls the inner loop, to 0. Because the `row` variable contains a value that is less than 3, the instructions in the inner loop are processed. The first instruction in the inner loop, `inFile >> num[row][col];`, reads the first number from the input file and stores the number in the num[0][0] element in the array. This is because both the row and col variables currently contain the number 0.

After storing the first number in the array, the inner loop increments the row variable by 1, giving 1. The row variable still contains a value that is less than 3, so the inFile >> num[row][col]; statement reads the second number from the input file and stores the number in the num[1][0] element. This is because the row variable currently contains the number 1, whereas the col variable contains the number 0.

After storing the second number in the array, the inner loop increments the row variable by 1, giving 2. The row variable still contains a value that is less than 3, so the statement inFile >> num[row][col]; reads the third number from the input file and stores the number in the num[2][0] element in the array because, at this point, the row variable contains the number 2 and the column variable contains the number 0.

After storing the third number in the array, the inner loop increments the row variable by 1, giving 3. Because the value in the row variable is not less than 3, the inner loop ends. At this point, the outer loop increments the col variable by 1, giving 1. The col variable's value is less than 3, so the outer loop instructions are processed again. Those instructions initialize the row variable to 0, and then read the next three numbers from the input file and store them in the num[0][1], num[1][1], and num[2][1] elements in the array. Figure 9-7 shows the values stored in the row and col variables and the num array after the inner loop completes each of its three processes. (The num array was initialized to 0 when it was created.)

Contents of row, col, and the num array after the inner loop is processed the first time

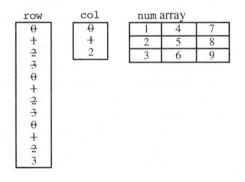

Contents of row, col, and the num array after the inner loop is processed the second time

Contents of row, col, and the num array after the inner loop is processed the third time

Figure 9-7: Illustration of the column-by-column entry of data into an array

You will now open a file that will allow you to observe how the row-by-row and column-by-column methods fill the num array with the data read from a file.

To open the array data-entry program:

1 Start Visual C++. Open the **LaProg01.cpp** file, which is located in the Cpp\Tut09\LaProg01 folder on your computer's hard disk. The array data entry program, which appears in the LaProg01.cpp window, is shown in Figure 9-8.

```cpp
//LaProg01.cpp
//this program demonstrates how to fill an array
//row by row and column by column

#include <iostream.h>
#include <fstream.h>

//function prototypes
void rowByRow(short [][3], short);
void colByCol(short [][3], short);
void displayArray(short [][3], short);

void main()
{
    //declare and initialize array
    short numbers[3][3] = {{0}, {0}, {0}};

    //fill array row by row
    rowByRow(numbers, 3);
    cout << "Array filled row by row" << endl;
    displayArray(numbers, 3);

    //fill array column by column
    colByCol(numbers, 3);
    cout << "Array filled column by column" << endl;
    displayArray(numbers, 3);

} //end of main function
```

declares and
initializes array

Figure 9-8: Array data-entry program (continues on next page)

enters data row by row

enters data column by column

displays contents of array

```cpp
//*****programmer-defined function definitions*****
void rowByRow(short num[][3], short numRows)
{
    ifstream inFile;
    inFile.open("numbers.dat", ios::in);
    if (!inFile.fail())
    {
        for(short row = 0; row < numRows; row = row + 1)
            for(short col = 0; col < 3; col = col + 1)
                inFile >> num[row][col];
            //end for col
        //end for row
        inFile.close();
    }
    else
        cout << "Error opening file." << endl;
    //end if
} //end of rowByRow function

void colByCol(short num[][3], short numRows)
{
    ifstream inFile;
    inFile.open("numbers.dat", ios::in);
    if(!inFile.fail())
    {
        for(short col = 0; col < 3; col = col + 1)
            for(short row = 0; row < numRows; row = row + 1)
                inFile >> num[row][col];
            //end for row
        //end for col
        inFile.close();
        cout << endl;
    }
    else
        cout << "Error opening file." << endl;
    //end if
} //end of colByCol function

void displayArray(short num[][3], short numRows)
{
    //display array row by row
    for(short row = 0; row < numRows; row = row + 1)
    {
        for(short col = 0; col < 3; col = col + 1)
            cout << num[row][col] << "  ";
        //end for col
        cout << endl;
    }//end for row
} //end of displayArray
```

Figure 9-8: Array data-entry program (continued)

You will notice that the program contains three programmer-defined void functions: rowByRow, colByCol, and displayArray. Each function is passed a two-dimensional Short Integer array and a value in the Short Integer range. When passing a two-dimensional array to a function, you leave the first set of brackets after the array name empty; recall that the first set of brackets represents the number of rows in the array. However, you must enter a value in the second set of brackets, which represents the number of columns in the array. In this case, the two-dimensional array passed to the `rowByRow`, `colByCol`, and `displayArray` functions will have three columns. The Short Integer value that is passed to each function will tell the function the number of rows in the array.

After declaring and initializing a two-dimensional Short Integer array named `numbers`, the `main` function calls the `rowByRow` programmer-defined function, passing it the `numbers` array and the numeric literal constant 3. The `rowByRow` function receives the array and the constant in its `num` and `numRows` formal parameters, respectively, and then opens the numbers.dat file, which is located in the Cpp\Tut09\LaProg01 folder on your computer's hard disk, for input. The numbers.dat file contains the numbers 1 through 9, with each number listed on a separate line in the file. If the numbers.dat file is opened successfully, the `rowByRow` function reads the nine numbers from the file and enters each into the array, row by row, before closing the file.

After the `rowByRow` function completes its task, the `main` function calls the `displayArray` function to display the contents of the array, after which the `main` function calls the `colByCol` function, passing it the `numbers` array and the numeric literal constant 3. The `colByCol` function receives the array and the constant in its `num` and `numRows` formal parameters, respectively, and then opens the numbers.dat file for input. If the file is opened successfully, the `colByCol` function reads the nine numbers from the file and enters each into the array, column by column, before closing the file. After the `colByCol` function completes its task, the `main` function calls the `displayArray` function to display the contents of the `num` array again. Execute the program to observe how the `rowByRow` and `colByCol` functions fill the `num` array with the nine numbers stored in the numbers.dat file.

As you learned in Tutorial 8, arrays in C++ are always passed, automatically, by reference. Recall that when you pass an array, the address of only the first array element is passed to the receiving function.

To observe how the `rowByRow` and `colByCol` functions fill the `num` array with data:

1. Build and execute the LaProg01 program. The contents of the `num` array, filled first row by row and then column by column, appear in the DOS window, as shown in Figure 9-9.

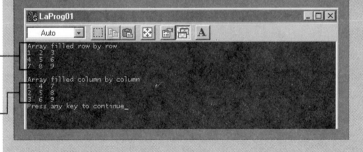

array filled row by row

array filled column by column

Figure 9-9: DOS window showing the `num` array filled row by row and column by column

2. Press the **Enter** key to close the DOS window.
    You are now finished with this program, so you can close it.
3. Close the Output window and the workspace.

In the remaining sections of Lesson A, you will either view or complete several programs that use a two-dimensional array. Begin by viewing a program that uses a two-dimensional Character array.

Using a Two-dimensional Character Array in a Program

Your computer's hard disk contains a program that uses a two-dimensional Character array to store the grades earned by three students on two tests. When you run the program, it will display the grades contained in the array and then allow you to change one or more grades. The purpose of this program is simply to make you comfortable with accessing the elements in a two-dimensional array. The IPO charts for the Character array demo program are shown in Figure 9-10.

`main` function

Input	Processing	Output

grades
answer
student number
test number
new grade
	Processing items:
	    three-row, two-column Character array
	
	Algorithm:
	1. display the grades stored in the array
	  (displayGrades function)
	2. get answer to "Do you want to change a grade?" question
	3. repeat while (answer is 'Y')
	    get the student number
	    get the test number
	    get the new grade and enter it into array
	    [student number][test number]
	    display the grades stored in the array
	    (displayGrades function)
	    get answer to "Do you want to change a grade?" question
	    end while
		new
		grade
		entered
		in array

`displayGrades` function

Input	Processing	Output

grades array
and number of
array rows from
main function
	Processing items:
	    row variable
	    column variable
	Algorithm:
	1. initialize row variable to 0
	2. repeat while (row variable is less than number of rows)
	    initialize column variable to 0
	    repeat while (column variable is less than 2)
	      display array element [row][column]
	    end while (column variable is less than 2)
	    end while (row variable is less than number of rows)
		grades

Figure 9-10: IPO charts for the Character array demo program

According to the `main` function's IPO chart, the program will use a Character array that has three rows—one for each student—and two columns—one for each grade. In other words, the first student's midterm grade will be stored in row 0, column 0 of the array, and his or her final grade will be stored in row 0, column 1.

Carefully study the `main` function's algorithm shown in its IPO chart. After calling a programmer-defined function named `displayGrades`, which simply displays the grades stored in the Character array, the `main` function will ask the user if he or she wants to change a grade. If not, the program will end; otherwise, the instructions in the `while` loop will be processed.

The first instruction in the `while` loop gets the number of the student whose grade the user wants to change. Recall that each student's grades are stored in a row in the array, so the valid student numbers are 0, 1, and 2 because these are the numbers that correspond to the row subscripts in a three-row array. If the user wants to change the first student's grade, then he or she will need to enter the number 0 as the student number.

The second instruction in the `while` loop gets the number of the test whose grade is to be changed. Recall that the test grades are entered in the two columns in the array. Therefore, the valid test numbers are 0 and 1 because these are the numbers that correspond to the column subscripts in a two-column array. If the user wants to change the final grade, for example, then he or she will need to enter the number 1 as the test number.

After the user enters both the student number and the test number, the next instruction in the `while` loop gets the new grade from the user. The grade will be stored in the array in the row specified by the student number and in the column specified by the test number. If, for example, the user enters the number 0 as the student number and the number 1 as the test number, then the grade will be stored in row 0, column 1 in the array.

After the grade is entered into the array, the next instruction in the `while` loop calls the `displayGrades` function to display the grades stored in the array. When the `displayGrades` function completes its task, the `main` function will ask the user if he or she wants to change another grade.

Figure 9-10 also shows the IPO chart for the `displayGrades` function. Notice that this function uses a nested repetition structure to display the contents of the `grades` array, which is passed to `displayGrades` by the `main` function, row by row. You will now open the two-dimensional Character array demo program to observe how it works.

You can tell that the displayGrades function is displaying the array row by row because the outer loop is controlled by the number of rows in the array.

To open the two-dimensional Character array demo program:

1   Open the **LaProg02.cpp** file, which is located in the Cpp\Tut09\LaProg02 folder on your computer's hard disk. The LaProg02 program appears in the LaProg02.cpp window, as shown in Figure 9-11.

```cpp
//LaProg02.cpp
//this program uses a two-dimensional Character array

#include <iostream.h>
#include <ctype.h>

//function prototype
void displayGrades(char [][2], short);

void main()
{
    //declare and initialize array
    char grades[3][2] = {{'A', 'A'}, {'B', 'C'}, {'D', 'B'}};

    //declare and initialize variable
    char answer  = ' ';
    short student = 0;
    short test    = 0;

    displayGrades(grades, 3);

    cout << "Do you want to change a grade? (Y/N): ";
    cin >> answer;
    cin.ignore(100, '\n');

    while (toupper(answer) == 'Y')
    {
        cout << endl << "Enter student number: ";
        cin >> student;
        cin.ignore(100, '\n');

        cout << "Enter test number: ";
        cin >> test;
        cin.ignore(100, '\n');

        cout << "Enter new grade: ";
        cin >> grades[student][test];
        cin.ignore(100, '\n');

        displayGrades(grades, 3);

        cout << "Do you want to change a grade? (Y/N): ";
        cin >> answer;
        cin.ignore(100, '\n');
    }//end while
} //end of main function
```

Figure 9-11: Character array demo program

```
//*****programmer-defined function definitions*****
void displayGrades(char studGrades[][2], short numRows)
{
    //this function displays the contents of the array
    cout << endl << "              0   1" << endl;
    for(short row = 0; row < numRows; row = row + 1)
    {
        cout << "Student " << row << ":   ";
        for(short col = 0; col < 2; col = col + 1)
            cout << studGrades[row][col] << "    ";
        cout << endl;
        //end for col
    } //end for row
} //end of displayGrades function
```

Figure 9-11: Character array demo program (continued)

You will notice that the `main` function uses a programmer-defined function named `displayGrades` and a two-dimensional Character array named `grades`. The `grades` array, which has three rows and two columns, is initialized to six character literal constants. The first set of constants, `{'A', 'A'}`, represents the midterm and final grades for the first student, the second set, `{'B', 'C'}`, represents the grades for the second student, and the third set, `{'D', 'B'}`, represents the grades for the third student.

After declaring and initializing the `grades` array, the `char answer = ' ';` statement declares and initializes a variable named `answer` that will store the user's response to the "Do you want to change a grade? (Y/N): " prompt. The `main` function also declares and initializes two Short Integer variables, `student` and `test`. The `student` variable will store the number of the student whose grade needs to be changed, and the `test` variable will store the test number.

Following the algorithm shown in Figure 9-10, the `main` function calls the `displayGrades` function and passes it the `grades` array and the numeric literal constant 3, which represents the number of rows in the array. The `displayGrades` function receives the array and the constant in its `studGrades` and `numRows` formal parameters, respectively, and then displays the contents of the array on the screen. When the `displayGrades` function completes its task, the `main` function asks the user if he or she wants to change a grade, and stores the user's response in the `answer` variable. The `while(toupper(answer) == 'Y')` clause compares the value stored in the `answer` variable to the character literal constant 'Y'. If the `while` *loop condition* evaluates to True, then the instructions in the `while` loop are processed.

The first six instructions within the `while` loop prompt the user to enter the student number and the test number, which are stored in the `student` and `test` variables, respectively. The user is then prompted to enter the new grade. You will notice that the `cin >> grades[student][test];` statement enters the new grade in the array element whose row location is stored in the `student` variable, and whose column location is stored in the `test` variable. If the `student` variable contains the number 0 and the `test` variable contains the number 1, for example, then the new grade will be stored in the `grades[0][1]` element in the array. After assigning the new grade to the appropriate array element, the `main` function calls the `displayGrades` function to display the contents of the `grades` array, after which the user is asked if he or she wants to change another grade.

Now study the code in the displayGrades function, which is also shown in Figure 9-11. The displayGrades function receives the grades array and the number 3, which are passed to it by the main function, in its studGrades and numRows formal parameters. A nested for loop is then used to display the grades, row by row, on the screen. Execute the program to observe how it works.

To observe how the Character array demo program works:

1   Build and execute the program. The contents of the grades array appear in the DOS window, and you are asked if you want to change a grade.

2   Type **y** and press the **Enter** key. You are prompted to enter the student number. Change Student 0's final grade from A to B. Student 0's final grade is stored in row 0, column 1.

3   Type **0** as the student number and press the **Enter** key. You are prompted to enter the test number. Type **1** and press the **Enter** key. You are prompted to enter the new grade. Type **B** and press the **Enter** key. The program replaces the letter A stored in the grades[0][1] element with the letter B. You are now asked if you want to change a grade.

4   Change Student 2's midterm grade—which is stored in row 2, column 0—from D to C.

5   Type **y** and press the **Enter** key. You are prompted to enter the student number. Type **2** as the student number and press the **Enter** key. You are prompted to enter the test number. Type **0** and press the **Enter** key. You are prompted to enter the new grade. Type **C** and press the **Enter** key. The program replaces the letter D stored in the grades[2][0] element with the letter C. You are now asked if you want to change a grade. Figure 9-12 shows the current contents of the grades array.

column subscripts

new final grade for student 0

new midterm grade for student 2

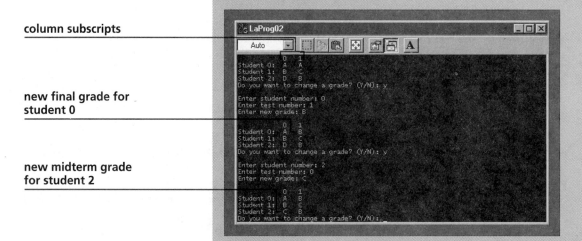

Figure 9-12: Current contents of the grades array

6   Type **n** and press the **Enter** key to stop the program, then press the **Enter** key to close the DOS window.

You are now finished with this program, so you can close it.

7   Close the Output window and the workspace.

In the next example, you will use a two-dimensional numeric array to store the sales amounts contained in a sequential access file.

Using a Numeric Two-dimensional Array in a Program

Conway Enterprises has both domestic and international sales. The company's sales manager has asked you to create a program that she can use to display the company's total sales during a six-month period. The program should also allow her to display both the total domestic and international sales for the period.

The six-month sales amounts for Conway Enterprises are stored in the sales.dat file, which is located in the Cpp\Tut09\LaProg03 folder on your computer's hard disk. Figure 9-13 shows the contents of the sales.dat file.

```
12000#10000
45000#56000
32000#42000
67000#23000
24000#12000
55000#34000
```

Figure 9-13: Conway Enterprises sales amounts entered in the sales.dat file

Notice that the fields in each record are separated by a # symbol.

Recall from Tutorial 7 that there is an invisible new-line character at the end of each record in the file.

The sales.dat file contains six records—one for each of the six months in the period. The first field in each record represents the domestic sales for the month, and the second field represents the international sales.

When analyzing this problem, you decide to use four programmer-defined functions: getMenuChoice, displayCompany, displayDomestic, and displayInter. You will have the getMenuChoice function display a menu with the following four choices: display company sales amount, display domestic sales amount, display international sales amount, and exit the program. The getMenuChoice function will be a value-returning function because it will need to return the user's selection from the menu. You will have the displayCompany function display the total sales amount for the company. The displayDomestic function's task will be to display the total domestic sales amount, and the displayInter function's task will be to display the total international sales amount. Since the displayCompany, displayDomestic, and displayInter functions will not need to return a value, you will make them void functions. The IPO chart for the main function in the Conway Enterprises program is shown in Figure 9-14.

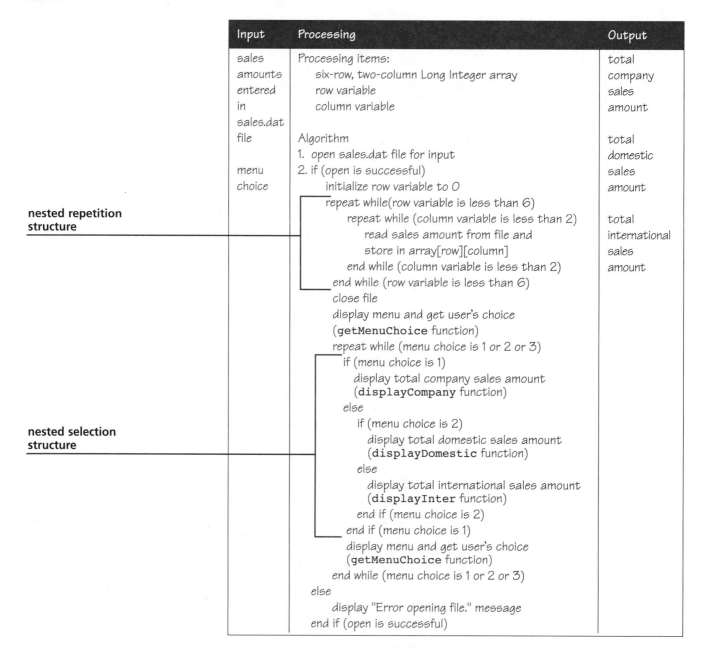

Input	Processing	Output

sales amounts entered in sales.dat file	Processing items:
	    six-row, two-column Long Integer array
	    row variable
	    column variable
		total company sales amount

menu choice	Algorithm
	1. open sales.dat file for input
	2. if (open is successful)
	    initialize row variable to 0
	    repeat while(row variable is less than 6)
	        repeat while (column variable is less than 2)
	            read sales amount from file and
	            store in array[row][column]
	        end while (column variable is less than 2)
	    end while (row variable is less than 6)
	    close file
	    display menu and get user's choice
	    (**getMenuChoice** function)
	    repeat while (menu choice is 1 or 2 or 3)
	        if (menu choice is 1)
	            display total company sales amount
	            (**displayCompany** function)
	        else
	            if (menu choice is 2)
	                display total domestic sales amount
	                (**displayDomestic** function)
	            else
	                display total international sales amount
	                (**displayInter** function)
	            end if (menu choice is 2)
	        end if (menu choice is 1)
	        display menu and get user's choice
	        (**getMenuChoice** function)
	    end while (menu choice is 1 or 2 or 3)
	else
	    display "Error opening file." message
	end if (open is successful)
		total domestic sales amount
		
		total international sales amount

nested repetition structure

nested selection structure

Figure 9-14: IPO chart for the **main** function in the Conway Enterprises program

According to the algorithm, the **main** function will begin by opening the sales.dat file for input. If the program encounters a problem when opening the file, the **main** function will display an appropriate message before the program ends; otherwise, a nested repetition structure will read the sales amounts from the file and store them in the array before the file is closed.

After storing the sales amounts in the array, the **main** function will call the **getMenuChoice** function both to display the menu and get and return the user's selection. The **main** function will use the value returned by the **getMenuChoice** function to determine whether the program should call another function or simply end. As the algorithm indicates, if the **getMenuChoice** function returns a menu choice that is not either the numbers 1, 2, or 3, the program will end. Otherwise, the main function uses a nested selection structure to determine which function to call. As the algorithm shows, the main function will call the displayCompany function if the menu choice is 1. However, if the menu choice is 2, then the main function calls the displayDomestic function. Lastly, if the menu choice is 3, the main function will call the displayInter function. After the appropriate function is called and completes its task, the main function will call the getMenuChoice function both to redisplay the menu and get another choice from the user.

On your computer's hard disk is a partially completed program that corresponds to the IPO chart shown in Figure 9-14. Open the program now.

To open the partially completed Conway Enterprises program:

1 Open the **LaProg03.cpp** file, which is located in the Cpp\Tut09\LaProg03 folder on your computer's hard disk. The Conway Enterprises program appears in the LaProg03.cpp window. The program's main function is shown in Figure 9-15.

```
//LaProg03.cpp
//this program displays the total company sales, the
//total domestic sales, and the total international sales
//for a six-month period

#include <iostream.h>
#include <fstream.h>

//function prototypes
char getMenuChoice();
void displayCompany(long [][2], short);
void displayDomestic(long [][2], short);
void displayInter(long [][2], short);

void main()
{
    //declare and initialize variable
    char  menuChoice = ' ';

    //declare and initialize numeric array
    long sales[6][2] = {{0}, {0}, {0}, {0}, {0}, {0}};

    //open file for input
    ifstream inFile;
    inFile.open("sales.dat", ios::in);

    //verify that open was successful
    if (!inFile.fail())
    {
        //enter sales into the array

        //close file
        inFile.close();
```

opens file

determines if
open was successful

missing instructions

Figure 9-15: main function in the partially completed Conway Enterprises program (continues on next page)

```
                //display menu
                menuChoice = getMenuChoice();

                while (menuChoice == '1' ||
                       menuChoice == '2' ||
                       menuChoice == '3')
                {
                    if (menuChoice == '1')
                        displayCompany(sales, 6);
                    else
                        if (menuChoice == '2')
                            displayDomestic(sales, 6);
                        else
                            displayInter(sales, 6);
                        //end if (menuChoice == '2')
                    //end if (menuChoice == '1')

                    //display menu
                    menuChoice = getMenuChoice();
                }//end while
            }
            else
                cout << "Error opening file." << endl;
            //end if (!inFile.fail())
        } //end of main function
```

displays message
if open failed

Figure 9-15: main function in the partially completed Conway Enterprises program (continued)

You will notice that the program contains the function prototypes for the four programmer-defined functions: getMenuChoice, displayCompany, displayDomestic, and displayInter. Only one of the functions, getMenuChoice, is a value-returning function; the other three are void functions. Notice that the three void functions will receive a two-dimensional Long Integer array, as well as a value in the Short Integer range, from the main function. This array will contain the Conway Enterprises sales amounts. The Short Integer value will tell each function the number of rows in the array.

The main function begins by declaring and initializing a Character variable named menuChoice. The main function will use this variable to store the value returned by the getMenuChoice function (recall that that value represents the user's selection from the menu). The main function also declares and initializes a six-row, two-column Long Integer array named sales. Each row in the array will represent one of the six months in the sales period. The first column in each row will store the domestic sales for that month, and the second column will store the international sales.

According to the algorithm shown in Figure 9-14, the main function should open the sales.dat file for input and then determine whether the file was opened successfully. You will notice that the code to accomplish both tasks is already entered in the program. If the open is not successful, then an appropriate message should be displayed. The cout << "Error opening file." << endl; statement in the if statement's false path handles this for you. If, on the other hand, the file is opened successfully, then the main function should use a nested repetition structure to read the sales amounts from the file and store them in the array. You will notice that the nested repetition structure is missing from the program.

When filling a numeric array with data, you must enter each value, one at a time, into the array. You will use a nested for loop to fill the sales array, row by row, with the 12 sales amounts stored in the sales.dat file. Because the sales array is a two-dimensional array, you will need one loop to keep track of the row number, and the other to keep track of the column number.

To complete the test score program's main function by entering the nested for loops:

1 Enter the nested for loops highlighted in Figure 9-16.

```cpp
//LaProg03.cpp
//this program displays the total company sales, the
//total domestic sales, and the total international sales
//for a six-month period

#include <iostream.h>
#include <fstream.h>

//function prototypes
char getMenuChoice();
void displayCompany(long [][2], short);
void displayDomestic(long [][2], short);
void displayInter(long [][2], short);

void main()
{
    //declare and initialize variable
    char  menuChoice = ' ';

    //declare and initialize numeric array
    long sales[6][2] = {{0}, {0}, {0}, {0}, {0}, {0}};

    //open file for input
    ifstream inFile;
    inFile.open("sales.dat", ios::in);

    //verify that open was successful
    if (!inFile.fail())
    {
        //enter sales into the array
        for(short row = 0; row < 6; row = row + 1)
            for(short col = 0; col < 2; col = col + 1)
            {
                inFile >> sales[row][col];
                inFile.ignore(1);
            } //end for col
        //end for row
```

enter this nested repetition structure

Figure 9-16: Completed main function (continues on next page)

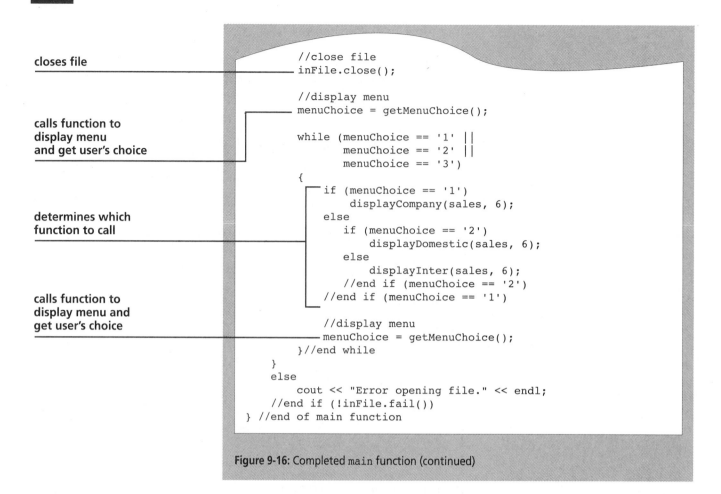

closes file

calls function to display menu and get user's choice

determines which function to call

calls function to display menu and get user's choice

```
//close file
inFile.close();

//display menu
menuChoice = getMenuChoice();

while (menuChoice == '1' ||
       menuChoice == '2' ||
       menuChoice == '3')
{
    if (menuChoice == '1')
        displayCompany(sales, 6);
    else
        if (menuChoice == '2')
            displayDomestic(sales, 6);
        else
            displayInter(sales, 6);
        //end if (menuChoice == '2')
    //end if (menuChoice == '1')

    //display menu
    menuChoice = getMenuChoice();
}//end while
    else
        cout << "Error opening file." << endl;
    //end if (!inFile.fail())
} //end of main function
```

Figure 9-16: Completed `main` function (continued)

The nested `for` loops highlighted in Figure 9-16 will read each sales amount from the sales.dat file and store each, row by row, in the `sales` array. The domestic sales amounts will be stored in the first column of the array, and the international sales amounts will be stored in the second column of the array, as shown in Figure 9-17.

domestic sales amounts stored in column 0

each row represents the sales for a month

international sales amounts stored in column 1

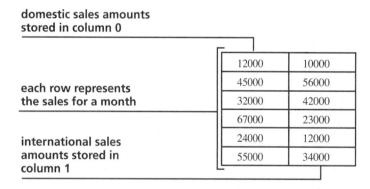

12000	10000
45000	56000
32000	42000
67000	23000
24000	12000
55000	34000

Figure 9-17: Domestic and international sales amounts entered in `sales` array

The next two steps in the algorithm shown in Figure 9-14 are to close the sales.dat file and call the value-returning getMenuChoice function both to display the menu and get the user's selection. The code to accomplish these tasks is already entered in the main function. You will notice that the main function assigns the value returned by the getMenuChoice function to the menuChoice variable.

According to the main function's algorithm shown in Figure 9-14, if the menuChoice variable contains a value other than the numbers 1, 2, or 3, then the program should end. Otherwise, the main function should use a nested selection structure to determine whether to call the displayCompany, displayDomestic, or displayInter functions. Recall that the main function will need to pass the sales array, as well as the number of rows in the array, to the function it calls. You will notice that the code to determine and call the appropriate function is already entered in the program.

The final task shown in the main function's algorithm is to call the getMenuChoice function to display the menu and get another choice from the user. The menuChoice = getMenuChoice(); statement in the program will handle this for you.

Now view the code in the getMenuChoice function, which is shown in Figure 9-18.

```
//*****programmer-defined function definitions*****
char getMenuChoice()
{
    //this function displays a menu and gets the user's choice
    char choice = ' ';
    //display menu
    cout << endl;
    cout << "Menu                                      " << endl;
    cout << "1  Display company sales amount       " << endl;
    cout << "2  Display domestic sales amount      " << endl;
    cout << "3  Display international sales amount" << endl;
    cout << "4  Exit the program                   " << endl;
    cout << "Enter your choice: ";

    //get user's menu choice
    cin >> choice;
    cin.ignore(100, '\n');

    return choice;
} //end of getMenuChoice function
```

Figure 9-18: getMenuChoice function

After declaring and initializing a local Character variable named choice, the getMenuChoice function displays a menu on the screen. The function then prompts the user to enter his or her choice, and then enters the user's response in the choice variable, whose value is returned to the main function.

Next, you will complete the displayCompany function.

The displayCompany Function

Recall that the displayCompany function should display the total sales for the company. To do so, the function will need to add together the values stored in each of the elements in the array. The IPO chart for the displayCompany function is shown in Figure 9-19.

Input	Processing	Output

sales array and number of array rows from **main** function	Processing items:
	    total company sales accumulator
	    row variable
	    column variable
	
	Algorithm
	1. initialize row variable to 0
	2. repeat while (row variable is less than number of rows)
	    initialize column variable to 0
	    repeat while (column variable is less than 2)
	        add sales amount from array[row][column]
	        to the total company sales accumulator
	        add 1 to column variable
	    end while (column variable is less than 2)
	    add 1 to row variable
	    end while (row variable is less than number of rows)
	3. display total company sales accumulator
		total company sales amount

Figure 9-19: IPO chart for the displayCompany function

The displayCompany function will use nested counter-controlled loops to add the value stored in each array element to the total company sales accumulator. After all of the values in the array are accumulated, the function will display the total company sales amount on the screen. You will now complete the displayCompany function in the current program by entering the code that will accumulate the sales amounts.

> To complete the displayCompany function:
>
> **1** Enter the nested repetition structure highlighted in Figure 9-20 in the displayCompany function, which is located in the programmer-defined section of the program.

```
void displayCompany(long saleData[][2], short numRows)
{
    //this function displays the total company sales
    long company = 0;

    //accumulate company sales
    for(short row = 0; row < numRows; row = row + 1)
        for(short col = 0; col < 2; col = col + 1)
            company = company + saleData[row][col];
        //end for col
    //end for row

    //display total company sales
    cout << endl << "Company sales: $" << company << endl;
} //end of displayCompany function
```

Figure 9-20: Completed `displayCompany` function

You will notice that the `displayCompany` function receives the two-dimensional `sales` array and the numeric literal constant 6, which are passed to it by the `main` function, in its `saleData` and `numRows` formal parameters, respectively. The nested repetition structure you entered will add together each of the values stored in the `saleData` array before displaying that value on the screen.

Next, you will complete the `displayDomestic` function.

The `displayDomestic` Function

Recall that the `displayDomestic` function should display the amount of the company's total domestic sales for the six-month period. To do so, the function will need to add together each of the values stored in the first column of the array—in other words, each of the amounts stored in column 0. (You can refer back to Figure 9-17 to see the location of the domestic sales in the array.) The `displayDomestic` function's IPO chart is shown in Figure 9-21.

Input	Processing	Output

sales array and number of array rows from **main** function	Processing items:
	    total domestic sales accumulator
	    row variable
	    column variable
	
	Algorithm
	1. initialize row variable to 0
	2. repeat while (row variable is less than number of rows)
	    add the sales amount from array[row][0] to the
	    total domestic sales accumulator
	    add 1 to the row variable
	  end while (row variable is less than number of rows)
	3. display total domestic sales accumulator
		total domestic sales amount

Figure 9-21: IPO chart for the `displayDomestic` function

The displayDomestic function uses a counter-controlled loop to add together the values stored in the first column of each row. The algorithm begins by initializing the row variable to 0. Because the row variable contains a value that is less than the number of rows in the array (6), the instructions within the while loop are processed. The "add the sales amount from array[row][0] to the total domestic sales accumulator" instruction adds the sales amount located in element [0][0] of the array to the accumulator. If you refer back to Figure 9-17, you will notice that the number 12000 is stored in the [0][0] element in the array. The next instruction in the loop, "add 1 to the row variable," updates the row variable by adding 1 to it, giving 1. When the loop is processed the second time, the "add the sales amount from array[row][0] to the total domestic sales accumulator" instruction adds the 45000 sales amount located in array element [1][0] to the accumulator. The "add 1 to the row variable" instruction then updates the row variable by adding 1 to it, giving 2. When the loop is processed the third time, the "add the sales amount from array[row][0] to the total domestic sales accumulator" instruction adds the 32000 sales amount located in array element [2][0] to the accumulator. The "add 1 to the row variable" instruction then updates the row variable by adding 1 to it, giving 3. During the fourth, fifth, and sixth processes of the loop, the "add the sales amount from array[row][0] to the total domestic sales accumulator" instruction will add the values stored in the [3][0] element, the [4][0] element, and the [5][0] element; those values are 67000, 24000, and 55000, respectively. Notice that the row number changes for each array element being added to the accumulator, but the column number remains at 0. The completed desk-check table is shown in Figure 9-22.

row	total domestic sales accumulator	number of array rows
~~0~~	~~12000~~	6
~~1~~	~~57000~~	
~~2~~	~~89000~~	
~~3~~	~~156000~~	
4	~~180000~~	
~~5~~	235000	
6		

Figure 9-22: Completed desk-check table for the displayDomestic function's algorithm

You can now complete the displayDomestic function in the current program by entering the counter-controlled loop that will add together the domestic sales amounts.

To complete the displayDomestic function:

1 Enter the repetition structure highlighted in Figure 9-23 in the displayDomestic function, which is located in the programmer-defined section of the program.

```
void displayDomestic(long saleData[][2], short numRows)
{
    //this function displays the total domestic sales
    long domestic = 0;

    //accumulate domestic sales
    for(short row = 0; row < numRows; row = row + 1)
        domestic = domestic + saleData[row][0];
    //end for row

    //display total domestic sales
    cout << endl << "Domestic sales: $" << domestic << endl;
} //end of displayDomestic function
```

Figure 9-23: Completed `displayDomestic` function

You will notice that the `displayDomestic` function receives the two-dimensional `sales` array and the numeric literal constant 6, which are passed to it by the `main` function, in its `saleData` and `numRows` formal parameters, respectively. The repetition structure that you entered will add together the company's domestic sales amounts, which are stored in the first column of the `saleData` array, before displaying that value on the screen.

Next, you will complete the `displayInter` function.

The `displayInter` Function

Recall that the `displayInter` function should display the amount of the company's total international sales for the six-month period. To do so, the function will need to add together each of the values stored in the second column of the array—in other words, each of the amounts stored in column 1. The `displayInter` function's IPO chart is shown in Figure 9-24.

Input	Processing	Output
`sales` array and number of array rows from `main` function	Processing items: 　　total international sales accumulator 　　row variable 　　column variable Algorithm 1. initialize row variable to 0 2. repeat while (row variable is less than number of rows) 　　　add the sales amount from array[row][1] to the total international sales accumulator 　　　add 1 to the row variable 　　end while (row variable is less than number of rows) 3. display total international sales accumulator	total international sales amount

Figure 9-24: IPO chart for the `displayInter` function

Refer back to Figure 9-17 to review the location of the international sales in the array.

The `displayInter` function uses a counter-controlled loop to add together the values stored in the second column of each row. The algorithm begins by initializing the row variable to 0. Because the row variable contains a value that is less than the number of rows in the array (6), the instructions within the `while` loop are processed. The "add the sales amount from array[row][1] to the total international sales accumulator" instruction adds the sales amount located in element [0][1] of the array to the accumulator. If you refer back to Figure 9-17, you will notice that the number 10000 is stored in the [0][1] element in the array. The next instruction in the loop, "add 1 to the row variable," updates the row variable by adding 1 to it, giving 1. When the loop is processed the second time, the "add the sales amount from array[row][1] to the total international sales accumulator" instruction adds the 56000 sales amount located in array element [1][1] to the accumulator. The "add 1 to the row variable" instruction then updates the row variable by adding 1 to it, giving 2. When the loop is processed the third time, the "add the sales amount from array[row][1] to the total international sales accumulator" instruction adds the 42000 sales amount located in array element [2][1] to the accumulator. The "add 1 to the row variable" instruction then updates the row variable by adding 1 to it, giving 3. During the fourth, fifth, and sixth processes of the loop, the "add the sales amount from array[row][1] to the total international sales accumulator" instruction will add the values stored in the [3][1] element, the [4][1] element, and the [5][1] element. Those values are 23000, 12000, and 34000, respectively. Notice that the row number changes for each array element being added to the accumulator, but the column number remains at 1. The completed desk-check table is shown in Figure 9-25.

row	total domestic sales accumulator	number of array rows
~~0~~	~~10000~~	6
~~1~~	~~66000~~	
~~2~~	~~108000~~	
~~3~~	~~131000~~	
4	~~143000~~	
~~5~~	177000	
6		

Figure 9-25: Completed desk-check table for the `displayInter` function's algorithm

You can now complete the `displayInter` function in the current program by entering the counter-controlled loop that will add together the international sales amounts.

To complete the `displayInter` function:

1 Enter the repetition structure highlighted in Figure 9-26 in the `displayInter` function, which is located in the programmer-defined section of the program.

```
void displayInter(long saleData[][2], short numRows)
{
    //this function displays the total international sales
    long inter = 0;

    //accumulate inter sales
    for(short row = 0; row < numRows; row = row + 1)
        inter = inter + saleData[row][1];
    //end for row

    //display total international sales
    cout << endl << "International sales: $" << inter << endl;
} //end of displayInter function
```

Figure 9-26: Completed `displayInter` function

Notice that the `displayInter` function receives the two-dimensional `sales` array and the numeric literal constant 6, which are passed to it by the `main` function, in its `saleData` and `numRows` formal parameters, respectively. The repetition structure that you entered will add together the company's international sales amounts, which are stored in the second column of the `saleData` array, before displaying that value on the screen. Build and execute the program to observe how it works.

To observe how the Conway Enterprises program works:

1 Save, build, and then execute the LaProg03 program. The program opens the sales.dat file for input and then reads the sales from the file into the `sales` array. The `getMenuChoice` function then displays a menu along with the "Enter your choice:" prompt. Use the program to display the total company sales amount.

2 Type **1** and press the **Enter** key. The DOS window indicates that the total company sales are $412000, as shown in Figure 9-27. The menu and "Enter your choice: " prompt redisplay.

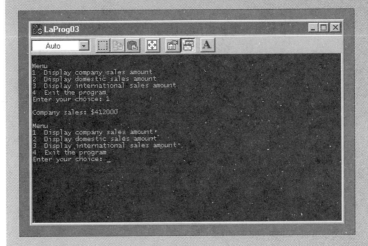

Figure 9-27: DOS window showing total company sales

Next, display the total domestic sales.

3 Type **2** and press the **Enter** key to display the total domestic sales. The `displayDomestic` function adds together the six sales amounts stored in the first column of the array, and then displays the total domestic sales amount of $235000. You will notice that this amount agrees with the desk-check table shown in Figure 9-22. The menu and "Enter your choice: " prompt appear on the screen again.

Now use the program to display the total international sales.

4 Type **3** and press the **Enter** key to display the total international sales. The `displayInter` function adds together the six sales amounts stored in the second column of the array, and then displays the total international sales amount of $177000. Notice that this amount agrees with the desk-check table shown in Figure 9-25.

Exit the program.

5 Type **4** and press the **Enter** key to exit the program, then press the **Enter** key to close the DOS window.

You have now completed this program, so you can close it.

6 Close the workspace and the Output window.

mini-quiz

Mini-Quiz 2

1. Assume a program declares a two-dimensional Character array as follows: `code[4][5]`. Write the statement that will assign the letter E to the element located in the second row, third column of the array.

2. Assume a program declares a two-dimensional Character array as follows: `code[4][5]`. Write the statement that will assign the string literal constant "H123" to the element located in the last row of the array.

3. Write a statement that stores the number 5 in the second row, third column of a two-dimensional array named `quantity`.

4. Write a `for` loop that sums the values stored in a two-dimensional Short Integer array named `quantity`. The array contains three rows and four columns. The accumulator variable is a Short Integer variable named `totQuantity`. Use `row` and `col` as the counter variables for the `for` loops. (You can assume that `totQuantity` has already been declared and initialized.) Sum the values row by row.

5. Write a statement that reads a number from `inFile` and stores the number in the first row, first column of an array named `quantity`.

You have now completed Lesson A. In this lesson, you learned how to declare, initialize, and access the elements in a two-dimensional array. You also learned how to add together the values stored in each of the array elements, as well as how to add together only the values stored in a column of the array. In Lesson B, you will learn how to update each element in a two-dimensional array. Before beginning Lesson B, you can either take a break or complete the end-of-lesson questions and exercises.

S U M M A R Y

An array is a group of related variables that have the same name and data type, but different subscripts. Each variable in the array is referred to as an element of the array. The most commonly used arrays in business applications are one-dimensional and two-dimensional. A one-dimensional array is simply a column of elements, whereas a two-dimensional array resembles a table in that the elements are in rows and columns.

The syntax for creating and initializing a two-dimensional array is similar to the syntax for creating and initializing a one-dimensional array. The two-dimensional array syntax, however, requires the programmer to provide two, rather than one, *nElements* values after the array name. The first *nElements* value represents the number of rows in the array, and the second *nElements* value represents the number of columns. As with a one-dimensional array, you can also initialize a two-dimensional array at the same time you create the array.

Just as each element in a one-dimensional array is identified by a unique number, called a subscript, each element in a two-dimensional array is identified by a unique combination of two subscripts. The first subscript represents the element's row location in the array, and the second represents its column location. C++ assigns the subscripts to the elements when you create the array. The first row subscript in a two-dimensional array is 0. The first column subscript is also 0.

After you create and initialize an array, you can then use a variety of methods to store other data in it. For example, you can use an assignment statement or you can enter data into the array from the keyboard. You can also read data from a file and store the data in the array.

You can refer to each row in a two-dimensional Character array simply by using the array's name followed by the row number. To refer to an individual element in a two-dimensional Character array, you use both a row and column number after the array name.

To fill a numeric array with data, you must enter each value, one at a time, into the array. You can use a nested repetition structure to do so. You can also use a nested repetition structure to add together the values stored in each element in the array. Adding the values stored in either a column or a row of the array, however, requires only one loop.

A N S W E R S   T O   M I N I - Q U I Z Z E S

Mini-Quiz 1

1. `short quantity[4][2] = {{0},{0},{0},{0}};`

2. `char notes[8][4] = {{"do"}, {"re"}, {"mi"}, {"fa"}, {"sol"}, {"la"}, {"ti"}, {"do"}};`

3. `char letters[3][4] = {{'A', 'B', 'C', 'D'}, {'E', 'F', 'G', 'H'}, {'I', 'J', 'K', 'L'}};`

4. 20

5. `quantity` sub one seven

6. 0, 5

7. 0, 2

Mini-Quiz 2

1. `code[1][2] = 'E';`
2. `strcpy(code[3], "H123");`
3. `quantity[1][2] = 5;`
4. ```
   for(short row = 0; row < 3; row = row + 1)
       for(short col = 0; col < 4; col = col + 1)
           totQuantity = totQuantity + quantity[row][col];
       //end for col
   //end for row
   ```
5. `inFile >> quantity[0][0];`

Q U E S T I O N S

1. C++ automatically passes two-dimensional arrays by _____ .
   a. reference
   b. value

2. If the `item[2][3]` element in the `item` array stores a Short Integer number, then the `item[3][4]` element in the `item` array _____ .
   a. can store either a Short Integer or a Float number
   b. can store either a Short Integer or a Long Integer number
   c. must store a Short Integer number

3. The first element in a two-dimensional array has a row subscript of _____ and a column subscript of _____ .
   a. 0, 0
   b. 0, 1
   c. 1, 0
   d. 1, 1

4. The individual elements in a two-dimensional array are identified by a unique _____ .
   a. combination of two subscripts
   b. combination of two names
   c. data type
   d. order
   e. subscript

5. `stock[2][4]` is read _____ .
   a. stock two sub four
   b. stock array two sub four
   c. stock bracket two bracket four
   d. stock sub two sub four
   e. stock sub two four

6. Which of the following statements declares a two-dimensional array named `item` that consists of four rows and three columns of elements, each of which can store the name of an item?
   a. `char item[0 to 4][0 to 3] = "";`
   b. `char item[3][4] = {{""}, {""}, {""}};`
   c. `char item[4][3] = "";`
   d. `char item[4][3] = {{""}, {""}, {""}, {""}};`
   e. `string item[4][3] = ' ';`
   ```

Use the following array, named `empName`, to answer questions 7 through 9. The array was created with the following statement: `char empName[3][5] = {{"Mary"}, {"Jean"}, {"Sue"}};`.

M	a	r	y	\0
J	e	a	n	\0
S	u	e	\0	

7. The statement `cout << empName[1]` will display _____ .
   a. J b. Jean c. M d. Mary

8. The `empName[0][3] = 'k';` statement will _____ .
   a. replace the letter r with the letter k
   b. replace the letter y with the letter k
   c. replace the letter k with the letter r
   d. replace the letter k with the letter y
   e. have no effect on the array

9. The `strcpy(empName[0], empName[2]);` statement will _____ .
   a. replace the letter M with the letter r
   b. replace the letter M with the letter J
   c. replace the letter M with the letter S
   d. replace the name Mary with the name Sue
   e. replace the name Sue with the name Mary

Use the following array, named `sales`, to answer questions 10 through 13. The array was created with the following statement: `short sales[2][5] = {{10000, 12000, 900, 500, 20000}, {350, 600, 700, 800, 100}};`.

10000	12000	900	500	20000
350	600	700	800	100

10. The `sales[1][3] = sales[1][3] + 10;` statement will _____ .
    a. replace the 900 amount with 910
    b. replace the 500 amount with 510
    c. replace the 700 amount with 710
    d. replace the 800 amount with 810
    e. none of the above

11. The `sales[0][4] = sales[0][4 − 2];` statement will _____ .
    a. replace the 20000 amount with 900
    b. replace the 20000 amount with 19998
    c. replace the 20000 amount with 19100
    d. result in an error

12. The `cout << sales[0][3] + sales[1][3];` statement will _____ .
    a. display 1300
    b. display 1600
    c. display `sales[0][3] + sales[1][3]`
    d. result in an error

13. Which of the following `if` clauses can be used to verify that the array subscripts called `row` and `column` are valid for the `sales` array?
    a. `if (sales[row][column] >= 0 && sales[row][column] < 5)`
    b. `if (sales[row][column] >= 0 && sales[row][column] <= 5)`
    c. `if (sales[row][column] >= 0 && sales[row][column] >= 5)`
    d. `if (row >= 0 && row < 3 && column >= 0 && column < 6)`
    e. `if (row >= 0 && row <= 1 && column >= 0 && column <= 4)`

Use the following array, named num, to answer questions 14 through 19. The array was created with the following statement: short num[4][2] = {{10, 5}, {7, 2}, {3, 4}, {1, 8}};. Assume that the total and count variables are declared as Short Integer variables and are initialized to 0. Assume that the avg variable is declared as a Float variable and is initialized to 0.

10	5
7	2
3	4
1	8

14. Which of the following will correctly calculate and display the average of the num elements?

```
a. for (short row = 0; row < 4; row = row + 1)
       for (short col = 0; col < 2; col = col + 1)
       {
             num[row][col] = total + total;
             count = count + 1;
       }//end for col
   //end for row
   avg = (float) total / (float) count;
   cout << avg << endl;
b. for (short row = 0; row < 4; row = row + 1)
       for (short col = 0; col < 2; col = col + 1)
       {
             total = total + num[row][col];
             count = count + 1;
       }//end for col
   //end for row
   avg = (float) total / (float) count;
   cout << avg << endl;
c. for (short row = 0; row < 4; row = row + 1)
       for (short col = 0; col < 2; col = col + 1)
       {
             num[row][col] = num[row][col] + total;
             count = count + 1;
       }//end for col
   //end for row
   avg = (float) total / (float) count;
   cout << avg << endl;
d. for (short row = 0; row < 4; row = row + 1)
       for (short col = 0; col < 2; col = col + 1)
       {
             total = total + num[row][col];
             count = count + 1;
       }//end for col
   //end for row
   avg = (float) total / (float) count;
   cout << avg << endl;
e. for (short row = 0; row < 4; row = row + 1)
       for (short col = 0; col < 2; col = col + 1)
       {
             total = num[row][col] + num[row][col];
             count = count + 1;
       }//end for col
   //end for row
   avg = (float) total / (float) count;
   cout << avg << endl;
```

Only one of the five groups of code shown in question 14 will display the average of the num elements. What will the other groups of code display? Record your answers in questions 15 through 19.

15. The code in question 14's answer a will display _____ .
    a. 0
    b. 2
    c. 5
    d. approximately 13.3333

16. The code in question 14's answer b will display _____ .
    a. 0
    b. 2
    c. 5
    d. approximately 13.3333

17. The code in question 14's answer c will display _____ .
    a. 0
    b. 2
    c. 5
    d. approximately 13.3333

18. The code in question 14's answer d will display _____ .
    a. 0
    b. 2
    c. 5
    d. approximately 13.3333

19. The code in question 14's answer e will display _____ .
    a. 0
    b. 2
    c. 5
    d. approximately 13.3333

E X E R C I S E S

1. Write the statement to declare a two-dimensional Character array named `words`. The statement should initialize the elements to the empty string. The array should be able to store six words. Each word should accommodate a maximum of nine characters plus the null character.

2. Write the statement to declare a two-dimensional Long Integer array named `population`. The statement should initialize the elements to 0. The array should contain 10 rows and four columns of elements.

3. Write the statement to declare a two-dimensional Long Integer array named `quantity`. Use a nested `for` loop to initialize the elements to 0. The array should contain 10 rows and four columns of elements.

4. a. Write the statement to declare a two-dimensional Character array named `firstName`. Initialize the elements to the empty string. The array should be able to store 20 first names. Each first name should accommodate a maximum of 15 characters plus the null character.

   b. Write the statement that will store the name Kevin in the first row of the array.

   c. Write the assignment statements that will store the name Susan, character by character, in the fifth row of the array.

5. a. Write the statement that will declare a two-dimensional Float array named `sales`. The statement should initialize the elements to 0. The array should contain four rows and six columns of elements.

   b. Write the assignment statement that will assign the number 10000 to the element located in the third row and last column in the array.

6. a. Write the statement to declare a two-dimensional Short Integer array named `quantity`. The statement should initialize the elements to 0. The array should contain 10 rows and five columns of elements.

   b. Write a programmer-defined function named `fillArray` that receives the `quantity` array, as well as the number of array rows, from the `main` function. The `fillArray` function should open a sequential access file named quantity.dat, which contains 10 records consisting of five numbers each, separated by the # symbol. The function should fill the `quantity` array with the data contained in the file and then close the file.

7. In this exercise, you will create a program that sums, by column, the contents of the elements in a two-dimensional array.

   a. Open the T9Ae07.cpp file, which is located in the Cpp\Tut09\T9Ae07 folder on your computer's hard disk.

   b. Create a program that sums, by column, the contents of the elements in the two-dimensional `numbers` array. Display the sum for each of the three columns. For example, the sum of the elements in the first column is 22 (2 + 6 + 7 + 4 + 3).

   c. Save, build, and then execute the program. When the program is working correctly, print the code. On the code printout, indicate the sum for each column in the array. Close the workspace and the Output window.

8. In this exercise, you will create a program that sums the numbers contained in a two-dimensional array.

   a. Open the T9Ae08.cpp file, which is located in the Cpp\Tut09\T9Ae08 folder on your computer's hard disk.

   b. Create a program that sums the numbers contained in the two-dimensional `numbers` array. Display the sum.

   c. Save, build, and then execute the program. When the program is working correctly, print the code. On the code printout, indicate the sum of the numbers in the array. Close the workspace and the Output window.

9. In this exercise, you will create a program that sums, by row, the contents of the elements in a two-dimensional array.

   a. Open the T9Ae09.cpp file, which is located in the Cpp\Tut09\T9Ae09 folder on your computer's hard disk.

   b. Create a program that sums, by row, the contents of the elements in the two-dimensional `numbers` array. Display the sum for each of the five rows. For example, the sum of the elements in the first row is 10 (2 + 3 + 5).

   c. Save, build, and then execute the program. When the program is working correctly, print the code. On the code printout, indicate the sum for each row in the array. Close the workspace and the Output window.

10. In this exercise, you will store values in a two-dimensional array.

   a. Open the T9Ae10.cpp file, which is located in the Cpp\Tut09\T9Ae10 folder on your computer's hard disk.

   b. Create a program that initializes the elements in a two-dimensional array to 0. The program should then use the repetition structure to store the even numbers from 2 through 10, along with their square and cube, in the two-dimensional array. For example, the first row in the array will contain the numbers 2, 4, and 8. Display the contents of the array.

   c. Save, build, and then execute the program. When the program is working correctly, print the code. On the code printout, indicate the contents of the array. Close the workspace and the Output window.

discovery ▶ **11.** In this exercise, you will observe how C++ initializes arrays.

   a. Open the T9Ae11.cpp file, which is located in the Cpp\Tut09\T9Ae11 folder on your computer's hard disk.

   b. Print and then study the code. You will notice that the program declares and initializes three arrays, and that not all of the arrays' elements are initialized. Also notice the difference in how the `item` and `state` arrays are displayed.

   c. Build and then execute the program. How does your C++ system initialize the uninitialized elements of a numeric array? How does your C++ system initialize the uninitialized elements of a two-dimensional Character array? Write your answers on the printed code from step b. Close the workspace and the Output window.

discovery ▶ **12.** In this exercise, you will create a program that calculates the average of the entries contained in a two-dimensional array.

   a. Use C++ to open the test.dat file, which is located in the Cpp\Tut09\T9Ae12 folder on your computer's hard disk. Print the contents of the file, then close the file.

   b. Open the T9Ae12.cpp file, which is located in the Cpp\Tut09\T9Ae12 folder on your computer's hard disk.

   c. Create a program that reads the scores from the test.dat file and stores the scores in a two-dimensional numeric array. The program should also calculate and display the average student test score.

   d. Save, build, and then execute the program. When the program is working correctly, print the code. On the code printout, indicate the average test score. Close the workspace and the Output window.

discovery ▶ **13.** In this exercise, you will create a program that allows the user to display the highest score earned on the midterm and the highest score earned on the final.

   a. Use C++ to open the test.dat file, which is located in the Cpp\Tut09\T9Ae13 folder on your computer's hard disk. Print the contents of the file, then close the file. The first score listed in the file is the midterm score and the second score is the final score.

   b. Open the T9Ae13.cpp file, which is located in the Cpp\Tut09\T9Ae13 folder on your computer's hard disk.

   c. Create a program that reads the scores from the test.dat file and stores the scores in a two-dimensional numeric array. The program should display the highest score earned on the midterm and the highest score earned on the final.

   d. Save, build, and then execute the program. When the program is working correctly, print the code. On the code printout, indicate the highest midterm and final scores. Close the workspace and the Output window.

discovery ▶ **14.** In this exercise, you will create a program that allows the user to display the average score earned on the midterm and the average score earned on the final.

   a. Use C++ to open the test.dat file, which is located in the Cpp\Tut09\T9Ae14 folder on your computer's hard disk. Print the contents of the file, then close the file. The first score listed in the file is the midterm score and the second score is the final score.

   b. Open the T9Ae14.cpp file, which is located in the Cpp\Tut09\T9Ae14 folder on your computer's hard disk.

   c. Create a program that reads the scores from the test.dat file and stores the scores in a two-dimensional numeric array. The program should display the average score earned on the midterm and the average score earned on the final.

   d. Save, build, and then execute the program. When the program is working correctly, print the code. On the code printout, indicate the average midterm and final scores. Close the workspace and the Output window.

discovery

15. In this exercise, you will count how many times a number appears in an array.

    a. Open the T9Ae15.cpp file, which is located in the Cpp\Tut09\T9Ae15 folder on your computer's hard disk.

    b. Create a program that counts the number of times each of the numbers 1 through 9 appears in the two-dimensional numbers array. Display the nine counts. (For example, the number 1 appears 2 times, the number 2 appears 2 times, and so on. (*Hint*: You can store the counts in a two-dimensional array.)

    c. Save, build, and then execute the program. When the program is working correctly, print the code. On the code printout, indicate the number of times each of the numbers from 1 through 9 appears in the array. Close the workspace and the Output window.

debugging

16. In this exercise, you will debug a program that uses a two-dimensional array.

    a. Open the T9Ae16.cpp file, which is located in the Cpp\Tut09\T9Ae16 folder on your computer's hard disk.

    b. Build and execute the program. The program should display the numbers 10 through 120, in increments of 10, as follows:

        10 20 30 40
        50 60 70 80
        90 100 110 120

    You will notice that the program is not working correctly.

    c. Debug the program. When the program is working correctly, print the code. On the code printout, summarize what was wrong with the program and circle the changes you made to the program. Close the workspace and the Output window.

debugging

17. In this exercise, you will debug a program that uses a two-dimensional array.

    a. Open the T9Ae17.cpp file, which is located in the Cpp\Tut09\T9Ae17 folder on your computer's hard disk.

    b. Save and build the program. Correct the syntax errors, then build and execute the program. The program should display the first and last names contained in both arrays. You will notice that the program is not working correctly.

    c. Debug the program. When the program is working correctly, print the code. On the code printout, summarize what was wrong with the program and circle the changes you made to the program. Close the workspace and the Output window.

More on Two-dimensional Arrays

Updating the Elements in a Two-dimensional Numeric Array

You learned how to update the contents of a one-dimensional array in Tutorial 8. You will learn how to update the contents of a two-dimensional array in this tutorial. The only difference between updating a one-dimensional array and updating a two-dimensional array is in the number of loops required to perform the update. As you may remember from Tutorial 8, you can use one loop to access each element in a one-dimensional array. A two-dimensional array, however, requires two loops, and the loops must be nested. You will update a two-dimensional array in the Earthware program.

The Earthware Program

Earthware Inc., which sells eight very specialized products, divides its sales territory into four regions: North, South, East, and West. Robert Gonzo, the sales manager, wants a program that will read the current year's sales from a sequential access file, then allow him to enter the projected increase in sales for the following year. The program will compute and display the following year's projected sales for each product within each region. On your computer's hard disk is a program that uses a two-dimensional array to solve Earthware's problem. Open that program now.

To view the Earthware program that updates a numeric array:

1 If necessary, start Visual C++. Open the **LbProg01.cpp** file, which is located in the Cpp\Tut09\LbProg01 folder on your computer's hard disk. The Earthware program appears in the LbProg01.cpp window. The `main` function is shown in Figure 9-28.

```cpp
//LbProg01.cpp
//this program updates a two-dimensional numeric array

#include <iostream.h>
#include <fstream.h>

//function prototypes
void displaySales(long [][4], short);
void updateSales (long [][4], short);

void main()
{

    //declare and initialize numeric array
    long sales[8][4] = {{0}, {0}, {0}, {0}, {0}, {0}, {0}, {0}};

    //open file for input
    ifstream inFile;
    inFile.open("sales.dat", ios::in);

    //verify that open was successful
    if (!inFile.fail())
    {
        //enter sale amounts into the array
        for(short row = 0; row < 8; row = row + 1)
            for(short col = 0; col < 4; col = col + 1)
            {
                inFile >> sales[row][col];
                inFile.ignore(1);
            }//end for col
        //end for row

        //close file
        inFile.close();

        //display sales
        displaySales(sales, 8);

        //update sales
        updateSales(sales, 8);

        //display updated sale amounts
        displaySales(sales, 8);
    }
    else
        cout << "Error opening file." << endl;
    //end if (!inFile.fail())
} //end of main function
```

Figure 9-28: Earthware program's `main` function

The `main` function uses two programmer-defined functions named `displaySales` and `updateSales`, and a two-dimensional Long Integer array named `sales`. You will notice that the `sales` array has eight rows—one for each of Earthware's products—and four columns—one for each region. After opening the sales.dat file, which is located in the Cpp\Tut09\LbProg01 folder on your computer's hard disk, the `main` function verifies that the open was successful. If the open was not successful, the selection structure's false path displays an appropriate message before the program ends. Otherwise, the `main` function uses a nested `for` loop to read the sales amounts from the sales.dat file. The amounts are stored, row by row, in the `sales` array. The `main` function then closes the sales.dat file and calls the `displaySales` function to display the contents of the `sales` array. After the `displaySales` function completes its task, the `main` function calls the `updateSales` function to update the values in the sales array. The `main` function then calls the `displaySales` function to display the contents of the updated array before the program ends.

Now view the code in the `displaySales` function. The code, which is already entered in the Earthware program, is shown in Figure 9-29.

```
//*****programmer-defined function definitions*****
void displaySales(long regSales[][4], short numRows)
{
    //this function displays the contents of the array
    cout << "Item North  South  East   West" << endl;
    for(short row = 0; row < numRows; row = row + 1)
    {
        cout << row << "      ";
        for(short col = 0; col < 4; col = col + 1)
            cout << regSales[row][col] << "   ";
        //end for col
        cout << endl;
    }//end for row
} //end of displaySales function
```

Figure 9-29: `displaySales` function

The `displaySales` function receives the `sales` array and the number of array rows, which are passed to it from the `main` function, in its `regSales` and `numRows` formal parameters, respectively. It then uses a nested `for` loop to display the sales, row by row, on the screen.

Next, view the code in the `updateSales` function. The code, which is included in the current program, is shown in Figure 9-30.

```
void updateSales(long regSales[][4], short numRows)
{
    //this function updates the contents of the array

    float rate = (float) 0.0;

    //get rate from user
    cout << endl << "Enter increase/decrease rate "
                << "in decimal form: ";
    cin >> rate;
    cin.ignore(100, '\n');

    //update each sale
    for(short row = 0; row < numRows; row = row + 1)
        for(short col = 0; col < 4; col = col + 1)
            regSales[row][col] =
                    (long) (regSales[row][col] * (1 + rate));
        //end for col
    //end for row

    //display updated message
    cout << endl << "Sales updated by "
        << rate * 100 << "%:" << endl;
} //end of updateSales function
```

Figure 9-30: updateSales function

Like the `displaySales` function, the `updateSales` function also receives the `sales` array and the number of array rows from the `main` function, in its `regSales` and `numRows` formal parameters, respectively. After declaring and initializing the `rate` variable, the `updateSales` function prompts the user to enter the rate by which the sales in the array should be either increased or decreased. The user's response is stored in the `rate` variable. You will notice that a nested `for` loop is used to increase (or decrease) each number in the `sales` array by the rate stored in the `rate` variable. When the `for` loops complete their tasks, the `updateSales` function displays a message indicating the rate by which each sales amount was updated. Program control then returns to the `main` function, which calls the `displaySales` function to display the updated contents of the array. Build and execute the program to observe how it works.

To observe how the Earthware program works:

1 Build and execute the program. The program opens the sales.dat file for input. It then reads the sales amounts from the file and stores them in the `sales` array. The program displays the eight item numbers (0 through 7) and sales amounts in the DOS window, along with the "Enter increase/decrease rate in decimal form: " prompt.

   Increase each price by 10 percent, or .1.

2 Type **.1** and press the **Enter** key. After increasing each number in the `sales` array by 10 percent, the program displays the appropriate message along with the contents of the updated array, as shown in Figure 9-31.

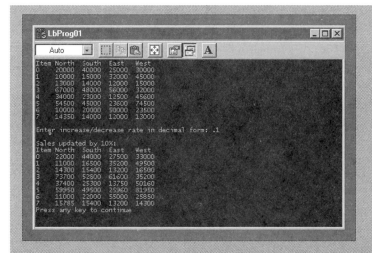

Figure 9-31: DOS window showing original and updated sales

You will notice that each updated sales amount is 10 percent more than its original sales amount—for example, 22000 is 10 percent (2000) more than 20000.

3 Press the **Enter** key to close the DOS window. Close the workspace and then close the Output window.

Next, you will learn how to search a two-dimensional array.

mini-quiz

Mini-Quiz 3

1. Write a `for` loop that increases, by 2, each number stored in a Short Integer array named `quantity`. The `quantity` array contains three rows and five columns. Use `row` and `col` as the counter variables for the `for` loops. Update the array, row by row.

2. Write a `while` loop that increases, by 2, each number stored in a Short Integer array named `quantity`. The `quantity` array contains three rows and five columns. Use `row` and `col` as the counter variables for the `while` loops. Update the array, column by column. (You can assume that the `row` and `col` variables have been declared and initialized to 0.)

Searching a Two-dimensional Array

As you may remember from the case outlined at the beginning of this tutorial, each year, Janet Hertel prepares the federal individual tax returns for many of her friends and relatives. To make her job easier, Janet would like a program that she can use to display the amount of federal tax an individual owes. The amount of tax is based on the individual's taxable net income and his or her filing status—either single, married filing jointly, married filing separately, or head of household—as indicated in the partial federal income tax table shown in Figure 9-32.

If line 38 (taxable income) is—		And you are—			
At least	But less than	Single	Married filing jointly *	Married filing separately	Head of a house-hold
			Your tax is—		
35,000					
35,000	35,050	6,603	5,254	7,129	5,511
35,050	35,100	6,617	5,261	7,143	5,525
35,100	35,150	6,631	5,269	7,157	5,539
35,150	35,200	6,645	5,276	7,171	5,553
35,200	35,250	6,659	5,284	7,185	5,567
35,250	35,300	6,673	5,291	7,199	5,581
35,300	35,350	6,687	5,299	7,213	5,595
35,350	35,400	6,701	5,306	7,227	5,609
35,400	35,450	6,715	5,314	7,241	5,623
35,450	35,500	6,729	5,321	7,255	5,637
35,500	35,550	6,743	5,329	7,269	5,651
35,550	35,600	6,757	5,336	7,283	5,665
35,600	35,650	6,771	5,344	7,297	5,679
35,650	35,700	6,785	5,351	7,311	5,693
35,700	35,750	6,799	5,359	7,325	5,707
35,750	35,800	6,813	5,366	7,339	5,721
35,800	35,850	6,827	5,374	7,353	5,735
35,850	35,900	6,841	5,381	7,367	5,749
35,900	35,950	6,855	5,389	7,381	5,763
35,950	36,000	6,869	5,396	7,395	5,777

Figure 9-32: Partial federal tax table

You will notice that the partial tax table shown in the figure has six columns. The first two columns list various ranges of taxable income amounts. The first column—the "At least" column—lists the minimum amount in each range, and the second column—the "But less than" column—lists the amount that a taxable income in the range must be less than. The remaining four columns in the table list the corresponding tax amounts, which are based on your filing status. To determine the amount of tax you owe, you first find your taxable income in a range shown in the first two columns of the table. A taxable income of $35,525, for example, is located in the $35,500 to 35,550 range. After locating your taxable income in the table, you then use your filing status to determine which of the remaining four columns contains your tax. If, for example, your taxable income is $35,525 and your filing status is "Married filing jointly," your tax is $5,329. If your filing status is "Single," your tax is $6,743.

Although the federal tax table uses two columns ("At least" and "But less than") to show each range of taxable income, you really need only search the "But less than" column to find the range in which a taxable income resides. When using only the "But less than" column to search for a taxable income, you stop the search when you encounter the first value in the column that is greater than the taxable income, because the taxable income will fall in that range. For example, assume that the taxable income is $35,125. The first value in the "But less than" column is $35,050, which is not greater than the $35,125 for which you are searching, so you must continue the search. The second value in the "But less than" column is $35,100, which is also not greater than $35,125, so you continue searching. The third value in the "But less than" column is $35,150, which is greater than the $35,125 for which you are searching. The $35,125 falls in this range.

The program that you will view in this lesson will store a portion of the federal income tax table—only the second through sixth columns for incomes of $35,000 to $36,000 shown in Figure 9-32—in a two-dimensional array. The program will allow the user to enter a person's net taxable income for the year, as well as his or her filing status. It will then determine the amount of federal income tax that he or she owes. Open the program now.

To open the tax program:

1 Open the **LbProg02.cpp** file, which is located in the Cpp\Tut09\LbProg02 folder on your computer's hard disk. The tax program appears in the LbProg02.cpp window. The `main` function is shown in Figure 9-33.

```
//LbProg02.cpp
//this program displays the amount of federal income tax owed

#include <iostream.h>

void main()
{
    //                      taxable, single,joint,separate,head
    long taxTable[20][5] = {{35050, 6603, 5254, 7129, 5511},
                            {35100, 6617, 5261, 7143, 5525},
                            {35150, 6631, 5269, 7157, 5539},
                            {35200, 6645, 5276, 7171, 5553},
                            {35250, 6659, 5284, 7185, 5567},
                            {35300, 6673, 5291, 7199, 5581},
                            {35350, 6687, 5299, 7213, 5595},
                            {35400, 6701, 5306, 7227, 5609},
                            {35450, 6715, 5314, 7241, 5623},
                            {35500, 6729, 5321, 7255, 5637},
                            {35550, 6743, 5329, 7269, 5651},
                            {35600, 6757, 5336, 7283, 5665},
                            {35650, 6771, 5344, 7297, 5679},
                            {35700, 6785, 5351, 7311, 5693},
                            {35750, 6799, 5359, 7325, 5707},
                            {35800, 6813, 5366, 7339, 5721},
                            {35850, 6827, 5374, 7353, 5735},
                            {35900, 6841, 5381, 7367, 5749},
                            {35950, 6855, 5389, 7381, 5763},
                            {36000, 6869, 5396, 7395, 5777}};
```

Figure 9-33: Tax program (continues on next page)

```
    //declare variables
    short row         = 0;
    short status      = 0;
    char  found       = ' ';
    long  taxableIncome = 0;

    cout << "Enter taxable income: ";
    cin >> taxableIncome;
    cin.ignore(100, '\n');

    while(taxableIncome >= 35000 && taxableIncome < 36000)
    {
        cout << "Enter status (1 Single, 2 Joint, "
            << "3 Separate, 4 Head of household): ";
        cin >> status;
        cin.ignore(100, '\n');

        if(status > 0 && status < 5)
        {
            row = 0;
            found = 'N';

            while(row < 20 && found == 'N')
            {
                if(taxableIncome < taxTable[row][0])
                {
                    cout << "Your tax is $"
                        << taxTable[row][status]
                        << endl << endl;
                    found = 'Y';
                }
                else
                    row = row + 1;
                //end if (taxableIncome < taxTable[row][0]

            }//end while (row < 20 && found == 'N')

            cout << "Enter taxable income: ";
            cin >> taxableIncome;
            cin.ignore(100, '\n');
        }//end if (status > 0 && status < 5)

    }//end while (taxableIncome >= 35000 && taxableIncome < 36000)
} //end of main function
```

Figure 9-33: Tax program (continued)

The main function begins by declaring and initializing a Long Integer array, named taxTable, which contains 20 rows and five columns. Compare the values assigned to the array to the values shown in Figure 9-32's tax table. The array records the amounts in only five of the six columns in the tax table. The amounts listed in the "At least" column of the tax table are not assigned to the array. The first column in the array, for instance, contains the values listed in the "But less than" column of the tax table. The second, third, fourth, and fifth columns in the array contain the tax amounts for taxpayers with a filing status of "Single," "Married filing jointly," "Married filing separately," and "Head of a household," respectively. At this point, you may be wondering how the program will be able to locate the range in which the taxable income amount resides without using the values in the "At least" column. As you did earlier, the program will search the "But less than" values (which are stored in the first column of the array), looking for the taxable income amount. When the program encounters the first value that is greater than the taxable income amount for which you are searching, the program will stop the search because the amount will be in that range.

In addition to the Long Integer `taxTable` array, the program also declares and initializes two Short Integer variables named `row` and `status`, a Character variable named `found`, and a Long Integer variable named `taxableIncome`. The `taxableIncome` variable will store the user's taxable income amount, and the `status` variable will store his or her filing status. The program will use the `row` and `found` variables when searching for the taxable income amount in the array.

After declaring and initializing the variables, the program prompts the user to enter his or her taxable income. The user's response is then stored in the `taxableIncome` variable. Because the array contains the tax amounts only for incomes in the $35,000 to $36,000 range, the `while` loop verifies that the user entered a number within that range. If the taxable income is valid, the user is prompted to enter his or her filing status—either 1, 2, 3, or 4.

The `if(status > 0 && status < 5)` clause in the program verifies that the user entered a valid filing status. If the filing status is valid, the first statement within the selection structure initializes the `row` variable to 0 so that each new search begins with the first row in the `taxTable` array. The second statement within the selection structure initializes the `found` variable to the letter N. Before the program processes the loop that searches the array, it will assume that the taxable income's range is not in the array.

The `while(row < 20 && found == 'N')` clause in the program tells C++ to process the loop instructions while there are array elements to search and the taxable income's range has not been found. The `if(taxableIncome < taxTable[row][0])` clause within the `while` loop compares the user's taxable income to the value stored in the first column of each row in the array. If the taxable income is less than the value in the current array element, the `cout << "Your tax is $" << taxTable[row][status] << endl << endl;` statement displays the appropriate tax, and then sets the `found` variable to the letter Y. Notice that the `status` variable determines which column in the array contains the applicable tax. If the status variable contains the number 1, which indicates a filing status of "Single," the program displays the tax amount stored in column 1 of the array. If, on the other hand, the status variable contains the number 2, which indicates a filing status of "Married filing jointly," the program displays the tax amount stored in column 2 of the array.

If the taxable income is not less than the value in the current array element, the `row = row + 1;` statement in the selection structure increments the row number by one so that the search can continue in the next row in the array. The `while(row < 20 && found == 'N')` loop will stop searching either when there are no more elements to search or when the taxable income's range is found in the array. When the loop stops, the user is prompted to enter another taxable income amount. Run the program to observe how it works.

To observe how the tax program works:

1   Build and execute the LbProg02 tax program.

Assume that your taxable income is $35,525, and your filing status is "Married filing jointly."

2 When you are prompted to enter a taxable income amount, type **35525** and press the **Enter** key. When you are prompted to enter a filing status, type **2** and press the **Enter** key. The DOS window shows that your tax is $5329. You are now prompted to enter another taxable income amount.

Now assume that your taxable income is $35,850, and your filing status is "Single."

3 Type **35850** as your taxable income and press the **Enter** key. When you are prompted to enter a filing status, type **1** and press the **Enter** key. The DOS window indicates that your tax is $6841, as shown in Figure 9-34.

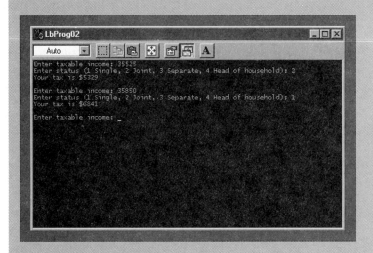

Figure 9-34: DOS window showing taxable income and tax

You can now end the program.

4 Type **0** as the taxable income amount and press the **Enter** key. Press the **Enter** key again to close the DOS window. Close the workspace and then close the Output window.

You have now completed Lesson B. You can either take a break or complete the end-of-lesson questions and exercises.

SUMMARY

The procedure for updating a two-dimensional array is similar to the procedure for updating a one-dimensional array. The only difference is that you use one loop to update a one-dimensional array, and you use a nested loop to update a two-dimensional array.

Recall from Lesson A that a two-dimensional array resembles a table in that the elements are in rows and columns. When searching a two-dimensional array for a specific value, you typically search for the value in the first column of the array. You then return one or more values located in the remaining columns of the array.

ANSWERS TO MINI-QUIZZES

Mini-Quiz 3

1.
```
for(short row = 0; row < 3; row = row + 1)
    for(short col = 0; col < 5; col = col + 1)
        quantity[row][col] = quantity[row][col] + 2;
    //end for col
//end for row
```

2.
```
while (col < 5 )
{
    row = 0;
    while (row < 3)
    {
        quantity[row][col] = quantity[row][col] + 2;
        row = row + 1;
    }//end while (row < 3)
    col = col + 1;
}//end while (col < 5)
```

QUESTIONS

1. Which of the following will correctly add 100 to each element in the `sales` array? (The `sales` array has two rows and five columns.)

a.
```
for (short row = 0; row < 2; row = row + 1)
    for (short col = 0; col < 5; col = col + 1)
        sales[row][col] = sales[row][col] + 100;
```
b.
```
for (short row = 0; row <= 2; row = row + 1)
    for (short col = 0; col <= 5; col = col + 1)
        sales[row][col] = sales[row][col] + 100;
```
c.
```
for (short col = 0; col < 5; col = col + 1)
    for (short row = 0; row < 2; row = row + 1)
        sales[row][col] = sales[row][col] + 100;
```
d. Both a and c will work correctly.

2. Assume that the `customer` array is a two-dimensional Short Integer array that contains 10 rows and two columns. The customer number is in the first column, and the customer's credit limit is in the second column. Which of the following can be used to display the credit limit for customer number 34? (You can assume that the `row` and `found` variables have already been declared and initialized to 0 and `'N'`, respectively.)

a.
```
while(row < 10 && found == 'N')
    if (customer[row][0] == 34)
    {
        cout << customer[row][1] << endl;
        found = 'Y';
    }
    else
        row = row + 1;
    //end if
//end while
```

```
b. while(row <= 10 && found == 'N')
      if (customer[row][0] == 34)
      {
           cout << customer[row][1] << endl;
           found = 'Y';
      }
      else
           row = row + 1;
      //end if
  //end while
c. while(row < 10 && found == 'N')
      if (customer[0] == 34)
      {
           cout << customer[1] << endl;
           found = 'Y';
      }
      else
           row = row + 1;
      //end if
  //end while
d. while(row < 10 && found == 'N')
      if (customer[0][1] == 34)
      {
           cout << customer << endl;
           found = 'Y';
      }
      else
           row = row + 1;
      //end if
  //end while
```

E X E R C I S E S

1. In this exercise, you will modify an existing program so that it updates only specific elements in a two-dimensional array.

   a. Open the T9Be01.cpp file, which is located in the Cpp\Tut09\T9Be01 folder on your computer's hard disk. You viewed this program in Lesson B.

   b. Modify the updateSales function so that it asks the user which array element (row and column) he or she wants to update before requesting the increase/decrease rate. (For example, if the user wants to update the sales amount stored in the first row, first column of the array, the user will enter the numbers 0 and 0.) Include a loop that will allow the user to modify as many sales amounts as he or she desires.

   c. Save, build, and then execute the program. Increase the sales amount located in the first row, first column by 20 percent, then increase the sales amount in the third row, first column by 25 percent, and then decrease the sales amount in the last row, last column by 15 percent. (*Hint*: To decrease a sales amount, enter a negative rate.) When the program is working correctly, print the code. On the code printout, circle all of the changes you made to the program. Also indicate the new sales amounts for the array elements that you changed. Close the workspace and the Output window.

2. In this exercise, you will modify an existing program so that it writes the contents of an updated array to a sequential access file.

   a. Use C++ to open the sales.dat file, which is located in the Cpp\Tut09\T9A\Be02 folder on your computer's hard disk. Print the contents of the file, then close the file.

    b. Use C++ to open the T9Be02.cpp file, which is located in the Cpp\Tut09\T9Be02 folder on your computer's hard disk. You viewed this program in Lesson B.

    c. Create a function named `writeUpdatedSales`. The `main` function should call the `writeUpdatedSales` function immediately after the `updateSales` function. The `writeUpdatedSales` function should write the contents of the updated array to the upsales.dat file.

    d. Save, build, and then execute the program. Update the sales amounts in the array by 15 percent.

    e. Print the code. On the code printout, circle all of the changes you made to the program.

    f. Use C++ to open the upsales.dat file, which is located in the Cpp\Tut09\T9Be02 folder on your computer's hard disk. Print the contents of the file. The sales amounts on this printout should be 15 percent higher than the sales amounts shown in the printout from step a. Close the data file, the workspace, and the Output window.

3. In this exercise, you will create a program that displays the number of students earning a specific score.

    a. Use C++ to open the scores.dat file, which is located in the Cpp\Tut09\T9Be03 folder on your computer's hard disk. Print the contents of the file. The file contains 20 records. Each record contains two scores: a midterm score and a final score. Close the file.

    b. Use C++ to open the T9Be03.cpp file, which is located in the Cpp\Tut09\T9Be03 folder on your computer's hard disk.

    c. Write a program that stores the contents of the scores.dat file in a two-dimensional Short Integer array. After filling the array with data, the program will allow the user to enter a score. The program will then display the number of students that earned that score on the midterm, and the number of students that earned that score on the final. For example, if the user enters the number 100, the program will display the number 2 as the number of students earning 100 on the midterm, and it will display the number 1 as the number of students earning 100 on the final.

    d. Save, build, and then execute the program. Use the program to answer the following questions:

    How many students earned 72 on the midterm?

    How many students earned 72 on the final?

    How many students earned 88 on the midterm?

    How many students earned 20 on the final?

    How many students earned 99 on the midterm?

    e. When the program is working correctly, print the code. On the code printout, write the answers to the questions from step d. Close the workspace and the Output window.

4. In this exercise, you will create a program that displays the number of students earning a score in a specific range.

    a. Use C++ to open the scores.dat file, which is located in the Cpp\Tut09\T9Be04 folder on your computer's hard disk. Print the contents of the file. The file contains 20 records. Each record contains two scores: a midterm score and a final score. Close the file.

    b. Use C++ to open the T9Be04.cpp file, which is located in the Cpp\Tut09\T9Be04 folder on your computer's hard disk.

    c. Write a program that stores the contents of the scores.dat file in a two-dimensional Short Integer array. After filling the array with data, the program will allow the user to enter a minimum score and a maximum score. The program will then display the number of students who earned a score within that range on the midterm, and the number of students that earned a score within that range on the final. For example, if the user enters a minimum score of 95 and a maximum score of 100, the program will display the number 4 as the number of students earning a score within that range on the midterm. It will display the number 6 as the number of students earning a score within that range on the final.

d. Save, build, and then execute the program. Use the program to answer the following questions:

How many students earned scores between 70 and 79, including 70 and 79, on the midterm?

How many students earned scores between 70 and 79, including 70 and 79, on the final?

How many students earned scores between 65 and 85, including 65 and 85, on the final?

How many students earned scores between 0 and 50, including 0 and 50, on the midterm?

e. When the program is working correctly, print the code. On the code printout, write the answers to the questions from step d. Close the workspace and the Output window.

5. In this exercise, you will use a two-dimensional numeric array.

Scenario: Jacques Cousard has been playing the lotto for four years and has yet to win any money. He wants a program that will select all six lotto numbers, ranging from 1 to 54, for him (an example of six lotto numbers would be 4, 8, 35, 15, 20, 3).

a. Create a console application named T9Be05 in the Cpp\Tut09 folder on your computer's hard disk. Write a program that uses the srand, rand, and time functions, which you learned about in Tutorial 5, to generate 50 groups of six random lotto numbers. (As an example, the six numbers 4, 8, 35, 15, 20, and 3 would be considered one group, while the six numbers 3, 54, 78, 21, 3, 1 would be considered another group.) Store the random numbers in a two-dimensional Short Integer array that has 50 rows and six columns, then send the 50 groups of random numbers to a file named T9Be05.dat for printing. The program should prevent a number from appearing more than once in the same group—in other words, each number in the same group should be unique.

b. Save, build, and execute the program. When the program is working correctly, print the code. Also use C++ to print the contents of the T9Be05.dat file. Close the data file, the workspace, and the Output window.

6. In this exercise, you will use a two-dimensional numeric array.

a. Create a console application named T9Be06 in the Cpp\Tut09 folder on your computer's hard disk.

b. Write a program that uses a two-dimensional Short Integer array that has 10 columns and three rows. Store the numbers from 1 through 10 in the first column of the array. Store the square of the numbers from 1 through 10 in the second column of the array, and store the cube of the numbers from 1 through 10 in the third column of the array. Use the pow function that you learned in Tutorial 4 to compute the square and cube of the numbers.

c. The program should prompt the user to enter a number from 1 through 10. It should also ask the user if he or she wants to display either the square or the cube of the number. The program should search the first column of the array for the number entered by the user. The program should then display the information entered in either the second column of the array (the square of the number) or the third column of the array (the cube of the number). Allow the user to display the square or cube for as many numbers as desired without having to execute the program again.

d. Save, build, and then execute the program. Test the program by displaying the square of the number 5, the cube of the number 10, the cube of the number 8, and the square of the number 7.

e. When the program is working correctly, print the code. Also indicate the answers displayed by the program in step d. Close the workspace and the Output window.

discovery ▶ 7. In this exercise, you will search and update the contents of a numeric array.

Scenario: Jacob Wynn, the inventory manager at Parklane Inc., wants an application that he can use to keep track of each inventory item's quantity on hand. The program should display a menu that allows Mr. Wynn to do the following:

- record the purchase of an item (increase an item's quantity on hand)
- record the sale of an item (decrease an item's quantity on hand)
- display an item's quantity on hand
- write the updated information to the invent.dat file
- quit the program

a. Use C++ to open and then print the invent.dat file, which is located in the Cpp\Tut09\T9Be07 folder on your computer's hard disk. This file contains the beginning inventory amount for the 10 items in Parklane's inventory. Each record contains two fields: the first field is the item's code, and the second is the beginning inventory amount for that item. Close the file.

b. Use C++ to open the T9Be07.cpp file, which is located in the Cpp\Tut09\T9Be07 folder on your computer's hard disk. The program should use a two-dimensional Short Integer array.

c. Write the program according to the scenario outlined at the beginning of the exercise. (*Hint*: While you are testing the program, you may want to write the updated information to a file other than the invent.dat file; by doing so, you ensure that the invent.dat file will remain intact during the testing phase.) When the program is working correctly, change the code to write the updated information to the invent.dat file.

d. Save, build, and then execute the program.

e. Use the program to record the following purchases:

Item code	Quantity purchased
11	50
78	100
22	50

f. Use the program to record the following sales:

Item code	Quantity sold
78	10
99	1
14	100

g. Use the program to display item 99's quantity on hand, then display item 78's quantity on hand.

h. Select the option that writes the updated information to the invent.dat file, then quit the program.

i. Print the code, then use C++ to open and then print the invent.dat file. Close the data file, the workspace, and the Output window.

discovery ▶ 8.   In this exercise, you will search a numeric array.

Scenario: If your taxable income for the year is less than $100,000, you can use the federal tax table provided by the Internal Revenue Service. If your taxable income is $100,000 or more, however, you must use one of the tax rate schedules (Schedule X, Schedule Y-1, Schedule Y-2, or Schedule Z) to compute your tax. A sample tax rate Schedule X, which must be used if your filing status is "Single," is shown in Figure 9-35.

Schedule X—Use if your filing status is **Single**

If the amount on Form 1040, line 38, is: Over—	But not over—	Enter on Form 1040, line 39		of the amount over—
$0	$24,650		15%	$0
24,650	59,750	$3,697.50 +	28%	24,650
59,750	124,650	13,525.50 +	31%	59,750
124,650	271,050	33,644.50 +	36%	124,650
271,050	....	86,348.50 +	39.6%	271,050

Figure 9-35

a.   Create a console application named T9Be08 in the Cpp\Tut09 folder on your computer's hard disk.

b.   Create a program that prompts the user to enter the taxable income. For this program, you can assume that the user's filing status is "Single." The program should display the appropriate tax based on the information shown in Figure 9-35's Schedule X. The program should allow the user to enter as many taxable incomes as desired.

c.   Save, build, and then execute the program. Test the program by entering the following taxable incomes, one at a time: 158000, 111500, and 274000.

d.   When the program is working correctly, print the code. On the code printout, indicate the tax amounts displayed in step c. Close the workspace and the Output window.

discovery ▶ 9.   In this exercise, you will use a two-dimensional array to code the hangman game.

Scenario: The hangman game is described in Exercise 10 in Tutorial 8's Lesson B. Rather than use two parallel arrays, as you did in that exercise, this exercise requires that you use a two-dimensional Character array. The first row in the array, which you will name word, will store the word that the student needs to guess. Each word can be a maximum of five characters plus the null character. The second row in the array will store a corresponding dash (hyphen) for each letter stored in the first row. As the student guesses correct letters, the program will replace the dashes in the second row of the array with the correct letters. Allow the student to make a maximum of six incorrect guesses before ending the game.

a.   Create a console application named T9Be09 in the Cpp\Tut09 folder on your computer's hard disk.

b.   Create a program that simulates the hangman game on the computer.

c.   Save, build, execute, and test the program. When the program is working correctly, print the code. Close the workspace and the Output window.

discovery ▶   **10.** In this exercise, you will use both a one-dimensional and a two-dimensional array.

Scenario: Gifts Express wants a program that it can use to display the state that corresponds to the area code entered by the user.

a. Create a console application named T9Be10 in the Cpp\Tut09 folder on your computer's hard disk.

b. Create a program that stores the following 10 area codes in a one-dimensional Short Integer array named `areaCode`: 201, 210, 214, 303, 310, 510, 516, 607, 619, and 706. The program should also store the following state abbreviations in a two-dimensional Character array named `state`: NJ, TX, TX, CO, CA, CA, NY, NY, CA, and GA. The state abbreviations correspond to the area codes stored in the one-dimensional array.

c. The program should prompt the user to enter the area code, then search the `areaCode` array for the area code. If the area code is in the array, the program should display the corresponding state from the `state` array. Otherwise, the program should display an appropriate message indicating that the area code is not in the array.

d. Save, build, and then execute the program. Test the program by entering various area codes. When the program is working correctly, print the code. Close the workspace and the Output window.

debugging   **11.** In this exercise, you will debug a program.

a. Use C++ to open the numbers.dat file, which is located in the Cpp\Tut09\T9Be11 folder on your computer's hard disk. Print the file, then close the file.

b. Use C++ to open the T9Be11.cpp file, which is located in the Cpp\Tut09\T9Be11 folder on your computer's hard disk. When the user enters a number from 1 through 9, the program should display the corresponding quantity.

c. Build the program. Debug the program. When the program is working correctly, print the code. On the code printout, summarize what was wrong with the program and circle the corrections you made. Close the workspace and the Output window.

TUTORIAL 10

Sorting, Searching, and Control Breaks

case ▶ Susan Li, the sales manager at Gifts Express, has asked you to write two programs. The first program will allow her to display a salesperson's annual sales amount simply by entering the salesperson's ID into the program. The second program will allow her to display a report showing the total sales made in each of the company's four sales regions during the month of January, as well as the total company sales for that month. Before you can create either program, you will need to learn how to sort data—in other words, how to arrange data in a particular order. You will also need to learn how to write an algorithm that performs a binary search, as well as one that produces a control break report.

Sorting and the Binary Search Algorithm

Sorting Data

In Tutorial 8, you learned how to store data in a one-dimensional array. As you may remember, programmers use arrays to store related data in the internal memory of the computer. One reason for doing so is to **sort** the data—that is, arrange it in either alphabetical or numerical order. When data is displayed in a sorted order, it allows a user to quickly find the information for which he or she is searching. For example, it is much easier to find a name in a list that is arranged alphabetically rather than randomly. Additionally, to work correctly, many programs require data to be in a specific sequence. For example, programs that use the binary search algorithm, which you will learn about in this lesson, require the program data to be sorted. Programs that use the control break algorithm, which you will learn about in Lesson B, also require the program data to be sorted.

You can sort both numeric and character data in either ascending (from smallest to largest or A to Z) or descending (from largest to smallest or Z to A) order, as illustrated in Figure 10-1.

Sorted numerical data		Sorted character data	
Ascending order	Descending order	Ascending order	Descending order
1	5	A	E
2	4	B	D
3	3	C	C
4	2	D	B
5	1	E	A

Figure 10-1: Illustration of numeric and character data sorted in ascending and descending order

Over the years, many different sorting algorithms have been developed. In this lesson, you will learn how to use one of those algorithms—the bubble sort—to sort the data stored in an array.

The Bubble Sort

The bubble sort provides a quick and easy way to sort the items stored in an array, as long as the number of items is relatively small—for example, less than 50. The **bubble sort** algorithm works by comparing adjacent array elements and interchanging (swapping) the ones that are out of order. The algorithm continues comparing and swapping until the data in the array is sorted. To illustrate the logic of a bubble sort, manually sort the numbers 9, 8, and 7 in ascending order. Assume that the three numbers are stored in an array named num. Figure 10-2 shows the num array values before, during, and after the bubble sort.

	Comparison	Swap	Result/Comparison	Swap	Result
Pass 1:					
num[0]	9 ⌐	Yes	8		8
num[1]	8 ⌐⌐		9 ⌐	Yes	7
num[2]	7		7 ⌐⌐		9
Pass 2:					
num[0]	8 ⌐	Yes	7		7
num[1]	7 ⌐⌐		8 ⌐	No	8
num[2]	9		9 ⌐⌐		9
Pass 3:					
num[0]	7 ⌐	No	7		7
num[1]	8 ⌐⌐		8 ⌐	No	8
num[2]	9		9 ⌐⌐		9

Figure 10-2: Array values before, during, and after the bubble sort

The bubble sort algorithm begins by comparing the first value in the array to the second value. If the first value is less than or equal to the second value, then no swap is made. If, on the other hand, the first value is greater than the second value, then both values are interchanged. In this case, the first value (9) is greater than the second (8), so the values are swapped as shown in Figure 10-2's Result/Comparison column.

After comparing the first value in the array to the second, the algorithm then compares the second value to the third. In this case, 9 is greater than 7, so the two values are swapped as shown in Figure 10-2's Result column.

At this point, the algorithm has completed its first time through the entire array—referred to as a **pass**. Notice that, at the end of the first pass, the largest value (9) is stored in the last position of the array. The bubble sort gets its name from the fact that as the larger values drop to the bottom of the array, the smaller values rise, like bubbles, to the top. Now observe what the algorithm does on its second pass through the array.

The bubble sort algorithm begins the second pass by comparing the first value in the array to the second value. In this case, 8 is greater than 7, so the two values are interchanged as shown in Figure 10-2. Then the second value is compared to the third. In this case, 8 is not greater than 9, so no swap is made. Notice that at the end of the second pass, the data in the array is sorted. However, the bubble sort algorithm will make one more pass through the array to verify that it is sorted.

In the third pass, the first value is compared to the second value. Because 7 is not greater than 8, no swap is made. The second value is then compared to the third value and because 8 is not greater than 9, no swap is made. Notice that no swaps were made during the entire third pass. This indicates that the array data is sorted, so the bubble sort algorithm stops.

On your computer's hard disk is a program that contains the code for the bubble sort algorithm. Open that program now.

To view the code for the bubble sort algorithm:

1 Start Visual C++. Open the **LaProg01.cpp** file, which is located in the Cpp\Tut10\LaProg01 folder on your computer's hard disk. The bubble sort program appears in the LaProg01.cpp window. The IPO chart and C++ code for the program's **main** function are shown in Figure 10-3.

Input	Processing	Output

four numbers	Processing items:
	   four-element Short Integer array named **number**
	
	 Algorithm:
	
	 1. display contents of unsorted array
	   (displayArray function)
	
	 2. sort array (**sortArray** function)
	
	 3. display contents of sorted array
	   (displayArray function)
		four sorted numbers

```
//LaProg01.cpp
//this program uses the bubble sort to sort
//the data in a numeric array

#include <iostream.h>

//function prototypes
void displayArray(short [], short);
void sortArray(short [], short);

void main()
{
    //declare and initialize array
    short number[4] = {3, 6, 2, 5};

    //display unsorted array
    cout << "Unsorted Array:      ";
    displayArray(number, 4);

    //sort array
    sortArray(number, 4);

    //display sorted array
    cout << "Sorted Array:        ";
    displayArray(number, 4);
} //end of main function
```

call function to display unsorted array

call function to sort array

call function to display sorted array

Figure 10-3: IPO chart and C++ code for the bubble sort program's main function

As Figure 10-3's code indicates, the main function uses two programmer-defined void functions named displayArray and sortArray, as well as a four-element Short Integer array named number, to which the main function assigns four numbers. You will notice that the values assigned to the number array—3, 6, 2, and 5—are not sorted in any particular order.

After calling the displayArray function to display the unsorted contents of the array, the main function calls the sortArray function, which contains the bubble sort code, to arrange the array values in ascending numerical order. The main function then calls the displayArray function to display the sorted contents of the array. Notice that the main function passes the number array, as well as the size of the array (the number of elements in the array), to both programmer-defined functions when the functions are called.

Next, view the code in the displayArray function, which is located in the programmer-defined functions section of the program. The function's IPO chart and C++ code are shown in Figure 10-4.

tip

As you learned in Tutorial 8, C++ passes arrays, automatically, by reference. As you may remember, the address of only the first element in the array is passed to the receiving function.

Input	Processing	Output
number array and array size from main function	Processing items: counter variable named x Algorithm: 1. initialize x variable to 0 2. repeat while (x is less than array size) display value stored in array element x add 1 to x variable end while	contents of array

display contents of array

```
//*****programmer-defined function definitions*****
void displayArray(short num[], short size)
{
    //this function displays the contents of the array
    for(short x = 0; x < size; x = x + 1)
        cout << num[x] << " ";
    //end for
    cout << endl << endl;
} //end of displayArray function
```

Figure 10-4: IPO chart and C++ code for the displayArray function

You will notice that the displayArray function receives the number array and its size in its num and size formal parameters, and then uses a for loop to display the contents of the array on the screen.

Now view the bubble sort algorithm in the sortArray function. The function's IPO chart and C++ code are shown in Figure 10-5.

Input	Processing		Output

number array and array size from **main** function	Processing items: Short Integer variable named **maxSub**
	 Short Integer variable named **temp**
	 Character variable named **swap**
	 counter variable named **x**
	
	 Algorithm:
	 1. initialize **maxSub** variable to highest subscript in the array
	 2. initialize **swap** variable to 'Y'
	 3. repeat while (**swap** variable contains 'Y')
	    set **swap** variable to 'N'
	    initialize **x** counter variable to 0
	    repeat while (**x** value is less than **maxSub** value)
	      if (value in array element **x** is greater than value in array element [**x** + 1])
	        set **swap** variable to 'Y'
	        assign value in array element **x** to **temp** variable
	        assign value in array element[**x** + 1] to array element **x**
	        assign value in **temp** variable to array element [**x** + 1]
	      end if
	      add 1 to **x** variable
	    end while (**x** value is less than **maxSub** value)
	  end while (**swap** variable contains 'Y')
			array containing numbers sorted in ascending order

swap values in adjacent array elements

highest subscript in the array

assume that no swap will be necessary

indicates that a swap was made

swap values in adjacent array elements

```cpp
void sortArray(short num[], short size)
{
    short maxSub = size - 1;
    short temp = 0;
    char  swap = 'Y';

    //repeat loop instructions as long as a swap was made
    while(swap == 'Y')
    {
        //assume that no swaps will be necessary
        swap = 'N';

        //compare array elements to see if a swap is necessary
        for(short x = 0; x < maxSub; x = x + 1)

            if(num[x] > num[x + 1])  //a swap is necessary
            {
                swap = 'Y';
                temp = num[x];
                num[x] = num[x + 1];
                num[x + 1] = temp;

            }//end if

        //end for

    }//end while (swap == 'Y')
} //end of sortArray function
```

Figure 10-5: IPO chart and C++ code for the sortArray function

Like the `displayArray` function, the `sortArray` function also receives the `number` array and the array size in its `num` and `size` formal parameters. The `sortArray` function also declares a Short Integer variable named `maxSub`, which is initialized to the value `size − 1`—in this case, it will be initialized to 3, the highest subscript in the four-element `num` array. The function will use the `maxSub` variable to control the processing of the `for` loop that determines if the values in adjacent array elements should be swapped.

The `sortArray` function also declares and initializes two other variables: a Short Integer variable named `temp` and a Character variable named `swap`. The `temp` variable, which is initialized to the number 0, will temporarily store the contents of a `num` array element so that a swap can be made. The `swap` variable, which is initialized to the character literal constant 'Y', will keep track of whether a swap was made during a pass of the array. As you learned earlier in this lesson, the bubble sort algorithm will stop only when no swaps are made for an entire pass.

Following the algorithm shown in Figure 10-5's IPO chart, the `while` loop, which is responsible for making the passes over the array data, will repeat its instructions as long as the `swap` variable contains the character literal constant 'Y'. The 'Y' value indicates that a swap was made and, therefore, the `while` loop needs to be processed again. Study the instructions within the `while` loop a little closer.

The first instruction within the `while` loop sets the `swap` variable to the character literal constant 'N'. When entering the loop, the algorithm assumes that no swaps will be necessary—in other words, it assumes that the array is already in sorted order. The next instruction in the `while` loop is a counter-controlled `for` loop, whose counter variable, `x`, will keep track of the array subscripts during each pass through the array. You will notice that the first instruction in the `for` loop is a selection structure that compares the values in the adjacent elements of the `num` array to see if one is greater than the other. If the `num[x]` value (the value in the current array element) is greater than the `num[x + 1]` value (the value in the next array element), then the `swap` variable is set to 'Y', indicating that a swap is necessary. The value in `num[x]` is then swapped with the value in `num[x + 1]`.

To accomplish the swap of two array elements—`num[x]` and `num[x + 1]`—the program first stores the `num[x]` value in the temporary Short Integer variable named `temp`. The `num[x + 1]` value is then assigned to the `num[x]` element. (If you did not store the `num[x]` value in the `temp` variable, the `num[x + 1]` value would write over the value in `num[x]`, and the value in `num[x]` would be lost.) At this point, the value in `num[x]` is the same as the value in `num[x + 1]`. To complete the swap, the program assigns the value in the `temp` variable to the `num[x + 1]` element. Figure 10-6 illustrates the process of swapping two array elements.

▶ Recall that the subscript of the first element in a one-dimensional array is 0. Because of this, the highest subscript in an array is always one number less than the number of array elements. The highest subscript in a four-element array, for example, is 3.

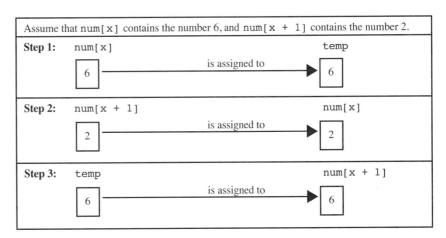

Figure 10-6: Illustration of the three steps necessary to accomplish a swap of two array elements

After the `for` loop completes the first pass through the array, the `while` loop again checks the value in the `swap` variable. If the value is 'Y', then the instructions within the loop are processed again. If, on the other hand, the value in `swap` is 'N', then the array is sorted and the bubble sort algorithm ends. Run the program to observe how it works.

To run the bubble sort program:

1 Build and execute the LaProg01 program. The `displayArray` function displays the contents of the unsorted array—the numbers 3, 6, 2, and 5. The `sortArray` function then sorts the array using the process shown in Figure 10-7. You will notice that the bubble sort makes a total of nine comparisons of the array data.

Pass 1:

	Comparison	Swap	Result/Comparison	Swap	Result/Comparison	Swap	Result
num[0]	3 ⌐①	N	3		3		3
num[1]	6 ⌐		6 ⌐②	Y	2		2
num[2]	2		2 ⌐		6 ⌐③	Y	5
num[3]	5		5		5 ⌐		6

Pass 2:

	Comparison	Swap	Result/Comparison	Swap	Result/Comparison	Swap	Result
num[0]	3 ⌐④	Y	2		2		2
num[1]	2 ⌐		3 ⌐⑤	N	3		3
num[2]	5		5 ⌐		5 ⌐⑥	N	5
num[3]	6		6		6 ⌐		6

Pass 3:

	Comparison	Swap	Result/Comparison	Swap	Result/Comparison	Swap	Result
num[0]	2 ⌐⑦	N	2		2		2
num[1]	3 ⌐		3 ⌐⑧	N	3		3
num[2]	5		5 ⌐		5 ⌐⑨	N	5
num[3]	6		6		6 ⌐		6

Figure 10-7: Bubble sort process used to sort the `num` array

After the `sortArray` function sorts the numbers in the `num` array in ascending numerical order, the `displayArray` function then displays the contents of the sorted array—the numbers 2, 3, 5, and 6.

2 Press the **Enter** key to close the DOS window, then close the Output window.

To help you understand how the bubble sort algorithm works, you will display the contents of the num array as the bubble sort is processing. To do so, you need simply to have the sortArray function call the displayArray function, passing it the num array, as well as the array size, when it does.

To display the contents of the num array as the bubble sort is processing:

1 Enter the additional code highlighted in Figure 10-8. Be sure to enter the opening and closing braces that surround the for statement's code block.

```
void sortArray(short num[], short size)
{
    short maxSub = size - 1;
    short temp = 0;
    char  swap = 'Y';

    //repeat loop instructions as long as a swap was made
    while(swap == 'Y')
    {
        //assume that no swaps will be necessary
        swap = 'N';

        //compare array elements to see if a swap is necessary
        for(short x = 0; x < maxSub; x = x + 1)
        {
            if(num[x] > num[x + 1])   //a swap is necessary
            {
                swap = 'Y';
                temp = num[x];
                num[x] = num[x + 1];
                num[x + 1] = temp;
            }//end if
            //display array while sorting
            cout << "Sorting the array: ";
            displayArray(num, 4);
        }//end for

    }//end while (swap == 'Y')
} //end of sortArray function
```

enter the opening brace →

enter these lines of code →

enter the closing brace →

Figure 10-8: Additional code to display the contents of the array as the bubble sort is processing

2 Save, build, and execute the LaProg01 program. The displayArray function displays the contents of the unsorted array—the numbers 3, 6, 2, and 5. The sortArray function then sorts the array, displaying the array's contents each time the instructions in the for loop are processed. The displayArray function then displays the contents of the sorted array—the numbers 2, 3, 5, and 6. See Figure 10-9.

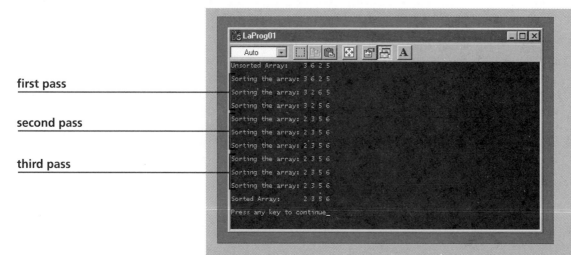

first pass

second pass

third pass

Figure 10-9: DOS window showing the contents of the array before, during, and after the bubble sort

Figure 10-9 illustrates the bubble sort process shown in Figure 10-7. Before the bubble sort begins, the array contains the unsorted numbers 3, 6, 2, and 5. During the first pass through the array, the bubble sort makes two swaps. First it swaps the number 6 stored in num[1] with the number 2 stored in num[2]. Then it swaps the number 6 stored in num[2] with the number 5 stored in num[3]. At the end of the first pass, the numbers in the array are in the following order: 3, 2, 5, and 6.

As Figure 10-9 shows, the bubble sort makes only one swap during the second pass through the array. It swaps the number 3 stored in num[0] with the number 2 stored in num[1]. You will notice that the bubble sort makes no swaps during the third pass through the array. The last line on the screen shows the contents of the sorted array—the numbers 2, 3, 5, and 6.

3   Press the **Enter** key to close the DOS window, then close the Output window.

Although the bubble sort you just learned is quick and easy, it is somewhat inefficient because it makes more comparisons than are necessary. For example, look closely at pass 1's third comparison in Figure 10-7. Notice that it compares and then swaps the last two elements of the array—the 6 and the 5. At the end of the first pass, therefore, the last two elements of the array are in their proper order. Notice, however, that the last comparison in both pass 2 and pass 3 also compares those two numbers to each other, which is unnecessary. You can improve the efficiency of the bubble sort algorithm by modifying the code. Instead of comparing items from the beginning to the end of the array, compare adjacent items from the beginning of the array only to the point where the last swap was made in the previous pass through the array. Since all the elements following the last swap are already in order, the algorithm does not need to compare them. The IPO chart for the modified bubble sort algorithm is shown in Figure 10-10. The changes from Figure 10-5's IPO chart are highlighted in the figure.

Input	Processing	Output

number array and array size from **main** function	Processing items: Short Integer variable named **maxSub**
	Short Integer variable named **temp**
	Character variable named **swap**
	counter variable named **x**
	Short Integer variable named **lastSwap**
	
	Algorithm:
	1. initialize **maxSub** variable to highest subscript in the array
	2. initialize **swap** variable to 'Y'
	3. repeat while (**swap** variable contains 'Y')
	    set **swap** variable to 'N'
	    initialize **x** counter variable to 0
	    repeat while (**x** value is less than **maxSub** value)
	        if (value in array element **x** is greater than value in array element [**x** + 1])
	            set **swap** variable to 'Y'
	            assign value in array element **x** to **temp** variable
	            assign value in array element[**x** + 1] to array element **x**
	            assign value in **temp** variable to array element[**x** + 1]
	            assign **x** value to **lastSwap** variable
	        end if
	        add 1 to **x** variable
	    end while (**x** value is less than **maxSub** value)
	    assign **lastSwap** value to **maxSub** variable
	end while (**swap** variable contains 'Y')
		array containing numbers sorted in ascending order

Figure 10-10: IPO chart for the modified bubble sort

To sort the values in descending order, simply change the selection structure's condition to "if (value in array element x is less than value in array element [x + 1])."

Now modify the bubble sort code in the sortArray function.

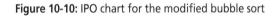

To modify the bubble sort code, then save and run the application:

1 Modify the bubble sort code in the **sortArray** function by entering the three statements and two comments highlighted in Figure 10-11.

```
void sortArray(short num[], short size)
{
    short maxSub = size - 1;
    short temp = 0;
    char  swap = 'Y';
    short lastSwap = 0;

    //repeat loop instructions as long as a swap was made
    while(swap == 'Y')
    {
        //assume that no swaps will be necessary
        swap = 'N';

        //compare array elements to see if a swap is necessary
        for(short x = 0; x < maxSub; x = x + 1)
        {
            if(num[x] > num[x + 1])   //a swap is necessary
            {
                swap = 'Y';
                temp = num[x];
                num[x] = num[x + 1];
                num[x + 1] = temp;
                //record position of last swap
                lastSwap = x;
            }//end if
            //display array while sorting
            cout << "Sorting the array: ";
            displayArray(num, 4);
        }//end for
        //assign position of last swap to maxSub
        maxSub = lastSwap;
    }//end while (swap == 'Y')
} //end of sortArray function
```

enter this statement → short lastSwap = 0;

enter this comment and statement → //record position of last swap / lastSwap = x;

enter this comment and statement → //assign position of last swap to maxSub / maxSub = lastSwap;

Figure 10-11: Modified bubble sort code in the sortArray function

When a swap occurs, the lastSwap = x; statement in the if statement's true path records the position of the array element that was swapped in the Short Integer variable named lastSwap. Each time the for loop completes an entire pass through the array, the maxSub = lastSwap; statement assigns the value stored in the lastSwap variable to the maxSub variable. The maxSub variable tells the for loop the array location at which to stop comparing. When you run the current program, the modified bubble sort will sort the num array using the process shown in Figure 10-12.

Pass 1:

	Comparison	Swap	Result/Comparison	Swap	Result/Comparison	Swap	Result
num[0]	3	N	3		3		3
num[1]	6 ①		6 ②	Y	2		2
num[2]	2		2		6 ③	Y	5
num[3]	5		5		5		6

Pass 2:

	Comparison	Swap	Result/Comparison	Swap	Result
num[0]	3 ④	Y	2		2
num[1]	2		3 ⑤	N	3
num[2]	5		5		5
num[3]	6		6		6

Figure 10-12: Modified bubble sort process used to sort the num array

If you compare both Figure 10-7 and Figure 10-12, you will notice that the modified bubble sort requires fewer steps to sort the data. With the addition of the three lines of code, only five comparisons, rather than nine, will be made. Run the bubble sort program to observe how the modified bubble sort works.

To observe how the modified bubble sort works:

1 Save, build, and execute the LaProg01 program. The `displayArray` function displays the contents of the unsorted array—the numbers 3, 6, 2, and 5. The `sortArray` function then sorts the array, displaying the array's contents each time the instructions in the `for` loop are processed. The `displayArray` function then displays the contents of the sorted array—the numbers 2, 3, 5, and 6. See Figure 10-13.

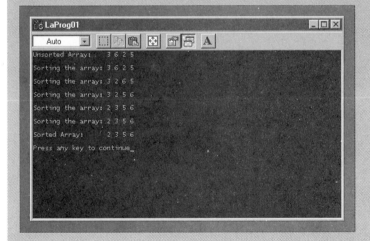

Figure 10-13: DOS window showing the contents of the array before, during, and after the modified bubble sort is processed

2 Press the **Enter** key to close the DOS window.

You have completed the bubble sort program, so you can close it.

3 Close the Output window and the workspace.

In the next section, you will learn how to use the bubble sort algorithm to sort the data stored in parallel arrays.

mini-quiz

Mini-Quiz 1

1. The process of arranging data in alphabetical or numerical order is called

_____ .

2. The bubble sort would compare the `code[x]` element to the _____ element.

3. When you use the bubble sort, the first step in swapping two of the elements in the `code` array is to _____ .

a. assign `code[x + 2]` to `temp`

b. assign `code[x]` to `temp`

c. assign `code[x]` to `code[x + 1]`

d. assign `temp` to `code[x]`

e. assign `temp` to `code[x + 1]`

4. After you complete step 1 in question 3, the second step in swapping two of the elements in the `code` array is to _____ .

a. assign `code[x + 1]` to `temp`

b. assign `code[x]` to `temp`

c. assign `code[x]` to `code[x + 1]`

d. assign `code[x + 1]` to `code[x]`

e. assign `temp` to `code[x + 1]`

5. After you complete steps 1 and 2 in questions 3 and 4, the final step in swapping two of the elements in the `code` array is to _____ .

a. assign `code[x + 1]` to `temp`

b. assign `code[x]` to `temp`

c. assign `code[x]` to `code[x + 1]`

d. assign `code[x + 1]` to `code[x]`

e. assign `temp` to `code[x + 1]`

Sorting the Data in Parallel One-dimensional Arrays

Gifts Express records each salesperson's annual sales amount in a sequential access file. The sales made in 1999, for example, are saved in the sales99.dat file, which is located in the LaProg02 folder on your computer's hard disk. Figure 10-14 shows the contents of the sales99.dat file.

```
621#141000
321#130000
204#200000
504#213000
303#150000
324#120000
411#310000
356#150000
222#455000
333#210000
444#180000
```

Figure 10-14: Contents of the sales99.dat file

Each record in the sales99.dat file contains two fields: the first is the salesperson's ID, and the second is his or her annual sales amount. Notice that the records are not ordered in any particular sequence. You will create a program that will sort the Gifts Express records in order by the salesperson's ID, and then save the sorted information in a file named sales99.srt. Figure 10-15 shows the IPO chart for the **main** function in the Gifts Express sort program.

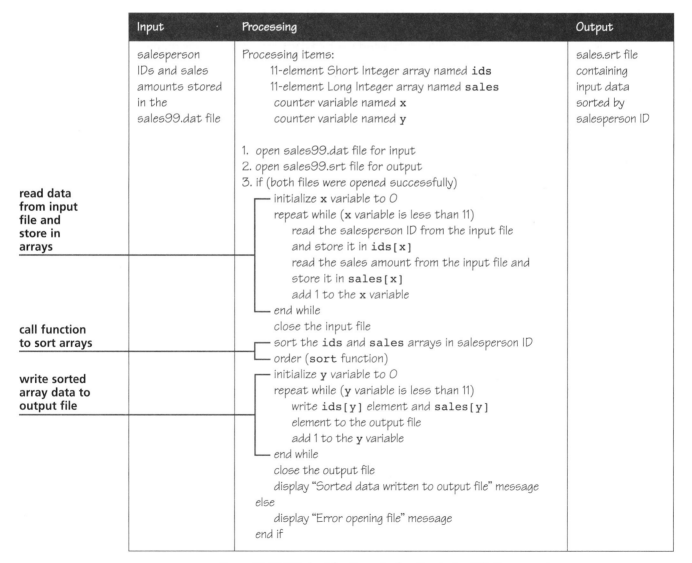

Figure 10-15: IPO chart for the **main** function in the Gifts Express sort program

As the IPO chart indicates, the main function's input is the data stored in the sales99.dat file—in this case, the salesperson IDs and sales amounts. The main function's output is a file named sales.srt, which will contain the input data sorted by the salesperson ID. Notice that the main function will use four processing items: an 11-element Short Integer array named ids, an 11-element Long Integer array named sales, and two counter variables named x and y. When the input data is read from the sales99.dat file, the main function will store each salesperson's ID in the ids array, and each salesperson's sales amount in the sales array. The ids and sales arrays are parallel because each element in the ids array corresponds to the element located in the same position of the sales array.

The main function will begin by opening the sales99.dat file, which contains the existing Gifts Express records, for input. It will also open the sales99.srt file, where the sorted records will be saved, for output. If both files are not opened successfully, the selection structure's false path will display an appropriate message. Otherwise, the instructions in the selection structure's true path will be processed.

You will notice that the selection structure's true path begins with a counter-controlled loop that reads each salesperson's ID and his or her sales amount from the input file. It then stores each in the appropriate location in the ids and sales arrays, respectively. The input file is then closed before the main function calls the sort function to sort the contents of both arrays in order by the salesperson ID. After the arrays are sorted, the main function uses a counter-controlled loop to write the contents of both arrays to the sales.srt output file before closing it. A message indicating that the sorted data was written to the output file is then displayed to inform the user that the program has completed its task. Open a partially completed program that corresponds to the IPO chart shown in Figure 10-15.

To open the partially completed Gifts Express sort program:

1 Open the **LaProg02.cpp** file, which is located in the Cpp\Tut10\LaProg02 folder on your computer's hard disk. The Gifts Express sort program appears in the LaProg02.cpp window. Figure 10-16 shows the program's main function.

```
//LaProg02.cpp
//this program sorts the contents of two parallel arrays

#include <iostream.h>
#include <fstream.h>

//function prototype
void sort(short [], long [], short);

void main()
{
    //declare and initialize arrays
    short ids[11]  = {0};
    long  sales[11] = {0};
```

Figure 10-16: main function in the Gifts Express sort program

open files

determine if files were opened successfully

read data from input file and store in arrays

call function to sort arrays

write sorted data to output file

display message if open failed

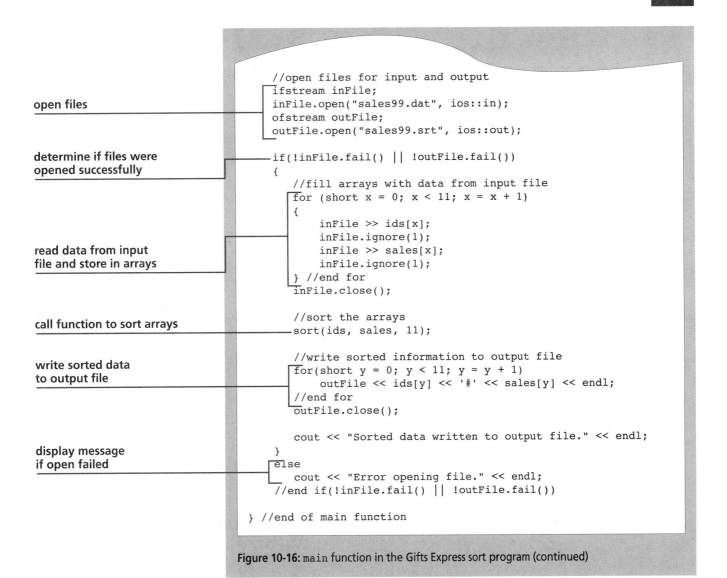

```
//open files for input and output
ifstream inFile;
inFile.open("sales99.dat", ios::in);
ofstream outFile;
outFile.open("sales99.srt", ios::out);

if(!inFile.fail() || !outFile.fail())
{
    //fill arrays with data from input file
    for (short x = 0; x < 11; x = x + 1)
    {
        inFile >> ids[x];
        inFile.ignore(1);
        inFile >> sales[x];
        inFile.ignore(1);
    } //end for
    inFile.close();

    //sort the arrays
    sort(ids, sales, 11);

    //write sorted information to output file
    for(short y = 0; y < 11; y = y + 1)
        outFile << ids[y] << '#' << sales[y] << endl;
    //end for
    outFile.close();

    cout << "Sorted data written to output file." << endl;
}
else
    cout << "Error opening file." << endl;
//end if(!inFile.fail() || !outFile.fail())

} //end of main function
```

Figure 10-16: main function in the Gifts Express sort program (continued)

Following the algorithm shown in Figure 10-15, the main function opens the sales99.dat file for input and the sales99.srt file for output. If both files are not opened successfully, the if statement's false path displays the message "Error opening file." However, if both files are opened successfully, then the main function uses a for loop to read each record from the input file, store the salesperson's ID in the ids array, and store his or her sales amount in the sales array. The main function then calls the sort function, passing it the ids and sales arrays, as well as the numeric literal constant 11, which corresponds to the size of the arrays. Recall that the sort function's task is to sort the contents of both arrays in order by salesperson ID. After the sort function completes its task, the main function uses another for loop to write the sorted contents of the arrays to the sales99.srt output file before closing it and displaying the message "Sorted data written to output file."

Next, view the IPO chart for the sort program's sort function, which is shown in Figure 10-17.

	Input	Processing	Output

two temporary variables	ids and sales arrays, as well as array size, from main function	Processing items: Short Integer variable named maxSub
		   ⌐ Short Integer variable named tempId
		   └ Long Integer variable named tempDollars
		   Character variable named swap
		   counter variable named x
		   Short Integer variable named lastSwap
			contents of both arrays sorted by salesperson ID

		Algorithm:	
		1. initialize maxSub variable to highest subscript in the array	
		2. initialize swap variable to 'Y'	

		3. repeat while (swap variable contains 'Y')
		    set swap variable to 'N'
		    initialize x variable to 0
		    repeat while (x value is less than maxSub value)
		      if (ID in array element x is greater than ID in array element [x + 1])
		        set swap variable to 'Y'	

swap salesperson numbers		⌐ assign ID in array element x to tempId variable assign ID in array element [x + 1] to array element x └ assign ID in tempId to array element [x + 1]	

swap sales amounts		⌐ assign sales amount in array element x to tempDollars variable
		   assign sales amount in array element[x + 1] to array element x
		└ assign tempDollars to array element[x + 1]
		      assign x value to lastSwap variable
		      end if
		      add 1 to x variable
		    end while (x value is less than maxSub value)
		    assign the value in lastSwap to the maxSub variable
		  end while (swap variable contains 'Y')	

Figure 10-17: IPO chart for the sort program's sort function

As the IPO chart indicates, the sort function will receive the ids and sales arrays, as well as the size of the arrays, from the main function. The sort function will then use the bubble sort to sort the contents of the arrays by salesperson ID.

If you compare the bubble sort algorithm shown in Figure 10-17, which sorts two parallel arrays, to the one shown earlier in Figure 10-10, which sorts one array, you will notice that both algorithms are almost identical. The main difference is in the inner loop's selection structure. In Figure 10-10, if the number in the current array element is greater than the number in the next array element, the algorithm simply swaps the numbers in both array elements. However, in Figure 10-17, if the ID in the current array element is greater than the ID in the next array element, then the algorithm swaps not only the IDs, but the corresponding sales amounts as well. Swapping the values stored in the corresponding locations in both arrays is necessary to keep both arrays parallel. To perform the swap, the algorithm uses two temporary variables rather than one. In this case, the Short Integer variable named `tempID` will temporarily store the salesperson's ID, and the Long Integer `tempDollars` variable will temporarily store the sales amount.

To complete the Gifts Express sort program, you will need to complete its `sort` function, which is located in the programmer-defined functions section of the program. The code that swaps the values in both arrays is currently missing from the `sort` function.

To complete the Gifts Express sort program, and then save and execute it:

1 Enter the eight statements highlighted in Figure 10-18 in the `sort` function's code, which is located in the programmer-defined functions section of the program.

enter these statements to declare the temporary variables

enter these statements to swap the array elements

```
void sort(short num[], long dollar[], short size)
{
    short maxSub      = size - 1;
    short tempId      = 0;
    long  tempDollars = 0;
    char  swap        = 'Y';
    short lastSwap    = 0;

    //repeat loop instructions as long as a swap was made
    while(swap == 'Y')
    {
        //assume that no swaps will be necessary
        swap = 'N';

        //compare array elements to see if a swap is necessary
        for(short x = 0; x < maxSub; x = x + 1)
        {
            if(num[x] > num[x + 1])   //a swap is necessary
            {
                swap = 'Y';
                //swap salesperson ids
                tempId = num[x];
                num[x] = num[x + 1];
                num[x + 1] = tempId;
                //swap corresponding sales amounts
                tempDollars = dollar[x];
                dollar[x] = dollar[x + 1];
                dollar[x + 1] = tempDollars;

                //record position of last swap
                lastSwap = x;
            }//end if
        }//end for
        //assign position of last swap to maxSub
        maxSub = lastSwap;
    }//end while (swap == 'Y')
} //end of sort function
```

Figure 10-18: Eight statements entered in the `sort` function

Execute the program to observe how it works.

2   Save, build, and execute the program. The `main` function opens the sales99.dat file for input and the sales99.srt file for output. It then reads the records from the input file and stores the salespersons' IDs in the `ids` array and the sales amounts in the `sales` array. The `main` function then closes the input file and calls the `sort` function, passing it the `ids` and `sales` arrays and the numeric literal constant 11. The `sort` function receives the arrays, as well as their size, in its `num`, `dollar`, and `size` formal parameters, and then sorts the contents of both arrays. When the `sort` function has completed its task, the `main` function writes the sorted array information to the sales99.srt file before closing the file and displaying in the DOS window the message "Sorted data written to output file."

3   Press the **Enter** key to close the DOS window.

Now open the sales99.srt file to verify that it contains the Gifts Express records sorted by salesperson ID.

4   Open the **sales99.srt** file. The contents of the file, sorted in order by the salesperson ID, are shown in Figure 10-19.

the file is sorted in ascending numerical order by the ID field →

```
204#200000
222#455000
303#150000
321#130000
324#120000
333#210000
356#150000
411#310000
444#180000
504#213000
621#141000
```

Figure 10-19: Contents of the sales99.srt file

As Figure 10-19 shows, the records in the sales99.srt file are sorted in ascending numerical order by salesperson ID. Also, because the bubble sort algorithm swapped the corresponding sales amounts each time it swapped the salesperson IDs, the `ids` and `sales` arrays are still parallel. For example, if you compare the unsorted records shown in Figure 10-14 to the sorted records shown in Figure 10-19, you will notice that the sales for salesperson 321 are 130000 in both the unsorted sales99.dat and the sorted sales99.srt files.

5   Close the sales99.srt data file.

You have completed the Gifts Express sort program, so you can close it.

6   Close the Output window and the workspace.

Now that you have sorted the annual sales records for Gifts Express, you can use the sorted records as input in another program. For example, you will use the sorted records as input in the program that allows Susan Li to display a salesperson's annual sales after entering the salesperson's ID. The sorted records will allow the program to perform an efficient search of the data—called a binary search.

The Binary Search Program

In Tutorial 8's Lesson B, you learned how to use a serial search to search for a specific value in an array. In a **serial search,** the program begins the search with the first array element. The program then continues searching, element by element, until either a match is found or the end of the array is encountered. A serial search is useful when the amount of data that must be searched is small. If you have a large amount of data, however, the serial search is extremely inefficient; in those cases, a binary search is a better option. For a binary search to work, the data in the array must be arranged in either alphabetical or numerical order. For example, if you are searching for a last name, then the last names in the array must be sorted in alphabetical order. If you are searching for a zip code, then the zip codes must be sorted in numerical order.

Assume that the Gifts Express salesperson IDs are sorted in numerical order and stored in an array named num. Also assume that you want to use the binary search to search for the number 411. Rather than beginning the search with the first array element, as a serial search does, the **binary search** algorithm begins the search in the middle of the array, as shown in Figure 10-20.

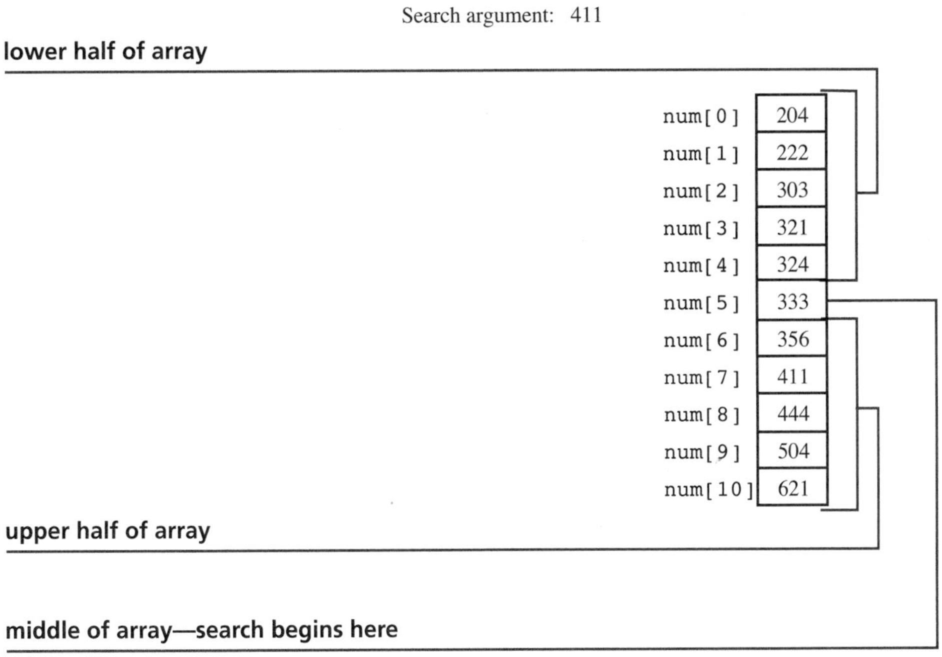

Search argument: 411

lower half of array

num[0]	204
num[1]	222
num[2]	303
num[3]	321
num[4]	324
num[5]	333
num[6]	356
num[7]	411
num[8]	444
num[9]	504
num[10]	621

upper half of array

middle of array—search begins here

Figure 10-20: Beginning of the binary search

If the **search argument**—the value for which you are searching—is equal to the value that is located in the middle of the array, then the search ends. If, on the other hand, the search argument is greater than the value located in the middle of the array, the search continues in the upper half of the array, where the values greater than the search argument are located. Otherwise, it continues in the lower half of the array, where the values that are less than the search argument are located. In Figure 10-20, the search argument (411) is greater than the value found in the middle of the array (the 333 stored in num[5]), so the search would continue in the upper half of the array.

Before continuing the search, the upper half of the array is halved again, as shown in Figure 10-21.

Search argument: 411

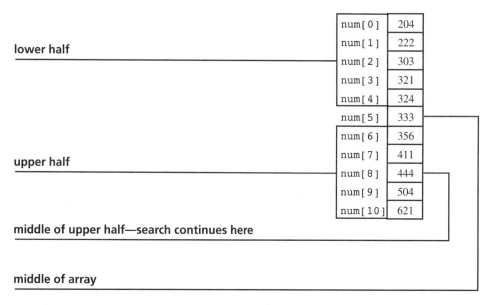

Figure 10-21: Upper half halved again

Here again, if the search argument is equal to the value in the array, then the search ends. If, on the other hand, the search argument is greater than the value in the array, the search continues in the array elements above the current one. Otherwise, it continues in the array elements below the current one. In Figure 10-21, the search argument (411) is less than the array value found in the middle of the upper half of the array (the 444 stored in num[8]). Therefore, the search would continue in the elements located between the middle of the array (num[5]) and the current element (num[8]). The binary search algorithm continues to halve the remaining array elements until it either finds a match or determines that no match exists. You will use the binary search in the program that allows Susan Li to display a salesperson's annual sales by simply entering the salesperson's ID. The IPO chart for the binary search program's main function is shown in Figure 10-22.

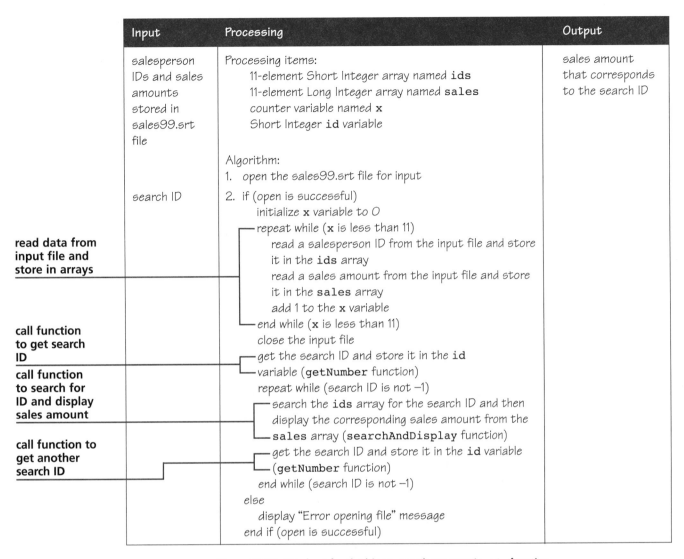

Input	Processing	Output

salesperson IDs and sales amounts stored in sales99.srt file	Processing items:
	    11-element Short Integer array named `ids`
	    11-element Long Integer array named `sales`
	    counter variable named `x`
	    Short Integer `id` variable
		sales amount that corresponds to the search ID

search ID	Algorithm:
	1. open the sales99.srt file for input
	2. if (open is successful)
	        initialize `x` variable to 0
	        repeat while (`x` is less than 11)
	            read a salesperson ID from the input file and store it in the `ids` array
	            read a sales amount from the input file and store it in the `sales` array
	            add 1 to the `x` variable
	        end while (`x` is less than 11)
	        close the input file
	        get the search ID and store it in the `id` variable (`getNumber` function)
	        repeat while (search ID is not −1)
	            search the `ids` array for the search ID and then display the corresponding sales amount from the `sales` array (`searchAndDisplay` function)
	            get the search ID and store it in the `id` variable (`getNumber` function)
	        end while (search ID is not −1)
	    else
	        display "Error opening file" message
	    end if (open is successful)	

read data from input file and store in arrays

call function to get search ID

call function to search for ID and display sales amount

call function to get another search ID

Figure 10-22: IPO chart for the binary search program's `main` function

The `main` function will begin by opening the sales99.srt file for input. Recall that the sales99.srt file contains the Gifts Express records sorted in ascending order by the salesperson ID. If the file is not opened successfully, then the selection structure's false path will display an appropriate message. If, on the other hand, the file is opened successfully, then the instructions in the selection structure's true path will be processed. You will notice that the true path uses a counter-controlled loop to read each ID and sales amount from the input file and store each in the `ids` and `sales` arrays, respectively. After the records are read and stored in the arrays, the input file will be closed and the `main` function will call the `getNumber` function both to get and return the search ID—the ID for which the user wants to search. If the user enters a −1 as the search ID, the program will end; otherwise, the two instructions in the `main` function's second `while` loop will be processed. You will notice that the first instruction in that `while` loop calls the `searchAndDisplay` function, whose task is to search for the search ID in the `ids` array and then display the corresponding sales amount from the `sales` array. The `searchAndDisplay` function will use the binary search algorithm to perform the search. The second instruction in the `while` loop will call the `getNumber` function to get another search ID from the user.

On your computer's hard disk is a partially completed binary search program for Gifts Express. Open the program now.

To view the partially completed binary search program:

1 Open the **LaProg03.cpp** file, which is located in the Cpp\Tut10\LaProg03 folder on your computer's hard disk. The binary search program appears in the LaProg03.cpp window. The program's main function is shown in Figure 10-23.

```cpp
//LaProg03.cpp
//this program uses the binary search to search an array

#include <iostream.h>
#include <fstream.h>

//function prototypes
short getNumber();
void searchAndDisplay(short, short [], long [], short);

void main()
{
    //declare and initialize variables
    short id = 0;

    //declare and initialize arrays
    short ids[11]   = {0};
    long  sales[11] = {0};

    //fill arrays
    ifstream inFile;
    inFile.open("sales99.srt", ios::in);

    if(!inFile.fail())
    {
        for(short x = 0; x < 11; x = x + 1)
        {
            inFile >> ids[x];
            inFile.ignore(1);
            inFile >> sales[x];
            inFile.ignore(1);
        } //end for
        inFile.close();

        //get a salesperson's number
        id = getNumber();

        while (id != -1)
        {
            //search for the salesperson's ID
            //display the sales
            searchAndDisplay(id, ids, sales, 11);

            //get another salesperson's ID
            id = getNumber();
        } //end while (id != -1)
    }
    else
        cout << "Error opening file." << endl;
    //end if(!inFile.fail())
} //end of main function
```

Labels pointing to the code:
- open file
- determine if open was successful
- read records from file and store them in arrays
- call function to get search argument
- call function to search for ID and display sales
- call function to get another search argument
- display message if open failed

Figure 10-23: Binary search program's main function

As Figure 10-23 indicates, the main function uses two programmer-defined functions named getNumber and searchAndDisplay. getNumber is a value-returning function and searchAndDisplay is a void function. The main function also declares and initializes a Short Integer variable named id, an 11-element Short Integer array named ids, and an 11-element Long Integer array named sales.

After declaring and initializing the variable and the arrays, the main function opens the sales99.srt file, which contains the Gifts Express sales records sorted by salesperson ID, for input. If the file is not opened successfully, then the if statement's false path displays an appropriate message. If, on the other hand, the file is opened successfully, then the if statement's true path uses a for loop to read each record from the input file. You will notice that the for loop stores the salesperson IDs in the ids array and stores the sales amounts in the sales array. After all of the records are read from the input file, the file is closed before the main function calls the getNumber function. Recall that the getNumber function's task is both to get and return the search argument—the ID for which the user wants to search. The main function assigns the value returned by the getNumber function to the id variable.

You will notice that the while (id != -1) clause in the main function uses the value in the id variable to determine whether to process the instructions in the while loop or simply to end the program. In this case, the program will end when the user enters a -1 as the search ID. If the user enters a search ID other than a -1, the first instruction in the while loop calls the searchAndDisplay function, which contains the code for the binary search algorithm. The second instruction in the while loop then calls the getNumber function, which simply gets and returns another ID.

Next, view the IPO chart and the C++ code for the getNumber function. Both are shown in Figure 10-24.

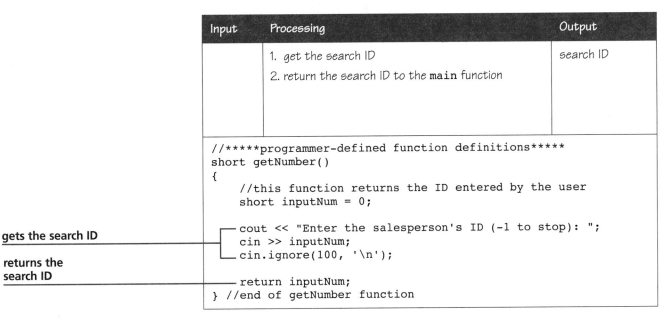

Figure 10-24: IPO chart and C++ code for the getNumber function

As Figure 10-24 indicates, the `getNumber` function simply gets the search argument—in this case, the salesperson's ID—from the user and returns it to the `main` function.

Next, view the IPO chart for the `searchAndDisplay` function, which contains the binary search algorithm. The IPO chart is shown in Figure 10-25.

Input	Processing	Output

search ID from **main** function
 	
ids and **sales** arrays, as well as array size, from **main** function
	Processing items:
	    Short Integer variable named `startSub`
	    Short Integer variable named `stopSub`
	    Short Integer variable named `middleSub`
	    Character variable named `found`
	
	Algorithm:
	1. assign 0 to `startSub` variable
	2. assign highest array subscript to `stopSub` variable
	3. assign 0 to `middleSub` variable
	4. assign 'N' to `found` variable
	5. repeat while (`found` is 'N' and `startSub` <= stopStop)
	        split array in half by assigning (`startSub` + `stopSub`)/2
	        to `middleSub`
	        if (ID in element `middleSub` is greater than search ID)
	            continue search in lower half of array
	        else
	            if (ID in element `middleSub` is less than search ID)
	                continue search in upper half of array
	            else
	                assign 'Y' to `found` variable
	                display sales amount from corresponding element
	                in sales array
	            end if (ID in element `middleSub` is less than search ID)
	        end if (ID in element `middleSub` is greater than search ID)
	    end while (`found` is 'N' and `startSub` <= stopStop)
	6. if (`found` variable is 'N')
	        display the message "This salesperson's number is not valid."
	    end if (`found` variable is 'N')
		sales amount corresponding to salesperson's ID

(Left margin annotations: **splits array in half**; **determines whether to stop searching or where to continue search**; **search ID is not in the array**)*

Figure 10-25: IPO chart for the `searchAndDisplay` function

According to the IPO chart's Input column, the `main` function will pass the search ID, as well as the `ids` and `sales` arrays and their size, to the `searchAndDisplay` function.

The binary search algorithm included in the `searchAndDisplay` function begins by initializing three Short Integer variables named `startSub`, `stopSub`, and `middleSub`, as well as a Character variable named `found`. The function will use the `startSub` variable to keep track of the first possible array position to search. The variable is initially given a value of 0—the first subscript in the `ids` array. The function will use the `stopSub` variable to keep track of the last possible array position to search. It is initially given a value of the highest array subscript—in this case, it will be initialized to 10, which is the last subscript in the 11-element `ids` array. The `middleSub` variable, which is initialized to 0, will be used to halve the array. The `found` variable, which is initialized to 'N', will keep track of whether the search ID was found in the array.

As Figure 10-25 indicates, the `searchAndDisplay` function will perform the `while` loop instructions only if the search ID has not been found (`found` is `'N'`) and there are still array elements to search (`startSub <= stopSub`). When either the ID is found or the entire array has been searched, the `while` loop ends. If, after the `while` loop ends, the `found` variable contains the letter 'N', then the function displays a message indicating that the salesperson's ID was not found. Study the `while` loop instructions more closely.

The first statement within the `while` loop splits the array in half by adding the first array subscript (`startSub`) to the last array subscript (`stopSub`), and then dividing that sum by 2. The result is assigned to the `middleSub` variable. In the current program, the `middleSub` variable will be assigned a value of 5, which is calculated by adding the `startSub` value of 0 to the `stopSub` value of 10, and then dividing that sum by 2.

The `while` loop then uses a nested `if` statement to determine if the middle element in the array contains a value that is either greater than, less than, or equal to the search ID. If the ID in the array is greater than the ID for which the user is searching, then the algorithm needs to continue searching in the lower half of the array only. (Recall that the IDs are sorted in ascending numerical order in the array. If the array value is greater than the search argument, then the search argument must be located in the lower half of the array; it cannot be located in the upper half, which contains even larger numbers.) If, on the other hand, the array value is less than the ID the user wants to find, then the algorithm needs to search the upper half of the array only. Lastly, if the array value is equal to the search ID, then the `found` variable is set to 'Y', indicating that a match was found, and the sales amount that corresponds to the ID is displayed. Figure 10-26 shows the C++ code for the `searchAndDisplay` function, which is located in the programmer-defined section of the current program.

```
void searchAndDisplay(short searchId,
                      short num[],
                      long  dollar[],
                      short size)
{
    //this function uses the binary search to search an array

    short startSub  = 0;
    short stopSub   = size - 1;
    short middleSub = 0;
    char  found     = 'N';

    while(found == 'N' && startSub <= stopSub)
    {
        middleSub = (startSub + stopSub) / 2; //split array in half

        if(num[middleSub] > searchId)          //search lower half
            stopSub = middleSub - 1;
        else
            if(num[middleSub] < searchId)      //search upper half
                startSub = middleSub + 1;
            else    //ID equals current element
            {
                found = 'Y';
                cout << "Salesperson " << searchId
                     << " sales are: " << dollar[middleSub]
                     << endl << endl;
            }//end if (num[middleSub] < searchId)
        //end if (num[middleSub] > searchId)
    } //end while (found == 'N' && startSub <= stopSub)

    if(found == 'N')
        cout << "This salesperson's ID is not valid."
             << endl << endl;
    //end if (found == 'N')
} //end of searchAndDisplay function
```

split array in half

continue search
in lower half

continue search
in upper half

array element's
value equals
the search argument

search argument
is not in the array

Figure 10-26: searchAndDisplay function's code

To understand how the binary search algorithm works, you will desk-check the
searchAndDisplay code shown in Figure 10-26 using a search argument of 321.
Figure 10-27 shows the values in the num and dollar arrays, as well as the values
in the searchId and size formal parameters, when the searchAndDisplay
function is called.

searchId	size
321	11

num[0]	204	dollar[0]	200000
num[1]	222	dollar[1]	455000
num[2]	303	dollar[2]	150000
num[3]	321	dollar[3]	130000
num[4]	324	dollar[4]	120000
num[5]	333	dollar[5]	210000
num[6]	356	dollar[6]	150000
num[7]	411	dollar[7]	310000
num[8]	444	dollar[8]	180000
num[9]	504	dollar[9]	213000
num[10]	621	dollar[10]	141000

Figure 10-27: Values in the searchId, size, num array, and dollar array formal parameters

The searchAndDisplay function begins by creating and initializing the startSub, stopSub, middleSub, and found variables, as shown in Figure 10-28.

startSub	stopSub	middleSub	found
0	10	0	N

Figure 10-28: Initial values of variables

After initializing the variables, the while loop determines if the loop instructions should be processed. In this case, the found variable contains the literal constant 'N' and the startSub variable contains a value that is less than or equal to the value in the stopSub variable, so the loop instructions are processed.

The first loop instruction splits the array in half by adding the startSub value of 0 to the stopSub value of 10, and then dividing that sum by 2. The result of 5 is assigned to the middleSub variable, as shown in Figure 10-29.

startSub	stopSub	middleSub	found
0	10	~~0~~ 5	N

Figure 10-29: New value placed in the middleSub variable

The first if statement in the while loop determines whether the middle array value—the value in num[middleSub]—is greater than the value for which the user is searching. If it is, the search should continue in the lower half of the array only. In the current program, the value in num[5] (333) is greater than the value in searchId (321), so only the array elements with subscripts from 0 through 4 should be searched the next time the loop is processed. As Figure 10-29 indicates, the startSub variable, which stores the position of the first possible element to search, already contains the correct value of 0. However, the stopSub variable, which stores the position of the last possible element to search, will need to be changed from its current value (10) to 4. You will notice that the stopSub = middleSub - 1; statement, which is located below the first if clause in the searchAndDisplay function, accomplishes that task. After the stopSub variable is assigned its correct value, the nested selection structure ends and the while statement determines whether the loop instructions should be processed again. At the end of the first time through the loop, the variables have the values shown in Figure 10-30.

startSub	stopSub	middleSub	found
0	~~10~~ 4	~~0~~ 5	N

Figure 10-30: Values in the variables after the while loop is processed the first time

Because the found variable contains the literal constant 'N' and the startSub value is less than or equal to the stopSub value, the loop instructions are processed a second time. The middleSub = (startSub + stopSub) / 2; statement halves the lower half of the array and assigns the result to the middleSub variable. In this case, middleSub will be assigned a value of 2, which is calculated by adding the startSub value of 0 to the stopSub value of 4 and then dividing that sum by 2, as shown in Figure 10-31.

startSub	stopSub	middleSub	found
0	~~10~~ 4	~~0~~ ~~5~~ 2	N

Figure 10-31: New value placed in the middleSub variable

The first if clause in the while loop determines whether the middle array value—the value in num[middleSub]—is greater than the value in searchId. In this case, the 303 stored in num[2] is not greater than 321, so the second if clause in the while loop then determines whether the middle array value is less than the value in searchId. In this case, 303 is less than 321, which means that the search should continue in the upper half of the halved array—the elements with subscripts 3 and 4. As Figure 10-31 indicates, the stopSub variable, which stores the position of the last possible element to search, already contains the correct value of 4. However, the startSub variable, which stores the position of the first possible element to search, will need to be changed from its current value (0) to 3. You will notice that the startSub = middleSub + 1; statement, which is located below the second if clause, accomplishes that task. After the startSub variable is assigned its correct value, the nested selection structure ends and the while statement determines whether the loop instructions should be processed again. At the end of the second time through the loop, the variables have the values shown in Figure 10-32.

startSub	stopSub	middleSub	found
~~0~~ 3	~~10~~ 4	~~0~~ ~~5~~ 2	N

Figure 10-32: Values in the variables after the while loop is processed the second time

Because the `found` variable contains the literal constant 'N' and the `startSub` value is less than or equal to the `stopSub` value, the loop instructions are processed a third time. The `middleSub = (startSub + stopSub) / 2;` statement adds the `startSub` value of 3 to the `stopSub` value of 4, and then divides that sum by 2. The 3.5 result is truncated to 3 before being stored in the `middleSub` variable, as shown in Figure 10-33.

startSub	stopSub	middleSub	found
~~0~~	~~10~~	~~0~~	N
	4	~~5~~	
3		~~2~~	
		3	

Figure 10-33: New value placed in the `middleSub` variable

The first `if` clause in the `while` loop determines whether the value in `num[3]`(321) is greater than the value in `searchId` (321). In this case, it is not. The second `if` clause then determines whether the value in `num[3]` is less than the value in `searchId`. In this case, it is not. If the `num[3]` value is neither greater than nor less than the `searchId` value, then the two values must be equal. In that case, the two statements within the second `else` clause are processed. The `found = 'Y';` statement sets the `found` variable to 'Y', which indicates that an ID matching the search ID was found in the array. The `cout << "Salesperson " << searchId << " sales are: " << dollar[middleSub] << endl << endl;` statement then displays the ID, as well as its corresponding sales amount from the `dollar` array. In this case, a sales amount of 130000 will display. After the `else` clause instructions are processed, the nested selection structure ends and the `while` statement determines whether the loop instructions should be processed again. At the end of the third time through the loop, the variables have the values shown in Figure 10-34.

startSub	stopSub	middleSub	found
~~0~~	~~10~~	~~0~~	~~N~~
	4	~~5~~	
3		~~2~~	
		3	Y

Figure 10-34: Values in the variables after the `while` loop is processed the third time

Because the `found` variable now contains the value 'Y', the `while` loop ends. The selection structure below the `while` loop then determines whether the search ID was found in the array. If the `found` variable contains 'N', then the search ID was not found and a corresponding message is displayed on the screen before the function ends.

Now desk-check the binary search code with an ID that is not in the array—for example, use the number 322. The `searchAndDisplay` function begins by creating the `startSub`, `middleSub`, `stopSub`, and `found` variables, and initializing them to 0, 0, 10, and 'N', respectively. The `while` loop then determines if the loop instructions should be processed. In this case, the `found` variable contains 'N' and the `startSub` variable contains a value that is less than or equal to the value in the `stopSub` variable, so the loop instructions are processed. (Recall that at this point the `startSub` variable contains the number 0 and the `stopSub` variable contains the number 10.)

The first loop instruction splits the array in half by adding the `startSub` value of 0 to the `stopSub` value of 10, and then dividing that sum by 2. The result of 5 is assigned to the `middleSub` variable. The first `if` clause in the `while` loop determines whether the middle array value—the value in `num[middleSub]`—is greater than the value for which the user is searching. If it is, the search should continue in the lower half of the array only. In the current program, the value in `num[5]` (333) is greater than the value in `searchId` (322), so only the array elements with subscripts from 0 through 4 should be searched the next time the loop is processed. At this point, the `startSub` variable, which stores the position of the first possible element to search, already contains the correct value of 0. However, the `stopSub` variable, which stores the position of the last possible element to search, will need to be changed from its current value (10) to 4. Recall that the `stopSub = middleSub - 1;` statement, which is located below the first `if` clause in the `searchAndDisplay` function, accomplishes that task. After the `stopSub` variable is assigned its correct value, the selection structure ends and the `while` statement determines whether the loop instructions should be processed again. At the end of the first time through the loop, the variables and formal parameters have the values shown in Figure 10-35.

searchId	size
322	11

startSub	stopSub	middleSub	found
0	~~10~~ 4	~~0~~ 5	N

Figure 10-35: Values in the variables and formal parameters after the `while` loop is processed the first time

Because the `found` variable contains the literal constant 'N' and the `startSub` value is less than or equal to the `stopSub` value, the loop instructions are processed a second time. The `middleSub = (startSub + stopSub) / 2;` statement halves the lower half of the array and assigns the result to the `middleSub` variable. In this case, `middleSub` will be assigned a value of 2, which is calculated by adding the `startSub` value of 0 to the `stopSub` value of 4, and then dividing that sum by 2. The first `if` clause in the `while` loop determines whether the middle array value— the value in `num[2]`—is greater than the value in `searchId`. Since 303 is not greater than 322, the second `if` clause in the `while` loop then determines whether the middle array value is less than the value in `searchId`. In this case, 303 is less than 322, which means that the search should continue in the upper half of the halved array—the elements with subscripts 3 and 4. At this point, the `stopSub` variable, which stores the position of the last possible element to search, already contains the correct value of 4. However, the `startSub` variable, which stores the position of the first possible element to search, will need to be changed from its current value (0) to 3. Recall that the `startSub = middleSub + 1;` statement, which is located below the second `if` clause, accomplishes that task. After the `startSub` variable is assigned its correct value, the nested selection structure ends and the `while` statement determines whether the loop instructions should be processed again. At the end of the second time through the loop, the variables and formal parameters have the values shown in Figure 10-36.

searchId	size
322	11

startSub	stopSub	middleSub	found
~~0~~	~~10~~	~~0~~	N
	4	~~5~~	
3		2	

Figure 10-36: Values in the variables and formal parameters after the `while` loop is processed the second time

Because the `found` variable contains the literal constant 'N' and the `startSub` value is less than or equal to the `stopSub` value, the loop instructions are processed a third time. The `middleSub = (startSub + stopSub) / 2;` statement adds the `startSub` value of 3 to the `stopSub` value of 4, and then divides that sum by 2. The 3.5 result is truncated to 3 before being stored in the `middleSub` variable. The first `if` clause in the `while` loop determines whether the value in `num[3]`(321) is greater than the value in `searchId` (322). In this case, it is not. The second `if` clause then determines whether the value in `num[3]` (321) is less than the value in `searchId` (322). In this case it is, so the search continues in the upper half of the array, with the element whose subscript is 4. At this point, the `stopSub` variable, which stores the position of the last possible element to search, already contains the correct value of 4. However, the `startSub` variable, which stores the position of the first possible element to search, will need to be changed from its current value (3) to 4. Recall that the `startSub = middleSub + 1;` statement, which is located below the second `if` clause, accomplishes that task. After the `startSub` variable is assigned its correct value, the nested selection structure ends and the `while` statement determines whether the loop instructions should be processed again. At the end of the third time through the loop, both the `startSub` and `stopSub` variables contain the number 4, and the `middleSub` variable contains the number 3. The loop is then processed again. At the end of the fourth time through the loop, the variables have the values shown in Figure 10-37.

startSub	stopSub	middleSub	found
~~0~~	~~10~~	~~0~~	N
	4	~~5~~	
~~3~~	3	~~2~~	
4		~~3~~	
		4	

Figure 10-37: Values in the variables after the `while` loop is processed the fourth time

Because the `startSub` variable now contains a value that is greater than the value in the `stopSub` variable, the `while` loop ends. The selection structure below the `while` loop then determines whether the search ID was found in the array. In this case, the `found` variable contains the literal constant 'N', which indicates that the search ID was not found. Subsequently, the message, "This salesperson's ID is not valid," is displayed before the searchAndDisplay function ends.

Run the binary search program to observe how the binary search code works.

To observe how the binary search code works:

1   Build and execute the LaProg03 program. When you are prompted to enter an ID, type **321** and press the **Enter** key. The DOS window indicates that this salesperson's sales are 130000.

Now try an ID that is not in the array.

2   When you are prompted to enter an ID, type **322** and press the **Enter** key. The DOS window displays the message, "This salesperson's ID is not valid."

3   When you are prompted to enter an ID, type **–1** and press the **Enter** key to end the program. Then press the **Enter** key to close the DOS window.

You are now finished with the binary search program, so you can close it.

4   Close the workspace, and then close the Output window.

Mini-Quiz 2

1. A(n) _____ search begins the search with the first array element.
2. A(n) _____ search begins the search with the element that is located in the middle of the array.
3. The data for which you are searching is called the _____ .
4. Trace the binary search code shown in Figure 10-26 using a search argument of 504. Use the num and dollar arrays shown in Figure 10-27.

startSub   stopSub   middleSub   found   size

You have now completed Lesson A. In this lesson, you learned how to use the bubble sort algorithm to sort the data stored in an array. You also learned how to use the binary search algorithm to search the sorted array data for a specific value. In Lesson B, you will learn how to use the sorted data in a report that displays subtotals. Before continuing to Lesson B, you can either take a break or complete the end-of-lesson questions and exercises.

S U M M A R Y

Sorting is the process of arranging data in either alphabetical or numerical order. When data is displayed in a sorted order, it allows a user to find quickly the information for which he or she is searching. You can sort both numeric and character data in either ascending or descending order. You begin by storing the data in an array. You can then use the bubble sort to sort the array data in the required order.

The bubble sort provides a quick and easy way to sort a relatively small number of items. The bubble sort algorithm works by comparing adjacent array elements and swapping the ones that are out of order. The algorithm continues comparing and swapping until the data in the array is sorted.

If you have a large amount of data to search, you should use a binary search rather than a serial search. A serial search begins searching with the first array element, then continues, element by element, either until a match is found or the end of the array is encountered. A binary search, on the other hand, begins the search in the middle of the array. If the search argument—the data for which you are searching—is equal to the value that is located in the middle of the array, then the search ends. If, on the other hand, the search argument is greater than the value located in the middle of the array, the search continues in the upper half of the array. Otherwise, it continues in the lower half of the array. The binary search continues splitting the array in two either until a match is found or until there are no more array elements to search. For a binary search to work, the field you are searching must be sorted in either alphabetical or numerical order.

ANSWERS TO MINI-QUIZZES

Mini-Quiz 1

1. sorting
2. `code[x + 1]`
3. b
4. d
5. e

Mini-Quiz 2

1. serial
2. binary
3. search argument
4.

startSub	stopSub	middleSub	found	size
0̶	10	0̶	N̶	11
6̶		5̶		
9		8̶		
		9	Y	

QUESTIONS

1. Sorting data means to arrange it in _____ order.
   a. alphabetical
   b. numerical
   c. either alphabetical or numerical

2. Data sorted from the largest value to the smallest value is sorted in _____ order.
   a. ascending
   b. descending

3. The _____ sort algorithm works by comparing adjacent array elements and swapping the ones that are out of order.
   a. alphabetic
   b. bubble
   c. compare
   d. list
   e. numeric

4. When you use the bubble sort, the first step in swapping two of the elements in the salary array is to _____.
   a. assign salary[x] to temp
   b. assign salary[x + 2] to temp
   c. assign salary[x] to salary[x + 1]
   d. assign temp to salary[x]
   e. assign temp to salary[x + 1]

5. After you complete step 1 in question 4, the second step in swapping two of the elements in the salary array is to _____.
   a. assign salary[x + 1] to temp
   b. assign salary[x] to temp
   c. assign salary[x + 1] to salary[x]
   d. assign salary[x + 2] to salary[x]
   e. assign temp to salary[x + 1]

6. After you complete steps 1 and 2 in questions 4 and 5, the final step in swapping two of the elements in the salary array is to _____.
   a. assign salary[x + 1] to temp
   b. assign salary[x + 2] to temp
   c. assign salary[x] to salary[x + 1]
   d. assign temp to salary[x + 2]
   e. assign temp to salary[x + 1]

7. Which of the following is false?
   a. A serial search begins with the first array element.
   b. A serial search continues searching, element by element, either until a match is found or until the end of the array is encountered.
   c. A serial search is useful when the amount of data that must be searched is small.
   d. For a serial search to work, the data in the array must be arranged in either alphabetical or numerical order.

8. Which of the following is false?
   a. A binary search begins with the middle element in the array.
   b. A binary search continues halving the array either until a match is found or until there are no more elements to search.
   c. If the search argument is greater than the value located in the middle of the array, the binary search continues in the lower half of the array.
   d. For a binary search to work, the data in the array must be arranged in either alphabetical or numerical order.

9. The value for which you are searching is called the _____.
   a. binary value
   b. key
   c. search argument
   d. serial value

10. Which of the following statements is used in the binary search algorithm to halve the array?

a. `middleSub = (startSub + stopSub) / 2;`

b. `middleSub = startSub + stopSub / 2;`

c. `middleSub = middleSub / 2;`

d. `middleSub = (stopSub − startSub) / 2;`

11. If the binary search algorithm determines that the search argument is in the lower half of the array, which of the following statements will set the appropriate variable to the appropriate value?

a. `startSub = middleSub − 1;`

b. `startSub = middleSub + 1;`

c. `stopSub = middleSub − 1;`

d. `stopSub = middleSub + 1;`

12. If the binary search algorithm determines that the search argument is in the upper half of the array, which of the following statements will set the appropriate variable to the appropriate value?

a. `startSub = middleSub − 1;`

b. `startSub = middleSub + 1;`

c. `stopSub = middleSub − 1;`

d. `stopSub = middleSub + 1;`

E X E R C I S E S

1. In this exercise, you will use the bubble sort to sort the 10 numbers contained in a sequential access file.

a. Use C++ to open and print the numbers.dat file, which is located in the Cpp\Tut10\T10Ae01 folder on your computer's hard disk, then close the data file.

b. Open the T10Ae01.cpp file, which is located in the Cpp\Tut10\T10Ae01 folder on your computer's hard disk. Complete the program as follows: The `fillArray` function should store the data from the numbers.dat file in a numeric array. The `displayArray` function should display the contents of the array. The `sortArray` function should use the bubble sort to sort the numbers in the array. The `writeToFile` function should write the sorted contents of the array to a file named numbers.srt.

c. Save, build, and execute the program. When the program is working correctly, print the code. Also, use C++ to print the contents of the numbers.srt file.

2. In this exercise, you will use the bubble sort to sort the 26 letters of the alphabet.

a. Open the T10Ae02.cpp file, which is located in the Cpp\Tut10\T10Ae02 folder on your computer's hard disk. Complete the `sortArray` function, which should use the bubble sort to sort the letters in the `alphabet` array.

b. Save, build, and execute the program. When the program is working correctly, print the code.

3. In this exercise, you will modify the bubble sort program you completed in Lesson A so that it sorts the numbers in descending order.

a. Open the T10Ae03.cpp file, which is located in the Cpp\Tut10\T10Ae03 folder on your computer's hard disk. Modify the `sortArray` function so that it sorts the numbers in the array in descending order.

b. Save, build, and execute the program. When the program is working correctly, print the code. On the code printout, circle any changes you made to the program.

4. Trace the binary search code shown in Figure 10-26 using a search argument of 303. Use the num array shown in Figure 10-27.

<u>startSub</u>   <u>stopSub</u>   <u>middleSub</u>   <u>found</u>

5. Trace the binary search code shown in Figure 10-26 using a search argument of 505. Use the num array shown in Figure 10-27.

<u>startSub</u>   <u>stopSub</u>   <u>middleSub</u>   <u>found</u>

6. In this exercise, you will use the binary search algorithm.

a. Open the T10Ae06.cpp file, which is located in the Cpp\Tut10\T10Ae06 folder on your computer's hard disk. Study the partially completed program. You will notice that the program stores the 26 letters of the alphabet in a Character array named `letters`. The `getLetter` function gets and returns a letter input by the user. The `searchAndDisplay` function, which is not complete, should search for the letter in the array. If the letter is in the array, its position in the alphabet should be displayed on the screen. For example, if the user enters the letter C (or the lowercase letter c), the number 3 should appear because the letter C is the third letter in the alphabet. If the letter is not in the array, an appropriate message should be displayed. Complete the program's code.

b. Save, build, and execute the program. To test the program, enter the letter z; the program should display the number 26. When the program is working correctly, print the code.

discovery ▶ 7. In this exercise, you will use the bubble sort to sort two parallel arrays.

a. Use C++ to open the T10Ae07.cpp file, which is located in the Cpp\Tut10\T10Ae07 folder on your computer's hard disk. The `code` array and the `number` array are parallel arrays—in other words, each letter in the `code` array corresponds to a number in the `number` array. For example, the first letter in the `code` array (L) corresponds to the first number in the `number` array (3). Complete the `sort` function, which should use the bubble sort to sort both arrays in ascending alphabetic order by the code stored in the `code` array. (*Hint*: Sort the `code` array. Whenever you swap values in the `code` array, swap the values in the corresponding positions of the `number` array. After you have sorted the arrays, the first letter in the `code` array should be A and the first number in the `number` array should be 6.)

b. Save, build, and execute the program. When the program is working correctly, print the code.

discovery ▶ 8. In this exercise, you will use the bubble sort to sort two parallel arrays.

a. Use C++ to open the T10Ae08.cpp file, which is located in the Cpp\Tut10\T10Ae08 folder on your computer's hard disk. The `code` array and the `number` array are parallel arrays—in other words, each letter in the `code` array corresponds to a number in the `number` array. For example, the first letter in the `code` array (L) corresponds to the first number in the `number` array (3). Complete the `sort` function, which should use the bubble sort to sort both arrays in ascending numeric order by the values in the `number` array. (*Hint*: Sort the `number` array. Whenever you swap values in the `number` array, swap the values in the corresponding positions of the `code` array. After you have sorted the arrays, the first number in the `number` array should be 1 and the first number in the `code` array should be B.)

b. Save, build, and execute the program. When the program is working correctly, print the code.

discovery ▶ 9. In this exercise, you will use the bubble sort to sort two parallel arrays contained in a record structure.

a. Use C++ to open and print the items.dat file, which is located in the Cpp\Tut10\T10Ae09 folder on your computer's hard disk, then close the data file.

b. Open the T10Ae09.cpp file, which is located in the Cpp\Tut10\T10Ae09 folder on your computer's hard disk. You will notice that the program defines a record structure named `itemInfo`, which consists of two five-element arrays named `number` and `price`. The `number` array and the `price` array are parallel arrays—in other words, each item number in the `number` array corresponds to a price in the `price` array. The `fill` function fills the arrays with the data from the items.dat file. When the arrays are filled with data, the first item number in the `number` array (1234) will correspond to the first price in the `price` array (45.67). Complete the `sort` function, which should use the bubble sort to sort both arrays in ascending numeric order by item number.

c. Save, build, and execute the program. When the program is working correctly, print the code.

discovery ▶ 10. In this exercise, you will use the binary search algorithm and the bubble sort algorithm.

a. Use C++ to open and print the dept.dat file, which is located in the Cpp\Tut10\T10Ae10 folder on your computer's hard disk, then close the file. You will notice that each record in the file contains two fields. The first field is the department field, and the next field is the salesperson number field. The file is not sorted in any particular order.

b. Use C++ to open the T10Ae10.cpp file, which is located in the Cpp\Tut10\T10Ae10 folder on your computer's hard disk.

c. The program should create a record structure that contains two member arrays; it should then read the dept.dat records into the arrays. The program should contain a menu that offers the user the following three options: "Search by department," "Search by salesperson's number," and "Exit the program."

If the user wants to search by department, the program should use the bubble sort to sort the array data by department; it should use the binary search to search the array. (Keep in mind that the user may enter the department in either uppercase or lowercase.) If the department for which the user is searching is in the array, then the program should display the salesperson's number; otherwise, the program should display an appropriate message.

If the user wants to search by a salesperson's number, the program should sort the array data by the salesperson's number. It should then use the binary search to search the array. If the salesperson's number is in the array, then the program should display his or her department; otherwise, the program should display an appropriate message.

d. Save, build, and execute the program. To test the program, select the option that allows you to search for a department, then enter the letter f; the program should display the number 45. Now select the option that allows you to search for a salesperson's number, then enter the number 40; the program should display the letter G.

e. When the program is working correctly, print the code.

debugging 11. In this exercise, you will debug an existing program.

a. Open the T10Ae11.cpp file, which is located in the Cpp\Tut10\T10Ae11 folder on your computer's hard disk. Build and execute the program. You will notice that the program is not working correctly. Debug the program.

b. When the program is working correctly, print the code. On the code printout, indicate what was wrong with the program and circle the changes you made.

debugging 12. In this exercise, you will debug a program.

a. Open the T10Ae12.cpp file, which is located in the Cpp\Tut10\T10Ae12 folder on your computer's hard disk.

b. Build the program, then debug the program. Save, build, and execute the program. If the program is not working correctly, continue debugging the program.

c. When the program is working correctly, print the code. On the code printout, indicate what was wrong with the program. Also circle the corrections you made.

Control Break Algorithms

Coding the Gifts Express Control Break Program

Recall from the case introduced at the beginning of the tutorial that Susan Li, the sales manager at Gifts Express, wants a program that will display a report showing the total sales made in each of the company's four sales regions (North, South, East, and West) during the month of January, as well as the total company sales for that month. Figure 10-38 shows the Gifts Express January sales records, which are saved in the jan.srt file on your computer's hard disk.

```
E#101#10000
E#204#20000
E#303#15000
N#204#9000
N#101#2000
S#321#13000
W#101#31000
W#321#15000
```

Figure 10-38: Contents of the jan.srt file

The .srt extension on the filename indicates that the data in the file is sorted.

Each record in the jan.srt file contains three fields: the region, salesperson's ID, and January sales. Notice that the records in the file appear in order by region field—for example, all of the East region records appear together. If you want to create a report that displays a subtotal for each region, then the records in the file must be sorted in region order. Figure 10-39 shows a sample sales report for Gifts Express (note that in the report, E stands for the East region, N for the North region, and so on).

report title

column headings

detail lines

subtotal

grand total

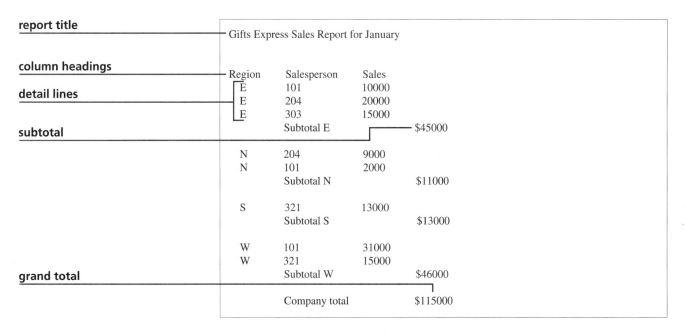

Gifts Express Sales Report for January

Region	Salesperson	Sales
E	101	10000
E	204	20000
E	303	15000
Subtotal E		$45000
N	204	9000
N	101	2000
Subtotal N		$11000
S	321	13000
Subtotal S		$13000
W	101	31000
W	321	15000
Subtotal W		$46000
Company total		$115000

Figure 10-39: Sample sales report for Gifts Express January sales

As Figure 10-39 indicates, the report contains a report title, column headings, detail lines, subtotals, and a grand total. The **report title** describes the contents of the report. In this case, the report shows the January sales for Gifts Express. The **column headings** identify the information listed in each column in the report. The **detail lines** in the report give you detailed information about the records used to process the report. A report will typically include one detail line for each record in the file. The detail lines in Figure 10-39's report, for example, show the values contained in each record's region, salesperson ID, and sales amount fields.

You will notice that the records in the report are grouped by region. For example, all of the East region records appear together. The field that controls how the records are grouped is called the **control field**. To produce a report that is grouped by the values in the control field, the records in the file must be sorted by that field. In the Gifts Express report, for example, the region field is the control field, so the records in the Gifts Express file must be sorted, in order, by region. Recall that the records in the jan.srt file are already sorted in region order.

The Gifts Express report also displays four subtotals. You will notice that a **subtotal** appears after the last record in each of the four regions, and it includes only the sales amounts for the records in that region. The subtotal for the East region, for example, is $45000, which is calculated by adding together the sales amounts in the three records that have E in their region field (10000 + 20000 + 15000). Reports that contain subtotals are referred to as **control break reports**. The term *control break* refers to the fact that a subtotal is displayed in the report each time the value in the control field changes.

In addition to including the subtotals, the Gifts Express report includes a **grand total**, also called a **summary total** or a **final total**, of the company sales. Grand totals, which are calculated by adding together the various subtotals in the report, typically appear at the end of the report.

The control break algorithm reads the sorted records from a file, one record at a time. As a record is read, the value in its control field is compared to the value in the prior record's control field. If the two values are equal, then both records belong to the same group. The group subtotals are then updated with the current record's information. In the Gifts Express report, for example, the three records with an E in their region field belong to the same group. The East region's subtotal includes the sales amounts for these three records.

If, on the other hand, the current record's control field differs from the prior record's control field, then a control break occurs. When this happens, the subtotal for the prior group is displayed in the report. In the Gifts Express report, for example, the first record with an N in the region field causes a control break, which displays the prior group's (the East region's) subtotal.

On your computer's hard disk is a partially completed control break program for Gifts Express. Before opening the program, study the **main** function's IPO chart, which is shown in Figure 10-40.

Input	Processing	Output

sales records in jan.srt file	Processing items:
	    Long Integer accumulator variable named **regionSubtotal**
	    Long Integer accumulator variable named **companyTotal**
	    Character variable named **control**
	    record variable named **sales**
	
	Algorithm:
	1. open jan.srt file for input
	2. if (open is successful)
	    display report title and column headings
	    read a record (**readRecord** function)
	    assign first record's region to **control** variable
	    while (it is not the end of the file)
	        if (the current record's region is not equal to the **control**)
	            process a control break (**processControlBreak** function)
	        end if (the current record's region is not equal to the **control**)
	        process the current record (**processRecord** function)
	        read another record (**readRecord** function)
	    end while (it is not the end of the file)
	    display last record (**processRecord** function)
	    display last subtotal (**processControlBreak** function)
	    display grand total
	    else
	        display an "Error opening file" message
	    end if (open is successful)
		report showing subtotals by region and a grand total by company

Figure 10-40: IPO chart for the control break program's main function

The `main` function will use four processing items: two Long Integer accumulator variables named `regionSubtotal` and `companyTotal`, a Character variable named `control`, and a record variable named `sales`. The `sales` record variable will contain a Character field named `region` and two Short Integer fields named `id` and `regSales`. When you code the program, you will use the C++ `struct` statement to define a record structure named `salesInfo`, which you will use to create the `sales` record variable.

After creating and initializing the variables, the `main` function will open the jan.srt file for input. If the file is not opened successfully, then the selection structure's false path will display an appropriate message. If the file is opened successfully, however, then the instructions in the selection structure's true path will be processed.

After the program displays the report title and column headings, the instructions in the selection structure's true path call the `readRecord` function to read the first record from the file, and then assign the value in the first record's `region` field to the `control` variable. The value stored in the `region` field of subsequent records will be compared to the value stored in the `control` variable to determine if a control break has occurred.

After reading the first record and assigning its region value to the `control` variable, the `while` clause will determine if the record indicator is at the end of the file. If the record indicator is not at the end of the file, the instructions in the `while` loop will be processed. Those instructions compare the value stored in the current record's `region` field to the value stored in the `control` variable. If both values are equal, then no control break has occurred. The `while` loop instructions then simply call the `processRecord` function to process the record before calling the `readRecord` function to read another record. If, on the other hand, the value in the current record's `region` field differs from the value in the `control` variable, then a control break has occurred. The program then calls the `processControlBreak` function to handle the necessary tasks prior to calling both the `processRecord` and `readRecord` functions.

When the record indicator is at the end of the file, the `while` loop ends. The `main` function then calls the `processRecord` function to process the last record read, and then calls the `processControlBreak` function to display the last group's subtotal. Lastly, the `main` function displays the grand total in the report before the program ends.

Now open the partially completed control break program for Gifts Express.

To open the partially completed control break program:

1 Open the **LbProg01.cpp** file, which is located in the Cpp\Tut10\LbProg01 folder on your computer's hard disk. The Gifts Express program appears in the LbProg01.cpp window. The program's `main` function is shown in Figure 10-41.

record structure

record variable

open file

display title and
column headings

read first record

initialize control variable

```cpp
//LbProg01.cpp
//this program produces a control break report

#include <iostream.h>
#include <fstream.h>
#include <iomanip.h>

//structure definition
struct salesInfo
{
    char region;
    short id;
    short regSales;
};

//function prototypes
void readRecord(ifstream &, salesInfo &);
void processControlBreak(salesInfo, char &, long &, long &);
void processRecord(salesInfo, long &);

void main()
{
    //declare and initialize variables
    long regionSubtotal = 0;   //region accumulator variable
    long companyTotal = 0;     //company accumulator variable
    char control = ' ';        //control variable

    //declare and initialize record variable
    salesInfo sales = {' ', 0, 0};

    //open file for input
    ifstream inFile;
    inFile.open("jan.srt", ios::in);

    //verify that open was successful
    if(!inFile.fail())
    {
        //display report title and column headings
        cout << "Gifts Express Sales Report for January"
            << endl << endl;
        cout << "Region  " << "Salesperson  " << "Sales"
            << endl;

        //read a record from the file
        readRecord(inFile, sales);

        //initialize control variable
        //to first record's region
        control = sales.region;
```

Figure 10-41: main function in the control break program for Gifts Express

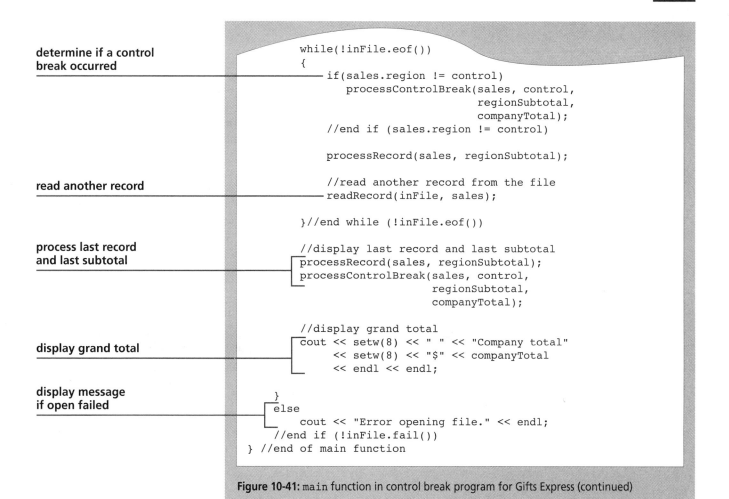

```
                         while(!inFile.eof())
                         {
determine if a control      if(sales.region != control)
break occurred                 processControlBreak(sales, control,
                                                   regionSubtotal,
                                                   companyTotal);
                            //end if (sales.region != control)

                            processRecord(sales, regionSubtotal);

read another record         //read another record from the file
                            readRecord(inFile, sales);

                         }//end while (!inFile.eof())

process last record      //display last record and last subtotal
and last subtotal        processRecord(sales, regionSubtotal);
                         processControlBreak(sales, control,
                                             regionSubtotal,
                                             companyTotal);

                         //display grand total
display grand total      cout << setw(8) << " " << "Company total"
                              << setw(8) << "$" << companyTotal
                              << endl << endl;

                      }
display message       else
if open failed            cout << "Error opening file." << endl;
                      //end if (!inFile.fail())
                   } //end of main function
```

Figure 10-41: `main` function in control break program for Gifts Express (continued)

As Figure 10-41 indicates, the control break program defines a record structure named `salesInfo`, which contains three fields: `region`, `id`, and `regSales`. The program also includes three programmer-defined functions: `readRecord`, `processControlBreak`, and `processRecord`. The `readRecord` function will simply read a record from the file. If the current record causes a control break, then the `main` function will call the `processControlBreak` function to process the control break. The `main` function will call the `processRecord` function to perform the tasks associated with processing each record in the file.

The `main` function begins by declaring and initializing three variables—`regionSubtotal`, `companyTotal`, and `control`—and a record variable named `sales`. The program will use the `regionSubtotal` and `companyTotal` variables to accumulate the values in each record's sales amount field. The `control` variable will be used to save the prior control field value so that the next record's control field can be compared to it. The program will use the `sales` record variable to store each record in the file, one record at a time.

After the variables are declared and initialized, the `main` function opens the jan.srt sequential file for input. If the file is opened successfully, the `main` function displays the report title and column headings. It then calls the `readRecord` function to read the first record in the file. When the `readRecord` function completes its task, the value in the first record's `region` field is assigned to the `control` variable. Subsequent records will be compared to the value in the `control` variable to determine whether a control break has occurred.

The `while` loop instructions in the `main` function will be processed for each record in the file. The loop instructions compare the value in the current record's `region` field to the value in the `control` variable. If the two values are not equal, a control break has occurred. The `main` function calls the `processControlBreak` function to process the control break. The `processRecord` function is then called. Notice that the `processRecord` function is called whether or not a control break occurs. Another record is then read and the `while` loop is tested to determine if the loop instructions should be processed again.

When the `while` loop ends, the `main` function calls the `processRecord` and `processControlBreak` functions to display the last record and the last subtotal. If both functions were not called when the `while` loop ended, both the last record and the last subtotal would not be displayed in the report. Lastly, the `main` function displays the grand total in the report and the program ends.

Next, view the IPO chart and the C++ code for the `readRecord` function, which is located in the programmer-defined functions section of the program. Both the chart and the code are shown in Figure 10-42.

Input	Processing	Output
jan.srt input file and **sales** record variable from **main** function	Processing items: none Algorithm: 1. read record from input file and store in the appropriate fields in the record variable	region, ID, and sales information stored in the record variable

```
//*****programmer-defined function definitions*****
void readRecord(ifstream &inFile, salesInfo &amounts)
{
    //this function reads a record
    inFile >> amounts.region;
    inFile.ignore(1);
    inFile >> amounts.id;
    inFile.ignore(1);
    inFile >> amounts.regSales;
    inFile.ignore(1);
} //end of readRecord function
```

Figure 10-42: IPO chart and C++ code for the `readRecord` function

As Figure 10-42 indicates, the `readRecord` function simply reads a record from the file. Recall that each record in the file contains three fields: region, ID, and sales. The value in each field is stored in a field in the `sales` record variable.

Next, view the IPO chart for the `processControlBreak` function, which is located in the programmer-defined section of the program. The IPO chart is shown in Figure 10-43.

Input	Processing	Output
`sales` record variable, `control` variable, `regionSubtotal` accumulator, and `companyTotal` accumulator from `main` function	Processing items: none Algorithm: 1. display prior region's subtotal line 2. add prior region's subtotal to company total 3. reset control variable to value in the current record's region field 4. reset region subtotal to 0	subtotal line in report updated company total accumulator new control field value reinitialized region accumulator

Figure 10-43: IPO chart for the `processControlBreak` function

When a control break occurs in the program, the `main` function calls the `processControlBreak` function, which should perform the four tasks shown in Figure 10-43. The `processControlBreak` function in the Gifts Express program is missing the statements that will accomplish tasks 2, 3, and 4. You will complete the function in the next set of steps.

To complete the `processControlBreak` function:

1 Scroll the LbProg01.cpp window, if necessary, until the `processControlBreak` function appears.

2 Modify the `processControlBreak` function by entering the three lines of code highlighted in Figure 10-44.

```
void processControlBreak(salesInfo amounts, char &control,
                         long &regSub, long &coTotal)
{
    //this function will be processed each time
    //a control break occurs

    //display subtotal line for prior region
    cout << setw(8) << " " << "Subtotal " << control
         << setw(11) << "$" << regSub << endl << endl;

    //add prior region's subtotal to company total
    coTotal = coTotal + regSub;

    //reset control variable to new region
    control = amounts.region;

    //reset regSub variable for new region
    regSub = 0;

} //end of processControlBreak function
```

enter these three lines of code

Figure 10-44: Completed `processControlBreak` function

Lastly, view the IPO chart for the `processRecord` function, which is shown in Figure 10-45.

Input	Processing	Output
`sales` record variable and `regionSubtotal` accumulator from `main` function	Processing items: none Algorithm: 1. add current record's sales amount to current region's accumulator 2. display detail line for the current record	updated region accumulator current record displayed in report

Figure 10-45: IPO chart for the `processRecord` function

The `main` function calls the `processRecord` function to process each record in the file. As the algorithm indicates, the `processRecord` function is responsible for adding each record's sales to the appropriate region's accumulator. It is also responsible for displaying the record information in the detail lines of the report. The `processRecord` function in the Gifts Express control break program is missing the statement that will accomplish the first task—updating the region accumulator with the value in the current record's sales field. You will complete the function in the next set of steps. You will also run the program to observe how it works.

To complete the `processRecord` function, then run the program:

1 Scroll the LbProg01.cpp window, if necessary, until the `processRecord` function appears.

2 Modify the function by entering the one line of code highlighted in Figure 10-46.

enter this line of code

```
void processRecord(salesInfo amounts, long &regSub)
{
    //add current record's sales to current
    //region's accumulator
    regSub = regSub + amounts.regSales;

    //display detail line
    cout << setw(3) <<  amounts.region
         << setw(8) <<  amounts.id
         << setw(15) << amounts.regSales << endl;
} //end of processRecord function
```

Figure 10-46: Completed `processRecord` function

3 Save, build, and execute the program. The January sales report for Gifts Express appears in the DOS window, as shown in Figure 10-47.

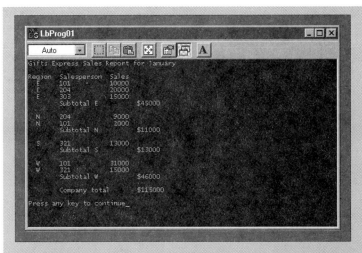

Figure 10-47: January sales report for Gifts Express shown in the DOS window

4   Press the **Enter** key to close the DOS window.

You are finished with the control break program, so you can close it.

5   Close the workspace and the Output window.

mini-quiz

Mini-Quiz 3

1. The field that controls how the records in a report are grouped is called the
    _____ .

2. A(n) _____ occurs when the value in the current record's control
    field does not match the value in the control variable.

3. A report typically includes one _____ for each record in the file.

4. _____ , which are calculated by adding together the various subtotals
    in the report, typically appear at the end of the report.

5. To create a report that shows subtotals, the data would need to be sorted in order
    by the _____ field, which is the field that controls how the records
    will be grouped.

You have now completed Lesson B. In this lesson, you learned how to display
subtotals in a report by using the control break algorithm. You can either take a
break or complete the end-of-lesson questions and exercises.

S U M M A R Y

To work correctly, programs that display subtotals in reports, referred to as control break reports, need the program data to be sorted. Control break reports
typically include a report title, column headings, detail lines, subtotals, and a
grand total. The logic for a program that produces a control break report is quite
simple. The program simply reads the sorted records from the file, one record at

a time, and totals one or more of each record's numeric fields. As a record is read, the value in its control field is compared to the value in the prior record's control field; if the two values are not equal, then a control break occurs. When a control break occurs, the subtotal for the prior control field is displayed; the program then begins totaling the numeric fields for the new control field's value.

ANSWERS TO MINI-QUIZZES

Mini-Quiz 3
1. control field
2. control break
3. detail line
4. grand totals, summary totals, or final totals
5. control

QUESTIONS

1. Which of the following types of programs would require the program data to be sorted in order for the programs to work correctly?
   a. programs that display department names in alphabetical order
   b. programs that display sales amounts in numerical order
   c. programs that display subtotals in reports
   d. programs that use the binary search algorithm
   e. all of the above

2. Which of the following describes the contents of a control break report?
   a. column headings
   b. detail lines
   c. report title
   d. summary totals

3. Which of the following shows each record's information in a control break report?
   a. column headings
   b. detail lines
   c. report title
   d. summary totals

4. The field that controls how records are grouped in a control break report is called the
   _____ .
   a. control field
   b. group field
   c. record field
   d. sort field

5. Assume that a file contains the following records:
   A Mary
   A Janice
   B Paul
   C Dave
   C Jean

6. Which of the records in the file will produce a control break?
   a. Janice's record only
   b. Paul's record only
   c. Dave's record only
   d. both Paul's and Dave's records
   e. Janice's, Paul's, and Dave's records

E X E R C I S E S

1. In this exercise, you will modify the Gifts Express program so that it also generates a report by salesperson.
   a. Use C++ to open the sales.dat file, which is located in the Cpp\Tut10\T10Be01 folder on your computer's hard disk. Print the sales.dat file. You will notice that each record in the file contains three fields: region, salesperson ID, and sales. Currently, the file is not sorted in any particular order. Close the data file.
   b. Use C++ to open the T10Be01.cpp file, which is located in the Cpp\Tut10\T10Be01 folder on your computer's hard disk. The file contains the same code as the LbProg01 program (the Gifts Express program) that you completed in Lesson B. Modify the code so that it contains a menu with the following three options: "Display report by region," "Display report by salesperson ID," and "Exit the program." The report by region should include a subtotal of each region's sales and a grand total for the company sales. The report by salesperson number should include a subtotal of each salesperson's sales, as well as a grand total for the company sales. In the report by salesperson, also include a grand total that displays the number of salespeople working for the company.
   c. Save, build, and execute the program. Test the program by displaying the two different reports. When the program is working correctly, print the code.

2. In this exercise, you will create a program that generates a control break report.
   a. Use C++ to open the grades.dat file, which is located in the Cpp\Tut10\T10Be02 folder on your computer's hard disk. Print the grades.dat file. You will notice that each record in the file contains one field, a grade, and that the file is sorted in ascending alphabetical order. Close the data file.
   b. Use C++ to open the T10Be02.cpp file, which is located in the Cpp\Tut10\T10Be02 folder on your computer's hard disk. Create a program that generates a control break report based on the grades in the grades.dat file. In other words, all of the A grades should appear grouped together in the report, as well as all of the B, C, D, and F grades. Count the number of A, B, C, D, and F grades earned; include the count in each grade's subtotal line. Also include a grand total line that shows the total number of grades processed.
   c. Save, build, and execute the program. When the program is working correctly, print the code.

3. In this exercise, you will create a program that generates a control break report.
   a. Use C++ to open the zips.dat file, which is located in the Cpp\Tut10\T10Be03 folder on your computer's hard disk. Print the zips.dat file. You will notice that each record in the file contains two fields: zip code and sales. The file is sorted in ascending order by zip code. Close the data file.
   b. Use C++ to open the T10Be03.cpp file, which is located in the Cpp\Tut10\T10Be03 folder on your computer's hard disk. Create a program that generates a control break report based on the zip codes in the zips.dat file. Accumulate the sales by zip code; also count the number of sales made in each zip code. Display both the accumulated sales and the number of sales in each zip code's subtotal line. Also include a grand total line that shows the total sales and the total number of sales.
   c. Save, build, and execute the program. When the program is working correctly, print the code.

discovery ▶ 4. In this exercise, you will generate a multilevel control break report.

a. In Lesson B, you learned how to generate a single-level control break report, which is a report that displays subtotals for only one field in each record. You would use a single-level control break to generate a report that displays subtotals by department within company. However, many reports, referred to as multilevel control break reports, must display subtotals for more than one field in each record. You would need to use a multilevel control break, for example, to generate a report that displays subtotals by salesperson within department and by department within company. To generate the report, you need to sort the data first by department, and then by salesperson within each department.

In this exercise, you will create a program that generates a control break report.

b. Use C++ to open the company.dat file, which is located in the Cpp\Tut10\T10Be04 folder on your computer's hard disk. Print the company.dat file. You will notice that each record in the file contains three fields: department, salesperson number, and sales. The file is sorted in ascending order by department; the records within each department are sorted in ascending order by salesperson number. Close the data file.

c. Use C++ to open the T10Be04.cpp file, which is located in the Cpp\Tut10\T10Be04 folder on your computer's hard disk. Create a program that generates a multilevel control break report. Accumulate the sales by salesperson number and by department. You should display subtotals by salesperson within department, and by department within company. Also include a grand total line that shows the total company sales.

d. Save, build, and execute the program. When the program is working correctly, print the code.

Classes

case ▶ Recently, three small businesses—Terney Landscaping, Martin Fence Company, and Pool-Time—have asked you to create programs for them. Terney Landscaping wants a program that its salespeople can use to estimate the cost of laying sod, and Martin Fence Company wants a program that will calculate the cost of a fence. Pool-Time, which constructs in-ground pools, wants a program that its salespeople can use to determine the number of gallons of water required to fill a pool—a question commonly asked by customers. While analyzing the three problems, you notice that each problem involves a rectangular shape. For example, in Terney Landscaping's program, you will need to find the area of the rectangle on which the sod is to be laid. In Martin Fence Company's program, on the other hand, you will need to find the perimeter of the rectangle around which the fence is to be constructed. Lastly, in Pool-Time's program, you will need to find the volume of a rectangle—the in-ground pool. To complete these programs, you first will create a programmer-defined class named `rectangle`. You will then use the `rectangle` class to create a rectangle object in the programs.

LESSON A
objectives

In this lesson you will learn how to:

- Create a class
- Use the public members of a class to manipulate the private members
- Create an object from a programmer-defined class
- Create a constructor function

Programmer-defined Classes

OOP Concepts

As you may remember from Tutorial 1, C++ is often considered a hybrid language because it can be used to create both procedure-oriented and object-oriented programs. In previous tutorials, you used C++ to create procedure-oriented programs. In this tutorial, you will learn how to use C++ to create simple object-oriented programs using objects that you create.

As you learned in Tutorial 1, the objects in an object-oriented program can take on many different forms. For example, the menus, option buttons, and command buttons included in many Windows programs are objects. An object can also represent something encountered in real life. For example, the `cin` object that you used in many of the programs created in previous tutorials represents the computer keyboard, and the `cout` object represents the computer screen. Examples of real-life objects typically found in a payroll program are a time card object, an employee object, and a date object. The idea behind object-oriented programming is to create reusable objects—in other words, to create objects that can be used with either little or no modification in more than one program. This saves programming time and money.

Every object in C++ is created from a class. For example, C++ creates the `cin` and `cout` objects from its `istream` and `ostream` classes, respectively. You use the C++ built-in `ifstream` and `ofstream` classes to create the input and output file objects, respectively, in your programs.

In addition to using the C++ built-in classes to create objects, you can also define your own classes from which you can then create one or more objects. Before learning how to create a programmer-defined class, you will review some of the OOP terms discussed in Tutorial 1. These terms will help you understand the components of a class.

Review of OOP Concepts and Terms

Recall from Tutorial 1 that object-oriented programming languages allow you to create a **class**, which is simply a pattern, or blueprint, for creating objects. Similar to the way a dress designer uses a pattern to create one or more dresses, or a car manufacturer uses a blueprint to create one or more cars, you use a class to create one or more objects.

tip

Recall that you do not need to make any modification to the C++ built-in `cin` and `cout` objects to use those objects in a program.

A class contains—or, to use an OOP term, it **encapsulates**—all of an object's attributes and behaviors. The **attributes** are the characteristics that describe the object. When you tell someone that your car is a blue Honda Accord, you are describing the car (an object) in terms of some of its attributes—in this case, its color, manufacturer, and model type.

An object's **behaviors** are the operations (actions) that the object either can perform or have performed on it. A car's behaviors, for example, include acceleration, braking, and steering.

Objects that you create from a class are referred to as **instances** of the class. Cars made from the same blueprint, for example, are instances of that class of cars. Keep in mind that a class is not an object; only an *instance* of a class is an object.

Some of a class's attributes and behaviors are hidden from the user, while others are exposed. In object-oriented programming, the term **abstraction** (or **data hiding**) refers to the hiding of a class's internal details from the user. Hiding those details helps prevent the user from making inadvertent changes to the object. Car manufacturers, for example, hide much of a car's internal details—engine, spark plugs, and so on—under the hood. Attributes and behaviors that are not **hidden** are said to be **exposed** to the user. For example, a car's steering wheel, gas pedal, and brake pedal are exposed to the driver. The idea behind abstraction is to expose only the attributes and behaviors that the user will need to use the object— everything else should be hidden. Try to keep these OOP terms in mind as you learn how to create your own C++ classes and objects in this lesson.

Defining a Class in C++

Before you can create an object in C++, you must first create a blueprint for it—in other words, a class. You create, or define, a class using the `class` statement. The syntax of the `class` statement is shown in Figure 11-1.

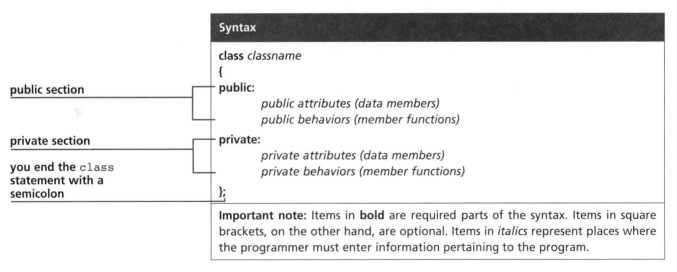

Syntax

class *classname*
{
public:
    public attributes (data members)
    public behaviors (member functions)
private:
    private attributes (data members)
    private behaviors (member functions)
};

public section

private section

you end the `class` statement with a semicolon

Important note: Items in **bold** are required parts of the syntax. Items in square brackets, on the other hand, are optional. Items in *italics* represent places where the programmer must enter information pertaining to the program.

Figure 11-1: Syntax of the C++ `class` statement

The difference between the `struct` statement and the `class` statement is that a `struct` statement's members are public by default whereas a `class` statement's members are private by default.

As Figure 11-1 shows, the `class` statement begins with the keyword **class**, followed by the name of the class. You enclose the attributes and behaviors that define the class in braces (`{}`), and you end the `class` statement with a semicolon (`;`). The attributes, also called **data members**, are the variables included in the class. The behaviors, called **member functions**, are the functions included in the class.

As Figure 11-1 indicates, a class can have a public section and a private section. You place in the class's private section the attributes and behaviors that you want to hide from the user, and place in the class's public section the attributes and behaviors that you want to expose to the user.

In most classes, you expose—in other words, you give the user access to—the member functions, and you hide the data members. In other words, you typically list the data members in the private section of the class, and you list the member functions in the public section. You hide the data members to protect them from being changed incorrectly by the program. To change a private data member, the program must use one of the public member functions. This idea of hiding attributes and exposing functions is nothing new to you. The electric company, for example, hides the electrical cables leading to your house. If you are having a problem with your electricity, you must call the electric company whose function it is to fix the problem.

The first class you will define will be a `date` class. You will use the `date` class to define a `date` object that can be used in any program that requires a date.

mini-quiz

Mini-Quiz 1

1. A pattern for creating an object is called a(n) _____ .
2. The characteristics of an object are called its _____ .
3. A class can contain _____ members, which are hidden from the user, and _____ members, which are exposed to the user.
4. A program cannot access a(n) _____ member of a class directly.

Defining a date Class

A **date** is an item of information used by many programs. For example, you will find hire dates in personnel programs, payroll dates in payroll programs, and departure dates in airline reservation programs. Rather than having each program manage the tasks associated with a date—for example, setting and displaying the date—you can create a date object that is capable of managing its own tasks. The date object can then be used in any program that requires a date.

Before you can create a `date` object, you first must use the C++ `class` statement to create a blueprint or pattern for the object—in other words, to create a `date` class. However, before you can create the `date` class, you need to determine a date's attributes and behaviors. As you know, a date consists of a month, a day, and a year. These three items are the attributes of a date. A date will typically be set (or changed) and perhaps displayed by a program; these are the behaviors that will be performed on a date. As mentioned earlier, you typically expose the object's behaviors and hide its attributes. You hide the attributes by listing them in the private section of the class, and you expose the behaviors by listing them in the public section of the class. The `class` statement you will use to create a `date` class is shown in Figure 11-2.

```
class date
{
public:
    //function prototypes - behaviors
    void setDate(short, short, short);
    void displayDate();

private:
    //variable declarations - attributes
    short month;
    short day;
    short year;
};
```

public section

private section

notice that the `class` statement ends with a semicolon

Figure 11-2: date class definition

You will notice that the private section of the `date` class shown in Figure 11-2 contains a variable declaration statement for the three attributes of a date: month, day, and year. Similar to the variable declaration statements you have used in prior programs, the variable declaration statements in a class must also include the data type and name of the variable. However, unlike the variable declaration statements used in prior programs, the variable declaration statements appearing in a class are not initialized within the private section. You will learn how to initialize each variable later in this lesson. The `month`, `day`, and `year` variables included in the `date` class are considered the data members of the class.

Because the data members listed in the private section of the `date` class cannot be accessed directly, you need some way of allowing a program both to set (change) and display the month, day, and year. Recall that setting and displaying the date are the two behaviors that will be performed on a date. To allow the program both to set and display the date, you will need to expose—or make public—two member functions: one to set the date, and the other to display the date. As Figure 11-2 indicates, you will name the member function that sets the date `setDate`, and you will name the member function that displays the date `displayDate`. To expose these functions, you simply include a function prototype for each one in the public section of the class. As with all function prototypes, the function prototypes in a class must include the function's data type and name, as well as the data type of any information the function will receive.

As Figure 11-2 indicates, the `setDate` and `displayDate` functions will be void functions, which means that neither will return a value. You will notice that the `setDate` function will receive three Short Integer values. The first value represents the month, the second value the day, and the third value the year. The `setDate` function will assign these values to the three variables listed in the private section of the class. Unlike the `setDate` function, the `displayDate` function will not need to receive any information from the program that calls it. The function simply will display the contents of the `month`, `day`, and `year` variables.

Before entering the function definitions for the `date` class's two member functions, you will enter the `class` statement in a programmer-defined header file.

Creating a Header File

By entering the `class` statement in a header file, you will be able to use the class to create objects in more than one program. To do so, however, you must be sure to include the header file in the program. You will enter the `date` class in a header file named date, which you will save in the *headers* folder on your computer's hard disk.

tip

Recall that the C++ built-in classes are defined in header files. For example, the `ifstream` and `ofstream` classes are defined in the fstream.h header file.

tip

Recall that you use the `#include` directive to include a header file in a program.

tip

The default name of each subsequent header file that you create in the same session will be H2, H3, and so on.

name of header file

enter these instructions

be sure to enter the semicolon

tip

You do not need to enter the .h at the end of the filename when you save the file. Because you opened a C/C++ Header File, C++ automatically saves the file with an .h extension on the file name.

To create a header file, and then enter the `date` class statement in the file:

1   Start Visual C++. Click **File** on the menu bar, and then click **New**. When the New dialog box appears, click the **Files** tab, then click **C/C++ Header File** in the list of file types, and then click the **OK** button. As the title bar indicates, C++ creates a header file with a default name of H1.

You should change the default name of H1 to a more meaningful name. This header file will contain the definition of the `date` class, so you will call the header file *date*.

2   Click **File** on the menu bar, then click **Save As**. When the Save As dialog box appears, open the **headers** folder, which is located in the Cpp\Tut11 folder on your computer's hard disk. Change the h1.h filename in the File name text box to **date**, then click the **Save** button. The title bar indicates that the file is now saved as date.H. (Recall that the .H stands for *header file*.)

You can now enter the definition of the `date` class in the header file.

3   Enter the `date` class definition shown in Figure 11-3.

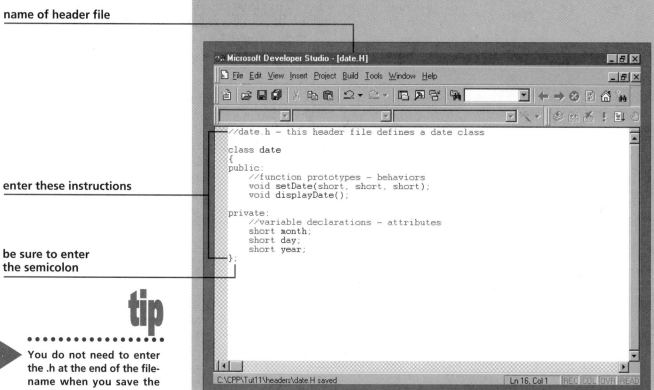

Figure 11-3: date class entered in the date.H header file

Now you need to enter the function definitions for the `setDate` and `displayDate` member functions.

Defining the setDate and displayDate Functions

The IPO charts for the setDate and displayDate functions are shown in Figure 11-4.

setDate function		
Input	**Processing**	**Output**
month number day number year number	Processing items: none Algorithm: 1. assign month number to the private **month** variable 2. assign day number to the private **day** variable 3. assign year number to the private **year** variable	values placed in private variables

displayDate function		
Input	**Processing**	**Output**
none	Processing items: none Algorithm: 1. display private **month**, **day**, and **year** variables separated by slashes	contents of private variables displayed

Figure 11-4: IPO charts for the setDate and displayDate member functions

As Figure 11-4 shows, the setDate function will be passed three numbers when it is called in a program. The first number will represent the month, the second the day, and the third the year. The setDate function will assign the three numbers to the variables listed in the private section of the class, thereby allowing the user to set the date. For example, if the user passes the numbers 3, 11, and 99, then the setDate function will set the month to the number 3, the day to the number 11, and the year to the number 99.

As Figure 11-4 also shows, the displayDate function will simply display the contents of the private variables, separated by slashes (/). Assuming the month, day, and year variables contain the numbers 3, 11, and 99, respectively, the displayDate function will display 3/11/99. Now that you know the tasks both functions will perform, you can begin entering their function definitions.

Recall that both the setDate and displayDate functions will be void functions because they will not need to return a value to the program that called them. As you learned in Tutorial 4, the syntax of a void function's header is **void** *functionname*([*parameterlist*])—for example, void displayDate() is a valid header for a function that does not belong to a class. If, however, the void function is a member of a class, you use the following syntax: **void** *classname::functionname*([*parameterlist*]). For example, if displayDate is a member of the date class, you would need to use the header void date::displayDate() when defining the displayDate function. You will notice that the only difference between the two versions of the syntax is that the class member function's header includes the class name followed by the scope resolution operator—two colons (::). The **scope resolution operator** separates the class name from the function name and tells C++ the class to which the member function belongs as well as the member function's name.

As you may remember, the `setDate` function will receive three Short Integer values. You will use the names num1, num2, and num3 as the formal parameters in the `setDate` function's header. The num1 parameter will receive the month number, num2 the day number, and num3 the year number. The `setDate` function will use three assignment statements to assign the values in the num1, num2, and num3 formal parameters to the private month, day, and year variables, respectively. Enter the `setDate` function's definition.

To enter the `setDate` function's definition:

1   Enter the `setDate` function definition highlighted in Figure 11-5.

enter these lines of code

```
//date.h - this header file defines a date class

class date
{
public:
    //function prototypes - behaviors
    void setDate(short, short, short);
    void displayDate();

private:
    //variable declarations - attributes
    short month;
    short day;
    short year;
};

void date::setDate(short num1, short num2, short num3)
{
    month = num1;
    day   = num2;
    year  = num3;
} //end of setDate function
```

Figure 11-5: setDate function definition entered in the date class

Next, enter the `displayDate` function definition. This function will not receive any information from the program that calls it; its only task is to display the contents of the private month, day, and year variables, separated by slashes (/).

To enter the `displayDate` function definition, then save the header file:

1   Enter the `displayDate` function definition highlighted in Figure 11-6.

```
//date.h - this header file defines a date class

class date
{
public:
     //function prototypes - behaviors
     void setDate(short, short, short);
     void displayDate();

private:
     //variable declarations - attributes
     short month;
     short day;
     short year;
};

void date::setDate(short num1, short num2, short num3)
{
     month = num1;
     day   = num2;
     year  = num3;
} //end of setDate function

void date::displayDate()
{
     cout << month << '/' << day << '/' << year;
} //end of displayDate function
```

enter these lines of code

Figure 11-6: displayDate function definition entered in the date class

2 Compare the code you entered in the date class definition with the code shown in Figure 11-6 and make any needed corrections, then save the date.h header file.

You can now close the date.h header file.

3 Click **File** on the menu bar, and then click **Close** to close the date.h header file.

Once a class is defined, you can then create an instance of it—in other words, an object—in a program. You will use the date class defined in the date.h header file to create a date object in the LaProg01 program.

Using a Programmer-defined Class to Create an Object

The LaProg01 folder on your computer's hard disk contains a partially completed program that will use the date class defined in the date.h header file to create an object that represents an employee's hire date. The program will allow the user to enter and then display the date. Open the hire date program and view its code.

To open the partially completed hire date program:

1 Open the **LaProg01.cpp** file, which is located in the Cpp\Tut11\LaProg01 folder on your computer's hard disk. The partially completed hire date program appears in the LaProg01.cpp window, as shown in Figure 11-7.

```
//LaProg01.cpp
//this program uses a date object whose class is defined
//in the date.h header file

#include <iostream.h>

void main()
{
    //declare date object

    //declare variables
    short hireMonth = 0;
    short hireDay   = 0;
    short hireYear  = 0;

    //get month, day, and year
    cout << "Enter the month: ";
    cin >> hireMonth;
    cin.ignore(100, '\n');
    cout << "Enter the day: ";
    cin >> hireDay;
    cin.ignore(100, '\n');
    cout << "Enter the year: ";
    cin >> hireYear;
    cin.ignore(100, '\n');

    //call public member function to set the date

    //call public member function to display the date
    cout << "The employee was hired on ";

    cout << "." << endl << endl;
} //end of main function
```

the statement that declares a date object is missing

gets the month, day, and year from the user

the statement that calls the setDate function is missing

the statement that calls the displayDate function is missing

Figure 11-7: Partially completed hire date program

After declaring and initializing three Short Integer variables named hireMonth, hireDay, and hireYear, the program prompts the user to enter the month, day, and year. The user's responses are stored in the hireMonth, hireDay, and hireYear variables.

To use the date class to create a date object, recall that you need to include the date.h header file in the program. When including a C++ standard header file in a program, you enclose the header file's name in angle brackets (<>); #include <iostream.h> is an example of a directive that includes a standard C++ header file in a program. As you learned in Tutorial 2, the angle brackets indicate that the file is located in the C++ *include* folder, which comes with the C++ system. However, if the header file is a programmer-defined header file that is not located in the *include* folder, as it is in this case, you enclose the header file's name, along with the full path to the file, in a set of double quotes (""). For example, you will enter the #include "c:\cpp\tut11\headers\date.h" directive in the current program.

2   In the line below the #include <iostream.h> directive, type **#include "c:\cpp\tut11\headers\date.h"** and press the **Enter** key. (If the full path to the date.h header file on your system differs from the one shown in this step, then change the #include directive to reflect the full path used on your system.)

Now use the `date` class, which is defined in the date.h header file, to create a date object named `hireDate`.

3   In the blank line below the `//declare date object` comment, type **date hireDate;** and press the **Enter** key.

After the user enters the month, day, and year that the employee was hired, the program should call the class's public `setDate` function, passing it the hire date information. The `setDate` function will assign that information to the private data members of the class—the `month`, `day`, and `year` variables.

4   In the blank line below the `//call public member function to set the date` comment, type **hireDate.setDate(hireMonth, hireDay, hireYear);** and press the **Enter** key.

Now use the public `displayDate` function to display the contents of the private variables on the screen.

5   Enter the statement highlighted in Figure 11-8.

```cpp
//LaProg01.cpp
//this program uses a date object whose class is defined
//in the date.h header file

#include <iostream.h>
#include "c:\cpp\tut11\headers\date.h"

void main()
{
    //declare date object
    date hireDate;

    //declare variables
    short hireMonth = 0;
    short hireDay   = 0;
    short hireYear  = 0;

    //get month, day, and year
    cout << "Enter the month: ";
    cin >> hireMonth;
    cin.ignore(100, '\n');
    cout << "Enter the day: ";
    cin >> hireDay;
    cin.ignore(100, '\n');
    cout << "Enter the year: ";
    cin >> hireYear;
    cin.ignore(100, '\n');

    //call public member function to set the date
    hireDate.setDate(hireMonth, hireDay, hireYear);

    //call public member function to display the date
    cout << "The employee was hired on ";
    hireDate.displayDate();
    cout << "." << endl << endl;
} //end of main function
```

verify that you entered
this line correctly

verify that you entered
this line correctly

enter this line of code

Figure 11-8: Current status of the hire date program

6 Save, build, and execute the program. When you are prompted to enter the month, type **7** and press the **Enter** key. When you are prompted to enter the day, type **3** and press the **Enter** key. When you are prompted to enter the year, type **99** and press the **Enter** key. The DOS window shows that the hire date is 7/3/99, as shown in Figure 11-9.

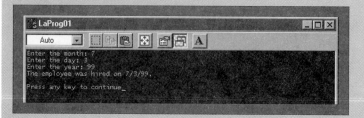

Figure 11-9: DOS window showing the results of the hire date program

7 Press the **Enter** key to close the DOS window, then close the Output window.

As you learned in Tutorial 3, you should always initialize the variables used in a program. If you do not, the variables will contain a garbage value—the remains of what was last stored at that memory location. In the next set of steps, you will determine if a variable in a class also contains a garbage value when it is not initialized.

To determine if a variable in a class contains a garbage value when it is not initialized:

1 Type **//** before the `hireDate.setDate(hireMonth, hireDay, hireYear);` statement in the program to tell C++ to treat the statement as a comment. By treating this statement as a comment, the program will not assign the values input by the user to the class's private variables, so the `displayDate` function will display the values stored in the uninitialized variables.

2 Save, build, and execute the program. When you are prompted to enter the month, type **12** and press the **Enter** key. When you are prompted to enter the day, type **23** and press the **Enter** key. When you are prompted to enter the year, type **99** and press the **Enter** key. The DOS window shows that the class's uninitialized variables contain garbage values, as shown in Figure 11-10.

garbage values stored
in uninitialized variables
(your values may differ)

Figure 11-10: DOS window showing garbage values in the uninitialized variables of the class

3 Press the **Enter** key to close the DOS window, then close the Output window.

As you just observed, you should initialize a class's variables to ensure that the variables do not contain garbage values. You do so by creating a constructor function.

Creating a Constructor Function

A **constructor function**, often simply called a **constructor**, is a member function that C++ calls automatically each time the class creates—or, to use an OOP term, **instantiates**—an object. The sole purpose of the constructor function, which has the same name as the class, is to initialize the class's variables. The constructor function for the date class, for example, would be named `date`. To initialize the date class's `month`, `day`, and `year` variables, you need simply to add the date constructor to the date class defined in the date.h header file.

You also can have multiple constructors in a class, and the constructors can be listed in the private section of the class. Both of these topics are beyond the scope of this book.

Although the constructor function cannot return a value, it can receive one or more values. As with other function prototypes, you list the data type of the formal parameters, separated by commas, within the parentheses following the function's name.

To add a constructor function to the date class defined in the date.h header file:

1 Open the **date.h** header file, which is located in the Cpp\Tut11\headers folder on your computer's hard disk.

You list the constructor function's prototype—in this case, `date();`—in the public section of the class. Unlike other function prototypes, the constructor function's prototype does not begin with a data type. Because the sole purpose of the constructor function is to initialize the class's variables, the function will never return a value, so no data type—not even `void`—is included in the prototype.

2 In the blank line below the `void displayDate();` statement, type `date();` and press the **Enter** key.

You must now enter the function definition for the constructor function. The function will simply assign the number 0 to each of the private variables in the class.

3   Enter the constructor function's definition, which is highlighted in Figure 11-11. After doing so, you will have completed defining the **date** class.

```
//date.h - this header file defines a date class

class date
{
public:
    //function prototypes - behaviors
    void setDate(short, short, short);
    void displayDate();
    date();

private:
    //variable declarations - attributes
    short month;
    short day;
    short year;
};

void date::setDate(short num1, short num2, short num3)
{
    month = num1;
    day = num2;
    year = num3;
} //end of setDate function

void date::displayDate()
{
    cout << month << '/' << day << '/' << year;
} //end of displayDate function

date::date()
{
    //this constructor initializes the private data
    //members of the class
    month = 0;
    day   = 0;
    year  = 0;
} //end of date constructor
```

verify that you entered
this line correctly

enter these lines of code

Figure 11-11: Completed date class showing the constructor function

4   Save the header file, then close the header file. The LaProg01 program should still be open.

Run the hire date program to ensure that the constructor initializes each of the class's variables to the number 0.

5   Save, build, and execute the LaProg01 program. When you are prompted to enter the month, type **3** and press the **Enter** key. When you are prompted to enter the day, type **2** and press the **Enter** key. When you are prompted to enter the year, type **99** and press the **Enter** key. The DOS window shows that the hire date is 0/0/0, which indicates that the variables were initialized properly.

6   Press the **Enter** key to close the DOS window.

You will now change the //hireDate.setDate(hireMonth, hireDay, hireYear); comment back to a statement by removing the //.

7 Delete the // that you entered before the hireDate.setDate(hireMonth, hireDay, hireYear); statement.

8 Save, build, and execute the program. On your own, enter a month, day, and year. The DOS window should show the month, day, and year, separated by slashes.

9 Press the **Enter** key to close the DOS window.

You have completed this program, so you can close it.

10 Close the Output window and the workspace.

mini-quiz

Mini-Quiz 2

1. Create a class named employee, which contains two private members and one public member. The private members should be a Character variable named code and a Float variable named hrlyPay. The public member should be a void function named getEmpInfo. The getEmpInfo function should assign, to the private members, the code and hourly pay passed to it by the program. Use the two formal parameters, id and money.

2. The scope resolution operator is _____ .

3. Write the constructor function prototype for the employee class created in question 1.

4. Write a constructor function definition for the employee class created in question 1.

You have now completed Lesson A. In this lesson, you learned how to create a programmer-defined class, and also how to use the class to instantiate (create) an object. You also learned how to create a constructor function that automatically initializes the variables in a class. In Lesson B, you will learn how to use value-returning functions in a class. For now, you can either take a break or complete the end-of-lesson questions and exercises.

S U M M A R Y

As you learned in Tutorial 1, a class is a pattern for creating one or more instances of the class—in other words, one or more objects. A class encapsulates all of an object's attributes and behaviors. An object's attributes are the characteristics that describe the object, and its behaviors are the operations (actions) that the object either can perform or have performed on it.

Some of an object's attributes and behaviors are hidden from the user, while others are exposed. In object-oriented programming, the term *abstraction* (or *data hiding*) refers to the hiding of an object's internal details from the user. Hiding those details helps prevent the user from making inadvertent changes to the object. The idea behind abstraction is to expose to the user only the attributes and behaviors that are necessary to use the object, and to hide everything else.

A class can have a public section and a private section. You place in the class's private section the attributes (variables) and behaviors (functions) that you want to hide from the user, and place in the class's public section the attributes and behaviors that you want to expose. Any program that contains an instance of the class can access a public member of a class. However, only another member of the class can access a private member of a class. The program cannot access a private member directly. The functions defined in the public section of the class allow the program to access the private members.

If you want to use a class to define an object in more than one program, you should place the class definition in a C++ header file. You then must include the header file in any program that will use the class to create an object.

You initialize the data members in the class by including a constructor function in the public section of the class. When the class is used to instantiate (create) an object, C++ automatically calls the constructor function. The constructor function has the same name as the class. Unlike other functions, however, it does not have a data type because it cannot return a value.

ANSWERS TO MINI-QUIZZES

Mini-Quiz 1

1. class

2. attributes

3. private, public

4. private

Mini-Quiz 2

1.
```cpp
class employee
    {
    public:
          void getEmpInfo(char, float);
    private:
          char code;
          float hrlyPay;
    };
    void employee::getEmpInfo(char id, float money)
    {
          code = id;
          hrlyPay = money;
    } //end of getEmpInfo function
```

2. :: (two colons)

3. employee();

4.
```cpp
employee::employee()
    {
       code = ' ';
       hrlyPay = (float) 0.0;
    } //end of employee constructor
```

Q U E S T I O N S

1. A blueprint for creating an object in C++ is called _____ .
    a. a class
    b. an instance
    c. a map
    d. a patterne
    e. a sketch

2. Which of the following statements is false?
    a. A class encapsulates all of an object's attributes and behaviors.
    b. An example of an attribute is the `minutes` variable in a `time` class.
    c. An example of a behavior is the `setTime` function in a `time` class.
    d. A class is considered an object.
    e. An object created from a class is referred to as an instance of the class.

3. To hide a data member from the program, you must declare the data member in the _____ section of the class.
    a. `concealed`
    b. `confidential`
    c. `hidden`
    d. `private`
    e. `restricted`

4. To expose a data member to the program, you must declare the data member in the _____ section of the class.
    a. `common`
    b. `exposed`
    c. `public`
    d. `unrestricted`
    e. `user`

5. A program can directly access the _____ members of a class.
    a. hidden
    b. private
    c. public
    d. both b and c

6. The program can access the private members of a class _____ .
    a. directly
    b. only through other private members of the class
    c. only through other public members of the class
    d. None of the above—the program cannot access the private members of a class in any way.

7. If you want to use a class to define objects in many different programs, you should define the class in a C++ _____ file.
    a. header
    b. program
    c. source
    d. text

8. Assume that the userclass.h file is located in the Cpp\Tut11\headers folder on the computer's C drive. Which of the following instructions will include this header file in a program?

    a. `#include <c:\cpp\tut11\headers\userclass.h>`

    b. `#include "c:\cpp\tut11\headers\userclass.h"`

    c. `#include "<c:\cpp\tut11\headers\userclass.h>"`

    d. `#include <"c:\cpp\tut11\headers\userclass.h">`

9. Which of the following is the scope resolution operator?

    a. `->`

    b. `::`

    c. `*`

    d. `.`

    e. `&`

10. The name of the constructor function for a class named `animal` is _____.

    a. `animal`

    b. `animalFunction`

    c. `conAnimal`

    d. `pet`

    e. All of the above could be used as the name of the constructor function.

E X E R C I S E S

1. In this exercise, you will use an existing class to create an object.

    a. Open the date.h header file, which is located in the Cpp\Tut11\headers folder on your computer's hard disk. (This is the file you created in Lesson A.) Print, then close the file.

    b. Open the T11Ae01.cpp file, which is located in the Cpp\Tut11\T11Ae01 folder on your computer's hard disk.

    c. Enter the appropriate `#include` directive to include the date.h header file in the program. (Recall that the header file is located in the Cpp\Tut11\headers folder on your computer's hard disk.)

    d. Enter the appropriate statements to create a `departDate` and an `arrivalDate` object. Create these objects from the `date` class defined in the date.h header file.

    e. The statements to set the departure and arrival dates are missing from the program. Enter the statement to set the departure date below the `//set departure date` comment. Enter the statement to set the arrival date below the `//set arrival date` comment.

    f. The statements to display the departure and arrival dates are also missing from the program. Enter both statements in the appropriate section of the program.

    g. Save, build, and then execute the program. To test the program, enter the number 2 as the departure month, the number 5 as the departure day, and the number 1998 as the departure year. Then enter the number 2 as the arrival month, the number 6 as the arrival day, and the number 1998 as the arrival year. The DOS window should show that the departure date is 2/5/1998 and the arrival date is 2/6/1998.

    h. When the program is working correctly, print the code.

    i. Close the workspace and the Output window.

2. In this exercise, you will modify both an existing header file and an existing program that uses a class defined in the header file.

    a. Open the T11Ae02.h header file, which is located in the Cpp\Tut11\headers folder on your computer's hard disk. (This code is identical to the code you entered in the date.h header file in Lesson A.)

    b. Modify the T11Ae02.h header file as follows. First, remove the setDate function prototype, as well as the setDate function definition. Then create three new public member functions named setMonth, setDay, and setYear. These functions should allow the user to set each private data member separately.

    c. Save the header file, then close the header file.

    d. Open the T11Ae02.cpp file, which is located in the Cpp\Tut11\T11Ae02 folder on your computer's hard disk.

    e. Enter the appropriate #include directive to include the T11Ae02.h header file in the program. (Recall that the header file is located in the Cpp\Tut11\headers folder on your computer's hard disk.)

    f. Enter a statement that uses the date class defined in the T11Ae02.h header file to create a date object named curDate.

    g. Modify the program so that it prompts the user to enter the month, day, and year. Store the user's responses in the curMonth, curDay, and curYear variables.

    h. In the program, enter the statements that will use the appropriate public function members to assign values to the private data members.

    i. In the program, enter the statement that will use the appropriate public function member to display the values in the private data members.

    j. Save, build, and then execute the program. To test the program, enter the number 2 as the month, the number 13 as the day, and the number 2000 as the year. The DOS window should show that today is 2/13/2000.

    k. When the program is working correctly, print the code for the header and program files.

    l. Close the workspace and the Output window.

3. In this exercise, you will create a class in a header file. You will also modify an existing program.

    a. Create a new header file. Save the header file as T11Ae03.h in the Cpp\Tut11\headers folder on your computer's hard disk.

    b. In the header file, create a class named time. The class should allow the user to set the hour and the minute individually. It should also allow the user to display the time. (*Hint*: You will need two private data members and four public member functions, which include the constructor.)

    c. Save the header file, then close the header file.

    d. Open the T11Ae03.cpp file, which is located in the Cpp\Tut11\T11Ae03 folder on your computer's hard disk.

    e. Enter the appropriate #include directive to include the T11Ae03.h header file in the program. (Recall that the header file is located in the Cpp\Tut11\headers folder on your computer's hard disk.)

    f. Modify the program so that it declares a time object. The program should prompt the user to enter the hour and the minute. Store the user's responses in the hour and minute variables.

    g. In the program, enter the statements that will use the appropriate public function members to assign values to the private data members.

    h. In the program, enter the statement that will use the appropriate public function member to display the values in the private data members. Display the hour, followed by a colon, and then the minute.

    i. Save, build, and then execute the program. To test the program, enter the number 10 as the hour and the number 15 as the minute. The DOS window should show that the time is 10:15.

> j. When the program is working correctly, print the code for the header and program files.
>
> k. Close the workspace and the Output window.

discovery ▶ 4. In this exercise, you will create a class in a header file. You will also complete a program.

> a. Create a new header file. Save the header file as T11Ae04.h in the Cpp\Tut11\headers folder on your computer's hard disk.
>
> b. In the header file, create a class named `item`. The class should contain two private data members named `partNum` and `price`. `partNum` is a Short Integer variable and `price` is a Float variable. The class should also contain public members that allow the user to set the part number and price individually, as well as display the part number and price individually. Additionally, the class should contain a public member that will calculate a new price by multiplying the original price by a percentage. The program that uses the class will provide the percentage in decimal form. For example, if the user wants to update the price by 10 percent, the program will pass .1 to the class. (*Hint*: You will need six public member functions, which include the constructor.)
>
> c. Save the header file, then close the header file.
>
> d. Open the T11Be04.cpp file, which is located in the Cpp\Tut11\T11Be04 folder on your computer's hard disk.
>
> e. Enter the appropriate directive to include in the program the T11Be04.h header file, which is located in the Cpp\Tut11\headers folder on your computer's hard disk.
>
> f. Modify the program so that it declares an `item` object.
>
> g. The program should prompt the user to enter the part number, the price, and the increase percentage, entered in decimal form. Store the user's responses in three variables.
>
> h. In the program, enter the statements that will use the appropriate public function members to assign values to the private data members.
>
> i. In the program, enter the statement that will use the appropriate public function member to display the values in the private data members.
>
> j. In the program, enter the statement that will use the appropriate public function member to update the price by the increase entered by the user.
>
> k. In the program, enter the statement that will use the appropriate public function to display the updated price.
>
> l. Save, build, and then execute the program. To test the program, enter the number 25 as the part number, the number 5 as the price, and the number .1 as the increase rate. The DOS window should show that the part number is 25, the old price is 5, and the new price is 5.5.
>
> m. When the program is working correctly, print the code for the header and program files.
>
> n. Close the workspace and the Output window.

debugging 5. In this exercise, you will debug a header file and a program.

> a. Open the T11Ae05.h file, which is located in the Cpp\Tut11\headers folder on your computer's hard disk. You will notice that the header file defines the `inventory` class, which has two private data members and three public member functions. The `inventory` constructor initializes the private data members. The `setItem` function allows the program to enter information into the private data members, and the `displayItem` function allows the program to display the information.
>
> b. Print and then close the header file.
>
> c. Open the T11Ae05.cpp file, which is located in the Cpp\Tut11\T11Ae05 folder on your computer's hard disk. You will notice that the program creates an `inventory` object named `item`. The inventory class is defined in the T11Ae05.h header file. Enter the appropriate `#include` directive to include the T11Ae05.h header file in the program. (Recall that the header file is located in the Cpp\Tut11\headers folder on your computer's hard disk.)

d. The program should prompt the user to enter the code and the quantity, and then assign the user's responses to the `item` object's private data members. The program should then display the values in the private data members. Build the program. You will notice that the program and/or header file contains some syntax errors. Debug the program and/or header file. (*Hint*: Correct the first error, then save and build the program again. You may find that by correcting the first error, you will also correct one or more of the subsequent errors.)

e. Save, build, and debug the program and/or header file until the program is working correctly, then execute the program. Enter the letter A as the code, and the number 45 as the quantity. The DOS window should display the code and the quantity.

f. When the program is working correctly, print the code for both the header and program files. On the code printouts, indicate what was wrong with the program and/or header file, and circle the changes you made to the original files.

g. Close the workspace and the Output window.

Using Value-returning Functions in a Class

Creating the `rectangle` Class

As you may remember from the case at the beginning of the tutorial, three small businesses—Terney Landscaping, Martin Fence Company, and Pool-Time—have asked you to create programs for them. While analyzing the three problems, you notice that each problem involves a rectangular shape. For example, in Terney Landscaping's program, you need to find the area of a rectangle on which sod is to be laid. In Martin Fence Company's program, on the other hand, you need to find the perimeter of a rectangle around which a fence is to be constructed. Lastly, in Pool-Time's program, you need to find the volume of a rectangular solid—an in-ground pool. To save time, you decide to create a class that contains the attributes and behaviors of a rectangle. You will use the class in each of the three programs to create an object that represents a rectangle.

As you learned in Lesson A, before you can create an object in C++, you first must create a blueprint or pattern for the object. You do so by specifying in a class the object's attributes, as well as the behaviors that the object either will perform or have performed on it. Before creating the `rectangle` class, consider what attributes a rectangular shape can have. All rectangles have a length dimension and a width dimension. If the rectangle is a solid, it also has a height (or depth) dimension. The length, width, and height dimensions are the attributes you will include in the `rectangle` class. You will use the variable names `length`, `width`, and `height`, and you will use the Float data type to declare each variable.

Now consider what behaviors the `rectangle` object will need either to perform or have performed on it. In this case, you will need the rectangle to calculate and return its area, as well as its perimeter and volume. You will include these three behaviors—calculate and return the area, calculate and return the perimeter, and calculate and return the volume—in the `rectangle` class. The formulas for calculating the area and perimeter of a rectangle, as well as the formula for calculating the volume of a rectangular solid, are shown in Figure 11-12.

Formula for the area of a rectangle:	length * width
Formula for the perimeter of a rectangle:	2 * length + 2 * width
Formula for the volume of a rectangular solid:	length * width * height

Figure 11-12: Area, perimeter, and volume formulas

As you may remember from Lesson A, you need a member function for each behavior listed in the class. The `rectangle` class, for example, will have three value-returning member functions, one for each of the three behaviors. The member function that calculates and returns the area of the rectangle, you will name `area`. The `area` function will need to know both the length and width of the rectangle, as the area formula shown in Figure 11-12 indicates. The function will need to receive this information from the program that calls it. The member function that calculates the perimeter of the rectangle, you will name `perimeter`. Like the `area` function, the `perimeter` function will also need to receive both the length and width of the rectangle. Lastly, the member function that calculates the volume, you will name `volume`. As the volume formula shown in Figure 11-12 indicates, the `volume` function will need to receive the rectangle's length, width, and height.

Now that you have identified the `rectangle` object's attributes and behaviors, you can begin creating the `rectangle` class. You will enter the `rectangle` class definition in a header file named rect.h, which you will save in the Cpp\Tut11\headers folder on your computer's hard disk.

To create the rect.h header file and then begin creating the `rectangle` class:

1 Start Visual C++. Click **File** on the menu bar, and then click **New**. When the New dialog box appears, click the **Files** tab, then click **C/C++ Header File** in the list of file types, and then click the **OK** button. Click **File** on the menu bar, then click **Save As**. When the Save As dialog box appears, open the **headers** folder, which is located in the Cpp\Tut11 folder on your computer's hard disk. Change the filename in the File name text box to **rect**, then click the **Save** button. The title bar indicates that the file is now saved as rect.H.

You can now begin entering the definition of the `rectangle` class in the header file. First enter the `class` statement.

2 Enter the `class` statement shown in Figure 11-13.

enter these lines of code

```
//rect.h
//this header file defines the rectangle class

class rectangle
{
public:
    float area(float, float);
    float perimeter(float, float);
    float volume(float, float, float);
    rectangle();

private:
    float length;
    float width;
    float height;
};
```

be sure to enter
the semicolon

Figure 11-13: `class` statement entered in the rect.h header file

3 Save the header file.

You will notice that the **class** statement's public section contains the proto-types for three value-returning functions. Each value-returning function represents a behavior that a rectangle object can perform. The public section also includes the prototype for the **rectangle** class's constructor function. As you learned in Lesson A, the constructor function's task is to initialize the class's variables. Also notice that the class statement's private section contains the three variables that correspond to the attributes of a rectangle: length, width, and height.

Now you need to enter the function definitions for the four member functions. Begin with the **rectangle** constructor function.

To enter the function definition for the **rectangle** constructor function:

1 Enter the **rectangle** constructor's function definition, which is highlighted in Figure 11-14.

these assignment statements will initialize the private variables

enter these lines of code

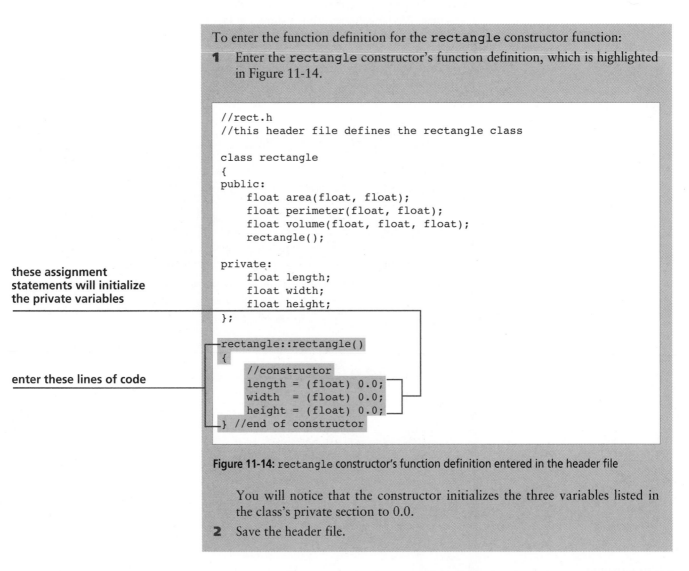

```
//rect.h
//this header file defines the rectangle class

class rectangle
{
public:
    float area(float, float);
    float perimeter(float, float);
    float volume(float, float, float);
    rectangle();

private:
    float length;
    float width;
    float height;
};

rectangle::rectangle()
{
    //constructor
    length = (float) 0.0;
    width  = (float) 0.0;
    height = (float) 0.0;
} //end of constructor
```

Figure 11-14: rectangle constructor's function definition entered in the header file

You will notice that the constructor initializes the three variables listed in the class's private section to 0.0.

2 Save the header file.

You can now enter the function definitions for the **area**, **perimeter**, and **volume** member functions. The **area** and **perimeter** functions will list two Float formal parameters in their function headers: one to receive the length of the rectangle and the other to receive the width. The **volume** function will list three Float formal parameters in its function header because it will need to receive the length, width, and height. Each of the three functions will return a value—either the area, the perimeter, or the volume—in the Float type range.

To enter the `area`, `perimeter`, and `volume` function definitions:

1 Enter the `area`, `perimeter`, and `volume` function definitions, which are highlighted in Figure 11-15. After doing so, you will have completed the `rectangle` class.

```cpp
//rect.h
//this header file defines the rectangle class

class rectangle
{
public:
    float area(float, float);
    float perimeter(float, float);
    float volume(float, float, float);
    rectangle();

private:
    float length;
    float width;
    float height;
};

rectangle::rectangle()
{
    //constructor
    length = (float) 0.0;
    width  = (float) 0.0;
    height = (float) 0.0;
} //end of constructor

float rectangle::area(float len, float wid)
{
    length = len;
    width  = wid;
    return length * width;
} //end of area function

float rectangle::perimeter(float len, float wid)
{
    length = len;
    width  = wid;
    return (float) 2 * length + (float) 2 * width;
} //end of perimeter function

float rectangle::volume(float len, float wid, float hgt)
{
    length = len;
    width  = wid;
    height = hgt;
    return length * width * height;
} //end of volume function
```

enter these lines of code

Figure 11-15: Completed `rectangle` class

2 Save the header file, then close the header file.

Now that you have defined the `rectangle` class, you can use it to create a rectangle object in the Terney Landscaping, Martin Fence Company, and Pool-Time programs. Begin with the Terney Landscaping program.

Completing the Terney Landscaping Program

Recall that Terney Landscaping wants a program that its salespeople can use to estimate the cost of laying sod. The IPO chart for this program is shown in Figure 11-16.

Input	Processing	Output

length of the rectangle, in feet
 	
width of the rectangle, in feet
 	
price of a square yard of sod
	Processing items:
	        `rectangle` object
	
	Algorithm:
	1. enter the length of the rectangle, in feet
	2. while (length > 0)
	        enter the width of the rectangle, in feet
	        enter the price of a square yard of sod
	        calculate the area in square feet (`rectangle` object's `area` function)
	        calculate the area in square yards by dividing the area in square feet by 9
	        calculate the total price by multiplying the area in square yards by the price of a square yard of sod
	        display the area in square yards and the total price
	        enter the length of the rectangle, in feet
	    end while
		area in square yards and total price

Figure 11-16: IPO chart for the Terney Landscaping program

You will notice that a `rectangle` object will be used as a processing item in the Terney Landscaping program. According to the algorithm shown in the IPO chart, the program will get the length of a rectangle, in feet, from the user. If the user enters a length that is not greater than 0, the program will end. However, if the user enters a number that is greater than 0, then the instructions in the `while` loop will be processed. Those instructions get the width of the rectangle, in feet, and also the price of a square yard of sod. The program will then call the `rectangle` object's `area` function to calculate the area of the rectangle, in square feet. The program will convert the value returned by the `area` function from square feet to square yards by dividing the return value by the number 9—the number of square feet in a square yard. The program will then calculate the total price by multiplying the number of square yards by the price per square yard of sod before displaying the area in square yards and the total price. The last instruction in the `while` loop will get another length from the user. The `while` loop's condition will then be evaluated to determine if the loop instructions should be processed again. Your computer's hard disk contains a partially completed program for Terney Landscaping. Open that program now.

To complete the Terney Landscaping program:

1   Open the **LbProg01.cpp** file, which is located in the Cpp\Tut11\LbProg01 folder on your computer's hard disk. The Terney Landscaping program appears in the LbProg01.cpp window. Only two instructions are missing from the program: the `#include` directive that will include the rect.h header file in the program, and the statement that declares a `rectangle` object named `lawn`. Enter the missing instructions, which are highlighted in Figure 11-17.

(If the full path to the rect.h header file on your system differs from the one shown in the figure, then change the #include directive to reflect the full path used on your system.)

your path may differ

```
//LbProg01.cpp
//Terney Landscaping program

#include <iostream.h>
#include <iomanip.h>
#include "c:\cpp\tut11\headers\rect.h"

void main()
{
    //declare rectangle object
    rectangle lawn;

    //declare and initialize variables
    float lawnLen    = (float) 0.0;
    float lawnWid    = (float) 0.0;
    float lawnArea   = (float) 0.0;
    float priceSqYd  = (float) 0.0;
    float totPrice   = (float) 0.0;

    //get the length
    cout << "Enter the length, in feet (0 to quit): ";
    cin >> lawnLen;
    cin.ignore(100, '\n');

    while (lawnLen > 0)
    {
        //get the width
        cout << "Enter the width, in feet: ";
        cin >> lawnWid;
        cin.ignore(100, '\n');

        //get the price per square yard
        cout << "Enter the price per square yard: ";
        cin >> priceSqYd;
        cin.ignore(100, '\n');

        //calculate the area in square yards
        lawnArea = lawn.area(lawnLen, lawnWid) / (float) 9;
        //calculate the total price
        totPrice = lawnArea * priceSqYd;

        //display the area and the total price
        cout << setprecision(2)
             << setiosflags(ios::fixed | ios::showpoint);
        cout << endl << "Number of square yards: "
             << lawnArea << endl;
        cout << "Total price of sod:  $" << totPrice
             << endl << endl;

        //get the length
        cout << "Enter the length, in feet (0 to quit): ";
        cin >> lawnLen;
        cin.ignore(100, '\n');
    }//end while
} //end of main function
```

enter these two lines of code

get the length

get the width

get the price

calculate the area and total price

display the area and total price

get the length

Figure 11-17: Terney Landscaping program

2   Save, build, and execute the program. When you are prompted to enter the length, type **120** and press the **Enter** key. When you are prompted to enter the width, type **75** and press the **Enter** key. When you are prompted to enter the price per square yard of sod, type **1.55** and press the **Enter** key. The DOS window shows that the area in square yards is 1000.00 and the total price is $1550.00. You are prompted to enter the length.

3   Type **0** (zero) and press the **Enter** key to quit the program, then press the **Enter** key to close the DOS window.

You are now finished with this program, so you can close it.

4   Close the workspace and the Output window.

You will complete the Martin Fence Company's program next.

Completing the Martin Fence Company Program

Martin Fence Company wants a program that will calculate the cost of a fence. The IPO chart for this program is shown in Figure 11-18.

Input	Processing	Output

length of the rectangle, in feet	Processing items:
	    rectangle object
	
	Algorithm:
	1. enter the length of the rectangle, in feet
	2. while (length > 0)
	    enter the width of the rectangle, in feet
	    enter the cost of the fence, per linear foot
	    calculate the perimeter (**rectangle** object's
	    perimeter function)
	    calculate the total price by multiplying the perimeter
	    by the cost of the fence, per linear foot
	    display the perimeter and the total price
	    enter the length of the rectangle, in feet
	    end while
		perimeter and total price

width of the rectangle, in feet		
cost of the fence, per linear foot		

Figure 11-18: IPO chart for the Martin Fence Company program

You will notice that a **rectangle** object will be used as a processing item in the Martin Fence Company program. According to the algorithm shown in the IPO chart, the program will get the length of a rectangle, in feet, from the user. If the user enters a length that is not greater than 0, the program will end. However, if the user enters a number that is greater than 0, then the instructions in the **while** loop will be processed. Those instructions get the width of the rectangle, in feet, and also the cost of the fence, per linear foot. Notice that the program will call the **rectangle** object's **perimeter** function to calculate the perimeter of the rectangle. The program will then calculate the total price by multiplying the perimeter function's return value by the cost of the fence, per linear foot. The last instruction in the **while** loop will get another length from the user. The **while** loop's condition will then be evaluated to determine if the loop instructions should be processed again. Your computer's hard disk contains a partially completed program for Martin Fence Company. Open that program now.

To complete the Martin Fence Company program:

1 Open the **LbProg02.cpp** file, which is located in the Cpp\Tut11\LbProg02 folder on your computer's hard disk. The Martin Fence Company program appears in the LbProg02.cpp window. Only two instructions are missing from the program: the `#include` directive that will include the rect.h header file in the program, and the statement that declares a `rectangle` object named `fence`. Enter the missing instructions, which are highlighted in Figure 11-19. (If the full path to the rect.h header file on your system differs from the one shown in the figure, then change the `#include` directive to reflect the full path used on your system.)

your path may differ

enter these two lines of code

get the length

get the width

get the price

calculate the perimeter
and total price

```
//LbProg02.cpp
//Martin Fence Company program

#include <iostream.h>
#include <iomanip.h>
#include "c:\cpp\tut11\headers\rect.h"

void main()
{
    //declare rectangle object
    rectangle fence;

    //declare and initialize variables
    float fenceLen    = (float) 0.0;
    float fenceWid    = (float) 0.0;
    float fencePerim  = (float) 0.0;
    float priceFt     = (float) 0.0;
    float totPrice    = (float) 0.0;

    //get the length
    cout << "Enter the length, in feet (0 to quit): ";
    cin >> fenceLen;
    cin.ignore(100, '\n');

    while (fenceLen > 0)
    {
        //get the width
        cout << "Enter the width, in feet: ";
        cin >> fenceWid;
        cin.ignore(100, '\n');

        //get the price per foot
        cout << "Enter the price per foot: ";
        cin >> priceFt;
        cin.ignore(100, '\n');

        //calculate the perimeter and the total price
        fencePerim = fence.perimeter(fenceLen, fenceWid);
        totPrice = fencePerim * priceFt;
```

Figure 11-19: Martin Fence Company program (continues on next page)

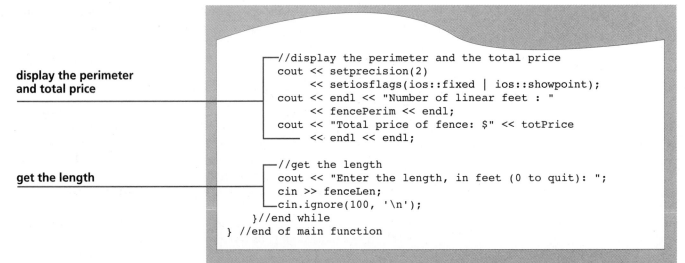

display the perimeter and total price

get the length

```
//display the perimeter and the total price
cout << setprecision(2)
     << setiosflags(ios::fixed | ios::showpoint);
cout << endl << "Number of linear feet : "
     << fencePerim << endl;
cout << "Total price of fence: $" << totPrice
     << endl << endl;

//get the length
cout << "Enter the length, in feet (0 to quit): ";
cin >> fenceLen;
cin.ignore(100, '\n');
}//end while
} //end of main function
```

Figure 11-19: Martin Fence Company program (continued)

2 Save, build, and execute the program. When you are prompted to enter the length, type **120** and press the **Enter** key. When you are prompted to enter the width, type **75** and press the **Enter** key. When you are prompted to enter the price per foot, type **10** and press the **Enter** key. The DOS window shows that the perimeter is 390 linear feet and the total price is $3900.00. You are prompted to enter the length.

3 Type **0** (zero) and press the **Enter** key to quit the program, then press the **Enter** key to close the DOS window.

You are now finished with this program, so you can close it.

4 Close the workspace and the Output window.

You have now completed Lesson B. In this lesson, you learned how to include a value-returning function in a class. You will complete the Pool-Time program in Lesson B's Exercise 1.

SUMMARY

Before you can create an object in C++, you must create a blueprint or pattern for the object; you do so by specifying the object's attributes and behaviors in a class. You will have a member function for each behavior specified in the class. The member functions can be either void or value-returning functions.

QUESTIONS

1. Which of the following statements is false?
   a. You typically use a public member function to change the value in a private data member.
   b. Because the constructor function does not return a value, you place the keyword void before the constructor's name.

c. The public member functions in a class can be accessed by any program that uses an object created from that class.

d. An instance of a class is considered an object.

2. You place the constructor's prototype in the _____ section of the class.

a. `confidential`

b. `hidden`

c. `public`

d. `private`

e. `restricted`

3. Which of the following creates an `animal` object named `dog`?

a. `animal "dog";`

b. `animal dog;`

c. `dog "animal";`

d. `dog animal;`

4. Which of the following tells C++ that the `displayBreed` function is a member of the `animal` class?

a. `displayBreed()->animal`

b. `displayBreed()::animal`

c. `displayBreed().animal`

d. `animal::displayBreed()`

e. `animal()->displayBreed()`

E X E R C I S E S

1. In this exercise, you will complete the Pool-Time program.

Scenario: Pool-Time, which sells in-ground pools, wants a program that its salespeople can use to determine the number of gallons of water required to fill a pool—a question commonly asked by customers. To calculate the number of gallons, you will need to find the volume of the in-ground pool. The IPO chart for this program is shown in Figure 11-20. (*Hint*: Because the pools built by Pool-Time are in-ground rather than above ground, the pool will have a depth dimension rather than a height dimension.)

Input	Processing	Output

length of the rectangle, in feet
 	
width of the rectangle, in feet
 	
depth of the rectangle, in feet
	Processing items:
	    rectangle object
	
	Algorithm:
	1. enter the length of the rectangle, in feet
	2. while (length > 0)
	    enter the width of the rectangle, in feet
	    enter the depth of the rectangle, in feet
	    calculate the volume (**rectangle** object's **volume** function)
	    calculate the number of gallons by dividing the volume by .13368
	    display the volume (in cubic feet) and the number of gallons of water
	    enter the length of the rectangle, in feet
	   end while
		volume (in cubic feet) and number of gallons of water

Figure 11-20: IPO chart for the Pool-Time program

a. Open the T11Be01.cpp program, which is located in the Cpp\Tut11\T11Be01 folder on your computer's hard disk.

b. Enter the appropriate #include directive to include the rect.h header file in the program. (Recall that you created this header file in Lesson B. It is located in the Cpp\Tut11\headers folder on your computer's hard disk.)

c. Enter the statement to declare a rectangle object named pool.

d. Enter the statement that calls the rectangle object's volume function to calculate the volume.

e. Enter the statement that calculates the number of gallons of water needed to fill the pool.

f. Save, build, and execute the program. Use 25 feet as the length, 15 feet as the width, and 6.5 feet as the depth.

g. When the program is working correctly, print the code. On the code printout, indicate the volume and the number of gallons of water from step f.

h. Close the Output window and the workspace.

2. In this exercise, you will create a header file and a program.

a. Create a header file that defines a class named triangle. Name the header file trian.h and save it in the Cpp\Tut11\headers folder on your computer's hard disk. The triangle class should have two value-returning member functions. One value-returning member function should calculate the area of a triangle and the other should calculate its perimeter. (*Hint*: The formula for calculating the area of a triangle is 1/2 * b * h, where b is the base and h is the height. The formula for calculating the perimeter of a triangle is a + b + c, where a, b, and c are the lengths of the sides.) Determine the appropriate variables to include in the class. Be sure to include a constructor function to initialize the variables.

b. Save the trian.h header file, and then close the header file.

c. Create a console application named T11Be02 in the Cpp\Tut11 folder on your computer's hard disk. Create a program that will display both the area and the perimeter of a triangle. Include the trian.h header file in the program. Also create a triangle object named tri. The program should prompt the user for the necessary information.

d. Save, build, and execute the program. Use the following information to calculate the area and the perimeter:

base: 10
height: 7
3 side lengths: 7, 10, 7

e. When the program is working correctly, print the code. On the printout, indicate the area and the perimeter from step d.

f. Close the workspace and the Output window.

discovery ▶ 3. In this exercise, you will modify an existing header file.

a. Open the T11Be03.h header file, which is located in the Cpp\Tut11\headers folder on your computer's hard disk. The header file defines a class named date. Print the code, then close the header file.

b. Open the T11Be03.cpp file, which is located in the Cpp\Tut11\T11Be03 folder on your computer's hard disk. Enter the appropriate #include directive to include the T11Be03.h header file in the program. The program uses the date class to create an object named today. Study the code. You will notice that the program prompts the user to enter the month, day, and year. It then uses the date class's public member functions (setDate and displayDate) both to set and display the date entered by the user. The program also uses a public member function named updateDate to increase the day by one. It then displays the new date on the screen.

c. Build and execute the program. Enter the number 3 as the month, the number 15 as the day, and the number 1998 as the year. The DOS window shows that today is 3/15/1998 and tomorrow is 3/16/1998, which is correct. Close the DOS window.

d. Execute the program again. Enter the number 3 as the month, the number 31 as the day, and the number 1998 as the year. The DOS window shows that today is 3/31/1998 and tomorrow is 3/32/1998, which is incorrect. Close the DOS window.

e. Modify the `updateDate` function in the header file so that it updates the date correctly. For example, if today is 3/31/1998, then tomorrow is 4/1/1998. If today is 12/31/1998, then tomorrow is 1/1/1999. (You do not have to worry about leap years; treat February as though it always has 28 days.)

f. Save, build, and then execute the program. Test the program four times, using the following dates: 3/15/1998, 4/30/1999, 2/28/1997, and 12/31/1999. The DOS window should show that tomorrow's dates are 3/16/1998, 5/1/1999, 3/1/1997, and 1/1/2000.

g. When the program is working correctly, print the header file's code. Close the workspace and the Output window.

ASCII Codes

Symbol	ASCII	Symbol	ASCII	Symbol	ASCII
(space)	0100000	?	0111111	^	1011110
!	0100001	@	1000000	_	1011111
"	0100010	A	1000001	a	1100001
#	0100011	B	1000010	b	1100010
$	0100100	C	1000011	c	1100011
%	0100101	D	1000100	d	1100000
&	0100110	E	1000101	e	1100101
'	0100111	F	1000110	f	1100110
(	0101000	G	1000111	g	1100111
)	0101001	H	1001000	h	1101100
*	0101010	I	1001001	i	1101001
+	0101011	J	1001010	j	1101010
,	0101100	K	1001011	k	1101011
-	0101101	L	1001100	l	1101000
.	0101110	M	1001101	m	1101101
/	0101111	N	1001110	n	1101110
0	0110000	O	1001111	o	1111111
1	0110001	P	1010000	p	1110100
2	0110010	Q	1010001	q	1110001
3	0110011	R	1010010	r	1110010
4	0110100	S	1010011	s	1110011
5	0110101	T	1010100	t	1110100
6	0110110	U	1010101	u	1110101
7	0110111	V	1010110	v	1110110
8	0111000	W	1010111	w	1110111
9	0111001	X	1011000	x	1111000
:	0111010	Y	1011001	y	1111001
;	0111011	Z	1011010	z	1111010
<	0111100	[	1011011	{	1111011
=	0111101	\	1011100	}	1111101
>	0111110	]	1011101		

Mathematical Functions Included in the math.h Header File

Mathematical Function	Returns
abs(*x*)	absolute value of *x*
acos(*x*)	arccosine of *x*
asin(*x*)	arcsine of *x*
atan(*x*)	arctangent of *x*
atan2(*y*, *x*)	arctangent of *y*/*x*
cos(*x*)	cosine of *x*
cosh(*x*)	hyperbolic cosine of *x*
exp(*x*)	exponential value of *x*
fabs(*x*)	absolute value of the floating-point *x*
fmod(*x*, *y*)	floating-point remainder of *x*/*y*
labs(*x*)	absolute value of the long integer *x*
log(*x*)	natural (base e) log of *x*
log10(*x*)	common (base 10) log of *x*
pow(*x*, *y*)	*x* raised to the power of *y*
sin(*x*)	sine of *x*
sinh(*x*)	hyperbolic sine of *x*
sqrt(*x*)	square root of *x*
tan(*x*)	tangent of *x*
tanh(*x*)	hyperbolic tangent of *x*

The case Selection Structure

The case form of the Selection Structure

As you learned in Tutorial 1, you use the selection structure when you want a program to make a decision and then take the appropriate action based on the result of that decision. Most programming languages offer three forms of the selection structure: if, if/else, and case. You learned about the if and if/else forms in Tutorial 5. Recall that you use the if form of the selection structure when you want the program to evaluate a condition and then perform a set of tasks only if the condition evaluates to True. You use the if/else form of the selection structure, on the other hand, when you want the program to evaluate a condition and then perform one set of tasks if the condition evaluates to True and another set of tasks if the condition evaluates to False.

C++ programmers often refer to the case form of the selection structure as the switch form because the C++ switch statement is used to implement the structure.

In some programs, you may need the selection structure to choose from several paths. Suppose, for example, that a program needs to display a message based on a letter grade that the user enters. The letter grades and their corresponding messages are shown in Figure C-1.

Letter grade	Message
A	Excellent
B	Above Average
C	Average
D, F	Below Average
I	Incomplete
W	Withdrawal
Other	Incorrect Grade

Figure C-1: Letter grades and messages

The case form of the selection structure is sometimes referred to as an extended selection structure.

As Figure C-1 indicates, if the letter grade is 'A', then the program should display the "Excellent" message. If the letter grade is 'B', then the program should display the "Above Average" message, and so on. Although you could use the if/else form of the selection structure to determine the appropriate message to display, it is often simpler and clearer to use the case form in situations where the selection structure has many paths from which to choose. Figure C-2 shows the flowchart and pseudocode for the case selection structure that would display a message based on the grade contained in a Character variable named grade.

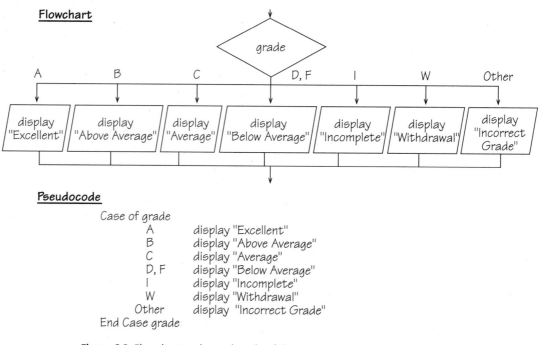

Figure C-2: Flowchart and pseudocode of the case selection structure

Notice that the flowchart symbol for the case form of the selection structure is the same as the flowchart symbol for the if and if/else forms—a diamond. Unlike the if and if/else diamond, however, the case diamond does not contain a condition requiring a true or false answer. Instead, the case diamond contains an expression—in this case, grade—whose value will control which path is chosen.

Like the `if` and `if/else` diamond, the `case` diamond has one flowline leading into the symbol. Unlike the `if` and `if/else` diamond, however, the `case` diamond has many flowlines leading out of the symbol. Each flowline represents a possible path for the selection structure. The flowlines must be marked appropriately, indicating which value(s) are necessary for each path to be chosen.

In C++, you use the `switch` statement to code the `case` selection structure.

The `switch` Statement

You use the C++ **switch** statement to code the `case` selection structure. Figure C-3 shows the syntax of the `switch` statement. It also shows the `switch` statement that displays a message based on the grade entered by the user.

Syntax	Example
switch(*selectorExpression***)** **{** **case** *value1:* *one or more statements* . . . **[case** *valueN:* *one or more statements]* **[default:**　　*one or more statements]* **}** *//end switch*	```switch (grade)
{
case 'A':   cout << "Excellent" << endl;
break;
case 'B':   cout << "Above Average" << endl;
break;
case 'C':   cout << "Average" << endl;
break;
case 'D':
case 'F':   cout << "Below Average" << endl;
break;
case 'I':   cout << "Incomplete" << endl;
break;
case 'W':   cout << "Withdrawal" << endl;
break;
default: cout << "Incorrect Grade" << endl;
} //end switch```
Important note: Items in square brackets are optional. Items in **bold** are required. Items in *italics* indicate places where the programmer must supply information pertaining to the current program.	

Figure C-3: The syntax and an example of the `switch` statement

The `switch` statement begins with the `switch` clause, followed by an opening brace and ending with a closing brace. As the syntax shows, it is a good programming practice to document the end of the `switch` statement with the `//end switch` comment. Between the `switch` statement's opening and closing braces are the individual `case` clauses. Each `case` clause represents a different path that the selection structure can follow. You can have as many `case` clauses as necessary in a `switch` statement. If the `switch` statement includes a `default` clause, the `default` clause should be the last clause in the statement.

Notice that the `switch` clause must include a *selectorExpression*. The *selectorExpression* can contain any combination of variables, constants, functions, and operators, as long as they evaluate to either a Boolean, Character, Short Integer, Integer, or Long Integer value. In the example shown in Figure C-3, the *selectorExpression* contains a Character variable named `grade`.

Each of the individual clauses within the `switch` statement (except for the `default` clause) contains a *value*, followed by a colon. The data type of the *value* must be compatible with the data type of the *selectorExpression*. In other words, if the *selectorExpression* is a numeric variable, the *values* in the `case` clauses must

tip

Although the `default` clause can appear anywhere within the `switch` statement, for clarity, it is recommended that you place it at the end of the `switch` statement.

be numeric. Likewise, if the *selectorExpression* is a Character variable, the *values* must be characters. In the example shown in Figure C-3, the data type of the *selectorExpression* (`grade`) is Character, as are the *values* in the `case` clauses—'A', 'B', 'C', 'D', 'F', 'I', 'W'—as indicated by the surrounding single quotes. The values in the `case` clauses can be literal constants, named constants, or expressions composed of literal and named constants.

Following the colon in each `case` clause are one or more statements. These statements will be processed when the *selectorExpression* matches that `case`'s *value*. Notice that the statements within a `case` clause are not surrounded by braces. The last statement in most `case` clauses is the `break` statement, which tells C++ to leave ("break out of") the `switch` statement at that point. After the appropriate `case` clause's instructions are processed, you will typically want to leave the `switch` statement without processing the remaining instructions in the statement. If you do not use the `break` statement to leave the `switch` statement, C++ will continue processing the remaining instructions in the statement. After the `break` statement is processed, the program will then process the instruction that follows the `switch` statement's closing brace.

When processing the `switch` statement, C++ compares the *selectorExpression*'s value with the *value* listed in each of the `case` clauses. If a match is found, C++ processes the instructions for that `case` until it encounters either a `break` statement or the `switch` statement's closing brace, which marks the end of the selection structure. C++ then skips to the instruction following the `switch` statement's closing brace.

If the *selectorExpression* does not match any of the *values* listed in the `case` clauses, C++ processes the instructions listed in the `default` clause. If there is no `default` clause, C++ simply processes the instruction following the `switch` statement's closing brace.

Exercises 1 and 2 will show you what happens when you do not use the `break` **statement to break out of the** `switch` **statement.**

Before opening a program that will allow you to observe how the `switch` statement works, look closely at the `case 'D':` clause shown in Figure C-3's example. Although a D grade should result in the "Below Average" message, you will notice that the clause does not appear to contain the necessary statements to display the message. It does not contain a `break` statement either. So, what, if anything, will display when the grade is a D?

Recall that, when the *selectorExpression* matches a `case` clause's value, C++ processes the instructions, beginning with that `case` clause, until it encounters either a `break` statement or the `switch` statement's closing brace. In this case, when the grade is a D, C++ will process the two instructions in the next `case` clause—`case 'F':`. Those instructions display the "Below Average" message, then break out of the `switch` statement. As this example shows, you can process the same instructions for more than one *value* by listing each *value* in a separate `case` clause, as long as the clauses appear together in the `switch` statement. The last clause in the group of related clauses should contain the instructions you want C++ to process when one of the *values* in the group is true. Only the last `case` clause in the group of related clauses should contain the `break` statement. Now open a program that will give you practice with the `switch` statement.

To observe how the switch statement works:

1   Open the **Prog01.cpp** file, which is located in the Cpp\AppC\Prog01 folder on your computer's hard disk. The grade program, which appears in the Prog01.cpp window, is shown in Figure C-4.

```cpp
//Prog01.cpp
//this program demonstrates the switch statement

#include <iostream.h>
#include <ctype.h>

void main()
{
    //declare and initialize variable
    char grade = ' ';

    //enter input item
    cout << "Enter a grade: ";
    cin >> grade;
    grade = toupper(grade);

    //display output
    switch (grade)
    {
    case 'A':   cout << "Excellent" << endl;
            break;
    case 'B':   cout << "Above Average" << endl;
            break;
    case 'C':   cout << "Average" << endl;
            break;
    case 'D':
    case 'F':   cout << "Below Average" << endl;
            break;
    case 'I':   cout << "Incomplete" << endl;
            break;
    case 'W':   cout << "Withdrawal" << endl;
            break;
    default:    cout << "Incorrect Grade" << endl;
    }   //end switch

} //end of main function
```

Figure C-4: The grade program

After declaring and initializing a Character variable named grade, the main function prompts the user to enter a grade. The user's response is stored in the grade variable, the contents of which are converted to uppercase. The switch statement compares the uppercase version of the grade to the values in the different case clauses, and then displays the appropriate message.

2   Build and then execute the program. When prompted to enter the grade, type **b** and press the Enter key. The cin >> grade; statement stores the grade you entered in the grade variable. The grade = toupper(grade); statement then converts the contents of the grade variable to uppercase. The switch statement tells C++ to compare the grade to the value listed in the first `case` clause—the character literal constant 'A'. Because you did not enter the letter A, C++ skips to the next `case` clause, where it compares the uppercase equivalent of the letter you entered to the character literal constant 'B'. Because both characters match, C++ processes the two statements within the `case` 'B': clause. In this case, the `cout << "Above Average" << endl;` statement displays "Above Average" in the DOS window, and the `break;` statement stops C++ from processing the remaining instructions in the `switch` statement. The program then ends.

3   Press the **Enter** key to close the DOS window.

4   On your own, run the program four times, entering the letters c, f, d, and t. The program should display "Average," "Below Average," "Below Average," and "Incorrect Grade."
    You are now finished with this program, so you can close it.

5   Close the workspace and the Output window.

tip

••••••••••••••••
▶ Recall that the `toupper` function returns the uppercase equivalent of the character in its actual argument.

You have now completed Appendix C. In this appendix, you learned how to use the C++ `switch` statement to code the `case` form of the selection structure.

Q U E S T I O N S

1. You can use the C++ _____ statement to code the `case` structure.
   a. `case`
   b. `case of`
   c. `struc`
   d. `switch`

2. Which of the following flowchart symbols represents the `case` selection structure?
   a. diamond
   b. hexagon
   c. oval
   d. parallelogram
   e. rectangle

3. If the *selectorExpression* used in the `switch` clause is the numeric variable `code`, which of the following `case` clauses is valid?
   a. `case '2':`
   b. `case "2":`
   c. `case 2:`
   d. `case = 2:`

4. If the *selectorExpression* used in the `switch` clause is the Character variable `code`, which of the following `case` clauses is valid?
   a. `case "2":`
   b. `case '2':`
   c. `case 2:`
   d. `case = 2:`

Use the following `switch` statement to answer questions 5 through 7. `id` is a Short Integer variable.

```cpp
switch (id)
{
case 1:    cout << "Janet" << endl;
           break;
case 2:    cout << "Paul" << endl;
           break;
case 3:
case 5:    cout << "Jerry" << endl;
           break;
default:   cout << "Sue" << endl;
} //end switch
```

5. What will the `switch` statement display if the `id` variable contains the number 2?
   a. Janet
   b. Jerry
   c. Paul
   d. Sue
   e. nothing

6. What will the `switch` statement display if the `id` variable contains the number 4?
   a. Janet
   b. Jerry
   c. Paul
   d. Sue
   e. nothing

7. What will the `switch` statement display if the `id` variable contains the number 3?
   a. Janet
   b. Jerry
   c. Paul
   d. Sue
   e. nothing

E X E R C I S E S

1. In this exercise, you will practice using the `switch` statement.
   a. Open the AppCe01.cpp file, which is located in the Cpp\AppC\AppCe01 folder on your computer's hard disk.
   b. Enter a `break;` statement in the `case 'D':` clause. Save, build, and execute the program. When prompted to enter a grade, type d and press the Enter key. On a piece of paper, write down what, if anything, the `switch` statement displayed on the screen and why this happened.
   c. Remove the `break;` statement from the `case 'D':` clause. Also remove the `break;` statement from the `case 'F'` clause. Save, build, and execute the program. When prompted to enter a grade, type d and press the Enter key. On a piece of paper, write down what, if anything, the `switch` statement displayed on the screen and why this happened.
   d. Put the `break;` statement back in the `case 'F';` clause. Save, build, and execute the program. When prompted to enter a grade, type d and press the Enter key. On a piece of paper, write down what, if anything, the `switch` statement displayed on the screen and why this happened.
   e. Close the Output window and the workspace.

2. In this exercise, you will practice using the `switch` statement.

a. Open the AppCe02.cpp file, which is located in the Cpp\AppC\AppCe02 folder on your computer's hard disk. This program uses the `switch` statement to display the names of the Christmas gifts mentioned in the song "The Twelve Days of Christmas."

b. Build and then execute the program. When prompted to enter the day, type the number 1 and press the Enter key. You will notice that the names of the gifts for the first through the twelfth day appear in the DOS window. Press the Enter key to close the DOS window.

c. Execute the program again. When prompted to enter the day, type the number 9 and press the Enter key. The names of the gifts for the ninth through the twelfth day appear in the DOS window. Press the Enter key to close the DOS window.

d. Modify the program so that it displays only the name of the gift corresponding to the day entered by the user. For example, if the user enters the number 4, the program should display "4 calling birds".

e. Save, build, and execute the program. When prompted to enter the day, type the number 4. The "4 calling birds" message should display. Press the Enter key to close the DOS window.

f. Print the code, then close the Output window and the workspace.

debugging **3.** In this exercise, you will debug a program.

a. Open the AppCe03.cpp file, which is located in the Cpp\AppC\AppCe03 folder on your computer's hard disk.

b. Print the code. A state code of 1 should display "Illinois," a state code of 2 should display "Kentucky," 3 will display "New Hampshire", 4 will display "Vermont", and 5 will display "Massachusetts." Debug the program.

c. When the program is working correctly, print the code. On the code printout, indicate what was wrong with the program. Also circle the corrections you made.

d. Close the Output window and the workspace.

A P P E N D I X   D
o b j e c t i v e s

In this appendix you will learn how to:

- Create and initialize a pointer variable
- Assign an address to a pointer variable
- Use a pointer variable to access the value stored in a variable
- Pass a pointer variable to a function

Pointers

Using Pointer Variables

As you learned in Tutorial 3, a variable is simply a memory location inside the computer where you can temporarily store data. In previous tutorials, you used variables to store data entered by the user at the keyboard and also to store the result of a calculation made by the computer. A **pointer variable**, typically referred to simply as a **pointer**, is a special type of variable. Rather than storing data, a pointer stores the memory address of a variable that contains data—in other words, a pointer tells you where the data is located in memory. As you will see later in this lesson, you can use a pointer to access the data stored in the variable to which it points.

Although the concept of a pointer may sound confusing, pointers are really nothing new to you; you have been using pointers since you were in elementary school. Think about the last time you looked up a topic in the index of a book. Once you found the topic, you used the page number that appeared next to the topic to locate the information in the book. In essence, the page number is a pointer to the information.

Before you can use a pointer, you must declare it. As with all variables, you should also initialize the pointer variables that you create.

Declaring and Initializing a Pointer

As you learned in Tutorial 3, the syntax to declare and initialize a variable that does not belong to an array, often referred to as a **simple variable**, is *datatype variablename = initialvalue;*. Recall that *datatype* is the type of data the variable will store, *variablename* is the name of the variable, and *initialvalue* is the beginning value assigned to the variable. The `short num = 0;` statement, for example, declares and initializes a Short Integer variable named num to 0.

The syntax to declare and initialize a pointer is similar to the syntax to declare and initialize a simple variable. The syntax to declare and initialize a pointer is *datatype *pointername = initialvalue;*. In the syntax, *datatype* is the type of data stored in the variable to which the pointer points. If, for example, the pointer will point to a Short Integer variable, then the pointer's *datatype* should also be Short Integer. Similarly, a pointer that points to a Character variable would be declared as a Character. If you attempt to store in a pointer the address of a variable that has a different *datatype*—for example, if you try to store the address of an Integer variable in a Short Integer pointer—C++ will display an error message.

pointername in the syntax is the name of the pointer and it must follow the same naming rules as for variables. The asterisk (*) before *pointername* in the syntax is called the **indirection operator** and it indicates that the variable being created

The rules for naming variables are shown in Tutorial 3's Figure 3-1.

In addition to the iostream.h file, you will find the NULL symbolic constant defined in many other header files.

is a pointer. The term "indirection" refers to the fact that the pointer can be used to refer, indirectly, to the variable to which it points.

initialvalue in the syntax is the beginning value for the pointer. As with an uninitialized variable, an uninitialized pointer contains an arbitrary number that could refer to a crucial location in memory. If your program changes the value stored at that location, your system could be corrupted and subsequently crash. To prevent this from happening, you should always initialize a pointer when it is created. Pointers typically are initialized to NULL—a C++ named constant defined in the iostream.h header file. When a pointer contains the NULL value, the pointer is pointing to nothing in memory, so the program cannot destroy, inadvertently, a critical memory location.

Figure D-1 shows examples of creating and initializing pointers.

Statement	Result
`short *numPtr = NULL;`	Declares and initializes a pointer named `numPtr` to NULL. The pointer can store the address of a Short Integer variable.
`float *salesPtr = NULL;`	Declares and initializes a pointer named `salesPtr` to NULL. The pointer can store the address of a Float variable.
`char *idPtr = NULL;`	Declares and initializes a pointer named `idPtr` to NULL. The pointer can store the address of a Character variable.

Figure D-1: Examples of declaring and initializing a pointer

The names of the pointers shown in Figure D-1 are `numPtr`, `salesPtr`, and `idPtr`, and not `*numPtr`, `*salesPtr`, and `*idPtr`. The asterisk (*) is not part of the name; rather, it tells C++ that the name that follows it is the name of a pointer.

Notice that the names of the pointers shown in Figure D-1 end with the three characters *Ptr*, which stand for *pointer*. Although you do not need to include those characters in the name, doing so makes it clear that the name refers to a pointer (which contains the address of a variable), rather than a variable (which contains data).

After you declare and initialize a pointer, you can then assign the address of a variable to it.

Assigning an Address to a Pointer

As you may remember from Tutorial 4, passing a variable's address to a function is called *passing by reference*.

Unlike a simple variable, which contains data, a pointer contains the address of a variable in memory. The syntax of a statement that assigns a variable's address to a pointer is *pointername = &variablename;*. As you may remember, you learned about the ampersand (&) operator, referred to as the **address-of operator**, in Tutorial 4. Recall that you use this operator to pass a variable's address to a function. Another use for the address-of operator is to assign a variable's address to a pointer. Figure D-2 shows examples of assigning values to the pointers declared and initialized in Figure D-1. You will notice that the data type of the variable whose address is being assigned must match the data type of the pointer.

Statement	Result
`numPtr = &number;`	Assigns the address of the `number` variable to the `numPtr` pointer. Because `numPtr` was declared as Short Integer, the data type of the `number` variable must also be Short Integer.
`salesPtr = &qtrSales;`	Assigns the address of the `qtrSales` variable to the `salesPtr` pointer. Because `salesPtr` was declared as Float, the data type of the `qtrSales` variable must also be Float.
`idPtr = &initial;`	Assigns the address of the `initial` variable to the `idPtr` pointer. Because `idPtr` was declared as Character, the data type of the `initial` variable must also be Character.

Figure D-2: Examples of assigning a value (an address) to a pointer

After assigning the address of a variable to a pointer, you can then use the pointer to access the value stored in the variable.

Using a Pointer to Access the Value Stored in a Variable

Assume that a program declares and initializes a Short Integer variable named **number** to 0. The program also declares a pointer named **numPtr**, to which it assigns the address of the **number** variable, as shown in Figure D-3. For illustration purposes, the letter A is used to represent the address of the **number** variable in memory.

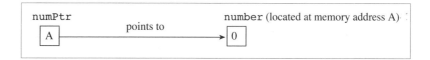

Figure D-3: Contents of the `numPtr` pointer and the `number` variable

Notice that the **number** variable contains the number 0, and that the **numPtr** variable contains the address of the **number** variable—in this case, address A. The **numPtr** variable tells you where the **number** variable—in other words, where the 0—is stored in memory.

Now assume that you want to display the contents of the **number** variable. You can do so by referring to the variable either directly, as you have done in previous tutorials, or indirectly, through its pointer. Recall that you directly refer to a variable simply by including the variable's name in a statement. The `cout << number;` statement, for example, would display the contents of the **number** variable—a 0. This method of referring to a variable is called **direct reference** because you are using the variable's name to directly access its contents.

You can also use a pointer to indirectly access the contents of a variable by using the indirection operator (*) followed by the pointer's name in a statement. For example, you could use the `cout << *numPtr;` statement to display the contents of the **number** variable. This method of referring to a variable is called **indirect reference** because, rather than using the variable's name to access its contents, you are using the address stored in its associated pointer. Figure D-4 shows examples of both reference methods—direct and indirect—using the `number` and `numPtr` variables. (Keep in mind that `numPtr` contains the address of the `number` variable.)

Reference	Statement	Result
Direct Indirect	`cout << number;` `cout << *numPtr;`	either statement can be used to display the contents of the `number` variable
Direct Indirect	`number = 5;` `*numPtr = 5;`	either statement can be used to assign the number 5 to the `number` variable
Direct Indirect	`cin >> number;` `cin >> *numPtr;`	either statement can be used to store the value entered at the keyboard in the `number` variable
Direct Indirect	`number = number * 2;` `*numPtr = *numPtr * 2;`	either statement can be used to multiply the contents of the `number` variable by 2 and then store the result in the `number` variable

Figure D-4: Examples of direct and indirect referencing of variables

You will notice that you can accomplish the same result using either direct or indirect referencing. For example, both the `number = 5;` (direct reference) and the `*numPtr = 5;` (indirect reference) statements can be used to assign the number 5 to the `number` variable. The `*numPtr = 5;` statement tells C++ to assign the number 5 to the `number` variable whose address is stored in `numPtr`. When referencing a variable indirectly, be sure to include the indirection operator before the pointer's name. If you do not, C++ will use the pointer itself, and not the variable to which the pointer points. The `cout << numPtr;` statement, for example, will display the address contained in `numPtr`, and not the value contained in the `number` variable. You will now open a partially completed program that will allow you to observe how a pointer works.

To open the partially completed program:

1 Start Visual C++. Open the **Prog01.cpp** file, which is located in the Cpp\AppD\Prog01 folder on your computer's hard disk. The partially completed pointer demo program appears in the Prog01.cpp window, as shown in Figure D-5.

```cpp
//Prog01.cpp
//this program uses a pointer to indirectly
//reference the contents of a variable

#include <iostream.h>

void main()
{
    //declare and initialize variable

    //declare and initialize pointer

    //assign address of variable to pointer

    //use the pointer to assign a value to the number variable

    //use the pointer to display the contents of the number variable
    cout << "The number variable contains the number: "
        << << endl;

    //display the contents of the pointer variable
    cout << "The numPtr pointer contains the address: "
        << << endl;
} //end of main function
```

Figure D-5: The partially completed pointer demo program

First, declare a Short Integer variable named number and initialize it to 0.

2   In the blank line below the //declare and initialize variable comment, type **short number = 0;** and press the **Enter** key.

Now declare and initialize a pointer variable named numPtr to NULL. Because numPtr will contain the address of the Short Integer number variable, you will need to declare it as a Short Integer.

3   In the blank line below the //declare and initialize pointer comment, type **short *numPtr = NULL;** and press the **Enter** key. Recall that the indirection operator (*) is necessary to tell C++ that numPtr is a pointer rather than a simple variable.

Next, assign the address of the number variable to the numPtr pointer.

The statement that assigns the address of a variable to a pointer must be entered after the statement that declares the variable; in other words, you cannot put the numPtr = &number; **statement before the** short number = 0; **statement.**

4   In the blank line below the //assign address of variable to pointer comment, type **numPtr = &number;** and press the **Enter** key.

Now assign the number 5 to the number variable using the indirect reference method—with the *numPtr = 5; statement.

5   In the blank line below the //use the pointer to assign a value to the number variable comment, type ***numPtr = 5;** and press the **Enter** key.

Now you will display the contents of the number variable using the indirect reference method. You will also display the contents of the numPtr pointer variable; recall that numPtr contains the address of the number variable in memory.

6 Modify the code by entering the highlighted instructions shown in Figure D-6.

```
//Prog01.cpp
//this program uses a pointer to indirectly
//reference the contents of a variable

#include <iostream.h>

void main()
{
    //declare and initialize variable
    short number = 0;

    //declare and initialize pointer
    short *numPtr = NULL;

    //assign address of variable to pointer
    numPtr = &number;

    //use the pointer to assign a value to the number variable
    *numPtr = 5;

    //use the pointer to display the contents of the number variable
    cout << "The number variable contains the number: "
        << *numPtr << endl;

    //display the contents of the pointer variable
    cout << "The numPtr pointer contains the address: "
        << numPtr << endl;
} //end of main function
```

modify these statements

Figure D-6: Completed pointer demo program

tip

. . . .

▶ Do not be concerned if the memory address shown in Figure D-7 looks confusing. Addresses in memory are specified using the hexadecimal (base 16) system rather than the decimal (base 10) system. In the decimal system, all numbers are formed using one or more of the ten digits from 0 through 9—for example, the number 125 is a combination of the numbers 1, 2, and 5. In the hexadecimal system, all numbers are formed using one or more of the following sixteen characters: 0, 1, 2, 3, 4, 5, 6, 7, 8, 9, A, B, C, D, E, and F. In the hexadecimal system, the letter A is equivalent to the number 10 in the decimal system, the letter B is equivalent to the number 11, and so on.

7 Save, build, and execute the program. The DOS window displays the contents of both the number variable and the numPtr pointer, as shown in Figure D-7. Do not be concerned if the address contained in numPtr differs from what appears in Figure D-7; your system may store the number variable, whose address is contained in numPtr, at a different location.

Figure D-7: DOS window showing the contents of the number variable and the numPtr pointer

You will notice that the number variable contains the number 5; the numPtr variable contains a memory address, specified in hexadecimal (base 16 notation), that tells where the number variable—in other words, where the 5—is located.

8 Press the **Enter** key to close the DOS window.

You have completed this program, so you can close it.

9 Close the workspace and the Output window.

In the next example, you will learn how to pass a pointer variable to a function.

mini-quiz

Mini-Quiz 1

1. Write a statement that declares a pointer named `quantityPtr`. Initialize the pointer to NULL. The pointer will be used to store the address of a Short Integer variable.

2. Write a statement that assigns the address of the Short Integer `quantity` variable to the `quantityPtr` pointer declared and initialized in question 1.

3. Write a statement that uses the `quantityPtr` pointer to assign the number 25 to the `quantity` variable.

4. Write a statement that uses the `quantityPtr` pointer to multiply, by 2, the value stored in the `quantity` variable. Assign the result to the Short Integer `doubleQuantity` variable.

5. Write a statement that displays the contents of the `quantity` variable. Use the direct reference method.

6. Write a statement that displays the contents of the `quantity` variable. Use the indirect reference method.

Passing a Pointer to a Function

Jerod Antiques needs a program that the store clerks can use to increase the price of each item in inventory by 10 percent. The IPO charts for the program's `main` and `calcNewPrice` functions are shown in Figure D-8.

main function		
Input	Processing	Output
old price	Processing items: none Algorithm: 1. enter the old price 2. calculate the new price (**calcNewPrice** function) 3. display the new price	new price

calcNewPrice function		
Input	Processing	Output
old price	1. calculate the new price by multiplying the old price by 1.1	new price

Figure D-8: IPO charts for the `main` and `calcNewPrice` functions

As Figure D-8 indicates, the `main` function will get the old price from the user, and then call the `calcNewPrice` function to calculate the new price. According to the `calcNewPrice` function's algorithm, the new price is calculated by multiplying the old price by 1.1; multiplying the old price by 1.1 will increase the old price by 10 percent. After the `calcNewPrice` function completes its task, the `main` function will display the new price on the screen.

Your computer's hard disk contains a partially completed program that corresponds to the IPO charts shown in Figure D-8. You will open that program now.

To view the Jerod Antiques program:

1 Open the **Prog02.cpp** file, which is located in the Cpp\AppD\Prog02 folder on your computer's hard disk. The Jerod Antiques program appears in the Prog02.cpp window, as shown in Figure D-9.

```cpp
//Prog02.cpp
//this program uses a pointer to pass the address of a variable

#include <iostream.h>
#include <iomanip.h>

//function prototype
void calcNewPrice();

void main()
{
    //declare variable
    float price = (float) 0.0;

    //declare pointer

    //assign variable's address to pointer

    //get the old price
    cout << "Enter the old price: ";

    cin.ignore(100, '\n');

    //call function to calculate new price

    //display the new price
    cout << setprecision(2)
        << setiosflags(ios::fixed | ios::showpoint);
    cout << "The new price is " << << "." << endl;
} //end of main function

//*****programmer-defined function definitions*****
void calcNewPrice()
{

} //end of calcNewPrice function
```

Figure D-9: The partially completed Jerod Antiques program

The main function begins by declaring and initializing a Float variable named price. The main function will need to pass the price variable to the calcNewPrice function for the calcNewPrice function to calculate the new price. Because the calcNewPrice function will need to replace the old price stored in the price variable with the new price, you will need to pass the address of the price variable to the function. As you learned in Tutorial 4, you can use the address-of (&) operator to pass the address of a variable to a function. In addition, you can also pass a pointer that contains the variable's address. In the Jerod Antiques program, you will pass a pointer that contains the address of the price variable to the calcNewPrice function.

Before you can pass a pointer, you first must declare, or create, the pointer; you should also initialize the pointer. Recall that the syntax to both declare and initialize a pointer is *datatype *pointername = initialvalue;*. Because the price variable is a Float variable, you will need to declare its associated pointer as Float. You will name the pointer pricePtr and initialize it to NULL.

To begin completing the Jerod Antiques program:

1 In the blank line below the //declare pointer comment, type **float *pricePtr = NULL;** and press the **Enter** key.

After declaring and initializing the pointer, you then assign a value to it. In this case, you will assign the address of the price variable.

2 In the blank line below the //assign variable's address to pointer comment, type **pricePtr = &price;** and press the **Enter** key.

Rather than entering the user's input into the price variable directly, you will use the pricePtr pointer to enter the input into the price variable indirectly.

3 In the blank line below the cout << "Enter the old price: "; statement, type **cin >> *pricePtr;**.

According to the main function's algorithm shown in Figure D-8, you now need to call the calcNewPrice function to calculate the new price. To give the calcNewPrice function access to the price variable, you simply need to pass pricePtr, which contains the address of the price variable.

4 In the blank line below the //call function to calculate new price comment, type **calcNewPrice(pricePtr);** and press the **Enter** key.

Now use the pointer to display the contents of the price variable.

5 Change the cout << "The new price is " << << "." << endl; statement as shown in Figure D-10. The modification you need to make to the statement is highlighted in Figure D-10, which shows the completed main function.

```
//Prog02.cpp
//this program uses a pointer to pass the address of a variable

#include <iostream.h>
#include <iomanip.h>

//function prototype
void calcNewPrice();

void main()
{
    //declare variable
    float price = (float) 0.0;

    //declare pointer
    float *pricePtr = NULL;

    //assign variable's address to pointer
    pricePtr = &price;

    //get the old price
    cout << "Enter the old price: ";
    cin >> *pricePtr;
    cin.ignore(100, '\n');

    //call function to calculate new price
    calcNewPrice(pricePtr);

    //display the new price
    cout << setprecision(2)
         << setiosflags(ios::fixed | ios::showpoint);
    cout << "The new price is " << *pricePtr << "." << endl;
} //end of main function

//*****programmer-defined function definitions*****
void calcNewPrice()
{

} //end of calcNewPrice function
```

Verify that you entered these four lines correctly

modify this statement

Figure D-10: Completed main function

To complete the Jerod Antiques program, you just need to complete the calcNewPrice function's prototype and definition. First change the function prototype to void calcNewPrice (float *). This prototype indicates that the calcNewPrice function will receive a pointer to a Float variable.

6 Change the void calcNewPrice(); function prototype, which appears above the main function, to **void calcNewPrice (float *);**.

7 Change the calcNewPrice function definition as highlighted in Figure D-11.

```
//Prog02.cpp
//this program uses a pointer to pass the address of a variable

#include <iostream.h>
#include <iomanip.h>

//function prototype
void calcNewPrice (float *);

void main()
{
    //declare variable
    float price = (float) 0.0;

    //declare pointer
    float *pricePtr = NULL;

    //assign variable's address to pointer
    pricePtr = &price;

    //get the old price
    cout << "Enter the old price: ";
    cin >> *pricePtr;
    cin.ignore(100, '\n');

    //call function to calculate new price
    calcNewPrice(pricePtr);

    //display the new price
    cout << setprecision(2)
         << setiosflags(ios::fixed | ios::showpoint);
    cout << "The new price is " << *pricePtr << "." << endl;
} //end of main function

//*****programmer-defined function definitions*****
void calcNewPrice(float *num)
{
    *num = *num * (float) 1.1;
} //end of calcNewPrice function
```

modify the function as shown

Figure D-11: Completed Jerod Antiques program

You will notice that the `calcNewPrice` function receives the pointer to the `price` variable, which is passed to it by the `main` function, in its `num` formal parameter.

8 Save, build, and execute the program. When you are prompted to enter the old price, type **25** and press the **Enter** key. The DOS window shows that the new price is 27.50.

9 Press the **Enter** key to close the DOS window.

You have now completed this program, so you can close it.

10 Close the workspace and then close the Output window.

mini-quiz

Mini-Quiz 2

1. Which of the following function headers can receive the address of a Float variable named **sales**? You can assume that the `salesPtr` pointer points to the `sales` variable.

   a. `void calcCommission(float &sales);`

   b. `void calcCommission(float salesPtr);`

   c. `void calcCommission(float sales);`

   d. `void calcCommission(float *salesPtr);`

   e. both a and d

2. Assume that a program includes the following function header: `void displayProfit(float *profitPtr)`. Which of the following function calls will pass the address of the `profit` variable to the `displayProfit` function? You can assume that the `profitPtr` pointer points to the `profit` variable.

   a. `displayProfit(profit);`

   b. `displayProfit(*profitPtr);`

   c. `displayProfit(&profitPtr);`

   d. `dislayProfit(profitPtr);`

You have now completed Appendix D. In this appendix you learned how to use pointers.

SUMMARY

A pointer variable, typically referred to simply as a pointer, is a special type of variable. Rather than storing data, a pointer stores the memory address of a variable that contains data. You can use a pointer to access the data stored in the variable to which it points.

Before you can use a pointer, you must declare it. You should also initialize the pointer variables you create. You can declare and initialize a pointer using the syntax *datatype *pointername = initialvalue;*. The *datatype* of the pointer must match the *datatype* of the variable to which it points. If, for example, a pointer will store the address of a Character variable, then the pointer must be declared as a Character. The asterisk (*) before *pointername* in the syntax is called the indirection operator and tells C++ that the variable being created is a pointer.

Because an uninitialized pointer contains an arbitrary number that could refer to a crucial location in memory, it is a good programming practice to initialize a pointer when it is created. Pointers typically are initialized to NULL—a C++ symbolic constant defined in the iostream.h header file. When a pointer contains the NULL value, the pointer is pointing to nothing in memory.

After a pointer is declared and initialized, you can then assign the address of a variable to it. The syntax of a statement that assigns a variable's address to a pointer is *pointername = &variablename;*.

If a variable has an associated pointer, you can use the indirect reference method to refer to the variable. You indirectly refer to a variable by using the indirection operator (*) followed by the pointer's name in a statement. You can also pass a pointer to a function.

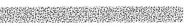

ANSWERS TO MINI-QUIZZES

Mini-Quiz 1

1. `short *quantityPtr = NULL;`
2. `quantityPtr = &quantity;`
3. `*quantityPtr = 25;`
4. `doubleQuantity = *quantityPtr * 2;`
5. `cout << quantity;`
6. `cout << *quantityPtr;`

Mini-Quiz 2

1. e
2. d

QUESTIONS

1. Which of the following is false?
   a. A pointer variable contains the address of a variable in memory.
   b. You should both declare and initialize a pointer before you use it.
   c. Pointers are typically initialized to the empty string (" ").
   d. A pointer's datatype must match the datatype of the variable to which it points.
   e. A pointer variable is typically referred to simply as a pointer.

2. Which of the following statements creates and initializes a pointer named `salesPtr`?
   a. `salesPtr = NULL;`
   b. `*salesPtr = "";`
   c. `float &salesPtr = NULL;`
   d. `float *salesPtr = "";`
   e. `float *salesPtr = NULL;`

3. Which of the following symbols is the indirection operator?
   a. `&`
   b. `*`
   c. `->`
   d. `<-`
   e. `>>`

4. Assume that a program includes the `short *agePtr = NULL;` statement. The name of the pointer is _____ .
   a. `*agePtr`
   b. `agePtr`

5. Which of the following symbols is the address-of operator?
   a. `&`
   b. `*`
   c. `->`
   d. `<-`
   e. `>>`

6. Which of the following statements will assign the address of the `age` variable to the `agePtr` pointer?

    a. `agePtr = &age;`

    b. `agePtr = *age;`

    c. `&agePtr = age;`

    d. `*agePtr = age;`

    e. `agePtr -> *age;`

7. Assume that a program creates and initializes a Short Integer variable named `age` and a pointer named `agePtr`, to which it assigns the address of the `age` variable. Which of the following statements will assign the number 21 to the age variable?

    a. `age = 21;`

    b. `*age = 21;`

    c. `agePtr = 21;`

    d. `*agePtr = 21;`

    e. both a and d

8. Assume that a program creates and initializes a Short Integer variable named `age` and a pointer named `agePtr`, to which it assigns the address of the `age` variable. The `cout << age;` statement uses the _____ method to access the `age` variable.

    a. direct reference

    b. indirect reference

9. Assume that a program creates and initializes a Short Integer variable named `age` and a pointer named `agePtr`, to which it assigns the address of the `age` variable. The `cout << *agePtr;` statement uses the _____ method to access the `age` variable.

    a. direct reference

    b. indirect reference

10. Assume that a program creates and initializes a Short Integer variable named `age` and a pointer named `agePtr`, to which it assigns the address of the `age` variable. The `cout << agePtr;` statement will display _____.

    a. the address of the `age` variable

    b. the value stored in the `age` variable

11. Which of the following statements will pass the `salesPtr` pointer to a function named `displaySales`?

    a. `displaySales(salesPtr);`

    b. `displaySales(&salesPtr);`

    c. `displaySales(*salesPtr);`

EXERCISES

1. Write your answers to this exercise on a piece of paper.

    a. Write the statement to declare and initialize a pointer variable named `partNumPtr` to NULL. The `partNumPtr` will need to store the address of a Short Integer variable.

    b. Write the statement that will assign the address of the `partNum` variable to the `partNumPtr` pointer.

    c. Write the statement that will assign the number 102 to the `partNum` variable. Use the direct reference method.

    d. Write the statement that will assign the number 333 to the `partNum` variable. Use the indirect reference method.

    e. Write the statement that will display the contents of the `partNum` variable. Use the direct reference method.

    f. Write the statement that will display the contents of the `partNum` variable. Use the indirect reference method.

    g. Write the statement that will display the address of the `partNum` variable.

    h. Write the statement that will add the number 1 to the contents of the `partNum` variable. Use the direct reference method. Store the result in the `partNum` variable.

    i. Write the statement that will add the number 1 to the contents of the `partNum` variable. Use the indirect reference method. Store the result in the `partNum` variable.

    j. Write the statement that will call a void function named `displayPartNum`, passing it, by reference, the address of the `partNum` variable.

    k. Write the statement that will call a void function named `displayPartNum`. Use the pointer to pass the address of the `partNum` variable to the function.

2. Write your answers to this exercise on a piece of paper.

    a. Write the statement to declare and initialize a pointer variable named `codePtr` to NULL. The `codePtr` will need to store the address of a Character variable.

    b. Write the statement that will assign the address of the `code` variable to the `codePtr` pointer.

    c. Write the statement that will assign the letter T to the `code` variable. Use the direct reference method.

    d. Write the statement that will assign the letter B to the `code` variable. Use the indirect reference method.

    e. Write the statement that will input a letter from the keyboard. Assign the uppercase equivalent of the letter to the `code` variable. Use the direct reference method.

    f. Write the statement that will input a letter from the keyboard. Assign the uppercase equivalent of the letter to the `code` variable. Use the indirect reference method.

    g. Write the statement that will display the contents of the `code` variable. Use the direct reference method.

    h. Write the statement that will display the contents of the `code` variable. Use the indirect reference method.

    i. Write the statement that will display the address of the `code` variable.

    j. Write the statement that will call a void function named `displayCode`, passing it, by reference, the address of the `code` variable.

    k. Write the statement that will call a void function named `displayCode`. Use the pointer to pass the address of the `code` variable to the function.

3. In this exercise, you will use a pointer to pass a variable to a function.

    a. Create a console application named AppDe03 in the Cpp\AppD folder on your computer's hard disk.

    b. Create a program that allows the user to input a number. Use a pointer to pass the number to a function named `squareAndCubeNumber`. The `squareAndCubeNumber` function should display both the square and cube of the number passed to it. (*Hint*: Use the `pow` function, which you learned about in Tutorial 4.)

    c. Save, build, and then execute the program. Test the program by entering the number 2. The numbers 4 and 8 should appear in the DOS window.

    d. When the program is working correctly, print the code.

4. In this exercise, you will use a pointer to pass a variable to a function.

    a. Create a console application named AppDe04 in the Cpp\AppD folder on your computer's hard disk.

    b. Create a program that allows the user to input one character. Use a pointer to pass the character to a function named `repeatCharacter`. The `repeatCharacter` function should display the character 10 times. For example, if the user enters the asterisk (*), the function should display 10 asterisks, on the same line.

    c. Save, build, and then execute the program. Test the program by entering the *. Ten asterisks should appear on the same line in the DOS window.

    d. When the program is working correctly, print the code.

5. In this exercise, you will use a pointer to pass a variable to a function.

  a. Create a console application named AppDe05 in the Cpp\AppD folder on your computer's hard disk.

  b. Create a program that allows the user to input a letter—either M for Monday, T for Tuesday, W for Wednesday, R for Thursday, F for Friday, S for Saturday, or U for Sunday. (The user can enter the letter in either uppercase or lowercase.) Use a loop to allow the user to enter as many letters as desired. Stop the program when the user enters the letter X, in either uppercase or lowercase.

  c. Use a pointer to pass the character to a function named `displayDay`. The `displayDay` function should display the day of the week that corresponds to the character passed to it. For example, if the user enters the letter R, the `displayDay` function should display the word Thursday.

  d. Save, build, and then execute the program. Test the program by entering the letter U. The DOS window should display the word Sunday.

  e. When the program is working correctly, print the code.

discovery ▶ **6.** In this exercise, you will use a pointer to point to a one-dimensional Character array.

  a. Open the AppDe06.cpp file, which is located in the Cpp\AppD\AppDe06 folder on your computer's hard disk. You will notice that the program declares and initializes a Short Integer variable named `x`, a Character array named `state`, and a pointer named `statePtr`. The program uses a `for` loop, along with the `statePtr` pointer, to display each character in the `state` String variable.

  b. Build and execute the program. The word Idaho appears in the DOS window. Press the Enter key to close the DOS window.

  c. Change the `char state[6] = "Idaho";` statement to `char state[15] = "";`. Modify the program so that it allows the user to enter the name of a state; store the user's input in the `state` variable. Have the program determine the length of the string contained in the `state` variable. (*Hint*: Use the `strlen` function, which is defined in the string.h header file.) Currently, the `for` loop will display only the first five characters contained in the `state` variable. Modify the `for` loop so that it displays every character contained in the `state` variable.

  d. Save, build, and then execute the program. To test the program, type Idaho as the state, and then press the Enter key. The word Idaho should appear in the DOS window. Close the DOS window, then execute the program again. Type Mississippi as the state, and then press the Enter key. The word Mississippi should appear in the DOS window. Close the DOS window.

  e. Print the code. On the code printout, circle the changes you made to the original program.

  f. Modify the `for` loop so that it displays every other character contained in the `state` variable. Save, build, and then execute the program. To test the program, type Mississippi and press the Enter key. The letters Msisipi should appear in the DOS window. Print the code. On the code printout, circle the changes you made to the program so that it now displays every other character.

  g. Modify the `for` loop so that it displays every character contained in the `state` variable backwards. Save, build, and then execute the program. To test the program, type Idaho and press the Enter key. The letters ohadI should appear in the DOS window. Print the code. On the code printout, circle the changes you made to the program so that it now displays every character backwards.

discovery ▶   7.   In this exercise, you will use a pointer that points to a two-dimensional Character array. (It may help to complete Exercise 6 before doing this exercise.)

a.   Open the AppDe07.cpp file, which is located in the Cpp\AppD\AppDe07 folder on your computer's hard disk. You will notice that the program declares and initializes a two-dimensional Character array named `state` and a pointer named `statePtr`.

b.   The program should use the pointer to display each of the four states on a separate line. The expected output is shown in Figure D-12 (notice the period at the end of each sentence).

```
The name of the state is Idaho.
The name of the state is Mississippi.
The name of the state is Michigan.
The name of the state is Louisiana.
```

Figure D-12

c.   Save, build, and then execute the program. The output shown in Figure D-12 should appear in the DOS window.

d.   When the program is working correctly, print the code.

discovery ▶   8.   In this exercise, you will complete a program that uses a pointer to point to a one-dimensional numeric array.

a.   Open the AppDe08.cpp file, which is located in the Cpp\AppD\AppDe08 folder on your computer's hard disk. You will notice that the program uses two programmer-defined functions named `getNumber` and `displayElement`. After declaring and initializing a five-element Short Integer array named `num` and a Short Integer pointer named `numPtr`, the program uses a `for` loop to fill the five-element `num` array with five numbers. The program also uses a `for` loop to display the contents of the `num` array. The code in both `for` loops, as well as the code in both programmer-defined functions, is missing from the program.

b.   Complete the `for` loops in the `main` function. Use the comments shown in the program as a guide.

c.   Code the `getNumber` function so that it prompts the user to enter a number. Use the pointer to store the number in the current element of the `num` array.

d.   Code the `displayElement` function so that it displays the current array element on a separate line.

e.   Save, build, and then execute the program. To test the program, enter the numbers 1, 2, 3, 4, and 5. The program should display each number (1, 2, 3, 4, and 5) on a separate line in the DOS window. Close the DOS window.

f.   When the program is working correctly, print the code. On the code printout, circle the changes you made to the program.

debugging   9.   In this exercise, you will debug a program that contains a pointer.

a.   Open the AppDe09.cpp file, which is located in the Cpp\AppD\AppDe09 folder on your computer's hard disk. Study the program's code. Build and then execute the program. Debug the program. When the program is working correctly, print the code. On the code printout, indicate what was wrong with the program and circle the changes you made to the program.

debugging   10. In this exercise, you will debug a program that contains a pointer.

a.   Open the AppDe10.cpp file, which is located in the Cpp\AppD\AppDe10 folder on your computer's hard disk. Study the program's code. Build and then execute the program. Debug the program. When the program is working correctly, print the code. On the code printout, indicate what was wrong with the program, and circle the changes you made to the program.

Index

D

E

O

P

S

V

W

Z